THE ILLUSTRATED DICTIONARY OF BRITISH HERITAGE

The Illustrated Dictionary of

BRITISH
HERITAGE

Edited by Alan Isaacs and Jennifer Monk

Published by the Press Syndicate of the University of Cambridge
The Pitt Building, Trumpington Street, Cambridge CB2 1RP
32 East 57th Street, New York, NY 10022, USA
10 Stamford Road, Oakleigh, Melbourne 3166, Australia

© Market House Books Ltd. 1986

First published in North America 1986
First published worldwide 1987

This edition published 1993
by the Promotional Reprint Company Limited
exclusively for Printwise Limited of Bolton

ISBN 1 85648 146 8

Printed in Hungary

CONTENTS

Editors:

Alan Isaacs
Jennifer Monk

Contributors:

Jennifer Drake-Brockman
Rosalind Fergusson
Marcus Gibson
William Gould
Janet Hammond
Patrick Hanks
Ian Harris
Robert Hine
E.M. Kirkpatrick
Tom McArthur
Charles Gordon Mosley
David Pickering
N.J. Priestnall
Judith Ravenscroft
B. Russell Davis
Doreen Sherwood
Dinah Verman
Edmund Wright

Compiled and prepared by Market House Books Ltd.

FOREWORD

I am delighted to be writing this foreword for the *Cambridge Illustrated Dictionary of British Heritage* because it fills a major gap in the books in our libraries dealing with our unique history. Previous dictionaries have now become out-of-date and few of them combine such a range – ACAS as well as Arundel Castle!

Today it is remarkable that English has become the major world language in diplomacy, trade, scientific research, and historical criticism. This is a result of our history; during the last three centuries we created, partly by design and partly by accident, a global empire through our command of the seas. And when, during my lifetime, we voluntarily gave it independence, the Commonwealth countries were very willing to continue our customs and language.

As is well known, our language is very rich, making it easy for our poets, because we have added the French of the Norman invaders to the language of the Saxons whom they conquered in 1066, and it is generally considered that this language emerged with our great poet Chaucer, who died in 1400. It has been continually enriched since, with words adopted from other countries, including India.

I have often pointed out that, although we are part of Christendom and have taken part in so many of the activities of our European neighbours, such as the Crusades and the Renaissance, our heritage of buildings (castles, palaces, country houses, cathedrals and, indeed, whole towns) has not suffered to the same extent from the destruction that took place across the English Channel owing to the wars and revolutions that have ravaged their lands. Many of our political, legal, educational, and economic institutions too, have survived for many centuries with little change. We can indeed be proud of our continuity, which is well illustrated by the fact that our Queen can prove direct descent from the Saxon King, Cerdic, who died in 534 AD.

I commend this book to all English-speaking peoples now living and their descendants.

Norfolk.

The Duke of Norfolk

PREFACE

The idea for this book came from an American friend resident in London, who protested that he frequently met words and phrases in the media that he could not understand and could not look up in a convenient book. Examples he gave not only included **Privy Purse, Black Rod**, and **Earl Marshal** but also **ACAS, MI5**, and the **Samaritans**.

Having accepted the need for a book to explain these terms to the foreigner, the next task was to design it so that it would be as interesting and useful to natives as it should be to visitors. The alphabetical format, rather than the thematic, was chosen because it provides the most simple and rapid access to the information. It also gives the most diverse and stimulating juxtaposition of entries for the browser – the eye can wander from the compassion of the **hospice movement** to the adjacent pageantry of the **Household Cavalry**, from the exclusive **peerage** to the mass-market **Penguin Books**, and backwards in time from the **Rolling Stones** to **Roman Britain**. Within the compass of a single page, the casual reader can swing from one extreme of British culture and history to another.

The prime task the editors set themselves was to encourage the contributors to be both accurate and interesting. If they have succeeded it is the contributors who should be praised – if they have failed the blame lies with the editors.

A.I.
J.M.

Note: An asterisk before a word in the text of an article indicates that further information can be gained at the entry for the asterisked word.

A

AA (Automobile Association) The world's largest motoring organization. Founded in 1905 with some 90 members and Sir Stenson Cooke (1874–1942) as its secretary, the Association's initial aim was to protect motorists from the increased use of police traps. (Policemen with stopwatches would hide behind hedges and time the unsuspecting motorists.) Subsequently the Association broadened its services, erecting warning signs at danger spots, village signposts with mileages, gradient and other road signs, and indeed, until the early thirties, providing the only countrywide signposting system. It also pioneered the provision of roadside filling stations. The first AA handbook listing appointed hotels and breakdown services was published in 1908, with the now universally recognized "star" ratings for hotels being introduced four years later. In 1910 it amalgamated with the Motor Union (*see* RAC) and by 1914 its membership had risen to 83,000. In 1986 its membership topped six million. Members benefit from breakdown, technical, and insurance services, legal representation and advice, and touring and travel information for the British Isles and abroad. It operates a chain of travel agencies, publishes books, guides, and maps, and campaigns on behalf of motorists at local, national, and international levels. As a founder member of the AIT (International Touring Alliance) it is closely involved in international road traffic and tourism matters.

ACAS (Advisory, Conciliation, and Arbitration Service) A government-funded, yet wholly independent, organization set up in 1974 to promote good labour relations, to resolve industrial disputes through conciliation, and to prevent such disputes through the provision of advisory services and codes of practice. The service was the idea of Jack Jones, head of the Transport and General Workers' Union (1969–78) and was formed by the then Secretary of State for Employment, Michael Foot. Since 1974 its negotiators have handled nearly 500,000 disputes ranging from national stoppages over pay to individual complaints about conditions of employment. In resolving collective disputes ACAS's conciliation procedures have resulted in a success rate of more than 80%.

accent The features of a person's pronunciation of English resulting from the interaction of such factors as place of birth, education, and social class of parents. Generally, the most influential factor in determining a person's accent is the language of his peer group as a child; children starting at a new school rapidly acquire features of the peer-group accent in the school, relinquishing earlier speech habits, even those of the parental home. Two people from quite different backgrounds who have attended public schools will probably have very similar accents; whereas two sons of farmworkers from the same village may end up with quite different accents if one stays on the farm and the other moves away at an early age. British English has a standard accent, called *Received Pronunciation (RP), which is used mainly by the middle classes, especially in the south. It has a high social status, being widely regarded as "more correct" than regional accents; it is this accent, therefore, that is taught to foreign learners and is the accent transcribed into the International Phonetic Alphabet (IPA) in the pronunciation guides of standard English dictionaries. However, while local variations of grammar and vocabulary may previously have been regarded as "ignorant" or "wrong" (*see* dialects), there is a growing tendency to regard a slight regional accent as acceptable and even fashionable. Indeed, there is a view that RP is not to be regarded as more "correct" than any other accent and that it is no more than one of many accents with which English is spoken in the British Isles.

There are two aspects to a person's accent: intonation and the phonetic quality of speech sounds. Each accent has its own set of characteristic "tunes", or intonation patterns, which is the aspect usually first seized on by mimics. It sometimes happens that a "question" intonation in one accent is similar to a "confirming" intonation in another, and this can lead to confusion. Differences between accents are standardly described in terms of the quality of the vowels and consonants, often with reference to the norm of RP. Some words are more informative than others about a speaker's local origins. The pronunciations of "face" and "boat" differ considerably from region to region of the British Isles, whereas such words as "kit", "dress", "goose", and "fleece" are pronounced much the same in most accents.

Some broad characteristics of regional accents can be listed. One of the most obvious is the short front vowel heard in "bath" in northern England and Scotland, as opposed to the long back vowel of the southeast and RP. A characteristically northern vowel sound occurs in such words as "cup", which is the same as that in RP "foot". In the south, the -u- is more open in words like "strut" and "cut"; but others, such as "put", are pronounced to rhyme with "foot". This distinction, which cannot be predicted from the spelling, is confusing for northerners and leads to mistakes when they try to adopt this feature of RP but apply it too widely. The open -u- in such words as "put" and "butcher" is neither authentic by the standards of the local accent nor correct by the standards of RP. A similar example is the southwestern English -o-, as in "lot", which is similar to the vowel of RP "bath". Londoners and other "grockles" (tourists or outsiders) usually assume erroneously that the southwestern -o- is always pronounced in this way; but words such as "cloth" are pronounced as in RP. To speak with a correct Devon or Bristol accent, one has to know which word belongs to which set.

Birmingham, lying on the boundaries of northern, southeastern, and southwestern accent areas, has an interesting mixture of vowel qualities. In "start", it uses the southern -a-, but in words with no -r- after the vowel, such as "bath" and "palm", Birmingham has the short northern -a-. In this accent, both the northern and southern -u- may be heard, varying freely in the accent of a single speaker. "Price", rhyming with "choice", is characteristic of a wide area of the West Midlands.

Another major distinguishing feature of accents of English is whether -r- is pronounced when it occurs before a consonant (e.g. start) or at the end of the word (e.g. cure). Scots and Irish accents are rhotic (that is, -r- in these positions is pronounced), but in England it is heard only in Bristol and the southwest, and in a small area near Manchester. A quite different -r- is heard in Scotland from the vowel-like English consonant; the Scottish -r- is generally quite strongly trilled, the English -r- varies phonetically from accent to accent. In many nonstandard accents of English, -t- between two vowels may be replaced by a glottal stop: "dau'er" for "daughter", "le'er" for "letter". This phenomenon is heard in places as far apart as London (Cockney) and Glasgow. Also, in most nonstandard accents, h- at the beginning of a word is dropped, and -ing at the end of words is pronounced as -in. Ironically, this last is a feature of extreme upper-class pronunciation too ("huntin', shootin', and fishin'"), though not of the middle-class RP. In Birmingham, by contrast, the -g- is given its full value as an independent speech sound, so that Birmingham "singer" rhymes with "finger". Other speech sounds may be characteristic of a very restricted locality. An example is Bristol's intrusive -l after vowels, so that in this accent "area" is pronounced identically to "aerial". "Bristol" itself was originally called "Bristow". In rural Devon, -oo in words such as "too" is sometimes pronounced like the vowel in French *tu* or German *für*.

The study of pronunciation and differences between accents is made more complex by the increasing mobility of the population, and by people's skill in changing, often subconsciously, from a local to a (more or less) standard accent, depending on the circumstances under which they are speaking, and the class and origin of the people they are addressing.

Accession Council A plenary session of the Privy Council that is convened as soon as possible after the death of a king or queen in order to proclaim the new sovereign. It is the successor to the old Anglo-Saxon council, the *witenagemot*. The Accession Council's business is in two parts: the first authorizes the proclamation of a new sovereign; the second, which normally follows immediately, hears the sovereign's declaration in which he or she swears to uphold constitutional government. (When Queen Elizabeth II succeeded to the throne in 1952, she was in Kenya and there was a delay of 48 hours between the first and second parts.) The Accession Council meets at St James's Palace, and those invited to attend include members of the House of Lords, both spiritual and temporal, the Lord Mayor of London, aldermen, and prominent citizens of the City of London, and (for the first time at Elizabeth II's accession) Commonwealth High Commissioners in London. They attend as onlookers, not participants, and only for the first part of the Council. The Privy Councillors used to take a fresh oath of allegiance to the new sovereign on this occasion and kiss his or her hand, a practice that ceased after 1910. During the Council the sovereign signs two copies of a declaration promising to maintain the Presbyterian government of the Church of Scotland – the only signatures necessary on this occasion.

Act of Parliament A document, also known as a statute, by which *Parliament (or, more accurately, the Queen in Parliament) either makes new law or reformulates the existing law. It originates as a *Bill, which undergoes various stages of consideration by both Houses of Parliament, and becomes an Act on receiving the *royal assent. Normally, this can be given only after both Houses have passed it, but the Parliament Acts of 1911 and 1949 made it sufficient for a Bill to have been passed by the House of Commons alone in certain circumstances. The 1911 Parliament Act was forced through Parliament by a Liberal government under Asquith, after the House of Lords had rejected a finance Bill giving effect to Lloyd George's "People's Budget" of 1909. Under this Act, any primarily financial Bill can, after passing the Commons, be submitted directly for royal assent if not passed unaltered by the Lords within one month; and under that Act as amended in 1949, other Bills rejected or blocked by the Lords may be similarly submitted after a delay of one year. Bills to extend the life of a Parliament are, however, excluded from these provisions.

Acts of Parliament are classified in a variety of ways. For publication by the Queen's printer, they are either public general, local, or personal, according to whether they relate to matters of public interest, to a particular locality such as the area of a local authority, or to a private individual or estate. Acts that make new law are described as "enacting", while those that restate existing law are either "consolidating" or "codifying" (the former if they merely pull together the existing Acts relating to a particular subject and the latter if they include case law). With reference to duration, they are either permanent or temporary (as for example, the Acts relating to the armed forces, which require annual renewal). An Act begins with a long title, summarizing its aims, which helps the courts with its interpretation; and it ends with a short title by which it is usually known. It comes into force at the beginning of the day on which it received royal assent unless, as is usually the case, it either specifies a later date or empowers the government to activate it by a commencement order.

Acts of Parliament constitute the most important form of legislation in the UK, but by far the greater volume of written law consists of subordinate legislation (or delegated legislation), i.e. law made by other bodies acting under the authority of Parliament. Parliament has neither the time nor the expertise to grapple with the minutiae of control, and a vast number of orders, regulations, rules, directions, and schemes, are made under powers delegated by statute to ministers, local authorities, the courts, and other officials and bodies. The substantive distinction between the two derives from the sovereignty of Parliament. As a sovereign body, Parliament itself can, in the words of an 18th-century commentator, "do everything but make a woman a man and a man a woman". It can enact any law that it pleases, and the validity of an Act cannot be questioned in the courts. Equally, as a sovereign body Parliament can have no rival, and it follows that subordinate legislation is always open to challenge. All subordinate legislation must be authorized by an Act of Parliament. If it is, it is *intra vires* (within the powers); if it is not, it is *ultra vires* (beyond the powers), and, on an application for judicial review, the courts will declare it null and void.

Admiral's Cup A yachting trophy competed for by international three-boat teams in waters to the south and west of Britain. The contest, which is one of the most important

3

events in the ocean-racing calendar, was initiated in 1957 by Sir Miles Wyatt, then admiral of the Royal Ocean Racing Club, with the purpose of encouraging competition in offshore sailing events by other countries in addition to the USA and Britain. The competition, which is held biennially, consists of four races, two inshore and two offshore, the best-known being the Fastnet Race, which is held during *Cowes week in August. In this race the yachts sail from Cowes (Isle of Wight) round the Isles of Scilly (off the coast of Cornwall), up to and round the Fastnet Rock (off the southwest tip of Ireland), and back to Plymouth – a distance of 968 kilometres (605 miles). Disaster struck this race in 1979 when force 11 winds blew up off southwest Ireland almost without warning and caught many yachts unprepared, leading to the deaths of 15 competitors. Amongst the expert sailors who have taken part in British Admiral's Cup teams are the former Prime Minister Edward Heath and Prince Philip, the Duke of Edinburgh.

Admiralty Court A court that forms part of the Queen's Bench Division of the *High Court of Justice and exercises the admiralty jurisdiction vested in that Division in 1970. It is concerned with all manner of marine disputes (e.g. claims relating to collisions at sea, and claims for salvage) and it deals also with questions relating to prize (*see* prize court). The court has special forms of procedure, the outstanding feature of which is the process by which a person's ship may be "arrested", i.e. impounded by the court, and detained to satisfy any damages for which he is held liable. The judges of the court are *puisne judges of the Queen's Bench Division nominated by the Lord Chancellor to be Admiralty judges; in suitable cases they may appoint lay specialists (nautical assessors) to help them. In a case involving questions of navigation or seamanship, assessors are always chosen from the elder brethren of *Trinity House.

adult education centres Centres offering a wide range of mainly practical or recreational courses for evening students. *Local Education Authorities maintain nearly 5000 of these centres, which are generally housed in schools or buildings used for other purposes during the day.

advocate A person (also called "counsel"), belonging to the *Faculty of Advocates, and thus entitled to practise law in Scotland. Advocates constitute the senior branch of the legal profession in Scotland, *solicitors or law agents forming the other; the functions of an advocate correspond closely to those of a *barrister elsewhere in the UK. The right of audience in the courts is shared by advocates with solicitors in the *sheriff courts and below, but is enjoyed exclusively in the *Court of Session, the *High Court of Justiciary, and (for the hearing of Scottish appeals) the *House of Lords. As with barristers, it is open to successful advocates to become *Queen's Counsel, and it is from amongst advocates that the majority of judicial appointments in Scotland are made.

In the broader sense an advocate is anyone who pleads the cause of another, and thus includes barristers, solicitors, and even laymen in the case of certain bodies whose procedure is largely informal (e.g. the *Employment Appeal Tribunal).

Age Concern A charity for promoting the welfare of elderly people. Founded in 1940, it currently coordinates the efforts of 1400 local groups, working with over 124,000 volunteers throughout Britain. It has a strong emphasis on community service, and among the benefits it provides are day centres, lunch clubs, visiting schemes, foot care, transport, and bereavement counselling. It has a training department for people working with the elderly and publishes information for professionals and volunteers including the quarterly magazine *New Age*. Its research unit is called upon to advise the government on legislation in matters affecting the elderly, although Age Concern itself is dependent upon voluntary help and contributions rather than official funding. It works closely with two other organizations: the Centre for Policy on Ageing, which provides research and information for policy makers, and Help the Aged, which is mainly active in fundraising.

agricultural show An annual exhibition of farming technology, stock, produce, and rural crafts and pastimes. Such shows are held throughout Britain during the summer months and are an integral part of British country life, appealing to a wide cross-section of people. They vary in size and importance from such national events as the Royal Smithfield Show, the Agricultural Machinery Exhibition at Earl's Court in London, the Royal International Agricultural Show at Stoneleigh in Warwickshire, and the Royal Welsh Show at Llanelwedd in Powys, to regional and county shows, as well as smaller events organized in market towns for the benefit of local areas. For farmers and landowners they serve a social as well as an economic purpose; they include displays of the latest techniques in husbandry, new agricultural equipment, and livestock competitions. For others, agricultural shows have numerous attractions, such as showjumping events, dog shows, and exhibitions of flowers, vegetables, and country produce.

Agriculture and Food Research Council A body created as the Agriculture Research Council under the terms of the Science and Technology Act 1965, to promote and finance research in agriculture and food science. This it achieves both through its own research institutes and by sponsoring projects in universities, colleges, and other organizations. The work of the Council is steered by its three research committees – on animals, food, and plants and soils. The AFRC institutes, such as the Institute of Animal Physiology at Babraham, near Cambridge, and the three food research institutes at Bristol, Norwich, and Reading, study a wide variety of topics concerning the basic biology of farm animals and plants, production systems, and the foods that are derived from them. In addition, a number of other research institutes are funded directly by the Ministry of Agriculture, Fisheries, and Food. The current chairman of the AFRC is Lord Selborne.

Albert Medal A civilian decoration instituted in 1866 to commemorate the Prince Consort (1819–61). It was designed to reward gallantry in saving life and subsequently could be awarded posthumously. In October 1971 all surviving holders of the Albert Medal

exchanged that decoration for the George Cross. Holders receive a £100 tax-free gratuity per annum.

Aldeburgh Festival An annual festival of music and the arts held in the Suffolk coastal town of Aldeburgh. Having spent most of the war in the USA, the composer Benjamin Britten (1913–76) returned to his native Suffolk and settled there with his lifelong friend, the singer Peter Pears (1910–86). In 1948 Britten, Pears, and their friends, including Imogen Holst (the daughter of the composer Gustav Holst), arranged the first of a series of annual festivals of music and the arts in Aldeburgh. From these small beginnings, the Aldeburgh Festival has become a major event in the musical calendar – operas, concerts, and some nonmusical events have been presented there each June for 35 years. Premières of Britten's own works, including the operas *A Midsummer Night's Dream* (1960) and *Death in Venice* (1973), were staged at the festival; the former was held in Aldeburgh's small British Legion hall, the latter in the fine concert hall built in the old Maltings at nearby Snape. The Maltings was a complex of riverside industrial buildings that for many years served as the centre of a thriving North Sea trade in barley. The decline of the Maltings Quay with the development of road transport left the buildings in considerable disrepair and in 1966 the festival directors courageously decided to ac-

ALDEBURGH FESTIVAL *Sir Peter Pears giving a master class.*

quire a lease on the largest brick building. An imaginative conversion was completed in 1967 but the building was gutted by fire on the first night of the 1969 festival. It was, however, rebuilt for the festival the following year.

The church at Orford (some ten kilometres (six miles) from Aldeburgh) is also used during the festival and has been used for premières of several Britten operas, including *Noyes Fludde* (1958) and *Curlew River* (1964).

alderman A senior official in local government. In Anglo-Saxon times, *ealdorman*, meaning "elder", was an honorific title applied to high officials, especially to the governor of a *shire. However, from the late 10th century, after the arrival of the Danes, this position was largely replaced by that of *earl, and with the passage of time aldermen gradually became civic dignitaries. In 1394 Richard II decreed that they should be elected for life instead of annually; in 1741, under George II, they became *justices of the peace. Today, the post is only actively maintained in the *City of London; elsewhere, it is a title conferred on a councillor in recognition of past services. Outside the City the rank was an active one until quite recently. The councillors of each local council elected a number of aldermen, who would share the same duties, but who held office for a longer period. The system was designed to make outside expertise available to councils, and to promote continuity; but it was opposed as undemocratic, and too open to manipulation for political advantage. The office was abolished in England and Wales generally in 1974, and subsequently in Greater London (except the City).

ale *See* beer.

A Level, GCE *See* school-leaving examinations.

All-England Lawn Tennis and Croquet Club The most famous lawn *tennis club in the world, founded in 1869. It adopted its present title in 1882. The first lawn tennis championships were held at the club's courts at *Wimbledon in southwest London in 1877, partly as a fundraising exercise to pay for the repair of the pony-drawn lawn roller. The All-England Club was the governing body of the sport in its formative years until the foundation in 1888 of the Lawn Tennis Association. The two bodies now cooperate in the running of the annual championships.

All Hallows Eve *See* Hallowe'en.

Alliance, the The electoral alliance formed in 1981 between the *Liberal Party under David Steel and the newly formed *Social Democratic Party under Roy Jenkins (now led by David Owen). The two parties have not merged, although there has been some pressure for this from the Liberals. Each party retains its identity, and there is agreement as to which party will fight which constituencies at a general election; there is also sufficient agreement on fundamental policy to enable them to form a united government if they should win. In that event, the leader of the party having the larger number of seats will become Prime Minister, and the other his deputy.

almshouses Dwellings built and endowed by private charity for the accommodation of the aged, infirm, and poor. Before the *Reformation, almshouses (or hospitals, as they were also called) were often attached to monasteries or convents and were places in which food, shelter, and medical aid were offered to the destitute (not necessarily only the elderly). The Hospital of St Cross, near Winchester (founded 1136), is a notable early example. After the Reformation laws were passed to deal with begging and vagrancy among the able-bodied poor, but those genuinely incapable of work were supported by a "poor rate", a tax levied on a parochial basis from those who had work or substantial property; those likely to prove "a burden on the parish" were moved on. To prevent such inhumane treatment befalling local people who became too old and infirm to support themselves, charitable gentry or tradesmen from the 16th to the mid-19th century founded almshouses, many of which still perform their original function of providing simple permanent accommodation for elderly members of the community who might otherwise be homeless. Architecturally, almshouses are often attractive examples of vernacular styles: identical small one- or two-storeyed dwellings built in a row or around a courtyard, often with a chapel, communal eating hall, and other additional facilities.

Amateur Athletic Association (AAA) The governing body of athletics in England and Wales. The Association is responsible for all official competitions in line with international rules agreed by the International Amateur Athletic Federation, to which the AAA is affiliated. The Association was founded in 1880 primarily to resolve a conflict between the athletes of Oxford and Cambridge universities, who preferred to train and compete in winter time, and those in the rest of the country, who had invariably treated athletics as a summer sport. Although the universities' athletes prevailed at first, the sport has developed into a fair weather one. Only at Oxford and Cambridge, where cricket, rowing, and examinations rule it out in the summer, is athletics seriously contested in winter out of doors: elsewhere competitors take part in an indoor season. By 1886, 154 athletics clubs representing some 20,000 athletes had joined the Association and national championships have been organized annually under its aegis. To compete in the "Three As" championships, which have long been regarded as the unofficial British championships, is the ambition of all top club athletes. Such contentious issues as ensuring the amateur status of competitors and the illegal use of drugs also come within the jurisdiction of the AAA.

amateur theatre The production of plays by unpaid enthusiasts in their spare time. The roots of amateur theatre may perhaps be traced to medieval liturgical drama and the *mystery plays; and it has always existed alongside the professional theatre (which began in the 16th century). Many of the best-known amateur companies were founded in the 19th century, when this form of entertainment reached the height of its popularity amongst the upper and middle classes. Such companies include The Old Stagers, founded in Canterbury in 1842, the Manchester Athenaeum Dramatic Society (1854), and the university companies – the ADC (Amateur Dramatic Club) at Cambridge and the OUDS (Oxford University Dramatic Society), founded in 1855 and 1885 respectively. The

variety of amateur productions is enormous, ranging from the annual school play to a full-scale season. The majority of groups, however, specialize in one-act plays. Many of the best are "Little Theatres", members of the Little Theatre Guild of Great Britain, founded in 1946. These include the Maddermarket theatre in Norwich, a replica of an Elizabethan theatre, built in 1919 to house the Norwich Players, and the Questors and Tower theatres, both in London. The National Youth Theatre, founded by Michael Croft in 1956, has had a powerful influence on the role of *theatre in education, sometimes revealing, like the university companies, the talents of young people who have later become professional actors. The work of the various university drama departments can be seen at an annual drama festival run by the National Union of Students, as well as at the *Edinburgh Festival.

Amateur theatre in England and Wales is fostered by the British Theatre Association (originally the British Drama League; founded 1919), which runs an annual festival with awards for the best amateur group and best new one-act play; and by the National Operatic and Dramatic Association (founded 1899). In Scotland it is overseen by the Scottish Community Drama Association, which runs its own festival. Scotland has several Little Theatre groups, which concentrate on three-act plays, of which the Traverse Theatre Club is probably the best known.

Amnesty International An independent voluntary worldwide movement dedicated to the release of prisoners of conscience, the fight against torture, and the abolition of the death penalty. Amnesty International, which began in 1961 as the result of a newspaper article by Peter Benenson, a British lawyer, is the world's largest international voluntary organization dealing with human rights. Awarded the Nobel Peace Prize in 1977 and the United Nations Human Rights Prize in 1978, Amnesty works for the release of men and women detained anywhere in the world for their "beliefs, colour, sex, ethnic origin, language, or religion who have neither used nor advocated violence". It has over 350,000 supporters in more than 150 countries and territories, national sections in some 40 countries, 3000 local groups in Africa, Asia, Europe, the Americas, and the Middle East, and maintains formal relations with the United Nations (ECOSOC), UNESCO, the Council of Europe, the Organization of American States, and the Organization of African Unity.

Anglican Communion The 28 autonomous provinces of the Anglican denomination throughout the world that are in communion with and recognize the authority of the *Archbishop of Canterbury. The Communion includes four British branches: the *Church of England, the *Church in Wales, the *Scottish Episcopal Church, and the *Church of Ireland. The Communion developed its links overseas in the 19th and 20th centuries as first bishoprics and then archiepiscopates of the Anglican Church were established throughout the British Empire. Initially under the control of the see of Canterbury, the main sees were in time granted their independence. The principal assembly of the Anglican Communion is the *Lambeth Conference, held every ten years and presided over by the Archbishop of Canterbury. The Anglican Consultative Council, instituted in 1968, is an assembly of bishops, clergy, and lay persons that meets every two or three years. The first such Council was held in 1971.

Anglo-Catholicism A movement within the Anglican Church that emphasizes its historical links with Roman Catholicism. It places a high value on the sacraments, the priestly office, and the apostolic succession in the episcopate as well as seeking re-union with Rome. It is distinguished from the High Church by its readiness to accept that the Roman Catholic Church is the true Catholic Church, whereas the High Church regards the Church of England as the only true bearer of Catholicism. Anglo-Catholicism is essentially a product of the 19th century, when the increased prominence of Low Churchmen and dissenters led some High Churchmen to take a more favourable view of Rome. Following the failure of the *Oxford Movement to reassert High Church dominance, Anglo-Catholicism became an influential attitude in the Church of England, which it still

remains, both at home and in other Anglican Churches.

Anglo-Saxon Britain Britain between the departure of the Romans (soon after 400 AD) and the Norman conquest (1066). The chronology of the settlement of England by the Angles, Saxons, and Jutes from northern Germany and Denmark is uncertain. Large-scale migrations appear to have begun around 450, and by 650 most of England had been settled so densely that it became the only one of the former Roman provinces to acquire a Germanic language (*see* English language). It is not certain what happened to the indigenous population: many, particularly those owning land, must have retreated to the Celtic. kingdoms in Wales, Scotland, and Cornwall, or to Brittany; others were absorbed into Anglo-Saxon society as slaves or semi-servile peasants; others conceivably died in the invasions, as it is reasonably clear that England's population shrank drastically in this period. Petty kingdoms developed (*see* map): Northumbria, *Mercia, and East Anglia were mainly inhabited by Angles; Essex, Sussex, and *Wessex by Saxons; while the Jutes settled in Kent and the Isle of Wight. These kingdoms fought for supremacy, with particularly successful kings being acknowledged as *bretwalda*, or "over-king". Northumbria was dominant in the 7th century and Mercia in the 8th, especially under Offa (r. 757–96), who conquered southeast England and regarded himself as the equal of his Frankish contemporary, Charlemagne. He was the first king to call himself "King of the English" (the name "England" did not emerge until the end of the 10th century). Wessex was briefly dominant in the early 9th century, before the Anglo-Saxon kingdoms were almost overcome by the **Viking invasions**. These began as raids from Denmark and Norway in the 790s but soon developed into another migration. By 878 the Vikings held most of England north of the River Thames; but in that year Alfred the Great of Wessex (r. 871–99) defeated them at Edington and halted their advance. In 886 a treaty between Alfred and the Danish leader Guthrum defined the limits of Viking control, the "Danelaw". The Anglo-Saxon resurgence continued, and in 926 all England south of the

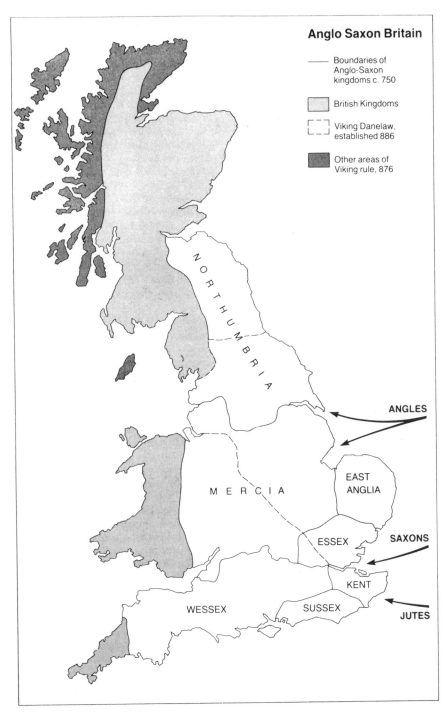

Anglo Saxon Britain

—— Boundaries of
Anglo-Saxon
kingdoms c. 750

British Kingdoms

Viking Danelaw,
established 886

Other areas of
Viking rule, 876

NORTHUMBRIA

ANGLES

EAST
ANGLIA

MERCIA

ESSEX

SAXONS

KENT

WESSEX

SUSSEX

JUTES

River Tees was united under Athelstan of Wessex (r. 924–40). The last Viking king of York, Eric Bloodaxe, died in 954. The Anglo-Saxon monarchy reached its height under Edgar (r. 959–75): contemporaries saw his reign as a peaceful period, and there were no challenges to his supremacy. At his coronation (973), his overlordship was acknowledged by eight "British kings", presumably Celtic tribal chiefs. However, renewed Viking attacks, conducted now by Swein Forkbeard, king of Denmark, with a highly-trained army, proved too much for Ethelred the Unready (r. 978–1016), who, as his nickname (derived from *unraed*, "no counsel") suggests, was a weak leader. In 1016 England was conquered by Swein's son Canute, who ruled a Scandinavian empire of Denmark, Norway, and England from 1019 until 1035. His sons failed to maintain his conquests, and the Wessex dynasty was restored with Edward the Confessor (r. 1042–66), son of Ethelred. After his death the succession was disputed between Harold II (1066) and William, Duke of Normandy, a dispute that led to the Norman conquest (*see* Norman Britain), the last successful invasion of Britain.

The instability seems not to have impoverished the land, nor did it impair the emergence in the 10th and 11th centuries of the strongest monarchy in Christian western Europe (*see* monarchy). The Danegeld, a tax imposed several times under Ethelred to buy off the Vikings, illustrates both points: no other kingdom had the authority or administrative capacity to levy a national tax; and it increased Britain's attractions to the Danes, confirming its reputation in Europe as a comparatively wealthy country. This tax was maintained and elaborated in the 11th century, being collected annually between 1012 and 1051. The Crown's authority was administered through the system of shires, which stabilized under Edgar into the form they retained until 1974. Under Ethelred the *sheriff emerged as the king's chief executive agent in each county, conducting his business through the county court. Each shire was further divided into hundreds, which had their own courts for purely local affairs. Hundreds may have existed in some places from as early as the 7th

century. These institutions survived the Norman conquest virtually unscathed, and formed the basis of future local administration. .

Culturally, the Anglo-Saxon heyday was in 7th- and 8th-century Northumbria. St Bede (c. 673–735), known as the Venerable Bede, is now remembered for his *Ecclesiastical History of the English People*, completed in 731, but in his own day his reputation embraced theology, grammar, saints' lives, and chronology. He was one of the greatest scholars England has ever produced. This tradition of learning reached its climax with the Northumbrian cleric Alcuin of York (735–804), who became master of Charlemagne's palace school at Aachen and played a significant part in the Carolingian renaissance. In the latter half of the 9th century Alfred the Great promoted the translation of Latin books into English so they could be more widely read and appreciated, and probably inaugurated the *Anglo-Saxon Chronicle* (891–1154), a record of events that forms an important historical source.

A lasting consequence of the invasions was a variety of local custom and law: Danish in the area of the Danelaw and Anglo-Saxon in the south and west, though with differences between Wessex and Mercia. The Norman conquest added a French element, and these differences persisted until the development of the *common law. Some variations endured into the Middle Ages: the laws of partible inheritance (i.e. division of estates between all sons) long observed in Kent have often been said to be of Jutish origin. Differences in local *dialects and *place names can also be traced back to these origins.

The Celtic areas remained largely separate from the Anglo-Saxon areas; indeed, the word "Welsh" was Anglo-Saxon for a foreigner or slave. The Welsh kingdoms of Dyfed, Powys, Gwent, and Gwynedd emerged in the 6th century. From the 9th century Gwynedd expanded to absorb them all except Dyfed. Cornwall held out against Wessex until 838. Scotland was divided among the Picts in the north and east; the Scots, who came from Ireland in the 6th century, in the west; and the Roman-influenced Britons in Strathclyde in the southwest. In the 9th century, the Vikings occupied the Hebrides and, less successfully, the western and northern mainland. The first step towards unification occurred around 843, when Kenneth MacAlpin, king of the Scots, gained the Pictish throne. A united Scotland emerged under Malcolm II (r. 1005–34). The organization of all the Celtic kingdoms, however, was tribal, and they lacked the centralized institutions developing in England. Macbeth, for example, king of Scotland 1040–57, was little more than a tribal chief and war leader.

The most significant British influence on the Anglo-Saxons was the ascetic and monastic Celtic form of Christianity (see Iona; Holy Island), which penetrated Scotland and England from Ireland in the 7th century and was largely responsible for the conversion of the Anglo-Saxons (see Church of England). Though the Roman Church (introduced by St Augustine into Kent in 597) asserted its authority, securing the rejection of some Celtic practices at the Synod of Whitby (664), the Celtic Church left its mark, particularly in the peculiarly Anglo-Saxon emphasis on monasticism.

The Anglo-Saxon period saw the emergence of a number of enduring features of Britain: many towns developed from the *burhs*, or strongholds, established by Alfred the Great and Edward the Elder (r. 899–924) to resist the Vikings, some on Roman sites (e.g. Winchester and Exeter) and some not (e.g. Oxford and Tamworth). The coinage used until decimalization in 1971 originated under Offa, who issued the first pennies (see sterling).

Antonine Wall A fortified wall built in 140–42 AD in Scotland under the Roman emperor Antoninus Pius (r. 138–61), relatively little of which remains today. It was designed to protect the newly extended frontier of the Roman province of Britannia with ancient Caledonia that had been established after the victorious campaign of Lollius Urbicus against the tribes of what is now Lowland Scotland. The wall ran for 59 kilometres (37 miles) from the Firth of Forth to the Firth of Clyde. The Antonine Wall was not as formidable as *Hadrian's Wall. Just over 3 metres (10 feet) high and constructed of cut turves on a stone foundation 4.5 metres (15 feet) thick, it was

protected by 19 small forts at intervals of two Roman miles (about 2200 metres, 2406 yards). A timber walkway ran along the top. There is evidence that Antoninus Pius wished to keep construction costs down; although the wall's chief purpose was to prevent restless northern tribesmen, whom he had deported to the south, from returning to their homelands, the wall also had an important symbolic value in marking where Roman control began and ended. During the principate of Commodus (r. 180–92) it was easily overrun in a revolt; and after the north had been pacified, the Romans abandoned it and retreated to Hadrian's Wall.

Stretches of the wall can still be seen at Bonnybridge and (most impressively) at Rough Castle fort; some stone foundations exist at New Kilpatrick. By far the most impressive part of the wall was the ditch to the north that was 14 metres (46 feet) wide in places and over 3 metres (10 feet) deep. Much of this can still be seen, particularly at Watling Lodge, west of Falkirk. Fort bath-houses have been found at Bearsden and Cramond, west of Edinburgh.

Archbishop of Canterbury The senior prelate and head of the Church of England, known as the "Primate of All England". Apart from administering his province of Canterbury, he is head of the worldwide fellowship of Anglican Churches, known as the *Anglican Communion, and also plays a major role in state ceremonies, crowning the sovereign and acting as the sovereign's spiritual adviser. He takes precedence after the royal princes but before the Lord Chancellor, is styled "Most Reverend and Right Honourable", and signs himself "Cantuar", from the Latin *Cantuariensis*, meaning "of Canterbury", after his Christian name. The present incumbent and 102nd Archbishop is Robert Runcie, installed in 1980.

His seat was established at Canterbury by Augustine, the first Archbishop, following his arrival from Rome in 596 AD, but the country remained under considerable Celtic influence until the installation of Archbishop Theodore in 668. He established new bishoprics and was the first really effective primate at Canterbury. Consequent rivalry with the *Archbishops of

ARCHBISHOP OF CANTERBURY *The earliest surviving representation of the murder of Thomas Becket, from a manuscript c. 1190–1200. It shows the knights of the royal household incited by Henry II's rage, murdering the Archbishop at the altar of Canterbury cathedral.*

York intensified under Archbishop Lanfranc (c. 1010–89), who attempted to assert Canterbury's authority over the northern province, and under his successor, Anselm (c. 1033–1109). Precedence and the title "Primate of All England" (as opposed to "Primate of England", the style enjoyed by the Archbishops of York) was finally conferred on Canterbury by Pope Innocent VI (1352–62). In the Middle Ages, successive Archbishops had to face the conflict of being papal representatives with the demands made on them by the Crown. This conflict was most intense between Henry II and **Thomas Becket** (c. 1118–70). Installed as Archbishop in 1162, Becket staunchly defended the rights of the Church against the wishes of the king, his former patron and friend. Becket took refuge in France, and on his return was murdered in his own cathedral by four knights, who believed they were acting according to Henry's wishes, on 29 December 1170. He was canonized in 1173 and his tomb was one of the major shrines of Europe until its destruction by Henry VIII in 1538.

A decisive point came in the 1530s under Archbishop Thomas Cranmer (1489–1556), who acquiesced with Henry VIII's breach with Rome (*see* Reformation) and the imposition of royal authority over the Church. In return, Henry bestowed upon the senior prelate certain privileges, including the right to confer so-called "Lambeth degrees" in divinity, and also in the arts, law, medicine, and music, a right which the Archbishop still has. Cranmer was a principal architect of the Anglican Church's liturgy, including the Prayer Books of 1549 and 1552. He was burnt as a heretic by Mary Tudor. Also executed was one of his more notable successors, William Laud (1573–1645), appointed Archbishop of Canterbury in 1633 under Charles I; it was his implacable hostility to Puritanism that sealed his fate at the hands of the Long Parliament (*see* Civil War, English). Subsequently, a greater breadth of opinion was tolerated within the Church. Following the suppression of Convocation by George I, the Archbishops were virtually deprived of any role in the state's political affairs.

Archbishop of Westminster   *See* Roman Catholic Church in UK.

Archbishop of York   The prelate who heads the smaller of the two provinces of the Church of England and is second only to the *Archbishop of Canterbury in the Church's hierarchy. York was originally a centre of the Celtic Church until the papal missionary Paulinus (d. 644) was installed as bishop in 625 AD. However, he was forced south in 633 and the Celtic influence briefly reasserted itself until the see was restored in 664 under Bishop Wilfrid (634–709), who introduced the Roman liturgy to much of the province. Archiepiscopal status was not attained until 735, under Egbert (d. 766), who also founded the cathedral school. The long-standing struggle for precedence with Canterbury was decided in favour of the southern province by Pope Innocent VI (1352–62), who gave the inferior title "Primate of England" to York.

The Archbishop is styled the "Most Reverend and Right Honourable" and signs himself "Ebor" (an abbreviation of *Eboracum*, the Latin name for York) after his Christian name. The present and 95th incumbent is John Habgood, installed in 1983.

areas of outstanding natural beauty Areas of special scenic beauty, designated as such by the *Countryside Commission. The Gower peninsula in South Wales was the first area to be so designated, in 1956, and there are now over 30 such areas. Special attention is given to planning control, public access, and general conservation measures, and some areas provide information services and wardens for the benefit of visitors. One of the chief problems facing such regions is the strain that tourism imposes on them, and the Countryside Commission sponsors various research projects to investigate this, often in conjunction with local authorities, nature trusts, farming organizations, and other interested bodies.

army In Anglo-Saxon times Britain's defence lay in the hands of a system of local militia (the *fyrd*) and the monarch's personal body-guard. However, after the Norman conquest, armies were raised through the feudal system in which vassals owed military service to their lords. Later results of this system were the private forces of retainers, which were used in the *Wars of the Roses, and the locally organized "trained bands", which were used by Oliver Cromwell as the nucleus of his red-coated New Model Army (1644). This developed into England's first professional armed force, which included infantry, cavalry, and artillery. In 1661 the New Model Army became the national army; it came under parliamentary control in 1689 as a result of the Mutiny Act, which laid down punishments for desertion. However, a healthy distrust of a standing army in peacetime (an Act of Parliament still has to be passed annually to approve it) ensured that the army remained small and harshly disciplined throughout the 18th century; when necessary, mercenaries were used to augment it in campaigns abroad, while home defence remained in the hands of local militia. Reorganized in the Napoleonic Wars, the regular army, which Wellington called "the scum of the earth", scored notable victories over the French. In the peace that followed, however, the army again declined, its weaknesses becoming public in the Crimean War, especially at Balaclava (1854). As a result of public anxiety many reforms were instigated in the last 30 years of the 19th century, inspired largely by Edward Cardwell and R. B. Haldane. These reforms included a new regimental structure, the abolition of purchased commissions, and the appointment of a general staff. From about 1900, khaki replaced the red coats throughout the army as a result of experience using it as camouflage in India. By 1914 there were 750,000 men in Lord Kitchener's army, from which the *British Expeditionary Force was drawn; four years later this figure had reached 5,585,000, after Britain had adopted conscription (in 1916; the last European country to do so). In World War II the emphasis switched from massive static armies and trench warfare to mobile tank warfare and the use of technologically advanced weaponry.

Conscription (reimposed in May 1939) ended in 1960; since then, the Army has consisted entirely of regular troops trained to act in coordination with both sea and air forces and supported by highly trained reserve (*see* reserve forces). The modern Army assists in the defence of the UK and fulfils roles with NATO, maintaining the *British Army of the Rhine (BAOR) and several overseas garrisons; it has seen active service in Korea, Cyprus, Northern Ireland, and the Falkland Islands. The British Army now consists of the cavalry, the Royal Armoured Corps, the artillery, the engineers, the infantry, and the signals, as well as such auxiliary services as the Royal Army Medical Corps and the Intelligence Corps. Since 1964 it has been administered by the Army Council of the Ministy of Defence. The current strength is 162,000 volunteers. *See also* women's services; infantry regiments; cavalry; Household Division.

Arthurian legend A collection of tales surrounding the legendary King Arthur, his knights of the Round Table, and their quest for the Holy Grail. In the earliest sources, such as Nennius' *Historia Britonum*, a British king named Arthur led the fight against the invading Saxons (*see* Roman Britain); some historians now believe that Arthur was indeed a 6th-century British lord who adopted Roman cavalry techniques and defeated the Saxons at the battle of Badon (?518 AD), the location of which is unknown. This historical figure was subsequently woven into the romantic history, *Historia Regum Britanniae*, written in Latin by the 12th-century historian Geoffrey of Monmouth, who associated the magician Merlin with Arthur and included pre-Christian mythical elements of ancient Welsh romances in which Arthur had appeared (*see Mabinogion*). The Norman writer Robert Wace of Jersey (c. 1100–75) used the *Historia* as a source for his Anglo-French *Geste des Bretons* (c. 1154) and introduced the Round Table into the legend. The first version written in English was a translation of Wace's poem by the 12th-century English priest Layamon, who added the now familiar themes of chivalry. Sir Thomas Malory's *Morte d'Arthur*, written in the mid-15th century, took as its sources Celtic, French, and English versions and blended them into a romance that has little historical evidence to support it. Many characters, notably Merlin, Arthur's wife Guinevere, and his half-sister Morgan le Fay, appear to have been inspired by figures from

ARTHURIAN LEGEND The Lady of the Lake telleth Arthur of the sword Excalibur. *A late-19th-century illustration for Sir Thomas Malory's* Le Morte d'Arthur *by Aubrey Beardsley.*

ancient Celtic mythology and other folk tales; the concept of Avalon, the island paradise to which King Arthur is taken at his death, may also have its source in Celtic literature.

According to legend, Arthur was the son of the King of All England, Uther Pendragon, and Igraine (wife of the Duke of Tintagel), who was bewitched by Merlin into believing that it was Tintagel rather than Pendragon who shared her bed on the night Arthur was conceived. Some years after his father's death the young Arthur established his right to the throne and ultimately set up his court at Camelot. On his marriage to Guinevere he was presented with the Round Table, which had originally been in the possession of King

15

Uther: the shape of the table ensured that none of those who sat round it would have precedence over any other. Accompanied by his band of knights and armed with his magic sword Excalibur, Arthur went on to win glorious victories at home and abroad. Returning from an expedition to France, he learnt that his son Mordred (the product of an incestuous relationship with Morgan le Fay), whom he had appointed to act as regent in his absence, had usurped his throne and raised a rebellion against him; at the ensuing battle Arthur was mortally wounded, and he was carried off to the island of Avalon.

Other elements of the legend deal with the adventures of the individual knights, notably Lancelot, Gawain, and Tristram; the actions of Merlin and the sinister Morgan le Fay; the adulterous affair between Sir Lancelot and Guinevere; and the quest for the Holy Grail, the chalice used at the Last Supper, supposedly filled with the dying Christ's blood and brought to England by *Joseph of Arimathea. Many of these themes were adopted from French romances. In the various retellings of the last, different knights are involved in the quest; in Malory's *Morte d'Arthur* it is Sir Galahad who finally achieves the Grail.

A number of towns and cities of southern England and Wales have become associated with the Arthurian tradition. Tintagel castle in Cornwall is alleged to be Arthur's birthplace and the Roman town of Caerleon in South Wales the site of his early court. The location of Camelot is disputed, the prehistoric hill fort of Cadbury castle in Somerset and the Hampshire city of Winchester being the two most likely contenders. Recent excavations at Cadbury castle indicate that it was probably occupied by a powerful leader in the 6th century. However, in the Great Hall at Winchester hangs an elaborately painted 14th-century round table, evidence that Winchester has been associated with Arthurian legend for many hundreds of years. Glastonbury in Somerset is generally identified with the island of Avalon and is alleged to be Arthur's burial place: in the late 12th century a group of monks claimed to have found Arthur's and Guinevere's remains in a grave at Glastonbury Abbey. The town has also been associated with other episodes in the legend and with the resting place of the Holy Grail.

Arts and Crafts movement An aesthetic and social movement of the late 19th century that arose from a dissatisfaction with the products of industrialism on account of their frequent poor quality and design. The movement's main proponents were the influential art critic John Ruskin (1819–1900) and the artist William Morris (1834–96); its activities centred around the firm of Morris & Co., founded in 1861 to produce handmade textiles, wallpapers, stained glass, and furniture. Advocating "truth to materials", the movement looked to medieval art for its ideal (*see also* Pre-Raphaelite Brotherhood) and to the social organization of medieval artists and craftsmen in guilds. Its aim was to combine art with old-fashioned craftsmanship in a bid to improve on the mass-produced imitations of artefacts of the pre-industrial era. The cost of implementing such nostalgic ideals in a machine age, however, was to prove prohibitive. Under Morris's influence, C. R. Ashbee, a leading artist, designer, and metal worker, founded the Guild and School of Arts and Crafts in 1888. The Century Guild for Craftsmen (1882) and the Arts and Crafts Exhibition Society (1888) were further offshoots of the movement. Morris's belief that art matters only "if all can share it" drew him to a form of socialism based on a utopian vision of an equal society, views that continued to influence the Labour movement until World War I. The curvilinear patterns favoured by the Arts and Crafts movement became typical of the emerging Art Nouveau style (c. 1890–1910).

Arts Council of Great Britain A nonpolitical body formed in 1945 to develop knowledge and practice of the arts and "to increase the accessibility of the fine arts to the public", by giving financial aid to groups in all fields of art. Its origins lie in the Council for the Encouragement of Music and the Arts, founded privately in 1939 to support the arts under wartime conditions. In 1940 the government began to contribute to the fund and the Board of Education took over the appointment of the CEMA committee. In 1945,

HERE BEGINNETH THE TALES OF CANTER-
BURY AND FIRST THE PROLOGUE THEREOF

The tendre croppes, and the yonge sonne
hath in the Ram his halfe cours yronne,
And smale foweles maken melodye,
That slepen al the nyght with open eye,
So priketh hem nature in hir corages:
Thanne longen folk to goon on pilgrimages,
And palmeres for to seken straunge strondes,
To ferne halwes, kowthe in sondry londes;
And specially, from every shires ende
Of Engelond, to Caunterbury they wende,
The hooly blisful martir for to seke,
That hem hath holpen whan that they were
seeke.

IFIL that in that seson on a day,
In Southwerk at the Tabard as
I lay,
Redy to wenden on my pilgrym-
age
To Caunterbury with ful devout
corage,

THAT Aprille with his shoures soote
The droghte of March hath perced to the roote,
And bathed every veyne in swich licour,
Of which vertu engendred is the flour;
Whan Zephirus eek with his swete breeth
Inspired hath in every holt and heeth

At nyght were come into that hostelrye
Wel nyne and twenty in a compaignye,
Of sondry folk, by aventure yfalle
In felaweshipe, and pilgrimes were they alle,
That toward Caunterbury wolden ryde.

ARTS AND CRAFTS MOVEMENT *A page from the Kelmscott* Chaucer, 1896, designed by William Morris *and Edward Burne-Jones. The Kelmscott Press, founded by Morris, produced 52 titles from 1891–98, of which the* Chaucer *is the most highly decorated. Morris favoured the idealized standards set by the medieval craft guilds, and his theory is reflected in the hand-printing with woodblocks, using very black ink on rough-textured hand-made paper, making the craftsmanship an integral part of the book.*

with Lord Keynes as chairman, the CEMA gained its *royal charter and became known as the Arts Council of Great Britain. The Chancellor of the Exchequer appoints the chairman and the members of the executive board, whose offices are voluntary and carry no salary; members of the Council act as chairmen to panels of experts in music, drama, the visual arts, and poetry, and advise the Council on the annual administration of grants in those fields, from money provided by the Treasury. Until 1985 the Council undertook to meet the losses of those groups it supported, but the companies themselves are now largely responsible for them. This, and the effective cut in the amount of money granted to the Council have brought protests from spokesmen for the arts and dissension within the Council itself. Its new policy is also intended to correct a bias towards London by assisting regional arts associations, theatres, and orchestras.

Arundel castle The ancestral home of the Dukes of Norfolk. Arundel castle stands on a chalk spur overlooking the River Arun, in West Sussex. The original Norman castle was begun in 1067 by Roger Montgomery, Earl of Shrewsbury, to command the strategic Arun valley. The old circular shell keep (c. 1135)

and the gatehouse with its two barbican towers, dating from 1295, remain, albeit much restored. Much of the castle was destroyed in the *Civil War, when Cromwell's troops bombarded it from the tower of the neighbouring St Nicholas's church in an attempt to subdue the garrison of the staunchly royalist Howard family. The 11th Duke lavished some £600,000 on a gothic reconstruction, much of which was dismantled and replaced by the 15th Duke between c. 1875 and 1903, again in a pseudomedieval style. He also built Arundel's delightful private chapel, with its stained glass by John Hardman Powell. The library houses a major collection of books and documents on Roman Catholicism, while in the east drawing room are mementos of Mary, Queen of Scots, including her prayerbook and the rosary carried by her at her execution in 1587. The nearby Fitzalan chapel occupies the chancel of the original parish church, built in 1380; it can only be entered from the castle grounds. The castle and its surrounding park are open to visitors.

Ascot races Horse racing at Ascot, near Windsor in Berkshire. The first races were initiated by Queen Anne in 1711. The most celebrated meeting is Royal Ascot, a four-day

ARUNDEL CASTLE *In West Sussex, home of the Dukes of Norfolk for over 400 years.*

event that takes place in June each year and is attended by the Queen and other members of the royal family. They open the meeting by arriving at the racecourse in splendid open horsedrawn coaches from Windsor castle, having travelled down the Royal Mile (sometimes in totally unsuitable weather). Royal Ascot enjoys a higher social standing than any other horse racing event and those who are permitted to enter the royal enclosure wear formal dress (grey top hats and tail coats for men, and elegant summer dresses and hats for women).

The most important race of the royal meeting is the Ascot Gold Cup run over 4 kilometres (2.5 miles), first run in 1807. However, the most valuable race is the King George VI and Queen Elizabeth Diamond Stakes, founded in 1951, which takes place in late July each year. The race, which is run over 2.4 kilometres (1.5 miles), imposes no age limit on the horses and thus frequently brings together the *Derby and other *Classics winners from two or more seasons. The winner can justifiably be considered the champion racehorse of the season.

Ashes, the The name of the trophy for which the *cricket teams of England and Australia compete. The first international (or test) match between the two countries took place at the Melbourne Cricket Ground, Australia, in March 1877. In September 1880 the Australian touring team played their first test match in England at the Kennington *Oval in south London. It was at the same ground that the story of the Ashes began in August 1882 when the Australians won a resounding victory. The *Sporting Times* printed the following mock obituary: "In affectionate remembrance of English Cricket, which died at The Oval on 29th August, 1882. Deeply lamented by a large circle of sorrowing friends and acquaintances. R.I.P. The body will be cremated and the Ashes taken to Australia."

Later in 1882 the Hon. Ivo Bligh led an English team to Australia on what he described as "a crusade to regain the Ashes". His mission was successful and after victory in the series was secured in the third test at Sydney Cricket Ground, a group of ladies burnt a bail and presented Bligh with the ashes in a small urn. That urn rests permanently at *Lord's Cricket Ground, even when Australia has actually won the series. The rivalry for the Ashes has produced many great matches and wonderful individual performances.

Ashmolean Museum A museum in Oxford, belonging to the university. Opened in 1683, it was the first public museum in Britain. Its origins lie in the provision made by Sir Thomas Bodley in 1602 for a gallery of antiquities as part of the *Bodleian Library. The Ashmolean's exhibits are based on the collection of the antiquary Elias Ashmole (1617–92), which he donated to Oxford University in 1675 and which was housed in a building designed by Thomas Wood, now used as the Oxford Museum of the History of Science. The present neoclassical building, designed by Charles Robert Cockerell, dates from 1845. The Ashmolean contains many of the finds made by the archaeologist Sir Arthur Evans (1851–1941) at Knossos, and its paintings include *Pre-Raphaelite works, Dutch genre paintings, and Paolo Uccello's *Hunt*. It also holds distinguished collections of prints, Greek vases and coins, and an unmatched collection of 17th-century Huguenot silver.

assizes Courts held before 1972 by judges of the *High Court of Justice and others of legal standing having commissions from the Crown to travel through the country on circuits and try cases. By royal commission they were authorized to deal with all serious criminal offences, the gravest of these being exclusively within their jurisdiction and the rest triable either by them or by *quarter sessions; and under a separate commission they were authorized to decide civil actions. Courts of assize were abolished by the Courts Act 1971, which established the *Crown Court to exercise their criminal jurisdiction, and transferred their civil jurisdiction to the High Court itself.

Astronomer Royal An honorary appointment made by the sovereign on the advice of the Prime Minister, who in turn is advised by the Science and Engineering Research Council. Although the post of Astronomer Royal is now separate from the directorship of the Royal Observatory (at which institution the incumbent was located until 1971), its holder is still able to represent British astronomy through the prestige of the office. The first Astronomer Royal was John Flamsteed who was appointed in 1675, the year in which the Royal Observatory was established at Greenwich, and served until his death in 1719. Edmund Halley, after whom the comet is named, served as Astronomer Royal, 1720–42. The present incumbent is the noted radio astronomer Professor Sir F. Graham Smith, appointed in 1982.

attainder A statutory process in which those condemned were put to death, and suffered "corruption of blood", by which the heirs of the person attainted were disinherited, particularly of any title held by the attainted person. Parliament acted as both judge and jury in such cases. The process was frequently used during the *Wars of the Roses and by the Tudor and Stuart monarchs. The last instance of attainder was that against Lord Edward FitzGerald in 1798 for his part in the Irish uprising of that year. Nearly all aspects of the attainder process were abolished in the 19th century.

attendance centre A place that an offender under 21 who, but for his age, would be liable to imprisonment, may be ordered by the court to attend for supervision, instruction, or occupation of a suitable nature. The court must be of the opinion that a custodial sentence is not called for, and that other penalties, such as a fine, would not be adequate. Attendance is for periods up to 3 hours at a time, to a maximum of 24 hours if the offender is under 17, and 36 hours otherwise.

Attorney General The chief law officer of the Crown for England and Wales. A political appointment, the Attorney General is a barrister and member of the House of Commons, who becomes a government minister (though not usually of Cabinet rank) and is customarily knighted and made a Privy Councillor. He has a variety of functions, both in and out of Parliament. He advises the government on important questions of law, answers questions of law in the House of Commons and steers complex government legislation of a legal character through the House. He is leader of the English *Bar, and, though not allowed to engage in private practice since 1895, appears

for the Crown in major civil and criminal cases. His consent is needed for certain prosecutions (e.g. for offences against the *Official Secrets Acts). He also acts on behalf of the public in a number of respects (e.g. at major tribunals of inquiry, and in the enforcement of public charitable trusts). He is assisted by the *Solicitor General. Since 1972, he has taken over the functions of the Attorney General for Northern Ireland. His counterpart in Scotland (though their functions do not correspond exactly) is the *Lord Advocate. See also Director of Public Prosecutions.

Automobile Association See AA.

Avebury An ancient monument in Wiltshire, in the south of England, consisting of a number of *stone circles, one within another, that constitutes one of the largest prehistoric monuments in Britain. The nucleus of the present-day village of Avebury lies within the site. The henge (see Stonehenge) was probably constructed in the early Bronze Age (about 1800 BC) under the influence of immigrants from Northern Europe, known today as the Beaker Folk (see prehistoric Britain). It covers some 11.5 hectares (28.5 acres) and consists of a huge circular bank and ditch, 12 metres (11 yards) deep and 9 metres (8 yards) wide, inside which are the remains of the largest stone circle known in Europe. Within this great circle of 100 stones stand two smaller circles, each with about 30 stones and a diameter of some 98 metres (89 yards). At the centre of one originally stood a tall stone surrounded by low boulders, while within the other was a U-shaped stone construction. There is also evidence of a third small circle within the large one.

Avebury Henge was built with rough sandstone boulders taken from the adjacent chalk downs. Its purpose is unknown. The interior of the henge was connected by the mile-long Kennet Avenue to a temple on a hill, known as the "Sanctuary", which was destroyed in the 18th century. The avenue was about 18 metres (16 yards) wide and was formed of pairs of stones that stood 25 metres (23 yards) apart. Once derelict, it has now been partially restored.

Avebury Henge was one of several sites of religious and political significance that centred on Salisbury Plain. Near it are Silbury Hill, the largest manmade prehistoric mound in Europe, the great West Kennet Long Barrow, and Windmill Hill, a Neolithic monument that dates back to about 2500 BC. The monument, the village of Avebury, and a museum on the site are now administered by the *National Trust.

B

badger-baiting A barbarous sport practised for many centuries in England, in which a badger was attacked by a terrier dog. The badger was shut in a box with the top covered by wire netting. A wooden tunnel some three metres (ten feet) long was attached to the side of the box. The terrier was released at the far end of the tunnel and on meeting the two animals fastened jaws, with the dog trying to draw the badger down the tunnel. Badgers are fierce fighters and the struggle was usually prolonged and the outcome uncertain. This gave great scope for betting, the main object behind the sport. The pastime was outlawed in about 1850; one of the last recorded cases was in 1897 at Preston, Lancashire. It is possible that similar practices still continue undetected in remote areas.

Badminton Badminton House, the ancestral seat of the Dukes of Beaufort. The house is a fine Palladian mansion built for the 1st Duke in 1682 and remodelled by William Kent around 1740. The 18th-century church in the grounds contains the family tombs. The estate of 6070 hectares (15,000 acres) is the territory for the foxhounds and riders of the famous Beaufort hunt and also the venue for the three-day Badminton horse trials, which have been held in April each year since 1949. This is one of the country's leading equestrian events and is often attended by members of the royal family.

In the 19th century, Badminton gave its name to a refreshing summer drink of claret, sugar, and soda water – the Badminton cup! Perhaps better known is the modern indoor court game of badminton, which is said to have orginated at Badminton House in the 1870s; it was probably derived from the ancient children's racket game of battledore and shuttlecock.

Ballet Rambert The oldest existing British ballet company, founded by the ballet teacher (Dame) Marie Rambert (1888–1982). The company emerged from the productions that she staged in 1926 at the Lyric Theatre in London. A season at the Mercury Theatre in Notting Hill, London, by her newly formed Ballet Club (1930) developed into regular Sunday matinées; the group subsequently became the first British ballet company and school. Alicia Markova was a member for four years. The Ballet Club was renamed the Ballet Rambert in 1935. The work of British choreographers has always predominated in the company's repertoire, though until 1966 it also performed the classics. Since then, after financial problems led to the company's reorganization and the appointment of choreographer Norman Morrice as associate director, a smaller company of 16–18 dancers has performed only ballets by contemporary choreographers, including Rudi van Dantzig (1933–) and Paul Taylor (1930–).

Balmoral A castle and estate of 9713 hectares (24,000 acres) located on upper Deeside, Grampian, privately owned by the royal family and used by them as a holiday home. The Balmoral estate dates from the 14th century but it was not until the 1830s that the tenant, Sir Robert Gordon, built the "pretty little castle in the old Scotch style" that caught Queen Victoria's eye. The royal family took over the tenancy when Sir Robert died and four years later, in 1852, Prince Albert bought it for £31,500. He engaged the Aberdeen architect William Smith (whose father John Smith had designed the existing castle) and together they completely rebuilt the castle on a larger scale, incorporating many of Albert's ideas.

Built from granite in the Scottish baronial style, the castle has a square tower 24 metres

BALMORAL CASTLE *In Grampian, Scotland.*

(80 feet) high. The gardens, which were laid out in the 1850s, contain many fine and rare pines and other trees and are regularly open to the public. While Albert's design for the castle has its detractors, for Queen Victoria it was "this dear paradise". The present royal family traditionally spend their summer holidays at Balmoral, from where they visit the *Highland Games held at nearby Braemar.

bank holiday Days on which banks in the United Kingdom are closed as provided for under the Bank Holidays Act 1871 and the 1875 supplementary Act. The term is now used more broadly to cover both public holidays and officially designated "bank holidays". England, Wales, Scotland, and Northern Ireland have bank holidays on New Year's Day, May Day (first Monday in May), the late spring bank holiday (last Monday in May), the late summer bank holiday (first Monday in August for Scotland and the last Monday in August for England, Wales, and Northern Ireland), and *Boxing Day, as well as holidays for the Christian festivals of Good Friday and Christmas Day. Easter Monday is a holiday in England, Wales, and Northern Ireland, while the day following New Year's Day is a bank holiday only in Scotland (*see* Hogmanay). St Patrick's Day (17 March) and the anniversary of the battle of the Boyne, 1690,

(12 July) are additional holidays in Northern Ireland. The Channel Islands have the same holidays as England, with the addition of *Liberation Day (9 May). When holidays designated by festivals or anniversaries fall on a Sunday, the Monday following becomes a holiday instead.

Bank of England The British central bank, incorporated in 1694 to formalize government borrowing, and to provide a properly regulated banking service. By the middle of the 18th century it was banker to most state departments, and was given the administration of the *national debt in 1751. In addition, it enjoyed a virtual monopoly of large-scale public banking from 1709 to 1826. With the subsequent growth of commercial banks (*see* banks), it retreated from general banking, consolidating its role as the nation's central bank (banker to the government and other banks, lender of last resort to the discount houses and supervisor of the monetary aspects of the economy). Its nationalization in 1946 brought it more closely under government control.

The Bank of England moved to its present site in Threadneedle Street in 1734, and the present building, designed by Sir John Soane, was begun in 1788. Its popular nickname "**The Old Lady of Threadneedle Street**" derives from a reference in Parliament by Richard Sheridan in 1797.

banks Institutions that provide financial services based on accepting deposits for safekeeping and making loans for interest. In Britain there are four main types of bank: the central bank (*see* Bank of England), commercial banks, savings banks, and merchant banks.

The lending of money for interest, although prohibited until 1545 and limited until 1854, has always been practised; but the regular acceptance of deposits for safekeeping was introduced in the 17th century by London goldsmiths. The first properly regulated bank was the Bank of England (founded 1694), which was virtually protected from competition by the introduction of a law in 1708 prohibiting any other bank from being set up with more than six partners. This did not, however, prevent many small provincial banks from being established. In Scotland, the Bank of Scotland was founded in 1695. A succession of failures among these led to the Bank Acts of 1826 and 1833, which opened up the market by permitting the establishment of joint-stock banks with any number of partners. A series of mergers led to the emergence in 1918 of the "Big Five" – Barclays (founded c. 1694), Lloyds (1765), Midland (1836), National Provincial (1833), and Westminster (1834). In 1968 the last two merged to form the National Westminster Bank. In recent years the facilities offered have expanded, especially into easy credit (using credit cards, first introduced by Barclays in 1966), mortgages, and insurance. This has brought competition from the building societies, which now offer some banking services, including cheque accounts paying a high interest rate, Saturday opening, and several other services that most commercial banks have failed to provide. Commercial banks are often called "clearing banks", although this term properly applies to members of the London Bankers' Clearing House, which includes all the major banks. The Post Office also provides banking services through the **National Girobank**, established in 1968. Originally it offered only a simple means of credit transfer, but personal loans and limited overdrafts were introduced in 1975 and legal obstacles to further expansion were removed in 1976.

Savings banks were founded to encourage thrift, by accepting small deposits into interest-bearing accounts. The largest is the **Trustee Savings Bank**, which originated in a non-profit making savings bank opened by the Rev. Dr Henry Duncan at Ruthwell, Dumfriesshire, in 1810. Savings banks were regulated by legislation of 1817 (1835 in Scotland), and obliged to invest in the *national debt, the government guaranteeing to pay their costs and interest. Recently, however, they have effectively been transformed into a single commercial bank, in which shares were issued in 1986. The other major savings bank is the National Savings Bank, founded as the Post Office Savings Bank in 1861. It is a government service, and its deposits count as part of the national debt.

Merchant banks originated among merchants who used their financial expertise and capital to offer specialized services to businesses. The most important of these is the provision of venture capital in return for a share in the equity of an enterprise. The services offered by merchant banks also include share management and dealing in gold and foreign currencies. Other types of institution, such as discount houses, specialize even further. The large commercial banks all have merchant banking departments.

Bannockburn, battle of (24 June 1314) A battle fought between English and Scottish armies that many Scots regard as "the greatest day in Scottish history". The conflict ended Edward II of England's hopes of uniting the four British nations and was the culminating victory in the campaign of Robert I of Scotland (Robert the Bruce) to rule an independent country. The arrival of an English army of about 20,000 men in Scotland was prompted by the siege of Stirling, by Robert's forces, which numbered only 10,000 men. The day before the battle was marked by a minor skirmish and a celebrated incident in which the commander of an English advance force, Sir Humphrey de Bohun, challenged Robert to single combat, only to have his skull split in two by the king's battle-axe. The following morning, the battle began with a charge by the

BATTLE OF BANNOCKBURN *With Stirling castle in the background, from a 15th-century manuscript.*

Scottish cavalry, which provoked a disastrous English counter-charge upon the superior defences of the Scottish position. The English horsemen were halted at a series of stake-lined pits dug in front of the Scottish ranks and were then easily dispatched by the Bruce's infantry. The English archers, their sights blocked by their own cavalry, were dispersed by the Scottish horsemen. A final charge by Robert's servants and retainers broke the English morale and precipitated a headlong flight, many drowning in the River Carse. Edward II himself fled to Dunbar and then by boat to Berwick. All the main features of the battlefield can still be seen and the site has become a focus of Scottish nationalism. A statue of Robert the Bruce was erected there in 1964.

Baptists Protestants who consider that the Christian revelation can only be received after the age of discretion (which they date variously) and who therefore reject baptism of infants. The present-day Baptist Church in Britain has evolved from two distinct origins: the Puritan separatist John Smythe (c. 1554–1612) established the first Baptist Church in Amsterdam in 1609; one of his followers, Thomas Helwys (c. 1550–c. 1616), returned to London to found the first congregation of General Baptists at Spitalfields. In 1633 a faction of the Calvinistic Separatist Church in London founded the Particular Baptists, who followed the Calvinist principle that only certain individuals are predestined for salvation. Many Baptists were persecuted as unorthodox Anglicans after 1660, among them the writer John Bunyan, but despite this, by the 18th century Baptist churches had been established in Wales, Ireland, and Scotland. The evangelical revival of the mid-18th century prompted some General Baptists to form the "New Connection" in 1770, while others turned to *Unitarianism. An offshoot of the Particular Baptists were the Strict Baptists, who allowed only their own members to the Communion table. They remain outside the main body of Baptists and have their own Strict Baptist Assembly. In 1812–13, the Particular Baptists formed the Baptist Union, with which the New Connection amalgamated in 1891.

The Baptist Unions of England, Wales, and Scotland now have a total of 2070 churches, 1490 pastors, and some 166,000 members. The Baptist Church is now well established in many other countries, particularly the USA. The Baptist World Alliance has its headquarters in Washington, DC.

Bar The collective name for counsel (see barrister) in the countries of the United Kingdom. The head of the Bar of England and Wales and the Bar of Northern Ireland is the Attorney General, and that of the Scottish Bar the Dean of Faculty (see Faculty of Advocates).

bara brith ("speckled bread") A type of rich fruit loaf traditionally made in Wales. Its ingredients include dried fruit and spices that have been soaked in cold tea before the eggs and flour are added and the cake is baked.

Barbican Centre for Arts and Conferences A complex in the Barbican development in the City of London. The architects Chamberlin, Powell, and Bon prepared the first plans for the redevelopment of the area in 1955, and the Barbican Centre was officially opened in 1982, by which time it had cost £153 million. It houses the largest exhibition gallery in London (1393 square metres, 15,000 square feet), three cinemas, a concert hall seating 2026 people, a wide "one-room" theatre seating 1166, and a studio space known as The Pit, seating 200, as well as a library and restaurants. Both the *London Symphony Orchestra and the *Royal Shakespeare Company are resident here.

bar billiards A variation of the game of *billiards, played mainly in public houses. For reasons of space, bar billiards is played on a table smaller than the traditional billard table and players use shorter cues. It would seem to be a derivative of a game described by Charles Cotton in *The Compleat Gamester* (1674), in which an ivory peg and an arch were placed on the table as obstacles. The aim of the game is to cause the balls to fall through holes in the table's surface and thus score the number of points allocated to each hole. Each time a player scores he has another shot, adding to his points each time and compiling a "break". He must avoid knocking over either of the two white pegs as that would cost him all the points of his break, or the black peg in which case he would lose his total score for the game. The time limit for a game is usually 15 minutes: the record score is believed to be 14,130, achieved by Mr Norman Day in 1974.

Bar Council *See* Senate of the Inns of Court and the Bar.

bard A Celtic minstrel-poet in Wales, Scotland, or Ireland after the Roman conquest. Bards sang to the harp from a store of traditional tales to which they themselves constantly added. In some regions they became a powerful hereditary order with religious and political significance; but their traditions and organization survived only in Wales (despite the tradition publicized by Thomas Gray that maintains that after Edward I's suppression of the Welsh rebellion, the king ordered all captured bards to be killed). Bardic assemblies took place as late as the 18th century; the modern *eisteddfod, however, dates from the 19th century.

It should be noted that "the Bard", thus capitalized, refers almost invariably to Shakespeare.

Barnardo's (Homes), Dr A charity concerned with the care of orphaned and needy children, supported by voluntary contributions. The Dublin-born physician Thomas John Barnardo (1845–1905) opened his first home for destitute boys in Stepney Causeway, London, in 1870 as an extension of his work among slum children in London's East End in the 1860s. A community for girls was established at Barkingside, Essex, in 1876, and in the 1880s Barnardo began sending groups of children to Canada for training and settlement there. Other Barnardo foundations included the Babies' Castle infants' home at Hawkhurst, Kent (1886), and a naval training school near Norwich (1901). In 1899 his many charitable enterprises were incorporated under the title "The National Association for the Reclamation of Destitute Waif Children". From its Barkingside headquarters, the present-day Dr Barnardo's is responsible for over 140 schools, hostels, youth centres, and other institutions, with branches overseas, for example, in Australia, New Zealand, and Kenya. It also runs an adoption and fostering service, and its emphasis falls increasingly on work with young people in the community, rather than residential care. It still adheres to the Christian principles upon which its founder's work was based. For many year "Barnardo boys" acted as ball-boys at the Wimbledon lawn tennis championships.

baron and baroness Holders of titles of honour, called baronies, lowest in rank and most numerous of the orders of *peerage in Britain. A barony may be either hereditary or conferred for life only. A baron, unless styled Baron or Lord X by courtesy because his father is a marquess or earl, is always the actual holder of the title. A baroness is usually the wife of a baron, but may also be a peeress in her own right – that is, the holder either of a life peerage or of one of the older baronies that may be inherited by female as well as male heirs. In Scotland the terms "baron" and "barony" mean something different: they refer to feudal territorial dignities (very roughly equivalent to the English lordship of the manor; *see* feudalism). The Scottish equivalents of English barons are "Lords of Parliament", a title that was conferred on Scottish nobles up to the union of English and Scottish parliaments in 1707. The term "baron" originally meant "man", in the sense of one who had done feudal homage to a great lord, particularly the king. Since all who held land direct from the medieval Crown were barons, some distinction was made between greater and lesser barons when summoning them to form the king's council. The House of Lords evolved out of the council of greater barons, whose members were summoned according to the royal will rather than according to the individual's land holdings. Such summonses were issued on an increasingly hereditary basis. Although later opinion has defined the first true parliaments as dating from Edward I's reign (1272–1307), earlier legal judgments had the effect of establishing some baronies before this period. Thus the premier baron is Lord De Ros, whose title dates from 1264.

Barons and baronesses, whether the latter are peeresses in their own right or barons' wives, take the style Right Honourable before their names, giving the form The Rt. Hon. the Lord or Lady X. The husband of a baroness derives no title from his marriage. Children of a baron or baroness in her own right may be styled "The Honourable". European and Japanese titles of baron or baroness confer no official precedence in the United Kingdom.

baronet A holder of a hereditary title of honour called a baronetcy, of which there are some 1350 in Britain. All baronets – but not necessarily holders of baronetcies (*see below*) – are male, being known by the form Sir A . . . B . . . , Baronet (usually abbreviated to "Bart" or "Bt"). Mary Bolles is the only woman ever to have been created a baronetess, in 1635. Baronets' wives are known as Lady B . . . (surname only unless she is the daughter of an earl, marquess, or duke, when the form is Lady C . . . B . . .). Normally the title is passed down through direct male descendants of the original holder; however, in a few special cases a baronetcy has been inherited through a female member of the family.

The Order of Baronets was established by letters patent on 22 May 1611, during the reign of James I. However, the term baronet is thought to have been used in the Middle Ages (e.g. in a statute of Richard II, to denote a noble who had lost the right of being summoned individually to Parliament in the way peers were). From the first, James intended recipients to pay three years' stipend to 30 soldiers at eight pence per man per day, to help to finance the colonization of Ireland. He chose the first 200 baronets himself, stipulating that they were to be gentlemen of good birth (that is, their grandfathers in the male line were bearers of a coat of arms), and have estates yielding a minimum of £1000 per annum.

When baronets were first introduced it was stipulated that no superior or equal degree should ever exist between their rank and the lowest order of *peerage. A little later it was stipulated that baronets should have precedence immediately after viscounts' or barons' sons.

Baronets used to be entitled to be knighted themselves and to demand that their eldest sons be knighted. This privilege was rescinded by George IV. However, as late as 1874 the son of a baronet was knighted on attaining the age of 21. No baronetcies have been created since 1964.

barrister A person (sometimes called "counsel") entitled to practise law in England and Wales or Northern Ireland by virtue of his having been called to the Bar by one of the *Inns of Court. (The bar in question is an imaginary line across a court of law from which the judge is addressed.) Barristers constitute one branch of the legal profession in these countries (regarded as the senior branch) and *solicitors the other. Their counterpart in Scotland is the *advocate.

A barrister's distinctive function is to represent people before the superior courts and other tribunals; but a barrister has the right to appear in every court in the system, from the lowest to the highest. In the *county court and *magistrates' courts, so too have solicitors; but in the *superior courts the right of the barrister is almost exclusive, the principal exception being that solicitors can appear in the *Crown Court in appeals from magistrates' courts. In all his functions a barrister never acts for a lay client directly, but must be instructed (or "briefed") by a solicitor, to whom the client must go in the first instance. A barrister cannot be sued for negligence for his conduct in court, but this immunity (based on public policy) does not extend to drafting or advisory work. Conversely, he cannot sue for his fees, though an instructing solicitor who defaulted on these would be subject to disciplinary action by the *Law Society.

A barrister is technically a **junior barrister** until he "takes silk" and becomes a *Queen's Counsel. (The senior rank from around the 14th century onwards was that of **serjeant-at-law**, and a barrister so appointed by the Lord Chancellor left his orginal Inn of Court and joined the exclusive **Serjeants' Inn**, from which all judicial appointments were made; but the rank fell into decline after that of Queen's Counsel was introduced, and died out completely in the last century.) A junior barrister will enable newly called barristers to gain practical experience by accepting them as "pupils" for a period. (Pupillage for 12 months after call is compulsory, though some of the time may now be spent under the guidance of a barrister working in industry or commerce.) Almost all judicial appointments are open only to barristers (though not confined to Queen's Counsel as was the case with the serjeants), but a solicitor may become a *recorder of the Crown Court, and thence a *circuit judge; solicitors may also be appointed stipendiary magistrates (*see* justice of the peace). *See also* Senate of the Inns of Court and the Bar.

barrows Earth or stone mounds covering ancient burial sites or serving as monuments to the dead. Often glimpsed as slight humps on the skyline, thousands of examples can be seen throughout England, particularly in southern and western counties. In Scotland and Wales such burial sites are known as cairns.

The earliest types are long barrows, dating from Neolithic times (4000–1800 BC). Constructed of earth or chalk, they are typically 30–90 metres (33–98 yards) long and 9–30 metres (10–33 yards) wide and are most common on the chalk downland of Dorset. The bodies of tribal chiefs, their families, and other notables, sometimes with food vessels, were placed in a mortuary enclosure of wood or stone, probably over a period of time. Then the barrow was built over the site, with the bodies (usually six or eight together) interred at the larger end.

Most round barrows were built during the Bronze Age (1800–550 BC), but they vary in size and content. Most commonly they are bowl-, bell-, or disc-shaped, 4–30 metres (4–33 yards) in diameter, and up to 6 metres (6.5 yards) high. Bronze Age burial practices varied considerably; sometimes the body was laid out on a platform in the centre of a ceremonial circle before being buried in a small grave on the spot, which then had a circular barrow constructed over it.

Barrows continued to be built sporadically during Roman and Saxon times (*see* Sutton Hoo), although they were not very common in the Roman period and disappeared entirely after c. 700–50 AD. Many barrows have been damaged or looted through the ages, particularly during the last 200 years. Many have simply yielded to time and the plough, although traces may remain. Aerial photography can reveal the persisting differences in soil associated with barrows and other ancient earthworks as patterns in crops.

Bath Festival A festival of mainly 18th-century music that takes place in Bath, Avon, for one or two weeks in June each year. Founded in 1948, with Ian Hunter as artistic director, the festival ceased to be held in 1956 because of financial difficulties. Three years later the violinist Yehudi Menuhin became closely involved with the event, and his recording orchestra became the Bath Festival Orchestra. The festival sustained its new lease of life after the departure of Hunter and Menuhin in 1968, when the orchestra was renamed the Menuhin Festival Orchestra. Subsequent artistic directors have included Sir Michael Tippet, William Glock, and - currently - Amelia Freedman. Chamber and orchestral concerts, and some opera and ballet, are performed at the Bath Festival, which commissions contemporary music and includes a few nonmusical events, such as art exhibitions and poetry readings.

Bath, Order of the A military order of chivalry created by George I in 1725 with the designation "Most Honourable" and consisting of the sovereign, a Great Master, and 36 Knights Companion. It was enlarged to three classes in 1815, and again in 1847 when civil Knights and Companions were added. The rules of the order have frequently been revised. Although the order was created in its present form by George I, there is an undocumented link with an earlier order, said to have been founded by Henry IV in 1399 at the Tower of London. According to tradition he conferred the honour on the 46 esquires who had attended him at his bath, the night before his coronation. The order consists of three classes, each of which has a military and civil division: Knights and Dames Grand Cross (who are called Sir or Dame and who put GCB after their names); Knights and Dames Commanders (who are called Sir or Dame and who put KCB or DCB after their names); and Companions (CB). Members of the civil division tend to be civil servants, recommended by the Prime Minister or the appropriate departmental minister; members of the military division are admitted on the recommendation of the Secretary of State for Defence. The Queen is sovereign of the order; the Great Master and first or principal Knight Grand Cross is the Prince of Wales; the dean of the order is the Dean of Westminster. Other senior positions are Bath King of Arms, a registrar and secretary, a genealogist, a Gentleman Usher of the Scarlet Rod, and a deputy secretary. The order numbers a maximum of 115 Knights and Dames Grand Cross, 328 Knights and Dames Commanders, and 1815 Companions other than honorary and additional members. The ribbon is crimson and the motto is *Tria juncta in uno* ("Three joined in one"). The chapel of the order is Henry VII's chapel in Westminster Abbey.

Battersea Dogs' Home A home for stray and abandoned dogs, founded in Holloway, London, in 1860 by Mrs Mary Tealby. It moved from Holloway to Battersea in 1871 following complaints about the animals' noise. At first the home was treated with some derision but it gradually acquired a high reputation for the service it performed and in 1884 the Prince of Wales became its patron. Queen Victoria followed him and Queen Elizabeth became patron in 1956. Some three million animals have been rescued by the home since it was founded.

Battle of Britain Day 15 September, the day on which is commemorated the struggle for air supremacy waged by Britain's Royal Air Force against the German Luftwaffe over southern England between August and October 1940. With the Germans losing 1733 aircraft and the British 915, the battle ended in a containment of German air power and the frustration of Hitler's invasion plans. A service of thanksgiving is held annually in Westminster Abbey, attended by members of the royal family or their representatives, to remember those who inspired Winston Churchill's memorable assertion: "Never in the field of human conflict was so much owed by so many to so few."

Battle of Flowers An annual flower festival that takes place in St Helier, Jersey, on the last Thursday in July. Initiated in August 1902, to celebrate the coronation of Edward VII and Queen Alexandra, the festival now attracts many thousands of visitors each year. The main procession consists of decorated floats with set pieces and working models made entirely from flowers: several million blooms are specially grown on the island for the occasion. The floats vary from year to year and often feature events in the island's history, notably the battle of Jersey in 1781; another float traditionally carries the reigning Miss Jersey amid a sea of blossom. At a given signal battle commences: the exhibitors and spectators bombard each other with flowers in a riot of fragrance and colour.

battle of the Boyne celebrations Annual celebrations of the defeat of James II (r. 1685–88), held in many towns and villages of Northern Ireland, notably Belfast, Londonderry, and Omagh, on 12 July. As a result of his Roman Catholic sympathies, James II had been forced to abdicate the throne in 1688 and flee the country, his Protestant daughter Mary and her husband William of Orange becoming joint monarchs in his place. James, anxious to regain the Crown, raised an army of French and Irish troops and met William's advancing forces at the River Boyne, near Dublin, on 1 July 1690. The battle of the Boyne was not an overwhelming defeat for James: 12 July, the date on which the celebrations now take place, is actually the anniversary of the battle of Aughrim, a more decisive victory for William's forces and the Protestant cause in 1691. The occasion is marked by elaborate and colourful Orange Lodge parades, with kilted troops, flags, banners, pipes, and drums (*see* Orangemen); on the following day the battle of the Boyne is re-enacted at Scarva, Co. Down. The celebrations of 12 July now tend to provoke hostility between rival Protestant and Catholic groups.

BBC (British Broadcasting Corporation) An organization that developed from the British Broadcasting Company, which began its daily broadcasts in November 1922. In 1927 it was granted a royal charter as the nation's sole broadcasting organization (motto: Nation shall speak peace unto nation). It has provided radio services ever since, being funded by the licence revenue agreed with the

BATTLE OF THE BOYNE CELEBRATIONS *Procession in Belfast on 12 July.*

Paymaster General (since 1974, the Home Secretary), who controls broadcasting in accordance with the many Wireless Telegraphy Acts. Since its inception under the directorship of J. C. Reith (later Lord Reith), the BBC has formulated a policy of impartiality deriving from an early awareness of the power and exceptional influence of radio.

The Corporation is managed by a board of 12 governors, whose chairman is appointed by the Queen in Council (on the advice of the Home Secretary); the board then appoints the director-general and the board of management. The BBC has no editorial policy and may neither accept advertising nor broadcast sponsored programmes, and it is the duty of the board of governors to ensure that the BBC is free of interference and that no untruthful or biased programmes are broadcast. The director-general is responsible for the day-to-day running of the BBC and, ultimately, is the editor-in-chief.

The social importance of the BBC grew throughout the twenties and thirties as more people acquired radios; George V made the first royal Christmas Day broadcast in 1932, and in 1936 Edward VIII gave his abdication speech over the air. During World War II it became a voice of freedom through its external broadcasts to Europe, which were listened to by millions of people, sometimes at great personal risk. At home, the wartime radio was the main channel of communication between the government and the people; listening to the news bulletins was a part of almost everyone's daily ritual, and Winston Churchill made some of his memorable speeches directly over the radio, rather than to Parliament. By the end of the war, the BBC was established as the world's most influential cultural institution and had gained an unrivalled reputation for high-quality radio broadcasting. Its influence on the development of centralized broadcasting systems throughout Europe was immense. The first high-definition television service was introduced by the BBC in 1936 but was suspended during the war years. After the war, the huge radio audiences that had developed transferred to television as it became widespread. (Twenty million people saw the Queen's coronation, televised in 1953; 100 million watched the World Cup football final of 1966; and an estimated 1000 million viewers saw the Live Aid concert of 1985.)

The BBC now has four national radio stations: Radio 1 for popular music, Radio 2 for light music and sporting events, Radio 3 for classical music, and, largest and most popular, Radio 4 for current affairs, news, and general features. The national regions, Scotland, Wales, and Northern Ireland, have their own radio stations, and there is also a network of local radio stations. BBC television has two channels, BBC-1 and BBC-2, which compete for audiences with each other and with the two independent channels. Additional services include Ceefax (a "teletext" information service), libraries of some 130,000 sound recordings and 20 million press cuttings, the Hulton Picture Library, and the weekly publication of the *Radio Times* and *The Listener*. Furthermore, 15 hours of educational and 36 hours of Open University tuition are transmitted on television each week; and the six BBC orchestras contribute to the 16,000 hours of music broadcast each year.

The domestic services of the BBC (national and local radio and all television services) are funded by income from 18 million licences (which brought in £703 million in 1983–84), together with £8 million derived from sales by BBC Enterprises. External services are not funded from licence-fee revenue, but by grant-in-aid from the Foreign and Commonwealth Office. By 1959 television was costing more than radio and now absorbs 72% of total expenditure.

BBC English *See* Received Pronunciation.

BBC Symphony Orchestra An orchestra founded by the *BBC in 1930 under the baton of Adrian Boult. It played regularly at the *Proms, and in 1935 became the first British orchestra to be conducted by Toscanini. Malcolm Sargent took over from Boult as principal conductor in 1950, and his successors have included Colin Davis, Pierre Boulez, and Gennadi Rozhdestvensky. Both the BBC Scottish Symphony Orchestra and the BBC Welsh Symphony Orchestra were founded in 1935.

bear-baiting A sport in which a bear was tethered to a post and whipped, taunted, and set upon by dogs. Bets were placed on which dog would survive the longest or die first. This practice was popular for hundreds of years in Britain (and throughout Europe) and was not made illegal until the 19th century, although,

BEAR-BAITING *In the 17th century.*

like all forms of animal-baiting, it always had its critics, especially among Puritans. It was a popular spectacle for the lower and middle classes although not confined to them: King Henry VIII ordered the first purpose-built bull- and bear-baiting theatre in Southwark, south London, and Queen Elizabeth I also enjoyed such entertainments. The phrase "bear garden" was the popular name for these places. Royal patronage lent the sport a measure of respectability and during the 16th and 17th centuries it became well organized with bears and dogs being bred specially for the purpose. These animals would then be taken round the country to provide entertainment at fairs. The growing towns provided larger audiences and therefore more profit for the organizers.

Bear-baiting was still popular in the late 18th century, although some changes had been introduced by this time, such as muzzling bears to give the dogs a better chance of survival. The first attempt at abolition was made in Parliament in 1802 and the sport was finally declared illegal in 1835.

beating the bounds A ceremony that takes place in various English villages, towns, and cities on Ascension Day. The custom evolved during the reign of Elizabeth I from the older ceremonies of Rogationtide, known as "Gang Days", which had been banned during the Reformation after becoming disorderly. Primarily a religious ceremony, beating the bounds was also a useful method of instilling the limits of the parish boundary into the minds of children and illiterate villagers in the days when maps were inaccurate and rare. The parson and his parishioners would walk around the parish boundary in solemn procession, stopping under certain oak trees to offer prayers for good crops. These became known as "gospel oaks". At places where the boundary changed direction unexpectedly a parish boundary stone was erected; in the early days the young boys of the parish were soundly thrashed beside these stones or ducked in a nearby ditch to ensure that their position would not be forgotten. The ceremony was also marked by feasting or the drinking of ale.

BEATING THE BOUNDS *Oxford.*

In places where the tradition survives today, the boundary stones, where accessible, are beaten with sticks carried for the purpose by young boys, often choirboys, in the procession. In Oxford there are 22 stones to be beaten, one of which lies under the floor of a pub, the Roebuck Inn, through which the procession must pass. The bounds of the *Tower of London are beaten every three years; in Lichfield the ceremony is conducted by the town sheriff on 8 September, in accordance with an ancient royal charter. In Scotland an equivalent ceremony is known as *riding the marches.

Beatles A rock group formed in Liverpool in the 1960s by John Lennon (1940–80), Paul McCartney (1942–), George Harrison (1943–), and Ringo Starr (1940–) whose style influenced a generation. The group (who composed their own material) originated in Lennon's Quarrymen (1955), but emerged in their final form in 1962 with their first record, "Love Me Do". In 1963 "Please Please Me" reached the top of the British charts, and was followed by very successful tours in Britain and abroad. The Beatles' tour

of the USA in 1964 announced the end of American domination of contemporary rock music, with the adulation of vast crowds and record sales in millions. "Beatlemania" became epidemic on both sides of the Atlantic; their clothes and hairstyles were copied everywhere. Two Beatles films, *A Hard Day's Night* (1964) and *Help!* (1965) were well received; in 1965 the group were awarded individual MBEs. After their last public performance in San Francisco the following year, they confined themselves to recording, coming to compose almost entirely in the recording studio with the help of the engineer George Martin. *Sergeant Pepper's Lonely Hearts Club Band* (1967) is probably their most important album, being the first ever to be planned thematically as a single musical entity rather than a collection of unconnected songs. A television film, *Magical Mystery Tour*, flopped in 1968, while a growing interest in Eastern mysticism made the group less accessible. Their association with drugs attracted controversy. Their last albums made before disbanding in 1970 were *The Beatles* (or *White Album*, 1968), *Abbey Road* (1969), and *Let It Be* (1970). Of the four, Lennon (until he was shot dead by a madman in 1980) and McCartney – one of the world's

THE BEATLES *1965.*

33

most popular singer-songwriters – were the most successful in their subsequent separate careers.

Becket, St Thomas *See* Archbishop of Canterbury.

beefeater *See* Yeomen of the Guard, Queen's Bodyguard of the.

beer An alcoholic drink made from malted barley, water, and hops. Until the introduction of hops into England from Flanders during the Hundred Years' War in the 14th century, the drink was brewed from barley sometimes flavoured with rosemary, yarrow, ground ivy, and other herbs, and known as ale; for some years afterwards the new "beer", with its foreign ingredients and bitter flavour, was disliked and disparaged by many ale-drinkers. Today, the term "ale" is synonymous with beer and it is the keg beer produced in bulk by the large breweries that is condemned by supporters of the Campaign for Real Ale (CAMRA), an organization founded in 1971. Traditional beer, or "real

ale", is made from natural ingredients and allowed to undergo secondary fermentation in the cask, whereas keg beer often contains added ingredients, such as wheat flour or chemical additives, and is filtered and pasteurized after the initial fermentation. Both types of beer are now sold in pubs and bars throughout the country. Further distinction is made between mild beer and bitter, the latter being lighter in colour, more bitter in flavour, and made with more hops. Stout is brewed from roasted barley and is very dark in colour; a similar drink, known as porter's ale or **porter**, was made in the 18th and 19th centuries. In recent years lager, which is a light, continental beer, has become increasingly popular; British lager is much weaker than the imported version, which is left to mature for a longer period.

BEF *See* British Expeditionary Force.

bell-ringing *See* change-ringing.

Bible, the The sacred writings of the Christian Church. By the 4th century AD, the au-

BEER *A family of Londoners hop-picking at the turn of the century. Every September the hop gardens of Kent were invaded by families of East Enders, who could afford no more than a working holiday. Hops were still being hand-picked in this way in the 1950s.*

thoritative content of both Old and New Testaments had been established, and around 400 St Jerome undertook the influential Latin translation since known as the Vulgate. Jerome worked from the original Hebrew and from early Greek and Old Latin translations. In England, portions of the Bible were rendered into the vernacular by such scholars as (the Venerable) Bede (c. 673–735) and Aelfric (c. 955–c. 1020), but after the Norman conquest, French and Latin versions became the standard. The first complete English translation of the Vulgate was inspired by John Wycliffe (c. 1330–84), although it was mostly the work of Nicholas of Hereford (d. c. 1420) and John Purvey (c. 1353–c. 1428), whose version, completed in 1388, was adopted by the *Lollards. The outstanding English translation was that of William Tyndale (c. 1494–1536). Because of official hostility to the project, Tyndale was forced to flee England for Germany where his New Testament was published at Worms in 1525. Translated directly from the Greek, Tyndale's New Testament had a new authority, and was widely used as a basis for later versions. Tyndale also translated parts of the Old Testament. Following the English *Reformation, Henry VIII permitted the publication of a complete English version by Miles Coverdale (1488–1568), based largely on the work of Tyndale and the German theologian Martin Luther. Further revised versions followed, including the Great Bible (1539), the popular Geneva Bible, published in Geneva in 1560, and the Bishops' Bible (1568). Also, the first major Roman Catholic English translation of the Vulgate was published – the New Testament at Reims (1582) and the Old Testament at Douai (1609–10).

In 1604 James I ordered a new translation and the resulting Authorized Version (1611) is the Bible that most people know today. A Revised Version was ordered by the Convocation of Canterbury in 1870 to accommodate changes in usage and developments in biblical scholarship. It was published in 1881 (NT) and 1885 (OT), but never matched the popularity of the King James Bible. In the 20th century there have been many attempts to produce versions in current English. Perhaps the best known are the *Revised Standard Version*, produced by a North American group (NT, 1946; OT, 1952; Apocrypha, 1957) and the *New English Bible* (NT, 1961; complete Bible, 1970), a project initiated by the Church of Scotland. Modern Roman Catholic versions include the translation by Ronald Knox (NT, 1945; OT, 1948–49) and the *Jerusalem Bible* (1966).

Big Ben The nickname for the clock tower and clock of the Houses of *Parliament. Originally the name referred only to the bell which tolls the hours, the heaviest cast in Britain at the time (1858). Following the tradition of naming bells (another example is Great Tom at St Paul's cathedral), it seems to have been named either after Sir Benjamin Hall who was first commissioner of works for the new Houses of Parliament (1855–58) or after the contemporary boxer Benjamin Caunt, both men of ample girth. Big Ben, 2.7 metres (9 feet) in diameter, and weighing 13 tonnes, was cast at Whitechapel bell foundry, which still exists today. After a number of difficulties which served to increase public interest, the clock (designed by E. B. Denison and made by Dent & Co), the quarter chimes, and the bell were finally set working in July 1859 in Barry's 96-metre (316-foot) tower. Within a couple of months the bell had cracked, but disaster was averted by turning the bell and reducing the weight of the hammer. Over the years the boom of the bell, the Westminster chime, and the sight of the illuminated clock faces at night came to symbolize London, and with the coming of radio in the 1920s the sound of Big Ben was broadcast round the country and later all over the world. During World War II nine strokes of the bell were heard, to announce the nine o'clock news. A light in the lantern above the clock indicates that the House of Commons is in session. A complete restoration of the tower was finished in 1985.

Bill A proposed *Act of Parliament during its passage through the legislative process from introduction into the *House of Commons or *House of Lords to *royal assent. This procedure originated in the 14th century, when Commons' petitions were presented to the king, who, with or without the advice of the

Lords, could accept or amend them, issuing the final version as a statute (a written statement of new law), or reject them outright. In the 15th and 16th centuries, it became established that a measure must be approved by both Houses separately and by the sovereign (who could only accept or reject, not amend, the proposal). Today, the process is complicated and lengthy (although the standing orders governing procedure can be manipulated to enable legislation to be rushed through in an emergency) and its exact form depends basically on whether a Bill is public or private. A **public Bill** relates to matters of general concern, and is normally introduced by a government minister. If its main purpose is not the expenditure of public money, however, it may be introduced by a backbencher, in which case it is known as a **private member's Bill**. By contrast, a **private Bill** relates to a particular local or individual interest and is promoted by the body or person concerned (e.g. a Bill by which a local authority or nationalized undertaking seeks additional powers).

Public Bills of a predominantly financial character must originate in the House of Commons, and other public Bills of major political significance normally do as well. Subject to this, public Bills may originate in either House, and parliamentary business is so arranged that government Bills (i.e. the great majority) are distributed as equally as possible between the two. (**Private members' Bills**, on the other hand, mostly originate in the Commons, where they have a very low priority compared to government business. Standing orders set aside just ten Fridays per session for private members, and a ballot is held at the beginning of every session to decide who shall have priority.)

In both Houses, a public Bill is presented to the House by the minister or other member in charge of it. This, its first reading, is a purely formal stage, authorizing it to be printed for the House and published. At its second reading the Bill is debated on its merits, normally by the whole House, but exceptionally (in the Commons) by a specially appointed second-reading committee or the Scottish *Grand Committee. Then comes the committee stage, when a *standing committee (or, in the case of

a very important Bill, a committee of the whole House) examines the Bill in detail, and makes amendments. At a subsequent report stage before the whole House, further amendments are often made, particularly to honour government undertakings given at the committee stage or to remove amendments carried at that stage against the government; and the Bill is then read a third time and passed. The third reading is normally formal but a debate can be demanded; the Speaker can also permit the making of minor verbal amendments. A Bill passed by one House is then sent to the other House, to go through similar stages there, and a Bill passed by both Houses is submitted finally for the royal assent. Under the Parliament Acts 1911 and 1949, it is also possible for a Bill to receive the assent after passing the Commons but foundering in the Lords (*see* Act of Parliament).

A **private Bill** is introduced by a petition, which the promoters must lodge with Parliament, together with a copy of the Bill, after public advertisement and the giving of specific notice to anyone whose interests are directly affected. This enables petitions to be made against the Bill. By contrast with public Bills, the second-reading debate is not concerned with the Bill's desirability but with whether its proposals are contrary to national policy. The committee stage that follows is the vital stage. The Bill begins with a preamble stating the facts that the promoters regard as justifying their proposals, and it is these facts that have to be proved in the committee stage. The promoters and any opponents of the Bill are entitled to be heard and to call evidence (for which purpose they are normally represented by counsel) and the views of any interested government department are also considered. If the preamble is rejected, the Bill falls. If it is accepted, the committee stage continues, and the report stage and third reading follow, in the same way as for a public Bill.

billiards An indoor game played with three balls on a rectangular table having cushioned sides and six pockets. Players use cues to strike their own ball against the others, scoring points for potting a ball in a pocket, or for striking both the other balls (a "canon"). The game's origin is not known, but it was mentioned by Shakespeare in *Antony and Cleopatra* (1606–07). The introduction of leather-tipped cues, chalk, slate beds, and India rubber cushions in the early 19th century revolutionized the game, and allowed professional champions to achieve extraordinarily high scores: in 1907, Tom Reece made an unfinished break of 499,135. By the late 19th century, the game was played throughout the British Empire. The Billiards Association was founded in 1885, but a single code of rules was only established after its merger in 1919 with the Billiards Control Club (founded 1909). Despite rules changes to prevent overlong breaks, public interest declined after the early 1930s as the champions still regularly made the game seem so simple as to be tedious. Joe Davis, one of the most accomplished players, abandoned billiards for *snooker in the late 1920s. Today, billiards still has its devotees, but they are few compared with snooker.

bingo A gambling game in which numbers are called out at random and players cover them on their individual cards, the winner being the first to complete a line, or the whole card, and call out "bingo!" The stake money is pooled and winners receive prizes or cash. Bingo is a variation of the children's game, "lotto", first recorded in the 18th century. It became popular during World War II with the armed forces and was known as "housey-housey" in the army, and "tombola" in the navy. It became a gambling craze in the 1960s after the Betting and Gaming Act 1960 permitted the formation of commercial bingo clubs. It was particularly popular with housewives and bingo halls sprang up all over Britain, often in former cinemas that had been unable to compete with television.

Birthday honours One of the two major occasions in the year when honours are conferred (*see also* New Year's honours). The date of the Birthday honours coincides with the Queen's official birthday, which is celebrated on a Saturday around the middle of June (*see* Queen's Birthday).

Black Death (1348–49) An epidemic of bubonic plague, part of the first major visitation of plague to Europe since 767 AD. With subsequent outbreaks in 1361–62 and 1369, it killed a significant proportion of the population; in the absence of reliable statistics estimates vary, suggestions ranging from 5% to 50%. This reduction caused considerable social and economic upheaval, replacing the earlier land shortage by an acute labour shortage. As a result wages almost doubled between 1340 and 1360, despite legislative attempts as early as 1349 to peg them, and during this period some landlords tried to reimpose feudal labour services (*see* feudalism). Resentment at these measures contributed significantly to the *Peasants' Revolt (1381). Many towns, too, suffered from the dislocation and decline in trade, experiencing a loss of both population and wealth.

Blackpool illuminations A lavish display of street-lights and illuminated tableaux staged by Blackpool Corporation during September and October every year. The idea originated from illuminated tramcars first used by the Corporation in 1897. In May 1912 a display of lights was erected to celebrate the visit of Princess Louise, daughter of Queen Victoria and Duchess of Argyll, and this proved so popular it was brought back in the autumn and again the following year. Discontinued during World War I, the illuminations were revived for the 1925 season and have since continued to grow in size and invention (with a break from 1939 to 1948 because of World War II).

A staff of 70 are required to design, erect, and operate the present display, which stretches for 9.5 kilometres (6 miles), incorporates 375,000 lamps and 120 kilometres (75 miles) of cable and wiring, and consumes 3 megawatts of electric power. Billed as "the greatest free show on earth", the illuminations attract some six million visitors annually, thereby extending the season of this famous seaside resort well into the autumn.

black pudding A type of sausage made from pig's blood, diced pork fat, cereal, and spices, all encased in a length of intestine, the ends of which are tied together to form a loop. The pudding can be boiled, baked, or split and fried with bacon and served as part of the traditional English breakfast. Recipes for the ancestors of today's black puddings were in-

BLACK DEATH Dance of Death *from a woodcut, 1493. Death and its mysteries were a recurrent theme in art and sculpture after the Black Death.*

troduced into England from France around the time of the Norman conquest; similar methods of utilizing the by-products of animal slaughter date back to Roman times. The traditional home of the black pudding is Lancashire, notably the town of Bury, where the puddings are often made from the blood of freshly-slaughtered beef rather than from pig's blood. The counties of Yorkshire and Wiltshire also boast a long-standing tradition of black-pudding making; similar types of blood sausage are eaten in the west country and in southern Ireland.

Black Rod The informal title of the Gentleman Usher of the Black Rod, whose office originated from the Gentleman Usher of the Order of the *Garter. This title derives from his staff of office, an ebony rod crowned with a golden lion. It was probably first created by Edward III in about 1348, with the order.

When the statutes of the order were redrafted by Henry VIII in 1522, Black Rod became an official of the House of Lords, responsible for maintaining order, and acting as the sovereign's personal attendant in the House of Lords. One of his chief ceremonial functions is as the official messenger from the Lords to the House of Commons: it is Black Rod who summons the members of the Commons to the Upper House to hear a speech from the throne or to witness the royal assent being given to a Bill. However, the Commons, jealous of their right to debate without interruption, do not give Black Rod free access to their chamber. In 1642 Charles I attempted to impeach five members of the Commons by personally entering the chamber, only to find that those he sought had fled. Thereafter the doors of the Commons' chamber have by tradition always been closed in the face of Black Rod and he is obliged to knock three times with his staff before being admitted.

Blenheim Palace One of the largest and most spectacular country houses in Britain, situated in the town of Woodstock, near Oxford. Blenheim Palace was given by the nation to John Churchill, 1st Duke of Marlborough, in gratitude for his victories over the French at the battle of Blenheim (now Blindheim, Bavaria) in 1704 during the War of the Spanish Succession. The architect Sir John Vanbrugh conceived the building as a triumphant baroque monument to the glorious duke, even though its construction took nearly 20 years (1705–24). Vanbrugh quarrelled with the duchess, Sarah Churchill, and resigned in 1716 leaving Nicholas Hawksmoor to supervise the completion.

The main block forms a complex mass of colonnades and pinnacles around three sides of the front courtyard, with the imposing central portico balanced by flanking towers. Inside, the heroic scale is sustained in the hall, saloon, and other rooms; the library, for instance, is approximately 56 metres (183 feet) long. The palace stands in 809 hectares (2000 acres) of landscaped park, mainly the work of "Capa-

BLENHEIM PALACE *The outstanding Oxfordshire setting, landscaped by "Capability" Brown in the 1760s, combines expanses of water, trees, and parkland to give an appearance of balanced naturalism.*

bility" Brown, who laid out the park and formal gardens according to the formations of the troops at the battle of Blenheim. The lake in front of the house is crossed by Vanbrugh's bridge, creating a sweeping vista to the statue of Marlborough standing on his column of victory in the park. Sir Winston Churchill was born at Blenheim and there is an exhibition of Churchilliana for visitors to the house and grounds.

Bloomsbury group A circle of writers and artists who, between the early years of the century and about 1930, formed an aesthetic milieu known, from the region of London in which many of them lived, as "Bloomsbury". Among them were the novelist Virginia Woolf and her husband Leonard, the painters Vanessa Bell (Virginia's sister), Duncan Grant, and Roger Fry (an influential theorist), the art critic Clive Bell, the biographer Lytton Strachey, and the economist John Maynard Keynes. Several had studied at *Cambridge University and had been inspired by the philosophy of G. E. Moore, whose *Principia Ethica* (1903) enshrined their beliefs, for example, that "By far the most valuable things are...the pleasures of human intercourse and the enjoyment of beautiful objects;...it is they...that form the rational ultimate end of social progress". While sharing broadly agnostic and progressive rationalist attitudes, and spending much time in discussion of these and their aesthetic implications, the group was never organized to any definite purposes; though the Omega workshop, in art, and the Hogarth Press, in letters, may be seen as its offshoots. Its fame exceeded its influence: and a wide public interest in the personalities of this circle is maintained by an apparently endless supply of letters, diaries, and biographies.

blue A sporting honour awarded by Oxford and Cambridge universities to students who represent their university against the other in the annual matches of certain sports. The first blues were awarded to competitors after the second *Boat Race in 1836. Originally, a blue was a strip of dark blue (Oxford) or light blue (Cambridge) ribbon, but now the holders are permitted to wear ties, blazers, or sweaters in the appropriate colour. Sports

for which blues are awarded include rowing, cricket, rugby union, association football (soccer), boxing, lawn tennis, golf, and athletics. Half-blues are awarded in several "minor" sports, such as squash, table tennis, fives, and rugby league.

Blue Cross A charity providing veterinary services for the pets of those unable to afford private veterinary treatment. Its work developed from that of Our Dumb Friends' League, formed in 1897, and it played a major part in the welfare of horses and dogs that accompanied the armies during World War I. The Blue Cross has homes and shelters for animals throughout the country, besides maintaining rest fields for horses and fully equipped animal hospitals in London and Grimsby.

Blue Riband An award for the fastest sea crossing of the Atlantic Ocean. First awarded in 1838, the Blue Riband of the Atlantic was named after the Blue Ribbon of the Order of the *Garter, (which by extension also refers to any recognized and coveted distinction). Rivalry for the award was most intense in the first 40 years of the 20th century and has been held by Britain, the USA, France, Italy, and Germany. It was held for many years by the British *Mauretania* (1909–29; 26.85 knots). Between 1930 and 1938 it was held by Germany, Italy, and France before being recaptured in 1938 by the British *Queen Mary*, which kept it for 14 years (31.96 knots). In 1952 America finally captured the Riband with the *United States* (35.59) but thereafter interest in the speed of liner crossings of the Atlantic lost their significance since the relative speed and cheapness of air travel diverted public interest (and funds) from sea travel; the few ships still plying the Atlantic now make a feature of their leisurely pace. In the 1980s a mild interest in the Blue Riband was revived by Richard Branson, who broke the record in a powerboat, although some regarded this as spurious as the Riband was intended for passenger-carrying liners and not speedboats.

Blues and Royals See Household Division.

Board of Green Cloth A committee and accounting department that audits the books

BOAT RACE *1985.*

of the royal household, of which it is a part, and acts as a bench of magistrates. Its functions are thought to date back at least to the reign of Edward IV (1461–83). The *Lord Steward nominally presides, but in practice the Board is convened under the Master of the Household, who is always a justice of the peace. The Chief Metropolitan Magistrate is customarily on the Board, which numbers four people in all. The name derives from the colour of the original covering on the table at which the medieval Board sat (although the tablecloth is now red).

The Board of Green Cloth formerly dispensed justice to malefactors within its area of jurisdiction or "verge" (from Latin *virga*, a rod or wand, a reference to the white wand of the Lord Steward). In medieval times this verge covered a circle of 12-mile radius centered on whichever royal residence was in use. As late as the 17th century Windsor had a separate verge, but by the 18th century there was one single verge having a 12-mile radius centered on Whitehall. The Board still issues liquor licences and has jurisdiction under the Gaming Acts for three public houses and several private clubs in an area of London covering the north side of the Mall, the northern part of Whitehall, and the north side of Trafalgar Square.

Boat Race An annual rowing race between the universities of Oxford and Cambridge, in which two eight-man boats (Cambridge in light blue colours and Oxford in dark blue) race over a distance of 6.8 km (4.25 miles). The Boat Race is the most popular rowing event in Britain – support for one of the teams does not necessarily involve any kind of connection with either university. It was first held

in 1829 at Henley, Oxfordshire, and since 1845 has taken place on the River Thames in southwest London, from Putney to Mortlake, in late March or early April. Oxford holds the record for the fastest time of 16 minutes 58 seconds, achieved in 1976. Up until 1986 Cambridge had won 69 races and Oxford 62, with one dead heat (1877). The tradition of crews being all male was broken in 1981 when a woman, Susan Brown, was chosen to cox the Oxford boat.

Bodleian Library The university library at Oxford, founded in 1598 by Sir Thomas Bodley (1545–1613), who restored the earlier, disused university library (first established in the 14th century) and laid the foundations of its now extensive holdings. Bodley was a student at Magdalen College, and then a university lecturer, before serving as a diplomat in The Hague. In 1609 he endowed the library with land in Berkshire and property in London, and in the following year obtained from Stationers' Hall the right of the library to receive a copy of every book printed in England. He replenished Duke Humphrey's li-

BODLEIAN LIBRARY *The 17th-century Schools Quadrangle.*

brary (founded 1480) and extended it with an annexe in the new Schools Quadrangle, which was later entirely given over to the library. The building (1613–36), attributed to Thomas Hold, is a mixture of gothic and Renaissance styles. More famous, however, is the Radcliffe Camera, James Gibb's circular science library of 1749, now incorporated into the Bodleian. The collection was subsequently enlarged by gifts, notably from Archbishop Laud and Oliver Cromwell, and acquisitions, such as John Selden's library (1659) and the Oppenheimer collection of Hebrew books (1829). It holds an important collection of oriental books and manuscripts. The new Bodleian building by Sir Giles Gilbert Scott was opened in 1946, and is connected to the old by a tunnel; the books are stored in enormous underground stacks and are moved from one library to another on a conveyor belt.

bonfire night   *See* Guy Fawkes Day.

Booker Prize   A prize for fiction inaugurated in 1969, and awarded annually in October. Sponsored by the engineering and trading company Booker plc, and administered by the *National Book League, the prize (currently £15,000) is awarded for what the judges regard as the best novel of the year. It must be written in English by a citizen of the UK, Commonwealth, Ireland, Pakistan, or South Africa. A short list of six novels is announced some weeks before the award is made, and speculation as to the likely or rightful winner gives the prize and, it is hoped, fiction generally, a great deal of publicity.

Book of Common Prayer (BCP)   The official service book of the Church of England, containing the authorized forms of service for morning and evening prayer, the ministration of Holy Communion, baptism, confirmation, marriage, burial of the dead, and other rites, as well as the psalter. The original Book of Common Prayer was formulated in 1549 by the Archbishop of Canterbury Thomas Cranmer, who also produced a second and more Protestant version in 1552. Suppressed during the reign of Mary Tudor, Cranmer's Book of Common Prayer was reinstated by Elizabeth I in 1559, with some amendments. However,

the Puritans continued to demand a more drastic revision along Calvinistic lines and it was again suppressed in 1645. After the *Restoration, a slightly revised version was authorized in 1662; it is still in use today. Efforts by the Convocations of the Church of England to introduce a new revised BCP were defeated by Parliament in 1927–28. But the use of alternative services was permitted in 1965 and these are now widely adopted. They were collected into the Alternative Service Book in 1980. Other Anglican Churches have produced their own versions of the BCP, notably the Scottish Episcopal Church in 1764 and the Church of Ireland in 1877.

Border, the (Scottish)   A line running from Berwick-upon-Tweed on the east coast to *Gretna Green on the Solway Firth. The border between England and Scotland was formerly one of the most disputed regions in the land with English and Scots forces struggling to occupy and reoccupy it. The line of the border was not fixed until the 14th century, giving scope for both national and local conflict. The town of Berwick, for instance, changed hands 13 times, until English control was finally established in 1482. Perhaps the most famous of the Border battles was fought in 1513 at Flodden Hill in Northumberland, when Thomas, Earl of Surrey led the English to victory over the Scots; James IV of Scotland and up to 10,000 followers were killed at a cost of only 1500 English soldiers. Apart from formal war, the inability of central government to maintain order in an area where jurisdiction was unclear allowed local English and Scottish Border families to indulge in frequent running battles among themselves. Their gangs, called reivers or mosstroopers, plundered the richer coastal plains during the conduct of their bitter feuds.

Not surprisingly, this constant disorder led to the building of many castles and other fortifications in the region. A good example is the 13th-century Hermitage castle near Hawick, which was once the home of the Earl of Bothwell, third husband of Mary, Queen of Scots. One popular means of protection was the pele tower – a squat thick-walled structure in which local inhabitants sheltered from marauders. Some, such as the "parson's pele" at

THE BORDER *Cattle-raiding: a scene from a 16th-century chronicle depicting the recurrent violence and disorder of the Border country.*

Ancroft, Northumberland, were incorporated into the parish church. Victims of the strife included the fine abbeys of Melrose, Jedburgh, Dryburgh, and Kelso, which were destroyed by the English.

The Border has inspired several famous writers and poets, notably Sir Walter Scott (1771–1832), who spent much of his life at Abbotsford House, near Melrose, and based many of his novels (e.g. *Waverley, Heart of Midlothian*) on the region's colourful past. Another local literary figure was James Hogg (1770–1835), the author of ballads and narrative poems and dubbed "the Ettrick shepherd".

The region has long been noted for its sheep and the prosperity of many Border towns is derived from the woollen industry, particularly the manufacture of tweed cloth and knitwear. Tourism is now a major industry. The Borders Region is a Scottish local government administrative region created in 1975 by amalgamating the former counties of Berwick, Roxburgh, Peebles, Selkirk, and southwest Midlothian.

borough A local government area that today exists only in *Greater London. Boroughs were originally derived from Anglo-Saxon settlements – *burhs* – fortified against the Vikings (*see* Anglo-Saxon Britain). Some later became markets, and by the 12th century were

granted certain rights of self-government by the king or his tenants-in-chief. By the late Middle Ages a borough had become a town that was represented in Parliament and had corporate status, enabling it to be governed by a municipal corporation. These were eventually regulated by various 19th-century Municipal Corporations Acts. Outside Greater London there were county boroughs and noncounty boroughs, the first being administrative units independent of the counties and the second subordinate to them: but all these disappeared with the structural reorganization effected by the Local Government Act 1972, under which the *county became the principal government unit everywhere outside Greater London and the unit below that of county was the *district. A district may, however, exercise the right to call itself a borough by royal charter.

borstal One of a number of custodial institutions to which young offenders aged 15 to 20 could formerly be sent instead of prison. Borstals took their name from the village of Borstal (near Rochester, Kent), where the first one was established in 1908. Their creation reflected the concern of the then Liberal government that young offenders should not be further corrupted by contact with hardened criminals. Accordingly, their purpose was to segregate young offenders from adults

43

and, in conditions far less strict than those in prisons, concentrate essentially on training and equipping them for a place in society. Sentences ranged from six months to two years, followed by a period under the supervision of a probation officer, during which the offender was liable to recall. Borstal training was ended by the Criminal Justice Act 1982. *See also* detention centre; youth custody centre.

Bosworth Field, battle of (22 August 1485) The culminating battle of the *Wars of the Roses, and the only occasion since the battle of *Hastings on which an English king has been killed on the battlefield. Having usurped the Crown in 1483, Richard III's hold on the throne had never been secure, many nobles being ambivalent in their loyalty. The Lancastrian claimant to the throne, Henry Tudor, Earl of Richmond, launched an invasion with French support in 1485, landing with 2500 men on 7 August at Milford Haven. He advanced into the Midlands, assembling an army of 7000 men. Richard mobilized his own force of 8000 men and marched north to Leicester. The two armies met a few miles from the town of Market Bosworth, Richard's army occupying a strategically superior position upon Ambien Hill. After an exchange of fire between the archers, the armies met in a headlong charge. At this point Lord Stanley, who had waited until the decisive moment before committing his own substantial force, unexpectedly attacked the king's flanks, throwing them into confusion. In desperation Richard charged with his bodyguard into the heart of the Lancastrians in an attempt to reach Henry Tudor. He was unseated, however, when his horse stumbled in marshland, and was cut down by enemy infantry, his crown reputedly rolling under a bush from where it was recovered by Lord Stanley and transferred to the head of the new king, Henry VII. The site of the battle is now marked by an exhibition centre and memorials to the dead king.

Bournemouth Symphony Orchestra An orchestra originating in the weekly symphony concerts conducted by Dan Godfrey in 1895 in Bournemouth, Dorset. From the first, Godfrey promoted English music, inviting composers to conduct their own work (in-

cluding Elgar, Stanford, and Parry). Godfrey's more recent successors include Charles Groves, Constanti Silvestri, and Paave Berglund. The Bournemouth Sinfonietta, a chamber orchestra, was formed in 1968. Both this and the symphony orchestra have toured widely in Britain and abroad.

bowls A game played on grass involving the rolling of heavy wooden balls – bowls or "woods" – so that they rest as close as possible to the target ball, the "jack". It was first recorded in the 16th century but the rules were not codified until 1849, by W. W. Mitchell, a Scots lawyer. (Players are also expected to conform to an unwritten code of behaviour and dress.) The Scottish Bowling Association was founded in 1892, its English counterpart in 1903, and the International Bowling Board in 1905.

There are two major bowling codes: flat green and crown green. In flat green bowls, the game is played in lanes on a flat lawn with two, three, or four players. In crown green bowls, the lawn is raised in the centre, producing all kinds of slopes that have to be taken into consideration. This game is generally played by two players. In both codes the woods have a built-in bias which causes them to move along a curving rather than a straight path. Bowls clubs are found throughout England, sometimes combined with another sport such as *cricket, and the game is generally popular with middle-aged and elderly people, being a gentle and sedate form of recreation. In recent years, with the increased television coverage of tournaments and the success of young players, there has been a growth in enthusiasm for the game amongst the younger generation.

boxing Fighting with fists in a roped-off square or ring. It is a sport of ancient origins, practised by the Greeks and Romans, that became popular in England in the late 17th century. In the 18th century, prize fights, fought between bare-knuckled pugilists for money until one could not continue, attracted huge crowds, who betted heavily on the result. The first rules were introduced by Jack Broughton in 1743, forbidding such practices as hitting a man below the belt or when he was down, and only permitting wrestling holds above the waist. However, prize fighting remained extremely brutal well into the 19th century. It was not until 1867 that a real attempt at reform was made, when the **Queensberry Rules** (so named from their endorsement by the 8th Marquess of Queensberry) stipulated the use of padded gloves (previously used only in practice), banned all wrestling, and declared the fight over when one contestant was unable to rise unaided after a count of ten. This marked the beginning of modern boxing, although prize fighting did not die out for another 30 years. In 1880 the Amateur Boxing Association was founded, and in 1891 the National Sporting Club was created to regulate professional boxing competitions. Weight classes, to make the sport fairer for smaller men, emerged at the end of the century but were not regularized until 1909. In 1892 the first heavyweight championship of the world, fought with gloves, took place between James L. Corbett and John L. Sullivan. In 1909 Lord Lonsdale, president of the National Sporting Club, presented belts to the winners of the British championships – the famous "Lonsdale Belts", which are still presented. The British Boxing Board of Control took over responsibility for professional boxing in 1929. Amateur boxers now fight over 3 rounds, professionals over a maximum of 15. Points are scored for clean hits with the knuckle of a clenched fist to the front or sides of the head or body above the belt, and for good defensive work. There have been some very successful British boxers at the lighter and middle weights (recently, Ken Buchanan, Jim Watt, Alan Minter, and Barry McGuigan) but the Americans have tended to dominate the heavyweights, especially since the 1940s. Boxing is a popular spectator sport amongst all classes, though its exponents tend to be of working-class origin. It has long been opposed in some quarters as dangerous, barbaric, and degrading; recently, as a result of a number of deaths and instances of brain-damage, medical opinion has become increasingly hostile and now wishes to see the sport banned.

Boxing Day The feast of St Stephen, celebrated on 26 December, and popularly known as Boxing Day. The name is derived from an old tradition of collecting Christmas offerings for needy parishioners in boxes placed in the church. On the day after Christmas, these were emptied and their contents distributed to the poor. Tradesmen and others who have rendered service during the year are still rewarded with Christmas "boxes" – traditionally a small gift or amount of money.

Through the ages St Stephen has been regarded as a benevolent influence in the equine world. The 17th-century writer John Aubrey recounted how on St Stephen's Day it was the custom for horses to be galloped, fed, and then bled by the farrier to ensure their good health in the coming year. This association continues with Boxing Day meets of foxhounds, race meetings, and other equestrian events.

Boys' Brigade A Christian organization for boys from 6 to 18 years of age, founded in Glasgow in 1883 by Sir William Alexander Smith. Its object is "the advancement of Christ's Kingdom among boys and the promotion of habits of obedience, reverence, discipline, self-respect and all that tends towards a true Christian manliness", it consists of some 3000 companies in the British Isles, each attached to one of the Protestant churches. There are also companies in over 60 countries overseas. Based on principles of Christian citizenship, physical activity, education, and service, the Brigade's programmes cover a wide range of activities including sports, drama, first aid, bands, drill, expeditions, and the *Duke of Edinburgh's Award scheme. The Brigade's badge is an anchor and cross with the motto "Sure and Stedfast".

Braemar Gathering A professional *Highland Games meeting held each year in August a few miles from Balmoral, the Scottish home of the royal family in the Grampian Highlands. The proximity of the castle has been important in the continuing popularity of this meeting: since the time of Queen Victoria, royalty have been frequent visitors to the Gathering. The usual range of running and throwing events associated with any Highland Games are held at Braemar, but the Gathering is particularly noted for its caber-tossing competition. The Braemar caber is 5.79 metres (19 feet) long and weighs 54 kilograms (120 pounds), and it was not until 1951 that

45

George Clark achieved the first completely successful tossing.

Brands Hatch A motor racing circuit near Farnham, Kent, in southeast England. Brands Hatch was used as a circuit for motorcycle club events in the 1920s. After World War II a hard surface was laid and in 1949 Formula 3 motor races were held over a distance of 1.6 kilometres (1 mile). The full Grand Prix circuit was opened in 1960 over 4.2 kilometres (2.5 miles). Its position between two hills makes it a spectacular and exciting course with a rapid succession of difficult corners, notably Paddock Hill bend, and variable undulations. The bottom straight is one of the few places where it is easy to overtake another vehicle. The British Grand Prix was first held at Brands Hatch in 1964, when it was won by Scotsman Jim Clark, and it is now held there every other year. Brands Hatch is also host to a variety of other motorsport events and is one of the most frequently used circuits in the country.

brass band A band made up entirely of brass instruments. The introduction to Britain from Paris of the cornopean (later called the cornet) and the development of saxhorn instruments, such as valve trumpets and trombones, were crucial to the emergence of brass bands in Britain in the 1830s. The cornopean provides an effective top line for the band, and saxhorns are particularly well-suited to open-air playing. The first brass band was probably that formed in 1832 at an ironworks at Blaina, in Monmouthshire (now in Gwent). By the end of the century some 20,000 bands existed, playing at all kinds of civic functions as well as on the bandstands in parks and public gardens where they are still a familiar sight. Among the best-known brass bands are the Besses o' th' Barn Band (formed in 1853) and the Black Dyke Mills Band (1855), but a better-known British institution is the Salvation Army's bands, which may still be heard on the streets on Sundays. Many of the 3000 brass bands now in existence compete in the National Brass Band Festival (dating from 1860), whose finals are held in the Royal Albert Hall.

The military bands differ from brass bands in that they consist of both brass and woodwind instruments.

Brethren, the (Plymouth Brethren; Christian Brethren) The Christian movement now known simply as the Brethren, which originated in Dublin but opened its first church in Plymouth, England, hence its popular name of Plymouth Brethren. At Trinity College, Dublin, in the 1820s, a group of students, who had become disillusioned with the absence of religious feeling in the proceedings of the Church of Ireland, started meeting in private to celebrate Communion. Among them were Anthony Norris Groves (1795–1853) and John Nelson Darby (1800–82), a priest who resigned from the Church of Ireland in 1827. Their disregard of denominational differences and their evangelistic outlook, coupled with a prophetic interpretation of scripture, rapidly gained them a following. Prominent among them was Benjamin Wills Newton (1807–99), who founded the Brethren's first church at Plymouth in 1831.

Differences between Newton and Darby caused a split in the movement, with Darby forming his breakaway Exclusive Brethren in 1848. These "Darbyites" later experienced further divisions, notably in the split by followers of the extreme doctrines of James Taylor. Meanwhile, the mainstream movement became the Open Brethren, disavowing the sectarian tendencies of its offshoot. Churches of the Open Brethren are known as gospel halls or evangelical churches and are governed by each autonomous congregation. Full-time pastors are rare, although certain members are trained as teachers or evangelists. From the outset, the Brethren have stressed missionary activity and the Brethren's "Christian Mission to many Lands" has over a thousand missionaries working in several continents.

Bristol Tolzey Court (Tolzey Court) An ancient court that, until its abolition in 1971, exercised within the city of Bristol a civil jurisdiction comparable to that of a *county court. In the 14th century a great deal of commercial business was transacted in fairs and markets, and many local courts developed to dispense speedy justice in disputes between the merchants who visited them. They were known as **piepoudre courts**, and the Bristol Tolzey Court was one of them. (The etymology of piepoudre is not entirely clear; it may refer to the dusty feet (*pieds poudrés*) of the traders and potential litigants.) The majority of piepoudre courts gradually died out, but the Bristol Tolzey Court became firmly established and, from 1710 onwards, operated under a charter granted by Queen Anne.

British Academy A learned society for the humanities and social sciences formed in 1901. Since 1982 it has occupied premises near Regent's Park, London. A maximum of 350 ordinary Fellows are elected to the Academy at any one time by virtue of their academic distinction. It also has some 250 corresponding, or overseas, Fellows. It aids 11 British schools and institutes abroad (e.g. the British School at Rome), and for this function it receives a government grant. Private funds are also administered by the Academy to finance awards, scholarships, etc. It publishes the *Proceedings of the British Academy*, which include biographies of deceased Fellows as well as transcripts of the Academy's annual lecture series.

British Airways Britain's chief airline and one of the world's foremost carriers of passengers and cargo by air. British Airways is a direct descendant of the former Imperial Airways (1924), which pioneered many international routes throughout the British Empire with its Handley Page Hannibals (passenger-carrying biplanes) and its flying boat service across the Atlantic. After World War II the configuration of airlines altered with the British Overseas Airways Corporation (BOAC) flying the long-distance routes and British European Airways (BEA) serving European destinations. The period was marked by a rapid expansion in airline business and by great technical developments, in which jets completely replaced propeller-driven commercial aircraft. In 1969 the Edwards Committee formed the National Holdings Board, later renamed the British Airways Board, in which BOAC and BEA retained their separate identities and routes. In 1974 BOAC and BEA were merged into one company, with the sole operating title of British Airways. Exactly ten years later, all responsibilities of the British Airways Board passed to British Airways plc, in which shares are planned to be sold publicly under the Conservative government's privatization scheme. In the early 1980s computerized flight booking and automatic landing systems on most aircraft were introduced. British Airways now operate 150 aircraft including 6 Concordes, and transports 230,000 tonnes of cargo annually.

British Army of the Rhine (BAOR) A corps of the British Army that forms part of the NATO forces for the defence of Europe. The BAOR developed from the British forces stationed in occupied Germany in 1945, and was originally intended as a permanent peacetime garrison continually on duty in the Federal Republic of Germany. The force currently represents one-third of the entire Army and is divided into three divisions, of which at least one is kept in Britain. With a total strength of about 56,000, the BAOR can also call upon support from the Territorial Army (*see* reserve forces), and is equipped with the most modern weaponry available, including Challenger tanks, Lynx helicopters, and tactical nuclear missile systems.

British Association for the Advancement of Science An organization founded to promote interest and progress in science, among both professional scientists and the general public. Membership of the British Association, as it is usually called, is open to all who have an enthusiasm for science. It was formed at York in 1831 by a group of scientists who were disillusioned with the elitist and conservative attitude of the *Royal Society during the early 19th century. The Association was incorporated by royal charter in 1928. The major event in the Association's calendar is the annual conference at which the social, political, and economic implications of scientific advances are considered. The Association cultivates contacts with other learned societies, the media, and government, as well as organizing a programme of lectures and conferences to help in its work of disseminating new scientific ideas. It sponsors several lectureships for young scientists in the physical, biological, and social sciences to encourage them to make their work known to wider audiences.

One of the most famous meetings of the British Association was held in Oxford in 1860, when the biologist T. H. Huxley won the celebrated debate with Bishop Samuel Wilberforce concerning Darwin's theory of evolution. The Association now has some 2000 members; its current president is Sir Hans Kornberg.

British Broadcasting Corporation *See* BBC.

British citizenship *See* citizenship.

British constitution The laws and conventions by which the UK is governed. They are concerned with the composition and functions of the organs of government, both central and local, and with the relationship between individual and state. Many nations have a written constitution establishing the organs of government, specifying their powers, and conferring on the country's subjects their fundamental rights, such as freedom of speech. The prime feature of written constitutions is that they are difficult to amend. In the USA, for example, there has to be a two-thirds majority in Congress and ratification by three-quarters of the States: as a result less than 30 amendments have been made in 200 years. As a consequence of these legal ramifications there has to be a court (in America, the Supreme Court) that has power to declare ordinary legislation invalid because it infringes in some way on constitutional rights. The British constitution is in this sense unwritten. Some of the matters usually dealt with by formal constitutions are to be found in *Acts of Parliament, so that it does contain written elements, but many others depend either on unwritten rules of the *common law or on unwritten conventions (which are not even law at all). Moreover, an Act that does have a constitutional character has no greater sanctity than any other Act. It is an ordinary Act that can be repealed or amended by another ordinary Act, and there is no court in the UK that can declare any Act of Parliament unconstitutional. Of the three elements in the British constitution (Acts of Parliament, common law, and

conventions) the first includes such milestones as the Bill of Rights 1689 (*see* Glorious Revolution); the Act of Settlement 1701 (responsible for devolving the Crown on the House of Hanover after the death of Queen Anne, and barring Catholics from the throne; it also established the independence of the judiciary); the Act of Union with Scotland 1707, and the Act of Union with Ireland 1800; the *Great Reform Act 1832 (the first comprehensive reform of representation in the House of Commons); the Parliament Acts 1911 and 1949 (securing the primacy of Commons over Lords in the legislative process; *see* Act of Parliament); the Statute of Westminster 1931 (the first Act to grant full independence to former colonies; *see* Commonwealth); and the European Communities Act 1972 passed when Britain became a member of the European Economic Community.

The constitutional contributions of the common law include the rule that the king (or queen) in Parliament constitutes the sole legislative authority in the land (statute law was recognized as superior to case law in the early 16th century; and by the decision of the judges in 1610, known as the Prohibitions del Roy, that the king could not personally judge any case, and that any case touching his interests should be decided by the judges), but its principal concern is with civil liberties and remedies for wrongful interference with them (e.g. *habeas corpus).

Conventions of the constitution are rules of conduct concerning public functions that do not have the force of law, but are nevertheless observed as faithfully as if they did. It is, for example, a convention that the executive powers of government, although legally still vested in the monarch, are exercised by her only on the advice of ministers who command a majority in the House of Commons. The *Cabinet and the *Prime Minister were created not by law, but by this convention and other subsidiary conventions. Again, it is by convention rather than law that Parliament is summoned at least once a year, and that the monarch does not refuse the *royal assent to a Bill passed by Parliament. Conventions are not enforceable in the courts; they are observed because they ensure the smooth functioning of government in accordance with the established practice of proven utility. Although they are unwritten, there are concealed sanctions behind the more important of them that would operate if they were breached. If, for example, Parliament were not summoned each year, the government would find itself without the annual authority needed to raise money by taxation and even to maintain the armed forces; if the Crown (except in very exceptional circumstances) did not follow ministerial advice, the survival of the *monarchy would be gravely imperilled.

British Council An independent nonpolitical organization set up in 1934, and incorporated by royal charter in 1940, to promote British culture, the teaching of English, and a knowledge of the UK abroad. The Council provides a point of contact with Britain for the peoples of 81 countries through its overseas staff and their wide range of educational, technical, and cultural activities. The director-general and 15 advisory councils manage the organization and its 4200 staff from its London headquarters. The Council's activities are funded by a Foreign and Commonwealth Office grant of £200 million in addition to fees paid by the Overseas Development Administration, and payments for the Council's services, which amounted to 26% of the Council's total expenditure in 1984. In the same year the Council organized English-language teaching for 53,000 students, 270 book promotion exhibitions, 330 artistic tours, and visits to Britain for 23,000 people. The demand for British culture also encouraged the Council to arrange a Turner exhibition in Paris, a display at the Los Angeles Olympic Arts Festival, and the British film archive festival in China. The membership queues that form outside Council libraries abroad are further evidence of the success of this form of cultural diplomacy.

British Council of Churches A London-based fellowship of Christian Churches in Britain, established in 1942 to promote Christian unity and joint action and cooperation. The Council includes 79 representatives drawn from over 20, mostly Protestant, Churches in England, Scotland, Ireland, and Wales, of which the largest are the Church of England, the Church of Scotland, and the Methodist Church. Associate councils include the Scottish Churches' Council, the Irish Council of Churches, and the Council of Churches for Wales, besides over 700 local church councils. The Council is financed by grants from member churches and subscriptions from associated councils. Its operations are conducted through various divisions, of which the best known is the development agency, *Christian Aid. The Conference for World Mission acts as a cooperative and consultative agency for missionary organizations in Britain, while its other divisions deal respectively with community, ecumenical, and international affairs. A week of prayer for Christian unity, held in January each year, is sponsored by the Council. Its president is the Archbishop of Canterbury.

British Dependent Territories citizenship *See* citizenship.

British Empire Britain's possessions overseas, which by 1914 covered over one-fifth of the world's surface, permitting the boast that the sun never set upon the British Empire. Colonial ambitions first emerged in the 16th century, when England made sporadic attempts to exploit the new territories being opened up by the Spanish and Portuguese. Newfoundland, claimed for England by John Cabot in 1497, soon became important for its cod fisheries and was formally annexed in 1583; the following year Sir Walter Raleigh established the first short-lived colony of Virginia (1584–c. 1590). However, the most profitable overseas activities were in illicit trade with the Spanish New World, especially in slaves (e.g. by Sir Francis Drake and Sir John Hawkins; *see* slavery). The first permanent overseas settlements established by the English were those set up in the 17th century in North America and the West Indies by trading companies or individuals seeking profit. However, these were often manned by emigrants escaping religious persecution in England (notably *Puritans in New England, after the voyage of the *Mayflower* in 1620, and Catholics in Maryland in 1634). Pennsylvania was founded in 1681 specifically as a refuge for Quakers. The intro-

BRITISH EMPIRE *Queen Victoria recommending the Bible to a native ambassador as the secret of Britain's greatness. By the end of the 19th century the Empire embraced almost a fifth of the global land mass and a quarter of the world's population.*

duction of sugar cane into the West Indies (c. 1640) made them the most important colonies, whilst in the east, the East India Company, incorporated by royal charter in 1600, began to develop trading links in India. This "first British empire", based on trade for the profit of the mother country, expanded through further foundations and conquests in the 17th and 18th centuries. With the foundation of Georgia (1732), Britain owned all the east coast of North America between Florida and Canada (the "13 colonies"); while the French were ousted from Canada and the Mississippi Valley between 1713 and 1763, notably after James Wolfe's victory at Quebec (1759). In India, the East India Company also ousted its French rival and began to acquire substantial territories, such as Bengal, which was effectively conquered by Robert Clive's victory at Plassey (1757) during the Seven Years' War (1756–63). This phase of empire building came to an end when resentment in

the 13 colonies (particularly the fact that colonists could be taxed without their consent) led to the American Revolution (1776–83). The loss of the 13 colonies signalled the end of this first empire and led to a reconstruction of Britain's colonial policy.

The pace of territorial expansion slowed amid scepticism of the long-term value of colonies. The Napoleonic Wars (1799–1815) added minor possessions appropriated from the French and their allies: Trinidad, Tobago, St Lucia, Mauritius, Ceylon, the Cape of Good Hope, and other territories. Britain was also responsible for the settlement of Australia when, following Captain James Cook's exploration (1770), the first convicts were transported to Botany Bay in 1788. New Zealand, first charted by Cook, was only systematically colonized from 1840.

Britain's second empire entered upon its greatest age in the second half of the 19th century with a new enthusiasm for imperialism. The

Indian Mutiny (1857–58) finally destroyed the East India Company and India was brought under the Crown with Queen Victoria assuming the title Empress of India in 1876 (*see also* British Raj). Britain also joined in a general European "scramble for Africa" from the 1880s, emerging with substantial territories in east and south Africa; its earlier trading influence in west Africa was also extended into direct rule. These advances were not made without some setbacks, however: the military establishment was humiliated in battle more than once in Africa, for example, at the hands of the Zulus and the Boers. In contrast, the white settled colonies of Canada, Australia, New Zealand, and South Africa all achieved "dominion status" (practical self-government) by 1910; and in 1931 full legislative independence was achieved by the Statute of Westminster. Since World War II, nationalist movements that are incompatible with colonial concepts have developed both in India and Africa. India gained independence in 1947, and Britain's African possessions were handed back to their indigenous populations between 1957 (Ghana) and 1980 (Zimbabwe). Britain's remaining colonies comprise a few scattered territories and islands, such as Belize, Bermuda, Gibralter, Hong Kong (to be returned to China in 1997), St Helena, and the Falkland Islands (the cause of a brief war with Argentina in 1982). Most of the former colonies have joined the *Commonwealth of Nations, a loose association headed by the Queen that emerged from the formal definition of dominion status in 1926.

British Empire, Order of the An order, awarded for service to the British Empire. The first honour granted to both sexes equally, it was instituted by George V in 1917, and has been enlarged and revised frequently since then. The Queen is the sovereign of the order and under her are the Grand Master (the Duke of Edinburgh), the prelate (Bishop of London), a King of Arms, a registrar, a secretary, a dean (Dean of St Paul's), a Gentleman Usher of the Purple Rod, a prelate emeritus, and a genealogist. There are five classes, with civilian and military divisions, and numbers admitted to each are limited. The classes are Knights and Dames Grand Cross (GBE, and addressed as Sir or Dame); Knights and Dames Commanders (KBE, DBE, and addressed as Sir or Dame); Commanders (CBE); Officers (OBE); and Members (MBE). Appointments are made on the recommendation of ministers, but recipients may come from all walks of life and not merely from public service. The order is designated "Most Excellent", and its motto is "For God and the Empire".

British Expeditionary Force (BEF) The seven British regiments that were sent to France at the start of World War I (1914). Comprising one cavalry regiment and six infantry regiments, the BEF suffered heavy losses and had to be heavily reinforced. The nickname **"Old Contemptibles"** came from a dismissive comment made about the force by the German Kaiser. The BEF was reinstituted in 1939 and ten divisions were sent to France once more, but had to be evacuated from Dunkirk and other ports in 1940.

British Film Institute (BFI) An organization founded in 1933 to "encourage the use and development of cinema as a means of entertainment and instruction" and to foster film-making as an art. It is located in London and funded by the government and members' subscriptions. The BFI aids film-makers and, together with Independent Television's Channel 4, helps to finance film and video workshops. It runs the National Film Theatre (founded after the 1951 Festival of Britain), which has at least 45,000 members, a National Film Archive (founded in 1935) of about 40,000 films and 10,000 television programmes, the National Film Library (founded 1938) for the hire of films and video cassettes, and an information service. In the regions it aids film theatres and the film activities of the arts associations. Every autumn the BFI stages the London Film Festival. Its equivalent in Scotland is the Scottish Film Council, and it operates in Wales through the Welsh Arts Council.

British Legion, Royal A nonparty nonsectarian national organization for ex-servicemen and women and serving members of HM forces. Formed in 1921 through the merging of four post-World War I ex-servicemen's associations, full membership was extended to those still serving in HM Forces in the Legion's diamond jubilee year (1981). Originally named the British Legion, it was granted its "Royal" prefix in 1971. The Legion endeavours to "perpetuate the memory of those who died in the service of their country" and to provide its members and their families with a wide range of social, welfare, and benevolent services. It runs five residential homes for aged or incapacitated ex-servicemen, three convalescent homes, and through its housing association provides housing for the elderly and disabled. It offers advice about disablement and war pensions. It runs sheltered industries for the disabled (the Legion is the largest private employer of disabled people), a London taxi training school, and through its Attendants Company provides employment for both the disabled and able-bodied in its 300 car parks and its security division. Combining its aims of remembrance and aid to ex-servicemen, its best-known task is that of providing poppies from its own factory for the annual November *Remembrance (or Poppy) Day appeal. In 1984 the Legion had 930,000 members, 1060 clubs, and 3500 branches, including 58 overseas branches.

British Library The national library, an amalgamation of the *British Museum Library, the National Central Library, and the National Lending Library for Science and Technology. Created by the British Library Act 1972, it has its main reading room in the British Museum. Lack of storage space has led to a new site for the library in Euston Road, London, in a building designed by Colin St John Wilson, scheduled to be in use in 1991. The library has three divisions. The reference division holds about 9.5 million printed books, 105,000 manuscripts, 18,000 seals, and 3000 papyri. Its collection of charters and papers dates from the 3rd century BC. It also holds the Lindisfarne Gospel (700 AD), some exquisite psalters and books of hours, as well as outstanding collections of Hebrew and Sanskrit manuscripts, some of which are on display. The lending division at Boston Spa, West Yorkshire, has about 4.5 million volumes for loan to libraries. The bibliographic services division publishes the *British National Bibliography*, the catalogue of British

publishing. In 1983 the library acquired the National Sound Archive.

British Medical Association (BMA) The major representative body of doctors and other members of the medical profession, which exists to safeguard the interests of its 70,000 members and to uphold standards of practice. It started in 1832 as the Provincial Medical and Surgical Association, founded by the practitioner and medical reformer Charles Hastings (1794–1866). Changing its name to the British Medical Association in 1855, the new organization's campaigns resulted in the Medical Act 1858, which established the General Medical Council, a statutory body charged with compiling a register of all qualified practitioners. As the BMA consolidated its position as the general practitioners' trade union, there was frequent rivalry between it and the powerful Royal Colleges, which traditionally had controlled the hospitals and specialists. The BMA pressed for changes in the Poor Law to improve doctors' conditions, but was less than satisfied with Lloyd George's National Insurance Act of 1911 (see national insurance). Further challenges faced the BMA in its negotiations with government concerning the establishment of the *National Health Service in 1948, particularly over preserving the traditional independence of doctors.

The BMA is now a registered trade union, with five autonomous committees representing *GPs, hospital consultants, junior hospital doctors, community health workers, and university teaching staff. Besides campaigning for improved pay and conditions for its members, the BMA has a powerful voice in all other aspects of the health service. Its main publications are the weekly *British Medical Journal* and the monthly *BMA News Review*.

British Museum (BM) The national museum of archaeology and ethnography in Bloomsbury, London. It was conceived along historical and scientific rather than aesthetic lines and until 1881 included the collection that became the Natural History Museum in South Kensington (see British Museum (Natural History)). The BM dates from 1753, when, upon the death of the physician and collector Sir Hans Sloane, his collection of "books, manuscripts, prints, drawings, pictures, medals, coins, seals, cameos, and natural curiosities" was acquired for the nation. To the Sloane collection were added two collections of manuscripts, forming the nucleus of the *British Library, which is still partly housed in the BM. £300,000 was collected by public lottery to fund the new museum, which was opened to the public in 1759. The present neoclassical building, designed by Sir Robert Smirke, was built (1823–47) on the site of the BM's original home, Montagu House. Its unique collections – probably the finest of their kind in the world – encompass a wide range of archaeological treasures from Egyptian mummies to Chinese ivories. Among its most famous exhibits are the Rosetta Stone from Egypt (196 BC), captured as plunder in 1801 after Bonaparte's defeat at Alexandria, and the Elgin Marbles from the Parthenon.

British Museum Library The library of the *British Museum, formed in 1753 from the Sloane collection, the Harleian collection of the Earls of Oxford, and Sir Robert Cotton's collection; in 1757 George II presented it with the royal library and with this came the right to receive a copy of every publication issued in Britain. It is now part of the *British Library. Its famous Reading Room dates from 1857.

British Museum (Natural History) Popularly known as the Natural History Museum, the present romanesque building in South Kensington, London, was built by Sir Alfred Waterhouse and opened in 1881 when the natural history exhibits acquired by the *British Museum were transferred from the Bloomsbury site. The collection had originally been built up around the scientific collections of the physician and naturalist Sir Hans Sloane (1660–1753), which were acquired by the nation on his death, and the major botanical collection bequeathed by the botanist and explorer Sir Joseph Banks (1743–1820). Unfortunately, many of the botanical items were lost during the air-raids of World War II. Among the museum's more famous exhibits are a reconstructed dinosaur, *Diplodocus carnegii,* which measures about 27 metres (85

feet), and a skeleton of a blue whale, about 28 metres (91 feet) long.

British Overseas citizenship *See* citizenship.

British Raj The period of British rule over the Indian subcontinent that began after the Great Revolt or Mutiny of 1857–58 and ended with independence in 1947 (*see* British Empire). During this period 562 native rulers continued to administer their own states (making up one-third of the country) with guidance from British advisers and with allegiance to the Crown through the Viceroy; in the ten provinces of British India itself (the presidencies of Bombay, Madras, Bengal, the Central and United Provinces, Assam, Burma, Bihar, Punjab, and the North West Frontier Province) the efficient and dedicated Indian Civil Service (ICS) administered reforms in law, finance, land systems, communications (especially railways), and education through district officers, supported by superintendants of police, public works engineers, inspectors of posts and telegraph, forest officers, and their assistants. Like the officers of the restructured Indian Army, all these officials and their families were British, supported in often gruelling circumstances by a sense of the importance of their work and the justice of British rule. The Durbars held in Delhi in 1877, 1903, and 1911, celebrated three successive monarchs as Empress or Emperors of India, amid glittering celebrations befitting Britain's greatest imperial possession.

The scattered British community was drawn more closely together by the development by British engineers of a railway system throughout India. By the 1880s a distinct lifestyle had evolved for the British in India, which lasted unchanged for half a century; it almost totally excluded the Indians, except as servants. In the provincial centres the British Raj, as it came to be called, could be pampered and snobbish; the cold weather season of polo, gymkhanas, hunting camps (including pig-sticking), tea dances, fancy-dress balls, and garden parties was followed by the hot weather season, when whole provincial governments move to such hill stations as Simla at the foot of the Himalayas, for a round of "duty and red tape,

BRITISH RAJ *British officer in India, c. 1870.*

picnics and adultery". For British families India brought great privileges, but it could also often involve considerable isolation and ill-health, with children away at boarding school in England and wives and husbands often separated for weeks on end.

Indian "nationalism" was always present, but achieved little until after 1919 when, on the one hand, the British will to hold India was weakened by India's increasing economic importance and, on the other, western education had created an articulate and organized class of nationalist leaders, such as Gandhi and Nehru. The stage was set for independence by degrees; the indianization of central government, of the ICS, and the upper ranks of the army was gradually achieved against a backdrop of civil unrest. The Raj's legacy to India and Pakistan in 1947 was the rule of law, an elected parliamentary government, a trained army, a civil service, a system of roads, railways, and irrigation, many civic and other buildings of considerable architectural merit, some industry, and English as a second language. For the British, India has been a great source of wealth as well as a dominant presence in Asia, with all

the attendant prestige and strategic advantages that this involved. The Raj also introduced hundreds of words into the English language: examples include bungalow, dinghy, pundit, pyjamas, sandal, thug, yoga, blighty, and kedgeree. Several novels (Kipling's *Kim*, E. M. Forster's *A Passage to India*, Paul Scott's "Raj Quartet" and *Staying On*) have been written about the experience of the British in India. Since independence about one million immigrants from India, Pakistan, and Bangladesh have settled in Britain, mainly in the industrial towns (*see* Commonwealth).

British Sports Association for the Disabled (BSAD) The coordinating body of sport for disabled people in the UK, founded in 1961 "to encourage sport and recreation among the disabled and so enable them to compete with one another and with the able-bodied". The headquarters of the BSAD are at the Stoke Mandeville stadium near Aylesbury, Buckinghamshire (*see also* Paraplegic Games (Stoke Mandeville)). There are 19 branches of the BSAD in the UK. It organizes conferences, exhibitions, and competitions, and provides information about all aspects of sport and outdoor pursuits for the disabled. The BSAD is affiliated to the International Sports Organization for the Disabled.

British Technology Group An organization formed in 1981 by the amalgamation of the **National Research and Development Corporation** (NRDC) and the **National Enterprise Board** (NEB) with the aim of improving the development and commercial exploitation of new technology in Britain.

The NRDC identifies potential commercially viable inventions and technologies as they emerge – mostly in universities, polytechnics, and government research establishments – supports their development, and undertakes the necessary patenting and licensing for commercial use. The NRDC currently holds some 600 licence agreements and receives royalties from such inventions as pyrethrin insecticides, developed at the *Agriculture and Food Research Council's Rothamsted experimental station in Hertfordshire, and alkali-resistant glass fibre, invented by the Building Research Station of the Department of the Environment. In addition, the NRDC invests in the development of products by commercial companies, in return for a levy on sales.

The NEB provides venture capital, usually in conjunction with the private sector, to establish new companies. These are typically operating in relatively new and often high-risk fields, particularly in electronics, information technology, and biotechnology.

British Tourist Authority The national tourist organization set up by the Development of Tourism Act 1969 to promote Britain overseas, to advise the government on tourism, and to improve tourist amenities in Britain. In pursuit of this last purpose, it cooperates with the **English, Scottish,** and **Wales Tourist Boards**, the three statutory bodies responsible for promoting tourism in their respective countries. (The Northern Ireland Tourist Board has a similar function.) In recent years the BTA has sought to encourage tourism outside the peak summer period, and to raise the standards of British catering; it has overseen the introduction of computerized reservation systems, and of training program-

mes, and has attended to simple but vital tasks, such as adequate signposting. It recommends the relaxation of British licensing laws and the laws on Sunday trading, and the provision of more accommodation for visitors in London. Tourism brought Britain a revenue of £5 billion in 1984, and is likely to become one of its largest assets by the end of the century.

British Waterways Board The public corporation set up to manage British waterways under the provisions of the Transport Act 1962, which gave it responsibility for 2000 miles of canals and rivers, 85 reservoirs, 15 freight depots, and a fleet of barges carrying five million tonnes of freight each year. In 1968 a further Act enabled the Board to register and levy fees upon the 23,000 unpowered and 5000 powered craft using the waterways. The chairman and up to 12 members of the Board are appointed by the Secretary of State for the Environment. The Board is responsible for the condition of waterways and their towpaths, tunnels, and embankments. It must also maintain water levels. For all these purposes it receives a government grant in addition to its earned income (mainly from leisure activities). Since much of the canal network is 200 years old, and estimates for its repair costs in 1985 totalled £150 million, there is a substantial backlog of work.

Broadmoor *See* special hospital.

Broads, the An area of lakes, waterways, and marshland centred principally on the rivers Bure and Yare and their tributaries in northeast Norfolk. Extending from the coast inland almost to Norwich, the Broads form an important habitat for wildlife, and the outstanding beauty of the area has made it a popular centre for boating, fishing, and birdwatching. The lakes (or broads) were formed as a result of peat-cutting for fuel that took place over several hundred years from the 12th century or earlier. Traditional Norfolk reeds are still harvested for thatching, but management of the willow and alder thickets (carrs) for poles and osier has largely died out. The waterways and vegetation of the Broads are under threat from the effects of modern farming methods and tourism: marshy areas are drained and reclaimed for arable crops,

THE BROADS *Cutting peat for fuel, a dying Fenland craft. The Broads are the product of intensive peat-cutting from around the 12th century, when blocks of the decayed marsh vegetation were used for domestic fuel in an area where alternative sources were scarce. The now flooded peat excavations are remarkable for their scale: over 1000 hectares (2500 acres) of peat were dug.*

fertilizers pollute the streams and rivers, and power boats damage river banks. Several nature reserves have been established, including Hickling Broad and Bure Marshes, in an attempt to protect the Broads and their wildlife.

Here, drainage is carefully monitored and vegetation managed, to preserve the traditional broadland features. Meanwhile, the often conflicting demands of farmers, holidaymakers, and naturalists are balanced by

THE BROADS

the Broads Authority, formed in 1979 to control development and land use throughout the Broads.

Brownie Guides   *See* Scout Association.

Buckingham Palace   The royal palace in which the Queen and Prince Philip reside when they are in London. A 600-room mansion set in 18 hectares (45 acres) of garden in the centre of London, it was started by John Nash on the instructions of George IV soon after his accession. As Prince Consort he had lived in Carlton House, a few hundred yards down the Mall, and had indeed spent a fortune improving and refurbishing it. However, once he became king he declared Carlton House to be no longer suitably imposing for the residence of a sovereign and ordered it to be demolished (Nash later built Carlton House Terrace on the site); a new palace was to be built for him on the site of Buckingham House (a large town house bought by George III from the Marquess of Buckingham), the home of his parents. In spite of pressure to build the new palace where Carlton House had stood, the king insisted that the large grounds of Buckingham House should be made use of and it was here that Nash built a three-sided court, open to the east, with the Marble Arch, as the main entrance, in the forecourt.

By 1830, when the king died, the palace had cost £700,000, against a sum of £200,000 authorized by the House of Commons. Nash was dismissed and the palace remained unused until Victoria's accession in 1837. Edward Blore was then appointed architect to complete the building and it was he who added the east front and removed the Marble Arch to its present position at the north end of Park Lane. However, the east front now visible from the Mall is a façade in Portland stone added by Sir Aston Webb in 1913. The south wing of the palace contains the Queen's Gallery, which is open to the public. The sovereign's personal flag, the Royal Standard, flies from the central flagpole when the Queen is in residence.

Buddhist Society   One of the oldest Buddhist organizations in the UK, which played a leading role in the development of Buddhism in Britain. The Buddhist Society was founded in 1924 by the lawyer Christmas Humphreys (1901–83) and his wife Aileen Faulkner and started life as the Buddhist Lodge of the Theosophical Society, becoming a separate society in 1926. Its journal *Buddhism in England*, founded in 1926, was renamed *The Middle Way* in 1945, a name derived from the first sermon of the Buddha as being the "noble eightfold path between all extremes which leads to enlightenment". Membership is currently in the region of 2500 and the Society's patron is the Dalai Lama.

There are over one hundred other Buddhist organizations in Britain. A Buddhist retreat (*vihara*) was established in London in 1926 and its modern successor, established in Chiswick in 1963, has a resident monastic community (*sangha*). The English Sangha Trust, formed in 1956, runs four *viharas*, including the Chithurst Forest Monastery in Hampshire and the Amaravati Buddhist Centre in Hertfordshire. All these cater for visitors who wish to learn more about Buddhism.

budget   *See* Chancellor of the Exchequer.

building societies   Financial institutions that provide mortgages for house purchase by lending to housebuyers funds that have been deposited with the society by savers. Mortgages are repayable over a long period, usually from 5 to 30 years. Building societies are non-profit-making, and income from interest is used to cover costs and pay interest to savers. Although normal deposit accounts with repayment on demand are available, most savers use "share" accounts, owning shares in the society equal to their balance. There are some restrictions on withdrawal, compensated by a higher rate of interest; but in normal circumstances repayment is made on demand. Special fixed-term deposits pay still higher interest. Some societies now also offer cheque accounts in competition with the banks.

Building societies originated in the 18th century, with small groups of people pooling their resources to build houses for themselves by paying a fixed monthly sum into a central fund. The society was dissolved when the work was complete. The modern permanent societies, which are not tied to particular investors or borrowers, emerged during the 19th century, with the right of incorporation being granted in 1874. Rapid growth followed: by 1919 their assets totalled £77 million. This figure now stands at £86,564 million, with the larger societies, such as the Halifax and the Abbey National, having a nationwide network of branches. However, there are still many small local societies, some with only one office. While building societies as such are unique to Britain, the idea behind them has spread abroad. The similar savings and loan associations in the USA date from 1831.

Burke's Peerage A reference guide to the aristocratic and titled families of Great Britain. It was the brainchild of the genealogist John Burke (1787–1848) who first published it in 1826 under the title *Genealogical and Heraldic Dictionary of the Peerage and Baronetage of the United Kingdom*. Its treatment of peers and baronets in alphabetical sequence by family name (instead of according to precedence) proved successful and it reached its ninth edition within Burke's own lifetime. Thereafter for many years it was published annually, reaching its 105th edition in 1970; it is still regularly updated. Entries take the form of a short biography of the current title-holder and his children, followed by an account of his ancestors (lineage), an illustration and description of the family coat-of-arms, the date of creation of the title, and the family residence. *Compare Debrett's Peerage.*

burning Judas An annual ceremony that takes place in a small area of Liverpool's dockland on Good Friday. The local children parade straw-stuffed effigies of Judas Iscariot from house to house, begging for money; later in the morning the effigies are burned on bonfires in the street. This potentially dangerous activity is frowned upon by the city's police force and the effigies are frequently confiscated. The ceremonial "punishing" of Judas, which originated and is still practised in Spain and some Latin American countries, is believed to have been introduced to this particular dockland area by sailors of the Spanish ships that were unloaded there in the 17th and 18th centuries.

burning the clavie A Scottish custom that takes place annually on 11 January (31 December under the old Julian calendar), in the fishing village of Burghead on the Moray Firth. Its origins are obscure, but it probably developed out of the lighting of fires at the winter solstice (21 December) or at the end of the year to drive out the evils of the old year, to ensure the fertility of crops, livestock, and people in the year ahead, and to remind the sun of its promise to return in the new year. It may also be linked to Norse fireworship. The clavie is constructed from half a tar-barrel, filled with pieces of wood and liberally covered with tar. By tradition, all materials used to make the clavie must be freely donated, not bought, and the nail that holds the structure together, made by a local blacksmith, must be knocked in with a flat stone rather than with a metal hammer. In the evening the clavie is set alight with a piece of burning peat and carried on the shoulders of a series of clavie bearers through the main streets of the town. The final destination is the top of a small hill, from which point the clavie is eventually sent rolling down, scattering fragments of charred wood that are eagerly gathered by the waiting villagers as tokens of good luck and charms against evil.

burning the old year out An annual celebration, with roots in Norse and Anglo-Saxon fire-worship, that takes place in Allendale,

Northumberland, on New Year's Eve. Late in the evening 40 or 50 local men, known as "guisers", parade down the main street wearing fancy dress and carrying flaming tar-barrels on their shoulders. At the stroke of midnight the barrels are thrown onto a huge bonfire in the market place to set it alight; with the assembled onlookers the guisers circle round the fire singing "Auld Lang Syne". When the fire has died down the guisers go "first-footing" – calling at nearby houses in the hope of receiving the traditional refreshments of wine and cake. A similar ceremony takes place at Comrie in Tayside, using huge torches instead of tar-barrels. A number of other Scottish towns, notably Biggar in Strathclyde and the northern town of Wick, perpetuate the ancient tradition of burning the old year out with communal bonfires. (*See also* Up-Helly-Aa.) Elsewhere in Scotland and northern England the arrival of the first guest after midnight on New Year's Eve, if he is a dark-haired man bearing symbols of plenty, is deemed lucky for the new year.

Burns Night An annual celebration that takes place throughout Scotland and among Scots around the world on January 25, the birthday of the Scottish poet Robert Burns (1759–96). The celebration takes the form of a banquet, known as the Burns Supper, followed by speeches, songs, recitations, and sometimes Scottish dancing, and was inaugurated in the early 19th century: the first Burns club was founded in Greenock in 1802 by a group of the poet's friends and admirers. At that time the main dish of the feast was a sheep's head; this was later replaced by the traditional Scottish dish *haggis. A flourish on the bagpipes heralds the arrival of the haggis at the banquet, and it is then carried in procession around the hall before being placed in front of the chairman. There follows a solemn recitation of Burns' "Address to a Haggis", after which it is ceremonially cut open and served. The toasts and speeches made during the course of the evening must, by tradition, include one to the "immortal memory" of Burns, another to "the lasses", reflecting the

BURNS NIGHT *The haggis arriving at the banquet.*

poet's fondness for women, and a loyal toast to the Queen.

Burrell Collection An art collection founded in Glasgow in 1944 by Sir William Burrell, a wealthy shipowner, and his wife Constance. The collection has a wide range of art treasures, including pottery and bronzes of ancient Egypt, Greece, and Rome, Oriental carpets and jade, as well as European tapestries and stained glass. It also includes European paintings from the 15th to early 19th century, the most notable being many fine works by Degas. The modern Burrell Collection gallery stands in Pollok Country Park and was opened to the public in 1983.

busking Entertainment by street musicians who play to queues and passers-by. The origin of the use of this word to denote street performances is obscure, but it seems to date from the 19th century. Buskers may claim distant antecedents in the earliest itinerant minstrels, but their true originals were the troupes of actors and entertainers with performing animals or freaks, who appeared at the medieval fairs and on the roads between them. Many acts which were later incorporated into circuses continued to be seen in the streets until the 19th century: clowns, rope dancers (remarked on by Pepys in the London of Charles II), acrobats, mime artists, and numerous others. The archetypal Victorian street entertainment was perhaps the barrel organ. Playing to queues is essentially a 20th-century practice. However, by-laws, increased traffic, and the rise of mass entertainment has greatly reduced the number of buskers, though they have never disappeared altogether (between the wars, groups of unemployed miners might be heard singing in London and Oxford); the one-man band has also survived. The closure to traffic of areas in cities throughout Britian has allowed street entertainers more of the scope which they enjoy, for example, in the London Underground stations and the restored piazza of Covent Garden.

by-election An election called to fill a vacancy in the *House of Commons, or in a local authority, that has arisen during its life (as the result of the death of an MP, for example). A warrant issued by the Speaker on the order of the House is required to call a parliamentary by-election, because of the Commons' exclusive right to control its internal affairs (*see* parliamentary privilege). The motion for this, to which no time limit applies, is traditionally moved by the chief whip of the party that formerly held the seat in question.

C

Cabinet The *Prime Minister and the group of senior ministers appointed by the Prime Minister, who are collectively responsible for the formulation and implementation of government policy. It is a body established not by law, but by constitutional convention (*see* British constitution) that the executive powers of the Crown are exercised only on the advice of a body that commands majority support in the *House of Commons. Originally, the principal officers of state were appointed by and answerable to the sovereign alone, and rarely acted in concert; a forerunner of the modern Cabinet emerged in 1696, when William III selected a ministry entirely from the Whig party then dominant in the Commons. It was, however, another century before the Cabinet became wholly independent of the Crown and was chosen and presided over by the Prime Minister. The Cabinet normally has around 20 members. Both this number and its precise composition are in theory decided by the Prime Minister, but there are certain restrictions: on one hand, statute limits to 20 the number of Cabinet salaries that may be paid, and on the other, practical considerations make it impossible to exclude the ministers in charge of major departments. The outstanding feature of Cabinet government is the doctrine of collective responsibility (again, purely a convention). Whilst every minister is individually responsible to Parliament for his own decisions and the conduct of his own department, the Cabinet is collectively responsible for its decisions. A member who cannot accept a Cabinet decision must resign, and if the government is defeated in the Commons on the issue, the whole Cabinet must resign. Since 1917 the Cabinet and its committees have been served by a *Cabinet Office.

Cabinet Office One of the most important departments of central government, consisting of the secretariat, the Central Statistical Office, the Management and Personnel Office, and about 135 special units and committees under the authority of the Secretary to the Cabinet. The secretariat provides administrative support for the Cabinet, drafting its agendas, taking the minutes of its meetings, informing other departments about its decisions, and providing the necessary background information for Cabinet ministers, including ministerial briefings prior to international conferences.

The Cabinet secretariat was formed in 1917 by Lloyd George, with Sir Maurice (later Lord) Hankey as the first secretary, in order to cope with the great demands of administration during World War I. Its continuation was recommended by the Machinery of Government Committee in 1918. Prior to 1917 the deliberations of Cabinet meetings were almost never recorded, since the Prime Minister took notes of the proceedings in order to report them to the sovereign. The minutes now taken merely summarize viewpoints and record decisions: verbatim records are not kept of Cabinet meetings. The secrecy which – sometimes incompletely – surrounds the Cabinet secretariat, and Cabinet decision making, remains a matter of fierce debate.

The Central Statistical Office, created by Winston Churchill in January 1941, coordinates a wide range of government statistics, in many cases working closely with the Treasury. The Management and Personnel Office is responsible for the recruitment, management, and organization of the civil service, and the development of comprehensive management development programmes under the authority of the Chancellor of the Duchy of Lancaster. The administration of the honours system is controlled by the Patronage Office, and the historical section is responsible for the writing of official histories. Units within the Cabinet, including temporary committees, may be set up to coordinate inquiries into major public

issues; permanent committees include the Joint Intelligence Committee, which analyses material from all sources for the most senior members of the Cabinet. In 1970 Edward Heath formed a Cabinet unit known as the Central Policy Review Staff or, informally, as the "think tank", which inquired into complex subjects crossing departmental boundaries in which every policy alternative was intended to be examined in depth – collective advice was then presented to the Cabinet. Its reports included one on Concorde and another on the devolution of government powers in 1975–77. The unit was disbanded in 1983, and replaced by the Downing Street Policy Unit.

Caernarfon castle One of a chain of Welsh fortresses built by Edward I to consolidate his successful military campaigns (1276–77 and 1282–83) against Llywelyn ap Gruffud, Prince of Gwynedd. Caernarfon castle stands southwest of Bangor, overlooking the Menai Straits (*see* castles of Wales for map). Building began in 1283 under the supervision of the architect James of St George, and continued sporadically until 1330 when the castle was left unfinished, much as it is today. The walls of the connected inner and outer wards are decorated by horizontal bands of coloured stone and punctuated by polygonal towers – a design said to have been inspired by Byzantine fortresses Edward had seen on the Crusade, before his accession. The Eagle Tower, the largest, named after the stone eagles on its triple turrets, is popularly supposed to have been the birthplace of Edward (1284–1327), who became the first non-Welsh *Prince of Wales in 1301 and later Edward II. The neighbouring Queen's Tower now houses a museum of the Welsh Fusiliers. Caernarfon castle has provided the setting for the investitures of two recent Princes of Wales – those of Prince Edward (later Edward VIII) in 1911 and HRH Prince Charles in 1969. The castle, which is open to visitors, is the strongest part of the fortifications that surround the historic town.

CAFOD (Catholic Fund for Overseas Development) An agency set up in 1962 by the Roman Catholic Church in England and

CAERNARFON CASTLE *The most sophisticated of Edward I's castles in Wales.*

Wales to promote overseas development. Raising its funds mainly from the Roman Catholic community, CAFOD now supports over 400 projects in some 70 countries of Asia, Africa, and Latin America, concentrating on food production, water supply, preventive medicine, and education. It works in conjunction with Catholic agencies within the recipient country as well as with British relief agencies, such as *Christian Aid and *Oxfam. Another important function is to promote awareness at home of third-world problems. In 1984 CAFOD's annual income was over £6 million.

Calvinistic Methodism *See* Presbyterian Church of Wales.

Cambridge Footlights A theatre company drawn from students at Cambridge University. Founded in 1883, the company's first production was an extravaganza, *Aladdin*, given in May Week. Since that time it has specialized in theatrical revues and has provided a starting point for some of Britain's leading comic artists. Until 1926 the Footlights were based at the Theatre Royal in Cambridge, af-

ter which they moved to the Arts Theatre, founded by Lord Keynes. The annual Footlights revue has become an important feature of Cambridge theatrical life and has successfully transferred to London's West End and other venues, such as the Edinburgh Festival. Among the many professional entertainers to have emerged from the company are the brothers Jack and Claude Hulbert, Jimmy Edwards, and Jonathan Miller, whose subsequent revue *Beyond the Fringe* (1961–64) included another former member of Footlights, Peter Cook.

Cambridge, University of The second oldest university in England, after Oxford (*see* Oxford, University of). Informal groups of scholars and masters were probably present in Cambridge at the end of the 12th century, and their numbers were swollen by students fleeing riots in Oxford in 1209. At first, all students lived in hostels and halls. The first college, Peterhouse, was founded in 1284. In 1318 the pope formally recognized Cambridge as a *universitas*, and further colleges were soon founded: Clare (1326), Pembroke (1347), Gonville (now Gonville and Caius) (1348),

UNIVERSITY OF CAMBRIDGE *The chapel of the most recently built college at Cambridge, Robinson College. Completed in 1980, the chapel is decorated with stained glass by John Piper.*

Trinity Hall (1350), and Corpus Christi (1352). Other 14th-century foundations were Michaelhouse (1324) and King's Hall (1337), both later absorbed by Henry VIII's Trinity College (1546). A further ten colleges were established by the end of Elizabeth I's reign, but then there was a hiatus until the foundation of Downing in 1800. The first women's colleges, Girton (1869) and Newnham (1871), pioneered university education for women, but were not given full university status until 1948. The 20th-century foundations include colleges for postgraduate students. A notable recent innovation is the admission of women students to most of the men's colleges.

The colleges are independent self-governing bodies; some, through accumulated endowments and property holdings, are enormously wealthy and have made important financial contributions to the university as a whole. Until the mid-19th century university affairs were run, in accordance with the Elizabethan code of statutes (1570), by the heads of the various colleges. Following royal commissions in 1850–52 and 1872–74, the MAs (Masters of Art) of the university – collectively termed the Senate – were given extended powers, and its members are still entitled to elect the chancellor (currently the Duke of Edinburgh) and formally confer degrees. The practical government of the university lies with the Regent House, a body of college and university office-holders.

Students apply for admission to individual colleges, which organize their tuition and accommodation. The examinations for the BA (Bachelor of Arts) degree are known as the *tripos. The MA degree is granted to BAs without further study or examination, when six years have elapsed after their matriculation. The university year consists of three terms (Michaelmas, Lent, Easter) with an unofficial long vacation term in July and August, when some students opt to stay in Cambridge. The linchpin of the Cambridge teaching system is the weekly supervision (tutorial period) during which the supervisor and usually one student read and discuss the latter's written essay. Besides these college-based tutorials, the university faculty boards organize lectures, demonstrations, and other classes for students from all colleges.

The highlight of Cambridge's social year is May Week (in fact now always in June), when college May balls are held and college rowing eights race on the River Cam. The eights also compete in the Lent Term in a series of races called the Lents (see Head of the River), and the university boat challenges its Oxford opposite number in the *Boat Race. Those chosen to represent the university against Oxford in rowing, rugby, cricket, and certain other sports are awarded their *blue – in Cambridge's case a light blue. More leisurely craft on the Cam are the punts, steered in Cambridge from the flat platform at one end, which is thus known as the Cambridge end (the other end is used at Oxford).

Many of the ancient colleges cluster along the east bank of the Cam opposite the grassy area known as the Backs; others are scattered around the town, and more recent foundations lie out in the suburbs. The college buildings exemplify architecture of every period from medieval to modern, ranged around courtyards called "courts" ("quads" at Oxford). Some particularly notable structures are the Wren Library (1677–92) and the Great Court of Trinity College, the so-called Mathematical Bridge (1749) from Queen's College over the Cam, and the great gothic chapel of King's College, built between 1446 and 1515.

The university museum, founded in 1816 by Viscount Fitzwilliam, has an extensive collection of antiquities and one of the country's finest collections of paintings (see Fitzwilliam Museum). Among other prestigious university institutions are the Cavendish Laboratory, founded in 1871, where many of the world's most eminent physicists, such as J. J. Thomson and E. Rutherford, have worked; *Cambridge University Press; and the University Library, one of the six copyright libraries, which can claim a copy of every book published in the UK.

Cambridge University Press (CUP) The printing and publishing house of the University of Cambridge, and an integral part of it. "Cambridge University Press" is the style under which the Chancellor, Masters, and Scholars of the University of Cambridge print and publish. The Press is a self-financing charitable enterprise, and its charitable objectives and its constitution and government are laid down in University Statute J which begins:

"There shall be in the University a University Press which shall be devoted to printing and publishing in the furtherance of the acquisition, advancement, conservation, and dissemination of knowledge in all subjects; to the advancement of education, religion, learning, and research; and to the advancement of literature and good letters".

Although John Siberch, a German printer, obtained a loan of £20 from the university to print a book in the city of Cambridge in 1521, he had no official connection with the university. The University Press originated in 1534, when Henry VIII granted the University of Cambridge in Letters Patent, the "lawful and warranted power to print there all manner of books approved by the Chancellor or his deputy and three doctors . . . and also to exhibit for sale, as well in the same University as elsewhere in our realm, wherever they please, all such books and all other books wherever printed". The university immediately appointed in 1534 the first of its unbroken succession of University Printers, although university printing operations did not actually begin until 1584, under Thomas Thomas (d. 1588), the eighth University Printer to be appointed. Since 1584, books under the university's imprint have appeared in each and every year.

CUP is the oldest press in the world, the oldest Bible printer and publisher in the world, and the oldest printer and publisher in the English language. The Press is also one of the oldest enterprises of any kind to have retained its constitutional identity intact throughout its history.

Since the late seventeenth century the "three doctors" of the Letters Patent have been replaced by the Press Syndicate, the governing body of eighteen senior members of the university. Before any new book, journal, or Bible, can be published by the Press, it must be considered and approved by the Press Syndicate.

A list of the Press's authors since 1584 includes (in the Humanities) Milton, Donne, Herbert, Bentley, Sir Thomas Browne, Samuel Butler, Doughty, Lord Acton, F. W. Maitland, G. E. Moore, Housman, Whitehead, Bertrand Russell, Quiller-Couch, Dover Wilson, Steven Runciman, Ventris and Chadwick, and F. R. Leavis. In the Sciences, Press authors include Newton, Harvey, James Clerk Maxwell, Rutherford, Eddington, Schrödinger, Jeans, Einstein, Gamow, Needham, Hawking, and Chandrasekhar.

The Press's publishing covers virtually every educational subject seriously studied in the English-speaking world, and now increasingly includes diversification into reference works, professional books, English Language Teaching publishing, software, and electronic publishing.

Over seventy per cent of the publishing output is exported, to over 150 countries. The Press complements and extends the research and teaching of the university by making available, worldwide, through its printing and publishing, an extensive range of academic and educational books, learned journals, Bibles and prayer books, and examination papers.

The United Kingdom operations of the Press are all based in Cambridge. The Pitt Building has been the headquarters of the Press since 1833, when it was built, financed by public subscription, in memory of William Pitt the Younger, for the use of the University Press.

The Publishing Division is housed in the Edinburgh Building, completed in 1980, and named in honour of the Chancellor of the University, The Duke of Edinburgh. It was opened by Her Majesty The Queen in 1981. The modern printing works which houses the Press's Printing Division was completed in 1963 and prints for many distinguished charitable organizations and institutions – as well as for the Publishing Division and the university in general. The American Branch, in New York and New Rochelle, was founded in 1949. The Australian Branch, in Melbourne and Sydney, was established in 1969.

The Press currently publishes well over 1000 new books each year, and maintains in stock some 8500 scholarly and educational titles, and nearly 600 different Bibles and prayer books. The two Divisions produce between them a total of 135 learned and scientific journals. CUP is one of the three English presses entrusted by the Crown with the printing of the Authorized Version of the Bible. The Press printed its first complete Bible – the Geneva version – in 1591, and has produced the Authorized Version since 1629. This unbroken tradition encompasses the Great Folio Bible printed by Baskerville in 1763, the Revised Version of 1881, the New English Bible, the New American Standard Bible, and the Revised Standard Version.

Camden Town group An association, mainly of painters, who gathered at the studio of Walter Sickert (1860–1942) in London's Camden Town after 1905. Formally established in 1911, the group included Harold Gilman, Spencer Gore, Lucien Pissaro, and the critic Frank Rutter. Their subjects were the ordinary streets and squares around them in north London, and the unglamorized domestic interiors within. In their treatment of these they introduced into England a form of postimpressionism. In 1913 most of the group's members were absorbed into the larger *London group.

Campaign for Nuclear Disarmament *See* CND.

canals A network of man-made navigable waterways forming a major feature of the English lowlands and parts of Wales. The Ro-

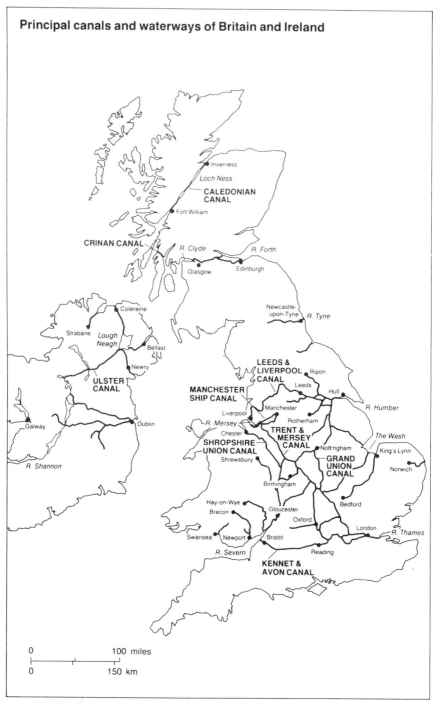

Principal canals and waterways of Britain and Ireland

Inverness
Loch Ness
CALEDONIAN CANAL
Fort William
CRINAN CANAL
R. Clyde
R. Forth
Glasgow
Edinburgh
Newcastle-upon-Tyne
R. Tyne
Coleraine
Strabane
Lough Neagh
Belfast
Newry
LEEDS & LIVERPOOL CANAL
Ripon
Leeds
Hull
ULSTER CANAL
MANCHESTER SHIP CANAL
Liverpool
Manchester
R. Humber
R. Mersey
Rotherham
Galway
Dublin
Chester
TRENT & MERSEY CANAL
The Wash
SHROPSHIRE UNION CANAL
Nottingham
King's Lynn
R. Shannon
Shrewsbury
GRAND UNION CANAL
Norwich
Birmingham
Hay-on-Wye
Gloucester
Bedford
Brecon
Oxford
London
Swansea
Newport
Bristol
R. Thames
R. Severn
Reading
KENNET & AVON CANAL

0   100 miles
0   150 km

mans probably built Britain's first canals, such as Car Dyke, which ran through Cambridgeshire and Lincolnshire, and Foss Dyke, connecting the rivers Trent and Witham, which is still in use. Thereafter, little canal construction took place until the late 18th century, with the notable exception of the Exeter ship canal, constructed in the 1560s to bypass an unnavigable stretch of the River Exe.

The great age of canal building started in the 1760s when James Brindley (1716–72) cut a canal connecting the Duke of Bridgewater's coal mines at Worsley with Manchester. Brindley followed this with a canal linking the Trent and Mersey rivers, a more ambitious project with much bolder use of cuttings, embankments, and tunnels. Brindley's enterprise and pioneering spirit was inherited by such engineers as Thomas Telford (1757–1835) and John Rennie (1761–1821). Their canals took more direct routes across the landscape, entailing great feats of engineering. Canal building increased as manufacturers came to regard this form of transport as rapid and safe, particularly for heavy goods, compared to the unsurfaced and sometimes impassible contemporary roads.

By the 1820s, around 3000 miles of canals had been constructed, largely by "navvies" employed by the private navigation companies. An entire culture developed based on the boatmen and the cargos they transported aboard traditional horse-drawn narrow boats between England's major industrial centres and the ports. The new prosperity brought by the canals was short-lived, however; by the end of the 19th century they were in decline, superseded by the railways, and in the 20th century many fell into disuse and dereliction. When the newly formed *British Waterways Board assumed control of Britain's canals and navigable waterways in 1963, only some 3200 kilometres (2000 miles) remained, much of it in disrepair. With the advent of motorways, the fate of the canals as trade routes ended for ever, but interest in the canal system was not entirely dead. Many of the old narrow boats have been restored and given gentler work as canal cruisers; and the canals themselves are now seen as an attractive amenity, not only for holiday cruising but also for fishing and for towpath walks. The wider ship canals continue to carry freight, but elsewhere the bridges, locks, and towpaths, with their canalside inns and cottages, have become scenic attractions for tourists and holidaymakers.

Candlemas The day on which the purification of the Virgin Mary and the presentation of Christ in the temple at Jerusalem are commemorated. Said to have taken place 40 days after his birth, it is now celebrated on 2 February. The name derives from the ceremonial procession and blessing of candles to be used in the coming year. Candlemas is the first of Scotland's *quarter days.

Canterbury cathedral *See* cathedral.

capital gains tax *See* tax system.

Cardiff Arms Park The most famous sportsground in Wales and the national rugby stadium. The Arms Park, as it is informally known, is the ground of Cardiff Rugby Football Club, one of Wales's most outstanding club sides, whose foundation in 1876 led to the formation of the Welsh Rugby Football Union (RFU) in 1881, the headquarters of which are also at Cardiff Arms Park. Since 1954 Cardiff Arms Park has been the venue for all of Wales's home international matches. For many years, during the summer season, the ground was used by Glamorgan County Cricket Club. In the late 1960s, after Glamorgan's move to the nearby Sophia Gardens, a programme was begun, which increased the seating capacity of the ground from 58,000 to more than 74,000.

Carnegie Trust for the Universities of Scotland A charitable trust founded in 1901 by the Scottish-born US steel magnate and philanthropist Andrew Carnegie (1835–1919). The Edinburgh-based trust allocates half its income for the improvement of research and other facilities in science, medicine, and certain arts subjects in the Scottish universities; the other half goes to pay the university fees of deserving students of Scottish birth or background.

castles of England The great age of castle building in England began with the Norman conquest (1066) and reached its conclusion

CASTLES OF ENGLAND *Leeds Castle, in Kent, was bought by Edward I in 1278 and given to his wife Eleanor of Castile. There is a striking contrast between this castle, set in landscaped parks, and the formidable strongholds built in Wales by the same king.*

during the reign of Henry VIII (1509–47), as the need for fortress-residences for kings and lords diminished. Of the numerous fortified houses and other structures that were built, some remain intact, some are now ruins, and some have disappeared.

The French "motte and bailey" layout, imported by the Normans, consisted of an earth mound (motte) and adjacent courtyard (bailey) surrounded by a timber palisade and a defensive ditch. The motte was reached by a moveable wooden bridge, and surmounted by a wooden tower. Since the buildings within the bailey were also wooden they were frequently destroyed by fire. Berkhamsted castle in Hertfordshire is an example of this type of structure; other motte and bailey sites were incorporated into later constructions, often with stone shell keeps replacing the wooden palisades (e.g. Carisbrooke castle in the Isle of Wight).

The Great Tower (or White Tower) of London (*see* Tower of London) is one of the earliest stone-built castles, dating from the 11th century. Greater protection was afforded by surrounding the bailey with a stone, or curtain, wall (as at Ludlow castle, Shropshire) and was necessary by the 12th century to withstand the improved siege machines. Walls were built higher, with projecting turrets and towers from which assailants could be repulsed. Characteristic of 12th-century castles are high rectangular keeps or "donjons", designed as an ultimate refuge. Examples are at Portchester castle, Hampshire, and Rochester castle in Kent.

The susceptibility of square-angled buildings to undermining in time of siege led to the greater use of buttressing and, in the 13th century, the introduction of curved walls and round towers, giving greater structural strength. Curtain walls were reinforced and the castle entrance was flanked by twin towers to form a gatehouse with portcullis and, typically, a moveable bridge across the moat (as at Pevensey castle, Sussex, for example). Concen-

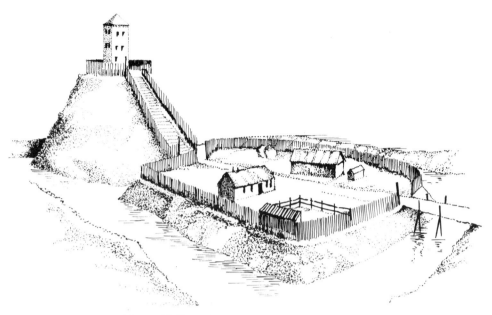

CASTLES OF ENGLAND *Motte and bailey castle.*

tric inner and outer curtain walls were employed in the latter half of the 13th century, a design exemplified by the castles built by Edward I (1272–1307) and his successors in North Wales (*see* castles of Wales).

The popularity of castle building reflected the internal instability of the country; thus the rise of centrally administered and strongly enforced justice (*see* common law) rendered the construction of highly fortified residences superfluous. The obvious exception to this was the Scottish *Border region, where stormy Anglo-Scottish relations have left some of the most striking examples of the 14th and following centuries, such as Alnwick, Dunstanburgh, and Workworth. The major residences built elsewhere in the later Middle Ages (e.g. Warwick, Kenilworth), although superficially impressive, played no part in the wars of the period (the *Wars of the Roses); and Tattershall Castle, Lincolnshire, was built of brick, hardly possessing the intrinsic strength of the earlier stone castles.

Manor houses largely replaced castles in the 15th century. Their high (thin) walls, narrow windows, and moats were evidently thought sufficient to cope with local crimes of violence (*see* country houses). Several castles underwent extensive adaptation of their internal accommodation to meet rising expectations of comfort (e.g. Arundel), or incorporated extra luxurious apartments (e.g. Castle Bolton). Despite many new developments in artillery, a few castles remained in effective occupation until the early 17th century, and stout resistance was offered to Cromwell from the castles at *Harlech, Pembroke, and Bolton.

The construction of castles in England did not end until the 19th century, when Martello towers (round towers with thick walls, in strategic places or at vantage points) were constructed to counter the Napoleonic threat. *See also* Arundel castle; Dover castle.

castles of Ireland Ireland's range of castles and other fortified dwellings reflect not only the country's long history of subjugation and settlement by the English but also reveal a distinctively Irish tradition. Norman mercenaries came to Ireland in the 12th century, initially at the behest of warring Irish chieftains, and brought with them the characteristically Norman motte and bailey castle (*see* castles of

69

CASTLES OF IRELAND *Late-12th-century castle of Carrickfergus, Co. Antrim, with a four-storey Norman keep.*

England). With the intervention of the English king, Henry II, the Normans extended their control to about half the country by 1200, consolidating their authority by constructing numerous castles. Designs paralleled those seen in England, with both rectangular keeps (e.g. at Carrickfergus, near Belfast) and round keeps (e.g. Nenagh Castle, Co. Tipperary); castles in which the rectangular keep had cylindrical turrets, or "flankers", at each corner represent a peculiarly Irish design – for instance, Carlow castle, Co. Carlow. The Norman castles were often taken over by the Irish nobility and used in their struggles with each other or against the Normans.

In 1429 Henry VI promised a £10 grant to anyone who would build a castle to his specifications – 20 feet long, 16 feet wide, and 40 feet high – in order to defend the border of the Pale – the English-controlled counties of Dublin, Meath, Kildare, and Louth, which were ruled from Dublin. The simple three-storey Donore castle, Co. Meath, is probably

one such £10 castle. This straightforward tower design was adopted by the Irish chieftains in other parts of the country and many good examples of the Irish tower house survive. The 15th-century Roodstown castle, Co. Louth, has four storeys with two turrets on top and a "murder hole" above the door, through which noxious substances, such as boiling oil, were poured onto intruders. Often the tower stood in one corner of a walled courtyard, or "bawn", which gave added protection and may have had corner turrets.

English settlers imported Tudor architecture in the late 16th and early 17th centuries; as defence became less of a priority, living accommodation developed on more spacious lines. At Ormond castle at Carrick on Suir, Co. Tipperary, for instance, the Earl of Ormond added an Elizabethan mansion to an existing castle in 1568. However, the Irish continued to build or adapt their long-established tower houses well into the 17th century, often retaining the name "castle" long after all pretence at fortification had been abandoned.

castles of Scotland Due in part to longer periods of internal strife, the fortified dwellings and defensive structures found throughout the Scottish mainland and on many of its offshore islands show a greater range both in age and design than is found south of the border. Although the English architectural styles were a major influence, uniquely Scottish elements are widely in evidence.

Dating from the 1st century, "brochs" were circular thick-walled masonry towers enclosing a central courtyard that was reached through a single low entrance. Following the extension of Anglo-Norman influence into Scotland, developments in English castle construction were exported northwards, and many motte and bailey castles were erected (*see* castles of England). The 12th-century remains of Norse strongholds are to be found on some of the northern and western islands, such as Cubbie's Roo on Wyre Island, Orkney, but the earliest surviving castle is probably Sween castle on Loch Sween, Strathclyde Region. It was built in the late 11th or early 12th century and consists of stone curtain walls surrounding

a courtyard where the original timber structures would have been protected.

In the 13th century, towers were added to this basic design, which can be seen at Inverlochy castle, Highland, (built 1270–80), where a rectangular enclosure is strengthened by round angle towers. This style of building, where the ultimate defensive strength lay in the keep or "donjon", is distinctive from that of the English and Welsh castles of Edward I, where the gatehouse was the stronghold. The combined residential quarters and gatehouse of the 14th-century castle at Doune, north of Stirling, foreshadow the development of the distinctively Scottish tower house that dominated from the late 13th to the late 16th centuries. Tower houses were square or rectangular thick-walled buildings of five or six storeys; their austere façades were surmounted by a parapet and wall, with possibly one or more turrets. Besides affording protection, they were symbols of power and authority for lairds and noblemen alike. Fine early examples are Borthwick (c. 1430) and Elphinstone (c. 1440), both in Lothian. After a lull in the early 1500s, the tower house tradition was revived between 1560 and 1600, often with two or

CASTLES OF SCOTLAND *Carloway broch, Isle of Lewis. Brochs are unique to Scotland.*

CASTLES OF SCOTLAND *Craigievar castle in Grampian; a spectacular seven-storey tower house.*

three towers combined in a Z-plan. Defensive features were now less of a consideration, however, and later examples, such as Glamis castle, were surmounted by a series of dormer windows elaborated into conical-roofed roundels. Craigievar castle, Grampian, completed in 1626, is held by many to be the apotheosis of the tower house. Its slim elegant façade with superbly balanced roundels and roof balustrade, make it one of the most traditionally Scottish of all castles. *See also* Edinburgh castle; Glamis castle; Stirling castle.

castles of Wales The large number of castles in Wales reflects its turbulent history in the Middle Ages. The Norman lords who sought to conquer Welsh lands from the 1060s onwards (*see* Welsh Marches) were responsible for building many of them, especially those in the east, south, and southwest, the chief areas of their penetration. One of the earliest was Chepstow, founded by William Fitzosbern, Earl of Hereford, shortly after the conquest. Its Norman keep is one of the finest of its type to survive. In 1090 Robert Fitzhamon founded a castle at Cardiff on the site of a Roman fort. His simple motte (*see* castles of England) was elaborated with a stone keep and fortification in the 13th century by the de Clare Earls of Gloucester. Pembroke castle was also founded in 1090, by Arnulf of Montgomery; again, the original timber and turf fortress was superseded by stonework including an impressive round keep in the late 12th and early 13th centuries. This story was repeated many times over. The most impressive Marcher castle, however, was a 13th-century foundation: Caerphilly, built (1266–72) by Gilbert de Clare, Earl of Gloucester, to secure land wrested from the Welsh. Covering 13 hectares (30 acres), it is the largest castle in Wales, and one of the largest and certainly the best defended in the British Isles. It was originally sited on an island in a lake, but this has now become marshy meadowland.

Castles were not a Norman monopoly, however. The earliest reference to castle building by Welsh lords comes from the early 12th century; but the most prolific builders were the Princes of Gwynedd in the 13th century. A notable survival (though restored in the 19th century) is Dolwyddelan, reputedly the birthplace of Prince Llywelyn the Great (1173–1240).

CASTLES OF WALES *Beaumaris castle, in Gwynedd, one of the last castles built by Edward I during his conquest of Wales. The castle is well preserved but incomplete, owing to shortage of money.*

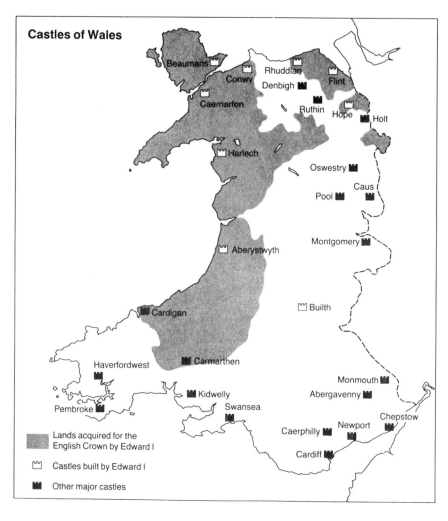

Castles of Wales

Beaumaris
Conwy
Rhuddlan
Denbigh
Flint
Caernarfon
Ruthin
Hope
Holt
Harlech
Oswestry
Caus
Pool
Montgomery
Aberystwyth
Builth
Cardigan
Haverfordwest
Carmarthen
Monmouth
Kidwelly
Abergavenny
Swansea
Pembroke
Chepstow
Caerphilly
Newport
Cardiff

Lands acquired for the English Crown by Edward I

Castles built by Edward I

Other major castles

The castles built by Edward I to consolidate his conquest of Gwynedd (*see* map) are perhaps the finest medieval fortifications in Britain. Between 1277 and 1304, the Crown spent £78,000 in Wales. There are substantial remains at Flint (begun 1277), Rhuddlan (1277), Aberystwyth (1277), Conwy (1283), Caernarfon (1284), Harlech (1285), and Beaumaris (1295). Criccieth, a Welsh castle dating from about 1230, was taken over by the king and expanded from 1285. In most cases, a fortified town populated by Englishmen was an integral part of the design, which was not merely to garrison but also to colonize Wales. At Caernarfon and especially Conwy, the town walls are still virtually intact. The most impressively situated of Edward's castles is Harlech, on a crag above the town, which serves as a landmark on the coast for many miles.

Some castle building continued after the conquest. Raglan dates from the 15th century (though it probably stands on an earlier site). However, the next major development is the "slighting", or demolition, of many castles captured from royalists during the *Civil War

(1642–51). Some examples of partial destruction are Rhuddlan, Monmouth, Raglan, and Haverfordwest; while Newcastle Emlyn, near Carmarthen, was almost completely razed, only one arch still standing. In later years a fashion for mock castles produced such examples as Cyfarthfa castle at Merthyr Tydfil, begun in 1790 by the Yorkshire-born ironmaster Richard Crawshay, and the ornate Castell Coch, built on the northern outskirts of Cardiff in the 1870s by the architect William Burges to a commission from the Marquess of Bute. The latter also extensively modified Cardiff castle, adding new towers and many neogothic flourishes. *See also* Caernarfon castle; Harlech castle.

cathedral The principal church of a diocese or archdiocese, deriving its name from the Greek *kathedra*, meaning "seat", since it was the obvious place to install the throne of the bishop or archbishop. During the Middle Ages the Church engaged the greatest craftsmen in Europe to produce these supreme devotional works of art, which are among the country's most splendid buildings. In England and Wales nearly 30 cathedrals have survived from that time, housing the seats of bishops, as many of the churches built before the Norman conquest were felt to be inadequate in this respect. A number of these medieval cathedrals (e.g. Rochester) had an associated monastic community, the bishop performing the additional tasks of the abbot and the monks serving as the cathedral chapter. At the Reformation this arrangement was changed; several large abbeys (e.g. Chester, an old Benedictine foundation) were converted into cathedrals for newly created dioceses and the monastic connections were severed. The chapters then consisted of a dean, as the head of the cathedral, and canons, who were Anglican clergymen rather than monks. Not many cathedrals were built in England or Wales after the Reformation until the second half of the 19th century, when there was a general shift of population towards urban centres. New sees then had to be created in such cities as Liverpool, Manchester, Birmingham, and Newcastle, where in many cases existing churches were converted into cathedrals (e.g. St Nicholas in Newcastle).

In Scotland the situation was somewhat different because the Reformation swept away episcopacy as well as Catholicism; as a result cathedrals ceased to exist. Many were allowed to fall into ruin (e.g. Elgin in Grampian) and some were relegated to parochial status (e.g. Whithorn in Dumfries and Galloway). This situation was not greatly altered by the later Stuart kings, who attempted to re-establish episcopacy. In some cases an important town kirk (e.g. the High Kirk of St Giles in Edinburgh) was designated a cathedral.

In Ireland the Catholic cathedrals were taken over by the *Church of Ireland. Catholics, both in Ireland and in England and Wales, were prohibited from building cathedrals until the 1830s. Thus most of the present Roman Catholic cathedrals were built in the 19th century, when Catholics could practise freely again.

Cathedral architecture in the British Isles has followed a range of styles, several of which are often apparent in the same building, since many medieval cathedrals have been altered, rebuilt, and added to over the centuries. The oldest surviving buildings for Christian worship in England are Saxon. The churches at Escomb (built c. 680 AD) and Bradford-on-Avon (built 800–900) are notable examples. With the arrival of the Normans in 1066, the Church was completely reorganized and buildings on a cruciform groundplan were introduced. The style of these buildings, called romanesque on the continent, was based on semicircular arches requiring heavy construction and small round-headed windows; Durham cathedral is the best-known example of a Norman building. From the middle of the 12th century, the gothic style, which originated in northern France, began to appear in the British Isles. The so-called early English form of gothic, which lasted until about 1280, was characterized by pointed arches and lancet windows; it reached its zenith in Salisbury and Lincoln cathedrals. The decorated gothic style that followed it continued until the mid-14th century, making use of greater ornamentation, with elaborately ribbed columns, carved exterior friezes, and more intricately decorated windows. Exeter and Wells cathedrals are perhaps the best examples of this style. The

CATHEDRAL *The nave of Durham cathedral. Begun in 1093, the cathedral is a fine example of Norman romanesque architecture, with massive columns, round arches, and one of the earliest rib-vaulted naves in Europe.*

uniquely English perpendicular gothic style followed the decorated style and lasted until the Reformation. It is the most common architectural style in ancient churches and is based on rectilinear window tracery (first used on a large scale in Gloucester cathedral). The windows are vast and enable spectacular use to be made of stained glass (as in **York Minster**, which demonstrates the mixing of all three

gothic styles), the walls are thinner, columns are long and slender, and great use is made of vertical lines and space. **Canterbury cathedral** and Winchester are fine examples of perpendicular architecture, although King's College chapel in Cambridge is perhaps the most breathtaking of perpendicular churches.

From the Reformation to the Civil War (1530–1642), very few churches and no

CATHEDRAL *The Roman Catholic cathedral in Liverpool, the most recently built cathedral in Britain, consecrated in 1967. The altar is in the centre of the building, beneath a huge lantern tower decorated with stained glass by John Piper and Patrick Reyntiens.*

cathedrals were built; internally, there were many changes to existing buildings – much of the religious statuary and carvings were destroyed, and many wall paintings obliterated. The first cathedral to be built after the Civil War was the replacement for the medieval **St Paul's cathedral** in London, which was destroyed in the *Fire of London. Sir Christopher Wren created in its place a baroque cathedral surmounted by a central lantern dome which still dominates the London skyline. In the 19th century the gothic style was revived, notably in the hands of Augustus Pugin (1812–52), who built the Roman Catholic cathedrals of Birmingham, Newcastle, and Southwark, and George Gilbert Scott (1811–87), whose work can be seen in virtually all major English cathedrals. His grandson Giles Gilbert Scott (1880–1960) designed Liverpool's Anglican cathedral. Completed in 1978, it took over 70 years to construct and is the largest church building in the country. By contrast, **Westminster cathedral**, the seat of

London's Roman Catholic archbishop, was constructed in a Byzantine style by John Francis Bentley between 1895 and 1903. With Liverpool's Roman Catholic cathedral (1962–67), architect Sir Frederick Gibberd made a complete departure from tradition, constructing what is essentially a concrete wigwam with its altar at the centre. Above rises a glass and concrete lantern surmounted by a fibreglass crown. Also in the modern style, next to the bombed-out ruins of Coventry's 14th-century cathedral church, is Sir Basil Spence's new cathedral. Opened in 1962, it contains works by several 20th-century artists, including John Piper, Graham Sutherland, and Jacob Epstein.

Catholic schools Schools providing an education for children of all ages based upon the tenets of the Roman Catholic faith. There are over 200 Catholic schools in England, 17 in Northern Ireland, 11 in Wales, and 6 in Scotland, run under the auspices of the Catholic Education Council, which numbers both clergy and teachers among its members. For historical reasons, Catholic schools are comparatively recent foundations. The dissolution of the monasteries under Henry VIII (*see* Reformation) put an end to the medieval monastic schools, and Roman Catholics who wished to preserve their children from Protestant teaching had to rely upon private tutors or send their sons to Catholic colleges on the continent. The latter practice was severely penalized by Elizabeth I since the seminaries at Rome and Douai (in northern France) became training grounds for missionary priests dispatched to win England back to the Catholic faith. Downside (founded 1814), one of the most prestigious boys' Catholic public schools in the country, traces its origin back to the school founded by the Benedictines at Douai in 1605: when the monks of Douai were expelled during the French Revolution (1795), they came to England and eventually settled at Downside in 1814. Jesuit-run Stonyhurst College (1794) began as a college for English boys founded at St Omer in 1592. In former times teachers were always monks and nuns, but most schools now have a proportion of lay staff.

cavalry Although in modern times the cavalry in the British army has been reduced to a ceremonial role, for many centuries mounted troops spearheaded British forces in battle. Used extensively by the Normans, the cavalry included many nobles; indeed charges were often led by members of the royal family. By Elizabethan times the cavalry had developed into three basic wings: the heavily armoured cuirassiers, carrying light lances; lightly armoured horsemen with coats of mail, lances, and a single pistol; and petronels, armed with primitive carbines. Over the next hundred years the increased use of gunpowder led to fundamental changes in cavalry tactics and formations. The light lance was replaced by carbines, pistols, and swords, and armour was gradually discarded. The petronels were replaced by a class of lightly armoured cavalrymen, able to fight either on foot or on horseback, called dragoons. At the same time the headlong charge was replaced by a more strategic approach, developed from the tactics of the Swedish king Gustavus Adolphus (1594–1632), and Oliver Cromwell's Ironsides. At the beginning of the 18th century Marlborough matched the British cavalry against the continental forces with considerable success. A hundred years later they held their own against the finest cavalry that Napoleon could field, establishing a reputation for bravado and arrogance in the face of daunting odds. The action of the Scots Greys at Waterloo (1815) and the charge of the Light Brigade at Balaclava (1854) reinforced this image; at the same time they reconfirmed the difficulty of maintaining discipline over mounted troops in battle. These limitations, combined with the advent of the internal-combustion engine and the machine gun, resulted in the inevitable mechanization of all the cavalry regiments and their merging with the rest of the army. The cavalry played a subsidiary role in World War I, and thereafter has occupied a purely ceremonial role (*see* Household Division).

ceilidh A Gaelic word meaning "visit", designating the social gatherings for story-telling, singing, dancing, and playing of such instruments as the bagpipes and fiddle, common in Scotland until the 20th century. Almost every town had a ceilidh house in which people from the surrounding district gathered for all-night sessions of music-making and the story-telling that enriches the Scottish oral tradition. Ceilidhs still take place occasionally in the Highlands, and have been staged at the *Edinburgh Festival. The word is now used throughout Britain to indicate an evening of traditional dancing.

Celtic crosses Ancient stone crosses found throughout Ireland and in parts of Scotland and northern England. They are enduring relics of the Celtic Christianity that held sway in those areas for most of the first millenium AD. The characteristic motif of the Celtic crosses is a circle enclosing the intersection of the cross. The upright, crossmember, and arcs of the circle are typically sculpted with figures, animals, and other ornamentation, often depicting biblical scenes. Their development is well illustrated by the many Irish crosses, ranging from the late 6th-century Carndonagh cross in Co. Donegal to the splendid cross of Muiredach at Monasterbolice, Co. Louth, which dates from the 10th century. In northeastern Scotland, the

CELTIC CROSSES *The High Cross at Donaghmore, Co. Tyrone: a high stone cross from the 9th or 10th century, carved with biblical subjects, including the Fall and the sacrifice of Isaac.*

Christian symbol evolved from early Pictish slabs, which were incised with symbols from that culture. Later examples, such as those at Meigle, Tayside, bear the familiar Celtic cross in relief on their rectangular surface. The crosses of southern Scotland and northern England, such as Bewcastle cross in Cumbria, are free-standing, like those in Ireland. Ruthwell Cross, near Dumfries, dates from the late 7th century and is inscribed with the Celtic poem *Dream of the Rood*, written in a runic alphabet. Celtic-style crosses were favoured in some parts until the medieval period.

Celtic languages The group of languages that were spoken in Britain from at least the 6th century BC until the coming of the Anglo-Saxons, and are still spoken in some areas of Wales, Scotland, and Ireland. There are two main groups of Celtic languages of which records, if not speakers, survive. These are known respectively as P-Celtic or Brythonic (*Welsh, *Cornish, and Breton) and Q-Celtic or Goidelic (*Irish, *Gaelic, and *Manx). In Roman times (1st to early 5th centuries AD), Brythonic and Goidelic were more or less neatly confined to Britain and Ireland respectively. Subsequently, however, the picture became more confused.

During the Roman occupation, the language used by Roman officials was Latin, and the vernacular was a Celtic language or rather a group of Celtic dialects, predecessors of modern Welsh. Very little is known about this tongue, which would have been the language spoken at the court of King Arthur (*see* Arthurian legend). In pre-Roman times, as the evidence of place names and some early records show, Celtic languages were spoken in many regions of Europe, particularly France and parts of Spain. Breton, however, is not a survival of one of these languages, but a re-introduction from Cornwall. Cornish settlers arrived in Armorica (later to be known as Brittany) in the 5th and 6th centuries AD. Descendants of some of these were eventually to return to Britain: there were many Bretons among the followers of William the Conqueror in the 11th century, and English people with surnames such as Brett (from Old French

bret "Breton"), Gough (in some cases at least from Breton *gof* "smith"), and Harvey (from the Breton personal name Haerviu) are among their present-day descendants. After the Angles, Saxons, and Jutes settled in what is now England, from the 5th century AD onwards (see *English language), the Celtic-speaking area shrank continuously for a millennium and a half, being pushed gradually westward, into the forbidding and more easily defended mountains of western Britain (now Wales).

The historical picture in Scotland and Ireland is more complex, but the end result is much the same. Scots Gaelic was brought to Scotland from Ireland in the 5th and 6th centuries AD. In medieval times, Irish and Scots Gaelic were under threat from other languages, at first Norse (the old Scandinavian language), and later Norman French. From the 16th to the early 20th century, Gaelic and Irish were both systematically eroded by English.

The pronunciation of Celtic languages, especially the Goidelic group, is complex, and hard for English speakers to learn accurately. In particular, a number of unfamiliar consonant distinctions are made. In Irish, for example, there are four varieties of -n-. Matters are further complicated by "mutations", changes to the initial consonants of words, determined by complex sets of rules based on syntax and vocabulary.

The Celtic languages now represent the remnants of once great cultures; they are spoken in the remoter western parts of Wales, Scotland, and Ireland, and most of those who use them are also competent in English. Attempts by enthusiasts to revive Welsh are, temporarily at least, meeting with some success, but elsewhere the long decline of Celtic languages continues. There remain 100,000 active speakers of Irish in Ireland, while Scottish Gaelic is spoken by around 80,000–90,000 people. The last speaker of Deeside Gaelic (the last of the eastern dialects) died in 1984, shortly before a party of philologists were due to visit her. The last speaker of Manx died in 1974. The last known speaker of Cornish died in 1777.

census *See* Population Censuses and Surveys, Office of.

Central Criminal Court A court (known informally as the *Old Bailey) that was established by Parliament in 1834 as a permanent *assizes for what is now Greater London, and also as the court of *quarter sessions for the City of London; it was converted by the Courts Act 1971 into London's principal *Crown Court. Its judges include the holders of two very ancient offices, the Recorder of the City of London (*see* recorder) and the *Common Serjeant. The Lord Mayor and aldermen of the City are also entitled to sit, but in fact do so only ceremonially.

Central Office of Information (COI) The official government information service, a branch of the civil service responsible for distributing information about Britain via domestic and foreign media. Roughly half the COI's staff of 900 are devoted to overseas publicity for the Foreign and Commonwealth Office or the British Overseas Trade Board, for information officers in British embassies, and for foreign journalists based in London. The remainder serve a wide range of home departments and agencies. The 1500 foreign officials who visit Britain each year are given planned tours organized by the COI, and briefings are given to British diplomats being posted abroad.

Ceremony of the Keys A ceremony in which the *Tower of London, formerly a fortress prison, is locked up for the night. Every evening at 9.55 pm the Chief Yeoman Warder, wearing a long red coat and Tudor bonnet and carrying a lantern, leaves the Byward Tower with an escort and locks the outermost gate, followed by those of the Middle Tower and the Byward Tower. He then proceeds to the Bloody Tower arch where, before he can enter the inner bailey (yard), he is challenged by a lone sentry. A staccato dialogue follows after which the keys, having been identified as the sovereign's keys of Her Majesty's Tower, are carried through the arch. The Chief Warder then encounters the rest of the Tower guard, formed up on the steps leading to the Broad Walk, and they present arms. He doffs his bonnet and calls "God preserve Queen Elizabeth", to which the guard responds "Amen!" The keys are finally carried by the Chief Warder to the resident governor in Queen's House on Tower Green, as the clock strikes ten and the "Last Post" is ·sounded.

The ceremony is reckoned to go back at least 700 years to the reign of Edward I (1272–1307) when the concentric castle was completed.

Certificate of Secondary Education (CSE) *See* school-leaving examinations.

chalk hill figures Giant figures of men or animals carved on chalk hillsides in southern England. Some are of considerable antiquity, others are more recent; the difficulty in keeping the exposed chalk outlines clear of vegetation has resulted in the obliteration of many figures. At Cerne Abbas in Dorset a naked giant represented in outline and brandishing a club stands 55 metres (180 feet) tall on the hillside above the village. A prominent feature of the carving is the large erect penis: the giant was for many years associated with fertility rites and a maypole set up in an early Iron Age earthwork above his head was the centre of local May Day festivities. One of the many theories concerning the giant's origin is that the figure was carved by the Romans in the 2nd century AD as a representation of Hercules; the banked enclosure, known as the Trendle or "Frying Pan" due to its distinctive round shape, may have been an Iron Age burial mound. A second giant, the Long Man of Wilmington, is carved on Windover Hill in Sussex, and is outlined by trenches and white-painted bricks. The figure stands nearly 70

CHALK HILL FIGURES *Aerial view of the Cerne Abbas giant in Dorset.*

metres (230 feet) tall and holds two staves, one in each hand: these may have originally been representations of spears or agricultural implements. Like the Cerne Abbas giant, the Long Man of Wilmington is believed to date back to Roman times or earlier.

Many of the surviving chalk hill figures represent animals: there are numerous white horses, notably those at Oldbury and Westbury in Wiltshire, and at Uffington in the Vale of the White Horse in Oxfordshire. The Wiltshire horses date back only to the late 18th century, although the Westbury horse may lie on top of a more ancient chalk figure; the Uffington horse, however, is believed to have been carved in the late Iron Age, perhaps as a cult object for the local Celtic tribe, the Belgae, and has inspired many imitations. Unlike the solid shapes of the other white horses, the Uffington horse is represented in a disjointed, stylized form: it is difficult to conceive how the original shape could have been laid out with such accuracy. A number of legends are connected with the figure – St George is alleged to have killed the dragon on a nearby hill – and the ceremonial seven-yearly scouring of the outline was once accompanied by games and festivities.

Chancellor of the Exchequer A senior government minister and member of the *Cabinet in charge of the Treasury (the principal department of state responsible for the management of the national economy).

The **Exchequer** was formed under William II or Henry I as the king's official debt-collecting agency. Its name was derived from the large chequered cloth used like an abacus for the public reckoning of royal debtors' accounts, so that observers could easily follow the proceedings. From these beginnings, it developed both into a full-scale court (*see* common law) and into the royal finance department, responsible for collecting all the king's income and paying out for authorized expenditure. This did not prevent revenue being diverted to other agencies, or appropriated directly by the king, and at various times in the Middle Ages the Exchequer was reduced to secondary importance. However, it was only finally superseded when the **Treasury** (originally the department that stored the king's

money) acquired an independent existence and control of newer, and more important, revenues in the 17th century. The Exchequer's business declined to insignificant levels, and its financial functions were transferred to the Treasury in 1833.

The Exchequer and Treasury were originally presided over by a lord high treasurer; but after 1714 by the lords commissioners of the Treasury ("lords of the Treasury"), who exercised his functions jointly. In the 18th century, whenever the First Lord was a member of the House of Commons, he was also Chancellor of the Exchequer; however, when he sat in the Lords, the Chancellor was the principal government financial spokesman in the Commons. As the office of First Lord of the Treasury came usually to be held by the *Prime Minister, his financial duties devolved onto the Chancellor – though as late as the 1840s Sir Robert Peel presented the budget as Prime Minister. The Chancellor, who is now always Second Lord of the Treasury, is responsible for the direction of economic and financial policy generally and, in particular, the raising of public revenue (primarily through taxation) and the control of public expenditure. He is also ex officio "master worker and warden" of the Royal Mint. Beneath him politically are the chief secretary to the Treasury (who deals with public expenditure, particularly departmental estimates for each year), the financial secretary to the Treasury (who assists him in the handling of financial business in the House of Commons), and one or more ministers of state. The proposals of the Chancellor with respect to taxation for the coming year are presented to the Commons in a March or April **budget**. After he has completed the budget speech containing these proposals (a closely guarded secret beforehand) the House confirms them by a series of formal resolutions that are given immediate (but temporary) legal effect by the Provisional Collection of Taxes Act 1968. A budget debate follows, spread over several days, and the proposals are then embodied in a finance Bill for enactment as an Act of Parliament.

Chancery Court of York *See* Court of Arches.

CHANCELLOR OF THE EXCHEQUER *Artist's impression of the Exchequer at work in the 12th century. On the furthest side are the king's ministers, facing the sheriff, whose accounts are being examined. The king's accountant did sums by moving counters from square to square in front of numerous witnesses. It was from the chequered cloth on the table that the Exchequer derived its name.*

Chancery Division *See* High Court of Justice.

change-ringing Bell-ringing according to a predetermined mathematical pattern. A custom found only in Britain and occasionally in the Commonwealth, change-ringing still takes place regularly at many churches. Between four and twelve bells – though the classic number may be said to be eight – are rung by teams of practised individuals. It is "method-ringing" – known informally as "ringing the changes" (hence the phrase) – the method being the permutations so arranged that in the succession of changes no consecutive two are alike. Methods vary in complexity: each has a two-part name, indicating firstly its intricacy (e.g. Grandsire, Treble Bob), and then the number of bells used (e.g. Singles: four, Doubles: five, Major: eight, Royal: ten). The pealing of bells has long been heard throughout Britain on Sundays.

changing the guard A daily ceremony usually involving footguards from one of the five regiments of the Household Division (*see* trooping the colour) at Buckingham Palace and St James's Palace, and the Household Cavalry at Horse Guards Yard, Whitehall. It has long been a tourist attraction, although when the Queen is not in residence at Buckingham Palace (as indicated by the absence of the Royal Standard on the palace roof) the ceremony there and in Whitehall is on a smaller scale.

After the Restoration of Charles II the responsibility for the daily protection of the sovereign passed from the Yeomen of the Guard to the Life Guards and the foot guards. Whitehall Palace was originally the official royal residence (until it was destroyed by fire) and it is for this reason that the ceremony for mounted guards takes place there; similarly the foot guards' ceremony starts at St James's Palace because that became the official royal residence before Queen Victoria moved to Buckingham Palace. At 11 am each morning the St James's Palace detachment of the old guard, bearing their colour, march up the Mall, led by their corps of drums; in the forecourt of Buckingham Palace they join the old Buckingham Palace guard, who are drawn up for inspection. The new guard arrives with regimental band and drums at 11.30 am; they present arms, the Palace keys are handed over, officers confer, new sentries are posted, and special orders are read out. After further military compliments, the old guard returns to barracks, led by the regimental band, while the St James's Palace detachment of the new guard marches to St James's Palace where the colour is lodged. A similar ceremony involving an old and a new guard – this time on horseback – is carried out in the more confined space of Horse Guards Yard in Whitehall where the Life Guards and Blues and Royals alternate on guard duties. Foot guards are also mounted at the Tower of London, Windsor castle, and Edinburgh castle.

Channel Islands An archipelago in the *English Channel 130 km (81 miles) south of the English coast. Owing allegiance to the British Crown, though not strictly part of the UK, they were attached to the Duchy of Normandy, which was brought into British hands by William the Conqueror. The islands were the only part of the Duchy not lost to Philip of France by King John in 1204. English has succeeded French as the everyday language, but an Anglo-Norman patois is even now spoken by a few local families, and island law students spend a year at a French university since legal documents are written in French.

The history of the islands has been relatively uneventful, save that during World War II their proximity to France and the difficulty in defending them led Britain to withdraw its forces in 1939, allowing the Germans to occupy the islands. They remained in occupation until 1945; the concrete gun towers and underground hospitals are maintained by the islanders as monuments of the occupation and to the many foreign slave labourers who died building them.

The islands are divided into two self-governing bailiwicks. The bailiwick of Guernsey, with its dependencies of Herm, Alderney, and Sark, is governed by a parliament called the States of Deliberation, while that of Jersey, with Les Minqueries and Ecrehou Rocks, is governed by the States of Jersey. Both have their own postal and monetary systems, based on those of the UK. Each has a lieutenant-governor and commander-in-chief, who has no vote in the elected assembly, but almost all enactments require the sanction of the Queen-in-Council. Bailiffs are appointed by the Crown as presidents of the assembly and of the royal courts of Guernsey and Jersey, and have a casting vote in the States. The legal system differs in minor respects from that of Britain and has allowed traces of feudalism to survive into the present day. In Guernsey, for example, until 1984 tenants had to pay a "congé" of 2% of the selling price of a house to the lord of the manor of their particular fief. In Sark, the head of the island is the seigneur or dame, and the Chief Pleas, or parliament, consists of 40 tenants and 12 elected deputies; there is no income tax and in accord with the wishes of the late dame, Sybil Hathaway, cars are banned.

chapel The word "chapel" is used in several senses. It may mean either a small church building or a consecrated building with no parochial status (e.g. the chapel of a university college). However, it also means a church of a *Nonconformist congregation, or even the congregation itself. In most parts of Britain, for every Anglican or Roman Catholic church, several chapels can be found nearby. Although generally of less architectural merit, they represent an enduring tradition of non-

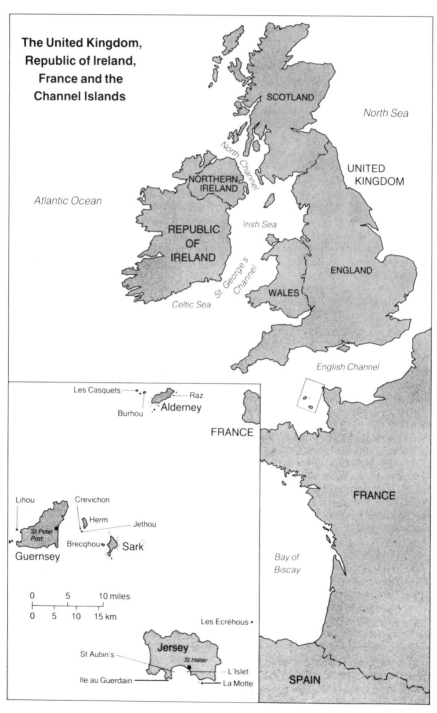

The United Kingdom, Republic of Ireland, France and the Channel Islands

SCOTLAND

North Sea

North Channel

NORTHERN IRELAND

UNITED KINGDOM

Atlantic Ocean

REPUBLIC OF IRELAND

Irish Sea

St. George's Channel

ENGLAND

WALES

Celtic Sea

English Channel

Les Casquets

Raz

Burhou

Alderney

FRANCE

Lihou

Crevichon

Herm

Jethou

St Peter Port

Brecqhou

Sark

Guernsey

FRANCE

0   5   10 miles

0   5   10   15 km

Bay of Biscay

Les Ecréhous

Jersey

St Aubin's

St Helier

L'Islet

Ile au Guerdain

La Motte

SPAIN

conformist worship that originated in the 16th and 17th centuries; in the following two centuries it led to a proliferation of denominations and sects, including the *Baptists, *Presbyterians, Unitarians, Congregationalists (*see* Unitarianism; United Reformed Church), and above all, the *Methodists.

These chapels embodied their founders' rejection of the ornament and ceremonial of the established Church and were constructed on a modest scale and in a simple and plain fashion. The majority of existing chapel buildings date from the 19th century, but nonetheless show a range of architectural variation on the basic rectangular plan. Façades typically have straightforward classical lines with a central door or porch and windows either side. Some later examples even have pillars or columns. Others yielded to the Victorian preoccupation with the neogothic. The interiors maintained the simplicity of the exteriors, with a rostrum and pulpit at one end, facing the pews for the congregation. Perhaps the oldest surviving example is the Congregational chapel at Horningsham in Wiltshire, which resembles a thatched cottage and has been in continuous use since its foundation in 1566.

The chapel is intended as the focus of the community, the scene not only of Sunday worship but also of instructional classes during the week; many have a strong musical tradition, with choirs and bands – the chapels of the Welsh valleys have produced some outstanding male-voice choirs (*see* Welsh male-voice choirs). In the industrial regions of South Wales and northern England particularly, the Nonconformist chapels were the catalysts for a broader social and political consciousness, in which rejection of Anglicanism was extended to include attacks on the gentry and the aristocratic structures with which Anglicanism was associated (partly because clergymen in the 19th century were often drawn from the upper middle classes). This sometimes led to participation in trade unions and the socialist movement.

chapter The governing body of a *cathedral, comprising the dean and his canons (i.e. constituent members of the chapter, paid by and usually resident at the cathedral, corresponding to the abbot and monks of a monastery, which a cathedral often succeeded). In old foundation cathedrals (medieval nonmonastic cathedrals), there are three principal canons: the precentor, in charge of choral services; the chancellor, responsible for the cathedral school and library; and the treasurer. In new foundation cathedrals, (monastic cathedrals given new constitutions by Henry VIII at the *Reformation), and those more recently established, the titles may vary and the chapter is usually headed by a provost. The greater chapter is a larger body comprising other canons of the cathedral. These may be permanent salaried staff of the cathedral or incumbents of parishes in the diocese who have certain duties and privileges connected with the cathedral (such as a personal stall in the choir). Many cathedrals now also have lay canons.

Charity Commission The body that oversees the administration of registered charities throughout England and Wales. Charity Commissioners were first appointed in 1853 but their present-day activities are regulated by the Charities Act 1960. The Commission maintains a complete register of charities at its London headquarters, with copies available elsewhere. The Commission's general aim is to promote the efficient operation of charities, to advise trustees (though it is not empowered to run charities), and when necessary to investigate reported abuses. Charities wishing to dispose of land or buildings usually have to seek the Commission's approval. The Official Custodian for Charities receives income from charities' land and investments and passes it to the respective charities free of UK income tax. This tax relief is of major benefit to charities and loss of charitable status is therefore a considerable blow. This has occasionally befallen organizations (e.g. certain fringe religious sects, for example, the Unification Church, or Moonies) whose activities and methods were deemed inappropriate for a charity.

Chartists Members of a movement (1838–48) for radical political reform, based around the "People's Charter" (1838). This was a set of six demands, drafted in the form of a parliamentary Bill, drawn up by the London Working Men's Association (founded 1836), and comprising annual parliaments, adult male suffrage, elections by secret ballot, equal electoral districts, the abolition of the property qualification for MPs, and the payment of MPs. None of these demands were new, having been in circulation since the late 18th century; however, the Charter presented them in a simple form calculated to attract wide support. From the beginning there was a division between the "moral force" Chartists, led by William Lovett (1800–77), who believed in constitutional persuasion, and the "physical force" Chartists, led by Feargus O'Connor (1794–1855), who were prepared to use direct action. Support for the movement fluctuated with the condition of the economy, being strong in times of depression. A national petition in support of the Charter was presented to Parliament in 1839 but made little impression. Its rejection split the movement, with a call for a general strike being first approved and then rejected. The only serious trouble occurred at Newport, Monmouthshire (now Gwent), where 14 demonstrators were killed by the militia and others were sentenced to transportation. A second petition, organized by O'Connor, was rejected in 1842. Chartism declined thereafter, apart from a brief revival in 1848, when a third petition was rejected. Since its demise, all the aims of the People's Charter have been enacted, except for annual parliaments; and the Chartists have acquired a place in the mythology of the *Labour Party and left-wing British politics.

cheese-rolling An annual contest that takes place on Cooper's Hill, outside the village of Brockworth, Gloucestershire, on spring bank holiday Monday (formerly Whit Monday); at one time it was one of a number of sporting events and festivities. Originally performed to maintain sheep-grazing rights on the common land of the area, the custom is believed to date back to the 16th century. The competitors line up at the top of the hill, beside a flagstaff that marks the point where the maypole once stood, while the starter, dressed in a white coat and top hat, prepares to launch the cheese; once it is on its way the perilous chase down the hillside begins. Any competitor who can catch the cheese before it reaches the foot of the hill is declared the winner and

keeps the cheese as a prize; if the cheese outruns its pursuers, as is invariably the case, the winner is the first person to reach the bottom. Competitors frequently fall headlong as they race down the one-in-three slope; the most unfortunate incident occurred in the 19th century when the triumphant winner, a young girl, is said to have dropped dead at the foot of the hill.

cheeses Many contemporary British cheeses were developed hundreds of years ago, although the expense of transport meant that they could rarely be enjoyed outside the district in which they were produced. The bulk of modern cheesemaking takes place in the creameries of the Milk Marketing Board, but a recent revival of interest in more traditional methods has made it possible to buy farmhouse cheeses from all over the country at specialist retailers in most large towns and cities. Cheddar is undoubtedly the most popular and best-known British cheese, although less than 1% of the Cheddar consumed in Britain today comes from Somerset, its traditional home; in fact a large proportion is imported from New Zealand, Canada, and elsewhere.

Caerphilly, a hard white cheese widely consumed by Welsh miners in the 19th century, is now made largely in England. Gloucestershire is the home of Single Gloucester and the creamier and better-known Double Gloucester; from Leicestershire come the hard red Leicester and Stilton, usually in its famous "blue" variety. The production of this internationally renowned blue cheese dates back at least to the early 18th century, when it was made at Quenby Hall in Leicestershire and known as "Lady Beaumont's cheese"; later it was sold from The Bell, a coaching-house at Stilton, some 50 kilometres (30 miles) from the village where it was made. Stilton is England's only protected cheese, its production being almost exclusively limited to the area around Melton Mowbray. Few other blue cheeses are to be found in Britain today, apart from the recently introduced Lymeswold, a soft blue cheese made in Somerset, and blue versions of such traditional cheeses as Wensleydale and Cheshire.

Cheshire is the oldest of Britain's named cheeses; it dates back to pre-Roman times and

CHEESE-ROLLING *Chasing the cheese down the perilous slope.*

was mentioned in Domesday Book. A hard white or coloured cheese with a crumbly texture, it is now produced throughout the county and in neighbouring Shropshire and Clwyd. White cheeses of a similar texture are made in Lancashire and in the Yorkshire Dales, notably Wensleydale. Cheeses from the Dales were originally made from ewes' milk by French monks who came to England after the Norman conquest; the name Wensleydale was not used until the 19th century, by which time the cheese had been made almost entirely from cows' milk for many years. Scottish cheeses include Dunlop, a hard cheese that originated in Ayrshire (now Strathclyde Region); a Scottish version of Cheddar; and two recently revived traditional soft cheeses, Crowdie and Caboc.

Chelsea Flower Show A show organized by the Royal Horticultural Society each May in the grounds of the Royal Hospital, Chelsea, in London. It was first held in 1913 and is now probably the greatest annual event of its kind in the world. The Royal Horticultural Society

was founded in 1804 by John Wedgewood (son of Josiah Wedgewood, the famous potter) to encourage the discovery, introduction, and propagation of new and rare flowering plants and vegetables. The numerous shows and exhibitions organized by the society, together with its publications, have stimulated public interest to such an extent that it is now considered the world's leading body in gardening and horticulture. Success at the Chelsea Show is the ambition of all competitively minded growers, and people come from all over the world to compete, or simply to admire the beauty and perfection of the exhibits.

Chelsea Pensioners Occupants of the Royal Hospital for old and disabled soldiers in Chelsea, London. Founded by Charles II in 1682 as a home for veteran soldiers, the Royal Hospital takes in about 420 men, usually aged over 65, and provides them with board, lodging, a weekly allowance, and medical attention. Chelsea Pensioners are organized into six companies, and wear distinctive uniforms, navy blue in winter and scarlet in summer.

87

The uniform also includes a three-cornered hat, which is worn on such ceremonial occasions as *Oak Apple Day.

Cheltenham Festival An annual festival of concerts held in Cheltenham, Gloucestershire, for one or two weeks in June or July each year. Conceived as a festival of contemporary British music, it opened in 1945 with a concert that included Benjamin Britten's "Four Sea Interludes" from the opera *Peter Grimes*, conducted by the composer. Opera itself is rarely performed because of the lack of a suitable theatre, but a wide range of orchestral, chamber, and solo concerts take place. In 1966 the work of foreign contemporary composers was introduced to the festival, and in 1974 the event was renamed the Cheltenham International Festival.

At the Festival of Literature held every autumn in Cheltenham, events include poetry readings and talks by writers.

Cheltenham Ladies' College *See* public schools.

Chequers The official country residence of British prime ministers, located in the Chiltern Hills near Princes Risborough, Buckinghamshire. The estate is mentioned in Domesday Book and belonged to the Cheker family as early as the 13th century. The son of Cromwell's youngest daughter married the heiress to the Chequers estate and the house still contains many of Cromwell's possessions, including his sword. The north façade dates from 1565 but the house was substantially remodelled between 1909 and 1912 by Lord Lee of Fareham, a Conservative politician and great admirer of Lloyd George, one of whose *Cabinet ministers he later became. Lee donated Chequers to the nation in 1921 as "a place of rest and recreation for her prime ministers for ever". Located close to London, the estate serves principally as the Prime Minister's weekend retreat but also as an out-of-town venue for top-level summit meetings.

Cheshire Foundation An organization devoted to the care of the mentally and physically handicapped, generally in the Foundation's own homes. The Foundation was set up in 1948 by Group Captain Leonard Cheshire VC (1917–   ), an RAF war hero, and man of deep religious conviction. Cheshire's original intention after the war had been to set up a series of cooperative settlements for ex-servicemen and women. However, after the first such community was disbanded because of financial difficulties, Cheshire became personally involved in the nursing of one of its former members who was terminally ill and homeless. He was soon inundated with requests to accept similarly helpless cases and in this way the first home came into existence. The organization is now worldwide, having affiliations with over 147 homes in 45 countries, in addition to the 75 homes and hostels in Britain. As well as residential care, the Cheshire Foundation also offers help to the handicapped in their own homes.

Chief Rabbi *See* Jews in Britain.

Chiltern Hundreds The "hundreds" of Stoke, Desborough, and Burnham in Buckinghamshire (a hundred being a small administrative unit, and subdivision of a *shire in Anglo-Saxon and Norman England). Their stewardship is an ancient public office in the gift of the sovereign, the holder of which is disqualified from membership of the *House of Commons, formerly because it ranked as an office of profit, and now because it is specifically listed as a disqualifying office in the House of Commons Disqualification Act 1957 (*see* Member of Parliament). The office has been a sinecure for centuries, but has been kept in existence (together with that of steward or bailiff of the Manor of Northstead in Yorkshire) as a means of enabling an MP to resign his seat. As there is no law or custom of Parliament allowing an elected member to resign, the member applies for one or other of these two offices. The office is granted as a matter of course, the MP loses his membership by automatic disqualification, and he then resigns the office to make it again available to others.

choir schools Schools associated with cathedrals or colleges, originally intended to provide a general education for their choristers. The majority of the schools in the Choir Schools Association (founded 1919) are *preparatory schools, but others cater for pupils up to the age of 18, and in these schools choristers

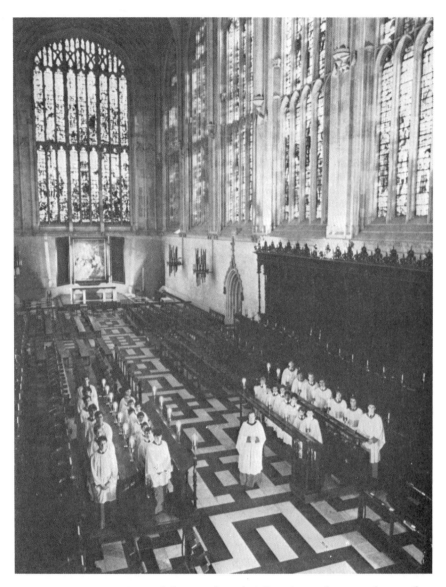

CHOIR SCHOOLS *The choirboys and choristers of King's College choir performing in the magnificent setting of King's College chapel, Cambridge.*

form a tiny percentage of the total membership. Applicants for choristers' places undergo voice tests, and the successful candidates are generally awarded scholarships, which they hold until their voices break. Although one or two schools are of ancient origin – King's

School, Rochester, and York Minster Song School both claim to have been founded in the 7th century – the education of choristers was largely neglected until Miss Maria Hackett (1783–1874) drew attention to their plight and provision was made for them in the Elementary Education Act 1870. The emphasis on musical training affords special opportunities for the musically gifted child or the boy with a fine singing voice, but otherwise the curricula and wider educational aims of choir schools are comparable to those of ordinary schools.

Christian Aid The organization set up by the *British Council of Churches in 1949 to coordinate the collection and distribution of donations for the needy overseas from the various Christian churches in Britain. It runs educational, agricultural, and health schemes in developing countries and operates a scholarship programme under which students from these countries can come to Britain. It also raises money for disaster relief, making no distinctions as to the religion, race, or politics of those it aids. Much of its work is done in collaboration with other relief agencies, especially Church-related organizations, such as the Catholic Fund for Overseas Development (*CAFOD). Within Britain it organizes lectures and other functions to raise public awareness of the needs of developing countries. The governing board of Christian Aid is appointed for a three-year term by the British Council of Churches.

Christian names The names given to children at birth or baptism that precede the surname. The set of ordinary Christian names in Britain and Ireland is surprisingly small: less than 1000 basic names for both men and women. To these may be added derivatives – affectionate forms, such as Kenny from Kenneth, and abbreviations, such as Tom from Thomas. Sometimes the connection between the two forms is not obvious, as in the case of Peggy, from Margaret. Surnames have from time to time been used: sometimes through their being the mother's maiden name, or the surname of an important family. Some of these, such as Dudley, Douglas, Rodney, and Shirley, have become standard Christian names. A few names are more or less confined to one family or clan, as is Sholto in the Scottish Douglas family.

There are two main sources of Christian names: Christian tradition, including Biblical names and those borne by early saints, and

names with a pagan (usually Germanic or Celtic) origin. The best-known Christian names are anglicized versions of those occurring in the New Testament: Simon, Peter, James, Thomas, Andrew, John, Philip, Mark, Matthew, and Paul. All of these names have cognates throughout Christendom, and have given rise to a number of derivatives. The girls' names Jane, Janet, Jean, Jeanette, and Joan are all derivatives of John. Not surprisingly the most common girl's name in Christendom is Mary. Ann (from the Hebrew name Hannah), Elizabeth, and Martha also derive from the New Testament. The Old Testament, similarly, has given rise to a number of popular Christian names. These are bestowed in honour of kings and heroes (David, Joshua), patriarchs (Adam, Joseph), and prophets (Samuel, Jeremy (Jeremiah)). Old Testament girls' names include Susan (Susannah), Sarah, Deborah, Abigail, Rachel, Rebecca, and Ruth. The Puritans in the 17th century particularly favoured the names of Old Testament prophets for boys; girls were often named after abstract virtues, such as Patience, Prudence, and Charity.

The Norman conquest (1066) brought a whole new set of names to the British Isles, virtually obliterating most of the Old English names, such as Wulfstan, Aethelred, and Aelfthryth. The few Old English names that have survived, notably Alfred, Edward, and Mildred, were borne by exceptionally heroic or saintly royal personages before the conquest, and are often 19th-century revivals. Norman names established among the new royalty and aristocracy in the 12th century include William, Henry, Richard, Robert, Ralph, Hugh, Jocelyn, Herbert, Raymond, and Reginald; Norman women's names include Alice, Evelyn, Maud, Rosamund, and Millicent. Norman and Old English names, for the most part, are both ultimately of Germanic origin, and generally are composed of two thematic elements. Thus, Roger is from *hrod* "fame" + *gari* "spear". Richard is from *ric* "rule" + *hard* "brave". Alfred is from Old English *aelf* "elf" + *raed* "counsel". Mildred is from *mild* "gentle" + *thryth* "power".

The most famous Celtic name is undoubtedly Arthur, and the names of several other characters from *Arthurian legend have passed into common use, notably Jennifer (Guinevere) and Gavin (Gawain). Less common are Lancelot and Percival. Other names of Celtic origin include Irish Brian, Neil, and Deirdre, and Scots Duncan and Kenneth. Alan is of Breton origin, apparently the name of an obscure saint; it is remarkably common for a name of such uncertain origin.

Use of a name by a member of the royal family has generally guaranteed its popularity: William, Henry, Edward, George, Charles, Elizabeth, and Alexandra are examples. Literary and, more recently, film vogues have also influenced the choice of Christian names. Miranda, Rosalind, Viola, and Imogen may owe much to Shakespeare, Emma to Jane Austen, Shirley to Charlotte Brontë, Wendy to James Barrie, and Tracy to Grace Kelly in the film *High Society*. Similarly, such modern names as Gemma, Lisa, and Wayne, have probably achieved popularity through the influence of the cinema. Finally, mention should be made of the "flower" and "gemstone" names for girls, such as Violet and Lily, Ruby and Beryl, introduced for the most part during the 19th century.

Christmas The feast of the nativity of Christ, now almost universally celebrated on 25 December, the first of the traditional 12 days of Christmas, which end with Epiphany on 6 January. The Christian feast replaced various pagan festivals held to celebrate the winter solstice, such as the Saturnalia of the Romans and the Scandinavian Yule. For many people in Britain, Christmas Day now marks the start of a week-long holiday lasting until after the *bank holiday on New Year's Day. Despite the increasing exploitation of the Christmas season by commercial interests, many people still attend church, either on Christmas Day itself or at the Christmas Eve "watchnight" service. Other traditions endure: greetings cards, decorated trees, carol singing, presents, and the customary *Christmas fare all continue to be important elements of the festive season.

The Christmas card was invented in 1843 by a civil servant, Sir Henry Cole, who commissioned a design from artist John Callcott Horsley. The idea may have been based on the

"Christmas pieces" produced by schoolchildren in the 18th century to demonstrate their handwriting skills. With the introduction of the penny post in 1840, the Christmas card soon became a popular way of sending greetings.

Christmas decorations, especially ivy, holly, and mistletoe, can be traced back to the evergreen symbols of life that featured in the pagan celebrations. Kissing under the mistletoe is a peculiarly British custom and recalls the ancient magical and sexual significance which the plant held for the *druids. The Christmas tree, however, was originally a Germanic custom, popularized in Britain by Queen Victoria's husband Prince Albert in the 19th century. Each year, Trafalgar Square in London is adorned by a huge tree, donated by the people of Oslo in Norway to commemorate their liberation in World War II. The streets of most towns and cities have their own Christmas decorations, with a notable display in the principal shopping streets of London's West End.

Carols, from the French *carole*, meaning a dance with a song, came originally from Europe, and became associated with Christmas in the 14th century. Most of today's popular carols were written in the 17th and 18th centuries. In the 19th century, groups of carol singers, known as waits, toured the streets before Christmas, playing and singing in return for a seasonal drink or mince pie, a tradition known as *wassailing. This custom still flourishes, often with singers collecting for charity.

Gifts were exchanged by the Romans during their Saturnalia and the Christian Church conveniently married this custom with the story of the gifts brought to the infant Christ by the three Magi. More significant for children is Santa Claus, or Father Christmas, who on Christmas Eve brings presents to fill the "stockings" hung at the end of the bed. He is a conflation of various historical and legendary figures, including St Nicholas of Patara and Odin, the gift-bringer of Norse tradition.

Today, as ever, the Christmas feast is central to the occasion. Lunch on Christmas Day is followed by the Queen's Christmas message, a tradition started by her grandfather, George

V, with a radio broadcast in 1932. The first televised Christmas message was broadcast live in 1957. *Boxing Day and the following days may be marked by more energetic pursuits, such as a visit to the *pantomime.

Christmas fare Traditional food eaten throughout the country, with a few regional variations, during the Christmas period. Roast fowl has been the central feature of Christmas dinner for hundreds of years: before the farming of turkeys in the late 16th and early 17th centuries, the vast majority of the populace ate goose or chicken, while the nobility feasted on boar's head, garnished with a wreath of rosemary, or on such delicacies as swan or peacock. Today's roast turkey is traditionally garnished with bacon and sausage and served with a variety of stuffings (often chestnut) and sauces (usually cranberry). It is followed by the rich dark plum pudding, a steamed suet pudding made with dried fruit and spices, laced with brandy, and often containing one or more small coins or charms to be kept by the lucky finder. Brandy is poured over the pudding and lit just before serving. The modern plum pudding evolved from plum pottage, a meaty broth containing prunes and dried fruit that was a traditional item of Christmas fare until the 18th century.

A combination of shredded meat, spices, and dried fruit formed the basis of mince pies, which formerly were baked in an oblong shape to represent the manger, with a small doll or pastry "baby" lying on the top crust. Towards the end of the 17th century it was discovered that the mixture now known as mincemeat – dried fruit, apple, suet, spices, sugar, and brandy – could be made weeks before Christmas and stored in sealed jars. The shredded meat, which had to be added when the pies were prepared, was eventually omitted altogether. Christmas cake, like homemade plum pudding, is often made in the months preceding Christmas. Possibly a relic of former Twelfth Night fare, it is a rich dark fruit cake topped with a layer of marzipan and royal icing and adorned with holly, piped decorations, or a festive greeting.

Church Army An organization founded in London in 1882 by the Reverend Prebendary Wilson Carlile (1847–1942). The Church Army is a body of trained lay evangelists within the Church of England devoted to both evangelicalism and social work. Its officers (designated captains and sisters) assist the clergy in the parishes, work in prisons and amongst prisoners' families, and in collaboration with local authorities and voluntary organizations the Church Army provides accommodation for the young unemployed and single homeless. It is also concerned with the rehabilitation of drug addicts. Other activities include working with HM forces, providing facilities for rest and recreation. There are autonomous "daughter societies" in Australia, Canada, the Caribbean, East Africa, New Zealand, and the USA.

Church Commissioners The fiscal and administrative body that handles the affairs of the Church of England. It is chaired by the Archbishop of Canterbury and comprises 42 diocesan bishops, three Church Estates Commissioners, representatives of the clergy and laity appointed by the General Synod, four appointees of the Queen, four of the Archbishop of Canterbury, various officers of the government and judiciary, and representatives of the cities of London and York and of Oxford and Cambridge universities. The body was formed in 1948 by the union of the Ecclesiastical Commissioners (established in 1836) and Queen Anne's Bounty – a fund created in 1704 by Queen Anne to augment the stipends of poor clergy. Today the Commissioners' various committees disburse pay and pensions to the clergy, provide for the upkeep of Church property, and administer the Church's assets. Their income for 1983 amounted to £14.4 million, of which £2.3 million was derived from stocks and shares and £7.9 million came from land and other property. Expenditure on clergy pay and pensions totalled £3.5 million.

churches Britain's past is nowhere more apparent than in its churches. The variety of church buildings reflects a flux of styles that stretches back over a thousand years. Little remains of the churches built by the early Celtic and Roman missionaries in the 5th and 6th centuries AD. Probably the oldest intact church is the small stone-built Saxon church at Escomb in northeast England, which dates from the late 7th or early 8th century. As the Saxons built primarily in wood, however, most of their churches have disappeared. One outstanding survivor is the Saxon stave church at Greensted in Essex, with its walls of split oak trunks.

The impact of the Norman invasion on parish church design became evident during the 12th century – a time of great rebuilding throughout England. Many examples of Norman churches still stand, characterized by thick stone walls, high narrow windows, and semi-circular arches. Some were given a rounded apsidal east end to the chancel, but many retained the traditional English square east end. These early Norman features are often submerged by later additions, such as aisles flanking the nave, a clerestorey, and a tower over the west end. From the mid-12th century, elements of the gothic style of pointed arches and stone roof vaulting, were introduced, initially in the large cathedrals and churches, but later in the more humble parish churches. Three main phases of the gothic style are generally distinguished: early English, decorated, and perpendicular (see cathedral).

Churches were altered or rebuilt according to the fortunes of their patrons – either the local gentry or the parishioners themselves – and the prevailing architectural style. Between 1420 and 1540 many new churches were constructed, especially in the prosperous agricultural regions; the wool and cloth merchants of East Anglia and the Cotswolds erected a variety of splendid examples in this period (see wool churches). Even poor communities devoted considerable time and resources to the parish church, which, before the industrial revolution, was the focus of most communities' spiritual, social, and cultural life. Local craftsmen provided many of the interior furnishings, such as the altar, font, screens, pews, and stalls. Stained glass and murals became popular, although most of the latter were either painted over after the Reformation or have now faded.

Since the Reformation, little new church building was started until the 19th century. However, following the *Fire of 1666, replacement buildings in the Renaissance style, with columned porticoes, domes, and tiered bell towers were favoured by such architects as Sir Christopher Wren (1632–1723) and his pupil Nicholas Hawksmoor (1661–1736). By the 19th century, these classical styles still had their exponents, such as John Nash (1752–1835), who designed All Souls in Langham Place, London, but many of the new churches built by the Victorians to accommodate the growing populations of the industrial towns and cities harked back to the gothic style, particularly those built by Augustus Pugin (1812–52) and George Gilbert Scott (1811–87). In 1828, one million pounds was voted by Parliament to build 214 new churches, mostly in London. Of this total 170 were built in the style of the gothic revival. Some regard the Victorian "restoration" of medieval churches, also prevalent at the time, as a form of vandalism. The 20th century has seen some voguish designs inspired by the *Arts and Crafts movement and by Art Nouveau. Since the last war, modernism has also appeared in some church architecture. In several modern churches the traditional plan of nave and chancel has been forsaken for a central altar and remarkable use has been made of such materials as reinforced concrete, glass fibre, and plastic.

Church in Wales The autonomous Anglican Church in Wales. Unlike the Church of England in England, it is no longer recognized as the established Church. The Church in Wales is organized as a single province containing six dioceses: St Asaph, St David's, Swansea and Brecon, Bangor, Llandaff, and Monmouth. The Archbishop of Wales is elected from among the six bishops. The government of the Church consists of three orders: diocesan bishops, clergy, and laity. All members of the Church government are elected.

Wales was a stronghold of the Celtic Church until the 12th century, when it came under the domination of Rome and the Archbishop of Canterbury as a result of the conquest of parts of Wales by Norman lords from England. After the *Reformation, which was grudgingly accepted by the Welsh, the Anglican Church in Wales suffered from a lack of leadership among its English-appointed clergy and its influence steadily declined. Towards the end of the 18th century, many people turned to the new *Methodist movement and attended chapel rather than church. There was widespread discontent among these *Nonconformists over enforced payments to the established Anglican Church. This ultimately became a major factor in Welsh politics and in 1920 an Act of Parliament disestablished the Church of England in Wales. By the early 1980s the Church in Wales had a membership of about 150,000 with some 1000 ministers presiding over less than 2000 places of worship.

Church Missionary Society A society founded in 1799 as a result of the evangelical revival and dedicated to spreading the Christian gospel to all lands. Its missionaries, who include not only clergy but also doctors, nurses, agriculturalists, and teachers, are sent at the invitation of the local Anglican Church in the country concerned and now operate in 27 countries throughout Africa and Asia. The Society promotes its work in churches, schools, and other organizations at home, and publishes a monthly magazine, *Outlook*. Under its patron, the Archbishop of Canterbury, the Society operates from offices in London and currently has an annual budget of over £3.5 million. Similar societies exist in Ireland, Australia, and New Zealand.

Church of England The Church established by law in England. The sovereign, who is its legal head, is obliged to be a member, swears to uphold its doctrines, and appoints senior members of the Church (in practice, on the advice of the Prime Minister). The state retains ultimate control over the Church's affairs and all clergy swear an oath of allegiance to the Crown. The more senior of the two archbishops and effective leader of the Church is the *Archbishop of Canterbury. The country is divided into two provinces, southern and northern, the latter under the primacy of the Archbishop of York. Each province is subdivided into bishoprics (totalling 42), and each bishop is supported in turn by archdeacons, deans, etc. The bishoprics total some 13,500 parishes with usually a single vicar or

rector in charge of each parish. In 1970 the *General Synod superseded the Church Assembly as the Church's governing body.

The doctrines of the Church of England and its relations with the state have undergone considerable change during the long history of Christianity in Britain. Earliest evidence of an organized Church dates from the 4th century AD. The Synod of Whitby (664) was instrumental in resolving conflict between the indigenous Celtic Church of the north and west and the Roman doctrines established by Augustine following his arrival in 597. During the following centuries, the Anglo-Saxon Church, unified under Theodore of Tarsus (c. 602–90), had to contend with hostile Danish invaders, although Alfred's reign (871–99) gave greater security to the Church. European influences figured more prominently after the Norman conquest, many new churches were erected and papal power, both spiritual and temporal, increased, undeterred by the various scandals surrounding it.

By the 16th century, resentment and mistrust of the wealth and privileges of certain monastic communities were such that Henry VIII found enough popular support to enforce his far-reaching *Reformation of the Church. Denied an annulment of his marriage to Catherine of Aragon by Pope Clement VII, in 1531 Henry forced the *Convocations of Canterbury and York to recognize the sovereign as "supreme head on earth" of the English Church and began the process of severing ties with the papacy in Rome. With the transfer of power to the Crown, the monasteries were dissolved and their assets sequestered.

A distinctive doctrinal character for the reformed Church emerged during the reign of Edward VI, when Archbishop Thomas Cranmer produced the First and Second *Books of Common Prayer (1549 and 1552). A reconciliation with Rome and persecution of Protestants occurred under Mary I (1553–58) but the situation was finally reversed with the accession of Elizabeth I in 1558. During her reign, in spite of disaffection both from Puritans and Papists, the majority accepted both the Church of England's Prayer Book and the Thirty-Nine Articles of religion encapsulating the doctrine of the Church, finally agreed in

1571. However, the Church remained a target for Puritan hostility, and with the victory of Cromwell's parliamentarians in the *Civil War of 1642–51, the use of the Prayer Book was banned, many traditions of the Church abrogated, and clerics sacked. But the *Restoration of Charles II in 1660 saw the Church re-established on its former basis, with no concessions to the Puritans.

The somewhat dry style of worship in post-Restoration churches failed to satisfy the spiritual needs of many Christians and led in the 18th century to the evangelical revival. Some remained in the Anglican Church as a Low Church party, but another group could not be contained within Church order and became the *Methodist denomination. To add to the Church's problems, as a result of the industrial revolution, there was a drift of the population from the country, where the church was a focus of life, to the towns, where neither church buildings nor pastoral effort could keep pace with the population growth. By about 1830 a turning point seemed to have arrived. The *Oxford Movement attempted to rescue Anglicanism from evangelicalism, dissent, and unbelief by vigorously stressing Catholic (but not necessarily Roman) doctrine and ritual. This had a limited influence; it can be argued that the ecclesiastical commissioners (now the Church Commissioners), the episcopate, and the evangelicals were more effective in saving the Church, respectively by redistributing church funds to fit changed population patterns, by church extension, and by pastoral vigour.

Congregations in the Church of England have declined markedly as a proportion of the population during the present century. However, over one-third of all children born in England are still baptized as Anglicans and of these a significant but diminishing proportion are later confirmed. Sunday services are attended by some 1.2 million people. Cooperation with other denominations at a local level is considerable, but all attempts at formal re-union have hitherto failed.

Church of Ireland The Anglican Church of Ireland, dating from Henry VIII's *Reformation of the 1530s. At its first Convocation in 1615, the Church adopted the 104 articles of doctrine (as the Irish Articles). The Church constantly found itself involved in the political and religious turmoil of the country, especially the polarization between the militant Protestantism of the north and the staunchly Catholic south. The Church's links with the Church of England were strengthened by the 1800 Act of Union, but this was repealed by the Irish Church Act of 1869, which formally disestablished the Church of Ireland. The Church of Ireland is headed by the Archbishop of Armagh, who is Primate of All Ireland. The Archbishop of Dublin serves as Primate of Ireland. Currently comprising 12 dioceses and some 600 clergy, the Church is governed by a General Synod of archbishops, bishops, and representatives of the clergy, laity, and the diocesan synods.

Church of Scotland The largest denomination in Scotland, founded by the Calvinist reformer John Knox (c. 1513–72) and others, in the wake of the *Reformation of the English Church in the 1530s. It was Calvinist in doctrine, and Presbyterian in church government (that is, instead of being headed by bishops appointed by king or pope, it rested on a series of committees culminating in its General Assembly, elected by congregations and groups of congregations). When Charles I tried to impose the Anglican (episcopal) Book of Common Prayer in 1637, leading Scottish Presbyterians responded by subscribing to the National Covenant (1638), which abolished the episcopal system in Scotland. In the resulting "Bishops' War" the Covenanters defeated the king, who was then forced by financial necessity to summon the "Long" and "Short" Parliaments, an action which in turn precipitated the *Civil War.

The Church of Scotland's position was emphasized by the Solemn League and Covenant, agreed between the Long Parliament and the Scots to establish Presbyterianism throughout the land. Although episcopacy throughout England and Scotland was re-established under Charles II, the situation was resolved following the *Glorious Revolution of 1688 and the readoption of Presbyterianism in Scotland under William of Orange. The 19th century saw a rift in the Church over the rights of the laity to veto the appointment of ministers.

This culminated in the Disruption of 1843 and the secession of about one-third of the membership and clergy to form the (nonestablished and self-supporting) Free Church of Scotland. A series of unions between the smaller Presbyterian Churches, including the Free Church, resulted in the United Free Church (1900), which in 1929 reunited with the Church of Scotland.

The churches, known as kirks, each conduct their own court, or kirk session, comprising the parish minister and kirk elders, the latter elected by the congregation. The minister and one elder represent the parish at the regional court of presbytery and the provincial court of synod. Each of the 46 presbyteries elects two commissioners to sit on the principal governing body of the Church, the General Assembly. This meets annually, presided over by a Moderator – the head of the Church who is elected annually. The Lord High Commissioner represents the sovereign. The Church has some 1780 kirks and an estimated communicant membership of over 900,000.

CID (Criminal Investigation Department) The branch within each police force concerned with the detection and capture of criminals. The CID of the *Metropolitan Police – usually referred to as "*Scotland Yard" – is particularly well known, as are its specialized sections, such as the Flying Squad. The Metropolitan Police established a detective department in 1842, but within 20 years it had been nicknamed the "defective department"; and in 1878, after much corruption had been revealed, it was disbanded and replaced by the CID in approximately its present form. For a century it was almost autonomous, but now detectives working at local level are directed by the uniformed branch. At Metropolitan Police headquarters level it is controlled by C department, within which work the specialized squads - including, for example, those concerned with serious crimes (C1), the Fraud Squad (C6, established jointly with the City of London Police in 1945 to investigate banking and currency frauds and public corruption), the Flying Squad (C8), and the Antiterrorist Squad (C13, whose commanding officer is also the head of *Special Branch). Under a long-term reorganization begun in 1985, the head-

quarters departments of the Metropolitan Police are to be rearranged, and C department will disappear. Some of its squads (e.g. C1 and C13) will come under a new department to administer purely specialized policing, and others under one covering all territorial policing.

cider An alcoholic drink made from fermented apple juice. Cider has been made in warm fertile regions of southern England and Wales since its introduction from France around the time of the Norman conquest. Production was limited at first to the Kent and Sussex area but soon spread to the western counties, notably Somerset, Devon, and Hereford, where new strains of apple, developed specifically for cider-making, were grown in large orchards. Traditional methods for extracting the juice from the crushed apple pulp varied from county to county: some are still in use.

The vast majority of cider consumed in Britain today is clear and golden in colour, aerated, and relatively harmless in terms of its alcohol content: it is produced in large quantities by commercial cider-makers and graded as sweet or dry according to the amount of unfermented sugar it contains. A number of smaller enterprises produce the more traditional still dry cider, which is clear and palatable but can be surprisingly potent. The true "scrumpy" or rough cider is difficult to find outside a few local pubs in certain apple-growing areas.

Cinque ports A confederation of English Channel ports, probably dating from the reign

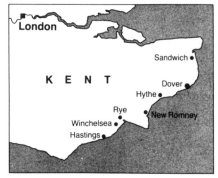

CINQUE PORTS

of Edward the Confessor (1042–66), that provided ships and men for the king in return for certain rights and liberties. The original five ("cinque") ports were Hastings, New Romney, Hythe, Dover, and Sandwich, to which were later added the ancient towns of Winchelsea and Rye, and many other towns became associate members (or "limbs"). The group totalled 39 at one stage. Their rights and duties were codified by Edward I in a royal charter of 1278. Their privileges included, among other things, exemption from certain taxes, the right to their own courts, ceremonial rights at the coronation, and the privilege of "den and strand" – namely, the right to land at Yarmouth to dry nets, and judicial authority over the court held annually at the Yarmouth herring fair! Administration was carried out by two bodies: the Court of Brodhull (for Kentish members) and the Guestling (for western ports). Their importance declined after the 14th century and of the original "cinque" only Dover remains a major port. The post of Warden of the Cinque Ports (who is also traditionally Constable of Dover Castle) is now entirely ceremonial and is currently held by Queen Elizabeth the Queen Mother; past Wardens include Sir Winston Churchill (1941–65) and the Duke of Wellington (1828–52).

circuit judge Since 1971, a trained lawyer appointed by the Crown on the advice of the Lord Chancellor to serve full-time as a judge in the *Crown Court and *county courts. Circuit judges, of whom there are some 400, may also be invited by the Lord Chancellor to sit in the *High Court of Justice.

Citizens Advice Bureaux (CAB) A national network of information offices, set up in 1939 to inform the public about the emergency wartime regulations. It has remained in operation since the end of the war in recognition of the need for an organization to provide free and confidential advice and information for the general public, particularly concerning the social services, housing, legal aid, consumer services, and family matters. Its 900 offices are supported by the National Association of Citizens Advice Bureaux from London and 22 branch offices. The CAB offices are staffed by

13,500 trained counsellors, 90% of whom are volunteers. Each office is self-governing under the leadership of an organizer, and is funded by the local authority, which often provides premises.

citizenship Status as defined by the British Nationality Act 1981, that came into force on 1 January 1983 and replaced the 1948 concept of citizenship of the UK and colonies, which was outdated by subsequent changes in the Commonwealth. The Act introduced three forms of citizenship: **British citizenship**, **British Dependent Territories citizenship**, and **British Overseas citizenship**. It relegated **Commonwealth citizenship** to secondary status.

On 1 January 1983 people became British citizens if, under the Immigration Act 1971, they enjoyed right of abode, and were not subject to any immigration control. Since that date there have been four ways in which British citizenship can be acquired:

1) By birth, i.e. by being born in the UK to a parent who is either a British citizen, or is ordinarily resident in the UK and not restricted under the immigration laws as to the period for which he or she may remain there.

2) By descent. This is acquired by people born outside the UK provided one parent is a British citizen; it is not enough (with a few minor exceptions) if the parent's citizenship is itself a citizenship by descent.

3) By registration, i.e. by application to the Home Secretary. Any minor may apply, but adults may only apply if connected in certain ways with the UK (e.g. enjoying one of the other new citizenships, and satisfying strict residential requirements). In some cases the Home Secretary must grant citizenship, in others registration is at his discretion.

4) By naturalization. Any adult may apply to the Home Secretary for a certificate of naturalization, but, in addition to satisfying residential requirements, must also offer proof of matters such as good character and proficiency in English, Welsh, or Scottish Gaelic, and the grant of a certificate is in all cases discretionary.

British Dependent Territories citizenship is acquired on grounds of birth, registration, or naturalization in a dependent territory, or of descent from a parent or grandparent who was a citizen of the UK and colonies by birth, registration, or naturalization in a dependent territory (for example, Anguilla, Bermuda, Gibraltar, Hong Kong). Citizenship by registration is more or less confined to minors, but otherwise the rules governing these four methods of acquisition are analagous to those for British citizenship.

Existing citizens of the UK and colonies acquired British Overseas citizenship if they were not entitled to either of the other forms. Since then, the Home Secretary has had a discretionary power to register minors as British Overseas citizens, but there are virtually no other ways of acquiring this form of citizenship.

Citizenship may be renounced under certain conditions, and the Home Secretary is empowered to deprive registered or naturalized citizens of their citizenship for certain misdemeanours, except in the case of British Overseas citizens.

Commonwealth citizenship is a secondary form held by anyone in one of the three primary categories, or by citizens of independent Commonwealth countries.

City livery companies Charitable and professional associations in the City of London that have their roots in the craft and trade guilds of the early Middle Ages. These guilds controlled production and quality in their respective trades as well as looking after the well-being, both material and spiritual, of their members. Their power and wealth became so formidable that by the 13th century they governed the City through the Lord Mayor, whom they elected, in return for financial and other support for the monarch (in this way municipal administration all over Britian has its roots in the guild organization). By this time the guilds were being chartered as companies and granted a livery or uniform to wear on ceremonial occasions. However, as trade expanded and developed, they lost their monopolies and some crafts declined. The livery companies themselves began to fall into abeyance during the 17th and 18th centuries and were only revived by the economic success and charitable zeal of the Victorians. They have flourished ever since.

There are now 94 livery companies of which 17 were founded after the 1930s, usually for such new professions as the actuaries, air pilots, and arbitrators. Although they no longer exercise control over a trade, as they once did, the gunmakers, apothecaries, fishmongers, spectacle-makers, and most notably the goldsmiths, still control standards in their particular areas. Some members of Companies have only a tenuous connection with their former trades, but there are still three ways of joining a livery company: by patrimony, apprenticeship, or the payment of a substantial entrance fee. Each company is headed by a master and wardens, elected by the liverymen, who number between 75 and 400 (depending on the company) and represent the employers. They are entitled to wear the company livery and are automatically freemen of the City, for which they pay a separate fee. The rank-and-file of the company are called the yeomanry of freemen; they do not receive these privileges unless they are elevated to the livery.

Some companies own magnificent dining halls (usually rebuilt and restored) as well as land and property, including almshouses, while others own virtually nothing and are maintained by fees and legacies. The guilds and companies have an established order of precedence, with the most recent coming last. However, although the saddlers' is the oldest guild and the weavers' the oldest company, neither is at the top of the order of precedence list. This is because craft guilds had less wealth and importance than the trade guilds that figure prominently among the 12 "great" companies (nominated in 1514): the mercers, grocers, drapers, fishmongers, goldsmiths, merchant taylors, skinners, haberdashers, salters, ironmongers, vintners, and clothworkers. Some of these are famous for their educational foundations as well as for granting scholarships, prizes, awards, and fellowships. Both "great" and "minor" companies combined together in the late 19th century to form the City and Guilds of London Institute, to work for the advancement of technical and scientific education, with a particular interest in their own craft or trade area.

Each company has evolved its own ceremonies to accompany the annual election and installation of new masters and wardens. This ensures that some of the ancient companies produce, at the grand election feast, embroidered "garlands", a custom dating from Tudor and Stuart times, to crown the new incumbents, as well as fine silver-gilt loving cups to pass around the assembled livery.

City of London The square mile on the north bank of the River Thames, roughly between Tower Bridge and Blackfriars Bridge. Probably a flourishing settlement at the beginning of the Christian era, London in 67 AD was already referred to by the Roman historian Tacitus (c. 55–c. 120 AD) as a trading city. Towards the end of the 2nd century AD, the Romans built a wall some two miles long round the city, which they called Londinium. After the Romans left Britain in 410, little is known about the fate of London until it was occupied by the Saxons in the 6th century. The Saxon king Ethelbert of Kent (c. 552–616), the first Christian king, founded St Paul's cathedral on its present site, and William the Conqueror built the Tower of London, immediately to the east of the city wall, soon after his arrival in 1066.

From the earliest times London was Britain's most important port. Standing at the lowest fordable point of the Thames, which gave it a large natural hinterland, it was the best site for communication with Europe. By the 11th century London was England's largest town, and in the late 14th century was probably the only city with more than 50,000 inhabitants. It was a natural focus for the activities of foreign merchants, especially Italians (*see* Lombard Street) and (later) Germans, who handled the majority of English trade until the 16th century.

In the late 13th century, when reliable figures become available in the form of customs records, London already dominated English trade, in particular the export of wool and (later) cloth; through the rest of the Middle Ages London's grip on exports tightened. A further stimulus was the gradual settlement of central government at nearby Westminster from the 12th century. The royal household, a lucrative customer, used London merchants as its principal suppliers and kings in need of cash turned to the wealthy merchants, English or

foreign, based in London, granting them aid and patronage in return. It was at this period in its history that London invested in its first stone bridge over the Thames; London Bridge was built in 1209 and it remained the only stone bridge until Blackfriars Bridge was built in 1769.

The opening, in 1571, of the Royal Exchange was a sign of the increasing volume and sophistication in London trade. When the explorations of the 16th century opened up the world beyond Europe, London was the only city in England wealthy enough to exploit the opportunities provided by world markets. Through monopoly companies, such as the Muscovy Company (founded 1555), the Levant Company (1581), and – greatest of all – the East India Company (1600), she extended her dominance.

In the 17th century, first the *Great Plague (1665) and then the *Fire (1666) between them destroyed much of the population and the buildings of the medieval city. Sir Christopher Wren's plan to rebuild London on more expansive lines was rejected by the City fathers on the grounds that it would cost too much and take too long. Nevertheless, Wren replaced the old gothic cathedral with the present baroque building and rebuilt 51 of the city's parish churches.

During the 17th and 18th centuries the population, docks, and trade of the city all expanded together – each meeting the needs created by the others. In this period the service industries grew up amid the increasing prosperity; for example, marine insurance was placed on a firm footing in *Lloyd's coffee house, *banks of integrity were established (*see also* Bank of England), and the foundations of a *Stock Exchange were laid. Growth continued as Britain conquered India and North America. By the end of the 18th century the docks and river in the city itself were so congested that expansion eastwards, down the river, provided the only workable solution to London's problems. This growth carried on throughout the 19th century, enabling the City of London to remain at the hub of a tremendous expansion of trade resulting first from the *industrial revolution and later from the development of the *British Empire. Thus during the first half of the 20th century, the City had become exclusively a commercial and financial centre providing the services required by the world's biggest and busiest port (*see also* Port of London Authority). As a centre for shipping, insurance, banking, and commodity markets, with a workforce drawn from London's sprawling suburbs and a tiny resident population, the City became a key factor in the British economy and the principal source of the invisible earnings required to maintain a favourable balance of payments.

Unfortunately, by the 1960s the port of London began to decline. Within the next 20 years its useful life came to an end, largely as a result of bad labour relations, lack of capital investment, failure to compete with foreign ports (such as Rotterdam), and the development of Tilbury, near the mouth of the Thames, as a port for the container trade. The entire dockland area is undergoing major redevelopment. The immense international importance of the City's financial institutions, however, continues.

See also Corporation of London; City of London streets.

City of London Police The police force for the City of London, established by Act of Parliament in 1839. A small force, currently numbering some 900 officers, it is provided and maintained by the Court of Common Council (*see* Corporation of London), in contrast to the *Metropolitan Police (the force responsible for the rest of the capital) which is the responsibility of the Home Secretary. Like the Metropolitan Police and all other forces in England and Wales (*see* police) it is, however, subject to the Home Secretary in matters of management, operational standards, and discipline. Headed by a commissioner appointed by the Common Council, it is wholly independent of the Metropolitan Police, but the two forces cooperate on many matters, such as traffic control, the policing of marches and demonstrations, and the investigation of fraud (*see* CID).

City of London streets London has grown from a village in Roman times to an enormous metropolis. The *City of London is now a mixture of medieval lanes and modern glass and concrete office blocks. Many of its street names reflect its history. The Barbican (*see also* Barbican Arts and Conference Centre) was a Roman street upon which a tower stood; it acquired its name in the 12th century from the Norman French *barbicane*, a tower. The Saxon influence is reflected in such names as **Cheapside**, originally called Westceape to distinguish it from Estceape (modern **Eastcheap**), from the Anglo-Saxon *ceap*, barter. Many of the streets derived their names from nearby churches, **Brides Lane** after St Bride's and **Bartholomew Lane** after St Bartholomew's, for example; others commemorate taverns – **Bear Alley** and **Beehive Passage** remain long after the Bear and the Beehive taverns have disappeared. Monastic life, too, has left its mark on the City. **Blackfriars Lane** and **Whitefriars Street** are obvious examples. **Carmelite Street** stands on the site of the 13th-century priory of the Carmelites (White Friars), while **Mincing Lane** reflects the Anglo-Saxon word for a nun (*minchen*), many of whom lived on this street in houses owned by the nearby St Helen's Priory. The **Minories** owes its name to the Sorores Minores, the little sisters of St Clare, an abbey for Spanish nuns founded in 1293. **Charterhouse Square** takes its name from the Carthusian priory, or *chartreuse*, founded there in 1371. Later, in the early days of the Reformation, the clergy of St Paul's used to walk in procession around the cathedral chanting the Lord's Prayer in what is now **Paternoster Row**, the Hail Mary in **Ave Maria Lane**, ending with the Amen in **Amen Court**.

Many names of City streets describe activities that took place there in medieval times. **Poultry** was the site of the poultry market, **Pudding Lane** (where the *Fire of London of 1666 started) was where the butchers of Eastcheap flung the guts and entrails (called puddings) of their carcass meat, and **Houndsditch** has even more unsavoury origins – the Saxon moat around the Roman wall was filled in by the 13th century, leaving a small ditch in which dead dogs were disposed of. **Love Lane** was once the red-light district of the old City.

civic insignia The robes, chains, badges, and other symbols of the authority invested in the civic dignitaries who serve in local authorities. They have their origin in medieval England when the principal towns gained the right by royal charter to conduct at least some of their own affairs, and followed the style set by the *City of London early in the 13th century. The Lord Mayor, sheriffs, and aldermen were invariably wealthy guildsmen (see City livery companies) and the Mayor's fur-trimmed velvet robes embellished with gold decoration, his gold chain, and later, his lace jabot and tricon hat with black ostrich feathers, would originally have been an outward show of personal wealth; in time they became a symbol of office. The Lord Mayor of London alone is entitled to wear what is called a "collar of esses" linked with knots and Tudor roses (a privilege shared with the *Lord Chief Justice and officers of the *College of Arms); in addition he has a badge of office in sardonyx and enamel encircled with diamonds, and six robes, including one used only for coronations. His escort of swordbearer, City marshal, and macebearer have their own special robes, as do the sheriffs and aldermen. The wealth of the City is further demonstrated by its possession of four ceremonial swords, a crystal sceptre, and the great mace, as well as ceremonial plate.

Although few boroughs can match the City in wealth, their mayors usually wear a robe of office for ceremonial occasions, either a black one with gold embellishments or a scarlet one trimmed with fur, together with a heavy gold chain, badge of office, and hat; the lady mayoress, the deputy mayor, the sheriff, and often the aldermen also wear robes and chains or badges, (for less important occasions the mayor will wear only the chain, or even the badge alone). The gold-plated mace is carried before the mayor by the macebearer, formerly a personal attendant or bodyguard; the mace itself was originally a weapon of war, gradually modified so that the handle grew into an ornate crown, representing the authority of the monarch invested in the mayor, and the head dwindled to a handle. The mace precedes the mayor into the council chamber and is laid on the table before him during a council session.

Civic Trust An independent charity founded in 1957 by Duncan Sandys, Minister of Housing and Local Government (1954–57), with the aim of protecting and improving the environment. It is based in London with regional associate trusts for the northwest (founded 1961), Wales (1964), the northeast (1965), and Scotland (1967). It functions through local amenity societies, buildings preservation trusts, and similar bodies of which there are about a thousand registered with the Civic Trust. The constituent societies remain independent, but are advised and assisted by the Trust in the realization of their schemes. Typical of the Trust's work is its concern with the impact of heavy lorries on the environment, schemes to regenerate and utilize urban wasteland, and the creation of *conservation areas under the Civic Amenities Act 1967, which it instigated. It advises the government on environmental issues and administers the Architectural Heritage Fund, which provides low-interest loans to enable charitable groups to buy and restore buildings that merit conservation. The Heritage Education Group (founded 1976), which it runs on behalf of the Department of the Environment, carries environmental issues into schools. It has a considerable library and photographic archive and also publishes a bimonthly magazine, *Heritage Outlook*.

civil list A payment from public funds for the maintenance of the royal household and family. Before the reign of William and Mary in the 1690s, no clear distinction was made between peacetime government expenses and the expense of maintaining the dignity of the sovereign. George III in 1760 made over the Crown Land revenues in exchange for a regular parliamentary vote of money but used civil-list money to buy parliamentary support. In 1782 such kingly patronage was limited, but it was not till 1831 that the remaining governmental expenses were removed from the civil list. A sum payable from the Treasury is fixed by Act of Parliament at the beginning of each reign; in exchange the new sovereign customarily surrenders to the Exchequer the revenues from the *Crown Estate. The civil-list payment covers the salaries of the household staff, travel, entertaining, and public engagements at home and abroad. Certain "civil-list pensions" are payable to distinguished scientists or practitioners of the arts at the discretion of the Prime Minister. Because of inflation the original sum provided in 1952 has been revised upwards from time to time. Annuities are made to the Queen, Queen Mother, Duke of Edinburgh, Princess Anne, Prince Andrew, Prince Edward, Princess Margaret, Princess Alice (Duchess of Gloucester), Duke of Gloucester, Duke of Kent, and Princess Alexandra. The last three are not specifically provided for by Parliament but since 1976 the Queen has refunded to the Exchequer the sums provided from public funds towards their official expenses, paying any shortfall herself. Part of the sums allocated to the royal family comes from the *Consolidated Fund, part comes via the royal trustees (the Prime Minister, the Chancellor of the Exchequer, and the Keeper of the Privy Purse). The royal trustees review the workings of the civil list every ten years.

For the year 1985–86 the civil list was fixed at £5,180,100, of which £3,967,200 was intended for the Queen.

civil service The permanent civil (i.e. non military) administrative body of government, excluding both elected and judicial office holders and some institutional staffs, such as the royal household. The civil service is responsible for the implementation of government policies, for the administration of the 95 major and 20 minor government departments, and for duties connected with organizations in the public sector. In running departments, advising ministers on the administration of policy, ensuring that statutory duties are fulfilled, and reacting to the changes introduced by newly elected governments, it performs an extraordinary variety of tasks. Some civil service departments (e.g. the Inland Revenue) are autonomous, and have functional responsibility to ministers.

In former times royal advisers and executive officers were directly selected through the sovereign's patronage. The first modern bureaucracy emerged in the late 18th and early 19th centuries, primarily to govern India without the corruption and scandal that existed during the rule of the East India Company. The acceptance of gifts and bribes was forbidden from 1765, and from 1813 recruits had to complete a period of study on India and produce a certificate of good conduct before taking up their post. Although standards were raised, further criticisms of the Indian administration culminated in the formation of a parliamentary committee (1835) under Lord Macaulay. A report published in 1854 on the British civil service, drawing on the work of the Macaulay committee, recommended the abolition of patronage, and recruitment by open competition. The Civil Service Commissioners were appointed in 1855 to supervise recruitment; over the next 30 years patronage was gradually eliminated.

Since World War II, the civil service has adapted to the expansion of the government's responsibilities in a number of fields: social policy, technology, the environment, and membership of many international organizations. The civil service now operates as a disciplined body, in theory both politically neutral and confidential (68,000 posts are subject to positive vetting). The service has an international reputation for being virtually incorruptible, particularly in the handling of contracts and acceptance of inducements. The Cabinet Office's management and personnel office, which superseded the Civil Service Department in 1982, deals with overall management, training, and organization, while the Treasury is responsible for manpower. Among government departments in 1985, the Ministry of Defence employed the largest number of civil servants. The Secretary to the Cabinet, who is also head of the home civil service, has an advisory role in the preparation of honours lists (see Birthday honours; New Year's honours), and concerning senior appointments and security within the service. At the head of each department is a permanent secretary and senior staff (popularly known as "mandarins"), supported by principal and other executive officers as well as clerical staff. The head offices of many government departments are located in or near Whitehall in London; the name is now synonymous with central government.

Since 1979 a programme of rationalization has led to significant staff reductions (from

733,000 to 600,000 during the period 1979–85), the devolution of departmental responsibilities to public-sector bodies, the increased use of computers, and the simplification of thousands of government forms.

Civil War, English (1642–51) A series of conflicts between the Stuart dynasty and parliamentarian forces. Relations between the Crown and *Parliament had deteriorated steadily during the reigns of James I (1603–1625) and Charles I; from 1629 the latter attempted to rule without Parliament. In this "eleven years' tyranny" he asserted the *royal prerogative more than any previous monarch, notably in collecting taxes (such as tonnage and poundage, and ship money from inland shires) without parliamentary consent. However, his attempts to recast the Presbyterian Scottish Church along Anglican lines led to two short wars with the Scots (1639–40), and his defeat and need for money forced him to negotiate with Parliament. The majority in the Long Parliament (1640–60) were in no

mood to compromise; but Charles, despite his weak position, was not prepared to abandon his absolutist pretensions. The attempted arrest in 1642 of five MPs, who included the influential John Hampden and John Pym, combined with the king's rejection of Parliament's demands, as set out in the Grand Remonstrance of 1641 and the Nineteen Propositions of 1642, made war inevitable. Many moderate parliamentarians joined the king rather than commit rebellion, which made the parliamentary cause more closely identified with political radicalism and religious Puritanism. Strongest in the north and west, Charles I set up his standard at Nottingham on 22 August 1642, while the parliamentarian forces based themselves in London. The first major battle was fought on 23 October 1642 at Edgehill in Warwickshire and, although indecisive, proved that, against expectations, Parliament could field a significant army. Charles then established his headquarters at Oxford and launched three separate campaigns, led by the

ENGLISH CIVIL WAR The Royall Oake of Brittayne, *c. 1649: an anti-Cromwellian allegory produced at the time of Charles I's execution in 1649. The engraving shows Cromwell supervising the destruction of a tree representing the British state.*

Duke of Newcastle in the north, by Sir Ralph Hopton in the southwest, and by the king himself in the Midlands, with the aim of uniting all three forces and marching on London. During 1643 the royalists (also known as cavaliers) made progress in the north and west; but the agreement in September of the Solemn League and Covenant between the parliamentarians (also known as roundheads due to their characteristically Puritan cropped hair) and the Scots Presbyterians, tilted the numerical balance against the king. Parliamentarian victories followed at Marston Moor (2 July 1644), where Oliver Cromwell's new "Ironsides" cavalry regiment distinguished itself, and Newbury (27 October 1644). In February 1645 a highly professional force, the New Model Army, was formed under the command of Sir Thomas Fairfax and Cromwell, and scored a decisive victory at Naseby (14 June 1645). By June 1646 Parliament had won control of the southwest and had taken Oxford. Later that year Charles I surrendered at Newark to the Scots, but was handed over to Parliament in 1647. A few months later, he took advantage of political rifts between the New Model Army and Parliament and, escaping to the Isle of Wight, negotiated the support of the Scots in exchange for a promise that he would introduce Presbyterianism into England. War erupted again in 1648 with royalist risings in Wales, Essex, and Kent, but was soon brought to an end by Cromwell, who defeated a Scottish army led by the Duke of Hamilton at Preston in Lancashire (17–19 August 1648). Charles was recaptured, and the army (now an independent political force hardly under parliamentary control) demanded his death. When Parliament attempted to negotiate with him, Colonel Pride purged the House of Commons of all but about 60 members (December 1648); a special commission was then established to try the king on a charge of tyranny, and he was beheaded on 30 January 1649.

The remaining members of the House of Commons, known as the Rump, abolished the monarchy and the House of Lords, and declared the **Commonwealth** of England (May 1649), in which supreme authority was vested in the House of Commons. Cromwell

went on to suppress rebellion in Ireland, becoming notorious there for the massacre of the 2500 defenders of Drogheda (11 September 1649), before fighting the final battles of the Civil War at Dunbar (3 September 1650) and Worcester (3 September 1651), against the Scots who now supported Charles's heir, Charles II. After Worcester, Charles escaped to the continent by means of disguise and his famous refuge from the roundheads in an oak tree. In 1653 Cromwell dismissed the Rump and replaced it with the nominated Barebones Parliament, which consisted largely of Cromwell's supporters. In December 1653 this parliament was dissolved and Cromwell became Lord Protector – in theory similar to a constitutional monarch, in practice akin to a military dictator. Executive power continued to rest in Cromwell's hands until his death in 1658, after which his son Richard was briefly Lord Protector. In 1659 he resigned after losing the army's support, and chaos ensued: the Rump was reconvened, then expelled; and then reconvened with those MPs excluded by Pride. The Long Parliament finally dissolved itself in March 1660, and a newly elected Convention Parliament set in train the arrangements for the return to England of Charles II, which was effected with the *Restoration of 1660.

clans Social groups into which the inhabitants of Ireland and the Highlands of Scotland were divided until after the Forty-five (see Jacobite rebellions), theoretically based on descent from a common ancestor. The Highland clan system evolved from an earlier division of the land into tribes based on patriarchal descent; on the partial introduction of the Norman feudal system in the 11th century these tribal groups regrouped into smaller clans, each in control of a particular territory. The isolating geography of the Highlands (high hills and narrow valleys) was ideally suited to such division of its people: clans grew up around lochs, in mountain glens, and on islands. At the peak of the clan system some 40 clans, such as the Campbells of Argyll, the Macleods of the Western Isles, the Mackays of Caithness, and the Stewarts of Appin, were in existence, together with numerous smaller groups or "septs" led by local chieftains. Membership of a clan did not necessarily depend on kinship and blood ties: each clan had its share of "broken men", who had sought the protection of the clan chief for one reason or another. The clan system did, however, foster very strong bonds of loyalty and devotion between fellow clansmen, regardless of class or rank, and their chief. The chief was the undisputed leader of the clan; he governed clan territory, dispensed the law with varying degrees of independence, and was responsible for the conduct of his followers. The very nature of the system tended to result in bloody and long-standing feuds between rival clans, such as that between the Macdonalds of Keppoch and the Mackintoshes. Smaller clans sometimes sought the protection of their larger and more powerful neighbours by a system known as "manrent".

After the accession to the English throne of the Protestant king William III in 1688, many clans supported the cause of the deposed Roman Catholic king James II and his followers (known as Jacobites) and participated in a number of unsuccessful rebellions. After the last Jacobite rising of 1745, with Bonnie Prince Charlie's supporters soundly defeated at the battle of Culloden in 1746, the Highland clan system was deliberately dismantled by the English as a part of their policy to prevent further rebellions. Many leading clansmen were executed or imprisoned and the wearing of the tartan, which had developed into a means of expressing loyalty to the clan (each tartan, being coloured with local herbs, was a territorial mark) was proscribed for some 40 years. The clan chiefs, deprived of their feudal rights over their clansmen and militarily impotent, became intent on making an economic living from their land, and took part in the massive "clearances" of the late 18th and early 19th centuries in which large sectors of the Highland population were evicted from their crofts and smallholdings to make way for the more profitable industry of sheep-farming, thus further breaking down the regional identity of the clans.

With the passage of time interest in the clan system has been revived among genuine descendants of exiled Highlanders and many more who claim "kinship" on the strength of a common surname. In fact, the concept of a clan surname is just one of the many myths associated with this aspect of Scottish culture. Until the 17th century, the majority of clansmen were known by patronymics, in which the name of the father would be indicated by the prefix "Mac-" or the suffix "-son". Over the years, as surnames came to be required for legal purposes, some opted to use the name of their clan chief, some adopted their own patronymic as a legal surname, and others chose names that reflected their occupation or physical characteristics. Thus the same surname was sometimes borne by members of different clans. A second myth is that each clan had its own distinctive tartan: many of the tartans worn today are inventions of the early 19th century or later. It is a fact that the belted plaid kilt was an important part of the Highland clansman's traditional dress (along with the sporran and the tam-o'-shanter), but the pattern of the tartan depended largely on the local weaver and the plant dyes available to him.

Classics The five principal flat horse races held in England. They are the **One Thousand Guineas Stakes,** the **Two Thousand Guineas Stakes,** the *Derby, the **Oaks,** and the **St Leger;** all are races for three-year-olds, the Oaks and the One Thousand Guineas being reserved for fillies. The St Leger is the oldest of the five, dating from 1776 when it was established by Colonel Barry St Leger, after whom it was named two years later. It takes place at Doncaster in September over a course of 1.75 miles. The Two Thousand Guineas (1809) and One Thousand Guineas (1814), are run in the spring over the Rowley Mile course at Newmarket (so called because Rowley was the nickname of King Charles II). The Oaks takes place at Epsom in June, over a course of 1.5 miles. It was inaugurated by the 12th Earl of Derby and took its name from a shooting box, "The Oaks", at his residence near Epsom. The last colt to win the "triple crown", the three Classics for which colts are eligible, was Nijinsky, in 1970, ridden by Lester Piggott, who has won more Classics than any jockey in history.

clerk to the justices A barrister or solicitor of at least five years' standing, appointed to a *magistrates' court to advise lay magistrates (*see* justice of the peace) on points of law and procedure. He is also referred to as a "magistrates' clerk". His advice is normally given in open court, but magistrates may request advice after they have retired to consider their verdict. He must not, however, influence them in any way in deciding questions of fact.

clipping the church An annual ceremony that takes place on 19 September or the nearest Sunday at Painswick, Gloucestershire, in association with the Feast of the Nativity of St Mary, and at other times of the year in a variety of English towns and villages. In this context "clipping" derives from the Old English *clyppan*, meaning "embrace"; it does not refer to the coincidental ceremonial trimming of the 99 yews in the churchyard at Painswick (according to local superstition the hundredth tree when it is planted always refuses to grow). The Painswick ceremony takes place in the afternoon: the children of the town encircle the churchyard, join hands, then advance towards the church and retreat three times, singing the traditional Clipping Hymn.

Now a religious occasion, the ceremony probably originated in a pagan ritual dance around a central altar bearing an animal sacrifice. A special cake, in which a small china dog is embedded, is traditionally baked in Painswick on Clipping Day; known as "puppy dog pie", it may be a gruesome reminder of the pagan origins of the occasion.

CNAA *See* Council for National Academic Awards.

CND (Campaign for Nuclear Disarmament) An organization founded in 1958 to campaign against all nuclear weapons. It grew out of the earlier National Council for the Abolition of Nuclear Weapons Tests, which began in 1957, and most famous of its former activities were the annual marches from Aldermaston to London (between 1958 and the early 1970s) led by such notable figures as Bertrand Russell and Canon Collins. After a lull in public interest during the seventies, the organization again came to prominence with its campaign against the neutron bomb in 1977–78. It possesses both a national structure and locally based campaign groups, and has links with such organizations as trade unions, community

CND *Rally in London, 1984.*

groups, local councils, churches, and the Labour, Liberal, Scottish and Welsh Nationalist parties. It endeavours to form alliances with other peace groups nationally and pursues its campaign for nuclear disarmament through "demonstrations, meetings, door-to-door canvassing, and nonviolent direct action", as well as through the lobbying of all political parties and candidates. Internationally it maintains close contact with the American Freeze Campaign and European peace groups. CND's symbol, white (for hope and creativity) on a black background (for despair and destruction), represents the semaphore signals for "N" and "D".

Coastguard service Her Majesty's Coastguard: the UK's maritime assistance organization. Its duties include saving life at sea, watching for vessels in difficulty or listed overdue, monitoring emergency radio frequencies, and coordinating rescue services during emergencies along the coastline and in the eastern part of the North Atlantic. It also keeps watch for dangerous chemicals being washed ashore. The office of the Chief Coastguard manages the 550 regular officers and 8000 part-time staff – all civil servants of the Department of Transport under the auspices of the Maritime Search and Rescue Organization. The Coastguard also manages the Channel Navigation Information Service on behalf of the Department of Transport, and performs a number of duties to combat pollution.

Before 1822 the coastguard was an auxiliary force designed to combat smuggling. It became a reserve body of the Royal Navy with the specialized role of saving lives under the provisions of the Coastguard Service Act 1856, a service deemed necessary because of the huge scale of maritime losses (2000–3000 per annum) in the 19th century. HM Coastguard participated in the saving of 20,000 lives from 1859 to 1909, and suffered severe casualties with the Royal Navy during World War I. The service was transferred to the Board of Trade in 1923, when a large network of coastal watch stations was established.

After 1979 the Coastguard underwent radical change; its staff and watch duties were reduced, and its resources were concentrated into six large rescue coordination centres at Aberdeen, Clyde, Swansea, Falmouth, Yarmouth, and Dover, with 20 substations around the UK. Each Coastguard officer must have a thorough knowledge of weather and the local area, and be familiar with the operational procedures for calling in lifeboats and helicopters. Some 95% of distress calls are received by telecommunication rather than visual observation, and most rescue missions take place during summer months. Some 8500 people were rescued in 1984.

cockfighting A sport in which two or more specially bred game-cocks fight, often to the death, and spectators bet on the outcome. It was introduced to Britain by the Romans but little is known about it before the Middle Ages. From the early 16th century to the 19th century it was a popular sport enjoyed by all classes of society and by several British monarchs: during the reign of Henry VIII a royal cockpit was built at Whitehall. Although cockfighting went on throughout the year, the most important events were associated with public holidays and fairs. Contests took place between two cocks or several. In the latter case bets were laid on which bird would survive the longest. The birds had beaks and claws filed to sharp points and razor-sharp spurs were attached to their legs; they were even fed on special diets.

The sport was still popular in the 19th century, particularly during the Regency, and was not outlawed until 1849 when a £5 fine was imposed for staging a cockfight. Since it was relatively easy to hold fights clandestinely and the takings by far exceeded the fine, many organizers continued to stage events. Indeed, despite a decline in interest in blood sports among most of the populace, cockfights still occasionally take place in secret.

Cockney A native working-class inhabitant of London, or the language spoken by such a person. In the 14th century the term "Cockney" denoted a misshapen egg – jocularly referred to as a *cokken ey* or cock's egg. From this it came to denote an absurd or squeamish person, and was often applied to town-dwellers by countrymen. In the 16th century, the "king of the cockneys" was a master of the revels chosen by law students at Lincoln's Inn to preside at Christmas merrymaking; at about the same time the word came to mean a Londoner born within the sound of Bow bells, those of the church of St Mary-le-Bow, Cheapside.

Cockney English differs from middle-class London English in a number of respects. It is especially rich in slang, in particular *rhyming slang, which seems to have been invented in London. Some characteristic Cockney speech sounds include -v- and -f- for -th- ("muvver" for "mother", "nuffink" for "nothing"), -r- for -t- between two vowels ("gerroff" for "get off"). The dropping of h- at the beginning of a word, pronunciation of -ing as -in ("'Allo darlin'"), and change of -t- between two vowels into a glottal stop are features shared with some other nonstandard accents (*see* accent).

Coldstream Guards *See* Household Division.

College of Arms (Heralds' College) A corporate institution to whose members the sovereign has delegated, since at least the 15th century, the right of granting arms. The officers of arms, or *heralds, undertake genealogical as well as heraldic work. The *Earl Marshal heads the College of Arms, which has jurisdiction in England, Wales, and Northern Ireland. The equivalent body in Scotland, is the *Court of the Lord Lyon. The chief heralds, or Kings of Arms, are Garter King of Arms, whose post was instituted in 1417, and who is attached to the Order of the Garter and has no regional responsibility; Clarenceux King of Arms, dating from either 1362 or c. 1417, whose jurisdiction covers England south of the River Trent and whose title commemorates either a 14th- or early 15th-century Duke of Clarence; and Norroy and Ulster King of Arms, who now combines the functions of Norroy King of Arms (from "*Nord Roy*" or the northern part of the kingdom) – originating perhaps as early as 1277 and with jurisdiction over England north of the River Trent – and of Ulster, created by Edward VI with a supervisory authority over the whole of Ireland.

There are six ordinary heralds: Richmond (whose post dates from either Edward IV's or Henry VII's reign), Somerset (whose post is said to date from the reign of either Henry VII or VIII), York (thought to have been instituted in commemoration of a Duke of York, son of Edward III, but which certainly dates from at least the time of the 15th-century Yorkist kings), Lancaster (originally founded in honour of Edward III's son John of Gaunt, Duke of Lancaster, later abolished, but then revived by Henry VII), Chester (probably instituted in honour of the Black Prince, who was also Earl of Chester), and Windsor (said to have been founded by Edward III, who was also known as Edward of Windsor).

Of lower rank than the heralds are the pursuivants, originally a form of probationary herald: Portcullis (the name commemorates the Tudor badge), Bluemantle (commemorating the blue field of the arms of France quartered with England's by Edward III), Rouge Croix (denoting the red cross of St George), and Rouge Dragon (denoting the Welsh emblem and appearing on the Tudor arms). Heralds first appeared in the 12th century. They understood the pictorial devices used to identify individuals wearing suits of armour. The College of Arms itself was instituted in 1484 but its present charter dates from 1555. Since 1671 it has been located in Queen Victoria's Street in the City of London. The College of Arms remains the official repository of genealogical records of English, Northern Irish, and Commonwealth families.

colleges of education Institutions for the training of teachers. The former teachers' training colleges, of which there were 153 at the time of the Robbins Report (1963), underwent a radical reform following the James Committee's Report (1972) and are now much more closely linked with the universities and offer university-style courses of three or four years' duration leading to the degree of BEd (Bachelor of Education).

command papers Documents prepared by the government, and laid before Parliament (formally, by royal command) for its consideration. They are of two types. A **white paper** either sets out the government's policy on a particular matter (e.g. Cmnd 9510 of May 1985, containing proposals for future legislation on public order) or explains the background to and contents of a *Bill that it is currently promoting in Parliament. A **green paper** merely sets out proposals and possibilities for public discussion (e.g. on the reform of the rating system, or on education). Command papers published before 1870 were numbered serially without any prefix. They were prefixed C from 1870 to 1899, Cd from 1900 to 1918, and Cmd from 1919 to 1956. Since then the prefix has been Cmnd.

Commercial Court A court that forms part of the Queen's Bench Division of the *High Court of Justice and hears cases of a commercial nature, such as those involving banking or insurance law, imports or exports, or charterparties. The judges of the court are *puisne judges of the Queen's Bench Division nominated by the Lord Chancellor, chosen by him for their experience in commercial matters. The flexibility of the court recognizes the need of the commercial sector for the speedy resolution of disputes.

Commission for Racial Equality The public body set up under the Race Relations Act 1976 to eliminate discrimination in the fields of housing, services, and employment, to promote equal opportunities, and to monitor the race laws. It superseded the Race Relations Board and the Community Relations Commission, and is funded by an annual grant from the Home Office. Its five divisions, dealing with employment, education, housing, field services, and legal and general services, carry out the work of the Commission in conjunction with local community relations councils. The Commission provides grants to these councils for projects aimed at furthering racial harmony.

Common Entrance (examination) An examination taken by candidates for admission to *public schools. It is taken mainly by boys in *preparatory schools at the age of 13+, but in 1947 a similar examination was established for girls' public schools. Common Entrance is not a public examination, but is run by the Headmasters' Conference and Incorporated Association of Preparatory Schools,

and candidates' scripts are marked at the public school to which admission is sought.

common law The body of English unwritten law formulated by the royal courts during the first few centuries after the Norman conquest (1066) as constituting the common custom of the realm. It remains today one of the three primary sources of English law, the others being *equity and legislation (*see* Act of Parliament).

Before the conquest, Saxon law was essentially a matter of local custom, administered in local courts, primarily the county courts. Afterwards there was no attempt to impose a continental legal system on the English (indeed, William the Conqueror undertook that Anglo-Saxon laws would be preserved, though canon law would now be adopted by the Church). The growth of a common law began in the 12th century, especially under Henry II (1154–89), and was facilitated by two developments in royal judicial practices.

Firstly, the central royal courts began to replace local courts. During the reign of Henry I (1100–35) there had developed from the personnel of the royal court (*curia regis*) a particular department of state concerned with the collection and administration of the royal revenues. It was called the Exchequer, from the chequered cloths used in the reckoning of accounts. Under Henry II it took on judicial duties too and became the first royal court – the **Court of Exchequer**, staffed by judges known as barons of the Exchequer, under the presidency of a chief baron. It dealt at first purely with revenue disputes between subject and Crown, but subsequently with monetary disputes between subjects. Later in the reign of Henry II, there developed out of the *curia regis* a second royal court – the **Court of Common Pleas**. This was a court based permanently at Westminster, a practice (confirmed by *Magna Carta in 1215) designed to remedy the inconvenience caused to litigants by a court that travelled around the country with the king. Its judges were appointed from those holding the senior legal rank of serjeant-at-law (*see* barrister), and it assumed jurisdiction to deal with all manner of disputes between subjects. These two royal courts were joined by a third (a further offshoot from the *curia* regis) in the following century: the **Court of King's Bench**. Presided over by the Lord Chief Justice, it exercised both a civil and a criminal jurisdiction, and also a supervisory jurisdiction over inferior courts. The gradual replacement of local courts by the three royal courts (referred to collectively as the courts of common law) was due mainly to the superior procedures and greater effectiveness of the latter, which were also less tainted by corruption. The second development promoting a common law was the system of circuit judges introduced by William the Conqueror and developed by Henry II. Henry sent out judges of the Court of Common Pleas on regular tours (known as circuits), during the course of which they officiated in local courts and hence gained knowledge of local customs. By collating, clarifying, and amplifying these customs to cover new situations by analogy, these judges (and those of the Court of King's Bench when they became circuit judges) gradually propounded the common law as the common custom of the realm.

Eventually, all three courts of common law sat in Westminster Hall, together with a fourth court – the Court of Chancery, which developed after them and administered the supplementary system of law called *equity. All four courts were moved in 1872 to the newly built Royal Courts of Justice in the Strand (the Law Courts). Three years later they were replaced by the *High Court of Justice, established by the Judicature Acts 1873–75.

The Scottish common law has remained distinct from the English, maintaining its many differences of detail and procedure. Unlike the English law, which is entirely based on the precedents of previous cases, Scottish law has been analysed and reduced to sets of coherent principles since the 17th century; some of these works, such as Viscount Stair's *Institutions of the Law of Scotland* (1681), have official standing within the legal system equal to that of the Inner House of the *Court of Session. In Wales, the Statute of Wales 1284 applied English criminal law in the Principality but not in the *Welsh Marches; and Welsh law was suppressed entirely in 1542. Northern Irish law is very similar to English law.

common riding *See* riding the marches.

commons Areas of open land in England or Wales over which adjacent owners and occupiers have certain rights in common with each other. Many commons were formerly the wastelands of medieval *manors, the commoners (i.e. those enjoying the rights over them) holding the adjacent lands as tenants of the lord of the manor. The principal rights are pasture (the right to graze animals, also known as pannage in the case of swine), piscary (the right to fish), turbary (the right to dig turf), and estovers (the right to take wood for repairs or firewood). Uncertainty as to the exact status of many pieces of land led to the passing of the Commons Registration Act in 1965, providing for the keeping of registers by local authorities. Compiled after the investigation of any disputes by commons commissioners, they show what lands in the realm are commons, and who owns them, and they set out the commoners' rights.

Common Serjeant The holder of an ancient judicial office in the City of London. A barrister appointed by the Crown (originally from those holding the most senior rank of serjeant-at-law; *see* barrister), the Common Serjeant ranks in precedence next to the Recorder of the City of London (*see* recorder); and, like the Recorder, has been a judge of the *Central Criminal Court since it was established in 1834, sitting originally as a commissioner of *assize, and now as a *circuit judge.

Commonwealth (1649–60) *See* Civil War, English.

Commonwealth An association of independent sovereign states, consisting of the UK and a majority of the countries that were once colonies or dependencies of the UK. Its members are united in recognizing the Queen as its symbolic head and committed (in the words of a 1971 declaration of heads of government) to consulting and cooperating in the common interests of their peoples and the promotion of international understanding and world peace. It currently comprises 49 members, and some 1000 million people of many races, religions, and languages, living in all the continents.

The oldest members of the Commonwealth are Canada, Australia, and New Zealand, three of the countries to which the UK first

The Commonwealth

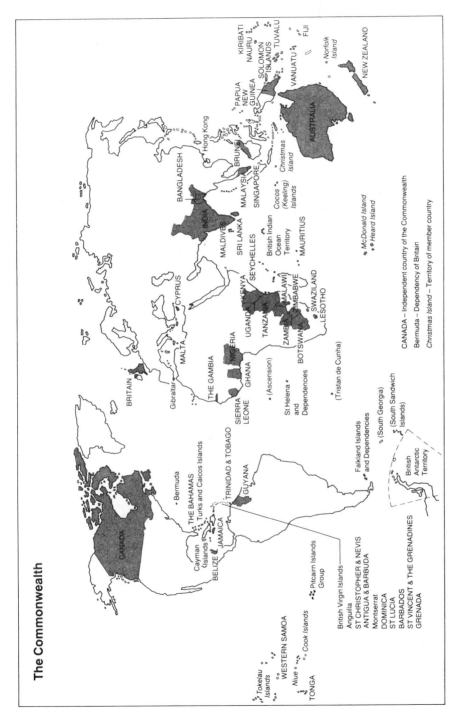

CANADA – Independent country of the Commonwealth

Bermuda – Dependency of Britain

Christmas Island – Territory of member country

granted independence by the Statute of Westminster 1931. (South Africa was also such a country, but left the Commonwealth in 1961.) They were known then as dominions, and their association with the UK was known as the British Commonwealth of Nations. After World War II, grants of independence became increasingly frequent, and an immediate problem was posed by India which, with Pakistan, had achieved statehood in 1947. India wished to become a republic yet remain within the Commonwealth, in which her citizens technically owed allegiance to the Crown. The Declaration of London 1949, confirming that her membership was to continue, pronounced that allegiance to the Crown was replaced by acceptance of the Crown "as the symbol of the free association of the independent member nations, and as such the Head of the Commonwealth". This Declaration heralded the beginning of the modern Commonwealth; the adjective "British" was dropped from its title, and the word "dominion" fell out of use.

The Commonwealth has no legal personality, no constitution, and no formal organs of government, legislative, executive, or judicial. Membership involves independence, recognition of the Queen in terms of the London Declaration, and acceptance by the other members. Membership is lost by voluntary withdrawal, by lapse (which occurs if a member becomes a republic, or a separate monarchy, and fails to get its membership confirmed on the new basis), or by expulsion. Pakistan withdrew in 1972, after the civil war, and Bangladesh was admitted. South Africa lapsed in 1961, on becoming a republic and having withdrawn its application for continued membership in view of the dissension that this was causing. There has been no case of expulsion, though South Africa would probably have been expelled if it had not withdrawn. Every two years, the heads of government meet (1983 in New Delhi; 1985 in Nassau, Bahamas) to discuss matters of mutual concern, and regional meetings also take place (in recent years between Canada and the Caribbean states and between Australia, India, and the Asian states). The 1965 conference agreed to set up a Commonwealth Secretariat at Marlborough House, London, which acts as a clearing house for information of interest to member countries and gives advice in connection with technical cooperation. The Secretary-General since 1975 has been Sir Shridath Ramphal, a former foreign minister of Guyana and member of the Brandt Commission on north-south economic problems.

Commonwealth citizenship *See* citizenship.

Commonwealth Institute An organization founded by statute in 1959 to replace the Imperial Institute, inaugurated by Queen Victoria in 1893. It is based in London and Edinburgh. The main activity of the Commonwealth Institute is the promotion of the heritage and cultures of its member nations through exhibitions, conferences, performing artists, educational courses, and its extensive library. The Institute in Kensington, London, was opened in November 1962. In addition to providing a regular meeting place for Commonwealth citizens, the Institute runs the Commonwealth poetry prize and organizes celebrations on Commonwealth Day (the first Monday in March). It is run by a board of governors, which includes the High Commissioners of its member nations.

Companies Court A specialist court within the Chancery Division of the *High Court of Justice, staffed by *puisne judges of that Division nominated by the Lord Chancellor, and exercising jurisdiction over matters arising under the Companies Acts 1947–81 (e.g. the compulsory winding up of a company unable to pay its debts). Within certain financial limits, the *county court also has a jurisdiction over company law, but it may be required by the parties to state any question of law arising during proceedings for decision by the Companies Court instead.

Companions of Honour, Order of the An award made to members of either sex for outstanding national service. It is a distinction entailing no acceptance of title, ranking of merit, or precedence. Recipients are styled A ... B ..., CH, and, in the event of a Companion holding several honours, the initials CH are placed immediately after the letters

GBE (*see* British Empire, Order of the). The Order of Companions of Honour was instituted in 1917 and the terms altered in 1919. It now consists of the sovereign and a maximum of 65 members. The ribbon is carmine in colour with gold edges.

comprehensive school *See* state education.

Confederation of British Industry (CBI) The association of British employers that acts as the spokesman for industry and commerce in discussions at the highest level; it produces economic forecasts and promotes the interests of business generally. The CBI was founded by royal charter in 1965 as a result of the amalgamation of the National Association of British Manufacturers (1915), the Federation of British Industries (1916), and the British Employers' Federation (1919). About half of the thousand largest companies in Britain are members, and they benefit from information services on business topics and an annual programme of conferences and seminars. As a pressure group, the CBI was successful in its campaign to abolish the national insurance surcharge, which cost industry £17,000 million over an eight-year period, a reduction in corporation tax to 35%, and limitations on commercial rates through rate-capping legislation. The CBI is represented on many other bodies concerned with trade and industry.

Congregationalism *See* United Reformed Church.

conservation area An area of architectural or historic interest that has been designated as such under the terms of the Civic Amenities Act 1967. Designation provides for planning control over the demolition of buildings, erection of hoardings, tree-felling, and other activities, so that buildings and any aesthetically important features may be protected and enhanced. Grants and loans may be available to encourage this process, for example, by assisting the maintenance and repair of listed buildings (*see* historic buildings and monuments). A wide range of places may be designated conservation areas, including towns, villages, hamlets, important houses, and even stretches of canal.

Conservative and Unionist Members' Committee (1922 Committee) The gathering of backbench Conservative MPs that meets periodically to debate party policies and strategy. Its name derives from its inaugural meeting at the Carlton Club in 1922, when it forced the withdrawal of the Conservatives from Lloyd George's coalition government. It elects annually as its chairman a senior and respected backbencher, who plays an influential role as a channel of communication between the back benches and the Prime Minister (by whom the Committee is addressed from time to time). It also elects annually an executive of senior backbenchers and a structure of subcommittees to examine specific areas of policy, such as defence, foreign affairs, education, and employment.

Conservative Party A major British political party, whose policies are distinguished by a cautious attitude to reform, encouragement of private enterprise, and a pragmatic rather than ideological approach to government. The Conservative Party emerged in the 1830s from the **Tory** party. This had governed the country since 1784 but had split in the late 1820s, and was in disarray after the defeat of the Duke of Wellington's Tory ministry in 1830 and the *Great Reform Act 1832, passed under a Whig ministry. The name originated in the writings of a John Wilson Croker in the *Quarterly Review* (vol. XLII, 1830), and seems to have been adopted by the Tories under Sir Robert Peel (Prime Minister 1834–35, 1841–46), as suggesting a philosophy of gradual reform within the framework of existing institutions and traditions.

The principal architects of Conservatism in the second half of the century were Benjamin Disraeli, later Earl of Beaconsfield (Prime Minister 1868, 1874–1880), whose novel *Sybil* (1845) drew attention in its much quoted subtitle to the "two nations of England", the privileged and the people; and Robert Cecil, Marquess of Salisbury (Prime Minister 1885–86, 1886–92, 1895–1903). During this period, the Conservatives and the Liberals (successors to the Whigs) alternated in power with fair regularity; the Conservatives were then kept out of full office by Liberal governments from 1905 to 1915, but figured in coalition governments from then until 1922. In the general election of that year, the Labour Party replaced the Liberals as the chief contender against the Conservatives, holding office briefly in 1924, and from 1929 to 1931. Since the coalition governments of World War II and the landslide Labour victory of 1945, Labour and Conservative governments have alternated, the Conservatives holding office from 1951 to 1964, 1970 to 1974, and again since 1979. The leader of the Conservative Party was formerly allowed to "emerge" from a process of behind-the-scenes consultations. However, since 1965, the leader has been elected by the parliamentary party. Party organization is in the hands of a chairman, who is appointed by the leader, and presides over the Conservative Central Office, which coordinates the activities of constituency associations throughout the country.

consistory court The ecclesiastical court of a diocese of the Church of England, presided over by a legally qualified chancellor appointed by the bishop. (In the diocese of Canterbury, however, the terms are commissary court and commissary-general.) The jurisdiction of consistory courts is twofold. They hear proceedings against priests for ecclesiastical offences not involving matters of doctrine or ritual (offences which do involve such matters being dealt with by the *Court of Ecclesiastical Causes Reserved); and they decide applications for faculties. A faculty, meaning licence, is required under ecclesiastical law for any alteration to consecrated land or buildings (including furnishings, ornaments, and decorations) and the court must take into account the views of all those interested (particularly the incumbent, his churchwardens and the parochial church council) and any relevant doctrinal or artistic considerations. Appeals from a consistory court are normally made to either the *Court of Arches or to the Chancery Court of York (see Court of Arches) depending on whether the diocese is in the province of Canterbury or York. Faculty decisions touching on questions of doctrine or ritual are, however, appealed instead to the Court of Ecclesiastical Causes Reserved.

Consolidated Fund The Exchequer account at the Bank of England, into which all tax revenue is paid and which is used for government expenditure. Its name originated in 1787, when the Prime Minister, William Pitt the Younger (1759–1806), consolidated the various funds in which the customs and excise revenues had previously been held (see tax system; Customs and Excise). With minor exceptions, the principle of a single account has been maintained ever since. The revenue sources are voted annually by Parliament in the Finance Act, and expenditure is approved by several Consolidated Fund Acts every year. The details of the latter are not challenged, but the debates are generally used by MPs to raise any subject they wish and frequently lead to all-night sittings.

Conspicuous Gallantry Medal A decoration instituted in 1874 and bestowed on warrant officers and men in the Royal Navy. Since 1942 the class of those eligible has been expanded to include persons serving in the Royal Air Force and Mercantile Marine. A holder of the decoration is entitled to the letters CGM after his or her name.

constituency An area of the UK for which a representative is elected to the *House of Commons or European Parliament. European constituencies consist of two or more House of Commons constituencies. The latter currently number 650 (523 in England, 38 in Wales, 72 in Scotland, and 17 in Northern Ireland), but vary to take account of population changes, variations being effected by Order in Council made on the recommendation of boundary commissions and approved by both Houses of Parliament. There are four commissions, one for each country of the UK, each chaired by the *Speaker of the House of Commons, and each including a senior judge amongst its members. They review the constituencies in their part of the UK at intervals of not less than 10 years and not more than 15 years, and make recommendations to secure convenient constituencies with electorates of similar size. There are, however, limitations on their powers. There must be no fewer than 35 seats in Wales, 71 in Scotland, and 12 in Northern Ireland, and the total for Great Britain as a whole must not be substantially more or less than 613.

Convocations of Canterbury and York
From Anglo-Saxon times the two provinces of the Church of England – Canterbury and York – have held assemblies, or convocations, to administer their affairs. Initially the convocations comprised only bishops, but in the 13th and 14th centuries, representatives of the clergy were admitted, resulting in the creation of the Upper and Lower Houses of Convocation in the 15th century. The power of the Convocations was severely curbed by the Submission of the Clergy exacted by Henry VIII in 1532 (*see* Reformation), although they retained responsibility for taxing the clergy until the early years of the Restoration, when meetings lapsed. Reconvened in 1700, the Convocations became the scene of heated exchanges between various factions in the Church and state, and meetings were suspended in 1717. After meeting again formally in 1741, they ceased for over a century until Canterbury met again in 1854 and York in 1861, since when proceedings have been relatively orderly. At the start of the 20th century, joint meetings of Convocation were initiated. The Synodical Government Measure of 1969 transferred powers held by the Convocations to the *General Synod, although the Convocations continued to exist in their own right. The Upper Houses now consist of the diocesan bishops and certain elected suffragan bishops, while members of the Lower Houses include deans, provosts, elected representatives of the clergy, and representatives of the armed services and certain universities.

Cooperative society An organization supplying goods and services, based on joint ownership, open membership, limited interest on capital, dividend in proportion to the use made of the services, democratic control, educational provision, and links with similar organizations. Such principles were a response to industrial workers to the exploitation they experienced in the mill towns of northern England, perhaps influenced too by the utopian ideas of the philanthropist Robert Owen (1771–1858). Various small-scale cooperative ventures were tried from the turn of the 19th century, but the real founders of the Co-ops were the Rochdale Pioneers, 28 artisans from Lancashire who pooled their resources in 1844 to rent a shop trading in such basic commodities as flour, sugar, and candles; the profits were shared amongst those who shopped there. The success of this experiment led to the development of the Cooperative movement in Britain, a complex organization including more than a hundred retail societies (with many shops each) all over the country: the Cooperative Wholesale Society, the Cooperative Union, the Cooperative Bank, the Cooperative Insurance Society, the Cooperative College, the Cooperative Party, and a number of associated productive societies and local federal societies. Although cooperative ideas spread elsewhere in the world, and have been applied particularly successfully in agriculture, Britain's developments have mainly been in consumer cooperation. The Co-op shop is as familiar a sight as the parish church or village pub.

The societies are run by a part-time management committee elected from and by the membership; all members have a vote regardless of the extent of their shareholding, but the dividend they draw depends on how much they have spent at the Co-op. Up to the end of World War II, almost a quarter of the British population were members of the Co-op and 20% of all retail trade passed through Co-op shops. With the expansion of retail trade once rationing ended, they failed to keep pace with their competitors. Now about 5% of British retail trade is accounted for by the societies as well as some 30% of all milk sales. Serving the societies are two national federations: the Cooperative Wholesale Society and the Cooperative Union. The CWS meets the societies' trading needs as manufacturer, buyer, importer, and provider of many services. It has about one hundred productive units and originated the "own brand" product in British shops. The Cooperative Union coordinates all the activities of the Co-op movement, such as finance, research, and education, and acts as spokesman and adviser on government policy. The Cooperative Party was founded in 1917 to determine and promote consumer interests and to ensure that the principles of cooperation were followed in the political sphere. There are usually about seven or eight Cooperative/Labour MPs in the House of Commons, about the same number of life peers in the House of Lords, and two Members of the European Parliament. The Cooperative, Labour, and trade union movements also meet together in a consultative committee known as the National Council of Labour.

The economic recession and steadily rising number of unemployed in Britain in the 1980s aroused much interest in the idea of cooperatives outside the established movement as a means of self-employment and genuine mutual ownership; housing, food, and service cooperatives formed all over the country, and in many cases received help and advice from the Cooperative movement.

coracle week, Cilgerran An annual festival staged during late summer in the ancient village of Cilgerran, in Dyfed, west Wales. The main feature of the festival, which always takes place during the week including 21 August, is a coracle race on the River Teifi, on the last day. The other days are devoted to football matches and fairs. Coracles are little tub boats, rowed with one paddle, and made of willow, formerly covered with calfskin (hessian is now preferred), coated with bitumen. Of remote origin, they have been used as fishing boats in some parts of Wales for many centuries, two boats rowing side by side with a fishing net stretched between them. A coracle rower is required by law to hold a special government licence; however, few licensed rowers survive, and indeed the number of people seeking licences has declined in recent years. The coracles used at Cilgerran coracle week are supplied by the only two surviving coracle makers in west Wales.

Cornish A *Celtic language, quite closely related to Welsh. It was spoken in Cornwall until the late 18th century; according to tradition, the last habitual speaker of the language was Dolly Pentreath, who died in 1777. Very few Cornish texts survive, and the spelling of those that do is highly variable. There are a few religious texts, including the Lord's Prayer and the Creed, some miracle plays (*see* mystery plays) translated from English, a couple of biographical pieces, and a Cornish grammar in E. Lhuyd's *Archaeologia Britannica* (London 1707).

The most striking relics of the Cornish language consist of the place names of Cornwall, some 85% of which are of Cornish origin. The most common recurring vocabulary elements in these place names are nouns and adjectives. Among the nouns are: *tre* "homestead", *pen* "hill", *pol* "pool", *porth* "port", *ty* or *chy* "house", *lan* "enclosure", *nans* "valley", *ros* "heath", *goon* "downland", *hal* "moor", *bod* "home", *celli* "grove", and *cos* "wood". The adjectives provide examples of the common phenomenon in Celtic languages of the initial mutation. Thus, the adjective *bean* "little" becomes *vean* when it occurs with a feminine singular noun. So, the name Porthbean means "little port"; the second syllable begins with b- because *porth* is a masculine noun. *Goon*, however, is a feminine noun, so the place name that means "little downland" takes the form Goonvean. Other common adjectives include *meor*, *veor* "big", *gwyn*, *wen* "white", *du* "black", *glas*, *las* "blue/green", *(g)wartha* "high", and *gollas*, *wollas* "low".

Cornish pasty A pastry case containing a mixture of meat and vegetables, usually potato, onion, and turnip. Originally prepared by Cornish farmers' wives to take out to the fields at meal times for the farmer and his hands, the pasties were much larger than those made today and their contents varied according to individual tastes. The casing was a round of shortcrust pastry, folded over the filling of cooked vegetables, chopped meat,

CORACLE WEEK *Coracle rower at Cilgerran.*

and seasoning, and sealed with a thick seam that could be held between the fingers of the farm worker while he consumed the contents, and then thrown away. The habit spread locally to fishermen and tin miners in the county. Some pasties also contained a sweet filling at one end to serve as a dessert.

coronation ceremony The formal investiture of a new monarch with the trappings of sovereignty. The ceremony is entirely organized by the *Earl Marshal, apart from the liturgy, which is the province of the *Archbishop of Canterbury. Much of the ceremony dates back to the 10th century when St Dunstan, as Archbishop of Canterbury, devised it for the coronation of King Edgar in 973; even then he made use of earlier pagan rituals, such as the enthronement and offering of symbolic objects, as well as Christian ceremonies, such as the anointing. St Anselm, Archbishop of Canterbury (1093–1109), refined the coronation

CORONATION CEREMONY *The coronation of 1953. The state procession in Westminster Abbey is led by Her Majesty Queen Elizabeth II.*

rite, which was further altered in the 14th century. The form of ceremony was then recorded in the *Liber Regalis* ("Kingly Book"), which was translated into English in 1603. Since two major revisions were made in the late 17th century, the ceremony has remained more or less unaltered; and since 1066 it has always taken place in *Westminster Abbey.

After the procession into the Abbey, the first part of the ceremony is the Recognition, in which the sovereign is presented to the congregation by the Archbishop of Canterbury, who asks whether they are willing to do homage and service, whereupon they cry, "God Save King (Queen) ...". The monarch then takes the coronation oaths, and a service of Communion follows. After the Creed is said, the monarch is divested of his or her crimson robe and, wearing a plain white gown, symbolizing humility before God, sits in King Edward's (Edward I) Chair and is anointed on hands, breast, and head by the Archbishop, who administers a blessing.

The monarch then retires to St Edward's (St Edward the Confessor) chapel to don the *colobium sindonis*, a white alb (a full-length, close-sleeved tunic), the *supertunica*, or gold cloth mantle, and a girdle. Next, he or she is offered certain royal ornaments: the gold spurs (which in 1953 the Queen merely touched; in the case of her male predecessors the heels of the monarch were touched with the spurs); the Sword of State and the Jewelled Sword, with which kings are usually girded but which in 1953 the Queen took in her hands and then laid on the altar; the armills (gold bracelets of sovereignty and wisdom); and lastly the Robe Royal (a semicircular cloak) and Stole Royal. These priestly vestments symbolize the monarchy's divine nature.

The monarch then sits in the Coronation Chair and briefly receives the Orb, the two Sceptres – one bearing a cross, the other a dove – and the coronation ring. Finally the Archbishop of Canterbury places Edward the Confessor's Crown on the sovereign's head. The moment the crown touches the head, trumpets sound, a salute is fired at the Tower of London, and the congregation cry "God Save the King (Queen)". After a blessing, the newly crowned monarch receives homage from the Archbishop (acting for all the bishops), and then from the royal dukes, and the other peers.

After the homage the monarch takes Communion and makes an offering before the altar; in 1953 the gifts were a gold ingot and an altar cloth. For the final part of the ceremony, known as the Recess, the monarch dons the royal robe of purple velvet and the Imperial State Crown, which is lighter than Edward the Confessor's Crown. Lastly he or she, holding the Sceptre with the Cross in the right hand and the Orb in the left, joins the procession to the west door of the Abbey, to the sounds of the national anthem and the pealing of bells.

coroner An officer of the Crown (traceable to the 12th century) whose principal function is to hold inquests into certain deaths occurring in his district. He also inquires into treasure trove. An inquest is held in the event of a violent or unnatural death. Its purpose is to establish the identity of the deceased, the time and place of death, and the cause of death. Proceedings are normally conducted entirely by the coroner, who must in some cases (e.g. death in police custody) sit with a jury, consisting of 7–11 members.

Treasure trove consists of gold or silver items that have been deliberately hidden and have no traceable owner. Such items belong to the Crown. It is for the coroner to decide whether they were hidden, or merely lost, in which case they would belong to the finder unless the owner can be traced. A finder of treasure trove normally receives some financial compensation if not permitted by the Crown to keep it. A coroner must be a barrister, solicitor, or medical practitioner of at least five years' standing, and many coroners are both lawyers and doctors.

Corporation of London The governing body of the *City of London, officially the "Mayor and Commonalty and Citizens of the City of London". The Corporation operates through three institutions: the Court of Common Hall; the Court of *Aldermen; and the Court of Common Council. The Court of Common Hall originated in a congregation of freemen of the City, summoned periodically for the election of municipal officers. Its membership has varied over the centuries, and it consists today of the liverymen of the City guilds (or *City livery companies). In September of each year, they choose two of the City's aldermen, who have previously served as sheriffs, for presentation to the Court of Aldermen as candidates for *Lord Mayor; and in June of each year, they elect a variety of dignitaries, including two sheriffs, a chamberlain, four bridgemasters (the City being responsible for Tower Bridge, London Bridge, Southwark Bridge, and Blackfriars Bridge) and seven aleconners (who were responsible for testing the quality of ale). The Court of Aldermen consists of 26 aldermen, each elected for life by the voters of one of the City wards (since 1975, however, they are expected to retire at the age of 70). It meets some 15 times a year, one function being to make a final choice between the candidates for Lord Mayor presented by the Common Hall, and others including the regulation of certain matters concerning the livery companies and the adjudication of disputes concerning elections to the Court of Common Council. Aldermen are also, by virtue of the charters of the City, ex officio justices of the peace. The **Court of Common Council**, which meets in the Guildhall, consists of the Lord Mayor, the aldermen, and 159 councilmen elected annually by the ward voters, and is the major governing body of the Corporation. The councilmen have no allegiance to any political party. Working through a large number of committees, the Corporation exercises all the ordinary local government functions of a London borough outside the City (see Greater London), likewise financing these out of general rates. Some offices still bear their traditional titles, such as the City Chamberlain, who is responsible for finance, the Comptroller, who is the City's legal adviser, and the Remembrancer, who is charged with certain ceremonial duties and acts as a parliamentary adviser. There are also ceremonial officers, including the swordbearer, the common cryer, and the City marshal. Funded by revenue from the City's estates, the Corporation also undertakes such special responsibilities as running its own schools (the City of London School, School for Girls, and Freemen's School), and for main-

taining the bridges and open spaces, such as Epping Forest, owned outside London by the City.

corporation tax *See* tax system.

Cotswolds A limestone-based upland region of southern England lying in a broad band between Banbury and Bath. The fertile valleys with their hamlets and villages and boundary walls of Cotswold stone give the area a distinctive appeal, and have made it a popular region for tourism. The ridge of the Cotswolds escarpment, known as The Edge, marks the boundary between the Thames basin and the river systems of the Midlands; the northwest facing scarp slope is divided by steep valleys while those of the southeastern slope are more gentle. The main industries of the region were for many years sheep-farming and the manufacture of woollen textiles, which prospered in the Middle Ages and again in the 18th century, with the weaving mills centred on the southwestern towns of Stroud and Bradford-on-Avon. Production of the famous Cotswold woollen broadcloth has now declined, although it is still used for the "green baize" familiar to snooker players and gamblers, as well as for military uniforms and hunting "pink". In the late Middle Ages, the wool trade was a considerable source of wealth. For example, William of Grevel, a 14th-century merchant, channelled his fortune into the rebuilding of Chipping Camden church (see wool churches). Following the dissolution of the monasteries in the 1530s, their lands passed to the wool merchants, who looted the abbeys and built themselves fine houses. Much of the Cotswold architecture dates from the 17th and 18th centuries and employs the local oolitic limestone, not only for walls but also as stone tiles for the roofs. With the Enclosure Acts of the 18th and 19th centuries (see enclosure, laws of) and a decline in the wool trade, farmers turned to producing lamb, beef, and grain. Most of the Cotswold sheep and their pastures have now been supplanted by acres of wheat and barley.

Council for National Academic Awards (CNAA) The organization that approves courses and awards degrees for institutions of higher education other than universities. Established as an autonomous organization with a royal charter in 1964, following recommendations in the Robbins Report (1963), the CNAA awards degrees and diplomas to students following approved courses at over 130 institutions, including *polytechnics, colleges of technology, services colleges, and colleges of art. Since the early 1970s it has increasingly been involved in setting the standards of teacher training through its supervision of BEd courses.

Council for the Protection of Rural England (CPRE) An independent charity, founded in 1926, that seeks to safeguard the quality of the rural environment. It was established at the instigation of Patrick Abercrombie (1879–1957), who had published a pamphlet entitled *The Preservation of Rural England* (1926), outlining what were to be the aims of the Council, which was later set up under the same name (it changed to the present name in 1969). The CPRE's first major campaign was against ribbon development, and it was active in promoting the Town and Country Planning Act 1932, the first legislation to acknowledge the importance of planning for the countryside. During World War II the CPRE supported development of the country's agricultural resources, but since the 1950s it has been increasingly concerned with the dangers of intensive agricultural methods that destroy wildlife and the variety of the countryside (for example, by the removal of ancient hedgerows). Other areas of concern over which it has, with varying degrees of success, lobbied the government, include coastline development, the impact of motorways upon the landscape, the damage caused in small towns and villages by heavy lorries, the reclamation of land after open-cast mining, the siting of reservoirs in areas of natural beauty, and development pressure on *green belt zones around cities.

Council for the Securities Industry A body set up in 1978 by the Bank of England and the Department of Trade and Industry to ensure that the highest standards of conduct are maintained by those operating in the securities industry. It reviews the rules of conduct laid down by the various financial insti-

tutions, and their arrangements for policing them, and initiates new policies and codes of practice as necessary. The Council meets as required, and at least quarterly. Its chairman and deputy-chairman are appointed by the Governor of the Bank of England, and its other members are also drawn mainly from the City, being the chairmen of bodies such as the Council of the Stock Exchange, the Issuing Houses Association, the Panel on Takeovers and Mergers, the Confederation of British Industry, and the Committee of London Clearing Bankers. The Governor of the Bank of England also nominates three lay members to represent the interests of the individual investor and the wider public.

Council on Tribunals An advisory body established by Parliament in 1958 to review the workings of tribunals. It reports annually to the Lord Chancellor and Lord Advocate. Most important administrative tribunals, but not domestic tribunals or courts of law, are under its supervision. The Council has two more specific functions: it may be required to consider matters that arise in connection with tribunals, and it has to be consulted before any changes or innovations are introduced by the minister responsible. The Council (which has a Scottish Committee to advise it with respect to bodies peculiar to Scotland) consists of between 10 and 15 members appointed by the Lord Chancellor and the Lord Advocate, together with the *Ombudsman as an ex officio member. Its chairman is salaried, but the other ordinary members receive fees only.

counsellors of state Individuals who act for the sovereign when he or she is abroad for more than a few days or seriously ill (but not totally incapacitated). Their powers are confined to routine business: they may sign Acts passed by Parliament and call meetings of the Privy Council, but they cannot create peers or confer other honours, dissolve Parliament, or appoint a new Prime Minister. Counsellors of state are appointed by letters patent under the Great Seal (letters from the Crown, sealed with the Great Seal of England), and have jurisdiction over the United Kingdom and dependent territories, but not Commonwealth countries. Under the terms of the Regency

Acts of 1937, 1943, and 1953 the counsellors of state are the sovereign's spouse, the four people next in line to the throne (unless disqualified from being a *regent for such reasons as being under age), and Queen Elizabeth the Queen Mother. Two counsellors make a quorum for the discharge of business.

countess The title given to the wife of an earl or, more recently, to a woman who is a peeress in her own right. It is also given to the wife of an earl by courtesy (e.g. as the daughter-in-law of a marquess or duke). The term countess, derived from the French *comtesse*, or wife of a *comte*, was absorbed into English usage unlike the male title *comte* (count), which never replaced the roughly equivalent pre-Norman conquest title "earl". Countesses in their own right are usually the holders of earldoms in the peerage of Scotland, which predates the union of English and Scottish parliaments in 1707, and in which females may inherit titles. An exception is the present Countess Mountbatten of Burma, who inherited her father's title, created in the peerage of the United Kingdom in 1947. Countesses, whether by marriage or inheritance, take the prefix "Right Honourable" and are usually referred to in the third person as "Lady A . . . ", where "A . . . " denotes the specific title. Women who are countesses by virtue of a continental European title have no official precedence in Britain.

country houses The stately homes of the English upper classes that reflect something of their lifestyle and idiosyncrasy. English society in the 16th century was less prone to military conflict than formerly; this was reflected in the architecture of the period, which paid less attention to fortification and more to domestic comfort. One of the first true country houses, and certainly one of the most picturesque, is Compton Wynyates in Warwickshire, built over a period of 40 years in the early 16th century. Constructed of brick and set in formal *gardens, it was originally moated and had an assortment of crenellated gables and turrets implying a lingering faith in fortification. By the latter half of the century, however, medieval influences had finally been shed and a truly Elizabethan style flowered; splendid

Tudor palaces in the new style included *Longleat in Wiltshire and Burghley House in Northamptonshire, both of which incorporate gothic and Renaissance elements.

The early 17th century saw the introduction of the Palladian classical style (after the 16th-century Italian architect Andrea Palladio), largely through its chief English exponent, Inigo Jones (1573–1652). But, with the interruptions of the English Civil War and its aftermath, it was not until the late 17th and 18th centuries that classicism found expression in numerous mansions. Meanwhile the heights of baroque extravagance were reached by Sir John Vanbrugh (1664–1726) at Castle Howard in Yorkshire and Blenheim Palace in Oxfordshire. The grounds surrounding these great houses were now elevated from being merely convenient reservoirs of game to the status of landscaped parks, in the hands of such men as Lancelot "Capability" Brown (1716–83) and Humphry Repton (1752–1818). The houses themselves also became repositories of the finest in European and oriental art, thanks to Britain's increasing wealth and the penetration of European seamen to most parts of the globe. Paintings, furniture, porcelain, silver, all demonstrate the wealth and taste of their owners and provide evidence of their lavish lifestyle. The houses were usually the centres of large estates comprising acres of woodland, a home farm, and several tenanted farms. Each estate employed hundreds of people in a strict hierarchic structure (*see* social class).

A revival of gothic architecture took place in the 19th century, together with a whole assortment of other influences, some picturesque, some vulgar. Sir Edwin Lutyens' (1869–1944) Castle Drogo in Devon, built 1910–30, is probably the last of the line – an austere throwback to the Norman fortress from which our ancestors were probably glad to escape. In the 20th century, the rising burden of *death duties and more recently inheritance tax (*see* tax system), together with increased maintenance costs, have undermined the finances of the great estates. Many, such as *Blenheim and Chatsworth, are open to the public; others have set up tourist attractions,

COUNTRY HOUSES *Compton Wynyates, Warwickshire, an example of early Tudor architecture. Built for comfort rather than security, as shown by the decorative twisting chimneys and broad mullioned windows, the battlement-style turrets nevertheless reveal a lingering medieval concept of defence.*

for example, the *Woburn Abbey safari park.

Country Life A weekly magazine founded in 1897 and bearing the rubric "*The* Journal for All Interested in Country Life and Country Pursuits". Its original title was *Country Life Illustrated* and it incorporated an earlier periodical, *Racing Illustrated*. Hunting reports have always been a regular feature, together with items on racing, polo, three-day events, and major horse shows. The magazine was originally devoted almost entirely to sport but has since broadened its range to cover such fields as gardening, travel, art, the sale-rooms, and architecture. *Country Life* preserves a unique illustrated record of Britain's large country

COUNTRY HOUSES *Castleward in Strangford, Co. Down, a mid-18th-century house built in a curious combination of classical and gothic styles. The classical front (shown here), with four Ionic columns rising through the upper storeys, contrasts starkly with the gothic face behind, which has battlemented parapets and pointed windows.*

houses, their history, and furnishings. These articles expanded from short notes in the first issue to major scholarly essays, a tradition started by (Sir) Lawrence Weaver (1876–1930), who was architectural editor from 1910 to 1916; and continued by the architectural historian Christopher Hussey (1899–1970), who edited the magazine from 1933 to 1940, and contributed hundreds of articles over a period of 50 years. In recent years *Country Life* has strongly identified itself with the conservation lobby.

country parks Special amenity areas that have been established throughout the country to provide people from urban areas with access to "pockets" of countryside. More than a hundred country parks now exist in England and Wales, mostly owned by local authorities, although a few are owned by the *National Trust and some are in private hands. Many parks have guides, nature trails, and even

study centres to provide information about the area and its wildlife.

Countryside Commission A department of the civil service set up by the Countryside Act 1968 to promote the interests and safeguard the beauty of the countryside. In 1982 it became an independent grant-aided body, with 12 members and 100 staff. The Commission proposes *areas of outstanding natural beauty for specific protection, and distributes both grants and expert advice to bodies undertaking conservation and recreational work. It also campaigns against the fencing of open uplands, the dumping of coal waste inshore, straw-burning by farmers, unnecessary land drainage schemes, further loss of broadleaved woodlands, and any loss of the *green belt around London. The Commission has inaugurated the Common Land Forum, and advisory groups on farming and wildlife, and has set up a number of model farms; its recent groundwork trusts have been involved with the urban fringes of towns in northwest England.

county An area of local government, being the Norman name for the Anglo-Saxon *shire. England (outside *Greater London) is currently divided into 45 counties, and Wales into 8, under the Local Government Act 1972, Of the 45 English counties, 6 are metropolitan (Greater Manchester, Merseyside, South Yorkshire, Tyne and Wear, West Midlands, and West Yorkshire – the major urban conurbations) and the remaining 39 are non-metropolitan (the so-called shire counties). The six former counties in Northern Ireland (Antrim. Armagh, Down, Fermanagh, Londonderry, and Tyrone) were divided into 26 administrative districts in 1973. In Scotland, under the Local Government (Scotland) Act 1973, the corresponding areas are known as regions. Counties (and the Scottish regions) are divided into districts; the responsibilities of local government, such as education, highways, fire services, and town and county planning, are divided between the county (or regional) councils and the district councils. In England, however, the Local Government Act 1985 provided for the abolition of the six metropolitan county councils in April 1986, transferring some of their functions to their individual districts, others to joint boards formed by their constituent districts collectively, and a remnant to a residuary body for each county. County and regional councillors are elected every four years. There is a lengthy list of disqualifications for election, in some respects similar to those for MPs. Unlike MPs, candidates for election must have a local connection, and after election can forfeit their seats for prolonged and unauthorized nonattendance.

county court One of a number of courts established in England and Wales by Parliament in 1846 to decide minor civil disputes (just as magistrates' courts deal with less serious criminal offences). There are some 400 county court districts, and their courts are grouped in circuits, normally presided over by a *circuit judge, and occasionally by a *recorder. Each court has a registrar (a solicitor of at least seven years' standing) who can hear certain cases himself if neither party objects; certain rare cases can be heard by a jury of eight members. Appeals against decisions lie to the Court of Appeal, or more rarely to the *Divisional Court of the Chancery Division of the High Court of Justice.

The general jurisdiction of county courts is governed by financial limits: they are empowered to decide actions in contract and tort in which not more than a certain sum is claimed; actions for the recovery of land not exceeding a certain rateable value; actions relating to mortgages and trusts up to a certain value; probate proceedings concerning estates below a certain value; and the winding up of companies having less than a certain share capital. They have an unlimited bankruptcy jurisdiction. County courts also decide on such specific matters as adoption, hire purchase, landlord and tenant, and race relations.

Two heads of county court jurisdiction are rather special: first, certain courts are designated as divorce county courts, and every petition for divorce must begin in one of these (defended cases being transferred to the High Court); secondly, since 1973 the courts have had a special power relating to "small claims", that is, actions involving amounts below £500 (or any other current figure). The registrar may order these to be decided by arbitration instead of in court, and the proceedings before him are private, informal, quick, and inexpensive. (In 1973 so-called **small claims courts** were set up in certain parts of the country, notably Westminster and Manchester. They were in fact arbitration bodies and were widely used, particularly in cases involving consumer complaints. As a result of the new power of county courts to force arbitration on the parties, the small claims courts have now ceased to exist.) County courts exist in Northern Ireland also, but not in Scotland (*see* sheriff court).

Courtauld Institute Galleries The art galleries of the Courtauld Institute of Art. The Institute, which, as part of London University, promotes the study of art history, was endowed by Samuel Courtauld (1876–1947), who donated his home in Portman Square, London, to serve as its premises. He also gave the Institute his collection of mainly French impressionist paintings, which was eventually housed in Woburn Square in 1958. The Courtauld collection has been augmented by various bequests, notably that of Count Antoine Seilern. It is hoped that it will eventually move to more spacious galleries in Somerset House.

Court of Appeal A *superior court of England and Wales created by the Judicature Acts 1873–75 as part of the *Supreme Court of Judicature, and consisting of two Divisions: the Civil Division and the Criminal Division. (The court was originally a single court, concerned only with civil appeals, but in 1966 it gained jurisdiction over criminal appeals, hitherto held by the Court of Criminal Appeal.)

The Civil Division of the court is presided over by the *Master of the Rolls, and the Criminal Division by the *Lord Chief Justice. The ordinary judges of the court are the *Lord Justices of Appeal, but any *puisne judge of the *High Court of Justice may be required to participate, and this frequently happens in the Criminal Division.

The Civil Division hears appeals from the High Court and the *county courts, and appeal is normally as of right. It also hears certain appeals from specialized courts and tribunals. Appeals are normally heard by three judges and decision is by majority.

The Criminal Division hears appeals from the Crown Courts, including the Central Criminal Court. Certain appeals (e.g. against sentence) can be brought only with the leave of the court. They are normally heard by three judges and only one judgment is delivered.

The Court of Appeal is, in a limited number of cases, a court of last resort. Normally, a further appeal lies to the *House of Lords, though only by leave of the Court itself or the House; in the case of criminal appeals, an important point of law must be seen to be at stake.

Court of Arches The ecclesiastical court of the Archbishop of Canterbury, which sits nowadays at Westminster, although it takes its name from its original location in the church of St Mary-le-Bow, Cheapside, the steeple of which was erected on arches. It hears all appeals from *consistory courts in the province of Canterbury other than appeals concerning faculties in which questions of doctrine or ritual are involved. These go instead to the *Court of Ecclesiastical Causes Reserved. The presiding judge of the court is the Dean of Arches, who also presides over the parallel court of the Archbishop of York – the **Chancery Court of York** – of which he is styled Auditor. A member of the Church of England, and a barrister of at least ten years' standing, he is appointed by the Crown on the advice of the two Archbishops, and sits with four other members, two in holy orders and two lay. Appeals from both courts lie to the *Judicial Committee of the Privy Council.

Court of Chancery See equity.

Court of Chivalry A court of feudal origin that retains a limited jurisdiction in ceremonial matters (e.g. over disputes concerning rights to use coats of arms, and rights of precedence) but has no power to enforce its judgments. The court is presided over by the *Earl Marshal (who also presides over the *College of Arms, or Heralds' College) or by a surrogate appointed by him. It originally sat regularly, but was considered obsolete by the late 18th century. In 1954, however, the Earl Marshal (the then Duke of Norfolk, in whose family that office has been hereditary for several centuries) reconvened it to decide a complaint by Manchester Corporation about the display of the city's arms by the Manchester Palace of Varieties.

Court of Common Council See Corporation of London.

Court of Common Pleas See common law.

Court of Ecclesiastical Causes Reserved A court established by the Ecclesiastical Jurisdiction Measure 1963 to exercise a twofold jurisdiction concerning matters of doctrine and ritual in the two provinces of the Church of England. (Other offences are dealt with by the *consistory courts of the individual dioceses.) It also hears appeals from consistory court decisions with respect to the granting of faculties where questions of doctrine or ritual have arisen (appeals in other faculty cases going instead to either the Court of Arches or the

Chancery Court of York; *see* Court of Arches). The court has five members – two of them judges or former judges, and three bishops or former bishops. It sat for the first time in 1984, to hear an appeal from the consistory court of Exeter concerning the placing in a church of an icon of the Black Madonna and a Roman lectionary. Findings of the court may be reviewed by a commission appointed by the Crown and consisting of Lords Spiritual (*see* House of Lords) and *Lords of Appeal in Ordinary.

Court of Exchequer See common law.

Court of Faculties An office of the Archbishop of Canterbury, the principal functions of which are to grant certain faculties, or licences, permitting alterations to consecrated land or buildings (a matter for which jurisdiction lies normally with the *consistory courts); to issue marriage licences, common and special (the former dispensing with the publication of banns of marriage, and the latter with certain other formal requirements as well). The office is presided over by the Dean of Arches and Auditor of the Chancery Court of York (*see* Court of Arches) as ex officio Master of the Faculties.

Court of King's Bench See common law.

Court of Probate A court established by Parliament in 1857 having jurisdiction over the proving of wills, and the granting of letters of administration on the death of a person intestate, and certain other testamentary matters. Before then, jurisdiction was exercised by ecclesiastical courts, a cause for resentment among non-Church members and in the legal profession, since these courts would only recognize lawyers who had obtained a doctorate in Roman law at Oxford or Cambridge University (the headquarters of these specialists, near St Paul's churchyard, being known as Doctors' Commons). The Judicature Acts 1873–75 abolished the Court of Probate, and transferred its jurisdiction to the *High Court of Justice (Probate, Divorce, and Admiralty Division).

Court of Protection The department of the *High Court of Justice dealing with the property of those declared of unsound mind.

Known originally as the Office of the Master in Lunacy, it derives its present name from the Mental Health Act 1959. Its judges are the Lord Chancellor and judges of the Chancery Division of the *High Court of Justice nominated by him, but its work is a matter primarily for a permanent Master and Assistant Masters. Appeals lie to the Court of Appeal and the House of Lords.

Court of Session A *superior court of Scotland, originating in the 15th century, exercising an unlimited civil jurisdiction comparable to that in England and Wales of both the *High Court of Justice and the *Court of Appeal. Currently, its judges are the Lord President (not to be confused with the Lord President of the Council), the Lord Justice-Clerk, and a number of Lords of Session (also known as Lords Ordinary, and not to be confused with *Lords of Appeal in Ordinary). It sits in two Houses. The Outer House consists of the Lords Ordinary other than the six most senior, sitting singly at first for the hearing of cases. The Inner House, which hears all appeals from the Outer House and all civil appeals from the *sheriff courts, consists of a First and Second Division, headed by the Lord President and Lord Justice-Clerk respectively, each sitting with three of the six most senior Lords Ordinary. Appeals from the Inner House lie to the *House of Lords.

Court of the Lord Lyon A body having jurisdiction over heraldic arms in Scotland. (*See also* College of Arms.) By a statute of 1677, claims to arms must be registered at the Lyon Office, so called after the Lyon King of Arms, a 14th-century herald. The Lord Lyon has under him four regular heralds, who are, in order or seniority, Islay, Marchmont, Albany, and a supernumerary herald known as Rothesay Extraordinary. There are two pursuivants, Unicorn and Dingwall. The Lord Lyon, who is also a judge, adjudicates on and issues decrees concerning clan chieftains and pedigrees.

courts of law Bodies established by the state either to adjudicate and apply the general law of the land or to exercise a more specialized jurisdiction. The ordinary courts exercise a criminal or civil jurisdiction, or both. In

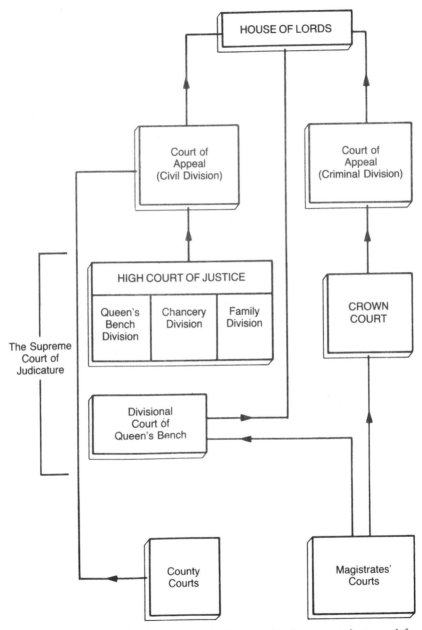

COURTS OF LAW *Diagram to show the courts of law in England and Wales. Arrows indicate appeals from lower to higher courts.*

England and Wales, criminal jurisdiction lies in the *magistrates' courts, the *Crown Court, the *Divisional Court of the Queen's Bench Division of the High Court of Justice, the

*Court of Appeal (Criminal Division) and the *House of Lords; and civil jurisdiction is in the magistrates' courts (to a very limited extent), the *county court, the *High Court of Justice (including its Divisional Courts), the Court of Appeal (Civil Division) and the House of Lords. For Scotland, the criminal courts are the district courts (which exercise a summary jurisdiction less extensive than that of the magistrates' courts in England and Wales), the *sheriff courts, and the *High Court of Justiciary; and the civil courts are the sheriff courts, the *Court of Session, and the House of Lords. The position in Northern Ireland corresponds broadly to that in England and Wales (*see* justice of the peace; Supreme Court of Judicature of Northern Ireland).

Courts of specialized jurisdiction include the ecclesiastical courts (*consistory courts, the *Court of Arches and Chancery Court of York, and the *Court of Ecclesiastical Causes Reserved); coroners' courts (*see* coroner); military, or more accurately service, courts (courts martial, and the Courts-Martial Appeals Court); the Restrictive Practices Court; and the *Employment Appeal Tribunal. *See also* Judicial Committee of the Privy Council. Many bodies that decide disputes involving such matters as employment, health, housing, and social welfare (e.g. industrial tribunals, mental health review tribunals, rent assessment committees, and supplementary benefit appeal tribunals) do not have the status of courts of law, and follow relatively informal procedures. These administrative tribunals are for the most part subject to the supervision of the *Council on Tribunals. There are also domestic tribunals, enforcing, for example, the rules and regulations of a profession, association, or club, and these are not legally relevant.

Covent Garden A square in central London known for the fruit and vegetable market that operated there for over two and a half centuries; it also gives its name to the *Royal Opera House close by. Once the garden of a convent in Westminster (hence its name), the site was developed in the 17th century by the Dukes of Bedford who commissioned the first buildings, some of which were designed by Inigo Jones (1573–1652). At first it was a fashionable area, but with the growth of the market and consequent noise and disorder, the wealthy families moved away and their large residences were turned into cheap lodging houses and offices. Coffee houses were opened and became popular meeting places for writers and artists. Various attempts were made, particularly in the 19th century, to run the market more efficiently. Proper halls were built, notably one designed by Charles Fowler in the 1830s, the Floral Hall in 1860, and the Jubilee Market in 1904. From the 18th century onwards there were suggestions that the market should find a more suitable site but this did not happen until 1974, when it moved to Nine Elms, Battersea. The area was then taken over by the Greater London Council, which undertook the restoration of the buildings, converting the market halls into shopping malls, restaurants, wine bars, and a street market at a cost of some £4 million. The elegance of the conversion has made the venture a great success, with both Londoners and tourists, who throng the area day and night to the delight of the street performers and buskers, giving the piazza an ambience unique in London.

Cowes week Nine days every August when international yachtsmen compete on the Solent, between the Isle of Wight and the mainland. The regatta is based on the Isle of Wight at the small twin towns of East and West Cowes. The first regatta, held by the Royal Yacht Club in 1826, consisted of two races followed by a ball and a firework party. Before long the races, classes of vessel, and competing clubs had proliferated. Ocean racing now predominates and some of the inshore events have been taken over by other regattas. During the first weekend the Channel Race from Cowes to Portsmouth takes place and on the second weekend, in odd-numbered years, there is the hazardous Fastnet Race to the southwest of Ireland and back to Plymouth. Both races form part of the *Admiral's Cup series. Cowes week's abiding position as the premier event of the yachting world is partly due to the town's breezy location, the challenges of the tidal courses, and the availability of mooring in the River Medina, and partly to the persistence of royal patronage and tradition from the days of the sailor-king William IV. The Prince of Wales and his father and brothers usually take part in some of the races (using the royal yacht *Britannia* as a base) and attend the evening celebrations held by the Royal Yacht Squadron.

crannog A lake dwelling built on an artificial island in a swamp or lake, creating a site easy to defend. Remains of crannogs are found in many parts of the British Isles, especially in Ireland, usually on sites of former lakes where drainage has revealed their presence. First used by lake dwellers of central Europe, waves of settlers imported the technique to Britain possibly as early as 3000 BC; the majority probably date from the late Bronze Age and Iron Age (500 BC onwards). A pile of tree trunks, stones, peat, and other materials was raised on the lake bottom and secured with vertical wooden piles. This provided the foundation for, typically, a single wooden dwelling surrounded by a palisade. Archaeologists often find wooden articles belonging to the crannog dwellers, such as canoes, well preserved in the damp conditions. Glastonbury and Meare in the Somerset marshes were among the first British crannog sites to be excavated. Some sites in Ireland were occupied through medieval times, even as late as the 17th century.

cribbage A card game for two or four people, popular in pubs and clubs. It was invented by the English poet Sir John Suckling (1609–42) and is probably based on an older game called noddy. *The Compleat Gamester*, published in 1674, described two games that were recognizably similar. The object of the game is to form various scoring combinations of cards, each player recording his or her points on a pegboard. Part of the appeal of "crib" is the quick completion of each hand and game, making it possible to involve many people in competitions and matches.

cricket An eleven-a-side bat-and-ball game, the object of which is to score more runs that the opposing team. The first certain references to the game date from the 16th century. At first there were many variations, but by the beginning of the 18th century the shape of modern cricket was evolving, with a batsman defending a wicket and attempting to hit the ball a sufficient distance to enable him to run to the other end of the pitch. In about 1760 the

Hambledon Club in Hampshire was founded, which did more than any other to popularize the game and produced the best team in England. Its last match was in 1793, by which time the focus of the game had switched to London and the Marylebone Cricket Club (*see* MCC), which had been founded in 1787. Thereafter the MCC became the most influential body in world cricket, remaining the ruling body of the game until 1969, when the Cricket Council took over this responsibility. Its ground, *Lord's Cricket Ground, is regarded as the world headquarters of the game. The county championship competition dates from 1864, with Yorkshire holding the record for the most wins. Test (international) matches began in 1877 with a game between England and Australia, played in Melbourne. The game quickly became popular throughout the British Empire, and test matches are now played between England, Australia, New Zealand, India, Pakistan, Sri Lanka, and the West Indies. (South Africa is currently suspended for political reasons.) Apart from these "first-class" matches, cricket is played throughout Britain at many levels. The minor counties (i.e. those other than the 17 first-class counties) have their own competition; both Lancashire and Yorkshire have a long tradition of high-class cricket leagues, mostly amateur but stiffened by a few professionals, sometimes overseas test players; villages almost invariably have their own teams; and cricket clubs proliferate, especially in the north of England. Some annual fixtures have become traditions in themselves, notably *Eton versus *Harrow and *Oxford University versus *Cambridge University, which have been played at Lord's since 1797 and 1827 respectively.

Cricket is unique in the length of time needed for a game (30 hours spread over 5 days in the case of a test match), which nevertheless often results in a draw; the fact that it is played and enjoyed by all social classes; the variety of statistics and records it generates (*see Wisden Cricketers' Almanack*); the quantity of literature, both serious and humorous, devoted to it; the extent to which cricketing metaphors appear in the general language; and in the fanatical devotion associated with it. This last is difficult to explain to nondevotees, who re-

CRICKET *Village cricket being played on the green at Lyndhurst, in the New Forest.*

gard it as slow and boring. Some attractions are the almost infinite variety and subtlety of tactics; the element of personal confrontation between batsman and bowler; and the appreciation of skilful play even if the match itself is dull. At the amateur level, it can be enjoyed by players of varying ability; it is slow enough not to interrupt good conversation, both on and off the field; and the inevitable session in the bar afterwards is often as enjoyable as the match itself.

Criminal Investigation Department *See* CID.

Crockford's Clerical Directory A reference book providing details of the ecclesiastical careers (but not full biographies) of the Church of England clergy and parts of the Anglican Communion overseas (though not the US Episcopalian Church). It has been published at intervals since 1858. It was the brainchild of Edward William Cox (1809–79), a lawyer with journalistic flair, but since the 1860 issue it has carried the name of Cox's clerk John Crockford, as Cox preferred not to put his name to the publication. Its overseas coverage has shrunk with the dwindling of the British Empire, but it may still be "reckoned amongst the National Institutions", as the 1937 preface writer claimed. The preface is a distinctive feature of the book; it is written anonymously and gives a survey of the state of the Anglican

Church and major religious events since the previous edition.

crofting A system of subsistence farming practised in the Scottish Highlands and islands. Traditionally the holdings are small – just a few hectares of land centred on the homestead (croft), possibly with access to "outfield" for rough grazing. Crops, such as oats, wheat, potatoes, roots, and vegetables, are grown principally to feed the crofter's family and livestock – a few sheep and cattle. Income may be supplemented by fishing or seasonal work in the tourist industry. Crofting was widespread throughout the Highlands until the clearances of the late 18th and early 19th centuries, when many landlords brutally evicted their tenants to make way for large-scale sheep-farming. Displaced crofters moved to often inhospitable sites on the west coast and islands and many communities were later abandoned, resulting in considerable depopulation of the Highlands. A series of Crofters Acts passed in the late 19th century gave some protection and in 1955 the Crofters Commission was set up to administer the system and channel funds into improving land, buildings, roads, and other aspects. There are currently nearly 17,800 registered crofts, the majority of which are still tenanted holdings.

croquet A game played on grass using wooden mallets to hit balls through hoops set in the ground. Croquet may derive from a

CROFTING *Croft on the Isle of Lewis.*

similar game played in the 16th century in Pall Mall, known colloquially as "pell-mell" or "pale-maille". In the 17th century Louis XIV of France played a game called *le jeu de mail.* The modern game came to England from France in 1852 and five years later John Jaques began to make and sell croquet sets and wrote a book about the game. Croquet became very popular over the next 30 years, especially with young people – not least because young ladies and young gentlemen could play together out of earshot, if not out of sight, of their chaperons. In 1867 the first championships, organized by Walter Jones-Whitmore, were staged at Evesham in Worcestershire (now Hereford and Worcester). From the 1880s the game began to decline in popularity due to the increasing enthusiasm for *tennis, despite the efforts of the Croquet Association and the All England Croquet and Lawn Tennis Club (which in 1882 nevertheless reflected this trend by changing its name to the *All England Lawn Tennis and Croquet Club). The Croquet Association now has its headquarters at The Hurlingham Club in southwest London. More people have taken up croquet in recent years, although it is not a spectator sport and is still limited to a few private clubs. However,

many people enjoy an informal version of the game on their lawns at home.

Crown Agents for Overseas Governments and Administrations A body offering services as a financial and commercial agent and adviser in the UK to overseas governments, both within and outside the Commonwealth, and to international organizations, such as the United Nations and the World Bank. It does not act for private individuals or commercial concerns in the private sector. The agency originated in 1833 as the Crown Agents for the Colonies, and its precise legal status and accountability were for a long time uncertain. In the early 1970s a number of ill-judged investments led to its financial rescue by the government and an inquiry into the conduct of its affairs; it now operates as a public corporation, regulated by the Crown Agents Act 1979.

Crown Court A *superior court of criminal jurisdiction established for England and Wales by the Courts Act 1971, primarily to try all indictable (i.e. more serious) offences. These involve trial by jury, and come before the Court after preliminary investigation by *magistrates' courts. The Court also hears appeals by people convicted by magistrates'

131

courts of summary offences (the less serious crimes), and sentences people convicted by magistrates' courts who have been committed to the Crown Court for that purpose. Forming part of the *Supreme Court of Judicature, and replacing *assizes and *quarter sessions, it sits at a number of centres throughout the country, which are designated by the Lord Chancellor and grouped into six circuits; there are currently some 400 component courts, with many more planned.

The judges of the Crown Court as a court of trial are visiting judges of the *High Court of Justice, *circuit judges, and *recorders. Some offences (e.g. murder) can only be tried by High Court judges, whilst others (e.g. manslaughter and rape) must be tried by them unless released to a circuit judge or recorder by the presiding judge assigned by the Lord Chancellor. Moreover, High Court judges visit only what are called first-tier and second-tier centres (the distinction between these being that first-tier centres are also High Court centres for civil proceedings). Third-tier centres are serviced purely by circuit judges and recorders. For the hearing by the Court of appeals from magistrates' courts and committals for sentence, two to four magistrates sit with the judge or recorder, and majority decisions are allowed. A person may appeal against his conviction or sentence by the Crown Court to the *Court of Appeal (Criminal Division); and either party to an appeal from a magistrates' court may appeal further on a point of law by requiring the Court to state a case for decision by the *Divisional Court of the Queen's Bench Division of the High Court. See also Central Criminal Court.

Crown Equerry The deputy to the *Master of the Horse. The Crown Equerry superintends the Royal Mews where the various means of royal transport are kept. He is responsible for the horses, coachmen, and grooms, and is helped by lesser equerries, a vet, and a comptroller of stores. He is ultimately responsible to the *Lord Chamberlain.

Crown Estate Property belonging by heredity to the sovereign "in right of the Crown". It is quite distinct both from the sovereign's personal property and the govern-ment's. The revenue from the Crown Estate is made over to the government at the beginning of each reign for the duration of the new sovereign's lifetime. (See civil list.) In the year 1983–84 this brought the Exchequer £19,000,000.

The Crown Estate originates in lands held by the Anglo-Saxon kings. Some property was once demesne land (private land not occupied by feudal tenants) of the medieval English and Scottish kings; some came to the Crown when Church and monastic lands were seized in the 16th century; some has been purchased over the last century and a half. Notable Crown properties in London are Regent's Park, parts of the West End in Regent Street, Lower Regent Street, Piccadilly, and St James's, and sites in Holborn, Trafalgar Square, Kensington, and Whitehall. The urban estates, which also include properties at Ascot, Portland, and Edinburgh, are by far the most lucrative. The Crown Estate comprises some 73,000 hectares (180,000 acres) in England, about 36,000 hectares (90,000 acres) in Scotland, and 260 hectares (650 acres) in Wales. Most of Britain's foreshore is included – the part of the coast lying between the mean high-water mark and the mean low-water mark (in Scotland it is between high and low spring tides) together with the seabed within territorial waters. Even beyond territorial waters any rights exercisable in regard to Britain's continental shelf other than oil, gas, and coal rights are vested in the Crown Estate. Certain fishing rights and investment in government securities make up the rest of the Crown Estate. Land revenues from Scotland were only put under the *Crown Estate Commissioners in 1833. Crown lands in Ireland paid revenue direct to the Exchequer's Consolidated Fund from 1820, but those in southern Ireland have been collected and administered by the Republic of Ireland since 1923.

Crown Estate Commissioners The managers of the *Crown Estate. Under the Crown Estate Act 1961 they are appointed by the sovereign on the advice of the Prime Minister and submit an annual report to Parliament. The first Commissioners (of woods, forests, and land revenue) were appointed at the end of the 18th century to manage the

Crown's English and Welsh estates. Later Crown revenues from Irish, Scottish, Manx, and Alderney estates also became their responsibility. The Crown Estate Commissioners have only been known by their present title since 1956; between 1924 and 1956 they were called Commissioners for Crown Lands and were the Secretary of State for Scotland, the Minister for Agriculture, Fisheries and Food, and a permanent Commissioner.

Crown jewels The regalia of English royalty used for coronations and state openings of Parliament. Since 1967 they have been displayed to the public in a semi-underground Jewel House at the Tower of London amid conditions of strict security. Before that they were on show at various sites in the Tower for over 300 years, narrowly escaping theft in 1671 (by an adventurer, Colonel Blood) and fire in 1841. Considering that the public were allowed to handle the jewels in the past it is remarkable that they have remained intact to this day.

In the Middle Ages and Tudor times the coronation ornaments were regarded as sacred relics of St Edward the Confessor (r. 1042–66) and kept at Westminster Abbey. Other crowns and sceptres were part of the royal treasure, to be pawned or sold as occasion demanded. In times of war they were pledged to wealthy subjects to raise immediate funds. When the monarchy was abolished by the parliamentarians in 1649 (*see* Civil War, English) nearly all the jewels were officially melted down or sold off. The gold **anointing-spoon** and eagle-shaped **ampulla** that contains the oil for anointing the sovereign during a coronation, dating from the 12th and 14th centuries respectively, were somehow preserved.

At the Restoration in 1660 a new set of regalia had to be made quickly and most of the regalia seen today date from this time. A great golden jewel-studded crown worn over a velvet cap, known as **St Edward's Crown**, was made for Charles II. In it was incorporated the remains of an old crown, supposed to be the Anglo-Saxon crown of Edward the Confessor. This reconstituted crown has been used for the ceremonial crowning at nearly every coronation since Charles II's. During the 19th century George IV and William IV preferred to wear the lighter **Imperial State Crown**, which was later remodelled for Queen Victoria and adapted for each of her successors; it is this crown that is worn for all other state occasions, including the procession after a coronation.

The Imperial State Crown is set with over 3000 precious stones, mainly diamonds and pearls, and displays several gems of outstanding historic interest – the Black Prince's ruby (said to have been given to the Black Prince by Pedro the Cruel of Castile after the battle of Najara in 1367, and later worn by Henry V at the battle of Agincourt in 1415), the Stuart sapphire which dates back to Edward IV's reign (1461–83), the Second Star of Africa (one of the nine stones cut from the huge Cullinan diamond in 1908), and four drop pearls, known as "Queen Elizabeth's earrings". In the uppermost cross of the crown is a sapphire which was almost certainly retrieved from Edward the Confessor's tomb in Westminster Abbey in the Middle Ages and would therefore be the oldest Crown jewel of all.

CROWN JEWELS *The Imperial State . Crown (viewed from the back).*

Also made for Charles II's coronation were a pair of **gold spurs** signifying chivalry, a pair of gold enamelled bracelets, the **armills**, signifying wisdom and sincerity, and the **King's Orb**, surmounted by a large amethyst and jewelled cross, which symbolizes the dominion of the Christian Church over the world. The **King's Sceptre with the Cross**, representing royal power (since 1909 containing the largest of the Star of Africa stones from the Cullinan diamond, at 530 carats the largest cut diamond in the world) and the **King's Sceptre with the Dove**, representing spiritual authority, also originate from this time. They are held in the monarch's right and left hand during the crowning ceremony: afterwards the Orb replaces the Sceptre with the Dove.

Five ceremonial swords also play a part in the ceremony. The most magnificent is the **Jewelled Sword of State** with diamonds, rubies, sapphires, and emeralds on the scabbard, forming the rose of England, the thistle of Scotland, and the shamrock of Ireland. This was made for George IV to replace Charles II's fine broadsword as the monarch's personal sword, which is briefly girded about him (or briefly held by a queen regnant when she is crowned) before being offered at the altar. This sword, as well as the **Sword of Justice to the Spirituality**, the **Sword of Justice to the Temporality**, and a **Sword of Mercy** with a broken blade, all dating from the 18th century, are carried before the monarch after the crowning ceremony. A sapphire and ruby sovereign's **ring**, made for William IV, and two **gold bracelets** given jointly by the Commonwealth countries in 1953 to signify the bond between sovereign and people, complete the ornaments used at the last coronation.

Among the Crown jewels are a smaller orb made for Charles II's niece Mary II (1689–94) who reigned as equal with her husband William III; three crowns made for queen consorts (Mary of Modena, James II's second wife, and the consorts of George V and George VI, Queen Mary and Queen Elizabeth the Queen Mother); a simple crown made for a Prince of Wales in the 18th century; a small diamond crown made for Queen Victoria in 1877; and the magnificent **Imperial Crown of India** made for George V to wear at the Delhi Durbar in 1912 when he was acclaimed Emperor of India. They are all set with numerous pearls, crystals, and hundreds of precious stones, the most famous being the Koh-i-Noor (meaning "mountain of light") diamond in Queen Elizabeth the Queen Mother's crown. This jewel was given to Queen Victoria in 1850 after the fall of the Sikh kingdom in the Punjab: previous owners had been Ranjit Singh, the ruler of the Sikhs, and Shah Jehan, the Mogul emperor who built the Taj Mahal. It is said that no man can wear the diamond without encountering disaster and no English king has ever worn it. Displayed with the Crown jewels are ceremonial maces, elaborate gold and silver plate, silver state trumpets, and coronation vestments.

Crown proceedings Civil actions against the Crown authorized by the Crown Proceedings Act 1947. It was a maxim of the common law that "the king can do no wrong". This royal virtue (the so-called "prerogative of perfection") originally meant, and still means, that no legal proceedings, civil or criminal, can be brought against the sovereign personally. However, when this immunity became extended to cover the Crown, including government departments and public bodies, there was clearly cause for concern. This was remedied in part by the petition of right, a special procedure that, while not legally enforceable, in practice enabled subjects to recover damages for breach of contract from the Crown. However, the petition did not extend to the law of tort. There was no way in which the Crown could be made liable for the breach of any common-law or statutory duty owed to its employees, or committed by them. The Crown Proceedings Act did two things: firstly, for matters such as breach of contract, it replaced petitions of right by ordinary civil actions; secondly, it imposed liability on the Crown for the first time. The Crown is now liable for the breach of any common-law duty to its employees, and for any breach committed by them in the course of their employment (*see* Crown servant). A person suing the Crown under the Crown Proceedings Act cites as defendant the appropriate government department or the Attorney General.

Crown servant A person employed by the Crown in the public service and paid wholly out of central government funds. Civil servants and members of the armed forces are Crown servants; police officers are not (*see* police). A Crown servant differs from a private employee regarding the law of contract in that he holds office only at the sovereign's pleasure, the implication being that the Crown thus avoids any fetter on its future actions, and the servant is dismissible at will. In practice, however, civil servants have always enjoyed a high measure of job security, and the employment protection legislation in force since 1971 was expressly extended to them and has made their contractual weakness largely academic. They are entitled to the statutory remedies for unfair dismissal available before an *industrial tribunal. This protection is not available to members of the armed forces.

Cruft's Dog Show The main event of the dog breeders' year in Great Britain, held each February at Earls Court, London. The show was initiated by Charles Cruft (1852–1938), who held his first dog show in Islington in 1886. Its organization is now in the hands of the Kennel Club of Great Britain, which was established in 1873 in response to the enormous increase in interest in dog breeding that took place in the second half of the 19th century. The Club now regulates all dog shows and is the supreme governing body of all dog breeders in Britain.

Cruft's is open to all breeds of pedigree dog recognized by the Kennel Club. From each breed a champion is chosen, a considerable accolade in itself. The best of breed animals are then grouped into six categories: hounds, gundogs, terriers, working, utility, and toy dogs. From each of these a best of group is chosen, and from these six the supreme champion of the show is selected. To achieve this honour a dog must not only be of the required build and appearance for its breed but must also carry itself correctly and display an appropriate character. Success at Cruft's is the greatest ambition of all dog breeders and a champion is immediately worth a great deal of money for breeding purposes. Dog lovers in large numbers attend the show, the latter stages of which are now televised.

Crystal Palace *See* Great Exhibition.

CSE *See* school-leaving examinations.

Cubs *See* Scout Association.

Culloden, battle of (16 April 1746) A battle, fought near Inverness, that effectively ended the *Jacobite rebellions. The "Young Pretender", Prince Charles Edward Stuart, and his mostly Highland army had spent a bitter winter in retreat before facing the challenge of a government army of 9000 men under the leadership of the Duke of Cumberland, a son of George II. On the night of 15 April Charles attempted a pre-emptive surprise assault while the enemy were asleep in their camp at Nairn; but this failed and he withdrew to Culloden Moor, 19 kilometres (12 miles) away. The following morning the exhausted Jacobite force, numbering in all about 5000 men, drew up in two ragged lines of battle opposite Cumberland's army, separated from it by undulating bogland. The chain of command amongst the Jacobites was confused. Cumberland's artillery was able to inflict heavy casualties upon the Jacobites before they finally launched forward in a general charge, lacking any real formation, against the three long red lines of the government troops, each line three men deep. Relatively few of Cumberland's force died; the Jacobite dead numbered about one thousand, the fleeing Highlanders being hacked down by cavalry. The dead clansmen, including 32 wounded men who were burnt to death in a barn, were buried in mass graves that can still be seen. The atrocities of the months that followed, when Cumberland's men ruthlessly pursued the fugitives, earned him the nickname "The Butcher". Their defeat marked the final end of Jacobitism and signalled the harsh suppression of the *clans. Culloden was the last land battle fought in Britain.

Cup Final The most famous *football match in Britain. It is the final game of the oldest football knockout competition in the world, organized each year since 1872 by the Football Association (hence the trophy name, the FA Cup). The first Cup Final was held on 16 March 1872 at Kennington Oval in south London between Wanderers and Royal Engineers; Wanderers won 1 – 0. In following years the Cup Final was held in various places, including Manchester and Liverpool, until in 1923 it moved to *Wembley Stadium where it has been held ever since. The most successful clubs in the history of the Cup Final are Aston Villa and Tottenham Hotspur, who have each won it seven times. Tottenham, indeed, have never lost a final although they have had to replay twice.

curling A Scottish national game played on ice with "curling stones" fitted with handles. It is said to have been introduced from the Low Countries in the 16th century. Two teams of four players alternately slide the curling stones across the ice some 36 metres (118 feet) into the "house", a series of concentric circles on the ice. For each stone finishing nearer the centre of the "house" than any of its opponents, the team scores one point. A feature of the game is that team-mates may sweep the ice ahead of a moving stone to remove any obstacles.

Customs and Excise The main collecting agency for indirect taxes levied in the UK. The department was established in 1909 through the amalgamation of the customs and the excise services, and it is now responsible to the Treasury under a Board of Commissioners.

Although considerable Crown revenues had been obtained from the importation of French wines during Norman times, Edward I (r. 1272–1307) founded the customs service by appointing "customers" to collect export duties on wool and hides. The excise office was established by the Long Parliament in 1643 to pay for the *Civil War by imposing duties on beer, spirits, soap, and other commodities; later, Charles II received all the excise revenue and introduced the first Board of Commissioners. An unpopular hearth tax on every fireplace in the land was imposed in 1662 but was later replaced by a tax on windows, which was retained for over 150 years.

Two functions now dominate the work of the Customs and Excise: the control of imported and exported goods to collect duties and statistics and impose prohibitions (especially on drug smuggling), and the collection of VAT

(*see* tax system) and other taxes on purchases. In 1983–84 a total of £31,000 million (40% of all taxation revenue) was obtained from VAT and taxes on petroleum, cars, alcohol, cigarettes, and betting. The UK is divided into 22 taxation areas, known as collections, controlled from the London headquarters with a total of 25,300 staff (1984). In 1971 the Customs installed a sophisticated computer at Heathrow Airport designed to handle the very large number of air cargo revenues. Cargo can be cleared through Customs within one hour of an entry being accepted by the computer.

cycling Cycling first became popular in Britain as a sport and form of recreation with the advent of the Rover "safety" cycle, designed by James Starley in 1885, and John Dunlop's pneumatic tyre (1888). The earlier penny-farthing cycle had been difficult to ride and dangerous, with the rider perched nearly 2 metres (5–6 feet) above the ground. The first official cycle race was held near Paris on 31 May 1868 and was won by an Englishman, James Moore. According to the records, the first race in England was held the next day, at Hendon in Middlesex. However, the development of cycling as a sport was hampered by the poor state of road surfaces, and special tracks began to be built in the 1880s and 1890s. This marked the division of the sport into two forms: track and road events.

Track events are staged either as sprints – usually over 1000 metres between two competitors – or as pursuits where two competitors race against the clock (although one loses if caught by the other). In contrast, there may be a hundred or more riders in an Olympic or professional roadrace. A race lasting more than one day is called a stage race or tour (*see* Milk Race). There are also time trials on roads, and cyclo-cross or cross-country races.

cymanfa ganu A marathon session of hymn-singing in Welsh. *Cymanfa ganu* is a custom that originated in west Wales, chiefly in Dyfed, and spread to other parts of Wales during the 19th century. The tradition has its roots in Welsh Nonconformism and has become a part of chapel life in many areas of the country, especially in the industrialized valleys of South Wales, the home of *Welsh male-voice choirs. The *cymanfa ganu* is held in most districts on an annual basis. It combines a chapel service with an entertainment, in which Welsh people sing their favourite hymns with great fervour. There is also a competitive element to these sessions. The *cymanfas* held by individual chapels involve contests in both singing and recitation of scripture passages. *See also* eisteddfod.

D

Dame Commander A woman holding the second highest class of any of four *orders of chivalry. The appropriate initials placed after the name are, in order of precedence, DCB (Dame Commander of the Order of the *Bath), DCMG (Dame Commander of the Order of *St Michael and St George), DCVO (Dame Commander of the *Royal Victorian Order), and DBE (Dame Commander of the Order of the *British Empire).

Dame Grand Cross A woman holding the highest class of any of four *orders of chivalry. The appropriate initials placed after the name are the same as for Knights Grand Cross of the respective orders.

Dartmoor An upland region of moor and forest in southern Devon, afforded *national park status since 1951, and one of the few remaining areas of wilderness in southern England. Dartmoor's heather-clad moors with their granite outcrops (tors), rushing streams, bogs, and rugged scenery attract many summer visitors. The highest of the tors is High Willhays at 621 metres (2038 feet) above sea level. The absence of intensive farming has preserved evidence of the past, including *stone circles and some of the earliest field boundaries and settlements in Britain, for example, at Grimpound, near Widecombe-in-the-Moor, dating from the early Bronze Age (1800–1400 BC) when the region enjoyed a flourishing agriculture. In Anglo-Saxon times Dartmoor was a royal forest, in the medieval sense of land reserved for hunting (*see* New Forest). The tin mines, which prospered in the Middle Ages, are now defunct, the granite quarries are fewer in number, and peat is no longer cut for fuel. Agriculture consists mainly of sheep and cattle grazing, while the famous Dartmoor ponies roam freely over the unenclosed moor. Dartmoor Prison at Princetown, which was built between 1806 and 1813 to house French prisoners during the Napoleonic Wars, holds many of Britain's most dangerous criminals.

darts A target game in which players throw three darts at a circular numbered board. The game may have originated in a medieval quasi-military activity: in bad weather archers continued their target practice indoors, taking aim at a sawn-off tree trunk. The modern game of darts is about one hundred years old, dating from the time when the circular numbered board and modern darts began to be used. In 1908 a case was brought at Leeds magistrates' court in which it was decided that, as a game of skill rather than chance, darts could be played in public houses, where it subsequently became very popular.

A standard board is 18 inches in diameter and divided into 20 numbered wedge-shaped sectors. There is an outer ring in which scores are doubled and an inner ring where they are trebled, so the highest possible score with three darts is 180. At the centre is a small circle called the bull, which is worth 50 points. The darts are about five inches long and are thrown from behind a slightly raised wooden strip on the floor – the oche (pronounced "ockey") – which is 7 feet 9.25 inches from the board. In the standard game two players attempt to score exactly 301 in a series of throws; they must start and finish with a double or a "bull's eye". Professional players tend to start at 501 and do not need a double to begin. In 1984 the English player, John Lowe, became the first to complete a game from 501 in the minimum possible of nine darts, in a televised competition.

David, Saint (Welsh: Dewi Sant) Wales's patron saint, who lived ?520–?588 AD. Of the four saints of the separate countries of Britain and Ireland, David is the only one associated with his nation by birth. Little is known of his early life, but an account written during the 11th century says that he was born near St Bride's Bay, the son of a chieftain of Ceredigion called Sant, and a woman named Non who later entered a convent. David was educated in southwest Wales and became a key figure in establishing monasticism there. He became abbot of the monastery of Mynyw, later known as St David's (or Tyddew in Welsh). He practised and enforced an austere regime both at St David's and in the many religious centres he founded. He is credited with having moved the centre of Wales's ecclesiastical government from Caerleon in Gwent to St David's. He was canonized in 1120 by Pope Calixtus II. His feast day, March 1, is celebrated in Wales by the holding of school *eisteddfods and the wearing of either of two emblems much associated with Wales – the daffodil and the leek.

D-Day 6 June 1944, the day on which was launched the Allied invasion of western Europe during World War II. The first forces landed on the beaches of Normandy, to begin the liberation of France and the eventual German defeat. The name was derived simply from D(ay)-day, and is now popularly applied to the start of any major operation.

death duties A tax on property that became payable at the owner's death. Also known as estate duty, it was introduced in 1894, replaced in 1974 by capital transfer tax, which was itself replaced by an inheritance tax in 1986 (*see* tax system). Its initial maximum rate was 8%, but in the 1970s estates worth more than £1 million were taxed at 80%. From the first the tax was opposed by landowners, and was a factor in the House of Lords' unprecedented rejection of Lloyd George's 1909 budget. To a large extent it was responsible for undermining the viability of large estates: in 1950, duty on the estate of the Duke of Devonshire amounted to £5 million and was not paid off until 1967. However, it was often regarded as a voluntary tax as there were many loopholes, especially through the judicious use of gifts and trusts. Many of these were removed with the introduction of *capital gains tax and capital transfer tax.

Debrett's Peerage A reference guide to the titled aristocracy of Great Britain. It is named after John Debrett (1752–1822), who in 1781 took over the business of a bookseller, John Almon, who had first published a peerage in 1769. The work was renamed after Debrett in 1802, appearing under the title *Debrett's Peerage of England, Scotland, and Ireland*; *Debrett's*

D-DAY *Infantry wading ashore carrying bicycles, part of the Allied landings of 1944.*

Baronetage appeared in 1808. This separation of peers and baronets is still maintained even in the present one-volume format (*compare Burke's Peerage*). Besides alphabetically arranged entries on titled families (including the royal family), giving information on coats-of-arms, residences, and ancestors, Debrett's also offers information on forms of address, precedence, and the wearing of decorations, and is considered an authority on arcane matters of etiquette. Since 1976, when a new publisher appropriated the title, the cachet of the Debrett name has also been appropriated for other works.

Derby, the The most prestigious of the English *Classic races and probably the most famous horse race in the world. This flat race for three-year-olds takes place over a 2.4 kilometres (1.5 miles) course on the Epsom Downs in Surrey in late May or early June. Even before the race's foundation in 1780, Epsom was a centre for fashionable society and horse racing; Samuel Pepys recorded how Charles II, accompanied by Nell Gwyn, watched racing on the Downs. The race was named after one of its founders, the 12th Earl

of Derby, apparently because he won the toss of a coin against the cofounder, Sir Charles Bunbury, whose horse, Diomed, provided some consolation to the baronet by winning the first Derby.

By the 19th century the race had become so important as an annual event that Derby Day was regarded as an unofficial public holiday; in fact, parliamentary business was suspended on the day from 1847 until the turn of the century. This festive atmosphere still continues, and not only as a social occasion for the grey-topper brigade; funfairs, *pearly kings and queens, and innumerable tipsters entertain the vast crowd of some half a million people that throng the Downs for a fine Derby. Quite apart from the money stakes on the course, millions of pounds are bet by punters throughout the country whose interest in horse racing is limited to a flutter on the Derby and the *Grand National.

detention centre A place to which a male offender aged 14 to 20 may be sent for a short period of disciplinary custody. He must have been convicted of an offence punishable by imprisonment in the case of a person aged 21

THE DERBY *Spectators on Derby Day. The world's most famous horse race, the Derby is an important event in the social as well as sporting calendar.*

or over, and the court must be satisfied that a custodial sentence is necessary either to protect the public or to reflect the gravity of the offence, or because he seems unwilling to respond to a noncustodial penalty. The sentence is from three weeks to four months, and the discipline is of the "short sharp shock" variety, with emphasis on parades and inspections, physical and general education, and personal cleanliness and effort. *Compare* youth custody centre.

dialects The regional varieties of English, especially those that are regarded as nonstandard. Unlike many languages, for example Swedish and Italian, British English is strongly standardized, in grammar and vocabulary as well as pronunciation, and regional peculiarities tend to have been stigmatized. Like all major languages, however, English has a large variety of different forms, both within and beyond the British Isles. Historically, the Northumbrian, Anglican, Saxon, and Kentish dialects have been distinct from each other ever since their introduction 1500 years ago (*see* English language). Midland and northern dialects were further influenced by the Anglo-Scandinavian speech of Viking settlements spoken alongside Old English from the 9th to the 11th centuries. In the course of time, however, these distinctions have become blurred. The Kentish dialect has more or less disappeared under the influence of neighbouring London, but southwestern, Midland, and northern dialects preserve some features that have differed from the standard language for over a thousand years. The Northumbrian dialect of Old English has direct descendants in *Scots and *Geordie, which is why historically-minded dialectologists refer to the speech of the industrial parts of Yorkshire and Lancashire as "north Midland" rather than "northern".

The majority of English speakers have at least a trace of an accent that suggests where they were brought up (*see* accent). However, although a slight accent can be fashionable, regional peculiarities of vocabulary may not be widely understood. Northern words such as "gradely" (excellent), and "mardy" (spoilt, of a child) are regarded as nonstandard, although they are widely used in everyday speech.

"While" meaning "until" is still used in the north. In matters of syntax, too, there are many regionalisms. Double negatives ("I don't want none"), nonstandard verb inflections ("I seen him"; "She gived it me"), and variations in the relative pronoun ("That's the man as shot our dog"; "That's the man what shot our dog") are features found in many dialects of English, but not in the standard language. In some dialects the reflexive pronouns "hisself" and "theirselves" are found, contrasting with standard English "himself" and "themselves". The dialect forms are logically more consistent with the forms "myself" and "ourselves", found in all dialects and the standard.

All dialects have been influenced to a greater or lesser degree over the centuries by the prevailing middle-class standard, and many dialect speakers nowadays, especially in the cities, can switch into more formal modes of speech when occasion demands.

Diploma of Higher Education (DipHE) A diploma, introduced in 1974, awarded by the *Council for National Academic Awards and some universities to students who have successfully completed a two-year (full-time) or three-year (part-time) course of study roughly equivalent in standard to that of the first two years of a degree course. The entry requirements are similar, and the DipHE can be seen either as a qualification in its own right or as a means by which students can then transfer to a degree course or a course leading to professional qualifications. DipHE courses in a wide range of subjects are offered by various colleges of higher education and *polytechnics.

diplomatic service The staff of the Foreign and Commonwealth Office that represents the UK abroad. Numbering 4700 in all, with 1600 staff holding diplomatic status, the diplomatic service is considered the intellectual elite of the civil service, attracting a high standard of applicants. The head of the diplomatic service is the permanent undersecretary at the Foreign and Commonwealth Office, who is responsible to the Foreign Secretary. The service represents Britain in 210 diplomatic missions (embassies, high commissions, and consulates) and in her delegations to international organizations (NATO, EEC, UN); it also administers the foreign policy of the British government, and gives expert advice to ministers on all matters affecting British interests abroad. One of the primary roles of the overseas diplomat is to keep the government informed of events occurring in the country to which he is posted and of likely developments in the future. The information and commercial attachés must know about forthcoming events, contracts, and business that would interest British companies and they must maintain close links with influential contacts. The consular service is concerned with assisting British citizens abroad and has statutory duties of registering births, marriages, and deaths as well as issuing passports and UK visas. The ambassador, with his deputy head of mission or head of chancery, first secretary, and other officers, maintains a position of considerable prestige at a high political level.

Before the 18th century political relations with foreign powers were mainly conducted through the resident ambassadors, the personal representatives of the monarch, who were given complete immunity from the law. The Foreign Office itself was founded in 1782; but the diplomatic service in its present form came into being in January 1965 by the amalgamation of the foreign service, the Commonwealth service, and the trade commission service, upon the recommendation of the Plowden Committee. The India Office and the Colonial Office were always separated from ambassadorial services and were both disbanded after World War II. Despite the decline in British military power and economic influence, and its decreasing scope for unilateral initiative in world affairs, the British diplomatic service is still highly regarded abroad for its incorruptibility and the high calibre of its officers.

Director of Public Prosecutions, England and Wales An official, appointed by the Home Secretary from barristers or solicitors of at least ten years' standing, to secure consistency of prosecuting policy in England and Wales. Before 1879, when the office was created by Act of Parliament, the question of whether or not a person be prosecuted was a matter for the local police investigating the case. However, the Act did not establish the Director to control an independent prosecution service, such as that in Scotland (*see* Lord Advocate); instead it required the police to report certain serious or difficult offences to him, giving him the power to institute prosecutions in these cases. He also had a duty to advise the police generally about prosecutions. The Prosecution of Offences Act 1985 does, however, provide for an independent prosecution service. The country is covered by a network of legally qualified Crown prosecutors appointed by the Director, and prosecution decisions rest with them rather than the police, except for a small number of cases that the Director must decide himself.

Discovery The ship built in Dundee, Scotland, in 1901 for Captain R. F. Scott's first polar expedition to the Antarctic. During the following decades, the *Discovery* was used as a carrier by the Hudson's Bay Company, as a supply ship during World War I, and for oceanographic research. During the years 1921–31 it once again took an expedition to the Antarctic, this time a joint British, Australian, and New Zealand venture. The *Discovery* was moored in London for many years, on the Victoria Embankment, where she was used by the Scout Association as a training ship, and then by the Royal Naval Reserve. She subsequently joined the historic ship collection at St Katharine's Dock, where she was repaired by the Maritime Trust. In 1986 the ship was returned to Dundee to form part of a major tourist development there.

Distinguished Flying Cross A decoration awarded to officers and warrant officers in the RAF for acts of gallantry performed during active service. Holders of the Distinguished Flying Cross may place the letters DFC after their names. The decoration was instituted in 1918 and eligibility was extended to officers and warrant officers of the Fleet Air Arm in 1941.

Distinguished Service Cross A decoration conferred on Royal Naval warrant officers and officers below the rank of captain. It was instituted in 1914 as a replacement for the

Conspicuous Service Cross, which had been introduced in 1901. Holders may add the letters DSC after their names.

Distinguished Service Order An order, admission to which is granted for special services performed in action by commissioned officers of the Army, Royal Air Force, Royal Navy, and (since 1942) merchant marine. It was founded in 1886 and has one class only, that of Companion. Holders are entitled to place the initials DSO after their names. A bar may be won by an additional act of service.

district An area of local government in the UK (except *Greater London): a subdivision of a *county, or in Scotland, a region. In England, the 6 metropolitan counties are divided into 36 metropolitan districts, and the 39 nonmetropolitan counties into 296 nonmetropolitan districts. Local government is shared between the county (or regional) councils and the district councils. Northern Ireland, however, has a single-tier system of 26 district councils. In England, the Local Government Act 1985 provided for the abolition of the metropolitan county councils in April 1986, and the transfer of their functions partly to the metropolitan district councils (which already had considerably wider functions than their nonmetropolitan counterparts), partly to joint boards established by those councils, and partly to residuary bodies for each county. The term of office of a district councillor is normally four years. In some districts, the whole council is elected in every fourth year, whilst in others an election of one-third is held in every year that is not a county council election year. A district can be called a *borough by royal charter, in which case its council is a borough council and its chairman a mayor.

Divisional Court A court consisting of two or more judges of the Divisions of the *High Court of Justice. A Divisional Court of the Queen's Bench Division hears appeals from magistrates' courts and certain tribunals, considers applications for *habeas corpus, and supervises inferior courts. A Divisional Court of the Chancery Division hears appeals relevant to the Division (e.g. relating to bankruptcy, land registration, etc.). A Divisional Court of the Family Division deals with matters of family law (e.g. concerning affiliation, maintenance orders, etc.).

Divisions of the High Court *See* High Court of Justice.

Dod's Parliamentary Companion An annual publication giving biographies of members of both Houses of Parliament and information about the organization of the government. It was first published in 1832, in the excitement generated by the reform of Parliament, and was compiled by an Irish journalist, Charles Dod (1793–1855). Its original title was the *Parliamentary Pocket Companion* and it retains an unusually small format to make it easily portable. Besides biographies of peers and MPs, the *Companion* lists parliamentary constituencies, the results of the last general election and any by-elections, the composition of ministries, and the structure of the royal household and government and public offices.

Doggett's Coat and Badge race An annual rowing race held on the River Thames, between London Bridge and Chelsea Bridge, on or around 1 August. The race was instituted in 1715 by the actor Thomas Doggett to commemorate the accession of George I. The winner was presented with a coat bearing an embroidered arm badge on the left sleeve; on his death Doggett bequeathed a sum of money, now held in trust by the Fishmongers' Company (*see* City livery companies), to provide a similar prize each year. Open to any Thames waterman who has completed his apprenticeship within the previous year, the race has been an annual event, almost without interruption, since its foundation. The boats are followed down the river by a barge bearing winners of earlier years, each proudly sporting his scarlet jacket with its silver badge.

Domesday Book A record of the lands of England, compiled around the year 1086 from detailed county surveys carried out during the previous five years by order of William I (the Conqueror). The name Domesday originates from the searches, which reminded people of "Doomsday", when Christ would call everyone to account. The Book, which is in Latin, comprises two volumes. One covers Essex,

IN REREDFELLE HVND.

Rex . W . teñ in dñio *REREDFELLE* . de feudo epĩ Baioc̃.
Goduin tenuit . 7 tc̃ 7 m̃ fe defd ,p . III . hid . T̃ra . ē
XXVI . car̃ . In dñio funt . IIII . car̃ . 7 XIIII . uilli cũ . VI .
bord hñt . XIIII . car̃ . Ibi . IIII . ferui . 7 filua de q̃t xx .
porc̃ de pafnag̃ . Parcus . ē ibi.
T . R . E . ualeb̃ . XVI . lib̃ . 7 poft:́ XIIII . lib̃ . Modo:́ XII . lib̃.
7 tam̃ redd . XXX . lib̃.

TERRA ARCHIEP̃I.   *IN MELLINGES HVND.*
.II. ARCHIEP̃S LANFRANC teñ C͠O *MELLINGES*.
  7 eft in Rap de Peneuefel . 7 T . R . E . defd fe ,p q̃t xx . hid.
  Sed m̃ n̄ hr̃ archiep̃s nifi . LXXV . hidas . quia comes
  moritonij hr̃ . V . hid ext hund . T̃ra toti C͠O . L . car̃.
  In dñio funt . V . car̃ . 7 cc̃ . 7 XIX . uilli cũ XXXV . bord
  hñt . LXXIII . car̃ . 7 XL.III . croft.
  Ibi . V . molini de . IIII . lib̃ 7 X . folid . 7 II . mil anguill.
  Ibi . cc̃ . ãc p̃ti . V . min̄ . 7 filua . ccc . porc̃ de pafnag̃.
  De herbagio . XXXVIII . fol . 7 VI . den̄ . 7 ccc.LV . porc̃ herbag̃.
  T . R . E . ualeb̃ . XL . lib̃ . Q̃do recep̃:́ XXX . lib̃ . Modo:́
  LXX . lib̃ . Hoc C͠O tenuit Godefrid ad firm̃a ,p . XC . lib̃.

In ROTHERFIELD Hundred
2 King William holds ROTHERFIELD in lordship, from the Holding of the
   Bishop of Bayeux. Earl Godwin held it. Then and now it answered
   for 3 hides. Land for 26 ploughs. In lordship 4 ploughs.
   14 villagers with 6 smallholders have 14 ploughs,
   4 slaves; woodland at 80 pigs from pasturage; a park.
   Value before 1066 £16; later £14; now £12; however, it pays £30.

---

2   LAND OF THE ARCHBISHOP

In MALLING Hundred
1a Archbishop Lanfranc holds the manor of (SOUTH) MALLING. It is in the
   Rape of Pevensey. Before 1066 it answered for 80 hides, but now the
   Archbishop has only 75 hides, because the Count of Mortain has 5 hides
   outside the Hundred. In the whole manor, land for 50 ploughs.
   In lordship 5 ploughs.
   219 villagers with 35 smallholders have 73 ploughs and 43 crofts.
   5 mills at £4 10s and 2,000 eels; meadow, 200 acres less 5;
     woodland, 300 pigs from pasturage; from grazing, 38s 6d;
     grazing, 355 pigs.
   Value before 1066 £40; when acquired £30; now £70.
   Godfrey held this manor at a revenue for £90.

DOMESDAY BOOK *Extract from* Domesday Book *(above in Latin, below in English). A hundred was an
administrative district within a shire; a hide was reckoned at 49 hectares (120 acres).*

Suffolk, and Norfolk; the other, the rest of the country except Durham, Cumberland, Northumberland, and Westmorland, which were excluded from the survey as being too remote. Some towns, including London and Winchester, were also omitted. Its aim was to describe the state of England after the upheavals of the Norman conquest (1066; *see* Norman Britain): it contained not only detailed information about landholdings (their size, value, ownership, and use), but also changes since Edward the Confessor's reign (1042–66). Whether it was designed to meet any immediate need, such as providing a basis for taxation, is unclear. However, by the early 12th century, it was being used as evidence in land and tenure disputes. Domesday Book is now kept in the Public Record Office, and is an invaluable historical source.

dominoes A table game, popular in public houses and clubs, in which small numbered blocks are matched and laid together. One face of each domino is divided in half, with each side bearing a number of dots, from nought to six. As there are no duplicates this produces a set of 28 pieces (some sets go up to nine dots, in which case a complete set consists of 55 pieces). Each player tries to use up all his dominoes before anyone else. The game is very old and is thought to have originated in China; the dominoes were said to represent all the possible combinations of a throw of two dice (there are no blanks in Chinese dominoes). The European game is much more recent, being first recorded in Italy and France in the 18th century, and probably introduced into Britain by French prisoners during the Revolutionary and Napoleonic Wars (1792–1815). The name is derived from the black and white cloaks called dominoes that were popular in France at that time; their appearance was suggested by the ebony and ivory blocks used in the game.

Dover castle A castle that looks out across the *English Channel from the southeastern corner of Kent, a frontline fortress against invaders since the 12th century, which remained in military occupation until recently. The keep and inner curtain walls were built by Henry II between 1180 and 1188. Constable's

Gate was constructed in the 13th century by Henry III, Dover's Constable being also Warden of the *Cinque Ports. The castle also features the remains of a Roman lighthouse (the oldest in Britain, dating from 43 AD) and a Saxon church. The castle is open to the public.

Downing Street A street in central London, off Whitehall, close to the Houses of Parliament; Number 10 is the official residence of the Prime Minister and Number 11 that of the Chancellor of the Exchequer. The street was created in about 1680 by Sir George Downing (1623–84), MP for Carlisle and for many years a diplomatic representative at The Hague. Of the original row of plain brick terraced houses only numbers 10, 11 and 12 remain, one side of the street having been replaced by the Foreign Office. The eastern part of Number 10 was acquired by the Crown in 1732, after which George II offered it as a personal gift to Sir Robert Walpole. Walpole accepted it in 1735 only in his capacity as First Lord of the Treasury, since when it has become the official residence of the Prime Minister (although some early prime ministers preferred to remain in their grander town houses and let Number 10 to relatives or colleagues). The building was altered internally in 1732–35 by William Kent and the western part was acquired in 1763. During further alterations in the 1950s and 1960s remnants of Roman pottery, of a Saxon wooden hut, and of the destroyed Whitehall Palace were discovered. Behind the modest façade lies a complex of rooms, including facilities on the ground floor for Cabinet meetings and a self-contained flat on an upper floor for the Prime Minister's private use. The western part of Number 11 was acquired by the Crown in 1805 and was intended for use as the Home Secretary's office. However, it has always been used by the Chancellor of the Exchequer. The eastern part was acquired in 1824. Number 12, Downing Street is occupied by the Party Whip's office.

Downs, the Areas of chalk upland that are a major feature of the landscape of southern England, the name being derived from the Old English *dun* ("hill"). The North Downs and South Downs form two roughly parallel east–west ridges marking the perimeter of the Weald region in the southeast. Both terminate at the coast in dramatic white cliffs: the North Downs at Dover and the South Downs at Beachy Head. Further west lie the Hampshire Downs, which rise to 297 metres (974 feet) at Walbury Hill, the Berkshire Downs, which include White Horse Hill at 261 metres (855 feet) and the Marlborough Downs in Wiltshire.

Traditionally, the lower slopes of the Downs were cultivated and the upper slopes and poorer soils devoted to grassland for grazing sheep. But now, with the encroachment of intensive arable farming, the areas of permanent chalk grassland are dwindling and with them their characteristic flora and fauna. The Downs were favoured sites for burial mounds (*see* barrows) and fortified settlements (*see* hill forts), and formed important ancient routes – some of which, such as the *Ridgeway along the Berkshire Downs, can still be followed. Traces of the ancient field systems also remain in places, particularly terraces in the hillsides formed by prehistoric ploughing. Perhaps the best-known features of the Downs are the huge figures cut into the hillsides (*see* chalk hill figures).

druids A high-ranking caste of learned holy men, who played a key role in Celtic societies of Britain and Gaul, until they were suppressed by the Romans in the 1st century AD. The association of druids with Stonehenge is a familiar part of British folklore, but one that is almost certainly spurious. As Celtic culture was predominantly based on an oral tradition, rather than a written one, knowledge of the druids' importance is derived from classical accounts (e.g. Tacitus and Pliny the Elder), and from Celtic vernacular texts (particularly Irish folk tales). In a society in which major figures were preoccupied with military prowess, the druids acted as the chief repositories of knowledge and were responsible for its oral transmission to young novitiates. They were both philosophers and theologians, displaying knowledge of astronomy and calendrical skills. They also had considerable judicial authority, settling disputes between individuals, judging criminal cases and arbitrating between rival tribes. Their most severe

sanction was to bar a person from attendance at sacrifices, making the offender a virtual outcast. Classical writers have referred to various forms of human and animal sacrifice performed by the druids, including lurid accounts of the ceremonial burning of wickerwork effigies filled with human victims. As leaders of the Celtic religion, the druids would have supervised religious ceremonies, including sacrifices. Pliny the Elder, in his *Natural History*, described the ceremonial cutting of mistletoe growing on an oak by white-robed druids using a golden sickle. The oak and mistletoe were potent symbols in druidic lore, and the name "druid" is possibly derived from the Greek *drus*, an oak tree. Many druidic rites were performed in sacred oak groves.

As the Romans conquered first Gaul and then Britain, the druids and their practices, both spiritual and secular, were suppressed as a danger to Roman order. Tacitus provides a graphic account of the druids' "last stand" in Anglesey in 61 AD, when they faced the Romans across the Menai Straits. The howled ritual curses of the unfortunate druids were of no avail: the Romans wiped them out and destroyed their sacred groves on the island. Celtic culture and the druids, however, persisted in Ireland, although after the first Christian missionaries arrived in the 4th and 5th centuries AD, their interests drifted more towards learning and poetry.

The druids were "rediscovered" by historians of the Renaissance. The English biographer and folklorist John Aubrey (1626–97) was the first to suggest (in 1649) that Stonehenge, Avebury, and other ancient stone circles were druid temples, thus creating the almost certainly erroneous connection between druids and the stone circles. This myth subsequently became embedded in national folklore. Elements of fantasy and fraud were introduced by Edward Williams (1747–1826), a Glamorgan stonemason who used the bardic nom de plume of Iolo Morgannwg. Williams fabricated documents purporting to demonstrate a link between Glamorgan's traditional bardic poets and the ancient druids; on 23 September 1792, he and a group of followers performed a ceremony on Primrose Hill, London, to celebrate the autumn equinox, the

DRUIDS *Druids on Primrose Hill, London.*

centrepiece of which was the *gorsedd*, or altar. In 1819 this entirely spurious ritual was repeated at a Welsh *eisteddfod, and thereafter became a permanent part of Welsh traditional culture.

Many other self-styled "druid" groups have sprung up, the oldest of which is the Ancient Order of Druids, set up as a secret society in 1781 by a London builder, Henry Hurle. Since the 19th century Stonehenge has been a natural focus for the activities of these various eccentric groups, leading occasionally to a contretemps with the owners or police, and some damage to the monument itself.

Duchy of Cornwall   The private estate of the eldest son of the sovereign, who is Duke of Cornwall from birth or from the moment his parent ascends the throne. The Duchy consists of some 52,000 hectares (130,000 acres) of land, mostly in Cornwall, Devon, and Somerset, with a smaller area in south London, which includes the Oval cricket ground. The Duchy dates back to 1337, when Edward III attached to it various lands in the West Country (including the forest and chase of Dartmoor, and the Stannaries (tin mines) in Devon and Cornwall) as well as several castles (such as Berkhamsted, Hertfordshire), in order to provide an income for his son the Black Prince. Under Henry V the Duchy acquired lands in Somerset, and under Henry VIII the holdings in Cornwall were increased. In the late 18th century much of the estate had to be sold to pay land tax and in 1863 the Duchy's management was regularized by Act of Parliament. It is now run by the eight members of the Council of the Duchy, who include the Prince of Wales (who is also Duke of Corn-

wall) and the Lord Warden of the Stannaries. During periods in which there is no Duke of Cornwall the annual revenues are paid into the Treasury. Before the present Prince of Wales was 18 the Queen donated eight-ninths of the revenues to the Treasury; thereafter until he was 21 a lesser, but nevertheless substantial, portion was given. This had been done by no previous sovereign; in fact, Prince Albert acquired the Sandringham estate for the future Edward VII out of Duchy revenues during Edward's minority. The Prince of Wales pays no tax on Duchy revenue, but before his marriage he donated half to the Treasury and since his marriage a quarter.

Duchy of Lancaster   An estate managed for the upkeep of the sovereign. The nucleus of the Duchy was created in 1267 by Henry III for his son Edmund (1245–96); it was subsequently much enlarged by their descendants. In 1399 when the last Duke of Lancaster became Henry IV, it was attached to the Crown, yet retained a separate administration. It continued to exercise criminal and common law jurisdiction in Lancashire until it was reformed in Victorian times under the Supreme Court of Judicature Act 1873. Even now, the High Sheriff of Lancashire and certain other holders of judicial office are appointed by the Chancellor of the Duchy of Lancaster, and not by the Lord Chancellor as elsewhere. Since revenue from the estate, which is not taxed, is paid straight to the Privy Purse (*see* Privy Purse, Keeper of the) the Duchy of Lancaster may be described as a public office or department of state, although it is not under the control of the Treasury. The office of Chancellor of the Duchy of Lancaster is a political appointment and is generally held by a member of the Cabinet. The Duchy lands consist of some 21,000 hectares (52,000 acres) of farmland and moorland, mostly in Yorkshire.

duke   A member of the most senior order of noblemen. (*See also* peerage.) The word duke comes from the Latin *dux*, a leader. In the Carolingian empire in 9th- and 10th-century western Europe, especially during its decline, the term duke came to denote a hereditary title, the holder of which possessed increasingly independent authority. Thus, the early Norman kings had, before the conquest of 1066, come to exercise sovereign rights as Dukes of Normandy. Probably because of this association with royalty, the early medieval kings of England were not prepared to make their subjects dukes. It was not till 1337 in England that the first dukedom in the peerage was created, for Edward III's eldest son the Black Prince (*see* dukes, royal). The first nonroyal duke was Robert de Vere, created Duke of Ireland in 1386. There are 26 nonroyal dukes, of which the premier is the Duke of Norfolk (title created 1483).

A duke is addressed as His Grace, and his wife, the duchess, as Her Grace. There have been instances of women being created duchesses in their own right, notably royal mistresses. There have also been dukedoms created for life only. A duke's eldest son is known, as a courtesy, by a subsidiary title possessed by the duke himself, usually a marquessate or earldom. Younger children are addressed as Lord or Lady, followed by Christian and surname.

Duke of Edinburgh's Award A scheme founded in 1956 designed to challenge "young people between the ages of 14 and 25, throughout the Commonwealth, to serve others, acquire new skills, experience adventure, and make new friends". Based on the ideas of Kurt Hahn (1886–1974), founder and headmaster of *Gordonstoun, the Duke of Edinburgh's old school, there are three categories of award: bronze, silver, and gold. At each level participants have to complete the requirements in four sections: service, expeditions, skills, and physical recreation. The scheme is not competitive: standards of achievement are related to individual ability, emphasis being placed on effort, ingenuity, and persistence. It is open to the able-bodied and the mentally and physically handicapped alike. Entrants participate through schools, youth organizations, employers, or the Award's operating authorities. The scheme operates throughout the British Isles and under various titles in some 40 countries both within the Commonwealth and outside. By 1983 over 1.5 million young people had taken part.

dukes of the blood royal See dukes, royal.

dukes, royal Usually sons of the sovereign who have been raised to the highest rank in the peerage. (Children of the sovereign are not peers or peeresses automatically apart from the eldest son, who becomes Duke of Cornwall at birth or as soon as his parent succeeds to the throne.) Those who subsequently inherit dukedoms originally conferred on royalty may also be regarded as royal dukes, even if they are only distantly related to the sovereign. (The Duke of Cumberland, until stripped of his title in 1919 for bearing arms against George V in World War I, was only a third cousin of the king through his descent from George III.)

A distinction exists between royal dukes and **dukes of the blood royal**. The Duke of Edinburgh was created a duke in 1947; he was granted the style, title, and attribute of Royal Highness; yet he is not strictly "of the blood royal" in the sense of being a descendant of a British sovereign in the male line, and is entered in the Roll of the Lords as a duke rather than as a royal duke. Grandsons of a sovereign in the male line have sometimes become royal dukes. George V was created Duke of York while his grandmother Queen Victoria still reigned, and his elder brother was created Duke of Clarence. There has been one case of a woman who was a duchess in her own right and entitled to be styled royally: Her Highness Princess Alexandra, granddaughter of Edward VII through her mother HRH Princess Louise.

The first royal duke was Edward III's son the Black Prince, created Duke of Cornwall in 1337; the second royal dukedom created was that of Lancaster, in 1351. The dukedom of Rothesay (1398) in the Scottish peerage is held by the Prince of Wales. The only other royal dukedoms extant are Cornwall, Edinburgh, Gloucester, and Kent. The second son of the sovereign has tended to be created Duke of York; other more recent royal dukedoms are Sussex, Cambridge, Cumberland, Albany, Clarence, and Connaught. If either of the Queen's younger sons were to be made royal dukes, certain titles (e.g. York or Sussex) are more likely than others; Clarence is thought to be unlucky, Connaught is the name of part of the independent Republic of Ireland, Cambridge is the name of an existing marquessate held by a cousin of the Queen, and both Cumberland and Albany might be revived if the heirs of their previous holders were to petition the Crown.

Dun Cow of Warwick A monstrous beast that is alleged to have terrorized the area around Dunsmore Heath in Warwickshire, destroying cattle and killing all who dared approach her. The cow was mentioned in works of the 16th and 17th centuries; an 18th-century account describes the animal as being "six yards in length and four high, with large sharpe horns and fiery eyes of a Dun Colour". All three books refer to the brave Sir Guy, Earl of Warwick, who finally succeeded in slaughtering the beast after a long and bloody struggle.

Dunmow flitch A side (flitch) of bacon presented to any married couple in the Essex town of Little Dunmow who will "swear that they have not quarrelled nor repented of their marriage within a year and a day after its celebration". The custom is mentioned by Chaucer and the first presentation of a flitch appears to have been made in 1244. However, the origin of the award is unknown, although it seems to have had some association with Dunmow priory, the remains of which are built into the parish church. The ceremony has been held on and off for over 700 years and still continues. The winners of the flitch are entitled to sit in a special chair in a place of honour in the chancel of the church.

Durham Miners' Gala A march through the city of Durham by coalminers and workers from other trades in Durham county, culminating in a rally. It takes place during the second week of July each year. The first Gala (pronounced locally to rhyme with "sailor") was held in 1871 and was associated with the growth of the trade union movement. On Gala Day men from each mine gather in the suburbs and march into the city, singing traditional songs to the accompaniment of drums and brass bands, watched by trade union and Labour Party leaders. The large banners representing the various pits depict scenes from the Bible, the work and lives of the miners, and portraits of past Labour leaders and working-class heroes. Black crepe around the edges of a banner indicates that a miner has been killed in that pit in the last year. If a pit closes, its banner is placed permanently in the trade union headquarters with great reverence and solemnity. The march wends its way to the riverside racecourse, which becomes a fairground for the occasion. The bands play, a favourite tune being "Gresford" written in 1936 by Robert Saint, a Hebburn miner, who left the copyright to the National Union of Mineworkers. Later the bands are silent as the crowd listens to speeches by union leaders and leading Labour Party politicians. When these are over the crowds march back to the cathedral for the Miners' Festival Service before they disperse. Pit closures, migration, and changing social habits in the northeast of England have reduced the significance of the Gala, but it still remains an impressive spectacle.

E

earl A member of the third most senior and second most numerous order of noblemen. (*See also* peerage.) The word comes from the Danish *jarl*, anglicized to *eorl*, and the title is the most ancient of all, dating from before the Norman conquest. Introduced in the reign of Canute (1016–35), the earl was a royal officer. He displaced the Anglo-Saxon official, the *ealdorman*, who administered a province on behalf of the king. An earl's area of authority might extend over several counties in whose courts he presided. After 1066 an earl's jurisdiction became confined to one county, but he continued to be awarded the "third penny" from the sheriff's court (that is, he received one-third of its profits) and to wear the sword of the county at investiture ceremonies. Over the same period the title became hereditary, and until the 14th and 15th centuries earldoms were similar to territorial fiefs in that the holders might, on occasion, be called upon to serve in Parliament. By the 14th century the title was no longer automatically linked with a county or county town, as had been the case with such earldoms as Essex and Oxford. However, when Edward III created several earls during his reign (1327–77), he also granted them lands to support their titles. In 1377 the first earl to hold the title for life only was created, and in 1383, Nottingham became the first earldom to be heritable by males only. An earl is addressed as Right Honourable, and his eldest son as Viscount or Lord X, where the viscountcy or barony is one of his father's subsidiary peerages. Younger sons are addressed as the Honourable A... B... (where A is the Christian name and B is the surname). An earl's daughter is addressed as Lady A... B.... The wife of an earl is a *countess. The premier earldom in Britain is Arundel, held by the Duke of Norfolk as one of his subsidiary titles. Earldoms were for long conferred on former prime ministers, and in 1984 the practice was revived when Harold Macmillan was created Earl of Stockton.

Earl Marshal The hereditary post held by the Howard Dukes of Norfolk. One of the *great officers of state, the Earl Marshal is at the head of the *College of Arms, and is also responsible for organizing state ceremonies. The Earl Marshal, or plain marshal as he was called in the early Middle Ages, originally commanded the king's cavalry, maintained order at court and during campaigns, and presided over the *Court of Chivalry. In the Middle Ages the post was intermittently hereditary. After 1483 it became increasingly identified with the Howard Dukes of Norfolk and was formally annexed to them from 1672. However, the post was often filled by a deputy after the *Reformation because most of the Howard family were Roman Catholics. The 16th Duke of Norfolk, who organized the coronation of Queen Elizabeth II, was universally praised for his skill at arranging state ceremonies. Not so Lord Effingham, (a Protestant Howard, who was deputy Earl Marshal for George III's coronation in 1761. He mislaid various items of the regalia, forgot the canopy and state chairs, and for a time lost the sword of state. His oversights caused the ceremony to drag on for six hours, with the result that the procession finally arrived at Westminster Hall in the dark, with the participants stumbling over each other. George III merely reprimanded Lord Effingham, who replied, "It is true, Sir, that there has been some neglect, but I have taken care that the *next* coronation shall be regulated in the best manner possible." The Earl Marshal's rod of office was originally wood, but changed to a golden rod with a black ring at each end in 1397. At its head are the royal arms, at its foot those of the Marshal. His coat of arms carries two batons in the form of a saltire cross. The Earl Marshal's stipend of £20 per annum has remained unchanged since it was fixed by Richard III in 1483.

East End, London An area comprising the neighbourhoods of Aldgate, Spitalfields, Whitechapel, Mile End, Bethnal Green, Wapping, Shadwell, Stepney, Limehouse, Poplar, and Isle of Dogs. The East End was traditionally an area of overcrowding and poverty: the *Great Plague of 1665 is thought to have started in Stepney. In the years after 1685, there was a large influx of French Protestants ("Huguenots"), fleeing persecution by Louis XIV. They settled especially in Spitalfields, and gave the area a reputation for fine quality silk. The poor were lured to the East End in their greatest numbers in the 19th century by the development of the docks, a great many of them being immigrants: Jewish, Irish, Chinese, and, more recently, Indian and Pakistani. Conditions in the area during the Victorian era were particularly harsh: in 1840 the average life expectancy was 16 years, half of the deaths occurring in infants under five years old. In 1888 Whitechapel was the scene of the Jack the Ripper murders that caused widespread terror in the capital. The East End was the most badly damaged area of London in World War II and subsequently many residents moved out. Industry also drained away from the district and in recent years efforts have been made to redevelop the docklands, now officially known as the borough of Tower Hamlets.

Despite its cosmopolitan makeup, the East End is a distinct community – self-contained but exuberant, a surviving stronghold of the traditional London *Cockney.

Easter Rising (1916) *See* Irish nationalism.

Economic and Social Research Council
A body founded by royal charter in 1965 to
encourage and carry out research in the social
sciences and to foster education and dissemi-
nate information on the subject. It was known
as the Social Science Research Council until its
change of name in January 1984. It is funded
by a grant from the Department of Education
and Science, most of which is disbursed in research grants and funds for postgraduate training in the social sciences. There are separate
committees for economic affairs, education
and human development, environment and
planning, government and law, industry and
employment, social affairs, and resources and
methods. Various research units are funded by
the Council, often in conjunction with other
organizations. For example, the Centre for
Urban and Regional Development Studies at
Newcastle University considers the social implications of changing patterns of industrial
activity and employment, while the Technical
Change Centre in London, set up in 1981,
surveys the impact of technological innovations on society. As well as fostering links with
social scientists in other countries, the council
sponsors seminars, conferences, and workshops.

Economist, The A weekly paper of financial
news, founded in 1843 and aimed at a professional and mercantile readership. Its original
subtitle "The Political, Commercial, Agricultural, and Free-trade Journal" indicated the
range of interests of its founder and first editor,
James Wilson (1805–60), who favoured free
trade and the repeal of the Corn Laws. In 1858
his eldest daughter married the economist and
journalist Walter Bagehot (1826–77) and the
following year Bagehot took over as editor of
The Economist. Under its first two editors,
with a circulation of around 3000, the paper
gained authority among bankers, businessmen,
and politicians, which it has never lost, principally on account of its statistical and analytical
approach. Wilson and Bagehot wrote much of
the paper themselves, assisted by a tiny staff.
The economist Nassau Senior (1790–1864)
contributed articles on foreign affairs and the
statistician William Newmarch (1820–82)
compiled an annual "Commercial History of
the Year" from 1863 onwards.

On Wilson's death *The Economist* was held in
trust for his six daughters, an arrangement
which lasted until 1928, when the last surviving daughter died. At its sale safeguards were
made to preserve its independence. An important editorship (1907–16) was that of Francis
Wrigley Hirst (1873–1953), who wrote every policy article himself, assembled a highly
efficient staff, and generally extended the paper's influence and scope.
Despite the bombing of its offices in 1941, *The
Economist*'s circulation topped 10,000 around
the time of its centenary. In the postwar period its influence has extended to an international readership. A sister company, the Economist Intelligence Unit, provides a worldwide
specialized research service for financiers.

Edinburgh castle A castle standing on
Castle Rock overlooking the city of Edinburgh that has served as a fortress and palace
since the 11th century. The building has been
sacked and rebuilt on several occasions; the
oldest surviving part is the tiny St Margaret's
Chapel, dating from the late 11th century and
built for Queen Margaret, wife of Malcolm III
(r. 1057–93) and sister of Edgar Atheling, the
king-elect of England. The chapel alone was
spared by Robert the Bruce after he captured
the castle from English forces in 1313. The
present palace buildings are grouped around
three sides of Palace Yard. The great hall was
built for James IV in the early 16th century as
a parliament house and banqueting chamber;
it now contains a collection of arms and armour. Beneath it are the "casemates", vaults in
which French prisoners were kept during the
Napoleonic Wars (1803–15). At Edinburgh
castle in 1566, Mary, Queen of Scots gave birth
to Prince James, who became King James VI of
Scotland in 1567, and James I of England in
1603. Since then the royal presence in Edinburgh has been restricted to occasional visits.
The stone-vaulted Crown Room contains the
state regalia of Scotland (*see* regalia, Scottish),
including the sceptre, sword, and crown.
These were last used in 1651 for the coronation of Charles II at Scone. The castle espla-
nade, long used as a drilling ground for troops,
is the scene of the annual military tattoo. In
the north side of Palace Yard is the national
war memorial, which commemorates the

100,000 Scots who died in World War I. Each weekday afternoon, in a tradition dating back to 1861, a cannon is fired from the castle ramparts at one o'clock precisely.

Edinburgh Festival An international festival of music and drama that takes place in Edinburgh for three weeks from mid-August every year. Founded in 1947, it was run by Rudolf Bing until 1950, when Ian Hunter became artistic director. The Earl of Harewood, Peter Diamand, and John Drummond have been among their successors. A range of orchestral and chamber concerts is given; opera, ballet, theatre, poetry readings, and art exhibitions are also staged. The Edinburgh *fringe offers a variety of lively "alternative" events. The festival has always been international in its scope, and many of the best foreign opera and theatre companies, performers, and orchestras have appeared there. It is probably the premier British arts festival, but the City of Edinburgh, which largely finances it, has not always been wholehearted in its support. The opportunity of building the opera house that Edinburgh lacks was passed over in the mid-1970s.

Edward Medal A decoration bestowed for acts of heroism by miners or quarrymen or by those who have risked their lives rescuing people employed in those occupations. It was instituted in 1907 and is named after Edward VII. Since October 1971 all surviving holders have exchanged the distinction for the George Cross.

egg-rolling (pace-egging) An Eastertide ceremony that takes place in a number of northern towns, notably Preston, Scarborough, and Barton-upon-Humber. Hard-boiled eggs, painted in bright colours, are rolled down a nearby grassy slope by groups of local children competing to see whose egg will reach the bottom first. The alternative name of "pace-egging" derives from the old English word Paschal, meaning Easter. In Midgley, Yorkshire, a pace egg *mummer's play is performed on Good Friday. The custom of egg-rolling is generally associated with the rolling aside of the stone from Christ's tomb on Easter morning; it may, however, have originated in pre-Christian times, the egg being a tradi-tional symbol of life and rebirth. At Dunstable in Bedfordshire a similar ceremony, in which oranges instead of eggs are rolled down the hillside, takes place on Good Friday.

eisteddfod A type of cultural festival originating in Wales, in which participants compete for prizes in public contests covering the fields of music, poetry and prose, drama, fine arts, and handicrafts. Eisteddfods are conducted mostly through the medium of the Welsh language and seek to preserve Welsh culture by providing a showcase for all aspects of it. The festivals range in scale from local and provincial events to the premier national competition, the *Royal National Eisteddfod of Wales.

The word *eisteddfod* means literally "session" or "assembly". As an institution, it belongs to the great bardic tradition found in Wales as in other Celtic countries. In the 6th century poets of the court of Prince Maelgwyn Gwynedd vied with one another in singing his praises, often to harp accompaniment, in bardic assemblies at his royal seat at Degannwy, North Wales. Bards practised their poetic gifts at other such assemblies throughout Wales, and the sessions also later included discussion of the craft of poetry. In 1176 the Lord Rhys sponsored a major bardic contest at Cardigan castle, at which prizes were awarded. In 1451 bards at Carmarthen fixed the rules for composing strict-metre alliterative verse that are still in use today. In 1568 Elizabeth I, herself a descendant of the Welsh family of Tudor, lent her patronage to an important eisteddfod at Caerwys, now in Clwyd, which staged competitions in both poetry and music and granted licences to bards.

Over the next hundred years eisteddfods almost disappeared but were revived in the 18th century as the growth of the *Romantic movement fostered an interest in diverse cultures. The first modern public national eisteddfod was held at Corwen in 1789. During the 19th century eisteddfods grew in popularity and absorbed much of the Welsh Nonconformist tradition. Hymn-singing in chapels, for example, led to the introduction of eisteddfodic choral competitions. Eisteddfods also became platforms for radical politicians and the founders of Welsh nationalism. In the

20th century they remained both political and academic. But themes for poetry compositions became more personal or more relevant to current society, while in music competitions, rock and other pop creations took their place alongside classical and traditional test pieces. *See also* International Musical Eisteddfod; Royal National Eisteddfod of Wales.

Eleanor Crosses Twelve roadside crosses erected by Edward I (r. 1272–1307) in memory of his wife Eleanor of Castile (1246–90). She married Edward when she was eight years old and bore him thirteen children. A devoted wife, she accompanied him on a crusade (1270–73). After her death at Harby in Nottinghamshire the bereaved king followed the cortege on its long journey to Westminster Abbey. Edward ordered crosses to be erected at each of the resting points along the way – at Lincoln, Grantham, Stamford, Geddington, Northampton, Stony Stratford, Woburn, Dunstable, St Albans, Waltham, West Cheap (Cheapside, in London), and the twelfth and most famous of all, at Charing Cross in London. The only crosses still standing are to be found at Geddington in Northamptonshire and Waltham Cross in Hertfordshire, although part of that at Lincoln still remains (near the priory of St Catherine where Eleanor was embalmed). Some of the crosses were quite elaborate, others less so. The Waltham cross, for example, cost £95, whereas the one at Charing Cross required several architects and two sculptors, who charged the king a total of £650. There is also some doubt as to why the cortege needed to stop at Charing, so close to Westminster Abbey. There was nearby a chapel of St Mary, belonging to the priory of Roancevall, and it could be that the procession waited here for the final preparations in the Abbey.

Most of Edward's devout and loving monuments came to a brutal end. In 1643 the Long Parliament ordered their destruction. Archbishop Laud commented in his diary, regarding the destruction of the cross in Cheapside, "The cross in Cheapside was taken down to cleanse that great street of superstition."

eleven-plus (examination) An examination formerly taken by all primary-school pupils at about the age of 11 in *Local Education Authority schools, to determine whether or not they should receive an academic secondary education. (*See* state education.) The break between primary and secondary education at this age was recommended in the Hadow Report (1926), and the examination itself was largely based on the now discredited theories of intelligence testing propounded by Sir Cyril Burt (1883–1971). The principal objections to the test were that the age of 11 is very young for a crucial decision to be made about a child's whole future, and could result in late developers being unfairly and irrevocably penalized; and that children who failed to achieve a place among the top 20%–30% selected for grammar schools could see themselves as failures, condemned to the "inferior" alternative of secondary modern schools. The eleven-plus, the bugbear of several generations of schoolchildren, is now generally abandoned by LEA schools in England and Wales, either because the comprehensive schools system prevails or because assessments are made less formally, based on teachers' appraisals and pupils' written work over a period. In Northern Ireland the eleven-plus takes the form of verbal reasoning tests in addition to work assessments.

Employment Appeal Tribunal A body established by Parliament in 1976, primarily to hear appeals, on points of law only, from *industrial tribunals. The tribunal (which ranks as a *superior court) replaced the National Industrial Relations Court, which a Conservative government had set up in 1971, and which trade unions had refused to recognize, even to the extent of disobeying its orders. The tribunal normally consists of a presiding judge and between two and four lay members, who must be experienced in industrial relations. Appeals against decisions of the tribunal lie to the Court of Appeal, but only with the leave of the tribunal or court.

enclosure, laws of Private Acts of Parliament that, after 1760, were the most common method of converting the medieval open fields and common lands into fields enclosed by hedges. In the open fields that formerly surrounded a *manor, land was divided into

LAWS OF ENCLOSURE *Enclosed fields at Padbury, Buckinghamshire. Aerial photography reveals the medieval ridge-and-furrow patterns formed by centuries of strip-farming, which are superimposed by the more recent pattern of straight hedgerows and large fields radiating from the village. These were created by parliamentary Act in 1795.*

small strips: a peasant farmer might work several strips, which did not necessarily adjoin each other, but which might lie right next to those of his neighbours. This made it difficult to farm efficiently or to experiment with new methods without infringing the rights of fellow farmers or the laws of the manor. In enclosed fields, with all common rights abolished, each farmer could act as he chose. Because of the complexities of land tenure and each landholder's rights, it was impossible to effect such radical changes in a manner satisfactory to all. A private Act of Parliament cut through the legal difficulties, while the use of local commissions to determine the exact terms and compensation for lost land and rights ensured (ostensibly at least) its fairness to all. As the pressure for change mounted, this approach became increasingly popular: from 1702 to 1760, 278 enclosure Acts were passed, contrasted with 1944 between 1760 and 1800.

In 1801 the General Enclosure Act simplified the procedure; but by this time all useful agricultural land had been enclosed. Enclosures favoured the existing larger landowners. Small landholders, even if adequately compensated by the commissions, found it impossible to compete in the new climate, and sold up. Those who had farmed through manorial rights, but had not owned land, were often simply expelled. Some became tenant-farmers or labourers on the new large farms, some became paupers, and many drifted to the towns, providing labour for the *industrial revolution.

English breakfast Traditionally a hearty meal eaten in many homes throughout the country, particularly at weekends and on other nonworking days. The central feature of the traditional English breakfast is a fried or grilled dish consisting of bacon, eggs, and such additional items as sausage, mushrooms, tomatoes, *black pudding, kidneys, and fried bread or potatoes; in some households a less substantial dish, such as kippers or boiled eggs, is preferred. This is usually preceded by *porridge, fruit juice, or some variety of commercially produced breakfast cereal, an early 20th-century innovation of US origin. Kedgeree, a mixture of flaked smoked fish, boiled rice, and chopped hard-boiled eggs, is a breakfast dish that originated in India. A foreign import of recent years is Swiss muesli, a mixture of rolled oats, nuts, apple, and dried fruit served with milk or cream. The cooked breakfast dish is followed, or sometimes replaced, by hot buttered toast and marmalade, a preserve that is usually prepared from bitter Seville oranges or other citrus fruits and has been enjoyed in Britain for many hundreds of years. For much of its early history marmalade was a dense solid jelly, too stiff to be spread and usually eaten as a sweetmeat; the addition of thin strips of orange or lemon rind to the preserve dates from the late 17th century.

The content of the English breakfast has varied considerably over the years, from the laden tables of medieval times to the delicate spiced cakes and bread of the 17th- and 18th-century nobility, according to changes in fashion, taste, and eating habits and the availability of particular food items. Modern influences include health- or weight-conscious diets and the shortage of time at the beginning of the working day in many family homes. Traditional breakfast beverages have also been subject to change: the popular ale or beer of the medieval period was superseded in middle-class homes of the late 17th century by coffee and chocolate and in the mid-18th century by tea; coffee and tea have retained their popularity to the present day.

English Channel The sea that runs between the south coast of Britain and the north coast of France, joining the North Sea to the east and the Atlantic Ocean to the west. At its narrowest point, in the Straits of Dover, it is only 34 kilometres (21 miles) wide, making it one of the busiest shipping lanes in the world. Swimming the Channel is a regular summer event, the first recorded successful swim being by Captain Webb in 1875. A bridge or tunnel across the Channel has been regularly discussed since it was first suggested by Napoleon in 1802. The digging of a tunnel by two private companies, one on each side of the Channel, began in 1882 but the British press campaigned vigorously against it on security grounds, forcing the government to intervene and stop the scheme in 1883. In 1964 the British and French governments revived the project and work began again on a tunnel in the early 1970s. This too was quickly abandoned, this time on economic grounds. In 1985 new plans for a tunnel rail link were agreed and work is now (1986) scheduled to begin on it again.

English Heritage (Historic Buildings and Monuments Commission for England) The *quango that superseded the Ancient Monument Board and the Historic Buildings Council under the provisions of the National Heritage Act 1983. It is also known as the Historic Buildings and Monuments Commission for England, the royal commissions on historic monuments for the national regions being excluded from the new organization. It is directly responsible for over 350 buildings and monuments formerly in the care of the Department of the Environment, and for protecting and preserving England's collection of 12,500 designated monuments and over 300,000 listed buildings (see historic buildings and monuments). It also advises the government about exemptions from inheritance tax, and determines preservation orders via the "listing" of buildings and the "scheduling" of monuments.

The first Act protecting ancient monuments was passed in 1882, but the first national survey of buildings for listing purposes did not take place until 1969. With a grant-aided budget of £54 million and 1100 staff, English Heritage is responsible for promoting existing sites and opening new areas of conservation (e.g. historic gardens; the archaeological excavation of Maiden Castle, Dorset), for protecting important monuments such as Stonehenge, and above all, for making new surveys of ancient buildings in England and Wales, with a view to listing a further 200,000. A membership scheme by the Historic Buildings and Monuments Commission has attracted 25,000 members.

The Historic Buildings and Monuments Board for Scotland, and Cadw (Welsh: heritage; formerly the ancient monuments branch of the Welsh Office), both have similar functions. Cadw, linked to the Wales Tourist Board, has the biggest task, since the sites in Wales are the least developed.

English language The language brought to Britain in the 5th century AD by Germanic tribes. One of the great international languages, it is the native language of approaching 500 million people, and a *lingua franca* for countless millions more. It is not only the native language of the British, the Irish, the Americans, Canadians, Australians, and New Zealanders, but also exists in distinct varieties that are native languages in such places as Liberia, the Philippines, Hong Kong, and the South Sea Islands. Scandinavian businessmen negotiate with Russians, Poles, and East Germans in it; Chinese and Japanese scientists write their technical papers in it; and English is also the language of international sport, travel, and leisure, as well as of business, aviation, shipping, pop music, computer technology, and learning.

It was not always so. After the Norman conquest English was a despised vernacular of the peasantry. Administration, the law, cultural activities, and philosophical learning in the England of Edward II were conducted in Latin and in Norman French (*see* Norman Britain). In Roman times the vernacular spoken in Britain was a variant of *Celtic. English was brought to Britain from across the North Sea Gradually it eroded Celtic languages everywhere except in the north, west, and southwest, but it was itself soon to be interfered with by further waves of northwest European invaders, the Norse-speaking Vikings. There were three main groups of dialects of Old English, or Anglo-Saxon, the language spoken and written in England up to the 12th century: Kentish, Saxon, and Anglian. In Kent and along the Sussex coast the Kentish dialect of the Jutes has left few traces on modern English. More influential was the Saxon group of dialects, in particular West Saxon, the language of King Alfred's court, in which a great body of Old English literature is preserved. Some features of West Saxon can still be heard in the rural dialects of Dorset and Devon. Modern standard English, however, is derived not from literary West Saxon, but from Mercian, one of the two divisions of the Anglian group of dialects of Old English. Mercian was spoken from the Thames northwards to a line stretching roughly between Hull and Liverpool; the Anglian dialects spoken north of that line, right up to Edinburgh and the old kingdom of Fife, are known as Northumbrian. The English of Scotland, historically speaking, is the northernmost of the Northumbrian dialects (*see* Scots).

The vocabulary of Old English had few borrowings. Learned terms were invented according to need. When Christianity came to Britain, the theological term "trinity" (Latin *trinitas*) was translated into Old English as *thrines* (literally "three-ness"). A disciple was a *leorningcniht* – a "learning youth". Borrowings from Latin were the exception rather than the rule at this period.

Both the Anglian dialect groups (Mercian and Northumbrian) were strongly influenced by Norse. From the 8th century onwards successive bands of Danish raiders and settlers appeared in Britain. King Alfred managed to keep them out of Wessex, but north of the Thames they took control and intermingled with the existing population. The effect on the language was to add to Old English a number of words of Norse origin; the Norse language itself died out in mainland Britain. Words such as "blunder", "blunt", "dirt", and "squeak" are from Norse. In many other cases, such as "blind", "gnaw", "goose", and "take", it is not really possible to say whether the modern English word is derived from Old English *blind* or Norse *blindr*, Old English *gnagan* or Norse *gnaga*, Old English *gos* or Norse *gas*, Old English *tacan* or Norse *taka*. Philologists traditionally derive these words from Old English, but mainly on the grounds that there were more speakers of Old English than Old Norse in England and that Old English in England is better recorded, rather than on any clear etymological evidence. It seems that it was much easier for speakers of Old English and Old Norse to learn each other's language than it is, say, for modern English speakers to learn Swedish or Danish. In a few cases, the

Norse influence on Old English has left us with doublets – two different words that are ultimately of the same origin. So, for example, "skirt" and "shirt" are ultimately derived from the same Germanic original; the former is the Norse word, the latter Old English.

The Norman invasion may not have had as profound an effect on English society as is sometimes supposed. Previous Scandinavian invaders had come to the British Isles, settled, intermarried, and taken over lands and power, even the Crown itself; the Normans did little more than repeat the pattern more thoroughly. However, the effect on the English language can hardly be underestimated. The word "Norman" means "Norse-man", but this particular group of Norsemen had settled in Normandy in France and had dropped their Germanic tongue in favour of a variety of French. The language of power and of culture was Norman French. According to one theory, the only reason that English survived at all was that the Normans employed local nursemaids for their children, thus accidentally ensuring that successive generations of the rich and powerful were exposed to it at an impressionable age. By the time it re-emerged as the literary language of Chaucer in the 14th century, English had changed dramatically. It had lost many of the inflections that are characteristic of Germanic languages, and had acquired a vast admixture of French and Latin words.

In Old English, for example, the adjective *god* ("good") could take any of ten forms (*god, godes, godre, godum, godne, gode, godra, goda, godan, godena*), the choice of form depending on whether the noun in question was masculine, feminine, or neuter; whether the case of the noun phrase was nominative, accusative, genitive, or dative; and whether or not the noun phrase was introduced by a determiner, such as "the". By the Middle English period the form of the adjective had been simplified: the basic spelling varied between *god, good*, and *guod*, depending partly on region, but the only trace of inflection was a vague -e, which was sometimes added, more or less at random, at the end of any of the basic spelling forms, and which may have reflected distinctions of pronunciation. Inflections were only a little more

durable in nouns and verbs. The main noun inflections were -en or -(e)s to indicate a plural (by Shakespeare's day -s had almost completely won this particular battle). Verbs have proved more obstinate, and today English still uses inflections to distinguish the third person singular, present tense (drives) from other persons in the present (I, you, we, they drive), and from the past tense (drove), as well as from the verbal adjectives, "driving" and "driven".

The debt of English to Latin is so immense that it is impossible to characterize with a few examples. Practically the entire learned and literary vocabulary of English came from Latin in the Middle Ages. Only much later, in the 17th and 18th centuries, did learned writers turn directly to Greek for their vocabulary: "psychology" and "physiology" are examples of such borrowings.

The Norman French influence was more social and cultural. Animals in the field are "sheep", "bulls" or "cows", and "swine" or "hogs" (words of Old English origin). By the time they have been "slaughtered" (another Old English word), they are "roasted", "boiled", or "fried" (Norman French) and served up as "mutton", "beef", and "pork" (all Norman French). Once again we find doublets: "display" is from Latin *displicare*; "deploy " is from the Old French verb *deployer*, which in turn comes from *displicare*.

The process of augmenting the basic vocabulary of English with words from French, Latin, and Greek continued unabated for some 500 years. In the 16th century the stylistic affectations of using "inkhorn terms" (English words consisting of Latin without inflectional endings) was so overused that Thomas Wilson, author of a popular and much-reprinted *Arte of Rhetorique* (1553), was moved to protest, "Some seeke so far for outlandish English, that they forget altogether their mothers language . . . . I know them that think rhetorique to stand wholie upon darke wordes, and hee that can catche an ynke horne terme by the taile, him they count to be a fine Englisheman, and a good rhetorician." The backlash against latinate borrowings in English simmered on throughout the 18th century, the great period of latinate elegance in English prose and verse, and raised its head again in the 19th century. The Society for Pure English was a scholarly body of medievalists, but it had its extremists: people who, so it was said, wanted to remove latinate phrases such as "impenetrability of matter" from English, and replace them with good Old English derivatives such as "ungothroughsomeness of stuff". The spread of English as a world language has had an impact on the language itself. English borrows easily from other cultures, and there are words in English derived from most of the world's languages – from "kayak" and "igloo" (from Eskimo, or Inuit) to "kangaroo" and "didgeridoo" (from Australian Aborigine). This flexibility guarantees its vitality. The tremendous wealth of literature written in English, coupled with its function as an international language, are sufficient to ensure its survival. Some spellings, for example the -gh- in "daughter", "bough", and "cough", represent sounds that have not been heard in standard English since the 16th century. Attempts at spelling reform, which have been proposed since at least the time of Shakespeare, have, however, found little favour.

English National Opera (ENO) An opera company, based at the Coliseum Theatre in London, that performs a wide repertoire of operas, usually sung in English. The origins of the ENO lie in the operas staged by Lilian Baylis (1874–1937), first at the Old Vic Theatre and later at *Sadler's Wells. In 1935 the Vic–Wells Opera settled at Sadler's Wells, and was renamed the Sadler's Wells Opera. In 1968 it moved to the Coliseum Theatre, and in 1974 took its present name. Norman Tucker's association with the company (1948–56) was particularly fruitful, with the production of several Janáček operas, some for the first time in Britain, and of operas by young British composers, including Richard Rodney Bennett (1936–) and Malcolm Williamson (1931–). Wagner was added to the company's repertoire in the late 1960s, and in 1973 Reginald Goodall (1905–) conducted a widely acclaimed performance of the *Ring* cycle. Musical directors of the ENO have included Colin Davis (1927–), from 1961 to 1965, Charles Mackerras (1925–),

from 1970 to 1977, and Mark Elder (1947–), from 1979.

English puddings Boiled, steamed, or baked sweet dishes served as the dessert course of the main meal. Until the 17th century, the cleaned-out intestines of slaughtered animals were the only available receptacles in which the soft pudding mixture could be cooked, and few sweet puddings were made. With the invention of the pudding-cloth, however, a wide variety of new recipes were devised and the familiar suet pudding soon became one of England's national dishes. The basic ingredients varied from recipe to recipe, the most common being flour, eggs, suet (the fat found around beef and lamb kidneys, shredded or rendered down), milk or cream, dried fruit, and spices; in poorer homes less expensive ingredients were used and the pudding was sometimes boiled in the same pot as the meat course. Puddings could also be baked, sometimes with a pastry crust, or the mixture divided into small balls and fried in butter.

Modern puddings are usually boiled or steamed in a heatproof basin or, in the case of milk puddings and some of the lighter sponge puddings, baked in the oven. With the advent of convenience foods, such as instant mixes and tinned fruit, and more health-conscious eating habits, the consumption of traditional English puddings has declined in recent years, but they are still enjoyed in many homes. Popular steamed puddings include the traditional plum pudding (*see* Christmas fare); jam roly-poly, in which the pudding mixture is spread with jam and rolled up before cooking; suet or sponge puddings flavoured with ginger, treacle, jam, or dried fruit; and fruit puddings, in which the basin is lined with suet pastry and filled with apples, plums, or other stewing fruit. Baked milk puddings are usually thickened with rice, semolina, sago, or tapioca; bread-and-butter pudding remains a popular way of disposing of stale bread.

English-Speaking Union A registered charity founded by Sir Evelyn Wrench (1882–1966) in 1918 with the purpose of "improving understanding about people, international issues, and culture through the bond the English language provides". The

Union is based in London and has branches in Britain, the USA, the Commonwealth, Europe, and other countries; in 1986 its membership numbered over 45,000. Its work falls into four main categories: "educational exchanges, the creation of an informed public opinion, the fostering of English as a means of international communication, and organized hospitality". It offers travel awards and scholarships and its activities include conferences, seminars, lectures, summer schools, and the publication of the quarterly *Concord*. Its Page Memorial Library boasts an extensive collection of American books, new British books being sent to the USA under its "Books-across-the-sea" scheme. The international centre of the Union is Dartmouth House in London's Mayfair.

English Tourist Board   *See* British Tourist Authority.

Episcopal Church in Scotland   *See* Scottish Episcopal Church.

Equal Opportunities Commission   An independent body established under the provisions of the Sex Discrimination Act 1975 "to work towards the elimination of discrimination against women". Its main function is the investigation of complaints derived from about 6000 enquiries each year. It assisted complainants in 797 cases in the period 1976–83, five cases going before the European Court of Justice. The Commission reports on such diverse matters of concern as sexual discrimination in school curricula, men-only areas in public places, intimidating behaviour towards women at work, the underpayment of women, the absence of women from top posts in public life, down to the use of the male/female pronoun in careers leaflets. By supporting well-publicized test cases the Commission hopes to encourage public adherence to the spirit as well as to the letter of the laws governing discrimination. It publishes the magazine *Equality Now*.

equity   A body of unwritten law, supplementary to the *common law in England, Wales, and Northern Ireland, that was administered from the mid-14th century onwards by the *Lord Chancellor, initially alone, and later in the **Court of Chancery**.

With the common law and legislation (*see* Act of Parliament) it remains one of the three primary sources of English law. "Equity" means justice. The word has acquired the secondary meaning of justice as contrasted with strict rules of law. Equity in this sense is the application of what seems right, as opposed to the application of a rule of law, which may not apply to a given circumstance or which prescribes what seems unfair.

By the mid-14th century, the common law had already begun to exhibit shortcomings. Its rules had become too rigid and many injustices resulted; and the principal remedy it offered to injured parties – the award of damages – was not always adequate. The practice had therefore begun of petitioning the king for special relief, but petitions soon became so numerous that responsibility for them was delegated to the Lord Chancellor, whose office issued the writs by which actions in the common-law courts were begun. At first, he issued decrees in the name of king and council, but by the end of the century, the Chancellor was making them in his own name as head of an independent Court of Chancery.

Until the fall of Wolsey (1529), Chancellors were usually eminent ecclesiastics, each tending to act according to his own concept of good conscience, unbound by the decisions of his predecessors. The rules of equity, it was said, "varied with the length of the Chancellor's foot". With the chancellorship of Sir Thomas More (1529–32), however, the office became almost exclusively a legal one; and, under More himself and equally outstanding lawyers, such as Lord Ellesmere (1596–1617) and Sir Francis Bacon (1617–21), equity increased in both scope and certainty. The greatest contribution of equity to substantive English law (though there are many others) is the law of trusts.

Not unnaturally, conflict arose between the courts of common law and the Court of Chancery. The latter would imprison people who exercised their common-law rights in defiance of its orders; and the common-law courts would then allow their release by means of *habeas corpus. In 1615 the dispute was put to James I in person, and he resolved it in favour of the Court of Chancery. From then on, in any case where common law and equity conflicted, equity was to prevail. For the next two hundred or so years, the rules of equity continued to develop to meet new needs; however, the Court of Chancery eventually fell into disrepute by reason of the vast backlog of work that successive Chancellors allowed to accumulate. In recognition of this problem, provision was made for a second judge (the *Master of the Rolls) in 1729, and a third (a Vice-Chancellor) in 1813. These additional appointments had only a limited impact, because a litigant dissatisfied with a decision by either of the new judges could apply to the Lord Chancellor for a rehearing of his case. Until 1872 the Court sat in Westminster Hall, alongside the courts of common law. In that year, all four courts were rehoused in the newly built Royal Courts of Justice in the Strand (the Law Courts). Three years later, under the Judicature Acts 1873–75, they were all replaced by the *High Court of Justice.

Equity does not exist in Scotland, where the different development of the common law did not create the same shortcomings as in England.

ERNIE *See* premium bonds.

Eton College The largest and most prestigious of the ancient English *public schools, situated on the north bank of the River Thames opposite Windsor. Henry VI founded both Eton and King's College, Cambridge, in 1440–41. William of Wayneflete, a former master at Winchester, was appointed the first provost of Eton in 1443, and in the same year Henry increased the number of "poor scholars" to be catered for to 70. An allowance was also made for some *commensales* (commoners), who today form the majority of the pupils. They are known as "Oppidans" because, unlike the "Collegers", they board in houses in the town (Latin *oppidum*, town). Until the first half of the 19th century Latin and Greek were the only subjects taught in the school, although tutors in other subjects were available outside school hours.

The school buildings, begun in 1441, were not completed for about 50 years. They were built

ETON COLLEGE *Many of the original medieval buildings dating from the 1440s are still in use, including the chapel and dining hall.*

around two quadrangles: the outer (known as School-yard) contains the chapel, and the inner contains the library, which houses a fine collection of manuscripts and rare books. An oddly shaped area on the north side of the chapel, between two of the chapel buttresses, gave rise to the ballgame known as Eton fives. These original buildings have been augmented greatly since the 19th century.

The "playing fields of Eton" were made famous by the remark, ascribed to the Duke of Wellington, that the battle of *Waterloo was won there. A form of football unique to Eton – the wall game – is played between Collegers and Oppidans on 30 November against the wall bordering the playing fields. The playing fields, however, are for "dry-bobs"; "wet-bobs" concentrate on rowing, for which Eton is famous. A procession of boats on the river forms a highlight of the annual Fourth of June festivities, held to honour the birthday of one of Eton's greatest benefactors, King George III. The association with the river is also celebrated in the school anthem, the "Eton Boating Song". Another venerable Etonian tradition is "Pop", an elite social and debating club formed in 1811.

The traditional school uniform has lent the school's name to two items of clothing: the Eton jacket (waist-length, with a V at the back) and the Eton collar (deep, stiffened, white, designed to be worn over an Eton jacket).

Evesham, battle of (4 August 1265) A battle that effectively decided the Barons' War (1264–67) with the death of the rebel leader Simon de Montfort (c. 1208–65). This uprising was triggered by Henry III's final repudiation (1264) of the Provisions of Oxford (1258), which had sought to transfer vital areas of royal authority to a council elected by the barons and to *Parliament. Under de Montfort's skilled command, the rebel barons unexpectedly routed a numerically superior royalist army at the battle of Lewes (14 May 1264) and took Henry III and his son, the future Edward I, prisoner. As the virtual ruler of England, de Montfort then summoned the first English *Parliament to include representatives of certain cities and *boroughs in order to ensure maximum support for his regime.

(This has assured him a place in popular mythology as the founder of democratic parliamentary government.) However, the experiment came to an end when Edward escaped and rallied the loyalists and those, such as the Earl of Gloucester, discontented with de Montfort's rule. The rebels and Edward finally met at Evesham in Worcestershire (now Hereford and Worcester), where the king's son, a brilliant tactician, cornered de Montfort in a curve of the River Severn. The bloody three-hour battle that followed was fought in a thunderstorm and cost the lives of some 18 barons, 160 knights, and about 4000 men-at-arms. Simon de Montfort himself was killed and his body hacked to pieces. Although some of the surviving barons held out at Kenilworth castle and on the Isle of Ely for another two years, the battle of Evesham doomed their cause; in October 1266, by the Dictum of Kenilworth, Henry III's rule was formally restored and all de Montfort's Acts made void. However, the Statute of Marlborough (1267) promoted reconciliation by reiterating *Magna Carta and adopting many of de Montfort's innovations, while not undermining the king's authority.

Exchange and Mart A weekly paper of trade and personal advertisements, founded in 1868. It was started by the lawyer and journalist Edward William Cox (1809–79), acting on an idea suggested in the correspondence columns of a women's journal of which he was the proprietor. From 1871 to 1928 it appeared under the title *Bazaar, Exchange and Mart*. Published from Poole, Dorset, it has northern and southern editions, with a total circulation of around 240,000.

Exchequer *See* Chancellor of the Exchequer; common law.

Exmoor An upland region and *national park in southwest England, extending inland from the Bristol Channel coast and straddling the Devon–Somerset border. Less bleak than neighbouring *Dartmoor, Exmoor's combination of heather moorland, pasture, and beautiful coastline attracts many visitors. The central sandstone plateau, rising to a height of

521 metres (1709 feet) at Dunkery Beacon, is the source of the rivers Exe and Barle and their tributaries. Their southwards-running valleys are gentler and wider than the deep wooded valleys (or combes) of the north-flowing waters. Exmoor has fewer prehistoric remains than Dartmoor, although several Iron Age forts can be seen. Following the Norman conquest, much of the central moor was held by the Crown as royal "forest", in the medieval sense of land reserved for hunting (*see* New Forest). (It was almost certainly treeless then as now.) In the 19th century, much of the marginal land was sold into private hands, enclosed, and improved for arable or pasture land.

F

Fabian Society A political organization founded in London in 1884 for the advancement of socialism by democratic means. Its founder members included the writer George Bernard Shaw as well as Sidney and Beatrice Webb (the economists and historians who also helped to found the *London School of Economics in 1895 and the *New Statesman in 1913). It took its name from the advocacy of gradual reform as opposed to revolution, from Fabius (Quintus Fabius Maximus), a Roman commander whose tactics of continually harassing Hannibal's armies without risking set battles earned him the title *Cunctator* (delayer). The Society first came to public notice with the publication of *Fabian Essays in Socialism* in 1889; it subsequently published a number of tracts, but became relatively inactive after World War I. It was revived in 1939 on amalgamating with a newer body, the New Fabian Research Bureau, and has been active ever since, with a considerable number of Labour MPs amongst its members.

Faculty of Advocates The governing body of *advocates in Scotland. Instituted in 1532, and having its home in the Parliament House in Edinburgh where the *Court of Session and the High Court of Justiciary sit, it is headed by an elected **Dean of Faculty**, and its other principal officers are the Vice-Dean, the treasurer, and the clerk of faculty. Students of the Faculty (known as intrants) are admitted to it and entered on the roll of advocates after examination in the main branches of the law and a period of practical training. Power to discipline members for professional misconduct by disbarring (removal from the roll), suspension, and censure is exercised by the Dean and a council of senior members.

fagging *See* public schools.

fairs Festive gatherings, with stalls, sideshows, and other amusements, that take place out of doors at various times of the year. Most modern English fairs have evolved from or are relics of ancient market or charter fairs. In the 13th and 14th centuries royal charters were granted establishing certain fairs as legal trading occasions, largely for the sale of livestock, dairy and agricultural produce, or other commodities relating to the locality; sideshows, games, and similar entertainments were a peripheral attraction. The Lammas Fair at Honiton in Devon is an example: the fair is still held annually on the Tuesday before the third Wednesday in July and is opened with a ceremony common to a number of West Country fairs. A glove, which once symbolized a guarantee of safe passage into and out of the town for medieval traders, is paraded on a decorated pole through the streets by the town crier, who proclaims: "The glove is up! The fair is open!" At this and other surviving market fairs, such as St Giles' Fair at Oxford, Pinner Fair, Trinity Fair at Southwold in Suffolk, and the Nottingham Goose Fair, the emphasis today is almost exclusively on amusement and entertainment, rather than on serious commercial trading. This shift from business to pleasure came about gradually over a long period and was partly responsible for the suppression of many fairs across the country, notably St Bartholomew's Fair in London, in the latter half of the 19th century.

A second category of fairs comprises the hiring or statute fairs, which originated in the 14th century at a time when there was a shortage of labour. All those seeking employment would line up at the fair wearing or carrying some symbol of their trade (shepherds, for instance, would carry a tuft of wool); employers scrutinized the ranks and selected workers for an initial period of 12 months. Over the years these fairs came to be used chiefly for the hiring of domestic servants and were known as Mop Fairs, probably from the mops carried by prospective maidservants. The most famous of these is the Stratford Mop Fair, which is still held annually on 12 October, although it is now strictly a festive occasion. Elements of the old traditions have been retained, notably the country-dancing displays and the ceremonial ox-roasting. A second fair is held about a week later: known as the Runaway Mop Fair, it originally provided an opportunity for any worker not happy in his or her new position to seek alternative employment.

Family Division   See High Court of Justice.

father of the House   The member of the House of Commons who, not holding ministerial office, has the longest period of continuous service in the House, irrespective of changes in the constituencies he may have represented. There are no duties attached to the position, but the father traditionally presides over the first business of every newly elected House, which is the choice of the *Speaker.

Fenian Society   See Irish nationalism.

Fens   A broad band of flat low-lying land in eastern England, extending from Boston, Lincolnshire, in the north almost to Cambridge in the south. Much of the region has been reclaimed from marsh and, with the average height only 4–6 metres (13–20 feet) above sea level, numerous drainage ditches and dykes intersect the area to prevent flooding.

The Romans were the first to construct an extensive drainage system of channels to divert water in the Fens but it was not maintained when they left. As the waters encroached once more, villages were abandoned leaving only the few dry "island" sites such as Ely, Axholme, and Medehamstede (now Peterborough). There were sporadic attempts at reclamation of siltlands in the 12th and 13th

centuries, but the peatlands remained untouched until the 17th century, when extensive drainage works were carried out by the Dutch engineer Cornelius Vermuyden. This caused some resentment amongst local people and the beneficial effects of the schemes were often short-lived. In some places, the drainage lowered the level of the peat by 2–3.7 metres (10–12 feet). In the 19th century, steam-powered pumps were installed.

The Fens are now one of the richest arable areas in England. The inland belt of peaty fen now grows sugar beet, potatoes, and cereals; the coastal silty fen is a major area for market gardening and glasshouse crops, with the towns of Spalding and Wisbech famous for their bulbs, flowers, and fruit. However, the waterlogged and marshy area of Wicken Fen, a National Trust reserve, gives an idea of what the Fens were like before Vermuyden.

Festival of Britain   An event organized in 1951 in commemoration of the *Great Exhibition of 1851. The intentions behind it were to reinvigorate the British people after the years of austerity during and following World War II, and to provide an exhibition of scientific and technological achievement that would be widely noticed. On the festival site on the south bank of the Thames between Waterloo and Hungerford bridges, the public enjoyed a variety of spectacles: the Dome of Discovery, the Skylon obelisk, pleasure gardens, the Tekkinema (an exhibition of the technical achievements of the cinema that developed into the *National Film Theatre). All these were temporary; but the Royal Festival Hall, a concert hall designed by Robert Matthews and Leslie Martin specially for the festival, was the nucleus of what became the *South Bank arts complex.

feudalism   The dominant social structure of medieval western Europe based on a man (and his heirs) holding another's land and exercising his rights in return for specific services (usually payment in money or kind, or religious or military service) and personal loyalty; in turn, the holder could regrant some or all of his holding to others. When repeated, this process created a pyramid-like network of re-

FENS *Men ricking bundles of Norfolk reeds at the turn of the century.*

lationships. The basic economic unit was the *manor.

Although earlier kings had rewarded their servants with grants of land, feudalism proper only emerged in France in the 9th and 10th centuries, when the collapse of central authority led to anarchy. The lands and rights of the kings and nobles were usurped, and in the ensuing confusion a tangled web of relationships emerged, with the king theoretically at the apex of a pyramid, but in practice powerless outside his own lands. One of the local potentates who profited from this system was William, Duke of Normandy, who conquered England in 1066. Not unnaturally he rewarded his followers with grants of land made on feudal tenures. The latter – "tenants-in-chief" – in turn rewarded their retainers similarly, creating a hierarchy of possession. However, because the system was transplanted, rather than spontaneously generated, there was greater uniformity in the terms of tenure than in France. Moreover, because the system was imposed as a result of

conquest, the monarch himself retained extensive lands and powers. This stable situation persisted, except during Stephen's reign (1135–54, when a disputed succession to the Crown undermined the king's authority), any bids for local independence being kept in check. Most important, as a result of the process of forfeiture and regranting that took place when the Anglo-Saxon nobility rebelled against William's rule, all land was universally acknowledged as ultimately the property of the king – a quirk that became established as the legal principle that only the Crown may own land.

In the 12th century, the slow revival in the European economy, which began in the late 10th century, reached a stage at which it began to undermine these structures. For example, many services were commuted to money payments; the king regularly preferred to levy *scutage* ("shield money") with which to hire highly trained mercenaries rather than rely on the conscripts provided by feudal obligations for military service; and under Edward I (r.

163

1272–1307), paid military service by contract became usual. As trade increased, significant markets appeared in goods and land. Parallel to this, the growth of a central administration and judiciary fostered the idea of a "community of the realm", with the nobility more concerned to influence royal policy than to assert their own independence. Finally, the development of parliamentary taxation in the 13th century reduced the king's feudal dues to a minor part of his income. Thus, by 1300, feudalism had become little more than a set of rules governing land tenure; and even they were being eroded. Restrictions on a lord's capacity to grant feudal subtenures were made in 1290, and in the 14th century legal devices allowing holders greater freedom to dispose of their land as they chose, regardless of the laws of feudal inheritance, became widespread. Feudal tenures lingered on until 1661, when they were abolished at the Restoration.

The basis of English land law is still feudal in many respects; still only the Crown may *own* land, the subject may only own an estate in land, which permits him to enjoy it as if he did own it.

Feudalism penetrated to Scotland from England, where it mixed with the native Celtic traditions to produce the two distinct social systems of the *Highlands (*see also* clans) and *Lowlands. Feudal tenures were not finally abolished in Scotland until 1914.

Fifteen, the   See Jacobite rebellions.

film industry in Britain   British cinema has its origins in the experimental work of a group of artists, known as the "School of Brighton", during the first decade of the 20th century. The group included Birt Acres (1854–1918), who invented the ciné camera and projector in 1895, and G. Albert Smith (1864–1959), who patented double exposure, the cut-in closeup, and Kinemacolor. Also involved was Cecil Hepworth (1874–1953), who published the first book of cinematography, *Animated Photography* (1897). Experimenting with many techniques, these innovators made a number of early films, which were both technically and artistically ahead of the American film-makers of the same period.

By the end of World War I, however, the situation was reversed and in 1927, to combat increasing American domination of the film industry, the British government introduced a quota system to ensure that more films were produced in Britain. This shortsighted piece of legislation unfortunately had disastrous results. Some 200 films a year – "quota quickies" – were produced in British studios (often by American directors) in order to fill the quota as quickly as possible. They were mostly third-rate comedies and thrillers that did very little for the reputation of the British cinema either at home or abroad. Among the few exceptional films made in Britain in this period in spite of the legislation were the historical productions of Alexander Korda (1893–1950), such as *The Private Life of Henry VIII* (1933) and *Rembrandt* (1937), and the thrillers of Alfred Hitchcock (1899–1980), including *The Thirty-Nine Steps* (1935) and *Jamaica Inn* (1939).

The years of World War II saw a sudden growth of interest in documentary film-making, which John Grierson (1898–1972) and Humphrey Jennings (1907–50) had pioneered in the 1930s. Films such as *London Can Take It* (1940) and *Target for Tonight* (1941) contributed greatly to Britain's prestige throughout the free world. Also produced during this period were a number of highly effective patriotic feature films, including Leslie Howard's *The First of the Few* (1942) and Noël Coward's *In Which We Serve* (1942) and *This Happy Breed* (1945).

After the war, British films (like British people and everything else British) were very much in demand abroad; David Lean supplied what was needed with his comedy *Blithe Spirit* (1945) and his stiff-upper-lip romance *Brief Encounter* (1946), while Carol Reed followed with *Odd Man Out* (1947) and the unforgettable *The Third Man* (1949). Unfortunately J. Arthur Rank's attempt to cash in on Britain's postwar popularity, with lavish Hollywood-style productions, was both ill-timed and misjudged. His disastrous *Caesar and Cleopatra* (1946), at a cost of £1.3 million, was then the most expensive British film ever made. However, these years also saw some excellent film adaptations of literary classics, notably David

Lean's *Great Expectations* (1946) and *Oliver Twist* (1948), and Laurence Olivier's *Henry V* (1945) and *Hamlet* (1949).

During the last few years of the 1940s and throughout the 1950s, the British film industry produced a steady stream of internationally successful films. From Ealing Studios came a number of comedies, including *Whisky Galore* (1948) and the *Lavender Hill Mob* (1951); Alec Guinness immaculately played eight parts in *Kind Hearts and Coronets* (1949), Henry Cornelius made *Passport to Pimlico* (1948) and *Genevieve* (1953), and the Boulting brothers introduced Peter Sellers to an international audience in *I'm All Right, Jack* (1959).

With the advent of the liberated 1960s a new group of documentary film-makers, including Tony Richardson, Karel Reisz, and Lindsay Anderson (who together had made *The March to Aldermaston* in 1959), sought to create more socially relevant films. A new approach to censorship enabled them to make more explicit films about the real lives of discontented and articulate people; examples of this new genre of British film include Richardson's production in 1959 of John Osborne's *Look Back In Anger*, Reisz's *Saturday Night and Sunday Morning* (1960), and Anderson's *This Sporting Life* (1963).

During the 1970s British films began to lose their originality and retreated into escapist spy thrillers, historical dramas, and musicals, which were almost indistinguishable from contemporary American productions. Moreover, the attractions of television and the rise in the cost of cinema tickets led to the decline of the local cinemas, many of which were closed or used as bingo halls. A levy on cinema tickets, introduced by Wilfred Edy in 1957, did not provide enough to finance many British films of quality, and for years British films failed to win the awards necessary to attract recognition and sponsorship. However, the remnants of the industry that survived the ravages of the 1970s have risen in the 1980s to produce *Chariots of Fire*, directed by David Puttnam, which won the Oscar for best film in 1982, Sir Richard Attenborough's *Gandhi*, which repeated this feat in 1983, and Sir David Lean's *A Passage to India* in 1985.

Fionn MacCumhaill (Finn MacCool) A legendary Irish giant of the 3rd century, hero of the Fenian cycle of Gaelic tales and ballads, father of the poet Oisin, and leader of the Fianna. The great fighting force of Ireland, the Fianna have been compared with the knights of the Round Table in *Arthurian legend: in addition to their extraordinary strength and skill, they were schooled in poetry and acquired certain magical powers from the fairies and wizards with whom they consorted. Fionn became their leader and many tales are told of his adventures, culminating in the final defeat of the Fianna. Fionn and Oisin, together with Fionn's wife Grainne, his friend Diarmuid, and his hound Bran, also appear in Scottish legend, their names usually anglicized to the more familiar Fingal and Ossian. In the early 1760s the Highland poet James Macpherson (1736–96) published a verse collection spuriously alleged to be translations of the poems of Ossian. An obvious connection between the Scottish and Irish legends is provided by the spectacular basaltic rocks of the Giant's Causeway in Ireland and the Scottish island of Staffa, thought to have once been a continuous formation: since the Irish believed Fionn to be the builder of the former, the Scots

FIONN MACCUMHAILL *Irish legend links Fionn with the dramatic rock formations at the Giant's Causeway, Co. Antrim.*

naturally associated Fingal with the latter – a possible derivation of the name of Staffa's most impressive cavern, Fingal's Cave (which inspired Mendelssohn's overture of that name).

Fire of London (1666) A fire that began accidentally in a bakehouse in Pudding Lane near London Bridge, and spread to two-thirds of the City of London, between 2 and 5 September 1666. The gothic St Paul's cathedral, 87 churches, many public buildings (including the *Royal Exchange), and over 13,000 houses were destroyed. Reconstruction began in 1667: Sir Christopher Wren's grand plans for wholesale redesign were not accepted, but the rebuilding work did incorporate wider streets and all-brick houses. The most famous landmarks of the period are Wren's St Paul's cathedral (*see* cathedral) and 51 new parish churches, symbols of the feeling that the fire was a judgment by God, to be appeased by emphasizing the importance of religious worship to the people of the capital. Many of these buildings survived until the second great fire of London, during the air raids of World War II. A monument (called The Monument), designed by Wren, was built (1671–77) exactly 202 feet from the bakehouse in Pudding Lane to commemorate the fire. Its height is also 202 feet, making it the world's tallest free-standing stone column.

fish and chips A "convenience food" that has been popular with the British for over one hundred years. It is so commonplace that almost every high street in the land has a fish-and-chip shop. The fish, often cod or plaice, is fried in batter and was formerly served (and eaten) from newspaper (now clean white paper). The fish and chips are usually sprinkled with vinegar, tomato ketchup, or some other sharp sauce. Use is made of the local fish-and-chip shop by all social classes in Britain when a quick take-away meal is required. Changing tastes have brought variety to the menu, and sausages, burgers, spring rolls, "mushy peas", and curry sauces are also usually on sale.

fishing (angling) A sport that has been practised from ancient times. The word "angle" is derived from the Old English *angul*, meaning a hook. The history of fishing as a popular pastime in Britain dates back to the publication in 1653 of the classic manual *The Compleat Angler* by Izaak Walton. The sport is now one of the most popular in terms of participators. It attracts people from all walks of life, using equipment of varying levels of sophistication to catch fish in lakes, canals, rivers, and the sea.

Freshwater fishing falls into two main categories: game fishing and coarse fishing. Game fishermen seek fish for eating, notably salmon and trout. They use artificial flies and spinners as lures, made to resemble the natural food of the fish. Game fishing is more expensive, particularly on rivers where the best stretches of water are normally privately owned, and it is therefore a sport traditionally associated with the landowning classes. Coarse fishing is the sport of the "common man" who catches fish not generally considered edible, such as pike, roach, or tench, and returns them to the water. The coarse fisherman uses all kinds of bait including bread, worms, maggots, and cheese. A particular branch of coarse fishing is "match fishing" – a competition between a number of anglers to catch the largest weight of fish in a given time. The sport is highly organized and yields substantial prizes. In recent years, however, there has been some erosion of the class boundaries between the two types of angling. This has largely come from commercial exploitation of reservoirs and large privately-owned lakes, which are stocked with rainbow trout (a non-native species). These are fished for using wet-fly lures and many coarse fishermen now go game fishing in this way. More recently still, reservoir fishing for salmon has been introduced. In order to protect fish during their spawning season, coarse fishing is prohibited in the UK from 15 March to 15 June, while salmon fishing is not allowed between 1 November and 31 January; trout fishing is not permitted from 1 October to the end of February.

Fitzwilliam Museum A museum in Cambridge, belonging to the university. It was founded in 1816, when the 7th Viscount Fitzwilliam bequeathed his collection to the university together with funds for a building to house it. The building was begun by the architect George Basevi in 1837 and completed in 1845 by C. R. Cockerell, who also designed the Ashmolean Museum in Oxford. The Fitzwilliam, which has been augmented by a series of bequests and donations, contains notable collections of Greek coins and pottery, some fine early Italian paintings, and a larger number of 18th- and 19th-century paintings.

fives A game in which a small hard ball is hit with the hand around a concrete court by four players wearing padded leather gloves. It originated in the English public schools in the 19th century and it is still in such schools and the universities of Cambridge and Oxford that the game is mainly played. There are three versions of fives – Eton, Rugby, and Winchester – each taking its name from its school of origin. There are considerable differences between the three: in Rugby and Winchester fives, the courts and walls are flat and plain and there is a back wall which comes into play. An Eton fives court has no back wall, a small downwards step right across it, and a buttress jutting out into the court. The extraordinary character of this court reflects the origins of the game in the space formed by walls and buttresses on the side of the *Eton College chapel. An informal ball game had been played there for many years before the Master had the first purpose-built courts erected in 1840.

flags The **Union Jack,** despite being universally recognized as the flag of the United Kingdom, and often flown from public buildings and waved on patriotic occasions, has never been officially designated the national flag. Its striking red, white, and blue design originates from 1603 when James VI of Scotland became king of England and a flag was needed for the royal warships (the term "Jack" is a nautical one and it has been argued that it is incorrect to use it ashore). For some 200 years or more English soldiers had displayed the cross of *St George (red on white) on their surcoats and pennants in battle, and Scottish soldiers the cross of *St Andrew (a diagonal white cross on blue): these were combined to form the basis of the present design. The first Union flag remained in use until 1801 when Ireland was brought into the Union of Great Britain. As the gold harp of Ireland, which Cromwell had used in his Commonwealth flag in the 1650s, was not considered an appropriate addition, a diagonal red cross of *St Patrick was devised and incorporated into the flag. At the same time a **Red Ensign** (popularly called the Red Duster by seamen) was designed for merchant navy ships, using the new Union flag in one corner; later similar flags were developed for other services.

Sharing the position of national flag with the Union Jack, and displaying the quartered arms of England, Scotland, and Ireland, is the **Royal Standard** (or Banner) of the United Kingdom, the monarch's personal flag that is flown from Buckingham Palace whenever the Queen is in residence. This is older than the Union Jack and even the cross of St George, although it has undergone various modifications over the centuries (*see* royal arms).

Wales is not represented in either the Union Jack or the Royal Standard because it is a principality and not a kingdom: the Prince of Wales's personal standard carries at its centre the arms of Wales, which are those of Llewelyn (d. 1282), the last native Prince of Wales. In the 1950s separate flags were approved for use in Wales and Northern Ireland; the **Welsh flag** bears a red dragon against green and white, while the **Northern Irish flag** bears the red cross of St George surmounted by a crowned six-pointed star (one point for each of the six counties) and the Red Hand of Ulster on its semiofficial flag.

Fleet Street A street in London between Temple Bar and Ludgate Circus, now the principal home of the newspaper industry. Fleet Street takes its name from the River Fleet, a tributary of the Thames that runs beneath Farringdon Street and New Bridge Street and is now used as a sewer. It was an important London thoroughfare even in medieval times but it was not until the early 16th century that printers and publishers began to establish themselves there. The first newspaper to be published in Fleet Street was the *Morning Advertiser*, whose offices were moved there from the Strand in 1825. Most of the national newspapers have offices in the area: the *Daily Telegraph* office and the glass-fronted *Daily Express* building are in Fleet Street itself, together with various organizations related to the newspaper industry, such as the National Union of Journalists, Reuter's, and the Press Association.

Floral Dance *See* Furry Dance.

follies Edifices generally constructed solely as ornaments; numerous towers, columns, arches, façades, and grottoes adorning the British countryside serve as testaments to the personal whims (and wealth) of those who built them. Most were erected in the 18th and early 19th centuries. Most popular was the sham-gothic tower or arch, built in the style of a medieval castle and usually sited on a hilltop. Another favourite was the classical temple, often constructed in a state of contrived and picturesque decay. Others recreated earlier styles with their pyramids, obelisks, and even replicas of prehistoric structures, such as Stonehenge. One of the most spectacular is the two-tiered Roman-style monument known as McCaig's Folly at Oban, Scotland, constructed

FOLLIES *Dunmore Park, Stirling. The "Pineapple", standing 15 metres (50 feet) high, was built as a garden retreat in 1761.*

by a local banker, John McCaig, as a monument to his passion for classical architecture. Waterloo Tower in Quex Park near Birchington, Kent, was built by a keen campanologist in the early 19th century. A peal of bells was installed, and the tower is surmounted by a striking cast-iron spire resembling the Eiffel Tower.
See also Portmeirion.

football An eleven-a-side field game, also called soccer, in which the object is to score goals by kicking or heading the ball from player to player and then into a netted goal. Games of kicking an object towards a target are recorded as long as 2500 years ago in China, and were popular in England in medieval times. Rules varied from place to place, but generally imposed few restrictions on the players; the resulting free-for-alls raised fears concerning public order, and several monarchs tried to ban the game. By 1800 it was played regularly only in the *public schools; again, each had its own rules, varying as to the degree of handling permitted. Steps towards common rules were first taken by Cambridge undergraduates in 1848. In 1863 the Football Association was founded and drew up its own set of rules; amid much controversy, handling was outlawed (except by the goalkeeper). The clubs that did not accept this formed the Rugby Football Union in 1871 to promote the handling game (*see* rugby). In 1872 the first Football Association (FA) Cup was won by the Wanderers, a club of ex-public school men.

The game rapidly spread from its southern base to the Midlands and north, and thence to Scotland. The challenge of the more working-class northern clubs soon became a domination, largely as a result of the employment of professionals. The FA legalized this practice in 1885 and the professional clubs have ruled the game ever since; in 1888 12 of them formed the Football League. The League Championship and the FA Cup (*see* Cup Final) have remained the two main competitions in England, and only four clubs have won both in the same season: Preston North End in 1889, Aston Villa in 1897, Tottenham Hotspur in 1961, and Arsenal in 1971. The Scottish FA was formed in 1873 with its own cup, and the

Scottish League followed in 1891. The first international soccer match took place between England and Scotland in 1872. Since then the game has spread all round the world, becoming the national game in many countries, particularly in Europe and South America. A world cup competition was inaugurated in 1930, and has been held every four years since, except during World War II. England has won it once, at Wembley in 1966. Leading British footballers have included Thomas Finney (1922–), (Sir) Stanley Matthews (1915–), and Bobby Charlton (1937–). All clubs have a core of loyal supporters, though attendances have declined in recent years. Unfortunately, matches have sometimes become the focus of gratuitous crowd violence, with some "supporters" attending mainly, if not entirely, to take on the opposing supporters verbally and physically.

football pools Postal betting on the results of English and Scottish soccer matches. It is estimated that some 12 million people in Britain do the pools each week. The pools first appeared in 1923 and were then relatively simple: an investor merely had to pick 8 matches that he thought would result in wins for the home side. However, this format yielded only low prizes and so a new system, known as the Penny Points, was introduced. Here the promoter selected, say, 12 or 14 games from the total and the punter had to forecast the correct result of all of them. This was much harder and with fewer winners the prize money was greatly increased. Interest in the competition snowballed and by 1939 the pools had become a familiar part of British life. In the early 1950s the Penny Points system was replaced by the Treble Chance as the most popular form of betting. In this system the object is to forecast 8 games that will result in "score-draws" – that is, games in which both sides score the same number of goals, as opposed to "no-score draws" in which neither side scores. This is more difficult if only 8 matches are selected so the punter may choose 10 or 12 or more, thus increasing his chances of winning and, of course, his stake. However, by being the only winner on the Treble Chance it is possible to win large prizes, now approaching £1 million.

From May to July each year, when football ceases in Britain, the results of Australian matches are used. In 1963 the winter was so severe that matches were cancelled for weeks on end and the pools could not continue. A panel of experts was appointed to decide what the results would have been if the games had been played – a practice that is still followed in bad weather.

foot guards *See* Household Division.

Foreign Secretary A senior government minister and member of the *Cabinet (in full, the Secretary of State for Foreign and Commonwealth Affairs) in charge of the Foreign and Commonwealth Office and responsible for Britain's relationships with other countries. In the 19th and early 20th centuries, it was a prestigious and specialized post. George Canning (1807–09, 1822–27), Lord Palmerston (1930–34, 1835–41, 1846–51), and Anthony Eden (1935–38, 1940–45, 1951–55) all made their names in foreign affairs before becoming Prime Minister; and Lord Salisbury was unique among Prime Ministers in being Foreign Secretary for almost the whole of his three premierships (1885–86, 1886–92, 1895–1907) rather than First Lord of the Treasury (*see* Chancellor of the Exchequer). In recent times, the prestige of the office has declined for several reasons: Britain's role as a world power has diminished since World War II; other areas of government activity, such as social and economic policy, have come into greater prominence; the efficiency of modern global communications has to some extent demystified foreign affairs; and Prime Ministers have assumed a greater role in diplomacy, with meetings between heads of government becoming commonplace. No modern Foreign Secretary could act like Palmerston, who pursued his own course in virtual defiance of his colleagues.

Forestry Commission The state authority responsible for the growth and management of forests in Britain. The Forestry Commission was set up in 1919 on the recommendation of the Acland Committee, with the purpose of creating reserves of timber. There had been severe shortages during World War I, due to immediate wartime needs and the reduction of Britain's forests in the 18th and 19th centuries when timber was required for many reasons by new industries. Until recently, fast-growing conifers were grown to supply the main timber market, which has always been for softwoods. Now more mixed woodlands are being planted because they are more suited to the soils of the areas concerned, and because woodlands are now being created for leisure purposes.

The Forestry Commission now manages 1.2 million hectares (3 million acres) of land under the Forestry Act 1967. The Commission and its 6750 staff are funded partly by the sale of timber products and partly by a grant. Until 1958 its main purpose was to grow forests, but its efforts are now devoted to producing raw material for industry (trees, sawlogs for British Coal, chipboard, etc.), to the sale of large areas of forest to private ownership in order to reduce its annual grant, and to considering the increasing significance of employment trends, and environmental and recreational factors to Britain's forests. The major tasks of the Commission are the management of existing forests and 4000 properties, the provision of grants for the creation of new forests in the private sector, the planning and plantation of trees on the Commission's own land (10,000 hectares (25,000 acres) in 1984), the felling or thinning of trees in other areas, and the training of foresters. The Commission must forecast the future supply and demand for timber, and encourage the mechanization of labour tasks. In the area of conservation, the Commission undertakes research to combat pests and disease (e.g. Dutch elm disease), and to curb pollution (e.g. acid rain).

Forty-five, the   *See* Jacobite rebellions.

Founder's Day, Chelsea Royal Hospital *See* Oak Apple Day.

foxhunting   A bloodsport practised in the countryside of Britain from November until April (the hunting season), in which huntsmen (and women) on horseback chase a fox with a pack of hounds. Described by Oscar Wilde as "the unspeakable in pursuit of the uneatable", foxhunting faces fierce opposition from those (especially the *League Against Cruel Sports) who regard it as cruel and de-

grading. Violent confrontations between hunters and protesters are not infrequent. Nevertheless it continues to attract considerable support in the countryside, mainly from the landowning gentry and farmers who defend their sport by claiming that the fox is vermin, which must be exterminated for the good of the community, and that opposition is misdirected since the animal always has a chance of escaping the hounds.

Foxes have been hunted throughout history but until about the end of the Stuart period were regarded as vermin, distinct from game (deer and hares were considered more "noble" game). With the enclosure of the common fields in the 18th and 19th centuries, hedges and fences added an element of excitement to the chase. In addition faster foxhounds were being bred, particularly by Hugo Meynell (of Quorndon Hall in Leicestershire), the father of modern foxhunting. With these new elements foxhunting became a favourite activity of the upper classes as well as with the farmers (whose livestock is endangered by foxes). Some of the glamour of the chase and the English countryside in which it takes place was captured by John Woodcock Graves in his song "D'ye ken John Peel", written in 1829 about his friend the Cumberland yeoman John Peel (1776–1854), who was master of a pack of foxhounds at Caldbeck for nearly half a century. Literature, too, has provided an interesting background to hunting. For example, the rumbustious exploits of Jorrocks, the fictional sporting grocer created by R. S. Surtees at the beginning of the 19th century, once described as "Dickens-and-horsedung", contrast with the more elegaic early-20th-century *Memoirs of a Foxhunting Man* by Siegfried Sassoon.

free churches   All Protestant Churches in Britain that are not established (i.e. supported by the state). This freedom they regard as essential in order properly to exercise their various forms of worship and church government. They include the Methodist Church (*see* Methodists), which is the largest, the *Baptists, and the *United Reformed Church. They are represented by the Free Church Federal Council, a body formed in 1940 by the union of the National Council of the Evangel-

FOXHUNTING *Near Elmley Castle, Hereford and Worcester.*

ical Free Churches (founded in 1896) and the Federal Council of Evangelical Free Churches (founded in 1919 by the prominent Baptist J. H. Shakespeare). This acts on their behalf and promotes unity among them.

Free Church of England (Reformed Episcopal Church) A small Protestant Church founded in 1843 by a dissident Church of England clergyman, James Shore. He founded its first church at Bridgetown in Devon because of a dispute with the High Church views of his local bishop in Exeter, who was a sympathizer with the *Oxford Movement. It is episcopalian in organization and adheres to an unusually strict interpretation of the Reformed doctrine. In 1927 it united with the **Reformed Episcopal Church**. It has some 33 churches.

freemasonry A movement claiming great antiquity, whose members are joined together in a fraternal association based on brotherly love, faith, and charity. It is nonpolitical, open to men of any religion, and is known for its rituals and signs of recognition that date back to ancient religions and to the practices of the medieval Roman Catholic craft guild of the stonemasons. The stonemasons' guild was probably formed in the 13th century when many large buildings in the gothic style were erected. Masons were itinerant, travelling the country as their skills were required, and consequently had to be able to recognize fellow craftsmen and exclude interlopers from their trade. During the 17th century the masons' clubs, or lodges, began to be attended by gentlemen who had no connection with the trade, but who in time came to outnumber the masons. Little is known about the movement in the years leading to the foundation of the Grand Lodge of England (1717), except that during this period the transformation from craft guild to a secret society for gentlemen apparently took place. Certain terms from the stonemasons' trade were retained: for example, the three grades of membership are apprentice, fellowcraft or journeyman, and master mason. The working tools of a mason also feature in the rituals of speculative freemasonry.

Grand lodges were formed in Ireland in 1725 and in Scotland in 1736; freemasonry also spread to the USA, the colonies, and European countries. The one essential qualification for membership is a belief in a supreme being. Freemasons are drawn mainly from the professional middle classes: lawyers, civil servants, doctors, accountants, etc. At his initiation, a new member is sworn to secrecy under threat of dire penalties (recently reduced in severity), and indeed, for this reason the movement is regarded with a certain mistrust in some quarters, and also because it is felt that members give covert help to their fellows, for example, in job appointments, business transactions, etc.

There are probably over 600,000 masons in England and Wales, 100,000 in Scotland, and 50,000 in Ireland. In England the Grand Lodge runs a hospital, a benevolent institution, and a school for orphans of former masons. Members of the royal family have from time to time been freemasons, the present Duke of Kent being currently Grand Master.

friendly society A traditional working-class association formed to provide financial aid for members. The statute of 1793 permitted such societies to be, "of good fellowship for the purpose of raising from time to time, by voluntary contributions, a stock or fund for the mutual relief and maintenance of all and every member thereof, in old age, sickness, and infirmity, or for the relief of widows and children of deceased members". Such societies had burgeoned during the preceding century, sometimes among such special groups of workers as the immigrant Huguenots, but usually based simply on the village inn. The 19th century saw the foundation of some large centralized societies, which had affiliated groups all over the country, such as the Foresters or Oddfellows. Since their members made relatively few demands on public relief, the authorities were happy to encourage friendly societies and by the end of the century various permissive Acts defining the limits of their activities had been passed. Their accounting methods improved and tables of sickness and life insurance were prepared on sound actuarial principles. With a membership of five million they were in a position to offer profes-sional insurance advice and cover. Thus societies that merely made door-to-door collections towards funeral expenses, for example, were not considered part of the movement and remained unregistered. Sickness benefit was the most popular feature of the friendly societies, but members could also contribute towards pension schemes, endowments, annuities, and medical treatment; the money either accumulated until it was needed, or interest and dividends were paid out from the surplus. In 1911 the government took over responsibility for the provision of *national insurance and used approved societies all over the country to help administer it. However, with the emergence of the welfare state after World War II it was felt that a central administration was needed and the friendly societies lost their key role. Although their membership is therefore now much reduced, they still offer various kinds of insurance, including endowments and special convalescence schemes, and have been active in the housing association field.

fringe theatre Theatre that exists outside the mainstream commercial and subsidized theatre because its form or content is unlikely to attract conventional audiences. The term was probably first applied to the theatre groups performing "on the fringe" of the *Edinburgh Festival. The focus of fringe activity in Edinburgh was the Traverse Theatre, founded under Jim Haynes in 1963. The Traverse discovered several well-known playwrights, foreign and British, among them C. P. Taylor and Tom Stoppard. Howard Brenton and David Hare were also first noticed in fringe theatre. Britain has almost 130 fringe theatres, often performing in temporary or converted premises. Among the best-known are the King's Head, Islington, the Orange Tree, Richmond, the Bush, at Shepherd's Bush, all in London; and elsewhere the Pip Simmons Theatre Group, Foco Novo, Welfare State International, Joint Stock, and 7:84.

Furry Dance (Floral Dance) An annual dance festival that takes place in Helston, Cornwall, usually on 8 May, the feast day of the Apparition of St Michael the Archangel. The Furry Dance is one of the oldest surviving English customs, said to be a celebration of the victory of St Michael, patron saint of Helston, in his battle with the devil (during which the huge stone that sealed the mouth of Hell landed at Helston, hence the name Hell's Stone); but it may well date back to earlier pagan rites. Also associated with the Roman Floralia, a festival in honour of the goddess Flora, it was known by the Victorians as the Floral Dance. The word "furry" is probably derived from the Latin *feria*, meaning "holy day" or "festival", or from the Celtic *feur*, meaning "fair" or "holiday". The festivities begin early in the morning, when the young people of the town dance through the narrow streets, which have been decorated for the occasion with flowers and bunting, and sing the ancient Furry Song, "Hal-an-Tow", the words of which suggest it is a relic of older May Day festivities. The principal dance, led according to custom by a Helston-born couple, begins at noon. To the accompaniment of the town band playing the more modern Furry Dance tune, the elegantly dressed couples dance through houses and shops, bringing good luck to the occupants.

G

Gaelic   The *Celtic language spoken actively by about 80,000–90,000 people in the Western Highlands and islands of Scotland, virtually all of whom are also able to speak English. Scots Gaelic (pronounced with a short a, as in "pan") is quite closely related to *Irish (which is also sometimes called Gaelic, but pronounced with a long a, as in "pain"). The two languages are no longer mutually comprehensible, mainly because of the Norse influence on Scots Gaelic in the Middle Ages. Gaelic was brought to Scotland from Ireland by invaders in the 5th and 6th centuries AD. Scots Gaelic was the language of the Scottish *clans, whose social structure was destroyed after the battle of *Culloden in 1746. The Highland clearances of the 19th century, in which aristocratic landowners cleared their

Scottish estates of human inhabitants to make way for deer and sheep, further eroded the Gaelic-speaking population. Some died; some migrated to Glasgow, Edinburgh, and elsewhere; others emigrated, especially to Canada, where Gaelic language societies now flourish. Surviving Gaelic speakers in Scotland are typically small farmers (*see* crofting), fishermen, and weavers.

The traditional forum for Gaelic poetry and music is the *ceilidh, an institution that has been copied by folk-music enthusiasts in other cultures. Historically, the great glories of Gaelic literature are Irish rather than Scots, although there was a brief independent flowering in the late 18th century, when Scots Gaelic poets, in particular Alasdair Macdonald (?1700–?80), mourned the destruction of their society. There has been a literary revival in Gaelic in the 20th century, in which poets such as George Campbell Hay (Deorsa mac Iaian Dheorsa, to give him his Gaelic name) figured prominently.

The pronunciation of Gaelic is complex, with a particularly large set of consonant distinctions, many of which escape an English ear. The situation is complicated further by the large variety of dialects and by the spelling, which tends to reflect the historical development of the language rather than pronunciation. The structure, too, is complex. As in all Celtic languages, the initial consonant of a word is subject to "mutation": that is, it may take any of up to four different sounds, depending on the words with which it occurs and the syntax of the phrase. Verbs and nouns also inflect, although the old case system is gradually disappearing. Numbering shares with French vestiges of a base-20 system: the Gaelic term for forty is *dà fichead*, literally "two twenties", sixty is *trì fichead*, eighty is *ceithir fichead*. The typical word order of a Gaelic sentence is verb-subject-object.

Gaelic football   A ball game played almost exclusively in Ireland. Its origins are obscure: the first direct mention of such a game was made in the 16th century. In the early 19th century it was especially popular in County Kerry, where it was known as *caid* (Gaelic for the oval ball used at that time); but by the 1860s it had degenerated into a violent game

English	Welsh	Scots	Irish	
one	ein	aon	aon	The four languages (and
two	dau	dà	do	most European languages)
three	tri	trì	tri	have some words in common.
four	pedwar	ceithir	ceathair	Here, as with many words, the
five	pump	cóig	cueg	Welsh use a **p** where the Irish and Scots have a **c** or a **q**.
Britain	Prydain	Bretain	Cruithin	These words have the same origin, although the terms Prydyn and Cruithni, referring to the inhabitants of Britain, came to be applied only to the Picts who lived in Northern Britain.
son	ap	mac	mac	The surnames Hewson, Pugh and MacHugh all mean "son of Hugh".

GAELIC *The national languages of Britain and Ireland.*

with few rules. New rules, aimed at revitalizing the sport, were introduced following the foundation of the Gaelic Athletic Association in 1884. The first All-Ireland championships began in 1887.

The ball used is like a football, but it may be punched as well as kicked. The goal posts are similar to those for rugby, though the lower part, beneath the crossbar, is netted. It is possible to score by sending the ball into the net or over the bar. There are 15 players on each side and a game lasts for 60 minutes. The ball is passed by kicking or punching it, or a player may proceed by "hopping" – bouncing the ball on the ground. Shoulder-charging is legal but all other forms of wrestling, tripping, and punching were outlawed in 1885. The game is played at a frenetic pace so stamina is as important as ball control and accuracy of passing. There is a considerable spectator following for Gaelic football in Ireland.

Gaming Board for Great Britain A board, under the control of the Home Office, charged with overseeing the gaming industry in Britain. The proliferation of gambling halls of all kinds in the 1960s, and fears of the opportunities they would provide for organized crime, led to the passing of the Gaming Act in 1968 and the establishment of the Gaming Board. It has control over the ownership, location, and running of licensed gaming clubs, the certification of gaming machine operators, and the licensing of casinos and *bingo halls. It is also responsible for enforcing other measures in the Act, such as the minimum duration of 48 hours membership for all casino clients prior to gambling (24 hours for bingo), the strict rules governing the acceptance of cheques, and the exclusion of live entertainment from licensed casinos. A team of inspectors maintains a close watch on all the licensed clubs. There is no appeal against the decisions of the Board, which does not have to disclose the information leading to its decisions. Under the Lotteries and Amusements Act 1976, certain lotteries must register with and submit their accounts to the Gaming Board. There are now some 120 licensed casinos and 2000 bingo halls in the country, with turnovers of £1483 million and £496 million, respectively.

garden city A town that has been planned to combine urban working and recreational facilities with an environment in which as many rural features as possible have been preserved. To achieve a perfect marriage of town and country was the aim of Sir Ebenezer Howard (1850–1928), who inspired Britain's first garden city, Letchworth, Hertfordshire, built in the early 1900s. His book, *Garden Cities of Tomorrow*, in which he set out his ideas for spacious attractive suburbs, was published in 1902. He wished to improve the quality of urban life, which had been eroded by the effects of the *industrial revolution in the 19th century. A few enlightened industrialists had built model villages for their workers during the late 18th and 19th centuries. Sir Thomas Salt's Saltaire, near Bradford, and Lord Leverhulme's Port Sunlight, on the Wirral, are two examples. In 1902 Howard formed the First Garden City Company; on an initial block of 1541 hectares (3800 acres) at Letchworth, architects Barry Parker (1867–1941) and Sir Raymond Unwin (1863–1940) began to build low-density housing in pleasing styles and materials amid congenial tree-lined avenues and parks. It was claimed that only a single tree was destroyed in the initial construction phase. These features were retained and evolved in Parker and Unwin's Hampstead Garden Suburb, built 1906–11; Welwyn Garden City, Hertfordshire, commenced in 1920 by Louis de Soissons; and Wythenshawe, Manchester, designed by Parker in the 1930s. Although high land prices mean that new garden cities are not feasible, they still provide inspiration and example for modern town planners.

gardens The British enthusiasm and talent for cultivating and planting their gardens, whether small backyards or large country es-

tates, has long been a national characteristic. Until the 15th and 16th centuries, gardens served largely to provide vegetables, fruit, and medicinal herbs. By Tudor times, the nobility, whose homes no longer needed to be defensible, began to enjoy gardens as places for recreation. Influenced by Italianate Renaissance styles, they laid out symmetrical hedges and borders and made extensive use of such features as knot gardens (intricate raised flower beds), arbours, and mazes. In the late 16th century explorers returned with new ornamental plant species from abroad; at the same time topiary became an established feature of the English garden. The fashion for geometrical layout persisted during the 17th century, with French influences increasingly in evidence – long straight walks, elaborately curved and patterned beds, and considerable use of lakes and canals. The accession of William and Mary in 1688 in its turn brought a Dutch influence to English garden design. However, many of these earlier designs were swept away by the move to a more naturalistic approach during the 18th century. William Kent (1685–1748) is usually accepted as the founder of the landscape movement, which drew much of its inspiration from the landscapes of the French painters, Claude Lorraine (1600–82) and Nicolas Poussin (1594–1665). Kent's lead was followed by such influential gardeners as Lancelot "Capability" Brown (1716–83), responsible for the grounds of *Blenheim Palace, Harewood House, and Burghley, among many others, and Humphry Repton (1752–1818), who coined the term "landscape gardening". They both laid out

GARDENS *Tudor knot garden, at the Tudor House Museum, Southampton.*

grounds and parks on a vast scale, creating an idealized English landscape, with vistas consisting of artificial lakes, copses, individual trees, and parkland grazing sweeping away to the horizon. The impact of these English landscape gardeners soon reached across the Channel into Europe. However, by the middle of the 19th century the style had been overplayed. The inevitable reaction was a resurgence of the Italianate designs: symmetrical layout, balustraded terraces, garden sculpture, and fountains. Technology also made its contribution; mechanical lawnmowers and heated greenhouses combined with an influx of new varieties and species of flowering plants and shrubs to create a fashion for smaller, more formal, gardens with manicured lawns and geometrically shaped beds of flowers.

This formality again inspired William Robinson (1839–1935) and his followers, including Gertrude Jekyll and the architect Edwin Lutyens (1869–1944) to become passionate advocates of "natural gardening" incorporating elements of both heath and woodland into the traditional English cottage garden. Many features of present-day gardens, notably herbaceous borders, were popularized by the Robinson school, whose ethos was more consistent with the limitations of scale imposed by the growth of the suburbs in the 20th century.

Garland Day An annual festival that takes place on or around 13 May in Abbotsbury, Dorset, once an important inshore fishing village. On Garland Day in Abbotsbury each family used to make a floral garland for its fishing boat; after a ceremony of blessing the garlands would be taken out to sea, to ensure a good harvest of mackerel in the coming season, and then either cast overboard or brought back to land. The picturesque custom has outlived the decline of the fishing industry: garlands of wild and garden flowers are woven in traditional designs and paraded by schoolchildren through the streets of the village, to be laid at the end of the day on the village war memorial. Sometimes one of the garlands is cast out to sea, in memory of Abbotsbury's past. A similar event takes place at Castleton in Derbyshire on 29 May (see Oak Apple Day).

Garter, Order of the The most ancient order of chivalry in Europe, by tradition founded by Edward III between 1344 and 1351. As the register of the order, known as the Black Book, was only compiled during the reign of Henry VIII (1491–1547), the early history of the order's first hundred years cannot be given with any certainty. It is said, however, that while Edward was at war with France, he was anxious to attract Europe's best soldiers into his service. He therefore planned a revival of King Arthur's round table (see Arthurian legend), arranging a grand jousting tournament at Windsor on St George's Day (23 April), 1344. A table 60 metres (200 feet) long was set up in Windsor castle and the gathered knights were regally entertained at the king's expense. Some reports say that it was at this event that Edward founded the Knights of the Blue Garter, with St George as their patron saint. This tradition accounts for the dark blue garter edged with gold, which is the order's principal emblem. It also accounts for the star of the cross of St George worn by knights of the order. The inscription in gold letters on the garter is the source of another legend. It is said that at a certain court festival the Countess of Salisbury dropped her garter, which was instantly retrieved by the king. Observing the knowing looks of the bystanders, the king tied the garter round his own leg, saying, "Honi soit qui mal y pense" (French for "shamed be he who thinks evil of it").

Another and altogether different account of the origin of the order relates to the battle of Crécy, at which, some reports say, Edward III displayed his garter as a signal for the battle to commence. Edward, presumably attributing the subsequent success of his army to this action, thereupon commemorated the event by instituting the Order of the Garter.

The officers of the order include Garter King of Arms (an office instituted in 1417) and the Gentleman Usher of the *Black Rod. Since 1805 there have been 25 Knights Companions of the order in addition to the sovereign, the *Prince of Wales, and the lineal descendants of George II (if elected). Knights are selected by the sovereign, since the reign of King George VI, without advice from the Prime Minister, and are installed in St George's Chapel, Wind-

ORDER OF THE GARTER *Edward III, founder of the Order, in Garter robes. Symbolizing mutual commitment of king and knights to the search for justice and fame through valorous deeds, the Order publicized the chivalric image he sought to project.*

sor. Here each Knight has his own stall in which his arms are permanently displayed.

GCE   *See* school-leaving examinations.

General Certificate of Education (GCE) *See* school-leaving examinations.

General Council of the Bar   *See* Senate of the Inns of Court and the Bar.

General Synod of the Church of England The governing assembly of the Church of England, which comprises the *Convocations of Canterbury and York joined together in a House of Bishops (53 members) and a House of Clergy (253 members), together with an additional House of Laity (250 members elected by the various local deanery synods). The General Synod meets at least twice yearly, with the Archbishops of Canterbury and York acting as joint presidents, to deal with both Church matters and other topics of religious or public interest. Motions dealing with doctrinal or liturgical matters can only be presented to the Synod by the House of Bishops. When parliamentary legislation is required, measures approved by the Synod are submitted to Parliament for its consideration. The Synod has a number of standing committees and permanent commissions, including a board of education and a board for "social responsibility". Among the major issues that have concerned Synod in recent years are the marriage of divorced persons in church and the ordination of women.

At local level, the affairs of each diocese are governed by a diocesan synod, comprising a House of Clergy, a House of Laity, and the bishop. Below these are the deanery synods, and at the base, the parochial church councils, which administer church affairs at parish level. This synodical system of government was introduced in 1969, when the General Synod took over the powers of the former Church Assembly and the Convocations, although the latter continued to exist in their own right.

Gentlemen at Arms, Honorable Corps of Noncombatant troops in attendance upon the sovereign for his or her personal protection. They provide an escort at coronations, state openings of Parliament, receptions during state visits, and royal garden parties; because of

their close proximity to the monarch, they are known as the "nearest guard". Although they carry axes, they are no longer considered full fighting troops and have never been subject to martial law.

The Gentlemen at Arms originated in 1509 when Henry VIII raised a bodyguard called variously "Gentlemen Spears" and "King's Spears". The corps then numbered 50 youths of noble birth who each bore a spiked battleaxe. They served both as foot soldiers and cavalry. In 1539 they were reorganized and named "Gentleman (*sic*) Pensioners" or "Band of Gentlemen Pensioners". The term Gentlemen at Arms was not applied solely to them till 1834. 1862 saw a further reorganization, and a minimum height and maximum age of 50 years on appointment were introduced.

The Gentlemen at Arms fought at the Battle of the Spurs against the French in 1513, which gained for Henry VIII the Normandy towns of Tournai and Thérouanne, and at the successful siege of Boulogne (1544). They also defended Queen Mary during Wyatt's Rebellion in 1554; accompanied Charles I on his abortive trip in 1642 to the House of Commons to arrest the Five Members (*see* Civil War, English); formed Charles's bodyguard at the battle of Edgehill in the same year, and also at Naseby (1645); and were ordered to attend George II when he raised the Royal Standard at Finchley Common in 1745 at the height of the Jacobite rising. In 1848 the Gentlemen at Arms guarded St James's Palace against imminent riot during the Chartist agitation.

Today corps members are chosen from officers in the Army or Royal Marines who have received decorations. Names of suitably qualified officers are put forward first to the Ministry of Defence, then to the Captain of the Gentlemen at Arms, then to the Lord Chamberlain, and finally, to the sovereign. The five officers of the corps are Captain, Lieutenant, Standard Bearer, Clerk of the Cheque (equivalent to adjutant), and Harbinger. (The Harbinger used to be sent ahead to arrange accommodation whenever the monarch was making a royal progress.) The captaincy became a party political appointment in the early 18th century; the incumbent is now invariably a peer and the government chief whip in the House of Lords. He receives a gold stick of office on appointment, in contrast to the other officers who carry silver staves. The present incumbent is Lord Denham. In the early years of the corps the Captain was often also Lord Chamberlain. The other officers' appointments are in the gift of the sovereign, and there are 27 ordinary members in the corps. Members now retire at the age of 70.

At official ceremonies the Gentlemen at Arms wear swallow-tail coats of scarlet with gold epaulets, plumed helmets, and brass box-spurs. By an order of James II, they are entitled to wear their hats in Westminster Abbey at coronations.

Geordie A native of the northeast of England, especially Newcastle upon Tyne, or the variety of working-class English spoken by such a person. Historically, Geordie is derived directly from the Northumbrian dialect of Old English, and has more in common with *Scots than with the language of Yorkshire. Geordie has a characteristic rising pitch in sentences, so that statements are sometimes mistaken for questions by outsiders. It also has a rich vocabulary of its own, together with characteristic syntactic patterns. Some of the expressions still common in Geordie may strike an outsider as old-fashioned, since they have long since passed out of other varieties of English. Examples include:

"How there, marra" = "Hello, mate."

"Howway, lads" = "Come on, lads."

"Aa canna bide yon chap" = "I can't stand that man."

"Gan yor ann gate" = "Go your own way."

Such expressions as "bonny lad" and "bonny lass", as terms of address, are familiar everywhere, but other typical expressions, for example "canny man", are less widely known. "Canny" is a favourite Geordie word, meaning kind, good, and gentle.

George Cross A decoration bestowed on civilians for conspicuous acts of the greatest heroism, or conspicuous bravery in circumstances of extreme danger, or on members of the armed forces for actions in which purely military honours are not normally granted.

The George Cross ranks second after the Victoria Cross. It was instituted on 24 September 1940 (amendments in the regulations governing its bestowal were made on 3 November 1942) and named after George VI. The George Cross is worn on the left breast by men and suspended from the left shoulder by women. Holders may take the initials GC after their names and since 1965 have been entitled to a tax-free annuity of £100.

George Medal A decoration instituted in 1940 by George VI and bestowed for acts of gallantry.

Gilbert and Sullivan The librettist and composer respectively of a series of operettas created between 1871 and 1896: W(illiam) S(chwenk) Gilbert (1836–1911) and Arthur Sullivan (1842–1900). "Sullivan and I," said Gilbert, "intend to produce comic operas to which any man may safely bring his mother and his aunts." Their first collaboration produced *Thespis* (1870, now lost). Impressed by their talent for whimsical comedy and memorable tunes, Richard D'Oyly Carte staged *Trial by Jury* (1875). He then leased the Opéra-Comique Theatre for the production of comic operas, specially those of Gilbert and Sullivan. *The Sorcerer* (1877), *HMS Pinafore* (1878) (an enormous success after Sullivan conducted extracts at the Covent Garden promenade concerts), *The Pirates of Penzance* (1880), and *Patience* (1881) were all produced there. *Patience* transferred to the greatly superior Savoy Theatre, built by D'Oyly Carte specifically for Gilbert and Sullivan. The members of the cast were called "Savoyards", a term that came to be applied to any enthusiast of the Savoy operettas. *Iolanthe* (1882), *The Mikado* (1884–85), *Ruddigore* (1887), and the *Yeomen of the Guard* (1888) followed, but during *The Gondoliers* (1889) Gilbert and Sullivan quarrelled. They were not reconciled until 1893, with *Utopia Limited*, but neither this nor *The Grand Duke* (1896) was successful. Sullivan was knighted in 1893, Gilbert in 1907. Although the annual D'Oyly Carte company seasons no longer take place, British enthusiasm for the operettas continues, and they are widely produced by amateurs.

gilt-edged securities Fixed interest stocks (*see also* Stock Exchange) issued by the government in units of £100 and so named because originally the stock certificates had gilt edges. They may be purchased through banks, the Post Office, or on the London Stock Exchange. Dated stocks are redeemable, usually at the issue price of £100 (par), on specified dates. Thus, for example, 7.75% Treasury Stock 1985–88 is a government stock paying 7.75% annual interest and is redeemable at £100 at a date, between 1 January 1985 and 31 December 1988, to be nominated by the Bank of England. Short-dated gilts (or shorts) are those with less than five years to redemption, medium-dated (mediums) have between five and fifteen years, and longs have over fifteen years to run. Some gilts, such as Consols (consolidated annuities, first issued as a result of the consolidation of the *national debt in the 18th century), are irredeemable. The price of irredeemable gilts moves inversely with the general level of interest rates, while with redeemable stocks this relationship weakens as the date of redemption approaches.

Girl Guides *See* Scout Association.

Girls' Brigade A Christian international and interdenominational organization formed in 1965 from the amalgamation of the Girls' Brigade (founded Dublin 1893), Girls' Guildry (Scotland 1900), and Girls' Life Brigade (England 1902), sister movements of the *Boys' Brigade. The document of union creating the present Brigade was signed in 1968. Open to girls from five years upward, its aim is "to help girls to become followers of the Lord Jesus Christ, and through self-control, reverence, and a sense of responsibility, to find true enrichment of life". The Brigade operates in over 50 countries and is comprised of local companies attached to a church or mission. Members attend church or Sunday school, participate in various activities including games, art, dancing, bands, camping, and such schemes as the Queen's Award and *Duke of Edinburgh's Award; they are also encouraged to express what they learn through services to home, community, and church.

Glamis castle The ancestral seat of the Lyon family since the 14th century, when Sir Robert Lyon built a castle on land granted to him by King Robert II of Scotland. The castle stands to the southwest of the town of Forfar in Tayside. Of the original building, only the old kitchen, Duncan's hall, and the crypt remain, incorporated into the existing castle. This was built by Patrick Lyon, Earl of Strathmore, in the 17th century and is a fortified house rather than a castle, its ornamentation inspired by the chateaux of France. The interior has some fine furnishings dating from the early 17th century and also a collection of paintings and armour. In the grounds is an elaborate sundial, 6.4 metres (21 feet) high, with 84 separate dials. The Queen Mother, daughter of the Earl of Strathmore, spent her childhood at Glamis, and Princess Margaret was born there in 1930.

Glasgow Herald A daily newspaper first published in Glasgow in 1783. Entitled the *Glasgow Advertiser* for about 20 years of its existence, the first edition of the paper was published and edited by John Mennons, a printer and almanac-maker. At the time of publication, as the first editorial indicates, Glasgow was "the foremost commercial city in Scotland", a city so trade-orientated that January 1783 also saw the rise of the Glasgow Chamber of Commerce. Despite their titles, neither the *Glasgow Herald* or its predecessor has ever restricted itself to Glasgow news or coverage. The *Glasgow Advertiser* was proud of the speed with which it published parliamentary news from London and had the distinction of printing an early scoop, details of the Treaty of Versailles (1783), which gave America its official independence. In modern times the *Herald* enjoys a wide circulation throughout the populous Strathclyde Region and other parts of Scotland. The *Glasgow Herald* and its sister paper, the *Evening Times*, are now printed and published by George Outram & Co.: the George Outram concerned was editor of the paper from 1837 until 1856, one of 18 editors to date, all of whom have made their mark on the newspaper and helped to preserve its editorial independence.

Glastonbury Thorn legend *See* Joseph of Arimathea.

GLAMIS CASTLE *Ancestral home of the Earls of Strathmore, Tayside. The present castle incorporates the remains of a much older stronghold dating back to the early 14th century.*

GLC (Greater London Council) *See* Greater London.

Glencoe, massacre of (13 February 1692) The killing of 38 members of the Macdonald clan in the pass of Glencoe, in the Scottish *Highlands. In an attempt to bring to an end the activities of Jacobite sympathizers after the *Glorious Revolution (1688; *see also* Jacobite rebellions), William III ordered all the Scottish clan chiefs (*see* clans) to swear an oath of allegiance to him, setting a deadline of 1 January 1692. The accidental failure of Macdonald of Glencoe, whose men were notorious Jacobites and troublemakers, to swear the oath in time resulted in the authorization of a punitive expedition, led by Captain Robert Campbell of Glenlyon (whose property had suffered badly at the hands of Glencoe men), to make an example of them. Having accepted the hospitality of the Macdonalds, the guests turned on their hosts after dark and murdered all they could find, including the chief, the survivors fleeing into the surrounding wilds to suffer the rigours of the Highland winter.

Glorious Revolution (1688) The largely peaceful replacement of King James II (r. 1685–88) by his daughter Mary II (r. 1689–94) and her husband William III (r. 1689–1702), ruler of the Netherlands. James fled the country without offering resistance,

throwing the Great Seal of England into the Thames in a futile attempt to paralyse government. His efforts to re-establish himself in Ireland were crushed at the battle of the Boyne (1690; *see* Jacobite rebellions; battle of the Boyne celebrations). This marked the definite failure of James to establish absolute monarchy and Roman Catholicism in Britain. The Bill of Rights (1689) curtailed the *royal prerogative, abolishing the power to suspend laws and severely limiting that to exempt individuals; it also declared illegal several of James's most objectionable acts, such as levying money without the consent of Parliament and maintaining a standing army in peacetime. The Bill of Rights is still regarded as one of the foundations of British liberty.

Historically, the Glorious Revolution might be regarded as a continuation of the Exclusion Crisis (1678–81), when strenuous but unsuccessful efforts had been made to debar James from succeeding his brother Charles II, because of his adherence to Roman Catholicism. After his accession, the rebellion of the Duke of Monmouth (an illegitimate son of Charles II, who would have succeeded had James been excluded), was easily put down (*see* Sedgemoor, battle of). However, James quickly alienated his subjects by his high-handed methods and by his advancement of Catholics. In 1688 virtually all political factions were united against him. After his removal from the throne, and once the memory of his reign had receded, many consciences were troubled at the deposition of an anointed monarch, and supporters of the Stuart line, the Jacobites, were a significant political force under Queen Anne (r. 1702–14). Their hopes of returning a Stuart monarch to the throne were effectively dashed with the accession of George I (1714) and the failure of the rebellion in favour of James's son (the Old Pretender) the following year.

Glyndebourne An estate near Lewes on the Sussex Downs, where an annual international opera festival takes place from May to early August. The Glyndebourne Festival Opera was founded by the estate's owner John Christie (1882–1962) in 1934, inspired by his wife, the soprano Audrey Mildmay. The opening productions were both works by Mozart – *The Marriage of Figaro* and *Così fan tutte* – and since then Glyndebourne has been devoted mainly to Mozart operas, although other operas, including works by Janáček and Hans Werner Henze, are continually added to the repertoire. The high standard of the performances owes something to the long rehearsal time, which was made possible in the festival's early days by Christie's personal fortune. Since 1954 the Glyndebourne Arts Trust has held financial responsibility for the festival. Fritz Busch was Glyndebourne's first musical director, with Carl Ebert its stage director and Rudolf Bing its manager. The first resident orchestra was the London Symphony Orchestra, which was succeeded by the Royal Philharmonic Orchestra and then by the London Philharmonic Orchestra. One of the main attractions of an evening at Glyndebourne is the long break for supper, during which visitors may stroll or picnic in the splendid grounds. In fine weather members of the orchestra traditionally play croquet on the lawn during the break. Glyndebourne makes its own recordings and has a touring company.

Godiva, Lady The wife of Leofric, Earl of Mercia, a powerful lord during the reigns of Cnut (1017–35) and Edward the Confessor (1042–66). Her story is related by the chronicler Roger of Wendover (d. 1236) in the *Flowers of History*, who places it in the year 1057. Lady Godiva is alleged to have ridden naked through the streets of Coventry on market day in response to a challenge issued by her husband: he promised to lift his oppressive taxes on the people of Coventry, as requested by his wife, on condition that she perform this immodest act. Fortunately, Lady Godiva's long flowing hair concealed most of her body from the eyes of the onlookers. Later versions of the legend maintain that the inhabitants of the town were instructed to remain indoors behind shuttered windows on the appointed day; all complied except a certain citizen called Tom, who peeped through the window and was struck blind on the spot. This element of the legend may have been derived from a blank-eyed wooden statue, possibly of pagan origin but alleged to be an effigy of "**Peeping Tom**", that now stands in a precinct in Coventry. For many years Lady Godiva's historic ride was re-enacted by modestly clad young ladies at the Coventry fair; the tradition is now carried on by local beauty queens at Coventry's annual carnival. The existence of Leofric and his wife is well documented, but the legend itself is of doubtful authenticity and has been associated with fertility rites and other rituals.

GOG AND MAGOG *Statue of Gog, in the Guildhall, London.*

Gog and Magog The two survivors of a mythical race of giants, descended from the daughters of Diocletian, who inhabited England before the arrival of Brut (the Trojan Brutus), the legendary founder of the British race. According to legend, Gog and Magog were taken to London as prisoners of Brut, who had destroyed the remainder of their race. There they were forced to serve as porters at the gate of the royal palace. Two effigies of the giants, three metres (ten feet) in height, have stood in London's Guildhall, said to have been built upon the site of Brut's palace, since the reign of Henry V (1413–22) or earlier. The original statues were destroyed in the Fire of London in 1666 and their replacements (1708) were destroyed in a World War II air raid; a third pair were installed in 1953. Two druid oaks (*see* druids) near Glastonbury Tor also bear the names Gog and Magog.

In ancient mythology Gog and Magog were associated with a moon-worshipping cult, Magog being the mother goddess and Gog her husband or son. In the independent tradition of the New Testament book of *Revelation* and other apocalyptic literature, Gog and Magog are hostile powers. attendants of Satan the Antichrist.

Gold Stick A post (formally, Gold Stick-in-Waiting) in the royal household whose incumbent acts as honorific bodyguard to the sovereign on routine ceremonial occasions, such as the state opening of Parliament. The post is held by two men who serve alternate months, only acting together for major state ceremonies. They are the colonels of the two *Household Cavalry regiments (the Life Guards and the Blues and Royals), and the name Gold Stick derives from the ebony stave or truncheon, surmounted by a gold head stamped with the royal cypher and crown, which the officer carries. The post was created in 1528, when it was decreed that Gold Stick should "wait next to His Majesty's person before all others". In 1678, at the time of the Popish Plot panic when there were fears for the king's safety, Charles II ordered that Gold Stick should be selected from "one of the King's captains".

In Scotland Gold Stick is the captain-general of the Royal Company of Archers. Gold Stick's deputies are known as Silver Sticks; in England this post is held by the lieutenant-colonel commanding the Household Cavalry and in Scotland by the second-in-command of the Royal Company of Archers.

golf A popular club-and-ball game played by millions of amateurs around the world, which also has a professional competition structure. Players attempt to hit their ball from a fixed starting point (the "tee") into a small hole in the ground 90–550 metres (100–600 yards) away in as few shots as possible. Most golf courses consist of 18 such holes with varying natural and man-made hazards. The earliest records of a recognizably similar game played in Holland date from 1296. By the 15th century it was widely played there and was introduced into eastern Scotland by Dutch traders. The earliest surviving written rules date from 1754, compiled at St Andrews for the club's inaugural competition. This game was played mainly with wooden clubs, but early in the 17th century the wooden ball was replaced by one known as a "feathery", which was hand-made from leather and stuffed with feathers. It was expensive and few could afford to play until the arrival in 1848 of the cheaper "guttie" made from a rubbery substance called gutta-percha. Golf clubs opened all over the country and the Empire and the sport spread to the USA in the 1880s. Golf matches were usually individual challenges with considerable betting interest until 1860, when the first Open Championship took place at Prestwick in Scotland. In 1885 the British Amateur Championship began and in 1894 the United States Golf Association was founded, which led to the first US Open and US Amateur Championships a year later. The first Ladies Championship was held in 1893. Many clubs were founded around the world over the next 30 years; in 1922 the first efforts were made to standardize the ball. The two famous team matches between the USA and Great Britain began in the 1920s – the Walker Cup (amateurs) in 1922 and the Ryder Cup (professionals) in 1927, now contested between the USA and Europe. In 1951 the Royal and Ancient Golf Club of St Andrews and the United States Golf Association, the governing bodies of golf on either side of the

Atlantic, cooperated to standardize the rules of the game.

Tournaments are played on either a strokeplay or a matchplay basis. In strokeplay each golfer records the exact number of shots taken to get round the course one or more times and the one with the lowest score wins. Most professional tournaments are over four rounds. In matchplay each hole is contested individually, and is won by the player taking the fewest shots, or "halved" if both take the same. The winner of the match is the player to take the greater number of holes.

As a guide for competitors, each hole is given a par figure, the number of shots which a good golfer should take to complete the hole. If a hole is rated a par four and a golfer gets down in three shots, or one under par, he is said to have scored a "birdie"; should he do so in two shots less than par he has scored an "eagle", and in three less, an "albatross". One shot over par is a "bogey". Golfers can acquire a "handicap", designed to enable players of different abilities to play together, or to measure their performances against par. A poor player will receive several shots' advantage each round from a good player; the exact number will depend on the course and the differential between them. Professionals are "scratch" golfers, which means they have a handicap of zero and are expected to go round a course in par. Golf can be an expensive game to play: good quality clubs are costly, the membership fees of golf clubs are frequently high, and the number of members often strictly limited. However, there are municipal golf courses (sometimes only nine holes) and practice driving ranges, which charge much less for their use. The beauty and quality of famous courses like Muirfield, St Andrews, Birkdale, and Wentworth are well known, but there are now many new well-designed courses of great character.

Gordonstoun A *public school on the Moray Firth in northeast Scotland. Gordonstoun was founded by the German educationalist Kurt Hahn (1886–1974) after his flight from Nazi Germany in 1933 and he remained its headmaster until his retirement in 1953. Hahn's educational theories emphasized the development of character, in particular the qualities of initiative and leadership through response to mental and physical challenges. The position of Gordonstoun House, a historic mansion set in a 120-hectare (300-acre) estate, allows pupils to participate in a variety of demanding outdoor activities: skiing and expeditions in the Cairngorms, canoeing and sailing on the Moray Firth, and gliding. The school has around 450 pupils and became fully coeducational in 1972. In the 1960s the Queen's sons, following in the footsteps of their father, were educated there.

GP (General Practitioner) A nonspecialist doctor who provides primary medical care to local patients. Although a small number of GPs are engaged exclusively in private practice, the vast majority, some 24,500, operate within the framework of the *National Health Service. Under the terms of that contract GPs are obliged to "provide all necessary and appropriate personal medical services" to the patients on their list and to refer patients to other NHS facilities as necessary. Most are in partnerships of two or usually more doctors, enabling the group to provide cover during holidays or illness. GPs receive fees made up of a capitation fee for each patient on their list and a basic practice allowance, plus various other payments to cover special services such as family planning, vaccinations, and "out of hours" working.

grammar school *See* state education.

Grand Almoner An hereditary office of the royal household, the Royal Almonry, which administers the monarch's charitable donations. The duties date from Richard I's reign when they entailed giving leftovers from the king's table to the poor, visiting the sick, reminding the king to give alms, and distributing to the poor the proceeds from the sale of the king's cast-off raiments. Medieval Grand Almoners had jurisdiction over offending paupers and lepers, even to the extent of being able to sentence them to death in certain circumstances. Later the Grand Almoner was supposed to hand out the blue cloth on which the sovereign had walked in Westminster Abbey during his coronation, and to collect money on a silver plate, which he was permitted to keep.

The post was traditionally held by the owners of the barony of Bedford, originally the Beauchamp family, but when the baronial lands became divided between a number of families, there were several claimants to the office. Since the coronation of James I it has become increasingly identified with the Cecil Earls and Marquesses of Exeter.

Grand Committees, Scottish and Welsh Committees established by the House of Commons to consider matters relating exclusively to Scotland and Wales. The Scottish Grand Committee consists of the 72 members for Scottish constituencies, together with between 10 and 15 other members to assist the political balance. Apart from debating Scottish matters that may be referred to it, the Committee may take the second reading stage of Bills certified by the Speaker as relating exclusively to Scotland, provided the House of Commons agrees to this.

The Welsh Grand Committee consists of the 38 members for Welsh constituencies and up to 5 others, and it has deliberative powers only.

Grand Falconer An hereditary post whose holder was formerly responsible for the sovereign's mews (where hawks were mewed, or kept) at Charing Cross. The present Grand Falconer is the Duke of St Albans whose family have held the post since 1688 (when the title was Master Falconer). The Grand Falconer shared with the royal family the exclusive privilege of being allowed to drive down Birdcage Walk (near Buckingham Palace) until 1828, when the thoroughfare was opened to the public.

Grand National Steeplechase The most famous English steeplechase and perhaps the most famous horse race in the world, watched on television by about 700 million people. Many people who otherwise have no interest in horse racing watch and bet on the Grand National. It takes place each year in March or April on the Saturday of the spring meeting at Aintree racecourse, near Liverpool. It is open to horses of six or more years, and they carry between 63 and 76 kilograms (10 and 12 stones) in weight according to a handicap system. The course is 7.2 kilometres (4.5 miles) long with 30 fences, 14 of which are jumped twice. The names of the most difficult jumps are well known: Becher's Brook, Valentine's Brook, the Chair, and the Canal Turn. Such is the gruelling nature of the race for both horse and jockey that many fail to complete the course.

The race was first held in 1836 when it was won by Captain Becher riding The Duke. In 1839, when it was first called the Grand National and run at Aintree, the unfortunate Becher fell at the fence that now bears his name. Seven horses have won the race more than once, but only two in the modern period – Reynoldstown in 1935 and 1936, and Red Rum in 1973, 1974, and 1977, the only horse to win three times. The race has produced many surprising results. In 1956 the Queen's horse Devon Lock fell on flat ground after the last fence, only 45 metres (49 yards) from the finish, to leave ESB the winner. In 1967 a loose horse careering across the face of a fence brought all the runners to a halt except one: Foinavon, which had been so far behind that it was unaffected by the incident, was able to pass the rest, establish an unbeatable lead, and win at odds of 100 to 1. In 1973 the favourite, Crisp, had led all the way and was some 15 lengths ahead at the last fence, but was so tired that the long run to the finish proved too much for him and Red Rum caught him at the line. The National was thought for many years to be too arduous a race for women; however, in 1977 Charlotte Brew became the first woman to enter, although no women have yet come near to winning. History was

GRAND NATIONAL STEEPLECHASE *The most gruelling test of horse and jockey.*

185

made in 1983 when Jenny Pitman became the first woman to train a National winner, Corbière.

In 1983 the future of the Grand National was in doubt when the owner of Aintree racecourse decided to sell it, possibly for commercial development. Following an appeal for money the course was bought by the *Jockey Club. The immediate future of the race and its continued ability to attract top horses and jockeys is assured by generous commercial sponsorship.

Gray's Inn   *See* Inns of Court.

Greater London   An area of local government constituted by the London Government Act 1963 and consisting of the *City of London, the Inner and Middle Temples (*see* Inns of Court), and 32 London *boroughs (12 inner and 20 outer boroughs). The boroughs cover not only the administrative county of London that existed previously under the London County Council, but also most of Middlesex, and parts of Kent, Surrey, Essex, and Hertfordshire. There is a council for each borough, which is elected every four years and is headed by a mayor and his deputy. The 1963 Act distributed most local government functions in Greater London between the borough councils (plus the corresponding body in the *City, the Court of Common Council) and the GLC (Greater London Council) which it established at County Hall. It gave the borough councils responsibility for housing and personal social services and the GLC responsibility for fire and ambulance services; town and country planning functions were divided between the two. Education was made a borough responsibility in the outer boroughs, but for the inner boroughs the Act established a single and virtually autonomous body, the Inner London Education Authority (ILEA). The Local Government Act 1985 provided for the abolition of the GLC in April 1986. Its functions were transferred to the borough councils, to joint boards established by the borough councils, and to government appointed *quangos. The ILEA is to continue in existence but is subject to review.

Great Exhibition   An industrial exhibition, a modern descendant of the medieval trade fairs, held in London from 1 May to 11 October 1851. "The Great Exhibition of the Works of Industry of all Nations, 1851" was inspired by Henry Cole (1808–82) and Prince Albert. To house the exhibition, Joseph Paxton (1801–65) designed an enormous glass building – dubbed "Crystal Palace" by *Punch* magazine in 1850 – covering 8 hectares (19 acres) of the site on the south side of Hyde Park. It was the world's first iron-framed and prefabricated building, and served to illustrate Britain's industrial supremacy. Over six million visitors saw the 100,000 objects, including engines, textiles, glass, cutlery, and jewels, shown by 7381 British and 6556 foreign exhibitors. The Crystal Palace was later re-erected at Sydenham, south London, where it was destroyed by fire in 1936. The gate money from the Great Exhibition, £356,000, was used to purchase 35 hectares (87 acres) in South Kensington on which a museum and college complex was built (*see* Science Museum; Victoria and Albert Museum; Imperial College of Science and Technology).

Great Famine (1845–48)   *See* Irish nationalism.

great officers of state   Holders of posts surviving from a time when the sovereign was effective head of government and the sovereign's directly appointed servants had an executive role. Subsequently such offices became hereditary. The great officers of state number seven. In order of precedence they are the *Lord High Steward, *Lord Chancellor, *Lord President of the Council, *Lord Privy Seal, *Lord Great Chamberlain, *Lord High Constable, and the *Earl Marshal. The second, third, and fourth of these are now political offices and their incumbents are members of the government.

Great Plague (1665–66)   The last major outbreak in England of bubonic plague, which had recurred at intervals since the *Black Death (1348). Beginning in April 1665, it reached its peak in September, and largely died out by the end of 1666. Its chief centre was London, where 68,576 people were recorded as victims, though the true total was probably nearer 100,000. All who could, fled the city, as crude countermeasures were largely ineffec-

GREAT EXHIBITION *This etching by Cruikshank shows people flocking from all over the world to this showpiece of Victorian Britain.*

tive, and many bodies were inadequately buried or rotted in the streets. Samuel Pepys, who remained in London throughout, recorded a graphic description of the plague's progress in his diary. Another badly affected area was Cambridge, where the university was closed; and at Eyam in Derbyshire, the villagers went into voluntary quarantine on discovering they had the plague, and all but two died.

Great Reform Act (1832) The Representation of the People Act 1832, which was the first comprehensive reform of the franchise and composition of the *House of Commons. Until this time, the medieval system had re-

mained largely unaltered; each county sent two "knights of the shire" and each town with a royal charter two "burgesses" to represent them in Parliament, as they had done since 1295. There were some exceptions that had grown up over the years: for example, Yorkshire and the City of London returned four MPs, Oxford and Cambridge universities sent two each, the Welsh counties and some boroughs sent only one, and the arrangements for Scotland and Ireland were contrived to suit the Acts of Union, which gave them a total 45 and 100 MPs respectively. By 1832 this system had become hopelessly unrelated to the distri-

GREAT REFORM ACT   *A typical piece of reform propaganda: King William IV floats with leading Whig and Radical politicians on clouds of glory, while down below the British lion, supported by Britannia, sends the Tories flying.*

bution of wealth, largely as a result of the *industrial revolution and the consequent shift of population from the shires to the towns. Over half the towns represented in Parliament at the

beginning of the 19th century had been represented under Edward I (r. 1272–1307); the last addition had been Durham in 1675. As a result the new industrial centres, such as

Manchester and Birmingham, were unrepresented in Parliament, while many small Cornish villages sent two members each. Some boroughs, known as "rotten boroughs", had decayed to the point of absurdity. The two most notorious were Old Sarum (near Salisbury, which had been deserted since the Middle Ages) and Dunwich, Suffolk (which had fallen into the North Sea through land erosion, but still had 30 freemen electors). Moreover, each borough had its own peculiar franchise qualification; a few allowed nearly all adult men to vote, many more had some restrictive qualifications (such as owning property), and some (the "nomination boroughs") were in the hands of small cliques, often dominated by a single man. In the shires the franchise was uniform; in England and Wales freeholders of land worth 40 shillings per year (as established in 1430) were allowed to vote, although the distribution of seats did not reflect the distribution of the population or wealth.

These idiosyncrasies had been criticized since the 17th century and reform began to be discussed seriously in the late 18th century as part of a wider movement to modernize the structure of Parliament. Pressure for reform came both from outside the political establishment and from some of those within it. Those outside felt excluded and those within were convinced that the worst anomalies could be removed without affecting their "legitimate" influence, and indeed should be, to ensure its continued acceptability. In 1785 William Pitt, then Prime Minister, had proposed a modest measure. The arguments against change were twofold. First, the existing system produced good government and no reform based on untested premises could hope to match the experience of centuries. It would upset the balance of the constitution as established by the *Glorious Revolution (1688) and could well result in disorder and revolution. Even the system's outdated aspects had their practical uses; nomination boroughs, for example, allowed their patrons to advance such young men of talent as William Pitt the Elder (MP for Old Sarum). Secondly, a vote was regarded as a piece of property and was related to a property qualification, so that any altera-tion in the value of a vote was an attack on legitimate interests.

The fear of radicalism generated by the French Revolution in the 1790s froze all attempts at reform for 30 years. The thaw began in the 1820s, although reform of Parliament, the central symbol of the old order, seemed imprudent to many. However, the breakup of the dominant government party after 1827 and the death of George IV in 1830, allowed a Whig government under Earl Grey to be formed in 1830. Grey had been an advocate of parliamentary reform since the 1790s and his government, spurred by its own weakness and the need to produce a rallying call, introduced a Reform Bill in 1831. This measure required three attempts to pass through Parliament; but under unprecedented pressure by popular feeling, the opposition gave way. In the general election of 1831 a strongly proreform Commons was returned. In 1831 and 1832 country houses were fortified and armed with cannon for the first time since the *Civil War against the threat of mob violence. The climax came in May 1832, when the Duke of Wellington failed to form an antireform government; most members of the House of Lords then dropped their opposition, allowing the third Bill to pass rather than oblige the king to create sufficient proreform peers to force it through, as Grey had demanded. The Bill received the royal assent on 7 June 1832.

The final Act was very moderate. In the distribution of seats it made adjustments, removed the worst abuses, but still retained wide variations. The more radical reforms suggested from outside Parliament, such as equal electoral districts, were resisted. The franchise was made uniform and some new classes of qualification introduced. The electorate approximately doubled to about 800,000, out of a population of about 24 million. (In Scotland, where the old system had been most oligarchic, the increase was spectacular, from about 4000 to 65,000.) The Act's greatest significance was that it had been passed at all. It established the principle that Parliament could reform itself when necessary and that existing vested interests could be overriden to that end. The second Reform Act (1867) destroyed any idea that 1832 was a once-and-for-all measure (as many of its supporters had suggested). Since then, the franchise has been progressively enlarged to include almost all adults (*see* House of Commons); moreover, the distribution of seats is now adjusted on a regular basis to take account of population changes.

Great Seal   *See* Lord (High) Chancellor.

green belt   A zone of open land surrounding a town or city on which building is prohibited. The purpose of the green belt is to prevent the uncontrolled spread of towns and the ribbon development along arterial roads that characterized suburban development in the 1920s and 1930s. The *garden cities, pioneered by Sir Ebenezer Howard at the beginning of the 20th century, provided the first practical application of a green belt, but it was not until the London County Council's work in the 1930s that London acquired its present green belt, formalized in the Green Belt Act 1938 and the subsequent Town and Country Planning Act 1947. However, since the war it has become apparent that although the concept has obvious merits, it also has serious shortcomings, perhaps the most important of which is that it confines the poorer sections of the community within an urban area of high population density, enabling the privileged members of the community to spread themselves within the green belt itself. As the demand for development land increases, particularly in southeast England, the existence of the green belt around London has created a problem for planners seeking new sites. Market towns and villages in the region have become the subjects of rapid peripheral expansion, often losing something of their character and quality of life in the process. Alternatively, new "greenfield" sites have been developed as new towns. However, neither of these solutions is considered adequate to cope with the projected expansion of population and industry by the end of the century, and many planners feel that the green belt should be reviewed.

Green Man   (Jack-in-the-Green)   A central character of spring and summer festivals; the bringer of luck and plenty. The Green Man's costume consists of a wickerwork cage, which completely covers the head and body, woven with branches, flowers, leaves, and other greenery. In the 19th century the Green Man was a prominent figure in the *May Day processions of chimney sweeps in London and other towns and cities; he still appears in certain May Day festivities, such as Knutsford's Royal May Day, and is depicted on numerous inn signs across the country. Similar figures appear in the folklore of other European countries; these and the Green Man himself may be relics of some form of tree-worship, possibly personifications of ancient tree spirits.

green paper   *See* command papers.

Greenwich   A London borough, lying on the south bank of the River Thames. Its name is derived from Anglo-Saxon and means "green village", or possibly, "village on the green". Greenwich Park was established in 1433, following the construction, by Humphrey, Duke of Gloucester, of a house that was the forerunner of Greenwich Palace. This palace became a favourite residence of the Tudors, Henry VIII, Mary I, and Elizabeth I all being born there. In the 17th century it fell into disrepair and was demolished in 1694 to make way for the Royal Naval College, designed by Sir Christopher Wren. In 1675 the foundation of the Royal Observatory (*see* Royal Greenwich Observatory), based in Greenwich until 1958, was laid; it is now part of the *National Maritime Museum. Until the 19th century Greenwich was the British navy's chief dockyard, but in recent years more diverse industries have become established there.

At Greenwich Pier the tea clipper *Cutty Sark* (built in 1869) is moored, alongside *Gypsy Moth IV*, the boat in which Sir Francis Chichester became the first man to sail around the world single-handed (1966–67).

Grenadier Guards   *See* Household Division.

Gretna Green   A Scottish border town where for many years young lovers from England fled to take advantage of the easier conditions of Scottish law and marry without parental consent. The ceremony required only a declaration in front of two witnesses and was performed in various local inns, at Gretna

Hall, and above all at the local smithy, where the famous "wedding anvil" is still on display. The law was changed in 1856 to require a three weeks' residence qualification for at least one of the parties and, in 1940, marriage by declaration was finally made illegal.

greyhound racing Racing in which greyhounds pursue a mechanical "hare" around an oval-shaped track. The sport evolved from rural hare coursing in which specially trained dogs chased hares over fields and rough country. This was not possible in built-up areas where enclosed courses were clearly necessary. The first recorded race in Britain took place in Hendon, north London, on 11 September 1876, with the hounds chasing the hare over a straight course 366 metres (400 yards) long. The event was enthusiastically received, but its appeal was shortlived as a straight track tested only the speed and not the skill of the dogs. Two modifications encouraged the growth of the sport: the circular track, and the introduction of betting at meetings. The former appeared in the USA around the turn of the century and the first such track was built in England in 1926 at Bellevue, Manchester, by Brigadier-General Alfred Critchley (1890–1964). To be successful on a course that includes curves and bends, a dog needs not only speed but also track craft, experience, and native ability. Greyhound racing rapidly became popular, and within a year of the Bellevue track opening, three more were built in London, at the White City, Harringay, and Wembley. In 1928 the National Greyhound Racing Club was formed to regulate the sport, which was liable to all manner of abuses, notably doping and substitution. The sport became something of a craze in Britain immediately after World War II, and although its popularity has declined, it retains a considerable following. There are a number of classic races, the best-known being the Greyhound Derby, run over 480 metres (525 yards) at the White City Stadium in west London every year from 1928 until 1984, when the White City was closed for demolition and the race was moved to Wimbledon Stadium. Mick the Miller, perhaps the most famous greyhound of all time, won the race in 1929 and 1930; he can now be seen preserved in the Natural History Museum in Kensington, west London.

grouse shooting A form of game shooting requiring great skill by the marksmen. The red grouse is native to the British Isles and found on high moorland, particularly in the north of England and Scotland. Grouse shooting became popular in the 1850s and 1860s due to the invention and subsequent improvement of the breechloading gun, and the growth of railways, enabling sportsmen to travel to Scotland from London in just a few hours. By the 1890s shooting parties were highly fashionable and often extravagant affairs sometimes patronized by the Prince and Princess of Wales (subsequently King Edward VII and Queen Alexandra).

Grouse shooting begins each year on 12 August, "the Glorious Twelfth", and the season lasts for four months. Informal shooting by one or two guns may be carried out by "walking-up" with a pointer dog, but the rewards are usually small. Nearly all grouse shooting takes place on formal shoots by the method known as "driving". A line of eight or ten grouse butts are constructed from stone and turf at intervals of 27–37 metres (30–40 yards) on a hillside, each butt occupied by a marksman and a loader. A party of beaters and specially trained dogs makes its way towards the butts driving the grouse from their cover and into the air. Grouse fly low and fast with a swerving flight, which makes them hard to hit. The most common type of gun is a 12-bore shotgun although a lighter 16- or 20-bore is often used instead. Part of the excitement lies in the unpredictable nature of the sport: not even the best gamekeeper will make confident predictions on the likely yield of a particular moor, however good or bad the previous season.

guinea An English gold coin bearing an impression of an elephant, first coined in 1663 from gold imported by trading companies from the coast of Guinea. In 1663 it was valued at 20 shillings, but for the next 148 years its value varied between 20 and 30 shillings. In 1811 the value was fixed at 21 shillings until 1817, when guineas ceased to be coined. The use of the term continued, however, by some

GROUSE SHOOTING *The birds, driven by the beater, fly low over the heather towards the butts, where the marksmen take aim.*

professional people, especially doctors, who continued to bill their clients in guineas until decimalization in 1971 when the term dropped from use.

Guinness Book of Records An annual reference book of facts and figures, first published in 1955. Its publishers, Guinness Superlatives, are a subsidiary of the well-known Irish brewery company. The book was conceived and compiled by twin brothers Ross (1925–75) and Norris (1925–) McWhirter, who had made their names as athletes and sports commentators. They produced it together until Ross was murdered by Irish terrorists. The book, giving details of almost every conceivable record – serious, sporting, or frivolous – was an immediate success, reaching five editions in its first year. By 1983 it was reckoned to have sold 48 million copies worldwide and had appeared in 189 editions in 24 languages, with people thinking up ever more bizarre stunts and competitions in order to have an entry in a book that has become a household name.

Gurkhas, Brigade of A division of the British army, recruited from the Gurkha ruling caste of Nepal. Renowned for their endurance and skill in battle, the Gurkhas were first recruited for the British army in 1815 and have long been regarded as its finest overseas troops. They were organized into separately numbered regiments after the Indian Mutiny and were divided between Britain and India upon Indian independence in 1947. Their motto is "Better to die than to live a coward".

Guy Fawkes Day An annual festivity celebrated by firework displays and bonfires followed by the burning of an effigy of Guy Fawkes. On 5 November each year the British remember the frustration of an attempt to blow up their Parliament nearly 400 years ago. Notwithstanding the celebrations, the story is a grim one. In 1605 a group of Roman Catholics felt that James I and his government were being increasingly and unacceptably oppressive to their coreligionists. They therefore resolved to blow up the Houses of Parliament, intending to destroy the buildings, the king,

GUY FAWKES DAY *The Gunpowder Plot conspirators, by an unknown artist, 1605.*

and most of his ministers in one devastating explosion. The instigator of the plot, Robert Catesby, believing that the assistance of a trained soldier to handle the explosives would be advisable, sent a special messenger to the Netherlands to enlist the help of a certain Guy Fawkes, a native of York, known to be a zealous Catholic convert. Fawkes was so appalled at conditions in Protestant England that he was then serving in the Spanish army. With apparently only the haziest notion of what was involved, Fawkes joined the conspiracy. The plotters rented a cellar below the Houses of Parliament and Fawkes managed to fill it with 30 barrels of gunpowder, which he concealed beneath coal and wood. However, as a result of an anonymous letter to Lord Monteagle, a relative of one of the conspirators, warning him not to attend Parliament on 5 November, the plot was discovered. Catesby was killed resisting arrest and Fawkes was captured. He was tortured, and with those of his fellows who had not been killed sword in hand, was executed in front of the Houses of Parliament on 27 January 1606, before a large crowd.

gymkhana An event at which there are various contests and activities on horseback, such as *show jumping, dressage, and horse trials. Gymkhanas were first held by the British army in India in the 19th century. Many gymkhanas in England are run by the Pony Club, which was founded in 1929 to promote good horsemanship among young people. The premier trophy, the Prince Philip Cup, has been awarded for the Pony Club gymkhana championship since 1957.

Gypsies A nomadic people found in every part of Europe, including Britain and Ireland. Gypsies are so called because they were originally believed to be "Egyptians". In fact, as has been ascertained from a study of their language (*see* Romany), they are of north Indian origin. They were first recorded in Britain around 1450. From their first arrival, they have been treated as a social nuisance and subjected to various forms of persecution. From time to time attempts have been made to persuade or force them – always unsuccessfully – to abandon their itinerant life style and settle in one place. In the 20th century they have exchanged horse-drawn caravans for ones drawn by lorries and cars, and they are to be found camped by the roadside or on waste ground. Otherwise little has changed. There are approximately 80,000 Gypsies in Britain today. Common occupations include working on fairgrounds and dealing in scrap metal and junk, as well as more traditional activities, such as selling clothes pegs and dealing in horses. The traditional Gypsy connection with clairvoyance is also assiduously maintained.

H

habeas corpus A writ for securing the prompt release of any person who is being unlawfully deprived of his freedom. It is a remedy of great antiquity (though not, as sometimes suggested, a child of Magna Carta) and was originally obtained by petitioning the Crown. Since 1679 it has been much regulated and strengthened by Acts of Parliament, and is now applied for to the *Divisional Court of the Queen's Bench Division of the High Court (where it takes priority over all other business) or, if the Divisional Court is not sitting, to any judge of the High Court, wherever available (even at his home if necessary).

Habeas corpus covers any detention, even if ostensibly official, that is invalid because of some jurisdictional or other irregularity. The applicant might be a convicted prisoner, or in custody pending trial, extradition, or deportation, or held as a mental patient. It also covers detention of a private character: for example, in 1772 the writ led to the freeing of a slave imported into England. The Latin name of the writ ("you have the body") is taken from its wording, commanding the person exercising custody to produce the detainee in court immediately, so that his case may be investigated. The writ is not actually issued nowadays, nor is the body produced. The applicant files an affidavit setting out the circumstances of the detention. If this establishes a prima facie case of illegality, the custodian is summoned to attend and show why the writ should not be issued; and if he fails to do so at this preliminary stage, a simple order is made for immediate release.

Habeas corpus is available in the courts in Northern Ireland, but has no direct counterpart in Scots law.

Hadrian's Wall A complex of fortifications built in northern England by the Roman emperor Hadrian (r. 117–38 AD). It stretches for 116 kilometres (72 miles) coast to coast from Wallsend near Newcastle upon Tyne to Bowness-on-Solway, and is the most enduring monument of *Roman Britain. After visiting Britain in 122 AD, Hadrian decided to strengthen the northern border that had been established in the time of Trajan (r. 98–117 AD) along a road, now known as the Stanegate, that ran from Carlisle to Newborough (and perhaps originally continued as far as Corbridge), which was defended by stone forts. Hadrian's new fortification, a few miles to the north of the Stanegate, consisted of six principal parts: a stone wall with a large ditch to the north formed the main part, and forts, milecastles, and turrets were built solid with this wall to accommodate the garrison; an earthwork, now known as the *vallum*, ran along the south side of the wall, marking the military zone. Roads ran on either side, forts and milecastles extended down the Cumbrian coast, and there were some outpost forts (e.g. Bewcastle) for extra defence. Whether the wall was primarily intended or used for offensive or defensive purposes is not clear, for documentary evidence is scanty.

Today the wall is still being excavated and together with its on-site museums is a popular tourist attraction. The most famous fort is at Housesteads, known to the Romans as Vercovicium ("hilly place"), where one can visit the military headquarters, or *principia*, granaries, barracks, a hospital, and well-preserved gateways that still show ruts from Roman cartwheels. Outside Housesteads are the remains of a large *vicus*, or civilian settlement. At South Shields a luxurious residence that probably belonged to the regional commander has recently been uncovered; a wooden sewing kit with needles still in place was found at Carlisle.

Hadrian's Wall has suffered great damage in the 14 centuries following the departure of the Romans. It has been plundered, covered by roads and partly destroyed by a quarry, though most of the destruction has been wrought by farmers since the 18th century. A plan to save it from erosion caused by tourists' feet, especially at Housesteads, involves a reconstruction, called Walltown, with replicas of parts of the wall and towers, as well as the development of other sites of interest to draw visitors to less endangered parts of the wall.

HADRIAN'S WALL *A section of the wall near Housesteads Fort, Northumberland, an enduring monument to 400 years of Roman occupation.*

haggis A Scottish dish consisting of a sheep's stomach stuffed with offal, suet, oatmeal, and seasonings, which is boiled for three or four hours and traditionally served with "neeps" (turnips) and "taties" (potatoes). A round sausage similar to haggis was enjoyed by the ancient Greeks and Romans; the Scottish haggis dates back to primitive times and is a central feature of Burns Night and Hogmanay banquets. Acclaimed by Burns as "great chieftain o' the puddin'-race", haggis remains a popular national dish and an important element of the tourist trade in Scotland.

Hallé Orchestra An orchestra based in Manchester. The Hallé originated in the weekly concerts conducted from 1857 in the Free Trade Hall, Manchester, by Charles Hallé (1819–95). Born Karl Halle in Westphalia, he became a pianist and conductor, and settled in Manchester in 1848. For 37 years Hallé conducted almost every concert given by his orchestra, often also performing in piano concertos. His policy of making available a large number of cheap seats to attract a wider public to his concerts came to be copied by other orchestras. During World War I Thomas Beecham (1879–1961) frequently conducted the Hallé, and from 1920 to 1933 its principal

conductor was the Irish composer Hamilton Harty (1879–1941). In the 20th century the Hallé has been identified above all with John Barbirolli (1899–1970), its conductor from 1943 until his death. Its principal conductor is at present Stanislaw Skrowaczewski (1923–   ).

Hallowe'en (All Hallows Eve) An annual festivity that takes place on 31 October, the eve of All Saints' Day. Hallowe'en has its roots in the pagan Celtic festival of Samhain: 31 October was the New Year's Eve of the Celtic calendar and was traditionally celebrated with bonfires and animal sacrifices. It was also the day on which the spirits of the dead were believed to revisit their homes and spells were chanted to ward off evil in the year ahead: these elements of the pagan festival are perpetuated in some modern Hallow'en traditions, in association with the Christian celebration of All Souls' Day on 2 November.

Children throughout the country celebrate Hallowe'en by dressing up as witches or ghosts, carving turnip or pumpkin lanterns in the shape of hollow heads with grotesque expressions, or taking part in such party games as duck-apple or bob-apple, in which competitors have to snatch with their teeth at apples suspended on a string or floating in a bowl of water. (In the USA children go from house to house demanding "Trick or treat?": any occupant who does not provide a "treat", usually in the form of a handful of sweets, is liable to be punished with a practical joke. Attempts have been made to introduce this custom to Britain.) At Hinton St George in Somerset, the last Thursday in October, which sometimes coincides with Hallowe'en, is Punky Night. A procession of children and adults parade around the village carrying "punkies" (lanterns made from hollowed-out mangel-wurzels) and singing for candles and money. Alleged to have originated in a specific event of the Middle Ages, this tradition has also been associated with the pre-Reformation custom of "souling": singing and begging alms for the souls of the dead.

Hampton Court Palace A royal residence situated on the banks of the Thames, 15 miles southwest of London. Hampton Court Palace was a favourite residence of British monarchs for centuries. Cardinal Wolsey (Lord Chancellor 1515–29) built and lived in it, until his fall in 1529, when it became the home of the court of Henry VIII. The king enlarged the palace and laid out some fine gardens. His successors, Edward VI, Mary Tudor, and Elizabeth I, all lived at Hampton Court, making alterations and conducting both private and state affairs there. The Great Hall is the oldest surviving Elizabethan theatre in Britain and Henry's covered tennis court is still in use. Charles I (r. 1625–49) extended the gardens and greatly added to the art collection in the house. Later he was imprisoned there by Cromwell, who also lived at Hampton Court until his death in 1658. Charles II (r. 1660–85) restored the palace to its former splendour but changes in taste led to major alterations by Sir Christopher Wren after 1688. George II (r. 1727–60) was the last monarch to reside at the palace, the cost of living on such a large scale proving inappropriate for subsequent rulers. Queen Victoria declared Hampton Court open to the public in 1851.

Hansard The official report of the debates and proceedings of the House of Commons

HAMPTON COURT PALACE *Constructed by Cardinal Wolsey, and used as a royal residence until the 18th century.*

and House of Lords. The publication is named after the Hansard family of printers, Luke Hansard (1752–1828) having printed the *Journals of the House of Commons* from 1774 until his death. His son Thomas Curson Hansard (1776–1833) began printing the *Parliamentary Debates* (initially compiled from newspaper reports) in 1803. As the result of a libel action brought against the company in 1837, it was established by statute in 1840 that the printers of government reports should enjoy the same immunity from prosecution for libel as the MPs whose statements they publish. In 1889 the name Hansard disappeared from the reports when Thomas Curson Hansard II sold off his interest in the business. However, the *Official Parliamentary Debates* continued to be generally referred to as *Hansard*, and in 1943 the name was reinstated on the title page. Parliament, which had supported the publication since 1855, took it over in 1909. It is not, strictly speaking, a government publication: it comes under the control of a committee in consultation with the Speaker and Clerk of the House of Commons. During parliamentary sessions *Her Majesty's Stationery Office publishes *Hansard* daily.

Harlech castle A castle perched on cliffs some 60 metres (200 feet) above the sea, in the Welsh coastal resort of Harlech (*see* castles of Wales for map). It was built for Edward I in 1283–89 by James of St George, who was appointed Constable in 1290. The walls and four corner towers of the inner ward remain largely intact. The twin-towered gatehouse facing the landward side, built as a self-contained retreat for the Constable, still stands. In 1404 Harlech fell to the Welsh rebel Owain Glyndwr, who assumed the title "Prince of Wales" and used the castle as his headquarters, before losing it to English forces in 1409. The popular song "Men of Harlech" was inspired by the terrible privations endured by the Lancastrian supporter Dafydd ap Ieuan and his followers, who held Harlech during the Wars of the Roses in the 15th century. In the English Civil War, Harlech was the last royalist-held castle to fall to the roundheads – in 1647.

Harley Street A street in the Marylebone district of central London in and around which leading medical specialists have consulting rooms in which they see their private patients. Dating from 1753, it takes its name from Edward Harley, second Earl of Oxford, and was a fashionable residential street before the doctors began to move in around the mid-19th century. The Duchess of Wellington and W. E. Gladstone were among its notable residents. The whole area, including Harley Street, Wimpole Street, and Devonshire Place, houses London's most prestigious private medical services, which include doctors, dentists, pathological laboratories, and nursing homes.

Harrow School A *public school in northwest London. Its founder, John Lyon (d. 1592), was granted a charter by Elizabeth I in 1571, allowing him to establish a "free *grammar school". Under the founder's statutes, fee-paying "foreigners" were admitted as well as local boys, and from the 1660s the increasing number of such pupils ensured Harrow's prosperity. To encourage them, part of the school's endowment was devoted to the upkeep of the London road. Until 1837 Latin and Greek were the only subjects taught, but in that year mathematics was introduced, followed by modern languages in the 1850s, with English and history in the late 1860s.

The first building, Old School, was begun in 1608. On the panelling of the Fourth Form Room, which dates from 1611, are carved the names of many famous Harrovians, including Byron and R. B. Sheridan. Winston Churchill was one of seven Harrovian prime ministers. Most of the school buildings date from Harrow's revival in the latter part of the 19th century. Besides the usual playing fields and pool (known as Ducker), the grounds include a working farm and new sports complex. Highlights of the school year include the cricket match at *Lord's against *Eton. Among Harrow's sartorial peculiarities is the tradition of tail-coats as Sunday dress for senior boys.

harvest festival An annual celebration and religious service that takes place throughout the country in September or October, when the year's harvest of crops has been completed. Harvest home feasts have been held in rural areas throughout England's agricultural history, but it was only in the mid-19th century that the festival became a regular event in the Church's calendar, believed to have been instituted by the Cornish poet and vicar Robert Stephen Hawker in 1843. The modern religious festival takes place even in industrial towns and cities, where offerings of flowers, fruit, vegetables, and other fresh (or tinned) produce are brought to church for subsequent distribution to the needy or for some other worthy cause. At the church of St Martin-in-the-Fields in London, the *pearly kings and queens hold a special costermongers' harvest festival on the first Sunday in October. Rural churches are usually decked for the occasion with sheaves of corn, loaves of bread, and other harvest gifts; in these areas many other customs relating to earlier harvest home traditions still survive. At Richmond in Yorkshire, on a specified Saturday in September, the first farmer to arrive at the market cross with a sample of new wheat is awarded a bottle of wine by the mayor. In some districts the traditional corn dolly is still fashioned from stalks of straw plucked from the last sheaf of corn to be cut. A representation of the Roman corn goddess Ceres, the corn dolly was once given pride of place at the harvest home supper and was eventually buried in the first furrow on *Plough Monday, to ensure the success of the next harvest.

Hastings, battle of (14 October 1066) A decisive battle that marked the start of the Norman era in Britain. King Edward the Confessor of England (r. 1042–66) had probably designated his cousin once removed, William, Duke of Normandy, as his successor in 1051. On his deathbed, however, he approved his council's choice of Harold Godwinson, his brother-in-law, as Harold II. William immediately began preparations for an invasion, and landed with 7000 men at Pevensey, East Sussex, on 28 September 1066. Harold was at this time in the north, having just repelled another invasion, by his brother Tostig and King Harold Hardrada of Norway, at the battle of Stamford Bridge (25 September). He hurried south, and the two armies met at Senlac Hill near Hastings. The English, lacking cavalry and archers but occupying the high ground, had little choice but to fight a defensive action. Their shield wall held fast against repeated and highly disciplined onslaughts until sunset, but finally broke after Harold fell, reputedly wounded in the right eye by a random arrow. The Bayeux Tapestry, which records the campaign, seems to show him being cut down by Norman knights. William "the Conqueror" subsequently took London and was crowned William I on Christmas Day 1066. The site of the battle was marked by Battle Abbey, founded by William, and by the town of Battle. *See also* Norman Britain.

Hatton Garden A street in central London, off Holborn, that has become the home of the diamond trade. It derives its name from Hatton House, built by Sir Christopher Hatton (1540–91), Lord Chancellor to Elizabeth I. This mansion was demolished in the 17th century to make way for what was described as "a little town", covering the area between Leather Lane, Saffron Hill, Holborn, and Hatton Wall. Until the early 19th century it was a favoured residential area providing pleasant views across Lamb's Conduit Fields up to Hampstead. Captain Thomas Coram established the Foundling Hospital in Hatton Garden in 1741 (though it moved to a larger site after four years). The buildings at numbers 52–53 once housed the notorious courtroom of Mr Laing, a magistrate whom Charles Dickens took as a model for Mr Fang in *Oliver Twist*. In 1696 a charity school opened in a converted chapel on the corner of Cross Street. Figures of children are visible on the façade that remains, although the rest was destroyed in World War II.

Jewellers moved into Hatton Garden during the 19th century and by 1880 it had become the world centre for diamonds. The London Diamond Club has its premises there and there is also a diamond laboratory.

Haxey hood game An annual contest that takes place at Haxey in Lincolnshire on January 6. The game is said to have originated in the 13th century, when a certain Lady de Mowbray lost her scarlet hood in a gale. A group of Haxey men retrieved it for her and as a token of gratitude she bequeathed to the parish a piece of land, whose revenue was to finance an annual hood game. On January 6 the 12 players, or "Boggans", accompanied by a Fool, parade through Haxey; although the traditional scarlet coats are no longer worn, an element of red is always included in their attire. The procession halts on the green near the church for the Fool to address the onlookers. A smoky fire is lit behind his back and this ritual of "smoking the Fool" has led to suggestions that the festivities now associated with the hood game may have originated in pagan rituals of fertility or sacrifice. The game takes place on a nearby hill: a mock sackcloth hood is thrown into the crowd and the Boggans try to prevent anyone from carrying it to one of the three pubs of Haxey and neighbouring Westwoodside, the goals of the game. After several sackcloth hoods have been fought over, the main hood – a length of rope wrapped in leather – is thrown up. The resulting free-for-all, known as the "sway", is even more boisterous and it may be two or more hours before the hood finally reaches a pub, whose landlord provides free drinks for the players and retains the hood until the following year.

Hayward Gallery An art gallery designed by Ove Arup & Partners and opened in 1968 at the *South Bank arts complex in London. Owned by the South Bank Board, the Hayward is rented by the *Arts Council of Great Britain, which used it as an exhibition space and as a place to store its art collection. The Arts Council mounts about eight exhibitions each year, the emphasis being mainly (though not exclusively) on 19th- and 20th- century European art of all forms, including photography. In recent years there have been major exhibitions of the work of Picasso, Matisse, Renoir, and Sickert, and displays of Islamic, Indian, and Romanesque art.

Head of the River The title gained by the winning team in rowing contests, known as "bumping" races (or "bumps"), held by Oxford and Cambridge universities amongst others. The boats start in a line (the starting order being determined by success in previous competitions), end-to-end, instead of side by side, and the object of the race is to catch up with, and bump into, the boat in front. The two boats involved then drop out and exchange places in the next race. At the end of

the series, the boat finishing at the top is declared the "Head of the River". The contests began in the 19th century and took the form they did because the rivers at Oxford and Cambridge were too narrow to permit racing side by side. One story traces their origin at Oxford to pleasure boats racing each other out of Iffley Lock. The main bumping races are Summer Eights and Torpids at Oxford, and the May and Lent races at Cambridge, all rowed in several divisions over four days with each boat racing once a day.

Head of the river races are held on rivers elsewhere, with crews striving to achieve the fastest time over the course, with no bumping. These races are held on open stretches of water where bends and currents must be taken into account. At important events, such as those on the rivers Thames and Trent, there may be several hundred crews competing for the title.

Hell Fire Club Any of several clubs founded for purposes of various debaucheries in the 18th century, especially the club that met in caves beneath the church at Medmenham, near West Wycombe, Buckinghamshire. The founder was Sir Francis Dashwood (1708–81), a former president of the Dilettante Society, Member of Parliament, and, very briefly, Chancellor of the Exchequer (1762–63); members included the notorious John Wilkes. The group which frequented the club were known as the Monks of Medmenham. The members of this club have been accused of a variety of orgiastic practices and satanic rituals, but most of these accusations appear to be unwarranted. The caves are now open to the public.

Henley Royal Regatta One of the most famous rowing events in the world, held at Henley-on-Thames during the first week of July. Although it attracts much publicity as a social event, it is nevertheless a serious competition, drawing leading British club, school, and university crews as well as many from overseas. The regatta was first held in 1839. Each race takes place over a straight course of 2.1 kilometres (1.3 miles), with two boats competing. There are competitions for every type of boat including the Grand Challenge Cup for eights, the Town Challenge Cup for fours, trophies for single and double scullers, and schools' trophies. The first overseas competitor was E. Smith from New York, who in 1872 took part in the Diamond Sculls, probably the most famous of the Henley trophies. The first overseas crew to win the Grand Challenge Cup came from Belgium in 1906. Important guests and oarsmen are entitled to enter the Stewards' Enclosure overlooking the finish and traditionally drink Pimm's or champagne. Men wear white flannels, boaters, and blazers, and women wear elegant dresses and hats.

heraldry The granting and designing of pictorial devices, originally used on the shields of knights in armour as a means of identification in battle. In the early 12th century these armorial devices became hereditary in Europe, used by successive generations of families through the male line of descent, though with occasional modifications.

The basic colour (called "tincture") or background of the shield is known as the "field". The field may be overlaid with heraldic signs ("charges"), which at their simplest are broad bands, such as the vertical one called a "pale", or narrower stripes, such as the horizontal one known as a "fess". The basic charges are called "ordinaries". More fanciful ones depict a vast range of subjects, from real and mythical creatures to scientific instruments. Ancillary heraldic devices include the helm, or helmet, which appears above the shield and denotes the rank of the bearer. A crest may be placed on top of the helm. Some coats of arms also have "supporters", either animals or human figures, on either side of the shield. The crest came into use in the 14th century and the use of supporters in the late 15th century.

Arms are regarded as insignia of honour and their unauthorized display is subject to legal sanction, being regulated by the *College of Arms in England and the *Court of the Lord Lyon in Scotland (whose heraldic rules are by no means the same as England's). Devices are "differenced" (subject to slight modifications in the design) in case of cadency (younger sons) or illegitimacy. A number of coats of arms properly inherited from different ancestors may be marshalled (arranged) by quartering, that is, the shield is divided into sec-

tions, each of which displays the arms of a particular ancestor. A husband may impale his wife's coat of arms by dividing the shield vertically down the middle, then placing his own on the dexter side (i.e. on the wearer's right) and his wife's on the sinister side (*dexter* and *sinister* being Latin for "right" and "left").

heralds Officers of arms. In addition to regular members of the *College of Arms and the *Court of the Lord Lyon, "extraordinary" officers of arms are occasionally appointed – for example, immediately before a coronation. Their duties are ceremonial. At present there are six heralds extraordinary – Norfolk, Wales, Surrey, Beaumont, Arundel, and New Zealand, attached to the College of Arms. Their titles are connected with the house of Howard, the family in which the post of *Earl Marshal, head of the College, has been hereditary for centuries. In Scotland there are three heralds of the nobility: Slains, first recorded in 1404, who is pursuivant (a lesser herald) to the Earl of Erroll; Endure, first recorded in 1454, who is pursuivant to the Earl of Crawford; and Garioch, first recorded in 1501, who is pursuivant to the Countess of Mar.

heritage coast Stretches of coast of great natural beauty that are protected and managed under the auspices of the *Countryside Commission. During the 1960s it became apparent that much of Britian's undeveloped coastline was threatened by increased building, tourism, and industry. Following reports on the problem published by the Commission in 1970, the government urged local authorities to define areas of heritage coast that would henceforth be carefully managed. Coordinators were appointed to take practical action locally (e.g. planting trees, mending fences and walls, improving footpaths), the cooperation of landowners was sought, and conservation bodies were encouraged to acquire important stretches of coast, often with funding from the Countryside Commission. There are now 38 such coasts established, totalling 1263 kilometres (785 miles), and 5 stretches still waiting to be defined. They often coincide with *national parks and *areas of outstanding natural beauty.

Her Majesty's Stationery Office (HMSO) A government department founded in 1786 to prevent overcharging by unscrupulous printers. For many years HMSO was the official printer for all government departments, for Parliament, and for many public bodies; it was also the purchasing agent for Parliament. It is responsible for the overnight production of *Hansard*, as well as many government forms, command papers, and reports. Though still the government printer, it lost its monopoly of supply to departments in 1982. With headquarters in Norwich, HMSO has a large number of printing establishments, warehouses, and bookshops. It had a total catalogue of 43,000 backlist titles and 7800 new titles in 1984, its annual sales approaching five million units. Its income from sales (around £21 million in 1984) is supplemented by an annual grant of approximately the same size.

Herne the Hunter The leader of the "wild hunt" in Celtic mythology. (This phantom host, which figures in legends throughout the world, is thought to consist of the restless ghosts of the dead.) Associated with the Norse god Woden, Herne and his followers are believed to have roamed the skies in the form of storm clouds, the noise of their hounds being represented by the thunder. Herne's ghost is alleged to haunt an ancient oak tree, blasted by his spirit into the shape of a great stag with huge horns, in the former royal hunting territory of Windsor forest, now Windsor Great Park; when this oak fell from natural decay in the late 19th century another was planted in its place. Shakespeare alludes to the legend in his play *The Merry Wives of Windsor*; similar characters appear in folk tales attached to the forest of Fontainebleau in France and the Black Forest in West Germany.

High Court of Justice A *superior court of England and Wales created by the Judicature Acts 1873–75 as part of the *Supreme Court of Judicature. It now consists of three divisions: the **Queen's Bench Division** (or, if the sovereign is male, King's Bench Division), the **Chancery Division**, and the **Family Division**. Its judges sit in the Royal Courts of Justice in the Strand (the Law Courts) and at certain provincial centres. The court originally consisted of five divisions: the Queen's Bench, Common Pleas, and Exchequer (from the courts of *common law); the Chancery (from the Court of Chancery, *see* equity); and the **Probate, Divorce, and Admiralty Division**. The latter replaced a number of courts (including the *Court of Probate) which had formerly dealt with the subjects indicated by its name (subjects summarized by the late A. P. Herbert as "wills, wives and wrecks"). In 1880 the Common Pleas Division and the Exchequer Division were merged into the Queen's Bench Division; and in 1970 the Probate, Divorce, and Admiralty Division was renamed the Family Division, its jurisdiction over probate matters being transferred to the Chancery Division, and its admiralty jurisdiction to the Queen's Bench Division.

The Queen's Bench Division is presided over by the *Lord Chief Justice. It hears a wide variety of civil cases, mostly actions in contract and tort, and certain appeals. It has jurisdiction over inferior courts and tribunals. Cases of a commercial nature are dealt with by a *Commercial Court which forms part of the division, and the admiralty jurisdiction is exercised by an *Admiralty Court.

The Chancery Division is presided over by a Vice-Chancellor. (The Lord Chancellor is the nominal head of the division, but he never in fact sits.) It hears cases concerning such matters as land, trusts, mortgages, the administration of estates on death, bankruptcy, and town and country planning. Matters relating to companies and to patents are dealt with by two special courts forming part of the division: the *Companies Court and the *Patents Court respectively.

The Family Division is headed by the President and is concerned with all disputes concerning marriage and children.

An ordinary judge of the High Court is known as a *puisne judge, and is assigned to a particular division by the Lord Chancellor. *See also* Divisional Court; Court of Appeal.

High Court of Justiciary A *superior court of Scotland, exercising an exclusively criminal jurisdiction both as a court of trial and as a court of appeal. Its judges are the same as those of the *Court of Session, but with the

Lord President presiding under the style or title **Lord Justice-General of Scotland** and the Lords of Session (or Lords Ordinary) styled Lords Commissioners of Justiciary. For trials, the individual judges sit regularly in Edinburgh, Glasgow, and other major cities, dealing with all of the most serious crimes and with some of the lesser ones that may equally be tried in the *sheriff courts. For appellate business, they sit in Edinburgh in benches of three, and hear appeals both from sheriff courts and justices of the peace and from other judges of the Court in their capacity as trial judges. By contrast with the Court of Session, and the *Court of Appeal in England and Wales, there is no further appeal to the House of Lords.

Highland Games Traditional athletics meetings, usually professional, that have been held in the Highlands of Scotland since the early 19th century. They are said to originate from the custom of *clan chiefs, dissatisfied with the speed of their messengers, of holding races among their retainers and rewarding the victors with money. Similar meetings were held in the south of Scotland (the Border Games) and in the Lake District in northern England (the Lakeland Games), but there is a unique prestige attached to the Highland Games, and particularly to the most famous meeting, the *Braemar Gathering.

All the Games include the standard athletic events, and are renowned for the high standards attained. In 1893 a triple jump of 15 metres (49 feet 9 inches) was achieved at the Border Games, which was not equalled by amateur athletes in Britain for nearly 50 years. However, the Games are noted for their unusual traditional events. The best-known is probably tossing the caber. This involves holding a tree trunk in a vertical position and launching it so that it lands with the base

HIGHLAND GAMES *Throwing the hammer, at the Grampian Aboyne Games.*

pointing away from the thrower, in the exact direction he was facing at the moment of throw. The size and weight of the caber make this difficult to achieve. By tradition, a caber may not be cut once it has been successfully tossed, although a new one can be shortened if no-one succeeds in tossing it. Other events include tossing the weight, in which the competitors are judged on how high and far they can toss a metal sphere with a chain and ring attached, weighing 25.4 kilograms (56 pounds). Some events, such as the hitch and kick, are no longer seen. This was a spectacular high jump, in which the competitor had to kick an inflated bladder or tambourine suspended over his head with his take-off foot. Heights of over three metres (ten feet) were recorded.

Highlands and Islands Development Board The public body set up in 1965 to coordinate and promote activities aimed at tackling the social and economic problems of northern and western Scotland. The area concerned lies to the west of a line running from Arran in the southwest to Forres in the northeast, and covers about half the total area of Scotland. During the last two centuries the Highlands have suffered population decline and economic recession, thanks partly to deliberate depopulation for sheep-farming purposes (the Highland clearances) and partly to the absence of industry. The Board has wide discretionary promotional powers of development and long-term planning, and operates a comprehensive programme of loans and grants to assist commercially viable projects in industry, tourism, farming, and fisheries. Since 1965 the Board has assisted in the creation of 35,000 jobs, many in areas of high unemployment. The Board also provides grants each year towards such projects as the building of community centres and the establishment of a new language body for the propagation of the *Gaelic language.

Highlands, the The upland region of Scotland that contains its highest mountains and some of its most spectacular scenery. The Great Glen, running between Fort William and Inverness, forms a natural divide between the Grampian or Central Highlands to the

south and the Northwest Highlands, which stretch northwards to Cape Wrath. The region is essentially a high ancient rock plateau, largely overlaid by sandstone, which has been etched and planed by successive glaciations and the many rivers of the area to form the present magnificent landscape of valleys (glens) and hills. The highest mountains are the resistant granite outcrops of the Cairngorm and Ben Nevis ranges; Ben Nevis itself, at 1343 metres (4406 feet) is the highest peak in Britain. The Northwest Highlands (and Western Isles) show evidence of former volcanic activity, in the form of ancient lava flows and plugs; the many swift rivers have helped create a greatly indented rocky coastline. Soils tend to be thin and acidic with accumulations of peat in places, although alluvial deposits in the valleys and lowland fringes are more fertile. Few fragments remain of the ancient oak and native pine woodland that once covered much of the Highlands, and the heather moorland and conifer plantations that now take its place are seen by many as a poor substitute.

Iron Age settlements have been found both on the coast and in lowland regions inland; field systems indicating a flourishing agriculture as early as 1000 BC occur in several parts of the Northwest Highlands, although this activity declined in the latter half of the millennium. The Highlands were the domain of the Picts, a Celtic tribe with their own language and distinct culture, of which few traces survive. By the 9th century they had been overwhelmed by the Scotic king, Kenneth of Dalriada, who imposed unity on the warring tribes. Meanwhile, from the 9th century onwards, Viking raiders founded their own Norse settlements around the coast of northern Scotland and the islands, for instance, at Jarlshof on Shetland. Under Anglo-Norman influence from the 11th century, the *clan system emerged, which formed the basis of Highland society until the 18th century. In contrast to the *Lowlands, the Gaelic language and culture remained strong, and the area was effectively outside the control of the Crown until the pacification of the Highlands after the battle of *Culloden (1746). During the Middle Ages, the forests were felled for fuel and timber or

THE HIGHLANDS *Highland cattle on the Isle of Skye.*

destroyed by fire, a common strategy for smoking out adversaries or criminals. The practice of widespread and shifting cattle-grazing gave way to a more settled and intensive system of arable farming and grazing. In the years following Culloden former Highland clan chiefs, many of whom now lived in the south, introduced large flocks of sheep to their lands, finding them more profitable than tenant farmers. Many of the latter were evicted in an often brutal and bloody campaign known as the Highland clearances and were forced to settle in new and sometimes inhospitable sites on the west coast (*see* crofting); others simply emigrated.

When the profitability of sheep declined, large areas were devoted instead to deer forest and grouse moors, especially in the northwest. These estates still rely on their sporting interests, not only shooting but also salmon and trout fishing. Fish farms are a relatively new venture, while deer are now reared as livestock for venison. Forestry is another major industry of the region and the clear waters of Highland rivers have long provided the crucial essence for Scotland's *whisky distilleries. But the principal industry nowadays is undoubtedly tourism, which depends on the Highlands' greatest assets – its noble hills and peaceful glens.

High Sheriff An officer of the Crown appointed annually for a county in England, Wales, or Northern Ireland, or for the whole of Greater London except the City (*compare* sheriff). The office of shire-reeve, the Crown's principal executive agent in a *shire, dates from Anglo-Saxon times (*see* Anglo-Saxon Britain), and was in the Middle Ages one of considerable power and profit, its duties including the maintenance of the royal authority, the management of royal estates, and the holding of courts of both civil and criminal jurisdiction. Most of these duties gradually passed to other officers, such as *coroners and *justices of the peace. The Sheriff's officers are still responsible for the execution of certain court judgments, and the levying of forfeited recognizances, but his own functions, apart from acting as returning officer at parliamentary elections, are primarily ceremonial. A High Sheriff is chosen by a method known as "pricking". Three names are selected by the Lord Chancellor, Lord President of the Council, Lord Chief Justice, and others, and the sovereign uses a silver bodkin to pick the successful candidate from their list. The choice was formerly made at random, but is now predetermined, the sovereign accepting the recommendations of his or her advisers.

hill forts Fortified hilltop settlements in the south of England, the borders of Wales, and Scotland, defended by ramparts and ditches. Some were permanently inhabited during the Iron Age; others were only occupied in times of crisis. Most of those that can be seen today in Britain were built in the Iron Age, the oldest of them dating from c. 1200 BC. The earliest of these settlements, known as promontory forts, relied largely upon natural defensive features, such as cliffs, but by 400 BC contour forts, where an entire hilltop might be enclosed by a bank and a ditch, were becom-

ing common. The greatest hill forts of this period were built in *Wessex, along the western frontier of their territory by a Celtic tribe known as the Western Belgae, and include the Hod Hill and Hambledon Hill forts near Blandford, and the huge Maiden Castle outside Dorchester, Dorset.

These hill forts were originally constructed as refuges or storage sites, or as residences of local chiefs. They were defended by multiple ditches and earthwork ramparts with timber palisades; later forts could only be entered through a series of maze-like approaches. Many enclosed circular huts of timber and thatch, up to 11 metres (36 feet) in diameter, and housed several hundred people. At South Cadbury in Somerset goldsmiths' and bronzesmiths' shops have been found, indicating that the inhabitants were fairly wealthy. Every fort seems to have had its shrine, in the form of a hut, often with a porch, usually surrounded by open precincts. At the entrance to

HILL FORTS *The Herefordshire Beacon hill fort in the Malvern Hills, one of a number of well-defended Iron Age strongholds along the Welsh border. Within the rampart and ditch defences are small depressions, which may indicate the sites of huts. The small earthwork on the summit is believed to be the later remains of a Norman castle.*

the shrine in Maiden Castle was found the body of a young child, possibly the victim of human sacrifice.

These forts were perhaps not quite large enough to protect the whole tribe; many members presumably lived in undefended hut villages. The forts may have had an important role as local capitals of a tribal farming system, where the harvest could be assembled, stored, and redistributed to the whole tribe; certainly they were most common where the contemporary population was most concentrated, for example, on such uplands as Salisbury Plain.

Other hill forts, especially those in southeast England, tended to be much smaller and more simply planned than those in the southwest. The hill forts of Wales were built by the hillmen of the borders, Monmouth, and Herefordshire, on the flat tops of steep rocky hills and mountains. The Welsh in Snowdonia and northwest Wales fought the Romans from such forts, which had strong stone ramparts. Traces can still be seen at Carn Boduan and Tre'r Ceiri in North Wales. Groups of huts represented the dwelling, workshops and storehouses of single families, together with a plot of land for cultivation.

The Roman occupation, however, brought a strong central government and hastened the settlement of unfortified lowland sites (*oppida*) and the decline of independent hill forts like the one at Danbury, Hampshire; those in areas outside Roman influence (e.g. in Ireland and the Scottish Highlands) probably continued in occupation for several more centuries. When the Romans left in the 5th century AD, some forts were reoccupied and restored by romanized Britons as a defence against the invading Saxons. Such forts were massively refortified and large timber buildings were erected inside. Probably the best-known hill fort is the Belgic stronghold of Maiden Castle in Dorset, which was partly excavated by the archaeologist Sir Mortimer Wheeler (1890–1976) and which is now the subject of new excavations under the auspices of the *English Heritage.

historic buildings and monuments
Britain's legacy of architecture and ancient monuments is amongst the richest in the world. The public body with responsibility for

sites in the care of the state is the Historic Buildings and Monuments Commission (since 1984 known as *English Heritage). Wales and Scotland have retained separate bodies for this function. The Commission may take sites into guardianship, purchase them outright, or administer grants available for their maintenance. It currently has in its direct care more than 350 monuments: they include prehistoric burial mounds (*see* barrows), Iron Age hillforts, Roman villas, many medieval castles and abbeys in various states of preservation, and a small number of later houses. The Commission also gives advice on archaeological excavation, undertakes research, and produces publications. There are approximately 300,000 **listed buildings** of special architectural or historic interest, for which grants or loans may be provided. Special consent from the local planning authority, or in extreme cases, the Secretary of State for the Environment, is required before listed buildings can be demolished or radically altered.

England's churches are not in the care of the state, except where in certain cases they have been declared "redundant". Their upkeep is the responsibility of the Church, which may be assisted by the voluntary Historic Churches Preservation Trust or its county subsidiaries. A wide range of voluntary organizations also helps to protect many of Britain's historic sites and buildings. Principal among these is the *National Trust; there are also the Society for the Preservation of Ancient Buildings, the Ancient Monuments Society, the Ulster Architectural Heritage Trust, the Victorian Society, and the Georgian Group. Additional resources may also be made available from the National Heritage Memorial Fund and the Architectural Heritage Fund.

HM Inspectorate The body responsible for maintaining educational standards in line with government policy in all schools and colleges in England and Wales other than universities. (A comparable body exists in Scotland.) The Inspectorate, about 450 strong, is recruited from the teaching profession. The state's right of inspection of schools dates from the late 1830s, when government funds were first made available for education. The 19th-century inspectors (of whom the poet Matthew Arnold is perhaps the most famous) were key figures in the reform and growth of education in the period after 1840, and the Inspectorate still fulfils an important function in liaison between the schools and colleges on the one hand and the Department of Education and Science, to which it reports, on the other.

HMSO *See* Her Majesty's Stationery Office.

hobby horse A stock character in *mummers' plays, *morris dances, and other folk traditions. The hobby horse takes a variety of forms: sometimes the horse, often wearing an elaborate and grotesque costume, is barely recognizable as the animal it is supposed to represent. A common feature is a pair of mechanically-operated jaws, which snap at onlookers and passers-by. The hobby horse appears at festivals throughout the year, notably around *May Day; two West Country towns, Padstow in Cornwall and Minehead in Somerset, have their own hobby-horse festivals at this time.

The Padstow hobby horse or "Obby Oss" is a fearsome monster, its "rider's" face hidden by a grotesque mask, that dances through the

HOBBY HORSE *The Padstow "Obby Oss".*

streets of the town on May Day morning, accompanied by a procession of "mayers" – dancers, singers, and musicians – performing a traditional song. Any young girl among the crowd of spectators runs the risk of being seized by the Oss; until recently she would have had her face blackened with soot as a token of fertility. From time to time the music swells to a climax then suddenly softens to a more dirgelike song; the Oss falls to the ground as if dead, only to spring up again at a crash on the drums to resume its former liveliness. The Minehead hobby horse, known as the Sailor's Horse, is boat-shaped and decked with coloured streamers and ribbons: the festival is believed by some to have originated in commemoration of a shipwreck off the Somerset coast, the tail of a dead cow washed ashore from the wreck being used as the tail of the first hobby horse. The horse appears in Minehead on 30 April and rampages around the town and surrounding districts, bowing to passers-by and begging for alms, until the evening of 2 May. After the final "booting ceremony", a relic of the former custom of beating nonpaying onlookers with a boot, the horse is returned to its "stable" until the following year. Both hobby horses are credited in legend with having frightened off foreign invaders, the Padstow hobby horse having scared off the French in 1346–47, and the Minehead hobby horse having repulsed the Danes in the 9th or 10th century.

Hogmanay New Year's Eve in Scotland, celebrated throughout the country by a variety of traditions and festivities. For many years the New Year has been a far more significant event in the Scottish calendar than in England, Wales, or Ireland. New Year's Day was a public holiday in Scotland long before the remainder of Britain decided to follow suit in 1972. Many of the Hogmanay festivities are relics of former Christmas or Hallowe'en customs, notably the tradition of "first-footing". The "first-foot" is the first person to cross the threshold of a house after midnight on New Year's Eve; in some areas bands of first-footers go from house to house during the early hours of New Year's Day, receiving a draught of whisky or other alcoholic drink at each one. According to superstition the first-foot should be a dark-haired man bearing gifts of food, drink, and fuel, usually a piece of coal; an empty-handed first-foot is generally considered to be a bad omen. The traditional gifts vary from region to region, red herrings being popular in the fishing villages of the east coast of Scotland and sheaves of corn in some rural areas.

Other surviving Hogmanay festivities include massed gatherings in the larger city centres, such as Glasgow and Dundee, and a number of traditional fire ceremonies (*see* burning the old year out).

holiday camps A camp or similar establishment in which families may spend a holiday and be accommodated relatively cheaply (compared with a hotel), often in a chalet. A wide range of communal activities and facilities are usually provided. The first was Dodd's Socialist Camp founded by J. Fletcher Dodd in 1906 at Caister-on-Sea, Norfolk; the facilities included beaches, gardens, sports pitches and equipment, shops, a library, function room,

and dining hall. Visitors slept in tents or chalets (which were more expensive). The food was frugal but wholesome, probably better than some of the urban working classes generally enjoyed. Rules laid down by Dodd demanded sobriety, punctuality, acceptable dress, silence at night, and communal labour. Dodd found no shortage of people willing to pay a guinea a week for this experience and after World War I his camps increased in number. By the 1930s other proprietors had entered the market, which had greatly expanded with the advent of paid holidays for most workers. The competition from Butlin's and Warner's camps improved the standard of facilities provided, although many of them retained the institutional character of Dodd's early camps. As holiday camps became more relaxed about rules, their popularity increased and they are now an integral part of the British summer scene. Nevertheless, holiday camps, or centres as they are now called, are less popular than they were in the 1950s and 1960s, although they have changed their im-

HOLIDAY CAMPS *Butlin's famous holiday camp at Clacton-on-Sea, in the 1950s. Holidaymakers enjoying a diving competition.*

age to meet demands for greater freedom of choice and more privacy. They are also far more luxurious than they used to be. However, it is the gregarious extrovert who will most enjoy the dancing, organized games, communal eating, and unflagging cheerfulness of the camp hosts.

Holy Grail   *See* Arthurian legend; Joseph of Arimathea.

Holy Island (Lindisfarne)   An island just off the Northumbrian coast, home of the community of Lindisfarne, which was formerly one of the most famous centres of religious learning and missionary activity in Britain. A church and monastery were founded there in 635 AD by St Aidan (d. 651) and a group of monks from *Iona. With the cooperation of the local chieftain Oswald and his heirs, Aidan reintroduced Christianity throughout Northumbria, setting up new monasteries at Melrose, Hexham, Whitby, and Coldingham. Under successive bishops, including St Cuthbert (685–87), Lindisfarne established a reputation for sanctity and scholarship that was celebrated throughout Europe. The Lindisfarne Gospels, an illuminated manuscript written by Eadfrid, bishop-abbot of Lindisfarne (698–721), survives as one of the finest early works of the English Church and is now in the British Library, London.

Danish raiders forced the monks to abandon the island in 875 when Eardulf, the last bishop of Lindisfarne, moved his seat to Chester-le-Street taking with him the remains of St Cuthbert. The community moved again to Durham in 995. However, a Benedictine priory was re-established on the island in 1093 by the prior of Durham, the remains of which can still be seen. The present parish church of St Mary the Virgin, beside the priory, may incorporate part of the original monastery. A modern statue of St Aidan stands nearby. The castle was built around 1500 and was converted to a picturesque dwelling by Edward Lutyens before 1914. At low tide the island and village of Lindisfarne can be reached from the mainland by a causeway.

Holyroodhouse, palace of   The official residence in Scotland of the reigning monarch. Its northwest tower was started in 1501, in the reign of James IV of Scotland, adjacent to 12th-century Holyrood Abbey (now ruined), about a mile across the old city from Edinburgh castle (known as the Royal mile). The palace was laid out according to the plans of James V, who added suites of apartments. Mary, Queen of Scots held her court there. The whole palace was badly damaged by fire on more than one occasion and was reconstructed in the 1670s in a French classical style by Sir William Bruce; his design incorporated the old tower on one side and balanced it with a similar one on the southwest side. A throne room, state rooms, and royal apartments were made ready for Charles II, but he never lived there. A long gallery hung with over a hundred portraits of Scottish kings by the Dutch artist De Wit was also prepared for his arrival. Shunned by the Hanoverian kings, Holyroodhouse finally came into its own in the reign of Queen Victoria, who loved all things Scottish. Her descendants, notably George V and Queen Mary, refurbished and redecorated the palace, and the present Queen and Prince Philip usually spend a week at Holyroodhouse at the beginning of July, carrying out official engagements in Scotland and holding a garden party. It is also occupied for a week every year in May by the Lord High Commissioner who represents the Queen at the General Assembly of the Church of Scotland. At other times it is open to the public.

Home Secretary   A senior government minister and member of the *Cabinet in charge of the Home Office (in full, the Secretary of State for the Home Department). The Home Office was established in 1782, and tended to administer new internal responsibilities of government until they in turn warranted separate departments. Many of the Home Secretary's present functions are concerned with law and order and security. He makes regulations with respect to the management, operational standards, and discipline of police forces in England and Wales (*see* police) and, in the case of the *Metropolitan Police, is responsible for maintaining and equipping it; he has overall responsibility for *prisons, the *parole system, and the *probation service; he has powers under the Public Order Act 1936 connected with the banning

PALACE OF HOLYROODHOUSE

of public processions, and powers under the Prevention of Terrorism (Temporary Provisions) Act 1976 to proscribe organizations and exclude individuals connected with terrorism; he controls firearms, poisons, and dangerous drugs; and he advises the sovereign on the granting of pardons in appropriate cases. He is also responsible for naturalization and the deprivation of *citizenship, for immigration control, and for extradition and deportation. A host of other miscellaneous responsibilities include the supervision of laws relating to gaming and lotteries, shops, and liquor licensing; the licensing of scientific experiments on animals; the making of rules governing the conduct of elections; functions connected with burials, cremations, and exhumations; and the scrutiny of bylaws made by local authorities.

Horn Dance A folk dance performed annually at Abbots Bromley, Staffordshire, on the Monday of the local *wakes week, which follows the first Sunday after 4 September. The naming of the dance is obscure, but may

have had some significance as a fertility rite. Six of the twelve dancers carry painted reindeer horns set in carved wooden heads; the other half of the group consists of an accordion player, a triangle player, a boy armed with crossbow and arrow, a jester, a man dressed as

HORN DANCE *The celebrated Horn Dance at Abbots Bromley.*

Maid Marian, and a *Robin Hood figure on a *hobby horse. The dance is performed at various points in the village and at nearby estates, notably Blithfield Hall, throughout the day. Reference was made to the Abbots Bromley Horn Dance in Robert Plot's *Natural History of Staffordshire*, published in 1686, at which time it was performed at Christmas, New Year, and Epiphany; the dance itself would seem to have altered little since then, apart from the addition of the now traditional costumes, modelled upon Tudor dress, which the dancers first wore in preference to their own clothes in the late 19th century. However, the fact that the horns used in the dance are genuine reindeer antlers of considerable antiquity, which have been kept in the parish church over the centuries, suggests that the dance could date back as far as the Anglo-Saxon period or earlier, and may commemorate the granting of hunting rights there.

Horserace Totalizator Board A body established by Act of Parliament in 1963 to operate totalizators at racecourses, and to provide off-course cash and credit offices. It replaced the Racecourse Betting Control Board. The totalizator (or Tote) system, whereby all the stake money is pooled and shared between the winners, after deductions for tax and expenses, has been in use in Britain since 1930. It provides punters with an alternative to betting with bookmakers, and generates money to support horse racing. The Tote contributed nearly £9 million to racing between 1929 and 1960. In 1960 the Betting and Gaming Act allowed the Tote to accept off-course cash betting, but until 1972 the Tote was forbidden to offer starting price bets. The three sections of the organization, betting shops at racecourses, the 120 high street betting shops, and Tote Credit, together gave £2 million to racing in 1985–86, derived from a turnover of £110 million. The chairman and seven other board members are appointed by the Home Secretary.

horse racing The so-called "sport of kings", horse racing is popular at all levels of society. For many wealthy people owning, breeding, and racing horses is a pleasure in itself, and the connection between horses and

the aristocracy is one of great antiquity in Europe, the Middle East, and many parts of Asia. Thoroughbred racehorses are a special breed descended originally from Arab horses imported in the Middle Ages. It is claimed that every thoroughbred in the world is in fact descended from the mare Old Bald Peg, born about 1659, and the earliest mare in the *General Stud Book* (*see* Jockey Club). Breeding horses is an expensive business but a successful racehorse can win large sums of money in prizes and also be worth huge sums for its breeding potential. For the vast majority of racing enthusiasts, however, the major interest is in betting, either at the racecourse itself or at off-course bookmakers or betting shops.

Horse racing in Britain is divided into two categories: flat racing and jumping (hurdles and *steeplechases). It has a very long history but arrived at something like its present form in the 18th century, with regular meetings organized all over the country and considerable royal patronage. In 1750 the *Jockey Club was founded as the governing body of horse racing in England. The most famous races and meetings have been running for over 200 years, among them the *Derby, St Leger, Oaks, One Thousand and Two Thousand Guineas on the flat (*see* Classics), the *Grand National and Cheltenham Gold Cup steeplechases, and the Champion Hurdle (Cheltenham). Each season there is competition for the title of champion jockey, a title won 26 times by (Sir) Gordon Richards between 1925 and 1953. The royal family has long been interested in horse racing; they own many top-class horses and frequently attend races, or visit stud farms, auctions, and sales in Britain and abroad.

hospice movement A movement dedicated to the provision of proper care for the terminally ill and support for their relatives. In pre-Reformation times hospices were attached to religious houses, and the care of the dying continues to be the concern of certain religious communities, for instance the Irish Sisters of Charity, who founded St Joseph's Hospice, London, in 1905. The modern hospice movement in Britain, however, derives its main impetus and inspiration from the work of Dame Cicely Saunders (1918–), who, from her experience as a medical social worker, realized that the physical and mental care of dying patients in hospital was frequently inadequate. In 1967 St Christopher's Hospice was opened in southeast London, with Dame Cicely as its founder-director. Her approach to nursing the terminally ill embraces not only the strictly medical aspects of cases, such as the relief of pain, but also teaching programmes for those involved in this work, and support for the families of patients. The hospice movement grew rapidly, particularly in the 1970s, and there are now about 70 hospice units in the UK, some independent, some within the National Health Service.

Household Cavalry *See* Household Division.

Household Division The seven regiments of guards, from which are drawn the sovereign's escort for ceremonial occasions. The division consists of two regiments of **Household Cavalry** and five regiments of **foot guards**. The Household Cavalry, with a strength of about 1600, is formed by the **Life Guards** and the **Blues and Royals** (created in 1969 when the Royal Horse Guards and 1st Dragoons were amalgamated) and maintains a mounted regiment of 300, quartered at Knightsbridge Barracks, as well as two armoured regiments, which alternate between Windsor and the *British Army of the Rhine. The foot regiments comprise the **Grenadier Guards**, the **Coldstream Guards**, and the **Scots Guards**, all formed in the 17th century, the **Irish Guards**, formed in the 19th century, and the **Welsh Guards**, formed during World War I. All the regiments are distinguished by resplendent dress uniforms, including breastplates for the cavalry and bearskins for the foot guards. Ceremonial events, in which these troops demonstrate precision drilling, sometimes with the Queen at their head in her capacity as their Colonel-in-Chief, include *trooping the colour, *changing the guard at Buckingham Palace, and other parades at St James's Palace and the Tower of London.

House of Commons The lower House of *Parliament, consisting of the elected representatives of the people. Each representative, known as a *Member of Parliament, or MP,

sits for a parliamentary constituency, and there are currently 650 members, representing 523 constituencies in England, 38 in Wales, 72 in Scotland, and 17 in Northern Ireland. These numbers can be varied not only by Act of Parliament, but also by constituency changes recommended by the boundary commission (*see* constituency).

A House of Commons is chosen as a whole at a general election, which follows the summoning of a Parliament by royal proclamation after the ending of one by dissolution or passage of time. Writs ordering the holding of elections in every constituency are issued by the *Lord Chancellor to returning officers throughout the country. A vacancy occurring in the House during the life of Parliament is filled by means of a *by-election. The conduct of elections is governed by the Representation of the People Act 1949. Voting is, and has been since 1872, by secret ballot; the result is, and has always been, by simple majority of seats (the so-called "first-past-the-post" system). Those entitled to vote are all *Commonwealth citizens aged 18 or over whose names are on the electoral register for the constituency in question as having been resident there on the qualifying date, and who are not under any legal disqualification. A new register of electors comes into force in each constituency every February, and the residential qualifying date is in the previous October. Those disqualified are peers and peeresses in their own right, the mentally ill, those in prison, and those having past convictions for corrupt or illegal practices at elections (such as bribery, intimidation, and spending more than the legal limit on an election campaign). Disqualification lasts for five years, and is sometimes national and sometimes for a particular constituency only. Until 1868 disputed elections were decided by the House itself as part of its right to control its own internal affairs (*see* parliamentary privilege), but an Act of that year transferred this jurisdiction to the ordinary courts. The validity of an election may now be questioned by an unsuccessful candidate or any registered elector by means of a petition presented within 21 days after the result to an election court consisting of judges of the High Court of Justice or Court of Session; the court

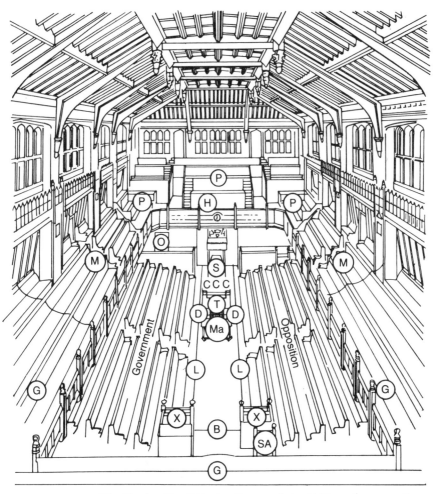

HOUSE OF COMMONS *The Chamber. Key: S, Speaker; P, press galleries; H,* Hansard *reporters; O, government official's box; C, Clerks of the House (when the House goes into Committee, the Speaker leaves the Chair, and the Chairman sits in the chair of the Clerk of the House, on the left); T, Table of the House; D, despatch boxes; Ma, Mace (when the House goes into Committee, the Mace is put "below the Table", on books); L, lines over which Members may not step when speaking from the front benches; B, Bar of the House; X, cross benches; SA, Sergeant-at-Arms; M, Members' galleries; G, public galleries.*

may declare the election null and void, and order a fresh one to be held.

The House is presided over by its *Speaker (or a deputy), who is assisted in the preservation of order by the *Serjeant at Arms. On matters of procedure, the Speaker is advised by the Clerk of the House (its chief permanent officer) and assistant clerks; he also has a legal adviser, the Speaker's counsel.

Although referred to as the lower House, the House of Commons is constitutionally the dominant House. The House of Lords does not participate (except formally) in the passing of financial legislation (*see* Parliament); it can delay legislation passed by the Commons, but cannot (whether it is financial or other-

213

wise) prevent its ultimate enactment (*see* Act of Parliament) in normal circumstances. Moreover, by convention, the Prime Minister and the majority of senior members of the Cabinet are members of the Commons, not the Lords.

House of Keys   *See* Tynwald.

House of Lords   The upper, and nonrepresentative, House of *Parliament, consisting of the **Lords Spiritual** and the **Lords Temporal**. The Lords Spiritual are the two archbishops of the Church of England, Canterbury and York, and 24 diocesan bishops – those of London, Durham, and Winchester as of right, and the 21 most senior of the others. Their eligibility to sit ceases on retirement. The **Lords Temporal** are hereditary peers and peeresses in their own right, peers and peeresses for life created under the Life Peerages Act 1958 (*see* life peerage), and the *Lords of Appeal in Ordinary who conduct the judicial business of the House (the latter are also life peers, although they are not referred to as such). A prince of the royal blood is not a member of the House as such and, apart from the heir to the throne, sits only if he holds a peerage conferred on him by the sovereign. The heir apparent sits as Duke of Cornwall, a title inherited by every sovereign's eldest son (*see* Duchy of Cornwall). The hereditary members of the House include the holders of titles created in the separate peerages of England and Scotland that existed before the union of the two countries in 1707, in the peerage of Great Britain that existed from then until the union with Ireland in 1801, and in the then established peerage of the UK. The Act of Union with Scotland provided for only 16 of the Scottish peers to sit, to be elected by all the Scottish peers for the duration of each Parliament. However, this restriction was removed by the Peerage Act 1963. The Act of Union with Ireland provided for the holders of titles created in the separate peerage of Ireland to elect 28 of their number to represent them in the House for life; however, the machinery for election lapsed with the creation of the Irish Free State in 1922. Peers of Ireland now have no right to sit, but by the same token are (unlike other

peers) eligible for election to the House of Commons (*see* Member of Parliament).

The House is presided over by the *Lord Chancellor as its speaker, and he is assisted in maintaining order by the Gentleman Usher of the *Black Rod. The chief permanent officer of the House is the Clerk of the Parliaments, who is appointed by the Crown but can only be removed at the instigation of the House.

The functions of the House of Lords are both parliamentary and judicial. Its parliamentary functions (legislative and deliberative) run parallel to the *House of Commons but it does not now exercise the dominant constitutional influence, even though it is referred to as the upper House. However, in its judicial functions it is unique. It is the highest court in the UK (except in a few limited cases that are reserved to the *Judicial Committee of the Privy Council) hearing civil and criminal appeals from the *Court of Appeal in England and Wales and the Court of Appeal of Northern Ireland (*see* Supreme Court of Judicature of Northern Ireland), and civil appeals from the *Court of Session in Scotland (in criminal cases in Scotland, there is no appeal beyond the *High Court of Justiciary). In law, all members of the House can participate in all its functions; there is no right of exclusion. In practice, however, there is a sharp distinction between the parliamentary and the judicial functions. The only restriction regarding the parliamentary function lies in a leave-of-absence procedure introduced in 1958 to discourage "backwoodsmen" (habitual nonattenders prone to appear unexpectedly in numbers sufficient to distort crucial votes). A peer who does not intend to be present during a session or other period is expected (but not obliged) to obtain formal leave of absence and not to attend during that period without giving notice. In its judicial function, however, the House as a whole adopts formally the majority opinion of one or two appeal committees; it is a firm convention that the only peers to take part in the proceedings of these committees are the Lords of Appeal in Ordinary, the Lord Chancellor and former Lord Chancellors, and others who hold, or have held, high judicial office.

Howard League for Penal Reform A charity dedicated to the cause of penal reform. Named after John Howard (1726–90), philanthropist, reformer, and author of *The State of the Prisons* (1777), the League grew out of the Howard Association, formed in 1866, and its amalgamation with the later Penal Reform League in 1921, when the present name was adopted. Its aims are to promote "public discussion about crime, its control, and its sanction" and "research into criminal justice"; it also maintains contact with offenders, their families, and the victims of crime. Internationally, it urges the United Nations to promote the standard minimum rules for the treatment of prisoners and campaigns for the abolition of corporal and capital punishment. Its publications include *The Howard Journal of Criminal Justice*.

Hundred Years' War (1337–1453) A series of wars between England and France, nominally over the right to the French throne. Charles IV of France died in 1328, leaving no direct male heir. Edward III of England (r. 1327–77) had a claim through his mother Isabella, Charles's sister; he was however, unable to press it effectively and the throne passed to Philip VI (Charles's cousin). Several factors caused Edward to review his claim in 1387. As the English monarchy was still under the shadow of Edward II's deposition and murder (1327), Edward III needed to demonstrate that he was a worthy king by conspicuous and continuous success. Since 1332 he had been attempting to conquer Scotland, following the example of his grandfather Edward I (r. 1272–1307), but with limited and temporary success; however, war with France – fought on French soil with the prospect of attractive plunder – was more to the liking of the nobility. In addition, relations with France were bedevilled by the status of the Duchy of Aquitaine, which English kings since Henry II had held by feudal tenure (*see* feudalism) from the king of France; the help France gave to Scotland was an additional source of antagonism. Thus when Philip VI confiscated the Duchy in 1337, Edward renewed his claim to the throne and declared war on France. In 1340 he incorporated the French fleur-de-lys into the English royal coat of arms. However, this claim

was primarily a negotiating ploy: Edward's priority was to end the French king's overlordship over Aquitaine.

The first phase of the wars lasted until 1388, when a truce began that was to last until 1415. The English strategy was to take an army to France and inflict as much damage as possible in the hope of bringing the French to battle, defeating them, and negotiating a favourable settlement. Spectacular victories were gained at Crécy (1346) and Poitiers (1356), where the French king, John II, was captured. This, and internal French troubles caused by the war, led to the treaty of Brétigny (1360), by which Edward gained a much enlarged Aquitaine, and Calais (captured in 1347) in full sovereignty. But, for all its apparent success, this strategy was flawed. Such raids (or *chevauchées*) were very expensive and hardly ever produced the expected booty. Also, they relied for their effect on the enemy being willing to do battle. These shortcomings were revealed by the ease with which the French recovered most of Aquitaine after 1369. Pitched battles were avoided and renewed English raids proved expensive and futile; by 1388 a virtually defeated England, suffering from internal political strife, secured a truce.

By 1415, when the second and final phase of wars against France began, the situation had been transformed. France, under the mad king Charles VI, was paralysed by civil war; whereas in England, Henry V, possibly the most capable of all English kings, had ascended the throne in 1413. In 1415 he captured Harfleur (modern Le Havre) and gained a crushing victory at Agincourt. In 1417 he started on a novel course, the systematic conquest of Normandy, which by 1419 was under secure English control. His primary aim was the acquisition of Normandy in full sovereignty; but in 1419 the assassination of the Duke of Burgundy drove his successor into firm alliance with the English, enabling Henry to secure the succession to the French throne and marriage to Charles's daughter Catherine, by the treaty of Troyes (1420). As the prior of Dijon charterhouse later put it, the English entered France "through the hole in the Duke of Burgundy's skull".

When Henry and Charles died within a month of each other (1422), Henry's son Henry VI succeeded to both countries. However Charles's son, Charles VII, continued to hold all of southern France except for Aquitaine. The tide began to turn in 1429, when the French, under the inspiration of Joan of Arc, raised the seige of Orléans and won the battle of Patay. In 1435 the Duke of Burgundy defected to Charles. Increasing English financial and political difficulties made recovery impossible; after several truces, Charles finally conquered all of France in 1453, with the sole exception of Calais. This was the end of any serious attempt by the English to conquer France. Later brief campaigns, by Edward IV and Henry VIII, while fought under the banner of the English claim, were minor affairs with political and financial goals not really related to their claim to the French throne. Calais was finally lost in 1558; but the title "King of France" was not removed from the English royal style until 1801 – after the French monarchy had been destroyed in the French revolution.

hurling A Gaelic stick-and-ball field game, also known as hurley, and traditionally regarded as the national game of Ireland. Hurling is played with 15 players to a side, who use a hurley, a curved stick with a broad blade, to drive a small hard horsehide-covered ball through the opposition's goalposts. Three points are scored when the ball passes under the crossbar, and one point when it passes over. The ball may be struck with or carried on the hurley and, when off the ground, can be struck with the hand or kicked.
Hurling is at least 3000 years old; players in Irish folklore included the legendary hero Cuchulain, and the pre-Christian Brehon Laws, the oldest Irish legal code, provided for compensation for any player injured in the game. Hurling has endured through the vicissitudes of Irish history, but declined in the 19th century. Following the foundation of the Gaelic Athletic Association (GAA) in 1884, one objective of which was to "bring the hurling back to Ireland", a competition structure was established. One of the fastest of all ball games, it is a popular spectator sport and the

All-Ireland Finals, controlled by the GAA, draw crowds of up to 70,000.

hurling the silver ball An ancient game played annually at St Ives and St Columb Major in Cornwall. The St Columb game takes place on Shrove Tuesday and the second Saturday afterwards, between teams (of perhaps 500 players) of Townsmen and Countrymen, in and around the main streets of the town. A small silver-coated ball, about the size of a cricket ball and inscribed with the motto "Town and country do your best, for in this parish I must rest", is hurled with considerable force from man to man towards one of the two goals, which stand two miles apart; once a goal has been scored the game is over. In St Ives, hurling the silver ball takes place in the public park on Feast Monday, the day after the festival of the town's patron saint, St Ia, and usually the first Monday in February. The ball is thrown by the mayor to the waiting crowd and passed or thrown from hand to hand; the person who happens to be holding the ball at the stroke of noon is declared the winner and receives a small prize. Both games are alleged to have originated in pagan rituals of sun-worship, the silver ball being a representation of the sun.

Hyde Park *See* royal parks.

I

Icknield Way A Neolithic track that linked Salisbury Plain (*see* Stonehenge) to the east coast of England. It has been an important thoroughfare since the Bronze Age (1800–500 BC) and parts of it now underlie modern roads. Like most other prehistoric paths (e.g. the Ridgeway, which joins it at the Thames from *Avebury), the Icknield Way follows natural routes along dry ground. It runs in a southwesterly direction along a chalk escarpment from the East Anglian ridge through the Chiltern Hills to the Berkshire Downs. Near Dunstable it doubles up to form the Lower and Upper Icknield Way, the former probably a later track.

In early times, the Icknield Way linked the Fens and the Thames valley, two areas of concentrated settlement as far back as the Bronze Age. The "road" consisted of bands of roughly parallel tracks, which may have been several kilometres wide in places. The Romans gravelled it and used it as a secondary road, but it was probably a main route for local commercial traffic. In the 5th and 6th centuries AD it may have been the route taken by early Saxon settlers. Although all roads in Britain deteriorated after the departure of the Romans, many remained serviceable. The 11th-century Laws of Edward the Confessor singled out the Icknield Way and the Roman Fosse Way, Watling Street, and Ermine Street, as *chimini regales*, or royal roads. These had to be wide enough for two wagons to pass or for 16 armed knights to ride abreast. Any assault committed upon one of these roads was considered a breach of the King's Peace and punishable by a fine of 100 shillings, at a time when a cow was worth two or three shillings. Fifty years later, Henry I founded the town of Dunstable to safeguard the meeting of the Icknield Way and Watling Street. This crossroads, which is still in use, had formed a nodal point in the network of *Roman roads.

Immigration Appeal Tribunal A tribunal operating under the Immigration Act 1971 to hear appeals against decisions by immigration officers (particularly, appeals against the refusal of entry into the UK, or the conditions attached to entry) and appeals against deportation orders made by the Home Secretary, except those made either on the recommendation of a court after a person's conviction of a criminal offence, or in the interests of national security. An appeal goes first to an adjudicator appointed by the Home Secretary, and from him to the tribunal with his or the tribunal's leave. There is no further appeal. The members of the tribunal are appointed by the Lord Chancellor, the president being a barrister, and a proportion of the others either barristers, advocates, or solicitors, and it is subject to the supervisory jurisdiction of the *Council on Tribunals.

Imperial College of Science and Technology A college of *London University formed in 1907 from the amalgamation of the Royal College of Science (founded 1845), the Royal School of Mines (founded 1851), and the City and Guilds College (founded 1884). It became part of London University the following year, and is situated on the South Kensington site developed after the *Great Exhibition of 1851. Considerably enlarged in the 1950s, Imperial College is one of the most important scientific academic establishments in the world, has numbered many Nobel Prizewinners among its professors (e.g. Sir Ernst Chain, Abdul Salaam, and Sir Denis Gabor).

Imperial Service Order A decoration conferred on civil servants. There is one class, that of Companion, and holders are restricted to 875 members of the home civil service and 670 members of the overseas civil service. The Queen is sovereign of the order, which was instituted in 1902.

Imperial War Museum A museum in London which houses information and artefacts relating to British and Commonwealth involvement in military operations since 1914. Intended as a memorial to those who died in World War I, the Imperial War Museum was founded in 1917 and established by an Act of Parliament in 1920 at the Crystal Palace (*see* Great Exhibition). From 1924 to 1935 the museum was based in the former Imperial Institute in South Kensington, before moving into the Royal Bethlem Hospital, popularly known as Bedlam, in 1936. These buildings were damaged during air raids in World War II and the museum was closed from 1940 to 1946, after which it was improved and extended (1962); it was later damaged by fire (1968). The museum now also houses a photograph collection, a reference library, aircraft, military insignia and badges, and administers the retired Royal Navy cruiser HMS *Belfast* (opened to the public in 1971) and the military aircraft museum at Duxford airfield in Cambridgeshire.

income tax *See* tax system.

Independent Broadcasting Authority (IBA) A public body responsible for the control of the independent television service, founded as the Independent Television Authority by the Television Act in September 1955; it became the IBA in 1972 under the provisions of the Sound Broadcasting Act in order to oversee both Independent Television (ITV) and the new Independent Local Radio service (ILR) (*see* local radio). Despite fears that ITV would lead to a decline in standards, the 15 independent companies and later the 50 ILR stations brought to broadcasting a considerable degree of innovation from the regions, which led to ITV becoming Britain's most popular television channel. The advent of competition compelled the BBC to improve its services.

Though the IBA does not itself make programmes, it controls the issue of franchises to the programme companies and regulates, monitors, and physically transmits the programmes they produce: an average of 105 hours per week by each ITV company. By statute, the IBA must ensure the exclusion from these broadcasts of inaccuracy, indecency, and gross bias; it publishes a code of practice called "Television Programme Guidelines". In 1984 10,300 television and 8200 radio scripts were checked against this code. Advertising also comes under scrutiny for similar faults, and some 18% of television advertisements are returned for amendment before being accepted for transmission. Other IBA responsibilities include the Independent Television News (ITN); Oracle, the "teletext" information service, started in July 1975; TV-am, the breakfast television service; Channel Four, the second independent channel – a wholly-owned subsidiary of the IBA; and the *Welsh language service, S4C. The IBA is financed by the programme companies and its 12 members are appointed by the Home Secretary. Its large engineering staff, apart from maintaining its transmitters, is also active in broadcasting research, and has achieved considerable success in work on digital television systems.

independent schools Schools that are independent of state funding. They include *preparatory schools, *public schools, Roman Catholic, Quaker and other religious foundations, and over a hundred former direct-grant grammar schools that opted not to merge with the state system under Labour educational policies in the 1960s and 1970s. They rely upon fees and endowments for their income; despite their high fees they account for around 5% of the school population.

Independent schools must register with the Department of Education and Science, but in 1978 the government decided that it could no longer afford to carry out inspections, recognizing them as efficient if they complied with the Department's criteria. Supporters of independent schools claim that they enable parents to choose the type of school they wish their children to attend, and that they provide a better education by being able to afford smaller classes, and higher salaries for their teachers. Many, but not all, independent schools also provide boarding accommodation, which very few state schools possess. Opponents of private education maintain that it is socially divisive and breeds elitism (*see* social class).

Independent Schools Joint Council (ISJC) An organization that represents the interests of the country's 2300 *independent schools and coordinates their actions when joint policies are desirable. It was constituted in 1974 from such bodies as the Headmasters' Conference and the Girls' Schools Association, primarily in response to the then Labour government's threats to abolish the independent sector in education. The ISJC also runs the Independent Schools Information Service (ISIS), which had been established in 1972 to improve public relations and to represent the views of its members.

Indian Empire, Order of the An order of knighthood (bearing the designation "Most Eminent"), admission to which is granted for services rendered to the Indian Empire. It was instituted in 1877 shortly after Queen Victoria became Empress of India, and was subsequently enlarged on several occasions. The order is divided into the sovereign, Knights Grand Commanders (who are called Sir and add GCIE after their names), Knights Commanders (who are called Sir and add KCIE after their names), and Companions (CIE). The ribbon is imperial purple in colour and the motto is *Imperatricis auspiciis* ("Under the auspices of the Empress"). Although the order still has members, it will eventually disappear as there have been no appointments to it since 1947.

industrial revolution The period during which Britain was transformed from an agricultural nation into an industrial nation. The first large country to cease to rely exclusively on an agricultural or maritime economy, Britain made use of the industrial revolution to become one of the world's primary political powers. By 1914 Britain owned some 40% of the world's capital investment and ruled over 20% of the world's population.

Several factors interacted to bring about this transformation; technological, social, demographic, and economic changes combined to provide a home market for industrial products and the means of exploiting it. Once industrial production was established, additional overseas markets were acquired to augment the home market. By far the most important factors in facilitating the industrial revolution were the technological innovations that made industrialization possible. Manpower, animal power, water- and windpower, the only usable energy sources known to the medieval world, were replaced by steampower, deriving from Newcomen's original steam engine (1712), as developed by Watt (1763). This new source of energy needed fuel in vast quantities, which was provided by the deep coal mines that steam-driven pumps made workable. Other British technical innovations included Darby's coke-smelting process (1709) for iron, and Cort's puddling and rolling process (1784) for producing wrought iron. In textiles, Kay's flying shuttle (1733), Hargreave's spinning jenny (1768), Arkwright's waterframe (1769), Compton's mule (1779), and Cartwright's powerloom (1785) transformed the Lancashire cotton industry and later the Yorkshire woollen industry. The economic factors contributing to the transformation included stable or even declining prices in the early 18th century, coupled with a rise

INDUSTRIAL REVOLUTION *A late-18th-century engraving of Ironbridge, Shropshire, the first iron bridge in the world (1779). Nearby Coalbrookdale, on the River Severn, is often regarded as the birthplace of the industrial revolution.*

in wages, which produced an increase in the purchasing power of the population. Enclosures (see enclosure, laws of) and agricultural innovations caused social upheaval in rural areas and provided a pool of labour to man the factories. At the same time improved communications (the repair of roads by local turnpike trusts from the 1730s and the construction of *canals from 1759) created an infrastructure enabling a mass market to develop at home, while overseas markets developed as the *British Empire expanded.

By 1820 large-scale factory manufacturing was to be found in some industries (notably cotton in Lancashire), which introduced the concept to other industries. The woollen industry, for long Britain's staple exporter, which had been spread throughout the land in small units, by 1860 became concentrated in factories on the West Yorkshire coalfield. Similarly, the small-scale iron foundries of the Weald vanished in the face of competition from the new works of South Wales (see Welsh valleys) and the Scottish *Lowlands.

Britain had thus gained a temporary advantage over other countries, which allowed her to build up an industrial pre-eminence in the first half of the 19th century. This advantage was not challenged until the end of the century when other countries (notably Germany and the USA) began to industrialize effectively. As a consequence, Britain quickly became the world's leading maritime nation, while the *City of London became the centre of world finance, banking, and insurance. All was not smooth progress, however. By 1851, when the *Great Exhibition was held, over half the population lived in industrial cities, whose rapid growth led to new social problems of urban squalor on a large scale. These problems were slowly tackled during the course of the 19th century. Working conditions, initially appalling, gradually improved, helped by regulatory legislation (e.g. the Factory Acts, from 1802, which placed limits on working hours and controlled the employment of women and children). Later, the emergence of *trade unions helped to make factory life more tolerable and political radicalism began to find support among the new urban proletariat. Early in the 20th cen-

tury this move towards radicalism among the factory workers, supported by the intellectual arguments of members of the *Fabian Society, led to the emergence of the *Labour Party.

industrial training boards (ITBs) Boards responsible for the provision and administration of training schemes for particular industries, with the object of improving both quality and quantity. Created under the Industrial Training Act 1964, the ITBs are usually constituted from representatives of the employers, employees, and trade unions in an individual industry, together with professional educationalists. They set up apprenticeship schemes, offer direct training services, formulate policies, and make recommendations regarding training; most have close links with colleges of further education. They report to the Training Services Division of the *Manpower Services Commission, by which they are financed from public funds.

industrial tribunal Any of a number of statutory bodies established to determine disputes relating to terms and conditions of employment. A primary function is the hearing of complaints of unfair dismissal under the employment protection legislation. The tribunal may order the employer to pay compensation to the employee, to reinstate him in his former position, or to re-engage him in other suitable work. Other matters dealt with by tribunals include disputes concerning redundancy pay, equal pay, maternity rights, race and sex discrimination in employment, industrial training, and health and safety at work. A tribunal is chaired by a barrister or solicitor of at least seven years' standing, who is assisted by two lay members. The latter must have industrial experience and are normally chosen from panels nominated by the Confederation of British Industry and the Trades Union Congress. The proceedings of a tribunal are informal, with the strict rules of evidence also dispensed with. Legal aid is not available. Appeals, on points of law only, lie in general to the *Employment Appeal Tribunal.

infantry regiments The oldest specifically designated infantry regiments date from Cromwell's formation of the "New Model Army" in the 17th century. Although a great many regiments have disappeared or been amalgamated with others since then, a number of regiments can list battle honours going back to the Napoleonic Wars and beyond. The modern army has nine divisions or brigades of infantry, including the Guards Division, the Scottish Division, the Queen's Division, the King's Division, the Prince of Wales's Division, and the Light Division. The Brigade of *Gurkhas form a further division, as do the *Parachute Regiment and the *Special Air Service (SAS).

Inner Temple *See* Inns of Court.

Inns of Court Voluntary unincorporated societies having the exclusive right to confer the rank of *barrister in England and Wales or Northern Ireland (a process known as calling to the Bar). For England and Wales, there are the four Inns that have existed in London since the 14th century – the Honourable Societies of the **Inner Temple**, the **Middle Temple**, **Lincoln's Inn**, and **Gray's Inn**; and for Northern Ireland, there is the Inn of Court of Northern Ireland, established in Belfast in 1926.

Of the English Inns, the Inner and Middle Temples lie between Fleet Street and the Embankment, on a site formerly occupied by the Knights Templar and still housing the famous Temple Church (one of four round churches built by the Templars in this country). Lincoln's Inn lies between Carey Street and High Holborn, with a 15th-century hall and a gatehouse onto Chancery Lane dating from 1512. Gray's Inn lies beyond Holborn, its main entrance in Gray's Inn Road, with Restoration buildings, and walks and gardens laid out by Sir Francis Bacon (1561–1626). Each is governed by a body of senior members (including judges) known as Masters of the Bench, or Benchers. Originally, they were organized on a collegiate basis, each training its own students by means of lectures and debates (known as moots); a student was called to the Bar on his production of a certificate that he had studied satisfactorily in the chambers of a practising member. In 1852, however, they established jointly the Council of Legal Education, which provides a system of lectures, practical training, and examinations common to all students. The Council now administers the Inns of Court School of Law in Gray's Inn under the general control of the recently established *Senate of the Inns of Court and the Bar; but the collegiate tradition remains in that to qualify for call, a student must not only pass the examinations, but also dine in his Inn three times in each of twelve legal terms (a process known as "keeping terms"). The other principal concern of the Inns has always been discipline, the Benchers having power to punish their members for professional misconduct by disbarring, suspension, and reprimand. The imposition of these penalties was originally a purely domestic matter, but comes now before the Senate of the Inns of Court and the Bar. Linked with the Inns of Court, and preparing very young students for admission to them, there were formerly some lesser societies known as the Inns of Chancery. They included Barnard's Inn, Clement's Inn, Clifford's Inn and Staple Inn, all of which were dissolved in the 19th century. There was also, at the other end of the scale, the exclusive Serjeants' Inn (*see* barrister).

International Musical Eisteddfod An annual competitive folk festival held for one week each July in the picturesque town of Llangollen, overlooking the River Dee in the Welsh county of Clwyd. The festival is a colourful spectacle, drawing singers, dancers, and musicians from many parts of the world. Founded in 1947, the eisteddfod is also a major tourist attraction and probably Wales's most widely known cultural event. As, however, it has no literary competitions and is conducted mainly in English, the Llangollen festival is not generally considered to be a properly Welsh eisteddfod. *See also* eisteddfod; Royal National Eisteddfod of Wales.

Iona The Inner Hebridean island of Iona, off the western coast of Scotland, that has for centuries been one of the most famous centres of Christendom. The modern Iona Community, founded by the Rev. George MacLeod in 1938, is the latest phase in a missionary tradition stretching back to 563 AD when St Columba (c. 521–97) arrived from Ireland to found a monastery. From their base on Iona, Columba and his monks converted the Celtic tribes of Scotland and northern England to Christianity. Indeed, one of Iona's most famous missionaries, St Aidan, established the equally renowned monastic community on *Holy Island in 635. Columba was buried on Iona but in 849, because of attacks by Norse raiders, his remains were moved to Kells in Ireland. The original monastery was burnt down but was rebuilt in the 11th century under the auspices of the now Christian Norse power based on the Isle of Man. In 1154 Iona became part of the see of Trondheim in Norway, but reverted to Scottish control in 1266. Meanwhile, in 1230, a Benedictine monastery and nunnery were founded. The fact that 4 Irish, 8 Norwegian, and 48 Scottish kings are buried on Iona, gives some indication of its reputation and importance up to the Middle Ages. Parts of the monastery were later incorporated into the cathedral church of St Mary, built in the 16th century. The monastery was suppressed following the *Reformation and the church fell into disrepair. Between 1899 and 1905 it was restored, following the acquisition of the island by the Church of Scotland, and since 1938 the Iona Community has restored the cathedral cloister and many monastic buildings, which now serve as a base for their missionary work in Scotland and abroad. All members of the Community undertake to spend part of each year on the island, helping with the restoration and maintenance of the buildings, which attract many visitors.

IRA *See* Irish nationalism.

Irish The *Celtic language still spoken in parts of Ireland. It is sometimes referred to as "Gaelic", but although Scots *Gaelic is derived from it, the two languages are no longer mutually comprehensible. Even though it is the national language of the Republic of Ireland, it is now spoken in only a few isolated regions (known as the Gaeltacht), in dialects that differ widely from one another, by little over 100,000 active speakers. The rapid decline of Irish since the 17th century may be attributed to the savage persecution of Irish speakers by English administrators from Cromwell onwards, coupled with such natural disasters as the potato famine of 1847–51, in which many thousands of Irish speakers died and thousands

more emigrated, mainly to America. By the late 19th century, when the Irish language became a powerful symbol for nationalists, it was already much decayed. Attempts to enforce Irish Gaelic as the medium of instruction in primary schools in the Republic have largely failed, not least because of a lack of Irish-speaking teachers. In some cases, Irish-speaking teachers from Dublin who went to teach in Donegal, for example, actually succeeded in discouraging local Irish-speaking children from using their own language, insisting that they should learn the "standard" language approved in Dublin – an artificial composite based on the dialect of Munster.

The literature of Irish Gaelic is extremely ancient, and flourished until the early 17th century, when English rule was finally imposed. The office of poet was hereditary at the courts of the various kings of Ireland, and many of the writings of these poets, including mainly heroic sagas (*see* *Irish legend) but also ballads and nature poems, are preserved. The best known of them is Dallán Forgaill (?6th century AD).

Irish has a very large inventory of consonant sounds, including four varieties each of -n- and -l-, three of -f-, and two of other consonants, including sounds unknown in English, such as a velar fricative (as found in the Scots Gaelic word *loch*). Traditional spelling reflects an ancient spoken variety of the language, so that many of the written letters have no spoken realization. As in Scots Gaelic, the initial letter of each word is subject to "mutation": that is, it may take a different sound depending on its position and meaning. Thus, the word *fear* "man" may also take the forms *fhear* and *bhfear*, and may also be inflected: *an fhir* "of the man".

Irish Guards *See* Household Division.

Irish legend Heroic stories found in the ancient literature of the *Irish language. Sagas relating episodes in the lives of heroes who lived in the 1st century BC are preserved in manuscripts dating from the 10th to the 15th centuries. One of the most famous of these is Cuchulain, hero of *Táin Bó Cúalnge* ("The Cattle Raid of Cooley"), who, taking a stand at a ford, defended the province of Ulster single-handed against the combined armies of the rest of Ireland. Another is the story of Deirdre, the betrothed of King Conchobar (Connor), who fled with her lover Naoise to Scotland. Conchobar enticed Naoise back to Ireland, murdered him and all his brothers, and Deirdre died broken-hearted on Naoise's grave. The legends of ancient Irish literature had a powerful influence both on medieval romance in other languages, including English, and on 20th-century Irish writers such as W. B. Yeats, who retold many of them in English verse and drama.

Irish nationalism The popular movement that resulted in the creation of the Irish Free State in 1921. The first English involvement in Irish affairs can be traced back to the reign of Henry II (r. 1154–89). The deposed Irish chieftain Dermot MacMurrough recruited the aid of Norman Marcher lords (*see* Welsh Marches) in 1169, in order to win back the kingdom of Leinster. On his death he left his lands to his son-in-law, the English commander Richard de Clare, Earl of Pembroke. There were thus a number of English adventurers in Ireland when Henry II visited the country in 1171 to assert his authority over them. During this visit the Irish chiefs were forced to submit to Henry, who had taken the precaution of securing a bull from the pope (in exchange for a promise of funds from the English clergy) granting him the lordship of the country. After Henry's visit many more English settlers crossed the Irish Sea to acquire new lands. The zenith of medieval English rule in Ireland was reached under Edward I (r. 1272–1307) when they controlled about three-quarters of the country. Thereafter the Irish gradually regained ground and the great Anglo-Irish earls flourished, paying little attention to the royal government, until by 1500 the area of secure English rule (the "Pale") consisted only of a small area around Dublin. The Tudors attempted to extend royal authority, first by offers of peaceful assimilation to the Irish under Henry VIII (who was declared King of Ireland in 1541), and then by conquest, with subsequent encouragement to new English settlers (the "plantation" of Ireland). The conquest was finally completed in 1603, after fierce Irish resistance; Ulster, the

most northerly Irish province, was then extensively planted with Presbyterian Scottish immigrant farmers (1608–12). In the 17th century a determined attempt was made to oust Catholic landowners in favour of Protestants, so that by 1703 only 14% of Irish land was held by Catholics, compared with 59% in 1641. The defeat (1688–91) of Irish Catholic support for James II in the *Glorious Revolution by William of Orange (*see also* Jacobite rebellions) exacerbated divisions; its events are still commemorated today in the *battle of the Boyne celebrations and form the basis of the doctrines of the Orange Order (*see* Orangemen). A subsequent attempt to eradicate Catholicism altogether by the savage Penal Code (1695–1727) failed.

The division between Catholics and Protestants thus persisted. However, the Protestants were not united. They were divided into two distinct groups: the Presbyterians of Ulster, who were excluded from effective political power, and a ruling elite of Anglicans, who held most of the remainder of Ireland, and whose estates were worked by Irish Catholic peasants. The Presbyterians and Catholics made common cause in the late 18th century to form the Society of United Irishmen in 1791. Founded by Wolfe Tone and other Protestant radicals, this society organized a rebellion in 1798, with French aid, with the object of establishing a republic in Ireland. The rising was finally crushed at the battle of Vinegar Hill and in 1801 Ireland was incorporated within the United Kingdom, with the abolition of the Irish parliament. The Union, however, was never accepted by the Catholics (nor was it accepted by some Protestants). In 1823 Daniel O'Connell, known as the "Liberator", founded the Catholic Association to fight for Catholic emancipation, which was achieved in 1829 (*see* Roman Catholic Church in UK). He went on to form the Repeal Association (1840) to fight for the repeal of the Act of Union. Many Catholics were dissatisfied with O'Connell's pacifist approach and in 1841 the Young Ireland Movement was founded. Its members, mostly under 30 years old, advocated armed rebellion. Their rising in 1848, however, collapsed after attracting little popular support. Meanwhile, the **Great Famine** of 1847–51, caused by the repeated failure of the potato crop, halved Ireland's population through starvation or emigration. This intensified the bitterness of the Catholic peasantry and many of the emigrants formed an influential anti-British Irish community in the USA, which still endures and still provides financial and other support for the nationalists in Ireland.

In 1858 James Stephens, a survivor of the Young Ireland Movement, founded the **Fenian Society**, a secret Catholic revolutionary organization committed to the establishment of an independent republic. An abortive Fenian uprising in 1867 alerted W. E. Gladstone, the Liberal statesman, to the need for some kind of reform in Ireland. In 1870 and 1881 he introduced land Acts that gave Irish tenants greater security. These, together with the introduction of the secret ballot for elections in 1872, allowed the nationalist Catholic peasantry to vote freely for the first time. In 1874 59 MPs were elected from the Home Rule Association, founded in 1870 by Isaac Butt to promote devolved self-government by the Irish, within the British Empire. They became more radical after Butt's replacement as leader by Charles Stewart Parnell in 1878. This assertion of the Catholics' voice, compounded by a Gaelic revival after 1880, provoked a reaction from the Protestants in Ulster: fearing domination by Catholics in any form of home rule, they became firmly attached to the Union. In 1886 Gladstone announced his conversion to home rule, but he failed twice to have Bills passed due to opposition in both Ulster and England. In 1905 the extreme nationalist **Sinn Fein** ("Ourselves") party, whose aims tended towards complete separation, was founded by Arthur Griffith. In 1914 a home rule Bill was finally passed, though Ulster secured special treatment after fierce opposition (1912–14) led by Sir Edward Carson. However, its implementation was delayed by the outbreak of World War I. Two years later the Irish Republican Brotherhood, a Fenian-type society founded in 1873, took the initiative by organizing the **Easter Rising** in Dublin, an event that has become an indelible landmark in Irish history. Under Patrick Pearse 2000 nationalists held the centre of the capital for

nearly a week before surrendering after being besieged in the central post office by British troops. Its injudicious suppression and the summary execution of 15 leaders swung Catholic opinion firmly behind the extreme nationalists. In the general election of 1918, Sinn Fein under Eamon de Valera won a majority of the Irish seats; he and his party withdrew from Westminster (1919) and set up their own parliament, the Dail. A new organization, the **Irish Republican Army (IRA)**, was formed and waged guerrilla warfare against the British until they conceded the establishment of the Irish Free State, a dominion within the British Empire, in 1921. It became a republic in 1937, and left the Commonwealth in 1949.

This was not, however, the end of Ireland's problems. Protestant Ulster had consistently refused to accept rule from Dublin by a Catholic majority. No sooner had the Irish Free State been formed than the six northeastern counties opted out, forming the British province of Northern Ireland with its own parliament (*see* Northern Ireland Assembly), at Stormont. This British province was, and remains, predominantly Protestant with a substantial Catholic minority. Ulster therefore became a new focus for nationalist feeling. The Irish republic did not recognize the status of Northern Ireland and this still remains the official position. A new IRA, outlawed and committed to the uniting of all Ireland, with Sinn Fein as its political arm, has used increasingly violent tactics in Northern Ireland and on the mainland of Britain to agitate for union. In 1968 this sectarian conflict, known as "the Troubles", intensified, leading to the arrival of British troops (1969) in Ulster to attempt to keep the peace when the basically Protestant *Royal Ulster Constabulary (RUC) failed to do so. In 1969 the IRA split into the Officials, seeking a socialist republic of all Ireland, and the Provisionals (**Provos**), whose sole aim is the expulsion of the British from Northern Ireland. In 1972 the Northern Ireland parliament was suspended and direct rule from London imposed. The position is now that the Protestant majority (the Unionists) in Ulster predominantly supports union with Britain, while the Catholic minority (the

Republicans), looks with more favour on union with the Irish republic. Britain, unwilling to abrogate its responsibilities to its Ulster citizens, has to attempt both to find a solution acceptable to these incompatible religious groups and to keep the peace. In 1985 agreement was reached with the Irish republic, giving it a consultative role in the running of Northern Ireland, in an attempt to reconcile the Catholics to British rule.

Irish Republican Army (IRA) *See* Irish nationalism.

Isle of Man Although situated in the Irish Sea so that, on a clear day, Ireland, Scotland, England, and Wales, are all visible, the Isle of Man has its own unique character and history. The land area of 588 square kilometres (230 square miles) comprises a central and southern upland region and a northern plain. Snaefell is the highest peak at 620 metres (2034 feet). On the eastern coast lies the island's capital, Douglas, seat of the Manx parliament – the *Tynwald. A Lieutenant-Governor represents the Crown and presides over a body of elected representatives, the House of Keys, and a Legislative Council – equivalent to the House of Lords. These bodies govern most of the island's internal affairs. The islanders enjoy lower rates of income tax and other taxes than those on the mainland.

Neolithic burial *barrows and the relics of Bronze Age and Iron Age inhabitants are evidence of early occupation of the island. Later it became a stronghold of Celtic culture, isolated from the Anglo-Saxon influence that spread throughout the mainland following the Roman withdrawal in the early 5th century AD. However, in the 9th century, the island was colonized by the Vikings who made an enduring impact, especially with the introduction of their legislature and legal system. Many place names, such as Ramsey, are of Norse origin. But Celtic culture persisted, including the *Manx language, which was in everyday use until the 19th century.

Allegiance to Norway ended with the last of the Scandinavian kings of Mann, Magnus (r. 1252–66), who accepted the authority of Alexander III of Scotland. Control of the island was disputed between Scotland and England from 1289–90 to 1333, when Edward III of England assumed suzerainty without difficulty. The title "King of Mann" fell to royal appointees and in 1403, after changing hands several times, the position was filled by John Stanley, whose heirs, the Earls of Derby, ruled for the next 350 years. The Isle of Man was eventually restored to the Crown in 1765.

The island's income now depends principally on tourism. Visitors are attracted by the mild but invigorating climate and picturesque scenery. Every year the famous Manx *TT (Tourist Trophy) motor cycle races are enthusiastically supported. Agriculture consists mainly of livestock farming, with dairy and beef cattle, sheep, and poultry. Other industries include fishing and textiles. A famous export is the tailless Manx cat – a breed associated with the Isle of Man for some 300 years.

J

Jacobite rebellions (1689–1746) Armed attempts by the supporters of James II (r. 1685–88; Latin name: Jacobus), deposed in favour of William and Mary by the *Glorious Revolution (1688), and his descendants to restore the Stuart dynasty. The Stuarts' natural supporters were Roman Catholics and Tories, who refused to accept the Revolution on the grounds that no resistance to the royal will was justified. To these were added hostile foreign powers, notably France, political opportunists, Catholic Ireland, and the Scottish *Highlands, especially after the massacre of *Glencoe (1692). An initial rising in Scotland (1689–90) collapsed despite the Jacobite victory at the battle of Killiecrankie, near Blair Atholl, Tayside (27 July 1689). Ireland had been held for James by the Earl of Tyrconnel, and he landed there in 1689. However, the Protestants of Ulster declared for William and Mary. James failed to take Londonderry after an epic siege lasting 105 days (1689); William's forces won the battles of the Boyne (1 July 1690), after which James fled to France,

JACOBITE REBELLIONS An Incident in the Rebellion of 1745, *by David Morier. The artist may have used Scots captured at Culloden as models for the Highlanders in his painting.*

and Aughrim (12 July 1690); and the Treaty of Limerick (1691) gave James's supporters the choice of submission or exile.

When James II died (1701), his son James Francis Edward Stuart (1688–1766; the "Old Pretender") became the focus of the cause. Recognized as the lawful king by both France and Spain, he made an early attempt to seize the throne in 1708 when he landed in Scotland, but he was soon forced to withdraw as the event turned into an ill-supported fiasco. The last years of the childless Queen Anne (r. 1702–14) saw an increase in Jacobite sympathy, and several members of her last Tory ministry (1710–14) favoured the succession of the Old Pretender. However, she was succeeded by the Hanoverian George I (1714). The Old Pretender determined to challenge the new regime, and the next year returned to Scotland to lead a rebellion, known ever since as **the Fifteen**. Before he could reach Scotland, however, a Jacobite rising in England was crushed at Preston (13 November 1715) and the more threatening Scottish revolt, under the command of the incompetent Earl of Mar, declined after the indecisive battle of Sheriffmuir on the same day. The Old Pretender, having landed in December, returned to France in February 1716. In 1719 a further

invasion attempt by the Duke of Ormonde came to grief; while the discovery in 1722 of a conspiracy, led by Francis Atterbury, Bishop of Rochester, marked the end of serious Jacobite activity in England.

It was not until 1745 that Jacobite fortunes lifted. Encouraged by France, then at war with Britain, Charles Edward Stuart (1720–88) James's elder son, the "Young Pretender", arrived in Scotland to lead a new rebellion, known ever since as **the Forty-five.** Having landed at Eriskay in July, "Bonnie Prince Charlie" proclaimed the Old Pretender king, gathered an army of about 3000 Highlanders, and installed himself at Holyroodhouse at Edinburgh. The government forces in Scotland numbered under 4000, and were commanded by Sir John Cope. The two armies met at Prestonpans, ten miles east of the Scottish capital, on 21 September 1745. The unexpected Jacobite victory, achieved in under five minutes, gave the Young Pretender control of all Scotland and encouraged him to march south. His army, now numbering some 5000, took Carlisle on 17 November. However, by the time the Jacobites had reached Derby, it was clear that they were going to receive little support in England, and Charles was reluctantly forced to retreat (6 December) in the face of three large Hanoverian armies, which would otherwise have encircled him. A long and wearying winter followed and despite a last victory at Falkirk on 17 January 1746, by April an English army under the Duke of Cumberland was approaching Inverness, where the Young Pretender had taken refuge. The ensuing battle of *Culloden (16 April) and the subsequent ruthless campaign to suppress the *clans – the "pacification of the Highlands" – ended all hopes of any further revival of the Stuart cause. Charles was sheltered by Flora MacDonald and other followers, finally escaping to Skye and then France. He spent the rest of his life overseas, dying a drunkard in Italy. The last royal Stuart, his brother Henry, died in 1807, a cardinal and a pensioner of George III.

jellied eels A popular dish that may have originated in the East End of London. The chopped eels are boiled in stock and the mixture left to set: as the liquid cools it forms a clear jelly around the pieces of fish. Jellied eels were more widely consumed in the days when eels could be readily fished from the Thames and provided a cheap form of nourishment for the working-class families of the area, but they are still available from fish stalls in the East End, in certain other parts of London, and at some seaside towns.

Jews in Britain There were an estimated 410,000 Jews in Britain in 1984, many of whom are prominent in political, cultural, and commercial life. However, over the centuries, Britain's Jews have experienced persecution and expulsion, although not on the same scale as in some other European countries. Reports of individual Jews in Britain go back to the Roman occupation although there was no Jewish settlement in Britain until the Norman conquest, when a number of Jews came to England from Rouen, providing a commercial and entrepreneurial expertise that feudal England lacked. The king, who levied a tax on these commercial transactions, found the presence of the Jews financially rewarding and consequently offered them his protection. By the 11th century communities of Jews were established in England, particularly in London and other major cities. They were disliked for

two reasons: their religious beliefs separated them from the Christian majority and their role as money-lenders made them the object of resentment, contempt, and envy. A mob attack on Jews attending the coronation of Richard I in 1189 sparked off a wave of anti-Jewish incidents throughout the country. By the time Edward I came to the throne the Jews were sufficiently impoverished to be of little further use to the Crown; in 1290 they were expelled from England.

For the next 365 years no Jewish communities existed in the British Isles. However, by the mid-16th century there was in London a small secret community of Marranos (Spanish and Portuguese Jews who had adopted Spanish-sounding names and who professed Christianity to avoid death at the hands of the Inquisition, although they practised Judaism in secret). These few families formed the basis of the Sephardi community, which was later augmented by many more Marrano families, who had been living in Amsterdam and Antwerp since their flight from Spain. Members of the Sephardi community petitioned Cromwell for permission to hold services and buy land for a cemetery; on account of their dislike of Catholicism, he granted their request. The first synagogue since the expulsion was opened in 1657, which was replaced in 1701 by a new building in Bevis Marks. This synagogue is still the centre of the Sephardi community in the UK and many of its present members retain the Marrano names with which their ancestors arrived in the 16th and 17th centuries: Henriques, Mocatta, Nabarro, and Alvarez are familiar examples.

Once the Jews were permitted to practise their religion in England, another branch of Jewry, the Ashkenazis of northern Europe, began to arrive. The Cossack uprising of 1650 had driven Polish and Lithuanian Jews westwards and some crossed the North Sea to England. Poor and practising an alien liturgy, they were not welcomed by the rich merchants of the Sephardi community. However, by the 18th century such illustrious Ashkenazi figures as Nathan Rothschild were contributing to London's development as a commercial and banking centre. In 1860, following the election of Lionel de Rothschild as MP for the City of

London, the parliamentary oath, which required a formal adherence to Christianity, was amended to accommodate Jews. The influx of Russian and Polish Jews after 1881 led to the growth of Jewish communities in several other cities. However, the immigration of European Jews escaping the Nazi persecutions in the 1930s brought many more Jews into the country; this wave of immigration was associated with some antisemitism, especially by British fascists.

The chief representative body of Britain's Jews is the Board of Deputies of British Jews. Established in 1760, it upholds the interests of Jews and ensures that their religious and other freedoms are preserved. The spiritual leader of the Ashkenazi community is the **Chief Rabbi**, a position held since 1967 by the Very Reverend Immanuel Jakobovits. He presides over the Beth Din (Court of Judgement), which arbitrates on religious matters and questions of Jewish law, relating to, for example, marriage and divorce. The Sephardis continue to maintain their own community and leader.

Jockey Club The governing body of British racing, both on the flat and over jumps (steeplechasing and hurdling). The Jockey Club is responsible for race meetings, the horses, riders, trainers, and officials at all races. It has some 90 members, including prominent figures from the racing world.

The Jockey Club was founded in 1750, with the aim of bringing order to British horse racing, which was at that time beset by corruption, bribery, doping, and other forms of malpractice. In 1752 it acquired some land at Newmarket racecourse, where it offered a kind of arbitration service. Since 1773 a member of the Weatherby family has been its secretary; over the years this post has developed into a full-scale service, with the family firm administering and keeping records and registers of horses, owners, jockeys, trainers, results, entries, producing the *Racing Calendar*, and maintaining the *General Stud Book*, the master record of thoroughbred racehorse breeding first published in 1791. The great strength of the Jockey Club, and its willingness and ability to uphold its rules with severe disciplinary sanctions when required, has earned respect for British horse racing throughout the world and guarantees its consistently high standard.

Jodrell Bank The site of one of the world's largest steerable single-dish radio telescopes, belonging to Manchester University's Nuffield Radio Astronomy Laboratories in Cheshire. The laboratory was founded in 1947, largely through the efforts of the astronomer Sir Bernard Lovell, who served as director at Jodrell Bank (1951–81). The construction of the Mk IA radio telescope, with its steerable parabolic receiving dish measuring 76 metres (250 feet) in diameter, was completed in 1957, just in time to track the carrier rocket of the first artificial satellite, launched by the Soviet Union on 4 October 1957. The Mk II telescope, with a 38 × 25 metre (125 × 82 foot) dish, came into service in 1964. Jodrell Bank has frequently collaborated with the American space agency NASA in tracking craft for the US space programme. Its main work, however, is the detection and analysis of radio waves and their sources, such as quasars and pulsars, in deep space. Linking it with other radio telescopes enables the mapping of radio sources and other astrometric observations to be performed with very high resolution.

A visitors' centre has been created at Jodrell Bank, featuring an exhibition of radio astronomy and a planetarium.

John Bull A personification of the typical Englishman, or of England itself. The character was developed by the writer John Arbuthnot (1667–1735) in his satire *The History of John Bull* (1712) and featured largely in political cartoons of the 18th and 19th centuries, representing a rather stout citizen oppressed by debt or taxation. Traditionally depicted as a short stocky figure, John Bull was renowned for his bluntness and obstinacy. His social status changed over the years: Arbuthnot showed him as an honest tradesman bringing a suit against Lewis Baboon (Louis XIV of France) for interfering with trade; in the mid-19th century he appeared as a prosperous citizen; and in the popular *Punch* cartoons he was sometimes a seaman of the Royal Navy, and most often a jovial countryman in a Union Jack waistcoat with a bulldog at his heels. In the political cartoons of the 20th century John

Bull tended to be replaced by caricatures of real people, notably Winston Churchill, but the character remains firmly established in British tradition.

Joseph of Arimathea (Glastonbury Thorn legend)   A New Testament figure who took responsibility for the burial of Christ after the Crucifixion. According to legend St Joseph travelled to Britain some years after the Crucifixion, bearing the Holy Grail (see Arthurian legend), with the intention of bringing Christianity to the pagan Britons. He rested on a hill near Glastonbury, now known as Weary-all Hill, and thrust his thorny staff, allegedly cut from the bush from which Christ's crown of thorns was made, into the ground. The staff miraculously took root and began to bud; St Joseph interpreted this as a sign that he had reached his destination and set about establishing England's first Christian church at Glastonbury. The Grail was buried at the foot of Glastonbury Tor at the site of a natural spring, now known as Chalice Well, the reddish waters of which were reputed to have healing powers.

The individual elements of this story belong to an assortment of legends dating from medieval times to the mid-18th century, and beginning with Robert de Borron's verse romance *Joseph d'Arimathie* (c. 1200). It is extremely unlikely that St Joseph ever came to Britain – this myth seems to date from the 13th century – and the true site of England's first Christian church is unknown. The thorn tree, however, has continued to blossom every year around Christmas time – out of season for the common hawthorn, to which it is apparently related. The original tree was cut down by a Puritan fanatic during the Civil War, but not before several successors, raised from cuttings, had been planted in the vicinity.

JP   *See* justice of the peace.

judge   A person appointed by the state to hear and determine legal proceedings in the courts, civil and criminal. (The parties to a civil dispute may, and frequently do in cases of a commercial nature, submit it instead to an impartial referee of their own choosing, known as an arbitrator.) The term is not quite exclusive to the *superior courts (in England

and Wales, for example, a *circuit judge sits in both the Crown Court and the county court) but it is not used of justices or magistrates (see justice of the peace). Judges are appointed almost exclusively from practising barristers, or in Scotland advocates, but a solicitor can be made a *recorder of the Crown Court and thence a circuit judge. Their independence is of fundamental importance and is secured in several ways: they hold office during good behaviour, and are not liable to removal by the government for political reasons; their salaries do not require the annual parliamentary approval necessary for most public expenditure; and they are immune from liability for anything said or done in the exercise of their functions. Judges are disqualified from membership of the House of Commons, and so too are sheriffs in Scotland, and stipendiary and resident magistrates.

Judges' Rules   Requirements drawn up by the judges of the Queen's Bench Division of the *High Court of Justice with respect to the questioning of suspects by the police, and the taking of statements from them. Questioning is governed by three main rules: a police officer must always caution a suspect before questioning him; he must caution him again before actually charging him; and any written statement must be made voluntarily. A formal caution runs thus: "You are not obliged to say anything unless you wish to do so, but what you say may be put into writing and given in evidence". (The words "against you" were formerly added at the end, but were dropped in a 1912 revision of the Rules.)

The Judges' Rules (which were last revised in 1978) are designed to ensure that confessions are voluntary. They are not, however, binding rules of law. A judge is always free to admit a confession as evidence even if they have been breached.

Judicial Committee of the Privy Council
A committee established by Parliament in 1833 to exercise the judicial functions of the *Privy Council, which consist primarily in the hearing of a limited range of appeals. Before then, any member of the Council, lay or legally qualified, could participate. Basically, the Committee consists of the Lord President of

the Council (who does not, in fact, sit), the Lord Chancellor, the Lords of Appeal in Ordinary, and any other Privy Councillors who have held high judicial office in the UK. The Council hears appeals from the highest courts of the colonies and other dependent territories, and of the few independent countries of the Commonwealth that have not abolished them, and judges of these courts may (if Privy Councillors) take part in these appeals. Other appeals which lie to the Judicial Committee are appeals from the Channel Islands and the Isle of Man, from the prize court, from ecclesiastical courts, and certain appeals assigned by Act of Parliament (e.g. appeals from the disciplinary committee of the General Medical Council). Appeals apart, the Committee may also be required by the Crown to give an advisory opinion on any legal problem of public concern. This advice is requested very rarely (e.g. to obtain advice on a question relating to disqualification for membership of the House of Commons).

jury A panel of lay people, chosen at random, who hear the evidence in legal proceedings, decide on the validity (or otherwise) of the facts presented to them, their interpretation of these, and give a verdict of "guilty" or "not guilty" based on the facts and on directions given by the judge. The judge usually decides what is admissible evidence and if the evidence is insufficient for a conviction. He also usually summarizes the evidence for the benefit of the jury and provides an explanation of any relevant points of law to enable the jury to arrive at their verdict. The judge usually decides on the sentence in criminal cases, although in civil cases involving claims for damages, the jury may be called upon to quantify the damages. Juries were introduced into England during the Saxon period, being first used by King Alfred, according to tradition. Their form, however, was greatly influenced by the inquisitorial system imported from Normandy in the 11th century; by the 13th century they feature in Magna Carta as a bulwark of the liberty of the people. It was not until the 15th century, however, that a clear distinction was drawn between the roles of counsel to present evidence and advocate its validity, the

jury to decide on the facts, and the court to administer the law.

Trial by jury spread throughout Britain and the USA, where the advantages of placing justice in the hands of unpaid ordinary people, rather than professional lawyers, has continued to recommend itself. (In Europe, despite its popularity as a symbol of democracy in the 19th century, it has largely been dispensed with.) Trial by jury in Britain is now largely restricted to criminal proceedings; in England and Wales, there are juries in Crown Courts, but not in magistrates' courts. There may also be a jury in a limited range of civil proceedings (e.g. actions for defamation in the High Court of Justice or a county court); there are also certain cases (e.g. a death in police custody) in which a coroner must sit with a jury. There are no juries in appeal proceedings. In criminal proceedings, there are 12 jurors to begin with, but as long as the number does not fall below 9, a trial may continue despite a juror's death or illness during its course. Before the jurors are sworn, the accused may object to up to 3 of them without giving reasons (a "peremptory challenge"); both sides may object to as many jurors as they wish for certain reasons (e.g. the likelihood of bias), the validity of which is decided by the judge ("challenges for reason"). Until recently verdicts had to be unanimous, but now majority verdicts are possible as long as there are at least 10 jurors. If 10, 9 must agree; if 11 or 12, 10 must agree. In civil proceedings, there are 12 jurors in the High Court (where the same majority rule applies), but only 8 in a county court (where 7 constitute a majority). There are 7 to 11 jurors in a coroner's court, and up to 2 may dissent.

To be liable for jury service, a person must be a registered parliamentary or local government elector aged between 18 and 65, and must have been ordinarily resident in the UK, the Channel Islands, or the Isle of Man for at least 5 years since becoming 13. Certain people are, however, ineligible, and certain are disqualified. The former include judges, barristers, solicitors, police officers, ministers of religion, and the mentally disordered; and the latter include anyone who has been imprisoned for three months or more in the previous ten years. In addition, certain people (principally,

MPs, members of the armed forces, and medical practitioners) have the right to be excused if they so wish.

justice of the peace (JP) A person appointed by the Lord Chancellor in the name of the Crown to exercise within a particular area of England or Wales a limited judicial jurisdiction (primarily criminal) and certain administrative functions. The majority of justices of the peace (of which there are over 20,000) are laymen, whose services are part-time and unpaid, although their expenses are reimbursed. They are also referred to as lay magistrates. Statute also provides for the appointment in London and the major provincial centres of qualified lawyers as stipendiary magistrates, who are full-time salaried magistrates also holding the office of justices of the peace.

The office dates from the 14th century, when the country commissions of the peace (which had previously been responsible only for pursuing and arresting criminals) began to take over some of the functions of royal judges in the shires. Their jurisdiction was fixed by statute in 1368, and included the determination of criminal offences. Subsequent statutes varied their duties and powers. The heyday of the justice of the peace was from the late 15th to the early 19th centuries, when they exercised most functions of local government outside the towns.

A magistrate must live within 15 miles of the area for which he is commissioned, but there are no other requirements for selection. Although not required to have legal qualifications, lay magistrates undergo training, and are assisted in court by a qualified official (*see* clerk to the justices). Stipendiary magistrates are appointed by the Crown on the advice of the Lord Chancellor and must be barristers or solicitors of at least seven years' standing. Magistrates, lay and stipendiary, may be removed from office by the Lord Chancellor at any time. At the age of 70, or earlier if they request, they are placed on a supplemental list and thereby usually cease to exercise any judicial functions. They normally preside in *magistrates' courts, but they also sit for certain purposes in the *Crown Court. Their administrative functions are largely regulatory,

for example, licensing in connection with the retail sale of alcohol, public entertainments, and public health.

In Scotland, there are also lay justices of the peace and stipendiary magistrates, but their judicial jurisdiction is criminal only, and it is not customary to speak of the former as "magistrates". In Northern Ireland, the position approximates to that in England and Wales, but the place of stipendiary magistrates is taken by resident magistrates.

K

Kaisar-i-Hind Medal A decoration awarded to men and women for special public service in British India, instituted on 10 April 1900. The name means "Emperor of India" in Hindi. There were three classes: gold, silver, and bronze; however, no awards have been made since 1947.

Kew gardens The popular name for Britain's most prestigious botanical institution, the Royal Botanic Gardens at Kew in Surrey. Situated on a 120-hectare (300-acre) site by the River Thames, the gardens contain a vast collection of herbs, trees, and shrubs gathered from all over the world. The gardens owe their existence chiefly to Princess Augusta, mother of George III, who in 1759 started a small botanic garden on her Kew estate. In 1760 George III inherited the neighbouring Richmond estate and, following his mother's death in 1772, took over Kew. The Botanic Garden flourished under the direction of Sir Joseph Banks (1743–1820), who sent collectors to South Africa, Australia, and the Pacific to gather specimens. In 1841 the Botanic Garden was given to the nation and Sir William Hooker was appointed its first official director. The gardens were enlarged and the scientific side expanded with the founding of the library, herbarium, and the department of economic botany. Further gifts of land from the royal family have brought the gardens to their present size.

One of the main tasks of Kew researchers is the identification of plant species of potential economic importance. The rubber plantations of southeast Asia were founded with seedlings of the South American rubber tree sent from Kew in the 19th century. Of most interest to visitors is the unmatched display of the gardens themselves, surrounding Kew Palace (1631), and Decimus Burton's famous Palm House, built between 1844 and 1848 and containing many varieties of tropical plants. Other glasshouses specialize in cacti, alpines, orchids, waterlilies, and a collection of Australian species. In 1965 the Royal Botanic Gardens extended its work by taking over the 187-hectare (462-acre) estate of Wakehurst Place in Sussex, which is also open to the public.

King's Counsel   *See* Queen's Counsel.

King's Medals   Two medals: the King's Medal for Courage in the Cause of Freedom and the King's Medal for Service in the Cause of Freedom. They were instituted on 23 August 1945 and were designed to reward foreigners for distinguished service in the Allied cause during World War II. Initially the decoration was intended for civilians, but later members of foreign armed services became eligible. Both sexes and all ranks could be considered for the decoration. The distinction between the award for courage and that for service is that the former was intended for those who had helped British servicemen in enemy territory, and the latter was for help in a civilian context. The medal itself is silver in both cases.

knight bachelor   A recipient of the honour of knighthood who does not belong to one of the *orders of knighthood. Knights bachelor derive from the earliest form of knighthood, which predates the introduction of orders. The honour is still awarded to men of distinction. The Old English word *cniht* originally meant a youth or retainer. By the mid-12th century *cniht* had come to mean something like the French *chevalier*, that is, a warrior on horseback. Under the feudal system (*see* feudalism) that developed in England after the Norman conquest, a knight was a soldier in the service of a lord, that is, he received certain benefits in exchange for a fixed number of days' military service each year. The term "bachelor" denoted a young landless knight and dates from the reign of Henry III (r. 1216–72). Before that time no special insignia had existed, but from 1257 registers were kept listing particulars of every knight bachelor for a given period. A formal register of knights bachelor was instituted by James I, but this lapsed. Not until 1908 was an association formed to continue these registers. It was called The Society of Knights and was officially recognized in 1912; in 1926 Georve V issued a warrant creating special insignia and permitting a badge to be worn on the left side of the outer garment by knights bachelor. The association changed its name by royal command to The Imperial Society of Knights Bachelor.

Knight Commander   The second highest male rank in various *orders of knighthood.

Knight Grand Commander   The highest male rank in the Order of the *Star of India and the Order of the *Indian Empire.

Knight Grand Cross   The highest male rank in various *orders of knighthood.

L

Labour Day   In Britain, as in the rest of Europe, the day on which trade unions and other labour organizations traditionally hold marches and rallies. It coincides with *May Day – declared an international labour holiday by the Second International (an international association of socialist parties) in 1889. May Day is properly 1 May but many Labour Day events take place on the first Monday in May, which has been a public holiday since 1977.

Labour Party   A major British political party, which advocates socialist policies. It

LABOUR DAY. An Offering for May Day 1894, *by Walter Crane. May Day festivities were adopted by socialists as a celebration of the Labour cause. Crane, a student of Ruskin, also provided cartoons for the socialist publications* Justice *and* The Commonweal.

traces its origin to the Labour Representative Committee (LRC) established in London in 1900 in response to a resolution made at the Trades Union Congress in 1899, which called for an independent working-class political organization. There were a few independent Labour MPs, such as Kier Hardie, in Parliament as early as 1892, but they lacked a common front. After the general election of 1900, when 12 Labour MPs were elected, the LRC was established to coordinate them. In the election of 1906 the LRC endorsed 50 candidates, of whom 29 were successful; as soon as Parliament assembled, it changed its name to the Labour Party and its MPs banded themselves together under elected officers and whips. The Labour Party's representation grew to 40 in the first of two elections in 1910, and to 42 in the second, but its real breakthrough came in 1922 (a Conservative victory) when, by taking 142 seats against the Liberals' 117, it established itself as the major opposition party. Labour held office briefly in 1924, and again from 1928 to 1931, under Ramsay MacDonald. After the prewar and wartime coalition governments, it swept to victory in 1945 under Clement Attlee, with a majority of 146 over all other parties. It lost power in 1951, but held it again from 1964 to 1970 and from 1974 to 1979.

The leader of the Labour Party was formerly elected by its parliamentary party. However, in 1980 the Blackpool party conference decided that election should be instead by an electoral college representing the three main sections of the movement (the unions, the constituency associations, and the parliamentary party). In 1981 a special conference decided that the unions should have 40% of the franchise, and the other sections 30% each.

ladies in waiting Female members of the royal household who attend the queen, whether regnant or consort. There are two ranks of lady in waiting, the senior consisting of two ladies of the bedchamber, who usually hold at least the rank of countess, and who attend the present Queen during the most important state functions, and occasionally on state visits abroad. In past centuries the position of lady of the bedchamber was frequently held by the king's mistress. Charles II ap-pointed Lady Castlemaine to attend Catherine of Braganza, his queen. Catherine Sedley, Countess of Dorchester, was mistress to James II and lady of the bedchamber both to his second wife Mary of Modena, and his daughter Queen Mary II, wife of William III.

The lower rank of lady in waiting consists of four women of the bedchamber; they are the Queen's full-time attendants, each serving for two weeks at a time. They fulfil the role of chaperone, companion, and secretary, and perform such duties as enquiring after people who are ill, making purchases from shops, and dealing with some of the Queen's private correspondence, such as the many letters written to her by children. They attend the Queen on all public and semiprivate engagements. Other female members of the royal family, such as the Queen Mother, are also attended by ladies in waiting.

The ladies in waiting used to be quasi-political appointments. In 1839 the partisan nature of the office was underlined by "the bedchamber crisis". The young Queen Victoria, who was obstinately attached to her Prime Minister, Lord Melbourne, refused to change her *Mistress of the Robes and ladies of the bedchamber when Melbourne's ministry fell. Sir Robert Peel, the potential Conservative Prime Minister, insisted on Queen Victoria replacing her Whig ladies as a mark of the Crown's confidence in his administration, but he was eventually obliged to yield and Melbourne resumed office. The episode is considered a landmark in British constitutional history. By the time Peel next attained office (1841), Prince Albert had arranged the resignation of the Whig ladies of the bedchamber, and subsequently ladies in waiting did not change with every ministry and were assumed to be politically impartial.

Lady Day The feast of the Annunciation of the Virgin Mary, celebrated in the Church calendar on 25 March, and popularly known as Lady Day – a name formerly applied to all festivals of the Virgin Mary. From the 14th century until 1752, Lady Day was considered the start of the new year and, being a *quarter day, was a time for payment of rent and other manorial dues (see manor). Old Lady Day (6

April) still marks the start of the fiscal year for accounting and tax purposes.

Lake District A region of hills and lakes in the county of Cumbria in northwest England, forming some of the loveliest landscapes in Britain, which has inspired many writers and artists (*see* Lake poets). The scenery of the Lake District, or Lakeland, is the legacy of a sequence of geological events. About 50 million years ago the region was dome-shaped with rivers radiating from the summit. During the Ice Ages that followed, the river valleys, called "dales", were carved out from the rock by glaciers; lakes formed in many of the valleys, while higher in the hills ("fells") smaller lakes or "tarns" are to be found. The landscape changes with the various types of underlying rock: the oldest, known as the Skiddaw slates, occur in the north of the region and have produced smooth rounded hills; whereas further south lies a belt of more rugged hills based on volcanic rock and including the craggy peaks of the Langdale and Scafell Pikes (England's highest point at 977 metres

(3206 feet)) and Sca Fell itself. Beneath the fells lie the lakes of Wast Water, Buttermere, Derwent Water, Thirlmere, Ullswater, and others. Between this region and Morecambe Bay to the south are the gentler hills around Windermere and Coniston Water, on more recent Silurian rock.

The first settlement of the region was probably on the flat sandy coastal strip during the Stone Age, with later migration into the more fertile valleys. Stone circles of late Neolithic and early Bronze Age can be seen at Castlerigg, near Keswick, and at Swinside, near Black Combe. The Romans built several forts in the area, including a spectacularly sited example in the Hard Knot Pass, in their efforts to quell the recalcitrant British tribe known as the Brigantes. Following the Romans' withdrawal in the early 5th century AD, the by then romanized British inhabitants faced incursions from the Angles, and in the 8th century Norse settlers from Ireland and the Isle of Man entered the region. The last king of Cumbria, Dunmail, was defeated by Edmund of Northumbria in 945 and control of the region passed

LAKE DISTRICT *Some of the highest peaks in England, including Great Gable (centre), reflected in Wastwater.*

235

Lake District National Park

COCKERMOUTH•

Bassenthwaite Lake

Skiddaw
△ 931m

△ Saddleback
868m

•PENRITH

Griesdale
Pike 790m
△

•KESWICK

Loweswater

Crummock
Water

Derwent Water

Ullswater

•WHITEHAVEN

Ennerdale
Water

Buttermere

Thirlmere

Red Tarn
△⊙
Helvellyn 950m

SHAP
•

Steeple △
841m

△Pillar 829m

Great △
Gable 899m

△Glaramara
780m

Griesdale
Tarn△
Fairfield 873m

High Street
829m △

Hawes Water

Scafell Pikes 977m △

Wast Water

△
Scafell
964m

△ Bowfell
902m

Langdale
Pikes 717m

Grasmere

•GRASMERE

•AMBLESIDE

△
Harter Fell
765m

Tarn Hows

Devoke Water

The Old Man of
Coniston 802m

Esthwaite
Water

WINDERMERE
•

Coniston Water

Windermere

•KENDAL

IRISH

SEA

ULVERSTON
•

GRANGE
OVER SANDS

0   5   10 miles

0   5   10   15 km

BARROW IN
•FURNESS

MORECAMBE

BAY

to the Scots king, Malcolm. The Normans conquered Cumbria in 1092 and established their castles and abbeys, although the region continued to be a cause of dispute between England and Scotland until 1157. Raids by the Scots remained a problem, especially in the 14th and 15th centuries.

Wool was for long the mainstay of the Lakeland economy, but the 16th century saw the start of mining – first copper and then lead. The forests, which once covered much of the fells, were cut down to provide fuel for smelting the ore. By the 20th century most of the mines had been abandoned. Livestock farming, especially sheep-rearing, is still the main agricultural activity. There are also now several commercial forestry plantations, largely conifers. The principal towns of Keswick and Kendal have some manufacturing industry but the region relies heavily on tourism. The Lakes provide splendid opportunities for mountaineering, fell-walking, and sailing. The whole area is a *national park and the National Trust is the biggest single landowner, facilitating public access to a great deal of the Lakeland countryside.

Lake poets The poets William Wordsworth (1770–1850), Samuel Taylor Coleridge (1772–1834), and Robert Southey (1774–1843), who chose to live and write in the beautiful Lake District of northwest England. The term "Lake School" was first applied by Francis Jeffrey in the *Edinburgh Review* (1817); it was contemptuously adapted by Byron, who called them the "Lakers". Wordsworth alone of the group was born in the district, at Cockermouth in Cumberland. In 1795 he moved to Somerset, where he became a close friend of Coleridge. In 1798 their famous joint collection, *Lyrical Ballads,* was published. The following year Wordsworth returned to Cumberland, settling with his sister Dorothy at Grasmere. From 1800 to 1804 Coleridge lived at Keswick, where Southey also settled in 1803. They had met in the early 1790s and planned, with little result, the establishment of a utopian community in America. Southey became *poet laureate in 1813, to be succeeded by Wordsworth, greatest of the Romantic poets (*see* Romantic movement), in 1843. A record of their lives in the Lake District is contained in Dorothy Wordsworth's *Grasmere Journal.*

Lallans The English or *Scots language as spoken in the central Lowlands of Scotland (including Edinburgh) and up the northeast coast to Aberdeen. In the 20th century, the term Lallans is associated especially with the Scots Language Society, whose journal *Lallans* offers prizes "for scrievin in the Scots tongue", and with the movement for the revival of literary Scots headed by the poet Hugh MacDiarmid (1892–1978), which started in the 1920s.

Lambeth Conference A meeting of bishops of the worldwide *Anglican Communion, held about every ten years, under the chairmanship of the Archbishop of Canterbury, traditionally at Lambeth Palace, to discuss doctrinal, liturgical, and other matters. Prompted by a proposal from Bishop Hopkins of Vermont, USA, the first Lambeth Conference was held in 1867 under the chairmanship of Archbishop Longley, but only about half of the 144 Anglican bishops attended. By 1968 attendance had risen to 462, with suffragan bishops also invited. This Conference initiated the establishment of an Anglican Consultative Council; this last met in Nigeria in 1984. The 1978 Conference, held at the University of Kent, (Canterbury), inaugurated biennial meetings of the primates of the Anglican Communion; the first such meeting was held in England the following November–December. Although Conference resolutions have considerable moral and spiritual authority, they are not binding on any member Church.

Lambeth Palace The official residence of the *Archbishop of Canterbury, near Lambeth Bridge on the south bank of the Thames in London. Part of the site was bought in 1190 by Archbishop Baldwin for a college of monks and the rest acquired by his successor, Archbishop Hubert Walter, who built Lambeth House around 1200. Only the present chapel crypt dates from this period. Archbishop Stephen Langton (1207–28) was the first primate to reside at Lambeth. As the seat of the Church's power, the palace has had a turbulent and often violent history, reflected architecturally by the many reconstructions and additions to the building. The Lollards' Tower, built as a water tower in 1432 and now converted to apartments, was so named because it was thought that *Lollards were held there by the archbishops. During the English Civil War and after, the palace was used as a prison and much of the fabric desecrated by the Puritans. With the *Restoration of the monarchy in 1660, the Archbishop returned to Lambeth and supervised the rebuilding of the 13th-century chapel and the Great Hall (1660–63), still one of the palace's main features. It is also the scene of the *Lambeth Conferences, which began in 1867.

Considerable reconstruction occurred between 1828 and 1834, at the hands of Edward Blore, who was a proponent of the gothic style. However, the fine red-brick Tudor gatehouse (1486–1501) was preserved. In 1900 some three hectares (nine acres) of the Palace grounds were given to London's municipal authority as a public park, known as Archbishop's Park.

Lammas Day   Observed on 1 August, and derived from the Anglo-Saxon *hlafmaesse*, literally "loaf-mass". In the early Church, this feast day of thanksgiving for the harvest involved a special mass in which bread made from the first-ripened wheat was consecrated. Lammas was first mentioned in the records of King Alfred (r. 871–99) and was widely observed in the Middle Ages. It is one of the Scottish *quarter days.

Land Registry   A body established by the Land Registration Acts 1925 and 1936 to operate a system of registration of title to land in England and Wales. Its headquarters are in Lincoln's Inn Fields, London, but actual registration takes place at district registries throughout the country. A proprietor's title is examined in depth, and, if established, he is registered as owner, and issued with a certificate of title by which the state guarantees his ownership. Subsequent transfers of the land are thereby rendered simple, quick, and relatively inexpensive. The aim is that all land be registered, but the labour involved is such as to make this a very long-term ambition. The Act provides that any owner may register his title

voluntarily, and that registration may be made compulsory by government order – but such an order merely means that registration of land in the area must take place when it is next transferred, and that may not be for many years. Progress is, however, being made, and a 1984 order (the first since 1978) specifying new compulsory areas for registration has the result that registration is now compulsory in areas containing 80% of the population. A further function of the Land Registry is the maintaining, in respect of unregistered land, of a register of land charges, that is to say, of rights over the land, such as restrictive covenants, owned by third parties.

Lands Tribunal   A body established by Parliament in 1949 to deal with disputes over land valuation. In an important appellate capacity, it decides questions as to value for rating purposes (e.g. concerning valuations by the Inland Revenue). It also considers the levels of compensation payable in the event of compulsory purchase orders, or of depreciation as a result of certain public works. Members of the tribunal are appointed by the Lord Chancellor. Its president is either a judge or a barrister of at least seven years' standing, and its other members must be either legally qualified or experienced in land valuation. It may sit anywhere in the UK. It is subject to the supervision of the *Council on Tribunals, and its decisions may be appealed to the Court of Appeal, but on points of law only.

lardy cake   A rich sticky cake traditionally made in Wiltshire and served warm from the oven. Lardy cake was originally made from scraps of bread dough left over from the weekly baking session and eaten, sliced and buttered, for Sunday tea. The bread dough is rolled out, spread with lard, sugar, and dried fruit, and folded; this procedure is repeated once or twice more before baking. To ensure its characteristic sticky texture, the cooked lardy cake is left to stand for a while before being turned out of the baking tin.

laver bread (Welsh: *bara lawr*)   A vegetable dish eaten in coastal parts of South Wales, particularly around Swansea and the Gower Peninsula. It is prepared from a seaweed, said to be rich in iodine, called laver (Welsh *lafwr* or *lawr*), which is boiled to a soft pulp. It is stored and sold out of large tubs by the pound in local markets. It is often coated in oatmeal and is fried. Bacon is commonly eaten with it. The Swansea-born poet Dylan Thomas (1914–53) obviously enjoyed it: "I was a stranger to the seatown, fresh or stale from the city where I worked for my bread and butter wishing it were laver bread and country salty butter yolk-yellow."

law centres Centres at a number of places in the UK, most of them in deprived urban areas, which provide free advice and representation, particularly in connection with education, housing, immigration, welfare rights, and matters outside the ambit of the statutory schemes for *legal aid and legal advice and assistance. The first centre was set up in 1970; and at the beginning of 1985 there were 54 of them, serving some 40,000 people a year. Thirty of the centres were funded by the Department of the Environment, fifteen by local authorities, seven by the Lord Chancellor's department, and one each by the Scottish Office and the Northern Ireland Office.

Law Commission A body established in 1965 to promote the development and reform of the law of England and Wales. It consists of a chairman and four other commissioners appointed by the Lord Chancellor. Commissioners must be the holders (present or past) of judicial office, or suitably experienced barristers, solicitors, or lecturers in law, and they hold office for up to five years, without prejudice to reappointment. The Commission produces consultative documents for discussion with the legal profession, government departments, and other interested parties; reports and recommendations; and draft legislation for enactment by Parliament. The Commission's function is to promote the modernization and simplification of the legal system: for example, by suggesting the abolition of obsolete legislation, or the consolidation of a number of Acts passed over time into one new Act.

There is also a **Scottish Law Commission**, established in 1965 for similar purposes in relation to Scots law. Its chairman and four other commissioners (who must be similarly qualified) are appointed by the Lord Advocate. It

was necessary to set up separate Commissions because the English and Scottish legal systems differ so fundamentally from each other in certain key areas such as property rights and criminal administration. The Commissions are, however, required to act in consultation with each other.

Law Lords *See* Lords of Appeal in Ordinary.

Law Officers The principal legal advisers of the Crown. For England, Wales, and Northern Ireland, they comprise the *Attorney General and the *Solicitor General; and for Scotland, the *Lord Advocate and the Solicitor General for Scotland (*see* Lord Advocate). The Law Officers' department, at the Royal Courts of Justice in London, is that which services the Attorney General and the Solicitor General, and for their Scottish counterparts it is the Lord Advocate's department, in the Crown Office, Edinburgh.

Law Society The governing body of *solicitors in England and Wales, established as the Incorporated Law Society by royal charter of 1831, and changing to its present name in 1903. The Society's functions include the education and examination of students, and their enrolment as solicitors after serving their "articles" (a period of apprenticeship with a solicitor of at least five years' standing) and passing their finals; the issue of the annual practising certificates to solicitors engaging in private practice; the making of rules governing professional conduct, and the supervision of solicitors' charges; the administration of the schemes for *legal aid and legal advice and assistance; and the hearing of complaints against solicitors. Complaints are investigated on behalf of the Society by a professional purposes committee, the work of which is monitored by a lay observer. The Society can order a solicitor to remit or refund fees in the case of substandard work, but cases of serious misconduct are referred to a disciplinary tribunal, which can order a solicitor to be struck off the roll, suspended from practice, or fined. There is an appeal from the tribunal to a *Divisional Court of the Queen's Bench Division of the High Court of Justice.

The Law Society of Scotland in Edinburgh, and the Incorporated Law Society of Northern Ireland in Belfast, have functions and powers broadly comparable to those of the Law Society in England and Wales.

leader of the House The minister appointed by the government to arrange the business of the House of Lords or the House of Commons. His prime concern is to carry through the government's legislative programme. He must, however, pay due regard to the legitimate requirements of the opposition parties; thus he and the government *whips function in close consultation with their opposition counterparts (the collective term being "the usual channels"). For both Houses, the leader is always a senior member of the Cabinet. Since 1964, the *Lord Privy Seal has normally led the Lords, and the *Lord President of the Council the Commons, but the roles are interchangeable.

leader of the opposition The leader of the opposition party having the greatest numerical strength in the House of Commons (any dispute being a matter to be decided conclusively by the Speaker). He would be invited by the Crown to form a government if the government in power resigned and would become Prime Minister; he is paid a salary out of public funds. He decides who among his parliamentary colleagues would become ministers, and together they form the **shadow cabinet**.

League Against Cruel Sports An organization set up in 1924 to campaign against the hunting of animals using hounds, hare coursing, and some forms of shooting. Its primary objective is to press for legislation to prohibit hunting with dogs and what it regards as "unnecessary" shooting of wild creatures. It elicits the support of landowners who are willing to prohibit such practices on their land, and purchases land for the creation of wildlife sanctuaries. In 1984 the League owned 33 sites covering some 800 hectares (2000 acres). It offers a legal advice service to farmers and to property and pet owners who suffer trespass, damage, or loss from hunts; in addition, it provides speakers, produces literature, and urges the adoption of the alternative sport of drag hunting in which a man-made trail is followed.

Leander Club The oldest amateur rowing club in the world, founded in about 1818 in London. Its boathouse is at Henley-on-Thames, Oxfordshire. Membership is a considerable distinction and many of its members are ex-Cambridge and Oxford oarsmen (*see* Boat Race). Leander has always been a leader in the sport but perhaps its strongest period was between 1890 and 1914, when the club won the Grand Challenge Cup at *Henley Royal Regatta 13 times. In those years Leander also won 17 other Henley events, the Olympic Pairs in 1908, and the Olympic Eights in both 1908 and 1912. Leander Club members are identifiable at Henley and other regattas by their scarves, ties, and blazers in cerise, the club colour.

LEAs *See* Local Education Authorities.

legal aid Professional help with civil or criminal legal proceedings that can be obtained at the public expense by people with limited financial resources, introduced in its modern form in 1949. The scheme for legal aid in civil proceedings in England and Wales is administered by the Law Society, in consultation with the Bar Council, and under the oversight of the Lord Chancellor; but the day-to-day running of the scheme (and, in particular, the issue of certificates authorizing aid) is in the hands of legal aid committees. It is available for cases in the High Court and the Court of Appeal, the House of Lords and the Judicial Committee of the Privy Council, county courts and magistrates' courts, and certain other bodies. For the purposes of the scheme, England and Wales are divided into areas, each under an area legal aid committee responsible for maintaining lists of practitioners participating in the scheme, and appointing local committees. A legal aid certificate, which must be obtained from a committee, authorizes the services of a solicitor, and of counsel where necessary. A person is eligible for legal aid if a means test shows his financial resources to be below certain limits. However, in addition to this means test the applicant must also satisfy the committee that he has reasonable grounds for bringing or defending the proceedings, and this has proved a highly effective screening process.

Legal aid in criminal proceedings is available for both trials and appeals, and, by contrast with civil aid (because there is little time for elaborate outside formalities), is a matter for the courts themselves. To obtain a legal aid order, an applicant must satisfy the court that he is unable to meet the costs himself. Once he has done this, the court *must* make an order in certain cases (e.g. murder) and may make an order in any other case where it seems desirable in the interests of justice.

A person whose financial resources exceed certain amounts may have to contribute towards the cost of either form of aid, and costs, damages or property recovered by him may also be used towards defraying the cost. Subject to this, the cost of aid is met from a legal aid fund maintained by the Treasury, or, in the case of criminal proceedings outside magistrates' courts, by the Lord Chancellor's department. Legal aid elsewhere in the UK is governed by provisions comparable to the above.

Legal advice and assistance may also be obtained at public expense by people of limited financial means, and cover such matters as correspondence, the drafting of documents, and the negotiating of agreements.

Liberal Party A British political party which, succeeding the Whigs after 1832, was a major force until the 1920s. After the *Glorious Revolution of 1688, Whiggism – which broadly stood for limited monarchy and toleration for Protestant Nonconformists – gradually became diluted in content, as Jacobitism ceased to be a political force (*see* Jacobite rebellions). Politicians were divided on issues of the day rather than on principle. In the late 18th century increasing numbers in the party began to favour reform of government and even of Parliament, and toleration for Roman Catholics. However, many were frightened by the excesses of the French Revolution after 1789; and in 1794 the party split, with many Whigs transferring their support to William Pitt's Tory administration. The remaining Whigs formed the opposition until the accession of William IV (1830): internal dissensions had already brought down the Tories, and the Whigs, under Earl Grey

(1764–1845) were admitted to office. In 1832 they secured the reform of Parliament by the *Great Reform Act. In the mid-century they enjoyed the majority of office, due largely to Tory disunity and weakness. During this time, with the widening of the franchise, the Whigs gradually broadened out into the Liberals, and the Tories likewise into the Conservatives. However, the conversion to Irish home rule of , the great Liberal statesman W. E. Gladstone (Prime Minister 1868–74, 1880–85, 1886, 1892–94) in 1886 again split the party, the Liberal Unionists eventually joining the Conservatives. The party regained power in 1905, and won a landslide election victory in 1906; social and political reform (*see* welfare state; House of Lords) followed under Campbell-Bannerman (Prime Minister 1905–08) and Asquith (Prime Minister 1908–16). This revival was dampened in its turn by Lloyd George's seizure of the premiership (1916–22) and alliance with the Conservatives, causing a party split that was not healed until Asquith's retirement in 1926. By this time the emerging Labour Party had outflanked the Liberals as the party of change. In Parliament since 1945, the number of Liberal seats has ranged from 6 in 1970 to 17 in 1983. In order to utilize the not inconsiderable popular support, which the party still enjoys, but which is not great enough to be reflected in the number of its parliamentary seats, the Liberals have formed the *Alliance with the *Social Democratic Party.

Liberation Day, Channel Islands The anniversary of the liberation of the Channel Islands from German occupation at the end of World War II, celebrated each year on 9 May by a public and bank holiday throughout the islands.

Life Guards *See* Household Division.

life peerage A title conferred for life only that permits the holder to sit in the *House of Lords. Since the Life Peerage Act 1958, life peers have the rank of baron, the lowest of the five ranks of the peerage. Originally, life peers could be granted higher rank. However, since the evolution of Parliament life peerages of higher rank have only been conferred on somebody already entitled to sit in the House of Lords, or ennobled women, who were not allowed to sit in the House of Lords before 1958 if life peeresses, and not before 1963 if peeresses in their own right. In consequence these earlier life peerages did not radically alter the composition of the upper chamber. Thus when in 1856 the Crown sought to make a commoner, the judge Sir James Parke, a life peer with the title Baron Wensleydale, the House of Lords rejected the attempt as invalid. After two further attempts to establish life peerages had failed, an Act was passed in 1876 permitting the creation of two Lords of Appeal in Ordinary with the possibility of two more additions. These "life peers" were to hold the rank of baron but could only sit in the House of Lords as long as they held their judicial appointments. In 1887 an Act permitted all retired Lords of Appeal to sit for life as members of the House of Lords.

The wife of a life peer is ennobled with her husband; however, the husband of a life peeress has no special title. Thus if Lord Smith and Baroness Jones were life peers, the Smiths would be known as Lord and Lady Smith, whereas the Joneses would be Baroness and Mr Jones. As with hereditary barons, life peers are entitled to the prefix Right Honourable and their children to that of Honourable.

Lilies and Roses, ceremony of An annual private ceremony that takes place at the Tower of London on 21 May, the anniversary of the death of King Henry VI (r. 1422–61, 1470–71). Although incapable of ruling effectively, Henry was a patron of learning and founded Eton College and King's College, Cambridge. He was allegedly murdered at the Tower of London in 1471 while praying in a small oratory in the Wakefield Tower, where he was held prisoner by Edward IV during the *Wars of the Roses: the ceremony of the Lilies and Roses commemorates this incident. Representatives of the two colleges, those from Eton bearing lilies and those from King's bearing white roses, attend a service conducted by the chaplain of the Tower, at the end of which the flowers are laid beside a marble tablet marking the spot at which Henry is said to have fallen. The flowers traditionally remain there for 24 hours before being taken away and burnt. The ceremony at the Tower was

inaugurated in 1923, although Eton has a long tradition of laying lilies on the tomb of Henry VI in Windsor.

Lincoln's Inn *See* Inns of Court.

Linnaean Society A learned society, named after the Swedish biologist Carolus Linnaeus (1707–78), and founded in London in 1788 by the naturalist Sir James Smith (1759–1828) for "the cultivation of the Science of Natural History in all its branches". It was incorporated by royal charter in 1802. Any professional or amateur biologist may be elected to fellowship of the Society, and through its journals and meetings members pursue discoveries and developments in all branches of biology. The Society's Piccadilly offices house Linnaeus' collection of books and botanical specimens, on which he based the system of taxonomic classification still in use. Smith bought the collection after Linnaeus' death and the Society purchased it from Smith's widow in 1828. The Society has numbered many prominent scientists among its fellows, including Charles Darwin (1809–82), Joseph Hooker (1817–1911), T. H. Huxley (1825–95), and Charles Lyell (1797–1875). It was at a Society meeting in July 1858 that the historic paper was read outlining the revolutionary ideas of Darwin and A. R. Wallace (1823–1913) concerning the evolution of species through natural selection. The Society now has some 1650 fellows.

Lion sermon An annual sermon preached on 16 October at the church of St Katharine Cree in Leadenhall Street, London. The date is the anniversary of Sir John Gayer's miraculous escape from a lion while travelling in the Middle East for the Levant Company. Hearing a lion's roar he prayed to God to keep him safe, and awoke next morning to find the sand around him covered with lion's pawmarks. After his return to England he eventually became Lord Mayor of London in 1647; among the many bequests on his death was one to the poor of the church of St Katharine Cree, where he worshipped, on condition that the story of his escape was retold every year and his gratitude to God recalled. So far there have been over 340 sermons.

listed buildings *See* historic buildings and monuments.

Liverpool Philharmonic Orchestra An orchestra formed in 1840, mainly of amateur players, by the Liverpool Philharmonic Society. In 1844 Jakob Zeugheer became the orchestra's conductor and, partly in response to competition from the *Hallé Orchestra in nearby Manchester, began to hire semiprofessional and professional players. Zeugheer's successors included Max Bruch, Henry Wood, Thomas Beecham, and, during World War II, Malcolm Sargent. Attracting distinguished soloists from bomb-threatened London (Liverpool was free of enemy action after 1942), Sargent greatly enhanced the orchestra's reputation. Charles Groves and Walter Weller are among its postwar conductors. The present Philharmonic Hall, designed by Herbert J. Rowse, opened in 1939 and is notable for Laurence Whistler's engraved glass panels in the entrance hall.

Lloyd's A society of underwriters. It insures nothing itself, but acts as a clearing house for its members, who are personally liable for the risks they undertake. The members (over 26,000 in 1984, also called "names") join syndicates organized by underwriters, who represent them at Lloyd's. Underwriters are not permitted to deal with the public except through brokers, represented at Lloyd's, who are engaged by prospective clients. Lloyd's is a unique institution, its procedures still reflecting its origins in the 1680s, when the coffee house owned by Edward Lloyd (d. 1726) became noted as a place for obtaining marine insurance. A society with fixed rules was established only in 1771, and was incorporated by Act of Parliament in 1871. It operated at the *Royal Exchange from 1774 until it moved to its own building, designed by Sir Edwin Cooper, in Leadenhall Street in 1928. In 1979 a controversial new building by Richard Rogers was begun, but the main entrance in the Leadenhall Street frontage has been preserved. Underwriters' "boxes", at which they transact insurance deals with brokers, are still reminiscent of the original tables and seats of Edward Lloyd's coffee house. One Lloyd's tradition is the ringing of the Lutine Bell, recovered from HMS *Lutine*, which sank in 1799. It is rung on ceremonial occasions and when announcements are made, but no longer whenever a ship is lost at sea.

In 1696, for the benefit of his customers, Edward Lloyd started publishing *Lloyd's News*, containing information about shipping and trade; this was the forerunner of *Lloyd's List*, which first appeared in 1726 and is London's oldest surviving newspaper. It is believed that the first issues of **Lloyd's Register of Shipping**, the oldest and largest international classification system of merchant shipping for insurance purposes, date from this period, although the earliest surviving volumes are those for 1764–66. Today, the Lloyd's organization, maintained voluntarily by the shipping community, employs a worldwide network of surveyors, who inspect ships under construction and subsequently check on their maintenance and condition; this information forms the basis of their classification at Lloyd's. The *Register*, an annual multivolume publication that is regularly updated, contains data on all merchant ships over 100 tons gross and is the internationally accepted authority, even in countries that have their own marine underwriting associations. The expression "A-1 (at Lloyd's)" is a popular reference to the soundest classification.

Lloyd's Register of Shipping *See* Lloyd's.

Local Education Authorities (LEAs) Bodies created under the Education Act 1902 to take charge of all state-provided education within a county or borough, below the level of the *universities. LEAs took over existing elementary schools from the old school boards and founded many new grammar schools to meet the growing demand for secondary education (*see* state education). They were funded by the government. Schools supported and controlled by the LEAs are known as "maintained schools" – as opposed to the *independent schools, or the direct-grant schools (abolished in 1976), which received their funding direct from the Department of Education. The voluntary-aided school is an intermediate category in which the LEA pays the running costs of the school while the voluntary body that founded it (usually a religious organization) pays part of its upkeep, and central funds the remainder. Under the Education Act 1944 the payment of fees by parents was abolished in LEA secondary schools. Since World War II the scope of the LEAs to determine their own policies within a national education strategy has varied with the prevailing political climate, particularly in such controversial matters as the introduction of comprehensive schools.

local radio The network of some 82 radio stations (BBC and independent), serving local regions, that were set up after 1970. The original stimulus for local radio came from the BBC, whose philosophy of fully integrating public broadcasting with the local community was accepted by the Pilkington Committee of 1962 and led to the establishment of nine radio stations, the first being BBC Radio Leicester in 1967. Licences for independent local radio (ILR) stations were issued following the Sound Broadcasting Act 1972.

The content of BBC local radio programmes is marked by more discussion and less pop music in comparison with its ILR counterparts. Regular news coverage is supplemented by features on local music, arts, sporting events, etc., and by daily "phone-ins" on social issues. Minority groups have been given special access: for example, there is a daily Asian programme on BBC Radio Leicester. Examples of special projects include the surveys of weather conditions produced by all stations during the severe winter of early 1985, Radio Humberside's coverage of the so-called cod war with Iceland, and Radio Bristol's information service to local people following an air disaster overseas. The BBC stations have a total weekly audience of nine million. The independent radio stations run by the *Independent Broadcasting Authority have a much larger revenue derived entirely from advertising. The most successful ILR station, Capital Radio in London, has a weekly audience of three million people. Funds permitting, the BBC plans to build and operate a network of 35 radio stations, while the IBA may set up a national radio network in the future.

Loch Ness monster A legendary creature that is believed by some to inhabit Loch Ness, one of Scotland's deepest lakes. Suggestions as to the nature of the monster are wide-ranging and often far-fetched: it may be a surviving prehistoric reptile; a type of giant eel or long-necked seal, hitherto unknown; some kind of psychic phenomenon, a hypothesis supported by the frequent failure of cameras to function in its presence; or a manifestation of evil, possibly the malicious *each uisge* or "water-horse" of Gaelic legend. Similar creatures are claimed to have been sighted in other Scottish lochs, such as Loch Morar, in Lough Nahooin in Ireland, in Canadian, Siberian, and Scandinavian lakes, and elsewhere. All these monsters share similar physical characteristics – a long dark body with a humped back and snakelike neck – but the Loch Ness monster, popularly known as "Nessie", is undoubtedly the most famous.

The earliest reference to the monster occurs in St Adamnan's 7th-century biography of St Columba, in which Columba is said to have banished an *aquatilis bestia* from the waters of Loch Ness. There were many accounts in the subsequent centuries. In the 1930s, after a fresh sighting, Nessie became a subject of worldwide fascination, and thousands of sightings followed, supported by photographs. Many were hoaxes; others were natural phenomena, sometimes distorted by atmospheric conditions but frequently embellished by the imagination. Interest in the monster was sufficient, however, to justify the setting up of a Loch Ness investigation bureau, which collaborated with two separate teams of scientists on sonar tests in the loch in 1968 and 1975. The first of these indicated the presence of "large animate objects" unlike any known fish; the 1975 tests appeared to confirm the existence of the monster with new photographic evidence. Although these findings were at first taken seriously, they were later rejected, and the controversy continues.

Lollards Followers of the radical theologian John Wycliffe (c. 1329–84), one of the most important English heretics of the late Middle Ages. The Lollards took their name from the Middle Dutch *lollen*, to mumble. An Oxford philosopher and theologian, Wycliffe

LOLLARDS *Wycliffe's translation of the Bible (the beginning of Acts): a copy made for the Duke of Gloucester before 1397. Wycliffe regarded the Bible as the infallible statement of God's law, and access to the Bible in the vernacular was therefore crucial. His ideas were echoed by many 16th-century Church reformers.*

criticized the worldliness of the Catholic Church and later attacked many of its fundamental tenets. Condemned by the pope in 1377, his immediate academic circle at Oxford was broken in 1382 by the Archbishop of Canterbury, William Courtenay. Wycliffe himself escaped charges of heresy, probably due to the protection of John of Gaunt, the king's uncle; he was, however, exiled to his rectory at Lutterworth until his death. Some of his followers – notably Nicholas of Hereford and John Aston – spread his doctrines on a more popular level and as a result groups of Lollards grew up in several towns.

Lollards are noted for having produced the first English Bible, originally produced in about 1384, with a preface by Wycliffe, and subsequently published in 1396 in a revised and improved edition by his secretary John Purvey. With the accession of Henry IV (r. 1399–1413) and the return from exile of the strongly anti-Lollard Thomas Arundel, as Archbishop of Canterbury, a more determined effort was made to eliminate Lollardy. In 1401 the statute *De Heretico Comburendo* permitted the burning of persistent heretics and forbade unlicensed preaching; in 1413 Arundel caused the prominent Sir John Oldcastle (c. 1378–1417) to be charged with heresy. After escaping from the Tower, Oldcastle attempted to lead a Lollard rising in January 1414, aiming to capture the king. However, only a very few rebels assembled and the king, who had learned of the plot in advance, had no trouble in routing them. Oldcastle was finally captured in 1417, and "hung and burnt hung". This failed and treasonable uprising heralded the end of Lollardy as a force of any significance, although it persisted underground, until subsumed by the *Reformation.

Lombard Street A street in the City of London that for centuries has been part of the capital's banking centre. The Lombards, who gave the street its name, were merchants, moneylenders, and bankers who came to London from Northern Italy in the 12th century. They remained until Elizabeth I banished them on account of their dishonest dealings. In medieval times Lombard Street was characterized by the elaborate metal banking signs hung out over the road. These were

banned as unsafe by Charles II and were not seen again until the occasion of Edward VII's coronation in 1901. In recent years major banks, such as Barclays, Lloyds, Glyn Mills, and Martin's had their head offices in Lombard Street.

London Central Mosque The spiritual focus for London's Muslims, near Hanover Gate, Regent's Park. A fund for a mosque was started by the Nizam of Hyderabad in the 1920s, and in 1944, following the acquisition of the site from the government, the Islamic Cultural Centre was opened. The present mosque (built 1974–77) was designed by Frederick Gibberd and Partners and includes a prayer hall, which is surmounted by a dome 25 metres (82 feet) high, and a minaret 43 metres (141 feet) high. There is also a library and residential accommodation.

London clubs Establishments in the West End of London, mostly in or around Pall Mall and St James's Street, which have traditionally served as meeting places for men. Two of the earliest clubs were the Friday Street Club, founded in the 17th century by Sir Walter Raleigh, which included Shakespeare, Donne, Beaumont, Fletcher, and Jonson among its members; and the Literary Club, which was founded by Joshua Reynolds and Samuel Johnson at the Turk's Head in the 1760s. Modern clubs have developed from the coffee houses of Pall Mall and each one is usually patronized by members of a particular profession, such as the theatre (the Garrick Club, founded 1831), or political persuasion (the Reform Club for the Radicals and the Carlton Club for the Tories, both founded in 1832). Other clubs elect members on the basis of university attendance (the United Oxford and Cambridge University Club, founded 1972), military service (the Cavalry and Guards Club, founded 1890), or purely by connection with current members. Perhaps the oldest and grandest of the St James's gentlemen's clubs is White's, founded in 1693 and including among its past members George IV, William IV, and Edward VII, as well as numerous prime ministers. Membership of such clubs as the Savile (founded 1868 for actors, writers, and lawyers), the Athenaeum (founded in

Brooke's Club, London: a late-18th-century illustration by Rowlandson.

1824 for the intellectual élite), and the Savage (founded in 1857 for writers and artists) is still prestigious, despite high subscriptions and entrance fees. In recent times the rules prohibiting women from joining the clubs or even, in some cases, entering them, have been gradually relaxed although many restrictions still apply. Most clubs offer meals, library facilities, and overnight accommodation, although financial pressures have led to some cutbacks and the closure or amalgamation of several establishments.

London Festival Ballet A ballet company founded in 1950 by Anton Dolin (1904–   ) and Alicia Markova (1910–   ). Its original name, the Festival Ballet (after the *Festival of Britain), was changed first to London's Festival Ballet and then, in 1968, to its present name. It holds London seasons at the Royal Festival Hall, the Coliseum Theatre, and the New Victoria Theatre and tours widely in Britain and abroad. From the first it set out to capture a wide audience with a popular repertoire in which the standard classics predominated. It has an enthusiastic following but has suffered many financial and management problems. The company's first artistic director, Dolin, was succeeded by John Gilpin

(1930–   ) in 1962. Gilpin left in 1964, and the Ballet's managing director from its inception, Dr Julian Braunsweg (1877–1978), resigned in 1965. Beryl Grey (1927–   ) was artistic director from 1968 to 1979, when John Field (1921–   ) succeeded her. Among its notable successes have been *Symphony for Fun* (1952), *Etudes* (1957), and *The Witch Boy* (1957).

London group A society of English artists formed in 1913 mainly from existing groups, such as the *Camden Town group, the Futurists, and the Vorticists. Many of its early members shared a strong interest in postimpressionism and the group attracted criticism in more conservative artistic circles for its "advanced" art. Among its many distinguished members were Wyndham Lewis, Jacob Epstein, and, after World War I, Roger Fry.

London Library A library in St James's Square, London. Its creation was inspired by the historian Thomas Carlyle (1795–1881), who in 1841 became exasperated by the delays in obtaining books ordered at the British Museum Library. He envisaged a library with a more academic and thorough coverage than the circulating libraries, in which, unlike the British Museum Library, the readers them-

247

selves might be allowed access to the shelves and to borrow books. The London Library opened, with Carlyle as president, at 49 Pall Mall in 1841. It moved to St James's Square in 1845. The founding library of 3000 books had grown to nearly a million by the early 1980s. Its members pay a subscription. Coverage of the humanities is as complete as Carlyle had hoped, but it does not aim to supply books on technical subjects, such as medicine or engineering. In addition to Carlyle, past presidents have included Tennyson, T. S. Eliot, and Lord (Kenneth) Clark.

London marathon The largest single sports event in Britain in terms of participants. The course, which is 42 kilometres (26 miles) long, starts in southeast London at Greenwich, crosses the River Thames, passes through the docklands, the East End, the City of London, and the West End, to finish in Hyde Park. The marathon was founded by Christopher Brasher, one of the runners who took part in Roger Bannister's famous four-minute mile

LONDON MARATHON *Participants appear as a solid mass as they set off on the 1984 London marathon.*

in 1954, and the 1956 Olympic 3000-metre steeplechase champion. After taking part in the 1979 New York marathon and seeing the interest generated by the ladies' marathon held in London in 1980, he determined to stage a full-scale event in 1981. He expected more entrants than had ever taken part in a marathon in the UK (750), but was astonished at the 21,000 applications he received. The number had to be limited to about 7000, of whom over 90% finished. In 1982 there were over 16,000 runners and in 1986 over 18,000. Competitors range from world champions and Olympic marathon runners to the very young and the very old, and include families, teams, and celebrities. Many are sponsored to raise money for charity.

London markets London has been renowned for its street markets since at least the Norman conquest. The earliest records of such markets date back to 1016, the date of toll regulations for the Billingsgate fish market; this market stood on the same site in Upper Thames Street by the river until 1982, when it moved to the Isle of Dogs. Smithfield was well known in the Middle Ages as a livestock market, from which it grew to be the largest meat market in the world. Once the scene of the Bartholomew Fair (from 1123), many royal tournaments, the death of Wat Tyler, leader of the *Peasants' Revolt in 1381, and numerous public executions, it was eventually rebuilt by Henry Jones and reopened in 1868 as the London Central Meat Market. The Royal Agricultural Hall (1861–62) was also built by the Smithfield Club for exhibitions of livestock and agricultural produce. Leadenhall market was established in the 14th century for the sale of poultry. It was burnt down in the *Fire of London (1666) after which it was rebuilt and its range extended. The present market was built by Sir Horace Jones in 1881. Perhaps the best known London market was the *Covent Garden fruit and flower market, designed by Inigo Jones in 1630 and operating under a charter of Charles II. Covent Garden developed into a lively and fashionable trading centre, written about by Charles Dickens, Edmund Burke, and George Bernard Shaw. In 1974 the market moved to Nine Elms in Battersea. The original site was later developed as a shopping area.

The most notable outdoor market for antiques is in Portobello Road, off Notting Hill Gate, which grew from a nearby horse market run by Gypsies in the 1870s. The Sunday market in "Petticoat Lane" (real name Middlesex Street) in the East End, has been selling clothing since the early 17th century. In nearby Brick Lane stalls offer furniture and electrical equipment, while in Club Row stalls deal in fish, birds, reptiles, and other pets. Notable markets that have disappeared or been replaced by new ones include the Stocks market (on the site of the present Mansion House), the Fleet market (a meat and vegetable market closed in 1827), and the Haymarket (now the site of theatres and cinemas). Other popular markets still in existence include Spitalfields (fruit and vegetables), the New Caledonian market (general goods), and Church Street market (general goods).

London Philharmonic Orchestra (LPO) An orchestra formed by Thomas Beecham in 1932. It became self-governing when Beecham went to the USA at the beginning of World War II. Subsequent principal conductors have included Adrian Boult, John Pritchard, Bernard Haitink, and (since 1979) Georg Solti. The LPO was the first British orchestra to tour the USSR and China. It became the resident *Glyndebourne orchestra in 1964.

London School of Economics and Political Science (LSE) A college of *London University. The LSE was founded in 1895, mainly on the initiative of the economists and historians Sidney and Beatrice Webb and the philosopher and statesman R. B. Haldane, using a legacy of Henry Hunt Hutchinson, a member of the *Fabian Society. Its purpose was to promote the study and advancement of economics and political science and other related subjects. The school became a part of London University in 1900. Its library, the British Library of Political and Economic Science, was founded in 1896; rehoused in 1978, it is one of the most distinguished collections of books on the social sciences in the world, containing almost three million items. The Shaw Library, with more general literature,

originated in a gift from the widow of George Bernard Shaw, who had himself been closely involved in the early plans for the school. Past lecturers at LSE have included Harold J. Laski (later chairman of the Labour Party) and Lionel (later Lord) Robbins. Ralf Dahrendorf was appointed director in 1974.

London season Formerly an important part of the year for English society, now a more subdued social round that serves to introduce the daughters of the upper middle classes to young people of a similar age and background, particularly to eligible young men. Until the 1950s being a "debutante" meant being presented by a suitable aristocratic lady to the reigning monarch (once the Lord Chamberlain had checked the family's credentials), attending Queen Charlotte's ball dressed in a white gown and long white gloves together with about 300 other girls, and accepting invitations to balls, parties, and sporting occasions throughout the summer and autumn. This process, known as "coming out", marked the transition of young girls into womanhood. Royal presentation parties ended in 1958, and Queen Charlotte's ball (started in the 18th century) in 1976. A modern "deb" attends one or two charity balls, (such as the Alexandra Rose ball in May), visits the Royal Academy Summer Exhibition and the fashion show at the Savoy – at which debs themselves model the clothes – and may accompany her parents to a *royal garden party.

London shops Many of London's famous shops have a long tradition of service and are renowned for their quality and variety. Fortnum and Mason started at the beginning of the 18th century as a small grocery business in Piccadilly, opened by a footman of Queen Anne (Fortnum) and his shopkeeper friend from St James's market (Mason) to meet the needs of the royal household. They imported tea and spices through the East India Company; they sent ham, dried fruit, honey, and cereals to British army officers serving abroad, and they developed a range of delicacies for the aristocracy and nearby London clubs. Among their specialities was "portable refreshment" – canned, potted, or concentrated food useful on long hunting, fishing, and

LONDON SHOPS *A branch of Sainsbury's, 1906. The tiled walls, marble counters, and mosaic floors reflect the store's origins as a dairy in Drury Lane.*

shooting trips, as well as to MPs and "gentlemen detained on juries". Their tradition of supplying food hampers, which is still maintained, began in 1851 when they provided for visitors to the Great Exhibition and later to the Derby, Ascot races, and Henley Regatta. Gradually the grocery shop expanded into a teashop and department store selling clothes and furniture; its present building dates from 1923–25. Hatchard's bookshop, further along Piccadilly, was started in 1797 by an intellectual philanthropist, John Hatchard, who encouraged his clients – often writers or politicians from the Albany across the road – to sit reading in his shop while their servants waited for them on benches outside. Burlington Arcade, on the west side of Burlington House (home of the Royal Academy of Arts since 1868), was designed by Samuel Ware for Lord Cavendish in 1819 in order to prevent the public from throwing rubbish into his gardens.

Harrods began as a small grocer's shop in Knightsbridge in 1849; 20 years later it had diversified into perfumery, stationery, and medicine and by 1900 it employed 100 staff (now it has over 3000). When a fire destroyed the store in December 1883 Charles Digby Harrod, son of the founder, wrote to all his customers: "I greatly regret to inform you that, in consequence of the above premises being burnt down, your order will be delayed in the execution a day or two. I hope, in the course of Tuesday or Wednesday next, to be able to forward it". All the Christmas orders arrived on time and the reputation of Harrods was made. By 1894, under new management, an advertisement could proudly proclaim "Harrods serves the world"; it still boasts the world's most comprehensive range of merchandise and special services. The present vast terracotta building, with its impressive tiled food halls, was completed in 1905.

Liberty's was started in 1875 by Arthur Lasenby Liberty as "East India House" in Regent Street, selling oriental goods and coloured silks, often hand-printed by Thomas Wardle, a friend of William Morris. These became widely fashionable after their appearance in Gilbert and Sullivan's opera *Patience*. Soon the shop began to promote *Arts and Crafts furniture, silver, pewter, jewellery, and wallpapers. It now consists of two linked buildings dating from the 1920s, one on Regent Street with a concave pillared façade, and the other in Great Marlborough Street with mock Tudor front and interior, built from the timbers of two old fighting ships. Other establishments whose success was based on fabric are Jaeger in Regent Street (originally promoting "Dr Jaeger's Sanitary Woollen System"), and Burberry's in Haymarket. Thomas Burberry developed a gabardine akin to the material used in Hampshire shepherds' smocks in that it was cool yet weatherproof in summer, and warm in winter, and then refined and proofed it to meet the market for travelling and sporting gear around 1900. Lillywhite's started even earlier, in 1863, as a supplier of cricket equipment and then moved into other sports. Hamley's toyshop is the longest established of all London shops, starting as "Noah's Ark" in High Holborn in 1760 before moving to Regent Street; it introduced several now well-established games, the best known being ping-pong, or table tennis.

Many of the famous London stores started as drapers (their "mourning departments" being particularly important) in the 19th century, and reached heights of elegance in the 1920s and 1930s. Selfridges was not opened until 1909, when the American, Gordon Selfridge, came to London from Chicago. Selfridges still remains, though many of the other Oxford Street department stores have now closed. Probably the most famous food-store chain is Sainsbury's, started as a dairy in Drury Lane in 1869, hence the tiled walls, marble counters, and mosaic floors, which became part of Sainsbury's image. Both Sainsbury's and Marks and Spencer (which originated as a penny bazaar in a Leeds market) are still family firms that have been eager to expand and innovate without lowering standards of quality, thus making an invaluable contribution to the retail business in Britain.

London Symphony Orchestra (LSO) The longest surviving orchestra in London, founded in 1904. The LSO was formed by a group of players from the Queen's Hall Orchestra, from which they resigned when its conductor Henry Wood demanded first call on their services. Hans Richter conducted the LSO's first concert and was its principal conductor until 1911. His successors have included Elgar, Pierre Monteux, André Previn, and Claudio Abbado. In 1912 the LSO became the first British orchestra to tour North America, and in 1964 the first to tour the world. It made some of the earliest recordings under the baton of Richard Strauss and Bruno Walter, and played at *Glyndebourne from 1934 to 1939. It is now resident at the *Barbican Arts Centre but remains self-governing, managed by a board elected from among its players.

London to Brighton Veteran Car Run An annual run of veteran motor cars from Northumberland Avenue in the centre of London to the Hotel Metropole in Brighton, Sussex, organized by the *RAC. It is held on the first Sunday in November each year. The event commemorates the "Emancipation Run" held on 14 November 1896 over the same route. Until that year motor cars were restricted to 4 mph and someone was required to run in front carrying a warning red flag. When, after repeated lobbying, Parliament agreed to raise the speed limit to 12 mph the motor engineer and businessman Harry Lawson, who founded the Daimler Motor Company, decided to celebrate by staging the run. To qualify to take part in the modern London to Brighton run a motor car must be of veteran status, that is, built before 1 January 1905. The run generally attracts some 250 entrants from around the world. It is not, and never has been, a race. The object of the exercise is to enjoy the ride and complete the course of 85 kilometres (53 miles). The run was popularized in the British film *Genevieve* (1953).

London transport The use of large horse-drawn carriages for public use was for a long time restricted in London because of traffic congestion and because they threatened the business of the hackney carriages that served

LONDON TO BRIGHTON VETERAN CAR RUN *Crossing Westminster Bridge near the start of the run.*

the city. However, there were so-called short-stage services, which ran from central London to outlying villages. The first horse-drawn omnibus, holding about 22 passengers, appeared in 1829 and ran between Paddington and the Bank of England, being introduced by George Shillibeer in imitation of a successful public service in Paris. The first regular motor bus came into operation in 1904, between Peckham and Oxford Circus, but horse-drawn buses continued to be used as late as 1914. In 1908, for example, there were still 2155 horse-drawn buses in London and about half that number of motor buses. Over the years, motor buses became more comfortable, with pneumatic tyres, roofs for the upper deck, and lower boarding platforms. Another form of public road transport was the horse-drawn tram or street railway as it was called, introduced to London by the American George Train in 1861. Train's experimental

horse-tram lines projected above the road surface and were a hindrance to other traffic; they were taken up within a year. The permanent horse-tram lines laid from 1870 onwards were flush with the road surface, with a special groove for the wheel flanges. Eventually a network of double-decker trams covered a large part of London, excluding the centre. Once they were electrified at the turn of the century, some services were powered by overhead cables and others by subsurface live rails, necessitating a change from one system to the other on longer routes. The trolleybus, which appeared in the 1930s, was similar to the tram in that it was powered by overhead lines, but it was quieter and ran on pneumatic tyres without rails. After World War II diesel-powered buses gradually replaced all others, the last tram being burnt in 1952.

The mid-19th century saw the introduction of an alternative to road transport. As London grew and congestion on the surface increased, the capital slowly built for itself a system of underground railways. It was started in 1863 with the opening of the Metropolitan line. Besides being commercial ventures, the building of these railways was a response to the wish of the prosperous middle classes to live away from the dirt and congestion of central London, and yet still have convenient access to their places of work. The early lines were built by cutting trenches, usually along the lines of existing roads; the first stretch to be built ran between Paddington and Farringdon Road. By the time the first section of the Northern line (then the City and South London Railway) was opened in 1890 between Stockwell and King William Street, special tunnelling shields were employed, huge frames that protected the labourers as they dug out the earth at a deep level behind the shield. The Northern line was also the world's first tube railway to be powered by electricity rather than steam. The tube was immediately popular with the public, being fast, convenient, and clean. The Central line (then the Central London Railway), running between Shepherd's Bush and Bank, opened in 1900 and charged passengers a flat rate of twopence. It featured smartly painted trains, clean white tunnels, and electric lifts. Despite the popularity of the underground railways, there was a reluctance to invest in such ventures, and many of the later electric lines (Piccadilly, Bakerloo, and extensions to the Northern line) were financed by an American, Charles Tyson Yerkes. The first escalator, initially regarded with mistrust by the public, was installed at Earl's Court station on the Piccadilly line in 1911.

The railway companies agreed in 1907 to use the distinctive "Underground" sign at all stations, and all the London underground railways except the Metropolitan had become part of the Underground Electric Railways of London Ltd by 1913. This company also ran the maiin bus company and three of the tram companies. In 1933 the whole system was taken over by the London Passenger Transport Board. During World War II the Underground was used for storage and as air-raid shelters for the public. Since the war, the Victoria and Jubilee lines have been built

(1962–72 and 1972–79), and the Piccadilly line has been extended westwards to Heathrow Airport (1977). The Underground is now run by London Regional Transport and is one of the largest systems of its kind in the world, covering 418 kilometres (260 miles).

London University A federation of colleges, medical schools, and research institutions established as a university in 1836. University College was founded first (1826), as a nonsectarian institute for higher education at a time when the universities of *Oxford and *Cambridge were open only to members of the Church of England. Although it was known as the University of London for a time, its status was opposed by the Anglican establishment, and King's College, a Church of England foundation, was awarded a charter in 1829. Eventually University College gained its charter (1836), but at the same time a charter was granted to a new body to be known as the University of London, which was empowered to examine students and award degrees. In 1878 its degrees were also made available to women. The University of London Act 1898 established the university in its present form, apart from subsequent financial arrangements and the constitutional changes of the University of London Act 1926. Apart from the internal students at colleges and other institutions affiliated to the university, there are considerable numbers of external students studying at provincial or overseas institutions, or privately, who sit the university's examinations. Among the teaching and research institutions forming part of the university, in addition to University College and King's College are the *Imperial College of Science and Technology (1907; school of university 1908), the *London School of Economics (1895; school of university 1900), the School of Oriental and African Studies (1916), Bedford College (1849; school of university 1880), Birkbeck College (1823; school of university 1920), Queen Mary College (1887; school of university 1915), Royal Holloway College (1886; school of university 1900), Westfield College (1882), Queen Elizabeth College (1908), Royal Veterinary College (1791; school of university 1949), and the medical schools of the London teaching hospitals. In the 1980s the university's structure is being altered – most notably by the amalgamation of Bedford and Royal Holloway colleges, and of King's, Queen Elizabeth, and Chelsea colleges, in 1985.

London Working Men's College An institution founded in London in 1854 by the theologian J. F. D. Maurice (1805–72) to advance the ideals of "Christian Socialism" amongst the working classes. In 1848 he had belonged to the group that founded the Christian Socialist Movement. Maurice himself was the first principal of the college, and he persuaded many distinguished men to lecture there on a voluntary basis. As the adult education movement spread (*see* adult education centres), the college became the model for similar enterprises in other cities.

Longleat A splendid Elizabethan country house and estate near Warminster in Wiltshire. The house was built between 1560 and 1580 by Sir John Thynne, steward to the Duke of Somerset and later a clerk comptroller of the royal household. Although Thynne employed Robert Smythson and Allen Maynard as head masons, much of the design was his own. Inspired by the Italian Renaissance, the symmetrical façades of Longleat are punctuated by 13 projecting bays, all with large mullioned windows. Above the balustraded parapet rise assorted pepperpot domes, turrets, chimneys, and statuary. The interior was substantially remodelled by the firm of Crace and Co. in the early 19th century and features ornate Italianate ceilings, particularly in the state dining room and breakfast room. The great hall has a fine Elizabethan interior, with a screen passage, gallery, and magnificent fireplace.

The original formal gardens were replaced by "Capability" Brown's (1716–83) landscaped parkland and lakes in the mid-18th century; these were later modified by Humphrey Repton (1752–1818). In 1947 Longleat became one of the first of Britain's stately homes to open its doors to the public, a move forced

LONGLEAT *This Elizabethan mansion, with its distinctive mullioned windows, derives its name from the long stretch of water, or leat, in the foreground.*

on Henry Thynne, 6th Marquess of Bath, by economic necessity. In the 1960s in another pioneering venture, a safari park was opened in the grounds, featuring the "lions of Longleat". Other attractions now include Victorian kitchens, a pets corner, a maze, and the remarkable "Leisureland". The erotic murals painted by Lord Weymouth, the present heir to Longleat, are also on view to visitors.

Lord Advocate   The chief law officer of the Crown for Scotland. A member of the Scottish *Bar, and normally, but not necessarily, an MP, he is appointed by the government, and his functions correspond in most respects with those of his English counterpart, the *Attorney General; he is not, however, the head of the Scottish Bar (a position held by the Dean of Faculty: *see* Faculty of Advocates). He is responsible for a centralized system of public prosecution that was formerly peculiar to Scotland. (For the position in England and Wales, *see* Director of Public Prosecutions.) The Lord Advocate is assisted by the **Solicitor General for Scotland**, who is also a member of the Scottish Bar, but quite frequently not an MP. He and the Solicitor are assisted by a number of advocates–depute, operating with them in the Crown Office in Edinburgh, and procurators-fiscal appointed for all parts of the country. The decision to prosecute is never left to the police: every case is reported by them to a procurator-fiscal, who either makes the decision himself, in accordance with guidelines laid down by the Lord Advocate, or forwards the case to the Crown Office for consideration.

Lord Chamberlain   The chief official of the royal household, overseeing all aspects of its management, and bearing responsibility for matters ranging from the care of works of art to the appointment of royal tradesmen. The office emerged under Edward II (r. 1307–27) as head of the chamber (the part of the royal household closest to the king). Until the abolition of censorship in 1968, he was also responsible for licensing dramatic performances throughout Britain. Although appointed on the nomination of the Prime Minister, he has no political functions. His assistant, the vice-chamberlain, is by contrast a government

*whip (whose duties include writing a daily report of Commons proceedings for the sovereign) as also are the treasurer and the comptroller of the household, and some of the *lords in waiting. *Compare* Lord Great Chamberlain.

Lord Chancellor   *See* Lord (High) Chancellor.

Lord Chief Justice   The presiding judge of the Queen's Bench Division of the *High Court of Justice, and of the Criminal Division of the *Court of Appeal. Among other duties, it is his task to give guidance to judges on the level of sentences they should impose. Ranking second to the Lord Chancellor in the hierarchy of the law, he is appointed by the Crown on the advice of the Prime Minister, but this does not signify that his appointment is political. The Attorney General, who is a political appointee, used to be considered to have a claim when the office fell vacant; but the person now appointed is normally a Lord Justice of Appeal or *Lord of Appeal in Ordinary. The Lord Chief Justice's tenure of office is, basically, as for a *puisne judge of the High Court. The Lord Chancellor can, however, declare his office vacant for incapacity only with the agreement of the heads of both the other Divisions of that court, or of one or other of these plus the Master of the Rolls.

Lord Great Chamberlain   A high office of state, stemming from the 11th-century chamberlain (head of the royal chamber, part of the king's household). This hereditary office was granted to the Earl of Oxford by Henry I in 1133, and has descended to the present Marquess of Cholmondeley. It probably never possessed any real influence in the chamber, which the king kept under close personal control; and today the duties of the office are largely ceremonial, for example, at coronations, where the Lord Great Chamberlain presents the new sovereign to the people, and in the House of Lords, where he introduces new peers and prelates when they first take their seats. *Compare* Lord Chamberlain.

Lord High Admiral   A honorary title connected with the defence of the realm at sea.

255

Records exist of nobles holding posts similar to that of Lord High Admiral from 1314 but the full title was not used until 1618. In that year George Villiers, Marquess (later Duke) of Buckingham, was appointed. James II (1633–1701) was Lord High Admiral both before his accession and during his reign, but subsequently the post tended to be held by civilians. After 1709 the post remained unfilled except for a brief period (1827–28) when the Duke of Clarence (later William IV) assumed the position. In 1964, with the reorganization of the armed services, the post of Lord High Admiral was assumed once more by the Crown.

Lord (High) Chancellor　A high officer of state, one of the four *great officers of state, whose office is a unique combination of the judicial, executive, and legislative functions of government. He is head of the judiciary; he is a government minister, normally of Cabinet rank; and he is Speaker of the House of Lords. The Lord Chancellor is appointed by the Crown on the advice of the Prime Minister, and is preceded only by the royal family and the Archbishop of Canterbury in the official order of *precedence. He is always a peer, or is so created on his appointment.

The office originated in the 11th century as the head of the king's writing office – the Chancery, which derived its name from the Latin for the screen (*cancelli*) behind which the king's clerks worked within call of their royal master. From the reign of Edward the Confessor (r. 1042–66) he was responsible for keeping the **Great Seal**, with which the king authenticated his writs (royal directives or proclamations) – though the two offices were not formally merged until 1562. The Seal was the pivot of early medieval royal bureaucracy, and its keeper the most important member. In the Middle Ages, the increasing scope of royal government, effected by writs issued from Chancery, gave him a jurisdiction over disputes arising from them; also, from the 14th century, petitions to the king for justice were referred to him; this was the origin of *equity. At the same time, the uses of the Great Seal had become rigidly defined and the king had acquired other seals for his personal use (*see* Lord Privy Seal), with the result that Chan-

cery's administrative freedom declined – though the Chancellor himself usually remained an influential voice in government as one of the de facto heads of the administration and (usually) a trusted adviser of the king. These factors resulted in increased emphasis on the judicial side, especially equity; the Court of Chancery (*see* common law) emerged in the 15th century, and was consolidated under Cardinal Wolsey (Chancellor 1515–29) and his successors. The change is reflected in the type of men appointed to the post. Until 1529, he was almost always a cleric; in that year, however, Sir Thomas More replaced Wolsey, and thereafter the Chancellorship came to be regarded as a legal appointment. After Wolsey, the executive role of the Chancellor rapidly declined. No ecclesiastic has held the office since Archbishop Williams of York (1621–25). His role in the House of Lords derives from deputizing for the monarch, who now never attends the House except at the *state opening of Parliament.

The judicial functions of the Lord Chancellor today are manifold. He is entitled to preside over both the *House of Lords and the *Judicial Committee of the Privy Council, and often does so; he is also a member of the *Court of Appeal, and nominal head of the Chancery Division of the *High Court of Justice, though he does not in practice sit in either court. He advises the Crown on the most senior judicial appointments, and appoints magistrates himself (*see* justice of the peace); he oversees court procedure and administration; and he is much concerned with law reform (*see* Law Commission) and the workings of administrative tribunals (*see* Council on Tribunals). The Chancellor's ministerial functions include responsibility for the statutory schemes for *legal aid and legal advice and assistance, and for such bodies as the Land Registry, the Public Record Office, and the Public Trustee. As Speaker of the House of Lords, the Chancellor presides over debates and other proceedings, and is responsible (with the assistance of *Black Rod) for maintaining order. His seat as Speaker is on the **Woolsack**, a large red hassock dating from the reign of Edward III (r. 1327–77) and stuffed with wool as representing England's staple trade. It is technically outside the precincts of the House, so that he must vacate it and step within the House if he wishes to take part in debate (which, unlike the *Speaker in the Commons, he is free to do).

He retains his ancient function of keeping the Great Seal, now the royal seal used on the most important state documents (*compare* Lord Privy Seal). In theory the Seal is carried in the purse still used at an opening of Parliament, but in practice it is kept in a safe. By tradition, it is defaced and given to the Chancellor when the sovereign dies, and a new one is made.

Lord High Constable One of the *great officers of state. The post is probably of Saxon origin and certainly existed before the Norman conquest. Initially the Constable commanded the monarch's armies or a garrison on behalf of the king. He was also Master of the Horse and, together with the *Earl Marshal, presided over the *Court of Chivalry or Court of Honour. In the Middle Ages the post was hereditary. However, when the 3rd and last Stafford Duke of Buckingham was appointed Lord High Constable at the time of Henry VIII's coronation (1509) it was for the day only. Not till 1514 did the Duke successfully claim the post as an hereditary right. After Buckingham's execution in 1521, the office lapsed. The practice of appointing a Constable for one day only (usually a coronation) reflects the almost dictatorial powers attached to the position. The most recent appointment was Field Marshal the 1st Viscount Alanbrooke for the coronation of Queen Elizabeth in 1953.

Lord High Steward One of the *great officers of state. The post is now a temporary one, only filled at the time of a coronation. Until 1948 a Lord High Steward was appointed to preside over trials of peers in the House of Lords, but the peers' privilege of trial by their fellows is now abolished. The last such occasion was the trial of the late Lord (26th Baron) de Clifford for manslaughter in 1935. The office is of uncertain origin but is known to date from before the reign of Edward the Confessor (r. 1042–66). Originally a Steward's duties were largely domestic. For special occasions, such as a coronation, a noble was appointed to discharge the ceremonial functions; eventually the post became hereditary. In the earlier Middle Ages the Lord High Steward was considered head of the realm during any interregnum. (He still has charge of St Edward's Crown on the day of a coronation.) Under Edward II (1284–1327) the Steward was recognized as second only to the king and highest judge in the court of Parliament. In the 15th century the permanent office of Lord High Steward ceased.

Lord Justice-General of Scotland See High Court of Justiciary.

Lord Justice of Appeal An ordinary judge of the *Court of Appeal. He is referred to as "Lord Justice A...." or (in law reports, etc.) "A...., L.J.", and the plural is Lords Justices (L. JJ.). A Lord Justice is appointed by the Crown on the advice of the Prime Minister and the *Master of the Rolls, and on appointment also becomes a member of the Privy Council. To qualify for appointment he must be either a barrister of at least 15 years' standing or, more usually, a High Court judge. A Lord Justice's tenure of office is as for a *puisne judge, except that the Lord Chancellor can declare his office vacant for incapacity only with the agreement of the Master of the Rolls.

Lord-Lieutenant The sovereign's permanent representative in a county, Greater London, or a part of one of the Scottish regions. Appointed by letters patent (granted on the advice of the Prime Minister) to be Her Majesty's Lieutenant for the area in question, his lordly prefix is by custom only. The office originated in temporary appointments under Henry VIII from 1539 and was then of a military nature. It was permanently established in a systematic fashion in 1551. The lieutenant was commissioned in times of civil unrest to raise a militia from local inhabitants to preserve order. The office is now one primarily of honour, but the Lord-Lieutenant retains a connection with the reserve forces, acting as president of territorial, auxiliary, and reserve associations. He also makes recommendations for the appointment of *justices of the peace.

Lord Mayor of London   The head of the *Corporation of London, by which the functions of local government are carried out in the *City of London. The office was established in 1191, in the reign of Richard I, and regulated by a royal charter of 1215 that required the election annually of a person "faithful, discreet, and fit for government". There is no bar against holding the office more than once, and its most famous incumbent, Richard Whittington, was in fact Mayor three times (1397–98, 1406–07, 1419–20). The Mayor is elected by the Court of Common Hall and Court of Aldermen every Michaelmas (*see* Corporation of London) and his swearing in takes place at the Royal Courts of Justice on the second Saturday in November (*see* Lord Mayor's Show). In addition to his local government functions, the Lord Mayor performs many ceremonial duties: for example, he attends on the Queen when she visits the City on state occasions, tenders the City sword as token of her authority, and retains it with her assent.

Lord Mayor's Show   An annual procession that takes place in London on the second Saturday in November. The newly appointed Lord Mayor of London travels, with considerable pomp, from the *Mansion House (his residence while in office) to the Strand, in a ceremony that dates from the time of King John (r. 1199–1216), for it was he who decreed that the Lord Mayor must present himself to the people as well as to his sovereign. The Lord Mayor first travels to the Guildhall, where addresses of loyalty are presented to him; the procession then makes its way to the Royal Courts of Justice in the Strand, where at exactly midday, in front of the judges of the Queen's Bench Division headed by the Lord Chief Justice (who represents the monarch), the new Lord Mayor promises to perform his duties faithfully.

Originally the Lord Mayor's journey was made on horseback but he is now borne in a magnificent state coach, built in 1757, and drawn by three pairs of shire horses. The paintings on the panels of this gilded coach have been attributed by some to the Florentine painter Giambattista (1727–85). The Lord Mayor, with a guard of honour provided by the Company of Pikemen and Musketeers of the City-based Honourable Artillery Company, brings up the rear of a mile-long procession of decorated floats presenting tableaux linked with the theme chosen by each new Lord Mayor for his show. In the evening of the Monday following the show the Lord Mayor's banquet is held at the Guildhall. By tradition the Prime Minister broadcasts a significant political speech after the dinner and the Archbishop of Canterbury proposes the toast to the hosts.

Lord President of the Council   The head of the *Privy Council since 1497. He is responsible for the Privy Council office, which prepares business for the Council and its committees, but his duties are not onerous; and though officially a member of the *Judicial Committee of the Privy Council, he does not in fact sit. It has long been the practice to appoint a senior member of the Cabinet to the post, leaving him free for other governmental duties as required. Since 1964 he has been frequently leader of one or other of the Houses of Parliament (*see* leader of the House).

Lord Privy Seal   A high officer of state from as early as the 14th century. As the uses of the Great Seal (*see* Lord (High) Chancellor) became more formal and circumscribed, the kings began to use another, smaller, seal for their personal needs. This "Privy Seal" was first definitely used during the reign of King John (r. 1199–1216). However, it too passed out of the king's hands, and from 1311, when a separate keeper was appointed, it became part of the royal bureaucracy, having less authority but more flexibility than the Great Seal. The Privy Seal became associated especially with the royal council, which developed as a governmental body in the 15th century. However, its significance declined in the 16th century with the rise of the *secretaries of state. It quickly lost all practical value, but its use was not discontinued until 1884. It has long been the practice to give the post of Keeper to a senior member of the Cabinet, who can then take on particular responsibilities on an ad hoc basis. Since 1964 it has been customary for him to be made leader of one or other of the Houses of Parliament (*see* leader of the House.

Lord's Cricket Ground The most famous cricket ground in the world, situated in northwest London, near Regent's Park. It is the home of the *MCC, which owns it, and Middlesex County Cricket Club, and is recognized as the administrative and spiritual headquarters of national and international cricket. It is named after Thomas Lord (1757–1832), who built his first cricket ground in Dorset Square in 1787. He was forced to move in 1811 and, after an abortive move to a site required for the Regent's Canal, settled at the present site in 1814. The freehold was purchased for £18,000 in 1866. It is now surrounded by stands constructed at various times since 1898, with the west side dominated by the pavilion, built in 1890. Its famous Long Room is a favourite meeting and vantage point for members. The library is now housed at the real tennis court behind the pavilion, near the Memorial Gallery of historic cricketing treasures, incuding the *Ashes. At the east end of the ground is a spacious practice area known as the Nursery, where minor matches are also played. The whole ground has a noticeable slope from north to south, which can assist skilful bowlers.

lords in waiting Junior officers of the royal household presided over by the *Lord Chamberlain. The permanent lord in waiting and certain of the others are chosen by the sovereign and undertake not to engage in any political activity. Three or more, however, the so-called political lords, are nominated by the government, and act as government *whips in the House of Lords.

Lords of Appeal in Ordinary (Law Lords) Persons who, under the Appellate Jurisdiction Act 1876, have been granted peerages for life to enable them to take part in the judicial business of the *House of Lords. Prior to 1876 appeals to the Lords could, theoretically, be heard by any three peers, regardless of whether they had any legal qualifications. This unsatisfactory state of affairs was brought to an end in 1873 when the appellate jurisdiction of the House of Lords was abolished by Gladstone's Liberal administration. When it was subse-

quently restored, under Disraeli, the Lords of Appeal were created. Lords of Appeal are also members of the *Judicial Committee of the Privy Council. They are appointed by the Crown on the advice of the Prime Minister and, to qualify for appointment, must have held high judicial office for at least two years, or have been practising barristers for at least 15 years. A Law Lord ranks as a baron, but his peerage is quite distinct from the nonjudicial peerages created under the much more recent Life Peerages Act 1958 (*see* life peerage).

Lords Spiritual *See* House of Lords.

Lord's Taverners A club of cricketing enthusiasts formed in 1950 and describing itself as "the charity with a sporting profile". HRH the Duke of Edinburgh became its patron and "twelfth man", while the actor Sir John Mills was its first president. Members are drawn from leading personalities in the professions, sports, stage, and show business. The charity has three main objectives: to enable the young to keep physically fit and mentally alert through the playing of team games, especially cricket; to build and run adventure playgrounds for underprivileged children through the auspices of the National Playing Fields Association; and to provide minibuses for handicapped children to enable them to escape from the confines of home and hospital. Funds are raised through sponsorship by companies and other organizations of such events as Sunday cricket matches, the Henry Cooper boxing evening, and the Harry Secombe golf classic.

Lords Temporal *See* House of Lords.

Lord Steward Titular head of the Master of the Household's department, which is responsible for royal entertaining and domestic matters. The Lord Steward is invariably a peer. The term "Lord Steward of the Household" dates from Elizabeth I's reign, though the office is at least 800 years old. He had a seat in the Cabinet till 1782 and remained a political appointment till 1924. He is now nominated by the Crown. He has a white stave as his emblem and carries it on various official occasions. He attends the monarch on state visits, the opening of Parliament, and state banquets (at which he presents guests to the sovereign). He walks backwards in front of the monarch when he enters the room in which the state banquet takes place.

In addition to these duties, the Lord Steward used to administer oaths to MPs and preside over his own court, known as the Lord Steward's Court. This exercised jurisdiction in both civil and criminal matters within a circle of 12 miles' radius centred on the sovereign's residence. From 1541 this was replaced by the **Marshalsea Court**, although the Lord Steward himself still presided. Its civil functions were not abolished until 1849. These courts heard cases in which the monarch's domestics were involved. The Palace Court, also under the Lord Steward, existed from 1612 to 1849 but differed from the Marshalsea Court in dealing with personal quarrels between disputants, not necessarily of the royal household. Its jurisdiction extended within a 12-mile radius of Whitehall.

Lowlands, the Opinions vary as to what constitutes the Lowlands of Scotland. Some restrict the title to the belt of low-lying land between the Firth of Clyde and Firth of Forth.

Others would include all parts of Scotland south of the *Highlands, from Kintyre and Fife in the north to the hills of Galloway, Tweedsmuir, and Lammermuir as far as the *Border.

After the introduction of *feudalism in the 12th century (*see* Norman Britain), the Lowlands came to replace the *Highlands as the core of the Scottish kingdom. Edinburgh replaced Perth as the capital of Scotland in 1437. The history of the Lowlands was turbulent after 1290, however, owing to English invasions, civil wars, and unrest (*see* monarchy in Scotland). In the 16th century the Lowlands embraced Presbyterianism (*see* Presbyterians) after the Scottish reformation (1560; *see* Church of Scotland), which caused friction with the Crown and unrest in the 17th century. The *Act of Union with England (1707) reduced Scotland's political importance, but did open up commercial opportunities. Glasgow expanded, first as a centre for trade with North America (especially in tobacco), and, after the *industrial revolution, as a centre of heavy industry. Iron and steel, engineering, and, most

THE LOWLANDS *Abbotsford, near Melrose, Sir Walter Scott's home on the banks of the River Tweed.*

important, shipbuilding, were fuelled by the Lanark coalfield. Recent decline in these industries has created high unemployment and other problems of urban decay. Edinburgh meanwhile continued to function as the Scottish capital and as a centre of learning, being the focus of a Scottish renaissance from the mid-18th century. Each year since 1947 the city has hosted the internationally renowned *Edinburgh Festival. Edinburgh and Glasgow and the land between them contain the bulk of Scotland's population and industry.

Across the Firth of Forth lies the low peninsula of Fife with its picturesque coastline leading round to St Andrews, home of Scotland's oldest university (*see* St Andrew's University) and the home of *golf. Its Royal and Ancient Golf Club was founded in 1754 and the old course dates back to the 15th century. To the west is Stirling with nearby *Bannockburn, the battlefield on which Robert the Bruce led his forces to victory over the English army of Edward II in 1314, establishing Scottish independence (*see* monarchy in Scotland). Loch Lomond, north of the Clyde, is Britain's largest lake. Outside the central belt of the Lowlands are many unspoilt corners, such as the inlets and peninsulas of Cowal and the westernmost point – the long Kintyre peninsula extending south past the isle of Arran. Further south is the countryside of Ayrshire (administratively part of Strathclyde), which was immortalized in the poetry of its most famous son, Robert Burns (1759–96), born at Alloway near Ayr (*see* Burns Night). Nearby Kilmarnock was the home of Johnnie Walker, founder of the whisky distilling business that still bears his name.

LSE *See* London School of Economics.

Luddites Groups of workmen who rebelled against the increased mechanization of textile production in the early 19th century by destroying the new machinery. The Luddites were named after the possibly mythical Ned Ludd, a simpleton, who is reputed to have destroyed machinery in a rage. Luddism began with the smashing of stocking frames in the textile factories of Nottinghamshire in 1811 and rapidly spread to other industrial areas; the Luddites claimed to be concerned not only with the threat to their livelihoods posed by the new machinery but also with the inferior quality of the machine-made goods. The government, fearing a revolutionary conspiracy, introduced ferocious penalties: to smash frames, damage property, or take Luddite oaths became capital offences. In January 1813 seventeen men were executed at York and six were transported. The movement temporarily died down, only to be renewed in a more organized form, and again repressed, some three years later.

M

Mabinogion, The An anonymous collection of Welsh folk tales written in prose and contained in several medieval manuscripts, the earliest of which dates back to the 13th century. *The Mabinogion* belongs to a rich heritage of stories that were transmitted orally by *bards over many generations, and that draw upon an amalgam of ancient Celtic mythology and folklore and early British history, extending back to Roman times. The 11 tales that make up the canon of *The Mabinogion* fall into three groups. The first consists of four tales known collectively as *Pedeir Keinc y Mabinogi* ("The Four Branches of the Chronicle of Youth"). These four stories share certain themes and may be the corrupted survivors of a cycle of legends about Pryderi, a mythical Welsh prince. The second group comprises four independent native tales, one of which, "Culhwch and Olwen", contains the earliest reference to King Arthur in Welsh literature. The last three tales are romances set against the background of Arthur's court and containing references to chivalry and other literary elements found also in the French sources of *Arthurian legend.

The name *Mabinogion* is not original but was given to the collection of stories by Lady Charlotte Guest, who completed the first English translation of them in 1849. Lady Charlotte took the word *mabinogen* to mean "children's stories". But it is a modern coinage based on a misunderstanding of the word *mabinogi*, meaning "a tale of childhood".

magistrates' courts Courts in England and Wales that exercise a limited local jurisdiction, chiefly criminal. They consist of two to seven lay magistrates, or a single stipendiary magistrate (*see* justice of the peace). There are no juries. Lay magistrates are assisted on points of law by a legally qualified officer of the court (*see* clerk to the justices). All criminal prosecutions in England and Wales begin in a magistrates' court, but the more serious offences (indictable offences) are sent to the *Crown Court for trial by jury after a magistrates' court has carried out a "preliminary investigation" to decide whether or not there is a case to answer. The magistrates' court itself tries the less serious offences (summary offences), but the penalties it can impose are limited; in certain cases it can commit the offender to the Crown Court for sentence. A person convicted by a magistrates' court may appeal to the Crown Court against conviction, sentence, or both; and either side may dispute any ruling by the magistrates on a point of law by requiring them to state a case for decision by the *Divisional Court of the Queen's Bench Division of the High Court of Justice.

The civil jurisdiction of magistrates' courts includes a limited range of domestic proceedings (e.g. for adoption, affiliation, and maintenance orders) and also the enforcement of local authority rates.

Magna Carta The great charter of liberties of 1215 and one of the most famous documents in the English-speaking world. It was proclaimed by King John at Runnymede after a rebellion by barons and churchmen against his ruthless exploitation of the ill-defined limits of royal power, which they felt to be encroaching on their rights and privileges. Although repudiated by John immediately after the event, it was subsequently confirmed on a number of occasions (as, for example, by the *Confirmatio Cartarum*, enacted in 1297 during the reign of Edward I). The charter required that the existing liberties, such as those of the Church and the towns, should be respected; and some of John's objectionable practices,

such as excessive fines and ruinous exploitation of his wards' lands, were specifically forbidden or limited. A committee of 25 barons was charged with supervising the king's observance of the law, with the right of legalized rebellion should he be found wanting. (This clause, with others especially detrimental to royal power, were omitted from the reissues.) The charter's lasting constitutional importance stemmed primarily from the very fact of its concession, which was used to argue that the rights of the Crown were not unlimited, and that subjects had a legitimate interest in their definition. Also, some of its clauses dealt with issues that came to be regarded as fundamental to constitutional government. In its two most famous clauses, it stated: "No free man shall be imprisoned ... unless by the lawful judgment of his peers, or by the law of the land", and "To none will we sell, to none will we deny or delay, right or justice". It was a rallying call for the parliamentarians in their 17th-century conflicts with the Crown (*see* Civil War, English); words from it found their way into America's Declaration of Independence of 1776; and it is still regarded as a symbol in man's struggle for constitutional government. Most of the Magna Carta has now been repealed, however, as having no specific legal operation. Of the four original copies that still exist, two are in the British Library, one is in Salisbury cathedral, and one in Lincoln cathedral.

maintained schools *See* Local Education Authorities.

manor The basic economic unit of *feudalism and of rural Britain from Roman times until the 18th century. The lord of the manor's land was worked by peasant farmers, who also cultivated their own plots, rented from the lord in return both for their labour on his land and various other services or money payments. The peasants, or serfs, were bound to the land in that they were not free to farm elsewhere, and some were also personally "unfree": that is, their status vis-à-vis the lord lay somewhere between that of a slave and a freeman; the lord had certain rights over them (e.g. they could generally be bought and sold) but he could not, for example, kill or maim them with impunity. In practice, however, all peasants were very much at the mercy of the lord.

The extent of the manorial system in Anglo-Saxon Britain is obscure, but it became the norm in lowland areas following the Norman conquest (1066), with the peasants becoming the base of the feudal pyramid. Their lot did not noticeably improve during the next 300 years. In the 12th century, many labour services were commuted to more profitable money rents, a trend that increased as the population grew and land became scarcer. The development of the *common law in the 12th and 13th centuries led to the emergence of a uniform class of unfree serfs, under which most peasants were subsumed. However, the *Black Death (1348–49) transformed the situation: because labour became scarce, wages rose, rents fell, and restrictions on the movements of serfs became unenforcible. Landlords tried to reimpose labour services and to preserve the status quo by legislation. However, this led to discontent, culminating in the *Peasants' Revolt of 1381, which demanded an end to serfdom. Although this rising was suppressed, serfdom disappeared for largely economic reasons in the 15th century, to be replaced by yeoman farmers, who worked their own land, and wage labourers. The manor continued to thrive until the agricultural revolution of the 18th century did away with the traditional communal agricultural methods and remodelled landholding patterns (see enclosure, laws of). At the same time, the manorial courts rapidly decayed; most of their powers were transferred to the royal courts, though they retained jurisdiction over some land tenures until 1925. The lordships of ancient manors still exist, and confer certain privileges on the holder, such as mineral and sporting rights, as well as the theoretical right to hold courts. These lordships are now often bought and sold for their curiosity value.

Manpower Services Commission (MSC) A body established by the Employment and Training Act 1973 to oversee public employment and training services. The primary role of the MSC is to ensure the effective utilization of manpower resources by trying to create employment opportunities and to reduce un-

employment. The MSC has three main divisions, responsible for employment, training, and for the Skillcentre Training Agency, which provides a variety of training courses. Besides finding suitable people for general positions, the MSC places thousands of disabled persons and long-term unemployed in work via its community programme, and maintains severely disabled people in sheltered employment. Furthermore, it provides grants and professional advice under its Enterprise Allowance Scheme for unemployed people who wish to start their own businesses. The MSC runs three main training programmes: its Youth Training Scheme, adult training, and a scheme to help special groups in the labour force, such as the disabled, ethnic minorities, and women. Its future plans include the expansion of its community programme, and the introduction of vocational education schemes in selected areas.

Mansion House The official residence of the Lord Mayor of London during his year of office. Originally Lord Mayors continued to live in their own residences during their term of office, but in the reconstruction after the *Great Fire (1666) it was decided that an official residence should be provided. George Dance designed a mansion to be built on the site of Stocks Market. Work began in 1739, and in 1752 Sir Crisp Gascoyne took up residence in the house, which had cost more than £70,000 to build. The original heavy portico of six Corinthian columns remains, but many alterations – including the removal of an extension known as the Mayor's Nest – subsequently transformed the interior. In 1845 a private entrance for the Mayor was built, as well as the justice room, which forms one of the City's two magistrates' courts. Ten cells were added beneath the court, including one for women (known as "the birdcage"), in which the suffragette Emmeline Pankhurst was once confined. Statues of distinguished national figures were installed in niches in the banqueting room (known as the Egyptian Hall), together with large stained-glass windows by Alexander Gibbs (1868). Most valuable of the treasures of the Mansion House is a set of chairs commemorating Nelson's victory at the battle of the Nile (1798). In 1936 the

Mansion House was presented with the millionth telephone to be produced (made of gold). The building was damaged during World War II, the Egyptian Hall not being reopened until 1950. Recent alterations have included the addition of a public gallery to the justice room (1962). State banquets are still held in the banqueting room, and on the second Saturday in November each year the Lord Mayor's Show begins at the Mansion House.

Manx The extinct *Celtic language of the Isle of Man, related to Irish. It was probably brought to Man from Ireland in the 4th century AD and it died out in the 1940s, although the last native speaker lived on until 1974. Surviving texts consist of traditional ballads, a translation of the Book of Common Prayer, a few religious texts, and a grammar by Edward Lhuyd (1707), who also wrote on Cornish. Manx is quite similar to *Irish and *Gaelic in its structure and phonology, although it looks quite different in writing, since the spelling is based on the values of English vowels and consonants. An example sentence is *cha vel mee toigal ny t'eh dy ghra*, "I can't understand what he is saying".

Marble Day The day on which the British marbles championship, an annual competition, takes place at Tinsley Green, Sussex. Marble Day traditionally coincides with Good Friday and marks the official end of the marble-playing season, which begins on Ash Wednesday. The game of marbles has been played by children throughout the country since Roman times; the Sussex championship, which is contested by adults, dates back to an incident in 1600. Rival suitors for the hand of a beautiful village maiden, too well-matched to resolve the matter by fighting, finally resorted to a game of marbles to decide the winner. In the modern competition each contestant is armed with a three-quarter-inch marble known as a "tolley", which he uses to knock as many marbles as possible out of the centre of the circular rink. The championship is taken very seriously and played to strict rules; similar contests have been established overseas.

Mari Lwyd A winter custom in Wales similar to *wassailing in England, or first footing (*see* Hogmanay) in Scotland. Mari Lwyd, meaning "Grey Mary" or perhaps "grey mare", still survives in Mid Glamorgan and western Gwent, particularly in the upland parish of Llangynwyd, in Mid Glamorgan. According to custom, a group of people goes from house to house carrying before them a horse's skull on a pole decorated with coloured ribbons – the Mari Lwyd herself – and at each house they sing a traditional song that takes the form of a request for refreshment and hospitality. The custom goes back several centuries and is probably a New Year tradition. It has an affinity with *Hallowe'en, which marked the end of the old year in the Celtic calendar.

Maritime Trust A charitable trust formed in 1969 to rescue, restore, and display British vessels of historical and technical interest. The Trust's "Historic Ship Collection", which opened ten years later, is on permanent display near Tower Bridge, London, in the East Basin of St Katharine's Dock. The *Kathleen and May*, a three-masted topsail trading schooner built in 1900, is now on show at St Mary Overy Dock, close to Southwark Cathedral on the south side of the Thames. The Trust also has on display at Greenwich the *Cutty Sark* (1869) and Sir Francis Chichester's *Gipsy Moth IV* (1966). Its other activities have included restoration work on Captain Scott's *Discovery* (1901), which has now been chartered to the city of Dundee, where she was built, and the provision of assistance and grants to allied organizations, such as the Mary Rose Trust (*see* Mary Rose) and various maritime museums.

market towns Towns that have been granted a borough charter to hold a weekly or biweekly market. Many new markets were created when Richard I (1189–99) and John (1199–1216) sold such charters to finance their wars. Originally held on Sundays, the artisan's free day, markets were transferred to weekdays after pressure from Pope Innocent III (1198–1216).

In early Anglo-Saxon times markets were probably only held in seaports. Inland, trade was restricted by lack of secure sites for commercial activity. However, King Edward the Elder of Wessex (r. 899–924) made certain villages into *burhs* (Anglo-Saxon for a fortified

MARKET TOWNS *Arcaded Jacobean market hall in the Cotswold town of Chipping Campden. "Chipping" derives from the Anglo-Saxon word* ceapen, *meaning to buy or barter, and is associated with market towns.*

place) as a defence against the Danes. Market towns grew up inside these new "boroughs" but were initially known as "ports" (e.g. Newport, in Shropshire, a market town lying far from the sea). Trade was restricted to borough markets since they could easily be defended and the concentration of trade in a market square enabled the owner – usually the king – to collect toll money with ease. Toll tariffs in a 12th-century market amounted to about twopence on a cartload of goods, one penny on a horse-load, and one halfpenny on a man's load, at a time when a sheep cost about sixpence.

Some markets were privately owned by nobles who had obtained a royal licence to hold a market in a town without a borough charter. The large tolls to be obtained from these markets frequently led to violence over the siting of new ones. For example, a force of 600 men sent by the abbot of Bury St Edmunds wrecked a new market, ruled illegal by the courts, that had been nevertheless set up by the bishop of Ely on a site that the abbot regarded as too close to his own.

The market towns continued to prosper as trade flourished during the Middle Ages, controlled by their own market guilds, but by 1500 trade had expanded to the extent that it was carried on on a national rather than local basis. The once self-sufficient medieval town was now but a part of a much larger economic unit and local markets began to decline. Evidence of the prosperity of the older market towns is provided by the elegant buildings around market squares, the ornate crosses erected by wealthy merchants, and medieval market halls, such as that at Chipping Campden. Some towns owe their name and existence to their market: Chipping Norton takes its name from the word *ceapen* (Anglo-Saxon for barter, buy. sell), while Market Harborough was created by Henry II (1154–89) specifically to be a market.

In modern times, the only important local markets left are those dealing in livestock. Many towns still hold their traditional markets – one has been held every Wednesday in Market Drayton for 700 years – to provide a flavour of the past and low-rental premises for the stall-holders.

marquess A nobleman holding a title in the second rank of the *peerage (or certain eldest sons of dukes who are known by courtesy as marquesses if one of their father's subsidiary titles is a marquessate). The order is scarcely more numerous than that of the dukes: there are only 30 marquesses. An alternative spelling is marquis, though marquess is usually preferred. The word derives from the Latin *marchio* and originally denoted a commander of a march, or frontier area, on the continent of Europe. However, in early Norman England the term was used in a purely descriptive sense of certain nobles, for instance earls or barons who guarded the Welsh or Scottish marches or border areas. In 1385 Richard II created the first marquess as a title of nobility: Robert de Vere, Earl of Oxford was made Marquess of Dublin. The present premier marquess is the Marquess of Winchester, whose title was created in 1551. A marchioness is usually the wife of a marquess, although Anne Boleyn was created Marchioness of Pembroke in her own right in 1532. A marquess is entitled to the prefix Most Honourable. His eldest son is known by courtesy by one of the marquess's subsidiary titles, usually an earldom or viscountcy. Younger children are known as Lord or Lady followed by Christian and surname.

Marshalsea Court *See* Lord Steward.

MARY ROSE *The only surviving contemporary picture of HMS* Mary Rose, *from the Anthony Roll, a list of Henry VIII's ships completed in 1546.*

Martinmas The feast of St Martin, 11 November, widely observed until the 19th century and coinciding with the slaughter and preparation of cattle for the coming winter. Indeed, in Scotland and northern England, the animals were called "marts", and in Northumberland, families joined together to form "marts" in order to purchase a beast at this time of year. A spell of fine weather around this time used to be known as a St Martin's summer.

Mary Rose A warship of Henry VIII's navy, which sank ignominiously with a crew of some 700 men in Portsmouth harbour in 1545, on her way to do battle with the French off the Isle of Wight. Built in 1509–10, she was one of the world's first purpose-designed warships. The cause of the accident is not known, but is thought to have been a combination of poor handling and overloading. Henry probably witnessed the sinking from Southsea castle. The ship sank with her equipment and crew more or less intact: guns, archery equipment, musical instruments, clothing, tableware, and coins were all preserved in the mud of the Solent for over 400 years. After underwater searches during the 1960s, the ship was located in 1967. In the following years the contents were raised, and in 1982 the hull itself was lifted and placed in a special dry dock in Portsmouth where it may be viewed by the public.

Master of the Horse The officer of the royal household nominally responsible for all matters concerning the sovereign's motor transport, horses, hounds, stables, coach houses, stud, mews, and kennels. His functions originated in the duties of the medieval constable and marshal; he is now always a Privy Councillor and peer. His duties, however, are part-time and unpaid (the *Crown Equerry superintends matters on a day-to-day basis). Before 1924 the Prime Minister nominated the Master of the Horse and prior to 1782 he was in the Cabinet. The post is now a nonpolitical Crown appointment.

The Master of the Horse rides immediately behind the sovereign in all state processions, since he is theoretically responsible for his or her safety while on horseback or aboard a carriage. When Queen Victoria first travelled by train, the holder of the office on that occasion even attempted to mount the engine, holding that it was his privilege to drive Her Majesty; but he was dissuaded by an engine driver telling him how much dirt was involved. At her coronation the then Master of the Horse, the Earl of Albemarle, rode in the same carriage, for Victoria was unmarried and therefore considered the more in need of protection (not that she acquiesced readily in his claim to accompany her). The danger of exceeding the bounds of delicacy when the sovereign was an unmarried woman had already arisen in Elizabeth I's reign. The Earl of Leicester (Master of the Horse 1558/9–87) was said to have handed the queen her clothes when she dressed. The office has been greatly coveted: the 2nd Duke of Buckingham bought the post for £20,000 from the Duke of Albemarle in 1668.

Despite the post's largely honorific nature, the incumbent occasionally carries out inspections of the royal stables and is consulted about the purchase of new horses.

Master of the Queen's Music An honorary position held by a composer. The post dates from the appointment in 1626 of Nicholas Lanier (d. 1666) as "master of the music" at the court of Charles I. Lanier's role was to direct the king's musicians, and only after 1700 did it involve composing music for such occasions as royal birthdays. In the 19th century the post became more or less a sinecure, and the Master of the Queen's (or King's) Music has had no official duties since the 1920s. Malcolm Williamson (1931–   ), who became Master in 1975, wrote the *Mass of Christ the King* for Elizabeth II's silver jubilee in 1978. His predecessors include William Boyce (1710–79), from 1755, Edward Elgar (1857–1934), from 1924, and Arthur Bliss (1891–1975), from 1953.

Master of the Rolls The presiding judge of the Civil Division of the *Court of Appeal. He is appointed by the Crown on the advice of the Prime Minister, but the appointment is not made on a political basis; and his tenure of office is, basically, as for a *puisne judge. The Lord Chancellor can, however, declare his of-

fice vacant for incapacity only with the agreement of the heads of two of the three divisions of that court. The office of Master of the Rolls originated as the guardian of all charters, patents, deeds, etc., entered upon parchment rolls in Chancery. They were stored from 1290 in a chapel called the Rolls, which had been founded by Henry III in 1233 for Jewish converts to Christianity. When the Jews were banished in 1290, the chapel was annexed to the office of the Master of the Rolls by patent, and there the rolls remained until they were moved to the Public Records Office in the 19th century. The first recorded Master of the Rolls was John de Langton (appointed 1286) but the office seems to have existed long before that. The Master of the Rolls also advised the Lord Chancellor in the judicial work of the old Court of Chancery and became a full judge of the court in 1729 (*see* equity). As his legal responsibilities have increased, his record-keeping duties have reduced. The Public Records Office has, since 1958, been under the direction of the Lord Chancellor, although there is an advisory council, which the Master of the Rolls chairs. He also admits solicitors to practice, and is responsible for appointing the members of the Solicitors Disciplinary Tribunal.

May Day An annual festival celebrated throughout the country, largely in rural areas,

MAY DAY *Choristers herald the arrival of May morning from Magdalen Tower, Oxford.*

on 1 May. Its roots lie in ancient pagan festivities, such as the Celtic festival of Beltane when bonfires were lit and animals were sacrificed to the sun god, in celebration of the coming of spring, with its associations of new growth and fertility. In the morning or on the eve of May Day young people would collect flowers, branches, and greenery to decorate their homes. Ancient May Day traditions that survive in some places, such as Elstow in Bedfordshire, Gawthorpe in Yorkshire, and Welford-on-Avon in Warwickshire, include colourful processions, *maypole dancing, the crowning of a May queen, and *morris dancing on the village green.

At Knutsford in Cheshire, May Day is celebrated on the first Saturday following 1 May. A feature of the Knutsford festival, known as Royal May Day since its patronage by the Prince of Wales in 1887, is the tradition of tracing mottoes and patterns in coloured sand on the streets of the town. King Canute (or Knut), crossing a nearby ford in 1017, is said to have sprinkled a few grains of sand from his shoes in the path of a passing bridal party as a token of good luck: from this legend sprang the name of the town, Knut's ford, and the custom of sanding the streets for weddings and on Royal May Day. Other traditions associated with May Day include the *hobby horses of Padstow and Minehead and the May morning singing at Magdalen College, Oxford. This takes place at six o'clock in the morning of 1 May, when the choristers of Magdalen College chapel assemble at the top of the College Tower and sing the Latin hymn *Te Deum Patrem Colimus*. A peal of bells follows the singing; the crowds of undergraduates that line Magdalen bridge for the ceremony and gather in punts on the river below are further entertained by morris dancers in the city streets and the city's pubs are opened. *See also* Labour Day.

mayor The chairman of the council of a *borough (including a *district that has the title "borough" by royal charter; *see also* parish). A mayor may, by royal charter, be styled lord mayor (*see also* Lord Mayor of London). The word comes from the Norman title *maire*, which was introduced by Henry II in the 12th century.

maypole A central feature of *May Day dancing and celebrations since Celtic times. In medieval England maypoles stood on nearly every village green and also in some city streets on May Day. Some were permanent fixtures – the original Celtic maypole was a live tree stripped of foliage – others were taken down after the annual festivities. Maypoles inevitably became the focal point of the more riotous May Day celebrations and were condemned by the Puritans, who had them uprooted throughout the country in the mid-17th century. After the Restoration some were returned to their rightful positions: their successors still stand on a number of village greens today. Often brightly painted with spiral stripes, they are traditionally decked with coloured streamers or ribbons that are woven into complicated patterns by the dancers as they skip around the pole to celebrate the coming of summer. Barwick-in-Elmet, Yorkshire, boasts the tallest surviving maypole in England: 26 metres (86 feet) high, it is re-erected during annual celebrations, which take place on Whit Tuesday rather than on 1 May.

MCC (Marylebone Cricket Club) The world's premier cricket club with headquarters at *Lord's Cricket Ground, London. It was founded in 1787 by a group of enthusiastic aristocrats led by the Earl of Winchelsea; its first game was played on Thomas Lord's ground in Dorset Square in 1788. The MCC revised the rules of the game and succeeded Hambledon (near Portsmouth, Hampshire; *see* cricket) as England's leading club. Indeed, it was accepted internationally as the ruling body of the game until 1969 when the Cricket Council took over this role. The MCC has done much for the development of cricket both in Britain and abroad through its organization of tours. From the advent of international (test) matches (1880) until 1982, all England teams touring overseas went officially as representatives of the MCC and they still wear the red and yellow club colours. In Britain scarcely a summer's day goes by without an MCC side taking the field against a club or school side. There are 12,000 members of the MCC and a very long waiting list to join.

Medical Research Council A body responsible for promoting and undertaking research to improve health, established by royal charter in 1920. It maintains its own research institutes and, in addition, funds research in universities and polytechnics. The three largest institutes funded by the Council are the National Institute for Medical Research and the Clinical Research Centre, both in London, and the Laboratory of Molecular Biology in Cambridge. The Council's work is divided into four major areas, each supervised by a separate board. The Neurobiology and Mental Health Board deals with both physiological and behavioural aspects of the neurosciences. Topics covered by the Cell Biology and Disorders Board range through biophysics, cell and molecular biology, genetics, cancer, and immunology. A great deal of attention is devoted to cancer research and the Institute of Cancer Research is funded jointly by the Medical Research Council and the Cancer Research Campaign. The Council also subscribes to the International Agency for Cancer Research. The Physiological Systems and Disorders Board is responsible for research into a wide range of human disorders, including cardiovascular disease and Acquired Immune Deficiency Syndrome (AIDS). Lastly, the Tropical Medicine Research Board investigates health problems of tropical countries.

Member of Parliament (MP) A person elected to represent a parliamentary constituency in the *House of Commons. On election an MP is required to swear loyalty to the Crown and to sign the Test Roll accepting the sovereign as head of the Church of England (*see* Test and Corporation Acts). This done, he has no legally enforceable duties to perform, and need not even attend the House again. Formerly, the House held occasional roll calls, and imposed fines for nonattendance but no fine has been recorded since one of £10 in 1831.

Elected to represent his constituency as a whole, an MP is normally committed to a particular political party, following its policy and subject to the discipline of its *whips. He may, however, gain election as an independent and he certainly cannot be prevented from switching party allegiance (known as "cross-ing the floor"). An MP's allegiance is a matter of public knowledge; of great concern, particularly in modern times, has been the unseen influence of MPs' financial and business affairs. In 1975 the House resolved to establish a register of members' interests, since when an MP is required to supply information about all matters that might influence him, including details of any ownership of land or shares of substantial value or quantity, of any company directorships, of any clients for whom he renders professional services related to his membership of the House, of any financial sponsorship (e.g. by a trade union), of any overseas visits subsidized otherwise than out of public funds, and of any benefits received from governments abroad. Registration is not compulsory, but any MP who fails to declare any interest, or gives false information, may be punished by the House for contempt (*see* parliamentary privilege).

There were at one time qualifications for election, such as the ownership of property and residence within the constituency, but these have long been abolished. The list of disqualifications has been reduced; nonclerical religious bars ceased in the 19th century and women became eligible in 1918 (Lady Astor became the first woman MP in 1919). Those who remain disqualified are: aliens (meaning, for this purpose, people who are neither *Commonwealth citizens nor citizens of the Republic of Ireland); minors (the age of majority remains 21 for parliamentary purposes); peers and peeresses in their own right other than those of the peerage of Ireland (*see* House of Lords); many clergy (but not all); convicted prisoners (a disqualification added in 1981 after the election of Robert Sands, an IRA prisoner on hunger strike); undischarged bankrupts and people convicted of certain corrupt or illegal practices at previous elections (e.g. bribery, intimidation, or overspending on campaign expenses); people suffering from severe mental disorder; and the holders of a large number of public offices listed in the House of Commons Disqualification Act 1975. This aims to exclude both government patronage and office holders whose duties are incompatible with active membership or require political impartiality; those principally af-

269

fected are judges; stipendiary magistrates; civil servants; members of the regular armed forces; full-time police officers; and the chairmen and members of many public boards, commissions, tribunals, and undertakings. There is nothing in the law or custom of Parliament that enables an MP to resign from the House. The only way in which he can cease to be a member during the life of a Parliament is by applying for the *Chiltern Hundreds (or the Manor of Northstead).

Mercia A former kingdom established in central England, mainly by Anglo-Saxons, from the late 5th century AD (*see* Anglo-Saxon Britain). They settled in the boundary area between the Anglo-Saxons in the east and the native Britons in the west, and took their name from Old English *merce*, which means "men of the boundary" or "march". They became strong under the pagan king, Penda (632–55) at the expense of Northumbria and the Welsh, but were at their most powerful in the 8th century under Ethelbald (716–57) and his cousin Offa (757–96; *see also* Offa's dyke), who extended his territory until it reached from the Humber to the English Channel and treated lesser English kings virtually as subjects. After his death, however, Mercian power declined and the kingdom fell to the Danes in 877. It was reconquered by the kings of Wessex in the 10th century and, although it ceased to be a separate kingdom, the name is occasionally used within the area of old Mercia to indicate the general region, for example, by the West Mercia Constabulary.

Merit, Order of A body of distinguished men and women for whom a title of honour, such as a knighthood, may not be appropriate. It was instituted by Edward VII on 23 June 1902 and is limited to 24 members. Foreigners may be made honorary members. There is a military class, for which the badge bears crossed swords, and a civil one, for which the badge bears oak leaves; the order's motto reads "For Merit". Members are entitled to the letters OM after their names.

metaphysical poets A number of 17th-century poets, never in their own time identified as a group, whose work is characterized by an intensely metaphorical style in the treat-ment of thought and emotion, and an occasionally extreme imagery. John Donne, the principal exponent of this, referred to it as "strong lines"; John Dryden, in 1693, wrote that Donne "affects the Metaphysics ... in his amorous verses, where Nature only should reign, and perplexes the minds of the fair sex with nice speculations of philosophy ..." Other poets associated with the style include George Herbert, Henry Vaughan, Abraham Cowley, Andrew Marvell, and Richard Crashaw. Dr Johnson, in writing of Cowley (1777), first used the term "metaphysical" directly to identify the group; but it was T. S. Eliot who assisted their reputation in the 20th century by praising their oneness of feeling and intellect in an essay of 1921. There are now several anthologies of metaphysical verse.

Meteorological Office The national weather organization, responsible for the collection of data on weather, the analysis of climatic conditions, and weather forecasting for the government, industry, and the public. The Meteorological Office, or "Met." Office, has a staff of 2600 and is administered by the Ministry of Defence. It was founded in 1854 as a department of the Board of Trade, as a result of growing international concern about losses of ships and the need for a telegraphic storm-warning service. The first weather reports were published, and by 1880 a network of weather stations had been established. A parallel group, the British Rainfall Organization, was absorbed by the Met. Office in 1919. During World War II, the Met. Office provided vital information for the RAF and the planners of major operations, especially D-Day in 1944.

Using computers, information is sent to the Central Forecasting Office at Bracknell in Berkshire from 114 field stations, 3000 amateur recorders, ships of the Voluntary Observing Fleet, aircraft and radar, weather satellites, and balloons. This data is supplemented by the four Thunderstorm Location Centres, the National Meteorological Library, the Radar Research Laboratory at Malvern in Hereford and Worcester, and the Met. Office's own specialized weather aircraft. The latest summaries are then disseminated, particularly through the London Weather Centre. The

Met. Office is considered the world authority on meteorology on account of its experience in predicting the notoriously rapid changes in British weather patterns; an 80% accuracy in forecasting has been claimed. Many industries are dependent upon the accurate forecasting of the weather, notably those of aerospace, shipping, agriculture, and construction.

Methodists Members of the largest of the Protestant *free churches in Britain, with over 450,000 adult members and some 2070 ministers. The movement originated from a group of devout Oxford students led by brothers John and Charles Wesley (1703–91; 1707–88) whose earnest and methodical approach to religious study and prayer earned them the nickname "Methodists". Returning from an unsatisfactory missionary trip to the American colonies, John underwent a spiritual conversion in May 1738 and embarked on a self-appointed evangelical mission to the nation. Although members of the Church of England, the Wesleys and their followers were often barred from pulpits by incumbents or bishops, and resorted to open-air meetings. But, with an often inadequate established Church, the Methodist alternative proved very popular. From the 1740s followers were organized into societies, and in 1744 John Wesley arranged the first national conference for his lay preachers. But only in 1795, after Wesley's death, did the Methodists secede from the Church of England.

The Calvinistic Methodists (see Presbyterian Church of Wales), who disagreed with Wesley's emphasis on the possibility of self-regeneration by the individual through faith and works, went their own way as early as 1741. The Methodist New Connexion split from the main body in 1797 over organizational differences. The Primitive Methodists, a sect which arose in North Staffordshire, formed their own Church in 1811 following the expulsion of their leaders, Hugh Bourne and William Clowes. In the next decades, a number of factions sprang up as a result of constitutional differences: the Protestant Methodists (formed 1827) joined the Wesleyan Methodist Association (formed 1835) in 1836. Some of the Wesleyan Reformers, who had been expelled in 1849, united with the Wesleyan Methodist

Association in 1857 to form the United Methodist Free Churches. Reconciliation between these groups came in the 20th century. In 1907 the New Connexion, Bible Christians, and United Methodist Free Churches amalgamated to form the United Methodist Church, which in 1932, along with the Primitive Methodists, rejoined the main Wesleyan movement to produce the modern Methodist Church. The *Wesleyan Reform Union, which derives from the Wesleyan Reformers of 1849, remains outside, as do various independent Methodist Churches.

The principal governing body of the Methodist Church is the annual conference of ministers and lay representatives. Much of the conference's work is done by its various divisional boards, such as the Home Mission Division, the Division of Social Responsibility, and the Division of Education and Youth. The conference also supervises the Methodist-run National Children's Home and the Methodist Publishing House. Each of the 32 administrative districts, including Cymru and Scotland, has its own synod of ministers and lay persons. Each district comprises various circuits, and the churches and chapels in each circuit share a team of ministers and lay preachers, headed by a superintendent. Circuit business is conducted by lay circuit stewards. The Methodist Church in Ireland has over 21,000 adult members, most of whom are in Northern Ireland. There are now Methodist churches throughout the world.

Metropolitan Police The police force for London (except the City, which is the responsibility of the *City of London Police). Known informally as the Met, and notable for being the first force to have been organized in the UK, it was established in 1829 by Sir Robert Peel (the then Home Secretary, after whom policemen were known colloquially as "bobbies" or "peelers") for an area ranging from four to seven miles around Charing Cross. Its area today (the Metropolitan Police District) has a 15-mile radius, covering Greater London and some bordering parts of Essex, Hertfordshire, and Surrey.

The Met is closely associated with the Home Secretary, being maintained by him and governed by his regulations concerning management, operational standards, and discipline. At its head is the Commissioner of Police of the metropolis (appointed by the Crown on the Home Secretary's recommendation) and under the Commissioner are four principal headquarters departments, each responsible for a particular field of activity. They are: A - uniformed operations; B - traffic; C - criminal investigation (see CID); and D - personnel and training. (*Special Branch is in C department.) The Met is divided into 4 areas and 24 districts; there is also a Thames division (the river police). This structure is being radically altered, however, by a long-term reorganization initiated by the Commissioner, Sir Kenneth Newman, in 1985. When it is completed there will be eight areas instead of four; the districts will have disappeared; and headquarters departments A to C will have been replaced by one responsible for territorial policing, and another for specialist policing. See also Scotland Yard.

MI5 and MI6   Britain's secret service comprises two principal intelligence departments: MI5, which deals with domestic counterespionage and countersubversion, and MI6, which gathers intelligence in other countries. The initials MI stand for "military intelligence" and the numbers for former specialist sections in the secret service. Ultimate control lies with the Prime Minister through a joint intelligence committee, which includes the heads of the four main intelligence services: MI5, MI6, military intelligence, and the naval intelligence department.

The activities of Britain's secret service were somewhat haphazardly organized until the late 19th century, when the value of accurate military intelligence became apparent, for instance, during the Franco-Prussian war (1870-71). A director of military intelligence was installed at the War Office in 1887, while in the same year, the Admiralty appointed its first director of naval intelligence. In 1909 a secret-service bureau was set up; its foreign section was to liaise between the military intelligence departments and British agents abroad while its home section was to undertake domestic counterespionage. In 1916 the home section became MI5 and the foreign section (otherwise known as the secret intelli-

gence service) was then renamed MIı(c), which in 1921 became MI6. The head of MI6 is traditionally known as "C" – after the department's first chief, Commander Mansfield Cumming. Before and during World War I, Cumming's team worked in conjunction with military and naval intelligence, gathering information abroad about German war plans. Meanwhile, at home, MI5's head, Vernon Kell, monitored German agents and sympathizers, with the assistance of Scotland Yard's Special Branch. During World War II the intelligence services were expanded, and in July 1940 the Special Operations Executive (SOE) was formed to undertake sabotage behind enemy lines. A vital intelligence breakthrough was achieved by the government code and cipher school at Bletchley Park, Buckinghamshire, which broke many German signals codes in the early stages of the war.

After the war, confidence in the British secret service was shaken by a series of spy scandals, particularly that involving Guy Burgess and Donald Maclean – Foreign Office officials who defected to the Soviet Union in 1951. Even more disturbing was the revelation in 1963 that Kim Philby, head of anti-Soviet counterintelligence in MI6 at the end of the war and later intelligence liaison officer in the British embassy in Washington, had been a Soviet spy for over ten years.

Michaelmas   The feast of St Michael and All Angels, celebrated in the Western Church on 29 September. The name is given to autumn academic and law terms, and in commerce, Michaelmas is one of the English *quarter days. The day was once celebrated with a feast, the centrepiece of which was the Michaelmas goose, usually in plentiful supply at this time of year. Michaelmas is the traditional date for the annual election of the Lord Mayor of London and similar ceremonies are held in other towns around this time.

Middle Temple   See Inns of Court.

Midsummer Day   Although the summer solstice and "longest day" is 21 June, Midsummer Day is celebrated on 24 June – the feast of the nativity of St John the Baptist. But the religious observances of the feast day were long preceded by the ancient rituals of Midsummer

Eve, which were often of pagan origin. Bonfires were lit to guard against witches and the smoke allowed to drift over the cattle penned nearby. Yellow-flowering St John's wort was hung up for added protection, the red flecks on its leaves symbolizing spots of the holy martyr's blood.

Military Cross A decoration bestowed on captains, lieutenants, and warrant officers (both first and second class) in the army, and formerly also in the Indian and colonial forces. It was instituted in December 1914 and holders may write the initials MC after their names.

Military Knights of Windsor Retired regular army officers who receive a small sum from the charitable foundation of the same name in addition to their service pensions. At present there are 12, under a governor, and their quarters are in Windsor castle. They represent the Knights of the Garter (*see* Garter, Order of the) at Sunday matins in St George's Chapel and lead the procession of Knights of the Garter on Garter Day from the grand entrance of the state apartments in the castle down to the choir in the chapel.
The order was founded by Edward III in 1348 to provide financial help for knights who had been captured by the French in the early part of the Hundred Years' War and who had had to pay crippling ransoms. Later the same year, Edward increased their number to 26 to match the number of Garter Knights, with whom they became associated. They were subsequently called "Alms Knights" or the "Poor Knights of Windsor". When Henry VIII died his will provided for only 13 pensioners. Elizabeth I established them by statute but it was not until 1833 that their present name and uniform were instituted. They wear scarlet tail coats, white cross sword belts, crimson sashes, cocked hats with feathers, and a badge consisting of the shield of St George with the Garter star. Elderly soldiers may apply for enrolment by writing to the military secretary at the Ministry of Defence.

milkman The British milkman is one of the few left in the world still to make doorstep deliveries. By tradition he has other functions: as a doorstep philosopher and as someone who can be relied on to lend an unhurried ear to those of his clients with a complaint that can be relieved by the attention of a caring listener. Unfortunately, in many cases his customers can buy their milk and dairy products more cheaply in the local supermarket. In commercial terms, therefore, he provides a minor convenience service at a small extra cost.

Milk Race The name given to the Tour of Britain amateur cycle race, inaugurated in 1951 with the support of the *Daily Express* newspaper, and sponsored by the Milk Marketing Board since 1958. The race, a tour of England and Wales, is over 2400 kilometres (1500 miles) long and lasts two weeks. It is a very testing event: many of the stages are over 160 kilometres (100 miles) and incorporate long climbs and steep sections. It attracts riders from many Commonwealth and European countries.

MIND (National Association for Mental Health) The leading voluntary mental health organization in England and Wales. It was established in 1946 as the National Association for Mental Health (NAMH) by the amalgamation of the Central Association for Mental Welfare, the Child Guidance Council, and the National Council for Mental Hygiene. Already these organizations had been responsible for several innovations (e.g. the provision of occupational centres for the mentally handicapped), and NAMH continued to encourage the growth of community services, as well as working closely with mental health professionals. The growing criticism of mental hospitals in the 1960s led it to adopt a more critical stance after 1964. Attacks on NAMH itself led to a reappraisal of policy, with a new name, MIND, being adopted in 1970. Its role as a pressure group was emphasized, and support of patients' families became a priority. The advisory service was expanded, with a legal and welfare rights department being established in 1975. MIND's activities include publishing relevant material, investigations into the quality of service, projects to develop new techniques, and a bimonthly newspaper, *Openmind*. It is financed by a government grant as well as voluntary donations.

minister A person appointed by the Crown, on the advice of the Prime Minister, to hold office in a government. Ministers are required by convention, not law, to be members of either the House of Commons or the House of Lords; there is a further convention that most senior ministers should be in the Commons, and so answerable to the elected representatives of the people. However, to prevent excessive patronage by the Prime Minister, the total number of ministers in the Commons is limited by the House of Commons Disqualification Act 1975 to 95. A senior minister in charge of a government department is normally called a *secretary of state, although sometimes the title minister is used (currently, for example, the Minister of Agriculture, Fisheries, and Food). Other senior ministers (e.g. the *Lord President of the Council, the *Lord Privy Seal, or a minister without portfolio) have no specific departmental responsibilities, and are available for other governmental duties as required. A minister in charge of a department is assisted by at least one deputy minister (called a **minister of state**); other junior ministers (including **undersecretaries of state** or **parliamentary secretaries**) assist primarily in a department's parliamentary work. In the Treasury the titles are different (*see* Chancellor of the Exchequer).

minister of state *See* minister.

miracle plays *See* mystery plays.

mistletoe A semiparasitic evergreen plant with poisonous white berries that plays a central role in one of the pagan ceremonies connected with *Christmas: that of kissing under a sprig of mistletoe hung from the ceiling or over a door. The custom dates back many years and has been associated with the ancient Celtic druid rite of cutting or plucking the mistletoe from the sacred oak. Magical and medicinal properties are attributed to mistletoe throughout European folklore; the tradition of hanging mistletoe over the door at Christmas and other times of the year and kissing beneath it is associated with its apparent powers of fertility. In parts of the country where mistletoe was hard to find, a "kissing bush" made up of other evergreens would of-

ten be hung in its place. In some areas the Christmas mistletoe is ceremonially burnt on Twelfth Night; failure to do so is believed to condemn all those who have kissed under it to lifelong celibacy.

Mistress of the Robes The principal female member of the royal household attendant upon the queen, whether the latter is regnant or consort. She is normally a duchess, although the present incumbent, the Duchess of Grafton, was appointed in 1967 when she was still Countess of Euston, three years before her husband inherited his dukedom. The Mistress of the Robes is responsible for organizing the roster of ladies in waiting and she attends the Queen on state occasions: it is her task to present ambassadors' and ministers' wives to the Queen.

The Mistress of the Robes once exercised considerable political influence, particularly when she served a queen regnant. Sarah, wife of the first Duke of Marlborough, was Mistress of the Robes from 1704 to 1710 and did much to maintain royal support for her husband's party. On her dismissal she refused to surrender the gold key, which had hitherto been the post's symbol of office. The modern badge of office is an oval pearl brooch in which is set a miniature of the Queen. The post became a nonpolitical appointment early this century. The Queen Mother also has a Mistress of the Robes attendant upon her, the dowager Duchess of Abercorn.

monarchy The British form of government is a constitutional hereditary monarchy. England was first unified under one king, Athelstan, in 926 AD (*see* Anglo-Saxon Britain). In the 10th century his rights and duties were vaguely defined: he was seen principally as a leader in war and as the upholder of the customary laws. However, in the background lay the Roman concept of monarch as legislator and unfettered repository of authority. How far the lists of laws issued by kings since the 7th century were new law, or deliberate revisions, or summaries of the existing situation, is unclear. In addition, religious concepts and ceremonial, especially the *coronation (as inaugurated by Edgar (973), were increasingly investing kingship with a spiritual aura. The

Norman conquest (1066) added to the monarchy's resources, but the basic structure remained.

The legal clarification of royal authority began in the 12th century; combined with the increased sophistication of the royal bureaucracy, this caused the nebulous edges of royal rights to be defined at the expense of those of the subject. This path was pursued too vigorously by John (r. 1199–1216) to finance his wars, which eventually led to the baronial rebellion and *Magna Carta. This has been seen as the first limitation of the king's powers. In the 13th century, the scope of the king's rule continued to expand, especially with the formulation of the *common law and its execution in the royal courts. The emergence of *Parliament as a forum for the king's subjects was also to the king's advantage as it provided a means for agreeing changes in the law and imposing new taxes. However, once the king came to rely on Parliament for finance, Parliament for the first time acted as a check on royal power. Equilibrium was maintained until the 15th century, when the incompetence of Henry VI (r. 1422–61) led to a breakdown of royal authority, and occasioned the dynastic struggles of the *Wars of the Roses (1455–85). Through disinheritance and forfeitures for treason, Henry VII (r. 1485–1509) held more land than his predecessors – a power base he ruthlessly expanded, subjugating even the greatest nobles.

Royal power reached its zenith under Henry VIII (r. 1509–47), who assumed the title "Head of the Church in England" after a conflict with the pope. He also used the opportunity to expropriate the land of the monasteries, although much of it was quickly sold and by the end of the century war and inflation had put royal finances under strain. Under the Stuarts Parliament took the opportunity of asserting itself, especially over financial matters, which the kings saw as a challenge to their kingship by divine right – a view of monarchy that was currently gaining ground all over Europe. Charles I (r. 1625–49), a strong adherent of this theory, attempted and failed to dispense with Parliament in the "eleven years' tyranny" (1629–40). His refusal to compromise his view of royal author-

ity, even after his defeat by Parliament in the *Civil War, led to his execution in 1649.

The monarchy was abolished; Cromwell's Commonwealth failed to provide a satisfactory alternative and Charles's son was restored to the throne in 1660 (see Restoration). However, its traditional mystique and authority had been destroyed. Charles II (r. 1660–85) was careful to manipulate rather than dominate; and James II (r. 1685–88), who attempted to revive an aggressive monarchy, fled at the first sign of revolution. This *Glorious Revolution (1688–89) signified the limitation by law of monarchical power, which never again sought to exploit its prerogatives. The monarchy remained at the centre of affairs throughout the 18th century, but its powers gradually fell into disuse or were taken over by ministers: the last monarch to reject legislation passed by Parliament was Anne (r. 1702–14); the last regularly to attend Cabinet meetings was George I (r. 1714–27); and the last to dismiss a government was William IV (r. 1830–37). The emergence of strong political parties in the 19th century reduced the monarchy's freedom to manoeuvre; Victoria (r. 1837–1901) finally withdrew from an active and constant role in politics. The monarchy thereafter became a focus of tradition and ceremonial; but it still exercises some rights (see royal prerogative), and its still considerable theoretical powers are now viewed as a safeguard against unconstitutional action by government or Parliament. See also monarchy in Scotland.

monarchy in Scotland The Scottish monarchy that emerged in the 11th and 12th centuries (see Norman Britain) wielded most authority over the east and central *Lowlands and the east coast south of the Moray Firth; its power was less in the eastern *Highlands, and nearly nonexistent in the west. In all areas, however, much local power, especially judicial functions, was in the hands of local nobles rather than royal officials, and central government remained weak. Royal authority depended, at first, largely on the individual ability of each king, and although by the time of David I (r. 1124–53) the monarchy could be said to have established control over all Scotland, apart from the western Highlands, the

Royal Family Tree

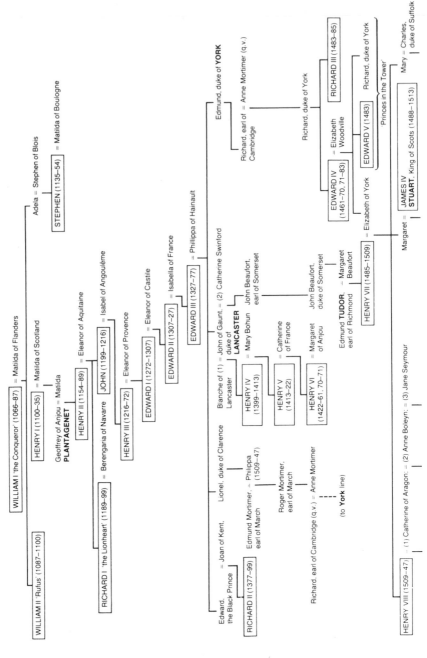

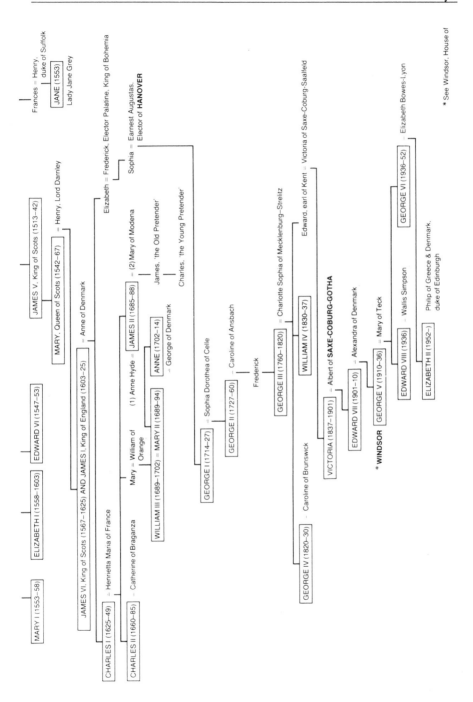

central government remained weak. Royal authority depended, at first, largely on the individual ability of each king, and although by the time of David I (r. 1124–53) the monarchy could be said to have established control over all Scotland, apart from the western Highlands, the central government remained weak, and from the 14th century onwards the monarchy itself suffered various setbacks, including a succession of elderly, weak, or infant kings in the house of Stuart, preventing the kings from establishing a continuous power base.

The Canmore dynasty died out in 1290 and there was an interregnum (1290–92) until a new king was chosen from the 13 claimants by Edward I of England, who took the opportunity to secure from them acknowledgement of his feudal overlordship over Scotland. From 1296 to 1307, and thereafter intermittently until 1337, England attempted to conquer Scotland on the pretext that the English king claimed feudal overlordship; from 1296 until the battle of *Bannockburn (1314) England exercised an uneasy military control over the Lowlands. From 1296 until Robert Bruce's coronation (1306), there was again no Scottish king. The English made further attempts at conquest in the 1330s, and in 1346 David II of Scotland was captured at the battle of Neville's Cross and held prisoner by the English until ransomed in 1357. Even then, the Scottish monarchy was not free from misfortune and was unable to subdue the nobles, who had exploited the confusion of the wars to increase their local independence. Until the end of the 13th century the monarchs in Scotland were ineffective; from 1406 until 1625, every monarch except James IV (r. 1488–1513) succeeded to the throne as a child, thus involving a regent; and again, from 1406 to 1424, the king (James I) was the captive of the English. However, the Scottish kings were by no means ciphers, and they commanded respect as the heads of a fiercely independent people; yet they were unable to expand their authority and curb the nobility. Thus by the late 15th century Scotland was an exception among European kingdoms, where the general trend was towards all-powerful monarchies. This was illustrated in the 16th century during the Ref-

ormation; in Scotland religion developed along self-governing Presbyterian lines having escaped from royal control in 1560. In this respect it differed from England and Europe, where the ruler was usually the dominant factor in determining the direction of religious observance. The Scottish monarchs' attempts (particularly those of Charles I) to impose a form of religion (usually episcopalian Protestantism on the model of England, sometimes Roman Catholicism) more to their personal taste and more amenable to control, provided the major source of conflict until the final victory of Presbyterianism in 1690 (after the *Glorious Revolution).

In 1603 the Scottish monarchy underwent a radical change when James VI (r. 1567–1625) inherited the English throne and moved south. He only once returned to Scotland (1617); from the reign of Charles I (r. 1625–49), Scotland was ruled by kings who were domiciled in England and had an English viewpoint. These absentee monarchs viewed their northern realm as little more than a troublesome province. The Scottish role in the English *Civil War was complex and divided, in the main opposing Charles I's policies: intermittent but vital support was given to the English Parliament, but the abolition of the monarchy (1649) in England was not accepted and Charles II was proclaimed king. However, after his defeat at the battle of Worcester (1651), Scotland was forcibly incorporated (1651–60) into the Commonwealth. At the *Restoration, the kingdoms were again separated. Charles II (r. 1660–85) turned out to be an authoritarian ruler in Scotland, in stark contrast to his careful manoeuvring in England, and, ignoring his promises on religion, caused a violent if unsuccessful rebellion in 1679. James VII (II of England, r. 1685–88) alienated most of the Scottish establishment by challenging their rights in the localities, and Scotland took advantage of the so-called Glorious Revolution to depose him. In 1707 Scotland and England were permanently united by the *Act of Union - a widely unpopular settlement, which only gradually gained support as economic growth in the 18th century brought prosperity. *Compare* monarchy.

MONASTERIES *The ruins of Whitby Abbey, North Yorkshire. This Benedictine foundation played an important role in a monastic revival in the north of England, after the Norman conquest.*

monasteries Abbeys, priories, and other religious houses that were important features of British life in the Middle Ages. Today most of them are in ruins. Monasticism developed in Britain from two directions: the Celtic missionaries of the north and west, who founded such communities as *Iona and *Holy Island, and the missionaries from Rome, the first of whom was St Augustine, who founded a Benedictine monastery at Canterbury in 598 AD. In addition to the Benedictines, from the 10th century onwards various other orders built monasteries in Britain. These benefited from grants of lands and tithes made by the Normans, following their invasion in 1066. Nine of the medieval English dioceses had

their seats in monasteries, the monastic church serving as the cathedral and the bishop acting as abbot.

The ancient Celtic monasteries were often located on bleak inhospitable sites, such as Tintagel in Cornwall and Whitby in Yorkshire. The monks lived in separate stone cells and had few communal buildings apart from the church. In contrast, most of their medieval successors were based on a common plan with the monastery buildings grouped around a cloistered square courtyard. The church filled the northern side of the square, with the dorter (dormitory) on the east side, the frater (refectory) along the south side, and the kitchens and storehouses to the west. Beyond

279

MONASTERIES *St Dunstan kneeling at the feet of Christ, from Eutychis's* Treatise on Grammar, *c. 950. The rejuvenation of the English Church and monastic life is particularly associated with Dunstan who, as Abbot of Glastonbury (c. 940), refounded the old Benedictine house there. Monastic life, largely extinguished by the early 10th century, flourished once more, only to come to an abrupt end with the dissolution of the monasteries in the 16th century.*

the cloister were the infirmary, the abbot's (or prior's) house, and guest quarters, as well as the garden and cemetery. This plan, established by the Benedictines (e.g. at *Westminster Abbey), the Cluniacs (e.g. Crossraguel in Strathclyde), and the Augustinians (e.g. Bolton Abbey in Yorkshire) was later used in a modified form by the Cistercians, for instance, at Rievaulx and Fountains abbeys in Yorkshire. Quite different were the Carthusian monasteries, known as charterhouses (from the French *maison chartreuse*), where the monks lived a virtually solitary life in individual cells or houses arranged round a cloister. Mount Grace Priory in Yorkshire is the best preserved.

The monasteries were centres of religion, learning, and pastoral care. But it was their material wealth, accumulated from the large monastic estates granted as endowments by the pious wealthy, that attracted Henry VIII. His Act of 1536 dissolved the smaller monasteries – those with annual revenue of under £200; the "greater monasteries" were suppressed in 1539. All monastery lands and other assets passed to the Crown and most were sold to raise revenue. The new owners, mainly gentry and nobility, plundered the abbeys and priories for building materials, leaving them to fall into ruin. The monks were pensioned off, with a few recalcitrants suffering execution for their resistance. Since the 19th century, several new monasteries have been founded in Britain, including the Benedictine abbeys at Buckfast in Devon, Prinknash in Gloucestershire, and Pluscarden in Grampian.

Monday Club A right-wing pressure group within the Conservative Party, founded in 1961 by the Marquess of Salisbury and others to press for the maintenance of what its members regard as traditional Conservative principles. So called because its meetings were originally held on Mondays, the Monday Club attaches particular importance to the rule of law, the sovereignty and national integrity of the United Kingdom, the right to own property, and the maintenance of liberty in "proper balance" with the duties of the individual. Implementation of these aims is sought by lobbying, both within the party and outside, and by means of occasional publica-

tions. Membership, restricted to party members, currently stands at around 1500 and includes several MPs.

Monopolies and Mergers Commission A statutory body of between 10 and 27 members appointed by the Secretary of State for Trade and Industry to investigate the effect of monopolies and mergers on the public interest. If the Director General of Fair Trading (*see* Office of Fair Trading) thinks that a "monopoly situation" exists in the supply of any goods or services in the UK (meaning that a single person or group has at least 25% of the market) he may refer the matter to the Commission. If the Commission finds that such a monopoly does exist and reports to the Secretary of State for Trade that it is detrimental to the public interest, the latter has wide powers to intervene. Large-scale mergers of business enterprises are referred to the Commission by the Secretary of State directly. Normally, referral is at his discretion, after taking the advice of the Director General. Certain newspaper mergers must, however, be referred, and are void unless he actually consents to them.

Monopolies have been subject to parliamentary control since the 17th century. The term was originally applied to grants from the Crown, for the exclusive right to make or sell particular goods. The practice became so onerous that Parliament objected and, in 1624, the Statute of Monopolies made all monopolies illegal, except those granted by Parliament.

morris dance A folk dance performed throughout England by local or visiting teams of morris men on a variety of festive occasions, notably May Day, Whitsun, and in the early summer. Probably one of the most popular and best-known folk traditions, the morris dance is the English version of the European *morisca* or Moorish dance, this association with the Moors possibly being derived from the dancers' former custom of blackening their faces to conceal their identity. The dance has its roots in pagan rituals connected with fertility in man, beast, and soil, and was already a well-established feature of spring and summer festivities among village folk when it became popular at the court of King Henry VIII. It is traditionally performed by six, eight, or ten men, dressed in white with bands of small bells tied around their shins, accompanied by a number of stock characters such as the *hobby horse, *Robin Hood, Maid Marian, and the Fool. The steps consist of vigorous hops and springs in a variety of formations; the waving of handkerchiefs or the striking together of wooden sticks are additional features of some of the dances. Well-known morris dances are "Bean Setting", "Constant Billy", "Country Gardens", and "Trunkles". Music is provided by a fiddler and an accordion-player; sometimes a solo jig is performed.

A number of teams of morris men are to be found in the Oxfordshire area, notably at Abingdon, Bampton, and Headington. The Abingdon morris men traditionally perform on the Saturday nearest to 19 June, when one of their number is elected mayor by the inhabitants of Ock Street. A ballot box is left outside the local pub until late afternoon, when the votes are counted and the new mayor is paraded up and down the street on the shoulders of his colleagues. At Bampton on spring bank holiday Monday (formerly Whit Monday) local teams of morris men dance at various points in the village throughout the day, and slices of cake are distributed by a swordbearer to the spectators. Annual gatherings of morris dancers from all over the country are held at various locations, notably Thaxted in Essex: it was here that the idea of a federation of morris clubs, known as the Morris Ring, originated in 1934. *See also* Horn Dance.

Mothering Sunday (Mother's Day) The fourth Sunday in Lent, the day on which servants were traditionally given leave to take gifts home to their mothers. It was formerly also called Simnel or Refreshment Sunday. Certain relaxations of the Lenten observances were permitted by the Church, such as the wearing of rose-pink rather than purple vestments and the consumption of *simnel cakes. The Christian occasion is now largely forgotten, and the day is generally marked by the giving of flowers and commercial Mother's Day cards.

MP *See* Member of Parliament.

mummers' play A play traditionally performed at Christmas in a number of towns and villages in England and Northern Ireland. Probably one of the oldest surviving Christmas customs, mummers' plays date back to medieval times or earlier, having links with early dumb shows and 16th-century Italian masquerading, and were passed on by oral tradition from father to son. There is some local variation in the names of the characters but the basic themes of the play remain the same: death and resurrection, the forces of light and darkness, and the triumph of good over evil. After the play has been opened by the "letter-in", or Father Christmas, the hero, usually *St George or King George, fights against the infidel Turkish Knight and is mortally wounded. (In some versions it is the Turk who is slain.) The Doctor, sometimes known as Doctor Good or Doctor Quack, enters with his magic potion and revives the dead man; the play ends with the character of Little Johnny Jack or his equivalent begging for alms from the spectators.

The mummers are sometimes dressed to represent the characters they are playing, but are perhaps more familiar in their formless shaggy costumes covered with fringes of cut paper (sometimes used to conceal the mummers' faces), streamers, or ribbons. Their faces may be blackened or hidden by masks. Surviving mummers' plays include those performed at Bampton in Oxfordshire and Overton in Hampshire on Christmas Eve, and at Marshfield, Avon, on Boxing Day. At Midgley in Yorkshire a mummers' play known as the Pace Egg Play (*see* egg-rolling) is performed on Good Friday; and the Cheshire custom of "soul-caking" – the performance of a mummers' play on or around All Souls' Day – is perpetuated at Antrobus.

Museum of London A museum at London Wall in the City, created from the former London and Guildhall museums and opened in 1975. It covers the history of London from prehistoric to present times. By such means as full-scale reconstruction and son-et-lumière it illustrates, for example, life in Roman Britain, the Fire of London (1666), and life during the Blitz. Amongst the other major exhibits are the Cheapside Hoard (probably the stock of a Jacobean jeweller), Victorian shopfronts, the bronzed lift-gates and panels (1928) from Selfridges department store, and the Lord Mayor's coach (1757).

music hall A form of entertainment, also called "variety", in which performers put on a number, or variety, of different acts, from singing and dancing, to conjuring and impersonations. Music hall (a term that strictly means a concert hall providing a mixture of music and comedy) developed from the "free-and-easys", the casual entertainments performed in taverns in the 19th century. In order to attract customers, landlords came to assign a room, called the saloon, for these evening entertainments, with a stage at one end, chairs, table, and a bar; a chairman presided over events. Saloons, such as those at The Grapes in Southwark Bridge Road and The Mogul (the "Old Mo") in Drury Lane, were renamed music halls around the middle of the 19th century, since from 1843 alcohol was banned from the legitimate theatre but not from the musical hall. Charles Morton, who became known as the "father of the halls", opened the Canterbury Music Hall next to his tavern, the Canterbury Arms, in 1852. Later, proper theatres, such as the Trocadero (1882) and the Empire (1887), were built specifically for this kind of entertainment. The passion for music hall spread from London throughout Britain, and continued into the 20th century. But its popularity was weakened firstly by the introduction of the licensing laws, forbidding drinking at performances, and then further when wireless and cinema became widespread. The stars of music hall were associated with particular acts or stereotypes. Sam Collins, a chimney sweep before going "on the halls", was the most famous of the "Irish comedians", and Harry Lauder the best known of the "Scottish comedians". The acrobat Jules Léotard (who wore what came to be called a leotard) was "the Daring Young Man on the Flying Trapeze". The Great Macdermott was famous for his patriotic songs, including "We don't want to fight, but by Jingo! if we do"

(hence "jingoism"). Morton was the first music-hall owner to employ women entertainers. The most popular was Marie Lloyd (1870–1922), whose attraction for music-hall audiences stemmed in part from her ability to suggest impropriety without vulgarity. At her last performance, in 1922, a few days before her death, she still sang her famous song "I'm one of the ruins that Cromwell knocked abaht a bit". The last great stars of music hall were George Formby and Gracie Fields. In the 1960s music-hall shows began to be performed again at the restored City Palace of Varieties in Leeds, and televised in the popular and long-running programme "The Good Old Days".

mystery plays Cycles of plays representing biblical events, which were performed between the 14th and 16th centuries. "Mystery" plays (from the French *mystère*, an event with mystical significance) derived from earlier liturgical drama, in which episodes from the life of Christ were performed during the Mass. However, mystery plays were performed, not in Latin, but usually wholly in the vernacular, in front of the church or in the market place. They emerged after the institution as a holy day in 1311 of the Feast of Corpus Christi, already celebrated since 1264 by a procession, which came to include the enactment of biblical scenes from the Creation to the Second Coming. At first they were performed on carts, but later, more sophisticated wheeled stages were used, and responsibility for each scene or play was allocated to one of the trade guilds. Performances were mounted not only at Corpus Christi but also at Easter and Christmas. Almost complete texts of the cycles at Chester, York, Wakefield, and Coventry are extant, and modern revivals of the plays have shown them to be not only exceptionally moving but also robustly humorous.

Mystery plays were forn rly known as **miracle plays.** Although t latter term refers strictly to plays about tne miracles of the saints, these occurred more commonly on the continent than in England, where the two terms tended to be interchangeable.

MYSTERY PLAYS *A play being performed at Coventry, 1745.*

N

naming a member   *See* Speaker.

national anthem   A solemn song entitled "God Save the Queen", sung to express patri-

otic sentiment. It is played or sung at important public occasions, and usually more than once when the Queen or a member of the royal family is present. There is uncertainty about who actually wrote the words and music. They are often attributed to Henry Carey who sang something on the lines of "God Save the King" at a banquet in 1740 (or so his son later claimed). He may have collaborated with an assistant of Handel, John Christopher Smith. Other discredited suggestions have been Handel himself, Purcell, and even Lully, because a similar song was apparently sung to Louis XIV by pupils at the royal convent at St Cyr in France. It would seem that scraps of the melody and some phrases had appeared from time to time for over 150 years in various folk songs and keyboard pieces, having their origins in the galliard, a popular dance in the 16th and 17th centuries. A version of "God Save the King" was certainly sung at Merchant Taylors' Hall by the Gentlemen and Children of the Chapel Royal to James I, less than two years after the discovery of the Gunpowder Plot (see Guy Fawkes Day). Dr John Ball (1563–1628), then organist of the chapel, probably set down the music for this "ayre". The manuscript is lost, but a later, much edited copy shows that it had a six-bar first part followed by an eight-bar second part, as has the national anthem. The librettist is unknown, but various phrases are drawn from Church sources.

What is certain is that "God Save the King", as we know it, was given its first public performance in 1745 at Drury Lane Theatre in an arrangement by Thomas Arne (1710–78) for three voices, at the height of alarm about the *Jacobite rebellions. Arne noticed an anonymous "old anthem" in a song collection, *Thesaurus Musicus*, published the year before, and shrewdly realized it had the stirring sound and sentiments needed at the time. The performance was a great success and encouraged the Theatre Royal in Covent Garden to present it too, in an arrangement by Dr Charles Burney (1726–1814). It continued to be sung for a full year after the suppression of the rebellion, which established it as a truly popular song. The words were slightly changed to their present form. By the end of the 18th century, under the influence of George III's popularity, concern about his recurring mental illness, and fear of a French invasion, the song had become a solemn national anthem – the first in the world. In 1982 there was a move in the Church of England to alter the nationalistic words of the second and third verses but this idea did not meet with enthusiasm.

Welsh speakers have their own national anthem (see Welsh national anthem), while the Scots have several patriotic songs, such as "Scotland the brave", which do not rank as national anthems but are sung on sporting occasions.

National Book League (NBL) An organization founded in 1925 to promote books and reading. Its offices are located in Wandsworth, London. The NBL, which has about 4000 members, runs a widely used Book Information Service, holds exhibitions, and administers awards. The Mark Longman Library of books about books is housed in the NBL, as well as a notable children's reference library.

National Childbirth Trust (NCT) A charitable organization founded in 1956, whose aim is to "help families achieve greater enjoyment in childbirth and parenthood". It organizes antenatal classes for expectant parents and through its branches and groups, of which there are over 320 (1984) throughout Britain, provides postnatal support, putting new mothers in touch with others who have babies and young children. It arranges training and study courses and its work in schools includes participation by members in parental skills or social studies courses. It encourages breastfeeding where possible and its counsellors provide advice to breastfeeding mothers.

National Consumer Council (NCC) A small independent body set up in 1975 to observe and investigate consumer affairs and report to the government, public bodies, and the general public. The NCC does not handle individual cases, but undertakes studies into a wide range of issues, such as the widening of choice for private investors, better terms for leaseholders, car-servicing problems, complaints against solicitors, and clarity in official language. The NCC argues on behalf of the disadvantaged in society, who least know their rights; it also promotes the free exchange of information, and fair competition. The NCC publishes two information booklets and the magazine *Clapham Omnibus*. The Scottish Consumer Council performs identical functions.

National Council for Civil Liberties An independent non-party-political body committed to the defence and extension of civil liberties in the UK, as well as the rights and freedoms recognized by international law. It campaigns against "injustice, intolerance, discrimination, and the encroachment of authoritarian government". The Council was founded in 1934 by its first general secretary, Ronald Kidd. E. M. Forster was its first president and among its many eminent early supporters were Harold Laski, Vera Brittain, Aldous and Julian Huxley, Bertrand Russell, Clement Attlee, H. G. Wells, A. P. Herbert, and A. A. Milne. It came into being because of what founding members saw as the hostile attitude of police and government to the hunger marches of unemployed workers in the thirties. On 25 February 1934 a gathering of unemployed workers in Hyde Park met the first of the Council's "vigilance committees", made up of independent observers. Since then it has campaigned on a wide range of issues including changes in the mental health laws, events in Northern Ireland, the administration of justice, censorship, discrimination on grounds of race or sex, and the right of police officers facing serious charges to be represented at disciplinary boards. In 1984 it comprised 30 local groups, 6000 members, and just under 1000 affiliated organizations.

national debt The accumulated state debt. The English national debt began in 1693 when a group of London merchants loaned £1 million to William III to finance the war against Louis XIV of France. Unlike previous loans to the Crown, this had no fixed date for repayment, and introduced the concept of deliberate deficit financing and a long-term or even permanent public debt, thus avoiding the cash shortages and credit crises previously inevitable in wartime. Despite early attempts to pay it off, it became a permanent feature of public finance.

In recent times, governments have borrowed to finance spending above revenue in peace as well as war. The annual shortfall is known as the **public sector borrowing requirement** (PSBR). Most money is now raised through credit facilities with fixed repayment dates, such as treasury bills, most *gilt-edged securities, and savings bonds. In 1984 the national debt stood at £142,885,181,539.

National Economic Development Council (NEDC) An organization founded in 1962 to promote economic debate and consultation between the three groups concerned with business: government, trade unions, and employers. It consists of a council of the most senior representatives of each party, the National Economic Development Office, a permanent secretariat serving the Council, with responsibility for research and for organizing conferences, and some 50 economic development committees, or study groups, for each industrial sector of the economy.

The NEDC meets monthly, under the chairmanship of the Chancellor of the Exchequer, to review Britain's economic performance and prospects. It provides a forum for industrial, trade union, and government leaders to debate vital issues and to develop a strategic view of the economy.

National Enterprise Board See British Technology Group.

National Film Theatre (NFT) The cinema administered by the *British Film Institute. The first BFI cinema, was originally the Tekkinema built for the *Festival of Britain. In 1958 it moved eastwards to its present *South Bank site under Waterloo Bridge. A second auditorium was added in 1970. Since 1957 the annual London Film Festival has been based at the NFT.

National Gallery An art gallery in London containing over 2000 pictures – the largest collection of paintings in Britain, and one of the finest in the world. The idea of a national gallery was first put forward by the journalist and politician John Wilkes (1725–97), outraged by the loss to the country of Sir Robert Walpole's collection, which was sold by the latter's grandson to Catherine the Great of Russia. Not until 1824, when Parliament purchased the collection of the late John Julius Angerstein, a Russian-born merchant and philanthropist, was a national gallery opened to the public, at 100 Pall Mall, Angerstein's former town house. Here was housed Angerstein's collection of 38 paintings, together with the collection of Sir George Beaumont, which he had offered to the nation in 1823. The gallery was administered from its inception by a board of trustees, and in 1855 its day-to-day administration was entrusted to a director. The present neoclassical building in Trafalgar Square was designed by William Wilkins and opened in 1838 to considerable criticism. The *Royal Academy shared these premises until 1869, and the *Tate Gallery was founded as an annexe to the National Gallery in 1897. Although the façade remains as Wilkins designed it, many additions have since been made, particularly to the interior of the gallery. An extension to the present building on an adjacent site is planned, and designs for this are under consideration.

Over half the gallery's contemporary collection of paintings have been acquired as gifts or bequests. Others have been purchased, and from as early as 1825 the Treasury provided money for this; since 1855 the gallery has received an annual purchase grant from Parliament. The purchasing policy of the National Gallery has been to represent in its collection the most important schools and periods of European art before modernism.

National Gallery of Scotland An art gallery founded in Edinburgh in 1859 and occupying a monumental neoclassical building erected for the purpose between 1850 and 1854 by Scotland's leading Greek revivalist, William Playfair (1790–1857). It contains European paintings, sculpture, drawings, and prints from the 14th to the 19th century, and Scottish art up to 1900. The collection includes paintings by Hugo van der Goes, Vermeer, Rembrandt, Titian, Raphael, and Rubens, and sculpture by Rodin and Degas. Among Scottish artists represented are Allan Ramsay and Henry Raeburn.

National Girobank *See* banks.

National Health Service (NHS) A nationwide service providing free primary health care (through *GPs, etc.) and hospital treatment to the whole population. It is the successor to the Board of Health set up in 1848 and the Ministry of Health founded in 1919, replacing the complex and inadequate health provision that existed previously. The NHS was proposed in the Beveridge Report (1942; prepared by the Liberal peer, Lord Beveridge) and greeted with considerable enthusiasm when it was introduced in 1948 by Aneurin Bevan, the Minister of Health in Clement Attlee's Labour government. It is operated by 192 district health authorities (DHAs) under the ultimate authority of the Secretary of State for Social Services and his counterparts in Scotland, Wales, and Northern Ireland. Of the total cost in 1984 of £16 billion, 85% was met by taxation, 11% by national health contributions, and 2% by various charges.

It employs over one million people, making it the largest single corporate employer in western Europe. The NHS provides a general practitioner service, 500,000 hospital beds, maternity and child welfare clinics, dental surgeries, and optical services. Additional treatment and support are supplied by 50 hospices for the terminally ill and their families, a blood transfusion service (relying on over two million donors), and treatment centres for abusers of drugs and alcohol.

The enormous demands for health care and limitation of resources mean that there are now waiting lists of some 800,000 people. This is largely because the expected fall in demand for health services after a high standard of care had been established failed to occur. Although after World War II the old diseases of diptheria, polio, and TB were virtually eliminated, new demands from the elderly and the chronically ill have arisen and extra requirements have been created by medicine's new power to treat hitherto fatal ailments. The NHS remains much admired in other countries for its provision of an extensive service to the entire population. However, some 6% of people take advantage of personal insurance schemes, sometimes organized by their employers, enabling them to be treated by private doctors, hospitals, and clinics.

national insurance A government insurance system based on the national insurance fund. All employees and employers, as well as the self-employed, contribute to the fund, from which employees derive a range of benefits. Benefits under the present national insurance scheme (now called *social security benefits) include the unemployment benefit (for up to 52 weeks), sickness benefit, retirement and widows' pensions, and grants for invalidity, industrial injury, and maternity. These benefits, which are annually adjusted in line with the *retail price index, are only paid if appropriate contributions have been made over a specified period. Employees may "contract out" of the state system by joining an approved private scheme.

Although Crown servants had enjoyed occupational pension schemes for some time (the Customs and Excise scheme was introduced in 1712; male civil servants have been similarly covered since 1834), insurance schemes were generally funded by friendly societies and trade unions in the 19th cer..ury: for many workers there was nothing between them and the workhouse, except for what they had managed to save. In 1909 Lloyd George, Chancellor of the Exchequer, put forward a "people's budget", a scheme increasing taxes for the rich, to pay for old age pensions and other welfare measures. The first national insurance Act was passed in 1911, modelled on Bismarck's welfare system in Germany of the 1880s. Liberal Prime Minister Asquith, Lloyd George, and Winston Churchill were primarily responsible for the Act, which established compulsory insurance against sickness and unemployment for manual workers, paid for by workers', employers', and state contributions. The system was extended by the Acts of 1920 and 1927 so that by 1937 some 12 million workers were insured. The Ministry of Health took over the administration of national insurance in 1919 and Churchill's Pensions Act 1925 expanded the system by introducing contributory pensions to private industry. The Act established that payments should begin at 65 and forced the Treasury to accept that it was responsible for that part of the scheme not met by contributions. In 1984 the national insurance fund obtained approximately 50% of its income (about £22 billion) from contributions from employees and employers, 8% from the Treasury, and the remaining 42% from general taxation.

nationalized industries Industries owned by the state. State control of the means of production is central to socialist thought although others regard public control as beneficial in certain cases – for example, where a nation-wide monopoly is the most efficient organization (e.g. postal services), or social or national considerations are more important than the profit motive (e.g. maintaining shipyards in areas of high unemployment). The nationalization of key industries was adopted as Labour Party policy in 1934 and implemented between 1945 and 1951; in this period, the Bank of England, electricity and gas supply, railways, road haulage, civil airlines, coal, and steel came under national ownership. Most have remained permanent public assets, but the succeeding Conservative administration denationalized road haulage and steel (1953). Steel was renationalized under a Labour government in 1967. Subsequent targets for nationalization have been airports (1965), buses (1968), aerospace, and shipbuilders (both 1977). The Post Office, previously a government department, also became a public corporation in 1969.

In the 1970s, more selective types of public ownership and investment emerged, designed to assist and guide private industry (*see* British Technology Group). After 1979, however, the Conservative government took a sceptical view of the merits of public ownership, selling off as much as possible into the private sector. Most notable was the sale of British Telecom (1984), the largest ever share issue; others include aerospace (1981 and 1985), road haulage (1982), and parts of British rail (hotels, 1983, and ferries, 1984).

National Library of Scotland A library in Edinburgh founded in 1682 as the Advocates' Library, by the king's advocate Sir George Mackenzie of Rosehaugh. Presented to the nation in 1924, the library adopted its present name in 1925. It is a copyright library, entitled to receive a copy of every book published in Britain. Possessing around 4,500,000 books, it is one of the country's four largest libraries. The letters and papers of some major Scottish writers – David Hume, James Boswell, Sir Walter Scott, and Thomas Carlyle – are housed here, together with a fine collection of illuminated manuscripts and early printed books.

National Library of Wales (Welsh: Llyfrgell Genedlaethol Cymru) The most important and comprehensive literary collection in Wales. It is located in the seaside resort and university town of Aberystwyth, on the west coast of Dyfed. It was founded in 1907, at the same time as the *National Museum of Wales in Cardiff. The National Library of Wales is one of the six copyright libraries in the UK. It accommodates more than two million printed books, 30,000 manuscripts, and well over three million documents. It houses one of Europe's finest collections of material relating to Wales and other Celtic countries. Its collection of 120,000 maps, topographical prints, and drawings is an outstanding feature of its value as a research establishment, and encompasses the work of such notable early map-makers as Humphrey Lhuyd (1527–68) and John Speed (1542–1629). Among items of importance to modern historians, the National Library houses the diaries and correspondence of David Lloyd George (1863–1945; Prime Minister 1916–22).

National Maritime Museum A museum founded at Greenwich, on the River Thames in London, housed partly in Inigo Jones's remarkable Palladian Queen's House (1616), built for Queen Henrietta Maria, wife of Charles I. The museum's exhibits illustrate the history of the Royal Navy and the Merchant Navy, as well as the development of marine technology. There is a special collection devoted to Admiral Nelson that includes Turner's painting of his ship *Victory*, and another commemorating Captain Cook, with a model of his ship *The Endeavour*, in which he discovered eastern Australia in 1770. The museum also houses an outstanding collection of globes, navigational instruments, and charts, and the state barge designed by William Kent in 1732 for George I.

National Museum of Wales (Welsh: Amgueddfa Genedlaethol Cymru) Wales's most important museum, situated in Cardiff's civic centre in Cathays Park. The National Museum, which received its charter in 1907, is primarily devoted to the sciences, but also has collections and exhibitions in archaeology, art, geology, and industry. The art section contains the Davies collection of French impressionist paintings and works by such Welsh artists as Augustus John. Archaeological material includes Romano-British remains from the legionary fortress of Caerleon in Gwent. The National Museum also houses the Reardon Smith Lecture Theatre, which is used for concerts and recitals as well as lectures and other museum events. The Welsh Industrial and Maritime Museum, sited in Cardiff's dockland area and housing collections that trace 200 years of industrial progress in Wales, and the *Welsh Folk Museum at St Fagans are both branches of the National Museum of Wales.

national parks Areas of special scenic or scientific interest, designated by the *Countryside Commission. There are ten national parks in England and Wales covering about 13,600 square kilometres (5250 square miles) or some 9% of the total land area. They include the *Peak District, *Lake District, *Snowdonia, *Dartmoor, Pembrokeshire Coast, *North York Moors, Yorkshire Dales (*see* Pennines), *Exmoor, Northumberland, and the Brecon Beacons. Each park is administered by a committee and has a team of officers and wardens who, in conjunction with the local authority, provide amenities for visitors. Special planning controls apply within national parks to help protect the landscape, and grants are available for such schemes as tree-planting and the removal of eyesores. But the major task of the park authorities is to reconcile the often conflicting needs of agriculture, forestry, tourism, and industry with the need to protect the natural beauty of the areas. *See also* national scenic areas (Scotland).

National Portrait Gallery A gallery of portraits of distinguished people in British history, opened in 1859. Housed first in Great George Street, then at South Kensington, and briefly in the Bethnal Green Museum, it moved to its present premises, in St Martin's Place, adjoining the National Gallery, in 1895. Of over 8000 portraits – paintings, drawings, and sculptures – and over 500,000 photographs, only a fraction can be displayed. The collection includes Holbein's portraits of Henry VII and Henry VIII; Sir Peter Lely's of Oliver Cromwell ("pimples, warts and everything as you see me"); self-portraits by Hogarth, Gainsborough, and Reynolds; Sir God-

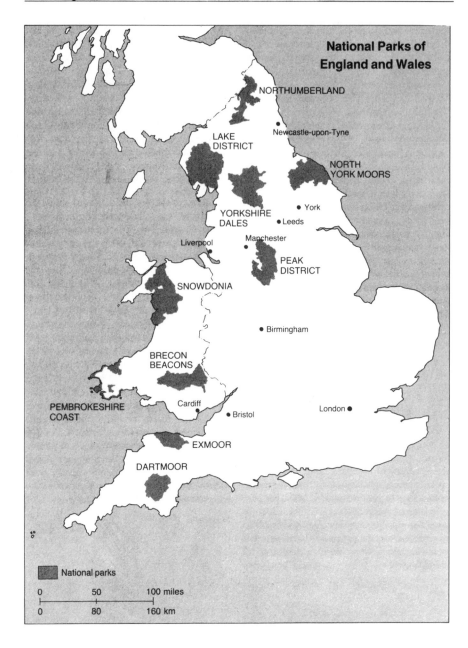

National Parks of England and Wales

NORTHUMBERLAND

Newcastle-upon-Tyne

LAKE DISTRICT

NORTH YORK MOORS

York

YORKSHIRE DALES

Leeds

Liverpool

Manchester

PEAK DISTRICT

SNOWDONIA

Birmingham

BRECON BEACONS

PEMBROKESHIRE COAST

Cardiff

Bristol

London

EXMOOR

DARTMOOR

National parks

| 0 | 50 | 100 miles |
| 0 | 80 | 160 km |

frey Kneller's Whig politicians; Sickert's portrait of Churchill; and numerous works by all the most important British portrait painters since the 16th century.

National Railway Museum (York)
Opened as an annexe of the Science Museum in 1975, the National Railway Museum in York contains one of the country's major collections of locomotives, rolling stock, and other railway memorabilia, housed in the former North York service shed. Engines dating from the earliest days of steam up to modern diesel-electric and electric locomotives can be seen, including such famous names as *Green Arrow* (1936) and *Mallard* (1938), the fastest of all steam locomotives. There is also a replica of George Stephenson's historic engine, *Rocket* (1829). Among the rolling stock are carriages from various royal trains, including a two-coach saloon built in 1869 for Queen Victoria. Other displays show developments in the technical aspects of the railways, such as track and signalling. Some of the museum's locomo-

tives are occasionally used to haul special trains.

National Research and Development Corporation *See* British Technology Group.

national scenic areas (Scotland) The 40 national scenic areas in Scotland, covering over 1,000,000 hectares (2,500,000 acres), are roughly equivalent to the *areas of outstanding natural beauty in England and Wales, and represent areas of outstanding scenic and/or scientific interest in which more stringent rules apply for planning and development than elsewhere. Examples are the Cairngorms, Upper Tweeddales, and Wester Ross. Special planning controls and incentives are operated, and potentially damaging activities, such as agriculture and forestry, are subject to consultation with the Countryside Commission for Scotland and the Scottish Secretary of State.

National Society for the Prevention of Cruelty to Children (NSPCC) The major British child welfare society. It was

NATIONAL RAILWAY MUSEUM (YORK) *Replica of George Stephenson's historic engine* Rocket *(see railways). The original locomotive was demonstrated on the Manchester–Liverpool line in 1829.*

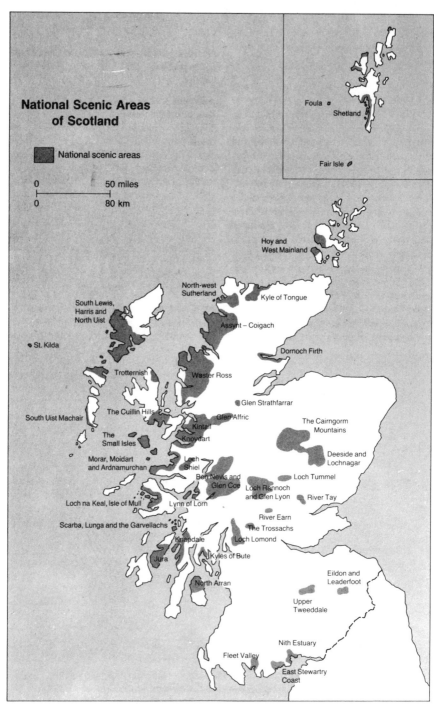

**National Scenic Areas
of Scotland**

National scenic areas

0   50 miles
0   80 km

Foula

Shetland

Fair Isle

Hoy and
West Mainland

North-west
Sutherland

Kyle of Tongue

South Lewis,
Harris and
North Uist

Assynt – Coigach

St. Kilda

Dornoch Firth

Trotternish

Wester Ross

Glen Strathfarrar

The Cuillin Hills

Glen Affric

South Uist Machair

Kintail

The Cairngorm
Mountains

The
Small Isles

Knoydart

Deeside and
Lochnagar

Morar, Moidart
and Ardnamurchan

Loch
Shiel

Loch Tummel

Ben Nevis and
Glen Coe

Loch Rannoch
and Glen Lyon

River Tay

Loch na Keal, Isle of Mull

Lynn of Lorn

River Earn

Scarba, Lunga and the Garvellachs

The Trossachs

Knapdale

Loch Lomond

Kyles of Bute

Jura

Eildon and
Leaderfoot

North Arran

Upper
Tweeddale

Nith Estuary

Fleet Valley

East Stewartry
Coast

founded in 1884 as the London Society for the Prevention of Cruelty to Children, with the backing of the philanthropists Angela Burdett-Coutts (1814–1906), the Earl of Shaftesbury (1801–85), and the author Hesba Stretton (Sarah Smith; 1832–1911). In 1888, through the efforts of Benjamin Waugh (1839–1908), it was established on a nonsectarian, nationwide footing with a constitution approved by Roman Catholic, Anglican, and Jewish dignitaries. Waugh, who became the society's first salaried director (1895–1905), promoted legislation between 1885 and 1908 that strengthened the legal rights of children and protected them from abuse, neglect, and exploitation. This was in line with the NSPCC's charter, granted in 1895, which undertook to prevent the private and public abuse of children and the corruption of their morals, and to see that laws concerning them were enforced. A similar organization was formed in Glasgow, also in 1884, thanks to the efforts of James Graham, a chartered accountant, who was much impressed by the work being done in London and also in Liverpool. This society eventually grew into what is now the Royal Scottish Society for the Prevention of Cruelty to Children.

The NSPCC has over 200 inspectors in England, Wales, and Northern Ireland who investigate reports of cruelty to and neglect of children. They are supported by a legal advisory service and are empowered to remove children from their homes if necessary, although in cases of child abuse they prefer to help the family as a whole. A child abuse register is maintained to monitor cases, and in 1974 the society set up the National Advisory Centre on the Battered Child. In the early 1980s the society handled about 70,000 cases a year, nearly half of which involved children under the age of five.

National Theatre A government-subsidized theatre company that, since 1976 has performed in its own building. Such a company had been projected by the actor David Garrick (1717–79) but was not founded until 1961. The National Theatre company opened at the Old Vic Theatre in London, and under the direction of Laurence Olivier (1907–) mounted a series of memorable productions of classics and contemporary plays in the 1960s. Olivier's most celebrated performance was as Othello. In 1973 Peter Hall (1930–) replaced Olivier and prepared for the company's move to its permanent home on the South Bank in 1976. The three theatres of Denys Lasdun's new building (begun in 1969) are the Lyttelton (opened 1976), with a proscenium stage, the Olivier (1976), with an open stage, and the Cottesloe (1977), a studio theatre often used for experimental plays and available to *fringe theatre groups. The foyer of the National Theatre is enlivened by musicians, who perform to theatregoers before performances and during intervals.

National Trust A charity founded in 1895 with the full name of "The National Trust for Places of Historic Interest and Natural Beauty". It acquired its first property, Dinas Oleu, 1.8 hectares (4.5 acres) of cliff land near Barmouth, Merioneth (now Gwynedd), in 1896, and from these modest beginnings has become the biggest private landowner in the country; yet all its properties have been obtained either by gift or by purchase with donated monies. Its membership stands at over 1.2 million, making it by far the largest and most influential conservation body in Britain. (Scotland has its own National Trust for Scotland.) While it works closely with government, it nevertheless prizes its independence. Before World War II the Trust mainly acquired small buildings, often of medieval origins. By the late 1930s taxation and rising costs were causing insuperable difficulties to owners of large *country houses, and in 1937 legislation was passed to allow the Trust to make the financial arrangements necessary to take over and run such properties. The Blickling Hall estate in Norfolk was the Trust's first acquisition under its "country house scheme". The government's decision in 1946 to accept suitable houses and land in payment of *death duties and to hand them over to the Trust brought a surge of acquisitions; its holding of country houses has grown steadily ever since. The Trust prefers the owner's family to continue living in the house while it assumes the management and financial burdens; because Trust property is inalienable, owners can be certain their houses will be maintained in perpetuity. Houses are usually handed over with a capital endowment, but where this is not possible the Trust has raised money by special appeals – as happened with the Dryden family home, Canons Ashby in Northamptonshire, acquired in 1980, restored with a grant from the National Heritage Memorial Fund, and opened to the public in 1984. Another post-World War II development was the Trust's "gardens scheme", which saved such outstanding gardens as those at Hidcote in Gloucestershire and Sissinghurst in Kent at a time when maintaining them would have been beyond the means of private individuals. Enterprise Neptune, launched in 1965, aimed to preserve what was left of Britain's unspoilt coastline from commercial exploitation; over 720 kilometres (450 miles) of *heritage coast, often acquired piecemeal in small lots, are now in the Trust's care. It also owns canals (e.g. the River Wey Navigation, Surrey), windmills (High Ham, Somerset), prehistoric sites (Avebury, Wiltshire), fenland (Wicken Fen, Cambridgeshire), moorland (the Derwent estate in Derbyshire and Yorkshire), islands (Lundy in the Bristol Channel), and natural curiosities (the Giant's Causeway, Northern Ireland).

The National Trust runs shops at some of its most popular sites, and its oak-leaf motif is familiar on an extensive range of products. It also publishes books and guides.

Natural Environment Research Council A body established by royal charter in 1965, responsible for promoting research into the physical and biological processes that shape the natural environment. It conducts research through its own institutes as well as funding projects in universities and other establishments. The Council is financed by a grant from the Department of Education and Science and by commissions received from other governments and agencies. In the physical and biological sciences, research bodies financed by the Council include the British Geological Survey (formerly the Institute of Geological Sciences), the Institute of Oceanographic Sciences, and the British Antarctic Survey. Marine biology is the concern of various Council-funded bodies, including the Institute for Marine Environmental Research, the Institute of Marine Biochemistry, the Marine Biological Association of the UK, and the Scottish Marine Biological Association. Work on fresh waters is the task of the Institute of Hydrology and the Freshwater Biological Association. Through its work, the Council aims to provide a better understanding of the effects of human impact on the environment so that effective environmental policies may be formulated.

natural gas *See* North Sea oil.

Natural History Museum *See* British Museum (Natural History).

Nature Conservancy Council An organization set up under the Nature Conservancy Council Act 1973 to oversee and coordinate nature conservation on a national scale in England, Scotland, and Wales (in Northern Ireland, these functions are discharged by the Department of the Environment for Northern Ireland). It succeeded the Nature Conservancy (established in 1949), and its functions were greatly enlarged by the Wildlife and Countryside Act 1981. The 14-member Council is responsible to the Secretary of State for the Environment and advises ministers on all matters affecting conservation. There are separate advisory committees on England, Scotland, and Wales, and on science, birds, and animals endangered in trade. Among its functions are the management of *nature reserves and more than 4000 sites of special scientific interest, and the education of the public in conservation techniques. It publishes pamphlets, information sheets, and visual aids, as well as an annual report and surveys on particular issues, such as river engineering and its bearing on wildlife.

nature reserves Areas of countryside in which the conservation of flora and fauna is made a priority. Apart from their importance as wildlife habitats, nature reserves are invaluable for education and scientific research. Some have nature trails and visitor centres. The 20th century has seen a dramatic increase in demand for land from agriculture, forestry, housing, and industry, resulting in the unprecedented loss of natural habitats and the decline of wildlife, and making nature conservation an urgent matter. Since its establishment in 1949 the Nature Conservancy (now the *Nature Conservancy Council) has acquired and administered national nature reserves in mainland Britain to serve as reservoirs of plants and animals in a wide range of habitats, including coastlands, woodland, grassland, heaths, freshwater, uplands, and peat. These now number over 200, with another 40 in Northern Ireland, where they are the responsibility of the Department of the Environment for Northern Ireland.

However, the vast majority of the 2000 or so reserves throughout the country are owned, rented, or leased by private and voluntary organizations, such as the *Royal Society for the Protection of Birds, the *National Trust, the Woodland Trust, the *Wildfowl Trust, and the 50 or so local conservation trusts, whose work is promoted by the Royal Society for Nature Conservation. These bodies are largely dependent on public subscription and the enthusiasm of volunteers to continue their work. Reserves require continual management if their value is to be maintained.

New Forest An area of heath, woodland, and marsh covering some 37,300 hectares (92,170 acres) of south Hampshire. It is the oldest of the great forests of England, and parts of it have changed little since William the Conqueror appropriated the area as his new "forest" in 1079. "Forest" formerly referred to an area set aside for royal hunting. When William I cleared the area, as many as 22 villages may have been destroyed. Game was rigorously protected by draconian "forest laws"; local inhabitants faced punishment by blinding for even disturbing the royal deer, were forbidden to enclose forest land, and found their grazing rights curtailed. For instance, pigs could graze only between September and November – the so-called "pannage season" – when the acorns were green and not suitable for the deer. The laws against disturbing deer were relaxed somewhat under Richard I (r. 1189–99). The pannage season still applies today, although the rules are less strict.

The forest bylaws are now administered by ten Verderers, the head Verderer being appointed by the Crown. They are assisted by Agisters, who patrol the forest on horseback and keep a check on the famous wild ponies that live there. Disputes are settled by the ancient Verderers' Court, which meets in Queen's House, Lyndhurst. The remaining ancient woodlands of the New Forest, which are now maintained by the *Forestry Commission, consist mainly of oak and beech trees. Visitors are drawn by the beautiful scenery, the picturesque villages in the area, and the wild ponies, whose presence was recorded in Norman times. There are still deer too (mainly fallow, roe, and sika, now that the red deer have become scarce).

Newgate Prison *See* Old Bailey.

newspapers The daily and weekly publications collectively referred to as "the Press" can be divided into national and provincial (or local) newspapers. The nationals are often colloquially called "Fleet Street" after the area of London in which many of their offices are situated. Their leading articles express editorial opinion on topics of national importance and tend to reflect a traditional affinity, despite changes in ownership, with a particular part of the political spectrum. Hence they attract a traditional readership: the *Daily Telegraph* middle-class and right-wing, *The Guardian* left-wing intellectual, etc. A distinction is sometimes made between the "tabloids", which present news in a condensed, often sensational, form, and the "qualities" (large format), which aim at a more serious and balanced approach. Few papers outside London would claim to influence national opinion; most are exclusively concerned with local news. Even more parochial are the free papers that are distributed within limited areas and are financed entirely by advertising.

London printers issued the first tentative news-sheets in the early 1620s. Such publications were officially suppressed in the following decade, and publication of domestic and foreign news only began in earnest with the many vociferously partisan *Diurnals, Mercuries*, and *Intelligencers* of the Civil War period (1640s). Strict control was reimposed by Oliver Cromwell in 1649, and continued after the Restoration of 1660. Among newspapers starting up in this period was England's longest surviving publication, the biweekly *London*

Gazette (first published in 1665 as the *Oxford Gazette*). With relaxation of censorship in the 1690s more newspapers appeared, including the first provincial.

In the early 1700s several distinguished literary figures were active journalists: Daniel Defoe ran his own paper, the *Review* (1704–13); Sir Richard Steele started the *Tatler* (1709–11) and joined forces with Joseph Addison to produce *The Spectator* (1711–12); Jonathan Swift was the most eminent contributor to the Tory *Examiner* when it commenced publication in 1710. Despite the financial burdens imposed by the Stamp Tax, a levy on various kinds of document including newspapers, from 1712, newspaper titles and circulations rose steadily in numbers throughout the century. Samuel Johnson's *Rambler* (1750) and *Idler* (1758) were notable landmarks on the literary scene; in the political sphere, the stir caused by John Wilkes's *North Briton* (1761) led to greater freedom of the press. In 1785 *The Times*, Britain's oldest surviving daily, was founded.

In the early 19th century improved printing technology, especially steam presses, speeded up production. In the years between reduction (1836) and abolition (1855) of the Stamp Tax newspaper circulation trebled as a substantial working-class readership was reached for the first time. The weekly *News of the World* (1843) was typical of papers catering for this new market, and the concept of "news in pictures" first took off with another weekly, the *Illustrated London News* (1842). Provincial newspapers also burgeoned; there were 81 in 1855, compared with 26 London papers. The influential *Manchester Guardian* (now *The Guardian*), founded as a liberal weekly in 1821, became a daily in 1855, as did Edinburgh's biweekly *Scotsman*. Afternoon or evening papers often far outsold their morning counterparts.

The first half of the 20th century, despite censorship and paper shortages suffered during the two world wars, saw the heyday of the mass circulation newspaper, thanks to increasing literacy after the Education Acts of the 1870s, and of press barons (press magnates who also received peerages to reward their political activities), such as Lord Northcliffe (who

started the *Daily Mail* in 1896) and Lord Beaverbrook (who took control of the *Daily Express* in 1922). After World War II changing social conditions and technological advances brought massive problems for the newspaper industry. Evening papers in particular suffered from the competition of television, and there were many mergers and closures. Production costs soared, while the printing trade unions, particularly in Fleet Street, resisted any changes that might threaten their members' wage levels. Among the casualties was (ironically) the popular radical newspaper associated with the Labour Party and Trades Unions Congress, the *Daily Herald*, which ceased publication in 1964. In the same year the *Sunday Times* and its weekend rival *The Observer* began issuing colour magazine supplements. Today, competition among the dailies is intense, with the tabloids conducting extravagant and highly publicized promotions in their "circulation wars". The financial vicissitudes of the newspaper industry have meant that many previously independent titles have become part of large commercial groups, some of which are not British-owned. This is viewed in some quarters as a threat to the integrity and freedom of the press, as it is thought that editors will be unable to resist the commercial or political pressures exerted by their foreign proprietors.

The freedom of the press is an important concept in the British mind. Since the abolition of the Stamp Tax, newspapers have been free of fiscal manipulation by the government, and legislation affecting their publication has not been extensive compared with that of many other countries.

New Statesman   A weekly socialist journal covering politics, literature, the arts, and science, founded in 1913. It was closely associated with the ideals of the *Fabian Society, although it did not adopt a party political line, and grew out of a campaign by Beatrice and Sidney Webb to replace the Poor Law by a system of national social insurance. The Webbs and their ally George Bernard Shaw were regular contributors.

The heyday of the *New Statesman* began in the 1930s with the appointment (1931) of Kingsley Martin (1897–1969) as editor. This was largely instigated by the economist J. M. Keynes (1883–1946), who had an interest in another publication, the *Nation*, which a few months later merged with the *New Statesman*. In 1934 the *New Statesman and Nation* took over the financially ailing *Weekend Review*, which had been founded in 1930 by Gerald Barry (1898–1968), and incorporated the *Review*'s "This England" feature. Progressive, anti-imperialist, and for a long time pacifist, the *New Statesman* under Martin built up a following among the intellectual Left; when he surrendered the editorship in 1960 its circulation had more than quadrupled to around 80,000. Besides Keynes, eminent writers associated with the *New Statesman* included J. B. Priestley (1894–1984), Harold Laski (1893–1950), and G. D. H. Cole (1889–1959).

After Martin, the editorship was held first by John Freeman (1915–   ) from 1962 to 1965, and then by Paul Johnson (1928–   ) from 1965 to 1972. This pattern of more frequent changes of editor has persisted since then, but the *New Statesman* continues to appeal to the core of its traditional readership. Its circulation fell to 30,000 in the early 1980s.

new towns The years since 1946 have seen the creation of 32 new towns throughout the United Kingdom: 21 in England; 2 in Wales; 5 in Scotland; and 4 in Northern Ireland. Examples include Harlow (Essex), Corby (Northamptonshire), Skelmersdale (Merseyside), East Kilbride (Strathclyde), and Cwmbran (Gwent). Most are based on a pre-existing village or town. The 1946 New Towns Act aimed to encourage the dispersal of people and industry away from the cities. The planning and building of each new town is administered by a development corporation, using a combination of public and private capital to fund projects. The new city of Milton Keynes in Buckinghamshire, started in 1967, is one of the largest and most ambitious, with great emphasis on incorporating the latest information technology in an attempt to attract industry. The success of the new towns has hinged on skilful coordination in the development of housing, industry, transport, and amenities in a pleasant environment. The concept of new towns was derived largely from the *garden cities built in the early 20th century. However, economies in construction, and neglect of detail have usually meant that they have failed to reach the same standard. Many have also experienced difficulties in creating a "community" where one did not exist previously; and crime, drug abuse, and vandalism have consequently compounded such failures.

New Year's honours Awards of various titles and decorations announced at the beginning of each year; it is one of the two main occasions on which awards are made. *See also* Birthday honours.

NHS *See* National Health Service.

Nonconformists Those who refuse to abide by the doctrines and policy of the established Church. In England and Wales, the Nonconformist Churches are Protestant but eschew the episcopal system of the Church of England or the Church in Wales. They include the *Methodists, *Baptists, *United Reformed Church, *Unitarians, *Quakers, and the *Brethren. In Scotland, where the established Church is Presbyterian, the *Scottish Episcopal Church is Nonconformist. The term was first introduced by the Act of Uniformity 1662 in referring to the Nonconformist "conventicles" (places of worship) used by the various dissenting groups opposed to the re-establishment of episcopacy under Charles II. About 2000 Presbyterian ministers, appointed during the Long Parliament and the Protectorate, refused to accept the 1662 Book of Common Prayer and were deprived of their livings. The Coventicle Act 1664 outlawed Nonconformist worship in gatherings of more than five people, and the Five Mile Act 1665 excluded Nonconformist ministers from within five miles of major towns or any community they had formerly served. Most legal sanctions against Nonconformist worship were suspended by the Toleration Act 1689, although Roman Catholics and Unitarians were excluded. However, certain disabilities remained in force until the 19th century; for instance, dissenters were barred from public office until 1828, and only in 1836 was marriage in a dissenting chapel made legal. *See also* free churches.

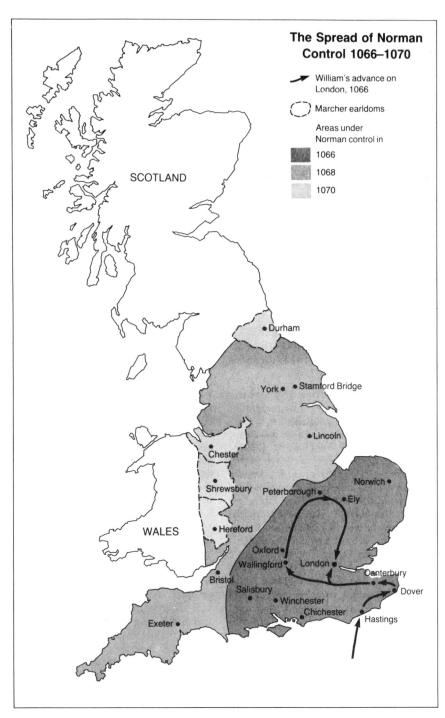

The Spread of Norman Control 1066–1070

➤ William's advance on London, 1066

◌ Marcher earldoms

Areas under Norman control in

▓ 1066

▒ 1068

░ 1070

SCOTLAND

WALES

Durham

York • • Stamford Bridge

• Lincoln

• Chester

Shrewsbury • Peterborough • • Norwich

• Hereford

Oxford • • Ely

Wallingford • • London

Bristol • Canterbury

Salisbury • Dover

• Winchester

Chichester

Exeter • Hastings

Norman Britain Britain during the two centuries following the Norman conquest of England (1066). By the end of this period Norman influence had spread to most of Britain (*see* map). William the Bastard, Duke of Normandy, claimed to be the heir of Edward the Confessor of England (r. 1042–66); at the battle of *Hastings he killed Harold II, successor of Edward the Confessor, and was crowned William I on Christmas Day 1066. In the early days of his reign upheaval was kept to a minimum: most Englishmen were allowed to retain their lands provided they submitted to William, the royal chancery continued to write letters in English, and the higher ranks of the clergy were permitted to retain their posts. However, English rebellions – for example, in the north under Edgar Aetheling (Edward the Confessor's great-nephew and claimant to the throne) in 1068 and 1069, and under Hereward ("the Wake") in the Fen country (1070–71) – obliged William to rely on his French followers. A harsher policy was inaugurated by the "harrying of the north" (1069–70), the systematic devastation of Yorkshire. The major English landholders were replaced by Frenchmen, who introduced continental *feudalism and often held lands on both sides of the Channel. By 1087, when *Domesday Book was compiled, more than 4000 former landholders had been replaced by less than 200 tenants-in-chief, of whom only two were English: Thurkill of Arden and Colswein of Lincoln. In 1070 Stigand, Archbishop of Canterbury, was deprived for pluralism and simony, and was replaced by Lanfranc; thereafter William did not appoint any English bishops or abbots. The English language was replaced by Norman French at court and in the higher ranks of society, and by Latin in the Church and royal bureaucracy. It was not until the end of the 12th century that the king addressed his letters to his "Faithful subjects" rather than to "French and English".

However, the Anglo-Saxon royal administration, perhaps the most sophisticated in Christian western Europe, was maintained and extended (*see* monarchy; Anglo-Saxon Britain). Indeed, it is doubtful whether any other kingdom could have produced Domesday Book.

As the most settled part of the king's domains, England was given the least attention. Between 1070 and 1087 William spent over half his time in Normandy, Henry II (r. 1154–89), who ruled much of western France, spent only 13 years in England during a reign of 35 years, and Richard I (r. 1189–99) no more than nine months in England, devoting himself to the Third Crusade to the Holy Land and to wars in France. Indeed, Richard's absence not only did not weaken the monarchy but was rather the occasion of rapid developments in the royal bureaucracy. The only major breakdown of royal government occurred under Stephen (r. 1135–54), in the special circumstances of a civil war over the succession between Stephen (Henry I's nephew) and Matilda (Henry's daughter).

The major tenants-in-chief, who later became the parliamentary peers, acquired an English identity sooner than the kings. Two main factors influenced them: the central administration that built up around the *common law, and the separation of Norman from English lands (fathers tended to leave Norman lands to one son and English lands to another). By the beginning of the 13th century, when Philip II of France had conquered Normandy, this awareness that England was a distinct realm found expression in *Magna Carta (1215), and later in the 13th-century precursors of *Parliament; it was also central to the barons' rebellion (1258–65) led by Simon de Montfort. Henry III's (r. 1216–72) preference for the company of Frenchmen, whom he appointed to important positions, by now was beginning to cause resentment. Yet Henry was not entirely immune to the developing mood of the country: he was the first king to give his sons English names (Edward and Edmund) and in 1259 he finally renounced his claims to northern France. His son, Edward I (r. 1272–1307), turned his attention to the conquest of Wales and Scotland; when in 1337 England attempted the conquest of France (*see* Hundred Years' War), it did so as a united nation.

In contrast, the Norman impact on Scotland was permanently divisive, because it failed significantly to penetrate the *Highlands. David I (r. 1124–53) spent almost 40 years at the

Anglo-Norman court before his accession, and he and his successors sought to replace the Celtic tribal structure of the kingdom with Anglo-Norman institutions. David's English and French followers were granted land by feudal tenure, and by 1200 the new tenants-in-chief had spread over much of the *Lowlands. The Church was reformed, with the establishment of fixed dioceses and the foundation of new abbeys; the royal administration was developed along English lines, with the division of the Lowlands into shires, the introduction of local sheriffs, and the extension of royal justice; the foundation of towns ("burghs") created outposts in the Celtic areas. By the 13th century, the southern and eastern Lowlands had been brought into the mainstream of European civilization and inroads had been made into the rest of the Lowlands and the eastern Highlands. However, the western Highlands, while absorbing some influences (see clans), remained predominantly Celtic. The Western Isles were Norse and were not acquired by Scotland from Norway until 1266. This division between Lowlands and Highlands deepened in the later Middle Ages, and to some extent persists to the present day.

Scotland's relationship with England was ambiguous. Although the border fluctuated until 1157, the English king's claim to overlordship in Scotland was asserted on occasions. This claim dated back to before the Norman conquest and was later complicated by the issue of the Scots kings' lands in England. Certain lands, such as the Earldom of Huntingdon, were held by feudal tenure of the English king, thus making the Scots monarch in one role his feudal inferior. It was not until the attempt of Edward I to acquire practical control of Scotland, on a slender legal pretext, that this issue became of central importance.

The Norman impact on Wales was immediate: William I granted his tenants-in-chief on the border (the "Marcher lords") special rights, and successive kings acquiesced in their private conquest of most of Wales. In the 12th century some adventurers moved on to Ireland. The last Welsh principality, Gwynedd, experienced a resurgence under Llewelyn the Great (1173–1240), and his grandson Llewelyn ap Gruffyd (1246–82) was recognized as Prince of Wales by Henry III (1267). However, Edward I finally conquered the principality in several short campaigns (1276–84).

Many of Britain's national institutions have their roots in this period of history. There are also many direct survivals of Norman influence: in *Christian names, *surnames, and *place names, *churches and *cathedrals, *castles, and in the Norman French used in the *royal assent. The last surviving parts of the Duchy of Normandy subject to the English Crown are the Channel Islands – leading to the whimsical claim, sometimes heard, that they conquered England.

Norn The extinct Scandinavian language of the Orkney and Shetland Islands. Shetland is halfway between Scotland and Norway and was administratively part of Norway until 1469. In medieval times the main language of both groups of islands was Norn, but it was supplanted by *Scots from the 15th to 17th centuries. Norn died out in the 18th century, but traces of it survive in the local vocabulary, particularly of Shetland, and especially in folk tales. The only extant text of any length is a ballad about the Earl of Orkney and the king of Norway's daughter, dating from the late 14th century, which was written down in 1774. The linguist Roman Jakobsen, in 1928, claimed to have heard in conversation a Shetlander saying, Fo me a dik "Get me a drink" – (compare Old Norse fá mer drykk). Other, more garbled, snatches are found in folk stories.

Northern Ireland Assembly A body established under the Northern Ireland Act 1982 as a potential vehicle for the redevolution of self-government. The country is now governed by direct rule from Westminster as it was before the partition of Ireland in 1920 (see Irish nationalism). On partition, the Government of Ireland Act (without abrogating the overall powers of the UK Parliament) established at *Stormont a parliament of Northern Ireland and an executive of ministers responsible to that parliament. However, in March 1972, with orderly government under threat, the constitution was suspended and direct rule resumed, with executive functions transferred to a Secretary of State for Northern Ireland. This emergency solution was interrupted briefly in 1974 after the Northern Ireland Assembly Act 1973 and the Northern Ireland Constitution Act 1973 created an elected legislative assembly in place of the former parliament and an executive based on power-sharing between the Roman Catholic and Protestant communities. The collapse of this executive after only five months led to the dissolution of the assembly and a return to direct rule. The Northern Ireland Assembly, elected by a system of proportional representation in October 1982, was conceived in terms of what was described as "rolling devolution". Its functions, initially, were to debate Northern Ireland affairs and scrutinize legislation proposed for Northern Ireland by Westminster. It was empowered to submit proposals to the Secretary of State for the restoration of a devolved system of government, legislative and executive, either as a single operation or by stages. Any such proposals required the support of 70% of the members of the Assembly unless the Secretary of State was satisfied that they commanded widespread acceptance throughout the community. No proposals emerged, and some members (those belonging to the *Social Democratic and Labour Party and Sinn Fein) declined to take up their seats. The Assembly was dissolved in 1986.

North Sea oil The oil deposits discovered beneath the North Sea in the 1960s of which Britain has the largest share. Although Britain was previously almost wholly dependent upon oil imports, the discovery of oil in the United Kingdom continental shelf in 1969 signalled the country's eventual emergence as the world's fifth largest oil producer. The closure of the Suez Canal in 1967 and the subsequent political crises in the Middle East increased the cost of imported oil and added new impetus to the development of Britain's offshore reserves. Huge oil platforms made of steel or concrete were installed in the inhospitable North Sea and connected to the east coast of Britain by 940 kilometres (750 miles) of pipeline. The production platforms themselves had to be capable of withstanding winds of up to 260 kph (160 mph) and waves of 30 metres (100 feet).

Even so, some rigs have been lost, notably the *Alexander Keilland* platform, which overturned in 1980 with the loss of 124 lives. Despite these difficulties, the first oil came ashore in 1975 to be processed at terminals, such as that run by British Petroleum on behalf of 30 companies at Sullom Voe in Shetland. By 1984 125 million tonnes of oil were being produced each year, compared with a world total production figure of nearly three billion tonnes per year. By 1983 there were 24 offshore fields producing crude oil and exploration for further reserves was continuing. Oil production probably reached its peak around 1985, when it accounted for 5% of Britain's gross national product – 40% of production coming from the Brent and Forties fields, two of the largest offshore fields in the world.

In 1975 the Labour government set up a public corporation, the British National Oil Corporation (BNOC), to regulate this huge industry and to exploit it on behalf of the nation. BNOC's exploration, development, and production roles were, however, transferred to a new private-sector company, Britoil, in 1982, as part of the Conservative government's policy of denationalization. The planned abolition of BNOC was announced in 1985; it will ultimately be replaced by a new Government Oil and Pipelines Agency. Another new organization set up by the government to transfer public interests in the oil industry to the private sector was Enterprise Oil, which was created from the British Gas Corporation and privatized in 1984. Besides these there are about 250 other companies dealing in North Sea oil, chief of which are British Petroleum (BP) and Shell Transport and Trading. British firms are also aided in the securing of orders for specialist offshore equipment by the Department of Energy's Offshore Supplies Office, which seeks to promote overall British involvement in the offshore fields.

The extensive supplies of **natural gas** in the North Sea, often associated with oilfields, have also been exploited since BP's rig *Sea Gem* first struck natural gas in the West Sole field in 1965. The first gas was piped ashore two years later and by 1982 over 38 billion cubic metres of natural gas were being extracted each year. The gas industry has been under public control since 1949 (*see* nationalized industries), and the British Gas Corporation was founded in 1973 to provide more centralized control; but steps are now being taken to transfer ownership into private hands. Conversion of the gas network to natural gas was completed in 1977.

Although North Sea oil has done much to improve Britain's balance of payments in a time of recession, significant supplies are not expected to last beyond the 20th century, and research is currently under way to find and develop new sources of energy, such as SNG (Substitute Natural Gas).

North York Moors An upland region of northeast England, rising from the Vale of Pickering and extending northwestwards to the summit of the Cleveland and Hambleton Hills. The sandstone plateau of the moors is divided by the southward-flowing rivers Derwent, Seven, Dove, and Rye and their tributaries, which have gouged steep-sided narrow valleys.

Human settlers first arrived in Neolithic times (4000–1800 BC), and during the Bronze Age (1800–500 BC) settlement extended to most parts of the region. The early settlers began to clear the oak forests, the last remnants of which were finally destroyed in the Middle Ages to provide grazing for the sheep on which the prosperity of abbeys, such as Rievaulx, was founded. The thin acidic soils now left support mainly heather and grasses, which are managed to provide cover for grouse. Some parts have been planted with conifers for forestry. With their underlying deposits of Cleveland ironstone, the moors supported one of the earliest iron industries in Britain. A complete Iron Age smelting furnace, dating from 550 BC, has been found on Levisham Moor. The remains of numerous ore workings and furnaces indicate a flourishing local iron industry until the mid-16th century. After a period of decline came a partial revival with the industrial revolution, although many ventures were short-lived. Alum, used in tanning and paper-making, was also mined from the end of the 16th century to the mid-19th century.

The region was designated a *national park in 1952 and tourists come to admire the wind-swept beauty of the moors. A more ominous sight is that of the glass-fibre domes of the Fylingdales ballistic missile early warning station.

noson lawen A party or entertainment popular in many areas of Wales. The term *noson lawen* means literally a "cheerful evening" and the occasion includes Welsh music and song, poetry recitation, the telling of stories and jokes, and folk dancing known as *twmpath dawns*. The *noson lawen* gives people living in isolated areas the chance of meeting each other socially; it is popular with young people and forms an integral part of the week's late-night "fringe" activities at the *Royal National Eisteddfod.

Notting Hill Carnival An annual street carnival with a Caribbean flavour held on the August bank holiday weekend in the district of Notting Hill in west London. Founded in 1966 as a small local festival, it now attracts some 250,000 people. The carnival began as the Notting Hill Fair, with events held in local halls and a small carnival procession. In the early 1970s, however, the organization of the festival was taken over by local West Indians and the carnival acquired its present form. On both days a procession of about 30 floats snakes through the streets from midday till 8 pm, eventually lining up in Ladbroke Grove, where judges select the best float of the event. Each float belongs to a band: steel bands, brass bands, or exotic costume bands, which play on and around their floats, while others play at fixed sites. The crowd is further entertained by sideshows, and traditional Caribbean food, such as goat curry and dumplings, is sold on street corners.

The carnival was nearly banned after ugly clashes between youths and the police in 1976, but in recent years these have been avoided.

NSPCC *See* National Society for the Prevention of Cruelty to Children.

nursery education Education for children below the age of five, when schooling becomes compulsory. Provision of educational facilities for children in the three to five age group takes three main forms. Areas with sufficient population may have a nursery school devoted entirely to the requirements of this group. In other places a nursery class may be attached to the Local Education Authority primary school or other junior school. Elsewhere, the "community playgroup", run usually with the assistance of parents and volunteers, now provides an informal introduction to education for a growing number of children.

nursery rhymes Verses recited or sung by adults to small children and then handed down from generation to generation. Although anthologies of nursery rhymes have existed since the early 18th century, the bulk of verses were, and still are, passed on by oral tradition. References in medieval texts suggest that some modern nursery rhymes may have been in existence for hundreds of years, and a considerable number date back at least to the 17th century. Nursery rhymes are sung or chanted. Some are lullabies, such as "Rock-a-bye, baby" and "Bye, baby bunting", some are songs to accompany children's games, such as "Oranges and lemons" and "Ring a ring o' roses"; while others are rhymes used by children for counting-out at the start of a game. The best known of these, "Eana, meena, mina, mo", exists in many forms and may have been derived from the dialect words used by East Anglian shepherds when counting their sheep. Some rhymes, accompanied by the appropriate mime, are used to entertain young children: popular examples of these include "This little pig went to market", "Ride a cock-horse to Banbury cross", "Round and round the garden, like a teddy bear", and "Pat-a-cake, pat-a-cake, baker's man". Many nursery rhymes were specifically written as children's poems or songs, although some have developed from other sources: "Lavender's blue" is based on a 17th-century ballad and "Hot cross buns" originated as a street cry.

Many attempts have been made to interpret nursery rhymes as allegories of specific historical events, or lampoons of political figures; most of these are of doubtful validity. "Mary, Mary, quite contrary" is alleged to refer to Mary, Queen of Scots, "Little Boy Blue" may have been Cardinal Wolsey, and the "fine lady" of "Ride a cock-horse" has been variously identified as Queen Elizabeth I, Lady *Godiva, and the 18th-century traveller, Celia Fiennes.

8
Sing a Song of Sixpence

Sing a Song of Sixpence,
A bag full of Rye,
Four and twenty
Naughty boys,
Bak'd in a Pye.

GRANDE

NURSERY RHYMES *A rhyme from the oldest surviving collection of nursery rhymes, 1744.*

O

Oak Apple Day An annual celebration on 29 May commemorating the *Restoration of King Charles II in 1660. Fleeing from the battle of Worcester in 1651, Charles hid from Cromwell's roundhead troops in the now famous Boscobel Oak: in the years following the Restoration, a variety of ceremonies and traditions associated with the oak were introduced or revived on Oak Apple Day, the anniversary of the king's birthday, to celebrate his escape. Pensioners at the Chelsea Royal Hospital, which was founded by Charles II in 1682 as a home for veteran soldiers, celebrate Oak Apple Day as **Founder's Day**. The statue of the king in the courtyard is decked

OAK APPLE DAY *Garland Day in Castleton, Derbyshire. The "Garland King" is seated on the horse, beneath the flowers, and the "Lady" is led behind. Two men help the horse to support the weight of the flowers. The "Queen" is the posy on top of the bell-shaped garland.*

with oak boughs for the occasion; at the ceremonial parade the Pensioners wear sprigs of oak leaves on their bright scarlet uniforms and give three rousing cheers for "our pious founder".

At Wishford Magna in Wiltshire, Oak Apple Day is celebrated with festivities that date back to the early 17th century, more than 50 years before the Restoration. In 1603 the people of Wishford were granted by royal charter the right to remove wood from nearby Grovely Forest and to graze their animals there. These rights were originally claimed each year at Whitsuntide; after the Restoration the ceremony was moved to Oak Apple Day and still survives in a modified form. Boughs are cut from the forest oaks, houses are decorated with greenery, and there is a grand procession through the village. One of the larger oak boughs is hung from the top of the church tower to bring good luck to all those who are married beneath it.

Garland Day at Castleton, Derbyshire, also coincides with Oak Apple Day and apparently has some connections with Charles II, although its origins are probably more ancient. The "Garland King" and his lady, dressed in Stuart costumes, ride at the head of a colourful procession through the village streets, accompanied by a silver band. The king carries over his head and shoulders a massive beehive-shaped garland of flowers topped with a small posy; at the end of the procession the garland is hoisted up to one of the pinnacles of the church tower, the others being decorated with boughs of oak, and the posy is laid on the village war memorial.

Oaks *See* Classics.

Offa's dyke A vast earthwork consisting of a ditch and a rampart up to 6 metres (20 feet) high, extending for some 225 kilometres (140 miles) from the north coast of Wales (near Prestatyn, Clwyd) to the mouth of the River Wye in the south (near Chepstow, Gwent). It was begun in the late 8th century at the command of Offa, King of *Mercia (r. 757–96 AD) and the most powerful of the tribal kings of England. Its structure and position suggest that the dyke was both a line of demarcation of the border between England and Wales and a defensive barrier to prevent incursions into English territory by Welsh tribesmen. The earthwork is not continuous: in some places the woodland that existed at the time, or rivers such as the Severn, provided sufficient obstacles to potential invaders. But on open ground or in upland areas, though some parts have been eroded by wind and weather, imposing remains are still visible. Some of the most spectacular and best preserved are be-

tween Presteign and Montgomery in Powys, and parts are also visible in the parkland surrounding Chirk castle in Clwyd. Wat's dyke, an earlier construction of the same type built in the reign of King Ethelbald (716–57), runs parallel to Offa's dyke to the east, from the Dee estuary in the north to the tributaries of the Severn south of Oswestry, Shropshire.

Office of Fair Trading A government agency established in 1973 as the headquarters of the Director General of Fair Trading, who monitors the supply of goods and services in the UK. The Office has three divisions: consumer affairs, consumer credit, and competition policy. In the field of consumer affairs, the Director's aim is the elimination of unfair consumer trade practices (e.g. the misleading use of small print, or unacceptable methods of salesmanship or enforcing payment). In connection with consumer credit, the Director's principal function is to administer a statutory licensing system governing businesses by whom credit facilities are offered, as introduced by the Consumer Credit Act 1974. As to competition, the Director is concerned with restrictive trade practices, and monopolies and mergers (*see* Restrictive Practices Court; Monopolies and Mergers Commission).

Official Secrets Acts Acts of Parliament of 1911, 1920, and 1939 that create a variety of criminal offences relating to spying and other conduct prejudicial to the national interest. The offences are prescribed mainly in sections 1 and 2 of the 1911 Act (which Parliament passed at great speed, reflecting the fear of supposed German espionage) and cover an extremely ill-defined field.

Section 1 offences (which carry up to 14 years' imprisonment) are described by the Act as "spying" and include such acts as obtaining, or passing on, information that might be useful to an enemy of the state. They also include, however, a far wider offence relating to "prohibited places" such as naval, military, and air force establishments. It is a crime simply to enter, approach, or even be in the neighbourhood of such a place if for a purpose prejudicial to the safety or interests of the state; and demonstrators who approached a nuclear bomber base in time of peace, with a view to immobilizing it by sitting on the runway, were held by the House of Lords in 1964 to have been rightly convicted of the offence, although there was no question of espionage.

Section 2 offences (carrying up to two years' imprisonment) relate to official information generally, and it has been estimated that the section's 450 or so words create well over a thousand separate crimes. To illustrate its breadth, it is an offence for anyone to communicate confidential official information to any other person unless disclosure is either authorized or in the interest of the state; and the recipient of such information would likewise be liable to prosecution. The unauthorized retention of official documents, even those not involving national security, and failure to take reasonable care of them, are also offences. The section has been described as a "catch-all". Apparently harmless knowledge disclosed to a journalist by a minor civil servant can rank as an official secret. In the words of a former head of MI5 (Sir Martin Furnival-Jones) when giving evidence to the Franks Committee that examined the operation of the Acts in 1971: "It is an official secret if it is in an official file".

The apparent ferocity of the Official Secrets Acts is to some extent mitigated by the fact that prosecutions can be brought only with the consent of the Attorney General (in Scotland, the Lord Advocate), and it has been, in general, government practice not to prosecute civil servants for harmless leaks. (This practice was departed from in 1985 when Clive Ponting, a senior civil servant, was prosecuted for disclosing nonsensitive information to an MP. He was acquitted despite the judge's guidance to the jury that the "interests of the state" were synonymous with those of the current government.) Nevertheless, the Franks Committee took the view in its report in 1972 that the state of the law is wholly unsatisfactory, and recommended the enactment of a new Official Information Act to bring the criminal law into play only as far as necessary for national security. Governments of various political complexions have subsequently agreed on the need for reform, but no satisfactory replacement has yet been drafted.

Official Solicitor An officer of the Supreme Court of Judicature whose principal function is to act in litigation by or against minors or mentally disabled people. Such people may not sue or be sued in their own name: they sue in the name of a "next friend", and are sued in the name of a "guardian *ad litem*" (meaning "for the law suit"); the court will instruct the Official Solicitor to act in either of these capacities if there is no other person (e.g. a parent or someone *in loco parentis*) competent and willing to do so. The court can also appoint the Solicitor to be a judicial trustee in the case of disputes concerning trusts. A further function of his is to represent the interests of people imprisoned for contempt of court.

Official Unionist Party The largest political party in Northern Ireland, which in the 1983 general election gained 34% of the province's vote, with 11 MPs elected to Westminster. The present party is a direct descendant of the Unionist clubs that were set up in the 1880s and 1890s to organize Protestant resistance to Gladstone's Home Rule Bills. In the early 20th century, under the leadership of such men as Colonel E. J. Saunderson, Walter Long, and Sir Edward Carson, the Unionist Party conducted a vigorous and successful campaign to keep the largely Protestant northern counties within the United Kingdom. In 1921, after the partition of Ireland, Sir James Craig became the first Prime Minister of the newly created Northern Ireland parliament, the first in a long line of Unionist leaders to hold the post. The Unionist Party remained the dominant political force in Northern Ireland until the introduction of direct rule from Westminster in 1972. Two years later, Unionist MPs at Westminster broke their long-standing allegiance to the British Conservative Party by ceasing to take the party whip. In the 1970s the Unionist Party lost members to the Democratic Ulster Unionists, led by Ian Paisley, the Unionist Party of Northern Ireland, a breakaway group formed by Brian Faulkner in 1974, and William Craig's Vanguard movement, which was later reabsorbed into the Official Unionists. Since 1979, the Official Unionists have been led by James Molyneaux. They maintain their ardent support for continued union with Britain, preferably with government of domestic affairs vested in an Ulster parliament or assembly; they reject any moves towards the reunification of Ireland.

Old Bailey A street in the City of London, running between Newgate Street and Ludgate Hill. On the corner with Newgate Street stands the Central Criminal Court, itself familiarly known as the Old Bailey. Originally, the bailey was an outwork outside the city wall from which the street took its name. The first criminal court was erected in 1539 beside the notorious **Newgate Prison**, first built in the 12th century. Destroyed in the *Fire of London (1666), Newgate was twice rebuilt and finally demolished in 1902 to make way for the present courthouse, designed by E. W. Mountford and opened in 1907. The bronze statue of Justice by F. W. Pomeroy surmounting the dome of this building has become a notable London landmark. The courts themselves were considerably extended in 1970. On certain occasions the judges carry small posies of flowers as a reminder of the appalling smell that used to permeate Newgate Prison. The odour was not only unpleasant; it was associated with the gaol fever (typhus) that in May 1750 infected and killed the Lord Mayor, an alderman, two judges, most of the jury, and many others who had attended the court. Outside the courthouse the street is at its widest, in order to accommodate the crowds that gathered here to watch the public executions that took place outside Newgate Prison (after the gallows at Tyburn ceased to be used in 1783). The last public execution in England took place in 1868, when Michael Barrett was hanged for attempting to blow up a prison. Only four years earlier some 50,000 onlookers collected to watch the hanging of Franz Müller (convicted of murder). The fascination of the processes of the criminal law continued to draw large crowds for the trials of such notorious criminals as Dr Crippen (1910), William Joyce ("Lord Haw-Haw", 1945), and Peter Sutcliffe (the "Yorkshire Ripper", 1981).

old boy network *See* public schools.

Old Lady of Threadneedle Street *See* Bank of England.

old school tie *See* public schools.

Old Trafford The home of Lancashire County Cricket Club and a venue for international (test) matches. It was first used as a cricket ground by Manchester Cricket Club in 1857 and Lancashire started to play there eight years later. It was first used for test matches in 1884. In 1940 and 1941 the ground suffered considerable damage from German bombs. After the war the pavilion and stands were reconstructed as a result of donations from all over the world and with the help of ex-servicemen and prisoner-of-war labour. Old Trafford has a reputation for bad weather, and in fact two of the only three test matches ever to have been abandoned without any play because of continuous rain were the 1898 and 1930 Old Trafford tests.

Ombudsman (Parliamentary Commissioner for Administration) An official appointed under the Parliamentary Commissioner Act 1967 to investigate complaints of governmental maladministration from the public. The official is appointed by the Crown on the advice of the Prime Minister, but his independence is secured by the fact that he can be removed from office only at the instance of both Houses of Parliament. The jurisdiction of the Ombudsman does not extend beyond the departments of central government, so that such bodies as local authorities, the nationalized industries, and the police cannot be investigated by him. Even within the field of central government, specific matters are excluded from examination, including the conduct of authorities in the National Health Service. In 1973, however, Parliament relented to some extent and appointed health service commissioners to investigate complaints against the NHS; in the following year it established commissioners for local administration to look into complaints against local authorities, the police, and the water authorities. Moreover, in July 1985 the government announced that, in deference to the recommendations of a House of Commons *select committee, legislation would be introduced to extend the Ombudsman's jurisdiction to some 50 *quangos whose impact on the citizen may well be as significant as that of an actual government department.

The citizen may only put his complaint to the Ombudsman through an MP (not necessarily his constituency MP) and it is for the MP to decide whether or not to refer it onwards. Furthermore, the Ombudsman is not obliged to investigate complaints: if he does so, the investigation takes place in private, and the parties named are invited to comment. The Ombudsman has no coercive powers (e.g. to alter any decision or award compensation) but he may recommend remedial action and must send a statement of his findings to the MP through whom the complaint was made. The Ombudsman's report for 1984 shows that the number of complaints referred to him was 837, of which around 200 were investigated and about 190 of these were found to be wholly or partly justified.

One Thousand Guineas Stakes   *See* Classics.

Open University   An organization providing further education on a nonresidential, part-time basis for adults whose lack of formal qualifications or other commitments would prevent them from taking up a place at a conventional university. Originally called the "University of the Air", the Open University was established in 1969 at Milton Keynes, Buckinghamshire, by Jennie Lee, then Minister for the Arts in Harold Wilson's Labour administration. A bold and imaginative step in adult education, the Open University has two principal means of communicating with its students: BBC radio and television programmes, and its own national network of tutors and counsellors. Students working for a degree take a number of courses based on the broadcast programmes and on specially written course books to accumulate the necessary total of course credits, usually over a period of four years. They submit written work to their tutors and also attend short but intensive summer schools to bring them into personal contact with tutors and other students. The Open University also offers a wide range of other adult education services; its techniques have been studied and often emulated in other countries.

Orangemen   Members of a Protestant organization, named after William of Orange, whose victories over the forces of the deposed King James II are commemorated in the *battle of the Boyne celebrations. In 1795 a violent confrontation between Protestants and Catholics in County Armagh – known as the Battle of the Diamond – led to the formation of the Orange Society, with a threefold purpose: to protect Protestants against Catholics, to support the Protestant religion, and to maintain the Protestant succession. A secret society originally modelled on *freemasonry, the order now has lodges throughout Northern Ireland, Great Britain (notably Liverpool), and various British dominions. Despite attempts by the House of Commons to restrain it, the order strengthened opposition in Ulster to the Irish Home Rule Bill of 1912, and has continued to exercise great influence over political affairs in Northern Ireland.

Oranges and Lemons service   An annual ceremony that takes place at the Royal Air Force church of St Clement Danes, in the Strand in London, on or around 31 March. The bells of the church, made famous by the *nursery rhyme "Oranges and Lemons", were restored in 1919, and the following year the Oranges and Lemons service was instituted. Children from St Clement Danes primary school attend the service, at the end of which the nursery-rhyme tune is played on handbells and every chi¹d receives an orange and a lemon. In the early years this fruit was donated by London's Danish colony. In fact, both the participation of the Danes and the association of the church with the Oranges and Lemons service are based on somewhat tenuous connections. The well-known nursery rhyme "Oranges and Lemons" contains the couplet:

Oranges and Lemons
Say the bells of St Clement's

However, the St Clement's referre l to is almost certainly the one in Eastche ip, which stands close to the wharves at which imported citrus fruit was traditionally unloaded and stored. The Danish connection, which is believed to be with the St Clement's in the Strand, probably goes back to the 9th century when Alfred the Great drove the Danes out of

England, permitting those that had married English women to remain in this part of London, where they built a church, then known as Ecclesia Clementis Danorum. The church suffered extensive damage during a World War II air raid, and the Oranges and Lemons service had to be suspended until restoration work was completed.

orders of chivalry A class of honours and distinctions, which includes the *orders of knighthood and in addition the *Distinguished Service Order, the *Imperial Service Order, the Order of the *Companions of Honour, and the Order of *Merit. The latter, together with the Orders of the *Garter and *Thistle and the *Royal Victorian Order, are completely in the sovereign's gift.

orders of knighthood Various orders, admission to which is made by the sovereign, according to certain qualifications other than those of birth. In the early Middle Ages knighthood was conferred for military or other services rendered and for feudal tenure of estates to a certain value. Until Henry III's reign the dignity, which carried with it also the obligation to perform military service, might be conferred not only by the king but also by great barons and princes of the Church. The only native medieval order still surviving is the Order of the *Garter. However, the English *langue* – roughly "chapter" – of the medieval Knights of the Order of the Hospital of St John of Jerusalem was never formally suppressed at the Reformation, and the order was revived in Protestant form during the 19th century. There is also a British association of the Sovereign Military Order of Malta, a Roman Catholic religious order, which includes certain members called by such titles as Knight of Justice, Knight Grand Cross of Obedience, and Knight Grand Cross of Honour and Devotion. Members of this association are drawn from the old Catholic nobility of Britain, and membership of the higher ranks requires proof of long-standing grants of coats of arms in a candidate's family. However, unlike the other orders, the Association has no official standing. Other orders of knighthood proper are the Order of the *Thistle, the Order of the *Bath, the Order of the *British Empire, the *Royal Victorian Order, the *Star of India order, the Order of *St Michael and St George, and the Order of the *Indian Empire. The two Indian orders have had no new entrants since that country's independence in 1947. There is also an Order of St Patrick, no knightly admissions to which have been made since Ireland's independence in 1922.

Ordnance Survey A national organization supplying maps for the armed forces, government planning departments, HM Land Registry, local authorities, civil engineers, and the general public. It was founded in 1791 to produce maps of southern England with a scale of one inch to the mile for the British army, then threatened by Napoleonic invasion. The use of the word ordnance derives from the parent body, the Board of Ordnance, which was the Crown body responsible for army engineering and which carried out the original survey. British cartography in the 18th century was inspired by the work of General William Roy, scientist and surveyor, who had produced a map of Scotland after the 1745 Jacobite rebellion.

Ordnance survey maps are now all based on a network of 20,000 triangulation stations for measuring distances, and some 500,000 bench marks for measuring height relative to mean sea level (a standard level is used in Cornwall). Aerial photography is now also widely used in the making of maps. The primary task of the organization is to update the three main map series (scales 1:25,000, 1:50,000, and 1:250,000). It is also committed to the gradual transfer of all maps, particularly the large-scale maps, to an electronic database using automated cartographic technology (digital mapping). This will greatly facilitate the future amendment and subsequent publication of these maps. Other services include transferring maps to microfilm, compiling height lists for engineers, and preparing special maps for archaeologists, bird watchers, and ramblers. The organization has also assisted in a survey of the North Sea. It now employs 2800 staff and has an annual budget of £40 million – 50% of which is derived from its commercial and copyright revenues.

Outward Bound Trust A charity that organizes a wide range of activities, mainly outdoor, designed to develop individual potential and an awareness of others through teamwork and service. The first outward bound course was held in Aberdovey in Wales in 1941 for merchant navy cadets faced with the demands of wartime service. After World War II such courses were included in the training programmes of various companies and organizations and in 1946 the Outward Bound Trust was formed. The Trust administers five rural centres (one in Scotland, two in Cumbria, and two in Wales) as well as the urban-based City Challenge. Navigation skills, rock-climbing, canoeing, expeditions, and rescue work, are just some of the outdoor activities covered by the centres, while City Challenge aims to promote self-awareness and self-discipline, as well as an awareness of social problems through community service. Certain courses fulfil the requirements for elements in the *Duke of Edinburgh's Award scheme. There are some 36 Outward Bound Associations, the voluntary arm of the Trust, throughout the United Kingdom. The Associations publicize the work of the Trust and raise money locally to sponsor deserving young people who would otherwise be prevented from attending courses.

Oval, the A cricket ground at Kennington, south London. One of the largest in England, it is owned by the *Duchy of Cornwall and is the headquarters of Surrey County Cricket Club. It is regularly used for test matches and the last match in any test series is traditionally played there. At the main entrance are the Hobbs Gates, erected in 1934 in honour of Sir Jack Hobbs, certainly Surrey's and perhaps England's finest batsman of the 20th century. The Oval was first used for cricket in 1845 and the first test match in England, against Australia, was played there in 1880. The ground was also frequently used for football cup finals at the end of the last century, and as a prisoner-of-war camp during World War II.

Oxfam An Oxford-based charity dedicated to alleviating poverty and distress wherever they occur. Most of its funds are used to provide long-term development aid to Third

World countries, but it also helps victims of natural or man-made disasters through emergency relief funds. Oxfam was founded as the Oxford Committee for Famine Relief in 1942 with the aim of helping starving civilians in German-occupied Greece; among those prominent in setting it up were the classical scholar Gilbert Murray (1866–1957), and Canon T. R. Milford (1895–), vicar of the university church, who became the organization's first chairman (1942–47). After World War II it became apparent that there was a continuing need for its relief work, and Oxfam put its organization on a more formal basis, appointing its first director in 1951. Soon it was assisting refugees from the Korean War (1950–53), the Hungarian uprising (1956), and the war in Algeria (1957–62). The abbreviation "Oxfam", already widely used, was officially adopted in 1965.

In the 1960s Oxfam moved into the field of development aid. Its emphasis has always been on small-scale projects with a large element of self-help on the part of the communities that will benefit from them. To provide the steady income necessary for this aid, fundraising in Britain became more professional, with regional organizers to coordinate it and a trading company set up (1965) to market Oxfam goods. By the early 1980s there were nearly 700 Oxfam charity shops, staffed by volunteers, selling second-hand goods and clothing, and handcrafts from developing countries. Oxfam's knowledge of local conditions gained through its development work makes it highly effective in dealing with disasters in developing countries. Among the relief operations for which it has quickly raised huge sums are those for victims of the Nigerian civil war (1967–70), the Guatemalan earthquake (1976), the war in Cambodia (1979), and, more recently, the intercommunal strife in the Lebanon, and the famine in northeast Africa.

Oxford English Dictionary, The The standard dictionary of the English language. The idea for such a work was first mooted in 1857 and the Philological Society (London) began drawing up plans for its compilation, but work on the dictionary only commenced in 1878 under an agreement made between the Society and the Delegates of the *Oxford University Press. In 1879 James Murray (1837–1915) was appointed first editor of the work, which was then known as *A New English Dictionary on Historical Principles*. The first of the 125 fascicules making up the ten-volume first edition appeared in 1884, the final one in 1928. The lexicographers' aim was to include all the words that have featured in English vocabulary from the earliest records to the present day, with information on their etymology, the evolution of their various senses and forms, and their pronunciation. Over 5 million quotations from English literature and records were amassed, many from voluntary contribution, of which around 1.8 million were selected for printing.

In 1933 Oxford University Press brought out a new twelve-volume edition of the work under its present title, which has formed the basis of numerous abridgements, such as the *Shorter Oxford Dictionary*. 1972 saw the publication of the first of the OED supplements, covering the development of the language in the 20th century. The last of this four-volume set was published in 1986. The amalgamation by computer of the original work with the supplements began in 1984.

Oxford Movement A movement started by a group of Anglican theologians and clerics based in Oxford in the 1830s, which sought to reassert traditional High Church doctrines in the Church of England. The Movement arose as a reaction to the increased numbers of Nonconformists and from a fear that the Low Churchmen in the Church of England would do little to resist them. It was effectively launched by John Keble (1792–1866), in a sermon entitled "National Apostasy", delivered before the university on 14 July 1833. Provoked by the suppression of ten Irish bishoprics by the government, Keble warned of a national spiritual decline; his sermon was followed by *Tracts for the Times*, a series of articles and pamphlets written by the Movement's followers from 1833, which caused the Movement's adherents to be dubbed "Tractarians". Prominent among them were R. H. Froude (1803–36) and J. H. Newman (1801–90), Fellows of Oriel College. Newman's *Tract 90* (1841) gave an interpretation of the Thirty-Nine Articles that was broadly in harmony

with the principles of Roman Catholicism, which he indeed embraced in 1845. Following Newman's withdrawal from active participation in 1841, leadership of the Movement was assumed by E. B. Pusey (1800–82). The Movement attempted to revitalize traditional doctrines and practices within the Church, in spite of opposition from the university authorities, the episcopacy, and the government. Its success was limited, and lay at the time mostly in creating a symbol of resistance for High Churchmen and Anglo-Catholics.

Oxford, University of The oldest university in Britain. It had its origins in informal groups of masters and students assembling at Oxford in the 12th century, attracted perhaps by the existence there of several monasteries and a royal palace (all now vanished). The closure of the University of Paris to Englishmen in 1167 accelerated Oxford's development into a *studium generale* or *universitas*. Affrays between scholars and townspeople in 1209 caused some of the former to migrate (*see* Cambridge, University of), and although a charter of 1213 required the townspeople to pay an annual fine to the university in perpetuity (the first university endowment), friction between "town and gown" remained a feature of medieval Oxford life.

In 1214 the great scholar and churchman Robert Grosseteste (c. 1175–1253) appears as the first chancellor of the university. Students lived in lodgings in the town, although the oldest of the halls of residence, St Edmund Hall (formally incorporated a college in 1957), may have been in existence in 1226. An endowment for theological students made in 1249 traditionally marks the foundation of Oxford's first college, University College, although its statutes date from around 1280. In the meantime Balliol (c. 1263) and Merton (1264) were founded. Merton's Mob Quad, containing the oldest library in the country (1371–79), was the prototype for all later Oxford quadrangles, as were its statutes for later collegiate foundations. These include Exeter (1314), Oriel (1326), Queen's (1340), New (1379; *see also* Winchester College), Lincoln (1427), All Souls (1438), Magdalen (1458), Brasenose (1509), Corpus Christi (1517), Christ Church (begun by Cardinal

UNIVERSITY OF OXFORD *Society of New College, Oxford, in 1463. In the background are the magnificent college buildings, including gatehouse, chapel, and hall. Their arrangement around a quadrangle or court is characteristic of Oxford and Cambridge colleges.*

Wolsey, 1525; refounded by Henry VIII, 1546), St John's (1555), Trinity (1555), Jesus (1571), Wadham (1612), and Pembroke (1624). The rate of foundation then slowed, with Worcester (1714) and Hertford (1740) the only 18th-century foundations. Keble (1868) inaugurated a number of new ones, including the first four women's colleges, beginning with Lady Margaret Hall (1878) and Somerville (1879). Among 20th-century colleges are several admitting postgraduate students only, for example, Nuffield (1937), Wolfson (1966), and Green (1979). The autonomy and traditions of the individual foundations are jealously preserved within the university structure despite considerable changes after World War II, not least of which was the decision of most colleges in the 1970s to become coresidential.

Under the chancellor, as honorary head, the university is run by the vice-chancellor (selected from among the heads of colleges in rotation and serving for a four-year period), the two proctors (serving for a year and concerned with university discipline), and the elected 18-strong Hebdomadal Council (so-called from its weekly meetings). Congregation is a body of resident dons and administrators that functions as a form of parliament. Convocation comprises all MAs and doctors who have kept their names on their college books; its members elect the chancellor and professor of poetry and may veto proposals that fail to obtain a two-thirds majority in Congregation.

Students are admitted to individual colleges, which organize their tuition and accommodation, and assign a "moral tutor" to oversee each student's studies and general welfare. Tutorials are augmented by lectures, practicals, etc., run by the university faculties. The BA Honours examination is divided into two parts – Prelims or Mods (Moderations) and Finals – and the MA is awarded automatically after a set period to BAs who supplicate (apply) for it at a cost of five pounds.

The university year consists of three terms: Michaelmas, Hilary, and Trinity. Trinity contains the main social events: the Eights Week boat races (*see* Head of the River), the Commem balls (*commem*orating the college founders), and the presentation of honorary doctorates at a ceremony known as Encaenia. The colours awarded to those who row for Oxford or represent the university against Cambridge University at some other major sport are dark blue (*see* Boat Race; blue); a "half-blue" is awarded for other less prestigious sports. Competitive rowing takes place on the Thames, called the Isis in its Oxford reaches; punting and naked bathing (for men only at the secluded spot called Parson's Pleasure) are sports for Oxford's other river, the Cherwell, which flows through the university parks and Christ Church Meadows to join the Isis. The university library is the *Bodleian Library, refounded in 1602 by Sir Thomas Bodley to revitalize the library begun in the 15th century by Duke Humphrey of Gloucester, brother of Henry V. Some of the university's most impressive buildings are the Old Bodleian (1613–26); the Clarendon Building, home of the *Oxford University Press from 1713 to 1829, now used mainly by the Bodleian; the Sheldonian Theatre, designed by Sir Christopher Wren and completed in 1669, scene of degree ceremonies; the Old Ashmolean Museum (1683); the circular Radcliffe Camera (1749), built as a science library, now part of the Bodleian; the neoclassical Ashmolean Museum and Taylor Institute complex (1841–45); and the neogothic University Museum (1855).

Oxford University Press (OUP) The first book printed in the city of Oxford, an exposition of the Apostles' Creed, appeared in 1478 (wrongly dated 1468 on the title page). It had no official connection with the university. The University Press originated in 1585, the year after the university loaned £100 to a bookseller, Joseph Barnes, to set up a press. Barnes and his successors were businessmen, and their links with the university were informal until 1629, when Chancellor William Laud (1573–1645), later Archbishop of Canterbury, drew up the blueprint for a "learned press" to be run under the university's control. He obtained Charles I's permission for the university to appoint three printers (1632) and in 1633 an 11-member Delegacy (committee) was established to select manuscripts from the Bodleian Library for printing. (The senior university members who govern OUP are still called Delegates and the executive head of the Press is known as the Secretary to the Delegates. In 1636 the university's "Great Charter" allowed it to print bibles, prayer-books, and grammars – all steady sellers which had hitherto been the monopoly of the Stationers' Company in London. Although OUP did not immediately start producing such works (preferring an annual subsidy from the Stationers to refrain from competition), this charter ensure the Press's future prosperity.

After the Restoration Laud's work was continued by John Fell (1625–86), Dean of Christ Church. In 1668 the Press acquired premises in the basement and roof space of the Sheldonian Theatre in Broad Street. Defying the London printers and financial losses, Fell, who ran the Press from 1672 until his death, established its reputation, publishing on average ten books a year. In 1692 the printers had to leave the Sheldonian as their heavy equipment had seriously damaged the structure. Opportunely, the Press published its first bestseller, Clarendon's History of the Rebellion and Civil Wars in England (1703–07), and on the proceeds a printing house called the Clarendon Building was built next to the Sheldonian. The first book was issued from there in 1713, although the Sheldonian imprint continued in use.

The phenomenal prosperity of the bible business in the 18th and 19th centuries laid the basis for OUP's expansion. In 1829 it moved to large new premises, built in the style of an Oxford college, in Walton Street; from here the output of the learned press, as distinct from the bible press, increased. In 1855 the paper mill at nearby Wolvercote was bought and re-equipped. In 1870 a bindery was acquired in London, and the Press's London interests grew into a full-scale publishing enterprise based at Amen House (1924–65) and Ely House (1966–76). It looked to a more general readership than the more academic Clarendon Press at Oxford, where, in 1906, the learned and bible presses at last merged. Overseas branches were set up – New York (1896), Canada (1904), India (1912), South Africa (1915) among them. In 1976 the London and

Oxford businesses were consolidated under one roof in Oxford. OUP has produced numerous monumental works of scholarship, notably the *Oxford English Dictionary*, the supplements to the Dictionary of National Biography, and many standard lexicons of ancient and modern languages. In conjunction with *Cambridge University Press, it published the Revised Version of the Bible (1881) and The New English Bible (1961–70). Editorially, its productions set a standard for excellence followed throughout the English-speaking world. The Oxford poetic anthologies, such as the Oxford Book of English Verse and the Oxford Companions (popular reference books), have become standard works in many homes, while its new series of concise special-subject dictionaries (Medicine, Law, Science, etc.) have set high standards of lexicography, and its more academic series, such as the Oxford History of England and the Oxford English Texts, embody the work of leading scholars. Its longest-running series, however, is the Oxford Almanacks, giving information about university terms, etc., and published continuously since 1676.

P

pace-egging   See egg-rolling.

pancake race   An annual contest that takes place on *Shrove Tuesday in a number of English towns, notably Olney in Buckinghamshire. The Olney race dates back to 1445, when a local woman is alleged to have rushed to church at the sound of the shriving bell, still clutching her frying pan. (The shriving bell traditionally called the faithful of the Church to confession.) The contest is open to any woman over the age of 16 who has been resident in Olney for a specified period; she must be dressed for the race in a skirt and must wear an apron and a headscarf. The pancakes are tossed three times over the quarter-mile course; the first competitor to arrive at the church receives a prayer book and a kiss. A pancake race has also been run in recent years

PANCAKE RACE *Race at Olney, Buckinghamshire.*

in the US town of Liberal, Kansas, and in the early 1950s the Olney women were challenged by their transatlantic counterparts. The two races were run under identical conditions and timed: the Olney team were declared the winners. *See also* Shrovetide football.

pantomime An entertainment for children based on the dramatic presentation of a fairy tale, such as *Cinderella, Aladdin, Jack and the Beanstalk*, or *Babes in the Wood*. A traditional Christmas entertainment, the pantomime incorporates songs, slapstick comedy, acrobatics, and audience participation.

A pantomime, or "player of all parts", was originally an actor in ancient Rome. The term was misapplied in the late 18th century to the harlequinade, a play featuring Harlequin, a comic character in the contemporary Italian popular theatre (*commedia dell'arte*). In the 19th century the opening scene of the harlequinade became an independent extravaganza or burlesque, with actresses playing the heroes' roles. Although women had taken the "breeches part" of the male lead in plays even as early as the 18th century, the tradition that

the pantomime principal boy should be played by an attractive young woman showing off her legs in tights was not established until the 1880s. Augustus Harris, manager of the Drury Lane Theatre in London, no doubt adopted this idea as a means of interesting his adult audiences. He also introduced music-hall acts into the pantomime, including the 'dame', who is played by a man, following 18th-century custom. Cinderella's ugly sisters and Aladdin's mother, Widow Twankey, are examples of women's roles played by male comedians. The current tradition is therefore approximately a century old.

Parachute Regiment A specialized division of the British Army. The Parachute Regiment, known as the **Red Berets** after the caps they wear, was formed in 1941 as an airborne strike force for use in all the theatres of World War II. Skilled in operations behind enemy lines, the regiment has operated from aircraft including gliders at Arnhem, and helicopters in the Falkland Islands. In the present Army the regiment comprises three battalions, based at Aldershot.

315

Paraplegic Games (Stoke Mandeville)
National competitions held annually since
1948 at Stoke Mandeville Hospital, near
Aylesbury, Buckinghamshire, for the paraplegic and tetraplegic. There are some 15 special
events in addition to a full range of track and
field athletics. Every fourth year since 1960,
International Paraplegic Games (Paralympics)
have been held to coincide with the Olympic
Games, taking place if possible in the same
country. The concept of sport for the disabled
was fostered by Dr (later Sir) Ludwig Gutt-
mann (1899–1980) during the years immediately following World War II. As a neurosur-
geon specializing in the treatment of spinal
cord injuries, he came to believe that rehabilitation through sport was an integral part of
any treatment giving patients some purpose in
life. He introduced his patients first to archery
and wheelchair polo, then wheelchair basket-
ball, and so on. The first Stoke Mandeville
games began on 28 July 1948 to coincide with
the London Olympics. The games have expanded since then, with over a thousand competitors from all over the world at the 1984
event. Sir Ludwig conceived the idea of a stadium for the disabled and an Olympic village
to house competitors at Stoke Mandeville. The
stadium, which now bears his name, was
opened by the Queen in 1969, and the village
in 1981, just over a year after Sir Ludwig's
death. Administration of sport for the disabled, the Stoke Mandeville games, the stadium, and village is the responsibility of the
British Paraplegic Sports Society. It is also responsible for fundraising, and in this field it
owes much to the support of the television
personality Jimmy Savile, who has raised
many thousands of pounds for Stoke Mandeville's National Spinal Injuries Centre.

parish A local government area in England
that is a subdivision of a *district. Denoting
the area served by a church, parishes date from
the 7th century. With the growth of the population they were enlarged but their number
was reduced. By the 15th century there were
some 10,000 parishes in England. Parishes became units of civil administration in the 16th
century, when parish registers were introduced (1538) by Thomas Cromwell, in spite
of considerable opposition from the people,
who feared that they were a device to facilitate
some new system of taxation. Although the
boundaries of civil and ecclesiastical parishes
were at first identical, they have since di-
verged, largely as a result of the complexities of
local government (see also beating the
bounds). Every parish has a parish meeting
(an assembly of local government electors to
discuss local matters) and many have parish
councils, which can exercise limited powers
for the benefit of their locality (e.g. the provision of such amenities as allotments, recreation
grounds, and bus shelters). A parish council
may pass a resolution styling its parish a town,
itself a town council, and its chairman the
town mayor. There are no parishes in Wales
or Scotland. In Wales the districts are divided
instead into communities, with community
meetings and councils exercising similar functions and powers to those of parish meetings
and councils. In Scotland also there are communities and community councils, but the
councils have no governmental powers. Their
function is primarily to coordinate local opinion about public services in their areas.

parks Originally the word "park" described any enclosure of land but came to be
applied particularly to areas set aside by medieval noblemen as game reserves. Later, more
emphasis was given to the aesthetic qualities of
the park as an attractive setting for a *country
house, and during the 18th century such men
as "Capability" Brown (1716–82) and
Humphrey Repton (1752–1818) created the
fashion of sweeping landscaped parklands surrounding large country mansions.
With the growth of urban populations during
the industrial revolution, and later in the 19th
century, many towns and cities began to provide parks for the public, following the example set by London's long-established *royal
parks. Among the first municipally owned
parks were Derby's Arboretum, opened in
1840, and Birkenhead Park (1847). Many
more were laid out in the years following,
with larger examples extending to 100 hectares
(250 acres) or more and containing lakes,
trees, playing fields, bowling greens, and
bandstands. Designs were strongly influenced
by the landscape movement (see gardens), but
in addition gave full expression to the Victo-

rian passion for elaborate formal displays of bedding plants, a tradition that still flourishes in most municipal parks. Britain's public parks remain largely intact, a valuable feature of urban life.

Parliament The supreme legislature of the UK, consisting of the monarch and the three estates of the realm – the Lords Spiritual and Lords Temporal, sitting together as the *House of Lords, and the commoners elected to the *House of Commons. The primary functions of Parliament are the making of law, the control of the public revenue, and the examination of government policy and public administration. The first of these is effected by *Act of Parliament, which normally requires the agreement of the sovereign and both Houses, but can in certain circumstances be enacted without being passed by the Lords. Parliament's financial control relates to both the raising of revenue and the way in which it is spent: money may be paid out of the Exchequer only on the authority of an Act and used only for the purposes named in the Act. For the examination of policy and administration, Parliament's main tools are debates, questions (oral and written) to ministers, and increasingly, *select committees to investigate the activities of government departments and specific topics of public concern.

The maximum life of any Parliament is, under the Parliament Act 1911, five years. (The first limit was three years, imposed by the Meeting of Parliament Act 1694, but this was increased to seven years by the Septennial Act 1715 and remained thus until 1911.) In practice Parliament is always dissolved earlier, by royal proclamation. The exact time at which Parliament is to be dissolved is decided by the Prime Minister, who naturally chooses an electorally propitious moment. The life of a Parliament is divided into sessions of about one year each, and the business of each House is conducted at sittings, normally of a day's duration. The ending of a session, known as the **prorogation of Parliament**, is effected either by the sovereign or (more usually) by royal commissioners, whilst sittings are terminated by simple adjournment motions. (*See also* state opening of Parliament.)

The exact date upon which Parliament in its present form emerged is difficult to give; it evolved slowly. Before the Norman conquest, the monarch of England held a council (*witenagemot*), consisting of his thegns, ealdormen, bishops, and abbots, that fulfilled the dual function of giving advice and acting as a supreme court in both criminal and civil cases. After 1066 both functions passed to the *curia regis*, the king's court, which in its widest sense was an assembly of the monarch and all his tenants-in-chief. In the 13th century this was

PARLIAMENT *From a 17th-century engraving showing the Palace of Westminster as it was before the fire of 1834. On the left is St Stephen's Chapel (Parliament House) where the Commons met. Built as a royal chapel, St Stephen's was secularized during the Reformation in the mid-16th century. Members sat in the former choir stalls, and the Speaker's chair was placed on the site of the altar.*

the natural forum in which to agree the grants of extraordinary taxation increasingly necessary to keep the monarchy solvent. *Magna Carta demanded that all tenants-in-chief should be summoned when grants of extraordinary taxation were to be made. However, as political ideas evolved, it came to be considered that their consent was not sufficient to bind the whole realm. Representatives of the lower nobility and towns began to be summoned; and after the "Model Parliament" of 1295 their representation was established at two knights for each shire and two burgesses from each city or borough. (Representatives of the lower clergy also attended until the mid-14th century.)

The function of the Lords – the great magnates of the realm and major ecclesiastics in their capacity as tenants-in-chief – was to advise the king: they were the men without whose cooperation he could not hope to govern the kingdom. They were summoned individually as a recognition of their importance and the power they wielded. In the 14th century the king asserted his right to summon whom he chose; but gradually, the right to be summoned became hereditary. By the end of the 15th century, therefore, the rules for membership of the parliamentary peerage were firmly established, which clearly separated its members from the lower nobility. The *Reformation and the dissolution of the *monasteries greatly reduced the numbers of Lords Spiritual, leaving the Lords Temporal in a clear ascendancy.

The main purpose of the Commons was to provide medieval kings with money; which power they quickly came to use as a bargaining counter to negotiate redress of their grievances. As early as 1309 a subsidy was granted only on condition that Edward II abided by certain articles (the Articles of Stamford), which were not drawn up by him or his counsellors. The Commons began to meet informally in private session during the 14th century, and elected their first recorded *Speaker (to formally represent their views to the king and Lords) in 1376. The recognized division into two "houses" dates from the mid-15th century, and a hundred years later it was firmly established that legislation (which had

originated as petitions to the king) should be passed separately by both houses before being submitted to the king.

Had English monarchs not suffered almost continual financial embarrassment, it is most unlikely that Parliament, and especially the Commons, would have acquired any substantial powers. The political power wielded by Parliament fluctuated over the centuries. In the late Middle Ages, parliaments met frequently but generally lasted only a few weeks, with the king, Lords, and Commons in general cooperating to reach a settlement of the outstanding business (which usually centred around a grant of taxation) acceptable to most parties. As the monarchy grew stronger in the late 15th century, the kings met Parliament less frequently. Yet even then it proved useful to them: at the height of the monarchy's power, under Henry VIII, Parliament was the instrument used to give legitimacy to the radical changes of the *Reformation; and it was in this period that statute law (law made in Parliament) was definitively recognized as superior to other forms of law. As the Crown weakened, especially regarding its financial position, Parliament, and in particular, the Commons, reasserted their power in the early 17th century. Charles I tried and failed to rule entirely without Parliament (1629–40), and lost the subsequent *Civil War. The *Glorious Revolution (1688) marked the decisive shift in power from monarchy to Parliament. (*See also* monarchy.)

Scottish and Irish parliaments were similar in origin and function to the medieval English parliament. The Scottish parliament never exerted as much influence on the conduct of government as its English counterpart, largely as a result of the creation of the Lords of Articles (1424), who prepared legislation that the parliament could accept or reject, but not amend. Legislative power therefore largely rested with the Lords of Articles, who in this sense resembled the old *curia regis* of England. However, the Scottish parliament did pass a considerable amount of legislation, which effectively laid the foundation of a distinctive *Scots law.

The Irish parliament was largely an institution for extracting compliance and money from the Irish, and for much of its spasmodic life was legally subordinate to the English parliament. Therefore when the English and Scottish parliaments were merged in the Parliament of Great Britain in 1707, and Scotland was accorded a relatively limited degree of representation (a state of affairs which persisted until 1882), there was a good deal of protest, but when the parliament of Ireland vanished into the Parliament of the United Kingdom of Great Britain and Ireland, there was little effective change. In terms of constitutional power the UK Parliament is a continuation of the English parliament, rather than those of Scotland or Ireland. (An assembly for Eire came into existence with the creation of the Irish Free State in 1921, and correspondingly there existed a parliament of Northern Ireland from 1921 to 1973, which regulated the internal affairs of the province under the Crown, until terrorist activity necessitated direct rule. Scottish nationalist discontent has been more limited; Scotland has enjoyed no indigenous legislature since 1707 and plans for a Scottish parliament as part of a scheme for devolution were rejeted in a referendum in 1979.) *See also* Westminster, Palace of.

Parliamentary Commissioner for Administration *See* Ombudsman.

parliamentary counsel A small group of civil servants with legal training (formerly all barristers, now barristers or solicitors) who draft government legislation (*see* Bill). Headed by the first parliamentary counsel, and responsible to the *law officers, they work on instructions prepared by administrators and lawyers in government departments. After a Bill has passed through many drafts and been finally introduced into Parliament, they prepare any amendments that may be required to correct or amplify it or to give effect to government undertakings given during its passage. They also draft the budget resolutions (*see* Chancellor of the Exchequer) and assist with private members' Bills to which the government is sympathetic. Bills that relate exclusively to Scotland are drafted in the *Lord Advocate's dèpartment under the legal secretary and first legal draftsman.

parliamentary privilege The body of special rights and immunities that are enjoyed by the two Houses of Parliament for the purpose of maintaining their authority and independence. They are conferred partly by the *common law and partly by *Act of Parliament; neither House may extend its privileges by its own resolution, however. The privileges of the House of Commons include three "ancient and undoubted rights and privileges" (access to the sovereign, freedom from arrest, and freedom of speech) that the Speaker claims for members at the opening of every Parliament, and two more besides (exclusive control over the internal affairs of the House, and the right to punish for the breach of any specific privilege or any other contempt of the House). The right of access to the sovereign is a collective right, exercised by members through the Speaker, and is not of very great significance today. Nor is the right of freedom from arrest, which protects members against civil arrest only for 40 days before and 40 days after a meeting of Parliament (the time allocated for the journey to and from Westminster in the days when travel was much slower). It had some importance before imprisonment for civil debt was abolished, but now relates to little more than arrest for disobedience to a court order made in civil proceedings. Freedom of speech is, by contrast, a very substantial privilege. Its existence as a common-law right was recognized in 1668 by the House of Lords, sitting as the highest court of appeal and quashing the conviction of members of the Commons for seditious words spoken in that House, and it was subsequently enshrined in the Bill of Rights 1689. It protects members against liability in the courts. They can neither be sued civilly (e.g. for defamation) nor prosecuted criminally (e.g. for sedition, blasphemy, or offences against the Official Secrets Acts) for anything said by them in the course of debates or any other parliamentary proceedings.

The right of exclusive control over internal affairs is another collective right. It enables the House, for instance, to sit in secret session, to decide by resolution the timing of by-elections, and to exclude any member from taking his seat for any reason whatever. The right to punish for contempt is again collective, and is very wide. Conduct that constitutes a contempt because it breaches one of the House's specific privileges is relatively limited in range. Obvious examples would include the issue of a writ for defamation in respect of privileged words, or the reporting of proceedings held in camera. Other contempts cover conduct that the House may consider prejudicial to its dignity or its proper functioning. Recorded examples have ranged from disorderly behaviour and drunkenness, to refusal to give evidence to a committee of the House and the premature publication of committee proceedings. The punishments that the House can impose (acting normally on the advice of a Committee of Privileges composed of 15 of its most senior members, irrespective of party) are suspension and expulsion in the case of members, and reprimand and imprisonment in the case of members and strangers alike. Imprisonment (last resorted to in 1800) ends automatically on prorogation (*see* Parliament). A power to fine formerly existed but was last exercised some 300 years ago and is now obsolete. The privileges of the Lords are in most respects the same as those of the Commons but there are a few minor differences. The right of access to the sovereign is not merely a collective right, but is one enjoyed by each peer individually; freedom from civil arrest applies at all times; imprisonment for contempt can be for a fixed term that is not cut short by prorogation; and there is power to fine for contempt.

parole The conditional release of a person serving a sentence of imprisonment before the expiry of his term. Also known as release on licence, it applies to both life and fixed-term sentences, and is distinct from remission, which is the cancellation of part of a fixed-term sentence for good behaviour in prison and results in unconditional release. In the UK a prisoner applies for parole to the prison's local review committee, which includes the prison governor, a member of its board of visitors, a probation officer, and two members of the public. If his sentence is for a fixed term, he must already have served one-third of it or 12 months, whichever is the longer. If the committee recommends parole, his case goes to the parole board (which includes a judge, a psy-

chiatrist, and people experienced in the care and treatment of offenders); if the board recommends parole, the case goes to the Home Secretary for final decision. Parole being a privilege, not a right, the decision is at the discretion of the Home Secretary in each case. He does, however, follow general principles that are publicly declared. For example, in 1983 the Home Secretary announced in Parliament that a person guilty of the murder of a police or prison officer, or of murder in the course of armed robbery, must normally expect to serve a minimum of 20 years before being considered for parole. A prisoner on parole may be recalled to serve the rest of his sentence for breach of any of the conditions on which it was granted, and his licence may also be revoked by the court on his conviction of any further offence punishable by imprisonment.

Patent Office Britain's sole office for the granting of patents – rights over new inventions. The English patent system has a longer continuous history than any in the world. The word "patent" is an abbreviation of letters patent (from the Latin *litterae patentes*, open letters), which were issued by medieval kings for all their subjects to read and which were therefore not sealed closed, though still prominently bearing the royal seal. These letters were used to grant monopolies for certain goods and inventions, often to encourage the development of a new industry. For example, in 1449 Henry VI granted a monopoly to John of Utynam for the making of stained glass for windows at Eton and other college chapels. Later monarchs found the fees charged for such privileges a useful means of raising revenue, and granted monopolies to suppliers of such basic necessities as coal, fruit, and soap, a practice that continued until well into the 17th century. The procedure for obtaining letters patent became very elaborate, as no document might bear the Great Seal without the sovereign's approval. The process took about eight weeks to complete, and then the letters patent applied only to England and Wales, separate patents being required for Scotland and Ireland. Until 1878 patents were still drawn up on parchment and bore the Great Seal in wax attached by a silken cord. Not only was it a costly business to obtain a patent, but any trials for infringement were also lengthy, being heard in more than one court, and thus incurring more expense for the inventor. An Act of Parliament was passed in 1852 that established just one office for issuing patents, under the authority of commissioners who included the Lord Chancellor, the Master of the Rolls, and the Lord Advocate, among other legal dignitaries. This system proved to be simpler, more efficient, and cheaper than its predecessor. The commissioners were replaced by a Comptroller following an Act passed in 1883, and various subsequent Acts have refined and modernized the system.

Patents Court A court established by the Patents Act 1977 to deal with such matters as, for example, claims concerning the infringement of patents, or the revocation of patents that were improperly granted. It also hears appeals from decisions of the Comptroller-General of the Patent Office. The Court, which forms part of the Chancery Division of the *High Court of Justice, is staffed by two *puisne judges of that Division nominated by the Lord Chancellor as having special experience of patent law, and an independent scientific adviser may be appointed to assist at any hearing. Those entitled to appear before the court include not only barristers, but also solicitors and patent agents (people who obtain patents on behalf of others, and who are registered with the Chartered Institute of Patent Agents).

PAYE (pay-as-you-earn) *See* tax system.

Paymaster General's Office The accounting office for government departments' transactions (with the exception of the Inland Revenue and the Customs and Excise). The Office was founded in 1836 by the amalgamation of separate pay offices (for the army, navy, etc.), under the provisions of the Paymaster General Acts of 1835 and 1848. It provides banking and statistical services, and the responsibility of its administration rests with the Paymaster General, who is a government minister. The money voted annually by Parliament for spending by government departments is deposited in the *Consolidated Fund. As the departments draw monies for expenditure purposes, the Office monitors the Fund and issues a monthly account to each department. A computerized system (APEX) records accumulated totals of departmental payments and receipts, feeding the results into the Treasury's financial information system and onwards to the Central Statistical Office. Responsible for the payment of 1.2 million public-service pensions, and acting as the paying agent for all government departments, the Office handles a total of 400 accounts with millions of payable orders each year. The Office and its 900 staff cost £12 million in 1985–86, and are based at Crawley, Sussex.

Peak District An upland region of northern England at the southern end of the *Pennines. The 1404 square kilometres (542 square miles) covered by the Peak District *national park extend from Ashbourne northwards almost to Huddersfield between the cities of Manchester and Sheffield. Nearly one-third of Britain's population live within 50 miles of the Peak's crags and dales, making it one of the most popular recreational areas in the country. Named after a tribe of early settlers, the Pecsaetans – "hill-dwellers" – the Peak District consists of a raised limestone plateau. The rivers Derwent, Noe, Wye, and Dove have carved deep narrow valleys, or "dales", of which Dovedale in the south is perhaps the most beautiful. The limestone contains many underground caverns, and rivers may run through subterranean channels along part of their course. The perimeter of the Low or White Peak is marked by a roughly horseshoe-shaped belt of millstone grit forming the High Peak, which rises to a height of 636 metres (2088 feet) at Kinder Scout. This is a landscape of bleak infertile moors with deep cuttings, known as "cloughs", gouged by streams and resulting in many spectacular crags and outcrops. Scattered regions of shale form the third major geological element in the Peak scenery.

Visitors come to enjoy the hill-walking, rock-climbing, and pot-holing. The spa town of Buxton provides its famous hot springs, the elegant Crescent (built by the Duke of Devonshire at the end of the 18th century to rival the popularity of Bath), extensive gardens, and the newly restored opera house. Thermal springs are also one of the long-standing attractions of Matlock, to the east, while the market town of Bakewell is famous for its almond-flavoured Bakewell tarts.

PEARLY KINGS AND QUEENS

pearly kings and queens Costermongers (street vendors) of London, whose traditional outfits are decorated with thousands of small pearl buttons. Their costume dates back to the 1880s, when the arrival of a cargo of Japanese pearl buttons is believed to have inspired the fashion among local street vendors after one of them sewed the buttons around the bottoms of his trouser legs. The Pearly Kings and Queens Association was formed in 1911. Pearly kings were originally elected by their colleagues to protect them against those who sought to drive them from the streets; the tradition is now perpetuated largely for ceremonial occasions and charitable activities, such as their *harvest festival at the church of St Martin-in-the-Fields. The buttons are sewn onto the suits, dresses, and hats of the "pearlies" in a variety of designs; each outfit weighs around 60 pounds and carries thousands of buttons.

Peasants' Revolt (1381) A widespread rebellion among the peasantry, demanding the abolition of serfdom (*see* manor), to be succeeded by fair rents and wages, and better government. Long-term causes included the social tensions and dislocation caused by the *Black Death and distrust of the government, which was held responsible for the current failures in the *Hundred Years' War. The immediate cause was oppressive taxation, especially the poll tax of 1380, which was levied on every male at one shilling per head regardless of wealth. These basic grievances were fanned by peasant leaders into a fundamental dissatisfaction with the structure of medieval society – summarized in John Ball's questioning of the hierarchy, "when Adam delved and Eve span, who was then the gentleman?"

The revolt began in June 1381 in Essex and Kent, and both groups quickly converged on London. On 13 June, after accomplices had let them into the City, they attacked what they regarded as the most oppressive institutions – notably John of Gaunt's Savoy Palace and the Temple, where they made a bonfire of many legal books. King Richard II, then only 14 years old, accompanied by his advisers, met the Essex rebels at Mile End, conceded to their demands, and persuaded them to go home. Simultaneously, however, the Kentish men broke into the Tower and lynched the Chancellor, Archbishop Simon Sudbury of Canterbury, and the Treasurer, Sir Robert Hales. This signalled a night of anarchy in the City, in which the London mob enthusiastically joined. On 15 June, the king met the Kentish men at Smithfield and managed to win their loyalty, despite the killing of their leader, Wat Tyler, by the Mayor of London. The rebels departed with most of their demands met. The revolt had spilled outwards from London, with Hertfordshire, Suffolk, Norfolk, Cambridgeshire, and Huntingdonshire all being affected. However, all the risings were brought under control by the end of June and the king's concessions were then rescinded. The rebels were treated leniently, only a few leaders being executed. The only immediate effect of the rebellion was the abandonment of poll taxes, although serfdom itself, which was to some extent undermined by economic forces, effectively vanished in the 15th century.

Peeping Tom *See* Godiva, Lady.

peerage Holders of the title of *duke, *marquess, *earl, *viscount, *baron or baroness (both hereditary or for life), who make up, in that order of precedence, the titled nobility of the British Isles. Many titles date from the time when Scotland and Ireland had their own separate peerages (i.e. in Scotland, before the Act of Union of 1707; in Ireland, before the creation of the United Kingdom in 1801). There were occasional additions to the Irish peerage even after the Act of Union (e.g. the Dukedom of Abercorn). Peers have the right to be summoned as Lords of Parliament (unless they are Irish peers). The word peerage derives from the Latin *pares*, meaning equals: the early tenants-in-chief of the Anglo-Norman kings were regarded as each other's equals, and from this usage the term survived after the development of the parliamentary system (*see* Norman Britain; Parliament). This was also the basis for such notable privileges as a peer's right of trial by his fellows in cases of treason and felony, a right that existed until 1948. Even now the holder of a peerage is exempt from jury service and enjoys immunity from arrest in civil cases for 40 days before and after a sitting of Parliament. Under common law, a peer remains "forever sacred and inviolable".

The Peerage Act 1963 permits a person inheriting a peerage to disclaim it for life provided he (or she) does so within one year (or one month if an MP – peers may not vote in parliamentary elections or sit in the House of Commons). The subsequent descent of the peerage is not affected.

peer of the realm A holder of a *peerage.

Penguin Books A publishing house set up in 1935 by Allen Lane (later Sir Allen Lane) to market first serious fiction and later nonfiction, in paper covers at a very low price (originally 6d per copy). The paperback revolution in the book trade that occurred in the 1940s and 1950s largely sprang from this venture. Penguin Books had become a large and influential British institution by the 1960s, when its publication of an unexpurgated edition of D. H. Lawrence's *Lady Chatterley's Lover* was challenged unsuccessfully by the Director of Public Prosecutions. The failure of this famous lawsuit was regarded as a landmark both in the decline of censorship and the evolution of postwar British mores.

Allen Lane was himself not an intellectual, but he managed to collect around him a band of editors who, with their distinctively recognizable Pelican series, Penguin Specials, and Penguin Classics, created a library of books that provided a new audience of readers with sources of intellectual stimulation that did not exist elsewhere.

Pennines The long narrow region of upland that extends from the Derbyshire *Peak District northwards to the River Tyne. Sometimes called the "backbone of England", the Pennines consist of eastwards-tilted rock formations bounded in the west by downfolding and faults. The northerly limestone region, where the Pennines reach their highest point at Cross Fell (893 metres; 2930 feet), is divided from the more recent millstone grit of the central Pennines by the Aire Gap, which runs roughly between Settle and Leeds and was formed when the land slipped between the Craven Faults some two million years ago. Upon this basic structure, glaciation and rivers have carved the present landscape: high plateaux and windswept moors in the north; rocky outcrops and crags further south; while the fells to the east overlook the valleys of the Yorkshire Dales, including Wensleydale and Swaledale, all part of the Yorkshire Dales *national park.

Sheep have long grazed the moors and wool formed the basis of a thriving cottage industry until the industrial revolution. The lime-free waters of the central Pennines were ideal for washing the wool and factories sprang up in the valleys, using first water power and then steam, raised from coal from the Yorkshire coalfield. Leeds, Bradford, Huddersfield, Halifax, Dewsbury, Batley, and other towns in the area, all owe their early prosperity to the wool industry. In contrast, the Lancashire towns of the western Pennines specialized in cotton weaving, particularly Rochdale, Blackburn, and Manchester. Haworth, near Bradford, was the home of the Brontë sisters, Charlotte, Emily, and Anne, whose novels strongly evoked the passions of their beloved

323

moors. The central Pennines have long attracted climbers, fell-walkers, and ramblers from the nearby industrial centres. The long-distance Pennine Way footpath, which traverses the 402 kilometres (250 miles) from Edale to the Scottish border, is one of many routes open to visitors. Pot-holing is another attraction, with many cavern systems in the limestone rocks. Gaping Gill, situated beneath Ingleborough Hill north of Settle, is the largest limestone cave in Britain, the main chamber of which is spacious enough to accommodate York Minster.

Pentecostalists Those who seek "baptism in the Holy Spirit" akin to that experienced by the apostles of Christ on the feast of Pentecost. This process is sometimes accompanied by "speaking in tongues", and those who have undergone true "spirit baptism" are said to acquire the powers of healing, of interpreting the "tongues", and of prophecy. Modern Pentecostalism developed in the USA at the turn of the century, particularly among the poor and black communities. In Britain, the two main Pentecostal Churches are the Assemblies of God − the offshoot of a US organization − and the Elim Pentecostal Church. Others include the Apostolic Church and the New Testament Church of God. There are also Pentecostalist movements within the Roman Catholic Church, the Church of England, and other Churches, known as the Charismatic Renewal or simply the Charismatic Movement. Pentecostalist services are noted for their emotional and physical content, with emphasis on rousing gospel singing and impromptu personal confession or testimony by members of the congregation. Some Anglican and Catholic churches now hold special healing services, at which members of the congregation are said to receive the gifts of the Holy Spirit.

permanent secretary The rank held by the head civil servant in many government departments (its equivalent in others being the permanent undersecretary). The appointment of a permanent secretary requires the approval of the Prime Minister; it is the senior post in the administrative grade of the service, which starts with the rank of principal and progresses through assistant secretary, undersecretary, and deputy secretary (in some departments these last two are assistant and deputy undersecretary respectively). One of the permanent secretaries has always been head of the civil service as a whole, originally the permanent secretary to the Civil Service Department. The title is now held by the Secretary to the Cabinet.

personal names *See* Christian names.

piepoudre courts *See* Bristol Tolzey Court.

piers, seaside Structures stretching out to sea from the shore, originally to permit disembarkation at high or low tide. The emergence of *seaside resorts for the wealthy seeking a "cure" or simply recreation posed certain towns with the problem of transferring visitors from ship to shore as decorously as possible. The first pier was built at Ryde on the Isle of Wight in 1813–14 and was later copied by many other towns. Landing piers were built at Brighton, Southend, Walton-on-the-Naze, and Herne Bay. Southend pier was extended to nearly 2100 metres (7000 feet) between 1835 and 1846 and it is now claimed to be the longest in the world.

However, the pier soon became an attraction in itself, as a promenade and amusement park. The Wellington Pier Company of Great Yarmouth, for example, opened its pier in 1853, charging admission fees of a penny for adults and a halfpenny for children. Southport pier (1860) was perhaps the first conceived primarily as a leisure pier; nearby Blackpool soon followed suit, opening its North Pier in 1863. Between 1870 and 1900, some 50 seaside piers were erected to attract the increasing numbers of holidaymakers. The pier decks offered various amusements: bands played, and some companies installed tramways to the pierhead amenities, which, towards the end of the century, tended to be housed in elaborate pavilions. Changing habits and rising costs stopped pier construction by the early 1900s, and damage and neglect during World War II put paid to many of them. Many of the 50 or so piers that now survive are regarded as fine examples of Victorian or Edwardian architecture and

SEASIDE PIERS *Blackpool Central Pier, Lancashire.*

efforts have been made to preserve threatened specimens, such as Brighton's West Pier.

pigeon-racing A form of racing in which pigeons are released from a central point and the time measured for each to return to its own home (hence the name "homing pigeons"). Times are recorded by removing a seal carried by a pigeon during a race and placing it in a clock, which marks it with the time of return. The winner is determined by adjusting these times according to the distance each bird has to travel. The length of races varies between 60 and 600 miles, although some endurance events are flown over thousands of miles. The average speed for a racing pigeon is 56–64 kph (35–40 mph) but in favourable conditions up to 145 kph (90 mph) has been recorded over short distances. The Belgians first used pigeons as racing birds in the early 19th century. The pastime became popular in Britain towards the end of the century and in 1896 the Royal National Homing Union of Great Britain was formed. The breeding and training of pigeons requires great skill and patience on the part of the owners, or

"fanciers". Whilst young, the birds must be encouraged, through careful handling and feeding, to develop an affinity with their own loft that will later draw them back to it, even from great distances. They are trained to tolerate travel in panniers and over a period of time are released at ever increasing distances from home in order to build up their stamina. The sport's popularity is indicated by the fact that the Royal National Homing Union issues two million registration rings to new birds every year. Pigeon-racing goes on throughout Britain, but traditionally is associated with the north of England.

place names Place names are remarkably durable and are an important source of evidence for the earliest history of the British Isles. In Scotland, for example, there are several names beginning with Pit-, such as Pitlochry and Pittenweem. In each of these names, the first element means "Pict", but the second element is Gaelic, indicating that these were places where Gaelic-speaking incomers from Ireland in the 6th century encountered surviving Pictish settlements. However, the Picts

325

seem already to have been in a minority by the time the Gaels arrived: these "Pict" place names are found alongside others which are clearly of *Celtic origin, but of Brythonic Celtic (*see* Welsh) rather than Gaelic. So, for example, the name elements *aber* "river mouth" (as in Aberdeen), *pert* "wood" (as in Perth), *lanerc* "clearing in a wood" (as in Lanark), and *pen* "hill" (as in Penicuik) have cognates in Welsh rather than Gaelic. This indicates that the language of central and east Scotland at one time was neither Gaelic nor Pictish, but a Brythonic language, more closely related to Welsh than to Irish.

Although the place names of England are mainly of Anglo-Saxon origin, names of natural features, such as rivers (e.g. Welsh *avon*), are often Celtic, taken over from the local inhabitants by the Anglo-Saxon invaders of the 5th and 6th centuries. The two communities must have coexisted at least long enough for the newcomers to learn the established names of rivers and mountains in the vicinity. The origin of some river names, such as Severn, is so obscure that it seems likely that they had already been borrowed by the Romano-British from earlier unknown inhabitants, before being taken over in turn by the Anglo-Saxons. The name of the River Thames is probably British, identical to that of the Taff in Wales, meaning "dark water". The Windrush in the Cotswolds probably gets its name from (*g*)*wen* "white" + *risc* "marsh". The great majority of English place names denoting human habitations are of either Anglo-Saxon or Viking origin. Place-name evidence confirms that Danish settlement was widespread in Norfolk and Lincolnshire, while further north Norwegian forms tend to predominate. Place names ending in -by and -thwaite, among other forms, denote Scandinavian settlements. Places called Walton, on the other hand, indicate settlements of British speakers that survived into the Old English period (from Old English *wealh* "Welshman" (i.e. Briton), "foreigner", or "slave" + *tun* "enclosure").

Place names sometimes give an insight into the daily life of our ancestors. Wardle is a place where once a lookout was stationed, from Old English *weard* "watchman" + *hyll* "hill".

Chiswick was once a dairy farm where cheese was made. The lord of the manor of Beaumont in Essex in the 12th century, no doubt a speaker of Norman French, gave it this new Norman French name, which means "beautiful hill"; its previous English name was Fulepet "foul pit". Many English place names preserve the name of the leader of the original settlers. Birmingham means "the settlement (*ham*) of the people of Beornmund". Nothing is known of this original Beornmund, as is the case with the hundreds of other place names containing the element -ing meaning "people of". Other Old English personal names are preserved more directly. Mawdesley, for example, is simply "Maud's lee", or "the clearing where Maud lived". *Lēah* "clearing in a wood" (originally just "wood") is one of the commonest elements in English place names, preserved in modern names as -ley, -ly, or Leigh. Others include Old English *tūn* "enclosure"; *hām* "settlement"; *stoc* (Stoke) and *stōw* "place"; *h(e)alh* (Hale) "nook, sheltered place"; *burh* (Bury) "fortified manor house"; *wīc* (Wick) "dairy farm"; *bere* "(outlying) barn"; *h(e)all* "hall, main residence"; *burna* (Burn) and *broca* (Brook) "stream"; *worth* "homestead"; *dūn* "hill"; *denu* "valley"; and *wudu* "wood".

Plaid Cymru (Welsh Nationalist Party) A political party arguing that Wales, as a distinct nation, should be a politically separate state, with its own legislature and with official status for its language. Plaid Cymru's intention, apart from securing self-government for Wales, is to safeguard its culture, traditions, and economic resources.

Wales came under the political and administrative control of England through Acts of Union passed during the period 1536–43 in the reign of Henry VIII. There was no active attempt to destroy Welsh culture, language, and traditions – indeed, a Welsh translation of the Bible was published in 1588 – but there was a gradual erosion. This accelerated in the 20th century: the 50% of the population who spoke Welsh in 1901 had declined to 37% by 1931. Plaid Cymru was founded in 1925, initially to protect the Welsh language, and adopted the aim of self-government in 1932. Its first leaders were Lewis Valentine, a clergyman, and the writer and academic Saunders Lewis (1893–1985), who was Plaid's president from 1926 to 1939. The party fought its first parliamentary election in 1929 but did not achieve a victory until 1966, when Gwynfor Evans (1912–   ), who was president of Plaid Cymru from 1945 to 1978, won the Carmarthen seat. The party's high point was between 1974 and 1979, when it had three MPs. However in 1979, in a referendum on devolution, proposals for limited autonomy were defeated in Wales by a four-to-one majority. At the 1983 general election, Plaid Cymru gained about 125,000 votes (0.4% of the total), and won two seats.

Being a separatist party, Plaid Cymru has suffered from the activities of extremists not directly connected with it. In 1936 Lewis and Valentine were involved in a sabotage attack on a proposed Royal Air Force bomber school at Rhos, near Pwllheli. Their motives were pacifist, but their violent protest has inspired occasional incidents of terrorist extremism, such as the explosion in 1963 at a dam, at Tryweryn in Clwyd, supplying water to Merseyside, and the many arson attacks on English-owned holiday homes in Wales during the 1970s. Extremist offshoots from the nationalist movement not constitutionally connected with Plaid Cymru have included the Free Wales Army and the *Welsh Language Society.

ploughman's lunch A popular lunchtime snack served in pubs throughout the country, consisting of a hunk of bread or a bread roll, cheese, and pickle, with a salad garnish. Based on the medieval farm labourer's traditional midday snack of bread and hard cheese, the modern ploughman's lunch may be prepared with any of a variety of cheeses and sometimes ham, beef, or other cold meats. The ploughman's lunch served in most modern pubs would be unlikely to sustain a real ploughman: however it appears to satisfy the rustic aspirations of many white-collar workers.

Plough Monday The first Monday after Twelfth Night, marking the traditional end of the Christmas holiday season and, for the farmer, the return to the plough. In recent years Plough Sunday has also been celebrated,

with the blessing of the plough at special church services at Chichester cathedral and other places, but the traditions relating to Plough Monday date back to much earlier times. In Yorkshire groups of young farm labourers, known as "plough bullocks" or "plough stots", would drag a plough from village to village, performing the traditional *sword dance at various points along the way and begging for money: those who refused to pay ran the risk of having their gardens ploughed up. Similar activities took place in other areas, often with the performance of a traditional play known as the Plough Play, and generally culminating in an evening feast presided over by Bessy, the festival queen. At Revesby, Lincolnshire, a Plough Play containing elements of the *mummers' play and the sword dance is still performed on or around Plough Monday; at Goathland in Yorkshire the old Plough Monday traditions were revived in 1923. They now take place on the first Saturday after Plough Monday, when a bullock is led around the district and donations are collected for the festival dance.

poet laureate The poet, appointed for life to the royal household, with the duty (no longer obligatory) of writing verse upon significant royal and national occasions. The word "laureate" refers to the crowns of laurel leaves given as marks of honour in classical Greece and Rome. Oxford and Cambridge universities bestowed the title "laureate" before its adoption by the Crown; and the first poet to be formally rewarded by the court, Ben Jonson (1572–1637), was not so styled. In 1670 John Dryden (1631–1700) became the first official poet laureate, but he was dismissed in 1688 for his adherence to Catholicism, and replaced by the much inferior Thomas Shadwell. This marked the beginning of the degeneration of the office into little more than a political sinecure – a status it retained throughout the 18th century, being refused by, among others, Thomas Gray. The appointment of William Wordsworth in 1843 restored its dignity; and he was succeeded in 1850 by Alfred, Lord Tennyson (1809–1892) who gave the post an influence unequalled before or since. Poets laureate this century have included John Masefield (1878–1967) from 1930, and Sir John Betjeman (1906–1984) from 1972. His successor is Ted Hughes (1930–   ).

point-to-point A horse race derived from *foxhunting in which amateur riders race horses that are regularly used for hunting and have a Master of Foxhounds certificate to prove it. It is a form of steeplechase, with artificial hedges and ditches to jump; it derives its name from the original practice of running the race from one point to another over open country. The first point-to-points were organized by local hunts in the 19th century, one of the earliest being the Atherstone hunt meeting of 1870. As other hunts followed the practice, the National Hunt Committee (formed 1866) stepped in to regulate meetings and prevent such frauds as the use of professional jockeys and racehorses. Most meetings now race over racecourses rather than open country, the minimum distance being 4.8 kilometres (3 miles). Some 200 point-to-point meetings are held in Britain each year between February and June. The meetings are informal "tweeds-and-wellies" occasions, making them family picnic outings at which the racing may not be the prime attraction.

Polari A pidgin language or cant that was much used among sailors, circus people, vagrants, and others from the 16th to the 19th century. Traces of it are found in modern English, both in the slang still used by some groups of homosexuals and in a few more widespread slang terms, such as *lingo* "language", *fake* "to make something, especially something counterfeit or fraud", and *scarper* "to leave in a hurry". The name Polari or Palyaree itself is probably derived from Italian *parlare* "to talk". Many of the words in Polari are derived from the *lingua franca* of the Mediterranean, and were undoubtedly brought back to Britain by seamen. It was the practice of the merchant navy in former times to discharge sailors at the first landfall in England: large numbers of sailors making their way home by road would naturally fall in with other habitual travellers, and the cants or jargons of the various groups intermingled. Polari thus also contains vocabulary elements from the old-established cant of thieves and

vagabonds (a variety of English deliberately contrived to defy understanding by more law-abiding citizens), and possible also from *Romany.

police The civil forces responsible in the UK for the maintenance of law and order, and the detection and prevention of crime. They are organized on a local basis, but are subject to a considerable degree of central control. The policing of London is carried out by the *Metropolitan Police and the *City of London Police. In England and Wales (outside London) there are 41 forces, of which 31 cover single counties and 10 are the combined forces of two or more (e.g. the Thames Valley Police, covering Berkshire, Buckinghamshire, and Oxfordshire). For each county or combination of counties there is an authority, known as the police committee, two-thirds of which consist of county councillors, and one-third of magistrates (*see* justice of the peace). Its general functions are to maintain an efficient force for the area, and to provide the necessary buildings, vehicles, and equipment. It appoints and dismisses the chief constable, his deputy and assistants, but is subject in each case to the Home Secretary's approval. The police committee is also the paymaster for the force, which is financed partly by central government and partly by rates. The committee has no operational control of the force, however. This is the responsibility of the chief constable, who makes all appointments and promotions to ranks below that of assistant chief constable, is responsible for discipline, and determines the policing policy for the area and the deployment of resources within it. Moreover, the Home Secretary has power under the Police Act 1964 to regulate the administration and conditions of service of police forces generally, and can prescribe general standards of policing and a basic code of discipline. In Scotland, for which there are eight forces, the position is similar to that in England and Wales: but the forces cover either regions (not counties) or combined areas, the police authorities are in turn either the regional councils or joint bodies, and the authority of the Home Secretary is replaced by that of the Secretary of State for Scotland. For Northern Ireland, *see* Royal Ulster Constabulary.

The highly organized and professional police forces that exist today emerged in the 19th century (the first was the *Metropolitan Police, in 1829) but the individual police officer, of whatever rank, holds the ancient office of constable, a man sworn under the *common law to keep the peace of his sovereign. He is not a Crown servant, since he is neither appointed by the Crown nor paid wholly out of central funds; nor, since they have no control over his activities, is he the servant of the police authority. The unique independence of the office, meant that, for a long period there was no-one liable at law for such offences as trespass or assault committed by an officer in the exercise of his duties. This injustice was remedied by the Police Act 1964, which makes his chief constable liable ex officio, with damages payable as part of police expenditure. *See also* CID; Special Branch.

polo A sport in which players on horseback try to score goals using wooden mallets and a wooden ball. The name comes from *pulu*, the Tibetan word for the willow root from which the balls are made. The earliest records of polo are from Persia, China, and Tibet in the 8th century, and India in the 13th century. It was here that the British learned the game in the 1850s and took it back to England and to Australia, New Zealand, and North and South America.

Each polo team has four players and a game has eight seven-minute periods or "chukkas", with a three-minute break between each. The pitch is some 274 × 183 metres (300 × 200 yards) and the goalposts are made of wicker so

POLO *Players pursuing the ball in the Rothman's Cup competition, 1984. The sport requires both first-class horsemanship and ball-playing ability.*

as to break easily in the event of a collision. Mounts are referred to as "ponies", although in fact they may be horses of any age or size that are fast and agile and have enough stamina. Polo is a game requiring two very different skills: first-class horsemanship and accuracy when striking the ball. A player must control his pony with his left hand and hold the stick in his right. The ball is not large and the head of the mallet quite small so considerable skill is required, especially as the game is played at very high speed. The demands are such that a player may change his pony several times during a match. It is therefore necessary to keep a string of polo ponies and this makes it an expensive sport and limits the number of players. It has long been a favourite of the royal family, with the Duke of Edinburgh being a regular player before he retired and the Prince of Wales continuing the tradition.

polytechnics Institutions providing higher education with an emphasis on courses that are relevant to vocational training while preserving academic standards. The polytechnic concept originated in France at the end of the 18th century, and spread to Germany and Britain in the 19th century. The opening of the Regent Street Polytechnic by the philanthropist Quintin Hogg (1843–1903) in 1882 marked the start of the system in Britain. However, the majority of the 30 polytechnics in England and Wales were only formally designated as such between 1969 and 1973. They provide a wide range of courses in the sciences, social sciences, and technology to both full- and part-time students, with many "sandwich" courses designed to allow students time for practical experience in industry or commerce. The degrees awarded by polytechnics are comparable in standard to those awarded by universities but are validated not by the polytechnics themselves but by the *Council for National Academic Awards.

Population Censuses and Surveys, Office of (OPCS) The main government agency for executing population surveys of England and Wales. Similar functions are carried out by the General Register Offices for Scotland and Northern Ireland. The availability of figures for population and manpower, and other data, allows governments to plan the socio-economic strategies of the future, e.g. demands for hospital beds, pensions, and school places.

The first attempt at a general survey was *Domesday Book in 1086, ordered by William I to assess his English possessions. In the following centuries enumerative lists were occasionally compiled, but usually for a specific purpose such as taxation or military service. The first efforts to obtain figures for marriages and deaths were encouraged by Thomas Cromwell in 1538, during the reign of Henry VIII. Later, during the *Great Plague of 1665, 55,800 deaths were recorded (though the estimated number of deaths is nearer 70,000).

In the 17th and 18th centuries general censuses were occasionally proposed but usually rejected on the grounds that they would be an infringement of individual liberty. In 1796 John Rickman wrote a paper pointing out the merits of holding a census, and his proposal was taken up by his MP. The first census was conducted in 1801: local lists were compiled by parish overseers, giving details of the sex and occupations of members of each household. The Births, Deaths, and Marriages Act 1836 established the General Register Office and began the systematic assembly of essential statistics. The reports of the Registrar General's chief statistician, Dr William Farr, on the four cholera epidemics of 1848–66 proved Dr John Snow's theory that a link existed between foul water and the incidence of disease. In 1841 the responsibility for conducting the census was given to specially appointed registrars (1861 in Scotland). In 1911 Dr T. H. C. Stevenson introduced the idea of grouping occupations into social grades, numbered I–V, in order to relate data on infant mortality and incidence of disease to employment. In somewhat modified form, this grading system is still in use.

The OPCS was set up in 1970 when the old General Register Office for England and Wales and the Social Survey department were merged. The OPCS records the statistics delivered by 416 registrar districts, by hospitals, and by local authorities. These include basic figures for births, deaths, and marriages, and also figures for divorce, adoption, immigration, and emigration. Figures relating to health, such as cause of death, incidence of cancer, congenital defects in babies, abortions, and hospital activity analyses, are also collected. The OPCS carries out several operations on behalf of government departments. Its general household survey records many different social trends, such as the decline in cigarette smoking, the increase in one-parent families, and the increasing numbers of people living alone. The surveys suggest a British willingness to impart all types of information – even contraceptive use – with the exception of financial information! Other surveys include the family expenditure survey and the national food survey. The largest task of the OPCS is the management of the modern ten-yearly censuses that provide much reliable data, since accurate form-filling is mandatory for householders. All personal details disclosed remain confidential for one hundred years afterwards, but the statistics derived are published as soon as possible. The information gathered fills 16 kilometres (10 miles) of shelving at the registry at Titchfield, Hampshire. The headquarters of the OPCS is now at St Catherine's House in London, since it severed its historic link (from 1837) with Somerset House in the early 1980s. *See also* registrars of births and deaths.

porridge A breakfast dish of Scottish origin, consisting of oatmeal boiled in water or milk with a little salt and served with cold milk, sugar, treacle, or extra salt. Well suited to poor soil and a relatively harsh climate, oats have been Scotland's most important cereal crop since their introduction into Britain in the Iron Age. Scottish porridge is generally made from medium-ground oatmeal and is traditionally stirred clockwise with a wooden stick rather than a spoon. In England, however, the oatmeal is often replaced with commercially produced rolled oats, which can be stored for longer periods and cooked in half the time taken to prepare oatmeal porridge.

port A fortified sweet red wine produced in the Douro region of Portugal and shipped from Oporto. In the years preceding World War II Britain held first place among the port-drinking nations of the world, a position it has now lost to France. Portuguese wine has been imported by Britain since the late 17th century, when it enjoyed a preferential rate of duty compared with that imposed on imported French wine. The Methuen treaty of 1703 between Britain and Portugal consolidated this advantage; a number of British merchants set up wine lodges in Oporto and Portuguese wine growers began to experiment, fortifying their product with brandy to make it more palatable, to make it travel better, and to increase the alcohol content. The brandy was originally added after the wine had finished fermenting, but it was soon discovered that by using the spirit to halt fermentation a sweeter wine could be produced. A further development was the change in bottling techniques that enabled vintage port to mature in the bottle for at least ten to fifteen years and often much longer.

Tawny port is aged for fifteen to twenty years in wooden casks, a process that turns red wines more amber and improves the flavour as long-term chemical reactions take place. It is drunk soon after bottling. Ruby port is a young and relatively cheap port, aged in its cask for two to five years, that forms the basis of the once-popular pub drink, port and lemon. Crusted port, an acceptable substitute for the more expensive vintage port (wine of an exceptionally good year that has been aged in casks for two years and aged in bottles for more than fifteen) is a blend of several wines of different ages matured in the bottle. Port was originally drunk throughout dinner in place of French claret; it is now consumed at the end of the meal, sometimes with the cheese course. A number of traditions are attached to port-drinking, the best-known being that of passing the decanter to the left so that it travels around the dinner table in a clockwise direction. There is an obvious connection between this tradition and the nautical term "port" meaning "left", but its true origin remains the subject of endless dispute.

porter See beer.

Portmeirion A resort in northwest Wales on a tree-clad peninsula about 3 kilometres (2 miles) southwest of Penrhyndeudraeth, Gwynedd. The Welsh architect Sir Clough Williams-Ellis (1883–1978) chose this secluded spot, between the rivers Glaslyn and Dwyryd, to build a showpiece village that attempts to recreate in Wales the spirit of the fishing port and holiday resort Portofino, in northern Italy. Having rebuilt a luxury hotel, Williams-Ellis planted cypress, eucalyptus, and palm trees and introduced many ingenious architectural fantasies into the area. These include an Italianate campanile, lighthouse, and castle. Some buildings are complete edifices, other are mere façades, making Portmeirion a cross between a village and a stage set. It also has an outdoor museum and wild gardens full of exotic plants. Sir Noël Coward completed his comedy *Blithe Spirit* at Portmeirion in 1941, and the television series *The Prisoner* was filmed there during the l960s.

Port of London Authority (PLA) A public trust constituted by Act of Parliament in 1910 to regulate and maintain London's port facilities for the River Thames as far as Teddington, 153 kilometres (95 miles) upstream. It was formed to take over the ailing private companies that had formerly managed the docks. For years it was housed in an impressive stone building overlooking Tower Hill. From the late 1960s the combined effects of container trade, the need for deeper berths, competition from the ports of Rotterdam and Felixstowe, the high incidence of strikes, and overmanning under the national dock labour scheme, forced the PLA to sell many of the Upper Thames docks to local authorities (and later to the London Docklands Development Corporation, in the period 1979–84). The PLA has suffered severe financial difficulties from these changes and the workforce has fallen from 10,000 in 1975 to 3000 in 1984. The PLA's building was sold to a firm of insurance brokers in 1971 and it moved to smaller offices in the World Trade Centre at St Katharine's Dock. However, the Thames still handles 25,000 vessel movements per annum. The primary role of the PLA now is managing Tilbury Docks, the main downstream port in the London Basin. The PLA also licenses dock employers, port workers, the watermen and lightermen, and collects port dues on the Thames. It provides a radar and river navigation service, and dredges up tons of silt and rubbish from the river each year. Although the PLA was responsible for the successful Thames Barrier scheme (to counteract the possibility of flooding), it faces an uncertain future.

Post Office The national postal service, with a monopoly on the movement of letters (except for certain categories). The Post Office consists of Posts (the Royal Mail and post office counters), and the National Girobank (*see* banks). In 1635 Charles I made his royal posts available to the public, and the new service became known as the General Post Office in 1657; a local "penny post" was started in London in 1680. Sir Rowland Hill's reforms of 1840 established the modern postal system by introducing charges based on weight and prepayable by the use of adhesive stamps. The invention of the pillar box has been credited to the novelist and civil servant Anthony Trollope. Dramatic reductions in delivery times resulted from the development of the railway, the steamship, and finally the world's first scheduled airmail service in 1911. The General Post Office ceased to be a government department in 1968 and became a nationalized industry.

In 1983–84 10.7 billion letters and 195 million parcels were sent to 23 million delivery points in the UK using a sophisticated postcode system. With a turnover of £2776 million in 1983 and employing 175,000 staff, the Post Office has made a profit without subsidy for the past decade, and has become the only profitable twice-daily postal service in the world. In addition to performing essential tasks, such as the payment of pensions and family allowances, and the issue of television licences, National Savings certificates, and national insurance stamps, the Post Office must cope with great fluctuations in mail volume: for example, the 114 million extra postal items caused by the 1983 general election. The network of 22,000 post offices is the largest retail organization in the UK and one of the highest ratios of post offices per head of population by international standards. Other functions include an express mail, facsimile service, a special bulk mailing service, a British postal consultancy service that has advised many countries on development of new postal services, and the

Philatelic Bureau in Edinburgh. In the future a network of 80 mechanized letter offices and new optical sorting machinery is planned, together with some reductions in the number of post offices.

poteen A rough spirit resembling Irish whiskey, illicitly distilled in Ireland from malted barley, oats, or any other ingredients that can be fermented, notably potatoes. The liquor has been produced in Ireland for hundreds of years; in poorer districts the sale of poteen often provided vital extra income for low-paid workers. Since 1770 the distillation of spirits, whether for private consumption or for sale, has been liable to tax; in the late 18th century military force was sometimes used to track down illicit stills and apprehend their operators. The offenders often displayed considerable ingenuity in concealing the evidence: a certain 19th-century distiller once rode to market beside a liquor-filled tin vessel made in the shape of a woman and dressed as his wife. Despite the threat of heavy fines and the poor quality of the liquor in comparison to relatively cheap Irish whiskey, poteen is still produced in some parts of Ireland and remains a profitable business for those who succeed in avoiding prosecution.

precedence The practice of ranking people in a given order. Although frequently thought of as a social practice (used, for instance, in the all but obsolete practice of deciding in what order men and women go into dinner and their placement at table in relation to the host), the official table of precedence has evolved according to a body of legislation. The exceptions to this are precedence in the royal family, which is laid down by the sovereign (royal children who are minors are not normally included except in the table of succession), precedence among the various secretaries of state, which is decided by the Prime Minister, and judicial precedence, which is for the Lord Chancellor's office to decide. Precedence still operates on official and ceremonial occasions. There is one table of precedence for England and Wales and another for Scotland. Men and women have different tables of precedence, except that in an otherwise all-male gathering the sovereign, although in this reign

Table of precedence

England and Wales

Men

The Queen
Duke of Edinburgh
Prince of Wales
Prince Andrew
Prince Edward
Duke of Gloucester
Duke of Kent
Prince Michael of Kent
Lord Linley
Archbishop of Canterbury
Lord Chancellor
Archbishop of York
Prime Minister
Lord President of the Council
Speaker of House of Commons
Lord Privy Seal
Ambassadors and High Commissioners by seniority of arrival in UK
Lord Great Chamberlain
Lord High Constable
Earl Marshal
Lord High Admiral
Lord Steward of the Household
Lord Chamberlain
Master of the Horse
Dukes
Eldest sons of dukes of the blood royal
Marquesses
Eldest sons of dukes not of blood royal
Earls
Younger sons of dukes of blood royal
Marquesses' eldest sons
Younger sons of dukes not of blood royal
Viscounts
Earls' eldest sons
Marquesses' younger sons
Bishop of London
Bishop of Durham
Bishop of Winchester
Other diocesan bishops by seniority of consecration
Suffragan, assistant, and retired bishops
Secretary of state if a baron
Barons (or Lords of Parliament in the peerage of Scotland)
Commissioners of the Great Seal
Treasurer of the Household
Comptroller of the Household
Vice-Chamberlain of the Household
Secretaries of state
Viscounts' eldest sons
Earls' younger sons
Barons' eldest sons
Knights of the Garter
Knights of the Thistle
Privy Councillors
Chancellor of the Order of the Garter (invariably held by the Bishop of Oxford since 1837)
Chancellor of the Exchequer
Chancellor of the Duchy of Lancaster
Lord Chief Justice
Master of the Rolls
President of Family Division of High Court
Lord Justices of Appeal
High Court judges
Viscounts' younger sons

Younger sons of barons and all sons of Lords of Appeal in Ordinary, life barons and life baronesses
Baronets
Knights Grand Cross of the Order of the Bath
Members of the Order of Merit
Other Knights Grand Cross/Commanders
Companions of Honour
Knights Commanders
Knights Bachelor
Vice-Chancellor of County Palatine of Lancaster
Recorder of London
Recorders of Liverpool and Manchester
Common Serjeant
Circuit judges
Master of the Court of Protection
Companions of the Bath
Companions of Star of India
Companions of St Michael and St George
Companions of Order of Indian Empire
Commanders of Royal Victorian Order
Commanders of Order of British Empire
Companions of Distinguished Service Order
Lieutenants of Royal Victorian Order
Officers of Order of British Empire
Companions of Imperial Service Order
Peers' oldest sons' younger sons
Baronets' eldest sons
Knights' eldest sons
Members of Royal Victorian Order
Members of Order of British Empire
Baronets' younger sons
Knights' younger sons

Women

The Queen
The Queen Mother
Princess of Wales
Princess Anne
Princess Margaret
Princess Alice, duchess of Gloucester
Duchess of Gloucester
Duchess of Kent
Princess Michael of Kent
Princess Alexandra
Lady Sarah Armstrong-Jones
Duchesses
Wives of eldest sons of dukes of blood royal
Daughters of dukes of blood royal
Marchionesses
Wives of eldest sons of dukes
Daughters of dukes
Countesses
Wives of younger sons of dukes of blood royal
Wives of eldest sons of marquesses
Daughters of marquesses
Wives of younger sons of dukes
Viscountesses
Wives of eldest sons of earls
Daughters of earls
Wives of younger sons of marquesses
Baronesses, wives of Lords of Appeal in Ordinary and wives of life barons
Wives of eldest sons of viscounts
Daughters of viscounts
Wives of younger sons of earls
Wives of eldest sons of barons
Daughters of barons, Lords of Appeal in Ordinary, life barons and life baronesses
Maids of Honour
Wives of Knights of Garter
Privy Councillors
Wives of younger sons of viscounts
Wives of younger sons of barons
Wives of baronets
Dames Grand Cross
Wives of Knights Grand Cross
Dames Commanders
Wives of Knights Commanders
Wives of Knights Bachelor
Companions of Order of Bath
Companions of St Michael and St George
Commanders of Royal Victorian Order
Commanders of Order of British Empire
Wives of Companions and Commanders
Lieutenants of Royal Victorian Order
Officers of Order of British Empire
Wives of Companions of Distinguished Service Order
Companions of Imperial Service Order
Wives of Companions of Imperial Service Order
Wives of eldest sons of younger sons of peers
Daughters of younger sons of peers
Wives of eldest sons of baronets
Daughters of baronets
Wives of eldest sons of knights
Daughters of knights
Members of Royal Victorian Order
Members of Order of British Empire
Wives of Members of Royal Victorian Order
Wives of Members of Order of British Empire
Wives of baronets' younger sons
Wives of knights' younger sons

Scotland

Men

The Queen
Duke of Edinburgh
Lord High Commissioner to General Assembly of Church of Scotland
Prince of Wales as duke of Rothesay
Prince Andrew
Prince Edward
Duke of Gloucester
Duke of Kent
Prince Michael of Kent
Lord Linley
Lord Lieutenants of counties
Lord Provosts of cities
Sheriffs Principal
Lord Chancellor
Moderator of General Assembly of Church of Scotland
Prime Minister
Secretary of State for Scotland if a peer
Keeper of Privy Seal of Scotland if a peer
Hereditary High Constable of Scotland

Hereditary Master of Household in Scotland
Dukes
Eldest sons of dukes of the blood royal
Marquesses
Eldest sons of dukes not of the blood royal
Earls
Younger sons of dukes of the blood royal
Marquesses' eldest sons
Younger sons of dukes not of blood royal
Secretary of State for Scotland if not a peer
Keeper of the Privy Seal if not a peer
Lord Justice-General
Lord Clerk Register
Lord Advocate
Lord Justice-Clerk
Viscounts
Earls' eldest sons
Marquesses' younger sons
Barons (or Lords of Parliament)
Viscounts' eldest sons
Earls' younger sons

Barons' eldest sons
Knights of the Garter
Privy Councillors
Lords of Session
Viscounts' younger sons
Younger sons of barons and all sons of Lords of Appeal in Ordinary, life barons and life baronesses
Baronets
Knights of the Thistle
Knights Grand Cross of the Order of the Bath
Other Knights Grand Cross/Commanders as in England
Knights Commanders
Solicitor-General for Scotland
Lyon King of Arms
Sheriffs Principal
Knights Bachelor
Sheriffs-Substitute
Commanders and Companions and the rest as in England

a woman, would still head the order of precedence (compare the practice whereby if the Queen visits an Arab country she is regarded as an "honorary man"), and the Prime Minister, when a woman, would take the same position in the table of precedence as if she were a man. If a woman (who is not royal) enjoys a position in a table of precedence on a hereditary basis, it is derived from her father or husband. Exceptions are peeresses in their own right and baronesses. Female holders of ranks in the orders of chivalry are listed by their personal distinctions; official or ecclesiastical positions held by husbands or fathers confer no precedence on the wives or daughters. By custom rather than official written code, which makes no mention of them, the Lord-Lieutenant of a county, then the High Sheriff, take precedence over all other people in that county during their terms of office since they represent the sovereign. For the same reason the Lord-Lieutenant, when present officially, takes precedence over a mayor of a borough or city when in that borough or city. However, the mayor always presides in the sense of acting as host at functions of the borough or city. At Oxford and Cambridge the High Sheriffs of the county take precedence over the university vice-chancellors.

prefect system *See* public schools.

prehistoric Britain Although the first known men came to Britain before 2,500,000 BC as hunters with crude stone tools and weapons, occupation advanced and retreated with the glaciers of the Ice Ages until temperatures stabilized around 8000 BC; Britain finally became an island only by 6500 BC. By 3500 BC new colonists had introduced farming and displaced the hunter-gatherers over the following centuries. They began to build earthworks around their settlements, including early *hill forts, such as Hambledon Hill, Dorset – the first man-made works to leave a lasting mark on the landscape. Their veneration of the dead resulted in elaborate burial rituals and large *barrows, cairns, and chambered tombs built of stone. After 2500 BC a greater variety of pottery (first introduced about 3500 BC) and tools appeared. Henge monuments (circular monuments, surrounded by a ditch and bank breached by one or two entrances) were built, probably for ceremonial rites. (*Stonehenge was begun about 2500 BC.) Around 2300 BC copperworking, the earliest form of metalworking, was introduced from Europe; by 1800 BC copper had been superseded by an alloy of tin and copper, bronze. About 2000 BC a series of large enclosures was built in southern England, including the massive *stone circle at Avebury. At about this time, a new style of finely made and decorated pottery appeared, associated with new immigrants who have been named after it – the Beaker Folk. Personal possessions seem then to have become important for the first time, an indication of which was the wide array of artefacts deposited in the tombs of this period. At the same time society became more settled: the expansion of Stonehenge after 1700 BC into a monument unique in Europe in its sophistication must have required considerable organization and ability to mobilize labour.

Around 1000 BC a change to a colder and wetter climate forced the abandonment of settlements on high ground, such as *Dartmoor and the *North York Moors. New weapons, such as the slashing sword, appeared from Europe, and a new form of bronze (using lead rather than tin) had spread throughout the British Isles by 700 BC. Soon afterwards ironworking began to penetrate Britain and had superseded bronze by 500 BC. Whether iron was brought by a new wave of immigrants, the Celts (who were at this time expanding in Europe), is uncertain. The distinctive Celtic style of art seems to have appeared in Britain around this time, but other theories place the Celtic occupation later, after 450 BC. However, it is likely that by the time of the Roman conquest (43 AD) most of Britain spoke Brythonic *Celtic. By the first century BC, trading links had been re-established with the continent, and in the following years southeast England developed close links with the lands across the English Channel. These connections and trade gradually drew Britain into the fringes of the Roman world. When Julius Caesar visited Britain in 55 and 54 BC he found and described a fairly sophisticated society, based around *oppida* (Latin: towns), with a distinct privileged class. Exports to the continent included corn,

PREHISTORIC BRITAIN *Stone-built Iron Age roundhouse on Jarlshof, Shetland. Radial partitions divide the interior into a series of compartments around a central hearth. A simple saddle-quern for grinding corn can be seen (centre left).*

cattle, gold, silver, iron, hides, hunting dogs, and slaves. For a century the Romans were content to exercise influence to keep Britain from threatening the Empire, establishing a network of clients among important tribes; but in 43 AD, the Emperor Claudius decided that conquest was necessary (*see* Roman Britain).

premium bonds A form of government lottery introduced in 1956. It consists of a government bond on which no interest is paid, the interest notionally due being distributed as prizes in a lottery based on bond serial numbers. Draws are made for both weekly and monthly prizes, ranging from £50 to £250,000, by a computer known as **ERNIE** (Electronic Random Number Indicator Equipment). All prizes are tax-free and bonds may be redeemed at any time.

preparatory schools (prep schools) *In-dependent schools that prepare children in the age range 7–13 for entry to *public schools. Historically, prep schools are a 19th- and 20th-century phenomenon, arising from the decision of the public schools not to admit boys under a certain age. Their aims and interests are coordinated by the Association of Preparatory Schools, founded in 1892. Unlike the public schools, prep schools are usually privately owned profit-making concerns. They charge high fees and try to offer a wider range of academic and social opportunities than is available in the state schools; many of them are boarding schools. Links between them and their "target" public schools are often informal but close, with the prep schools measuring their success by the numbers of pupils they manage to get through the *Common Entrance examination. They therefore exert strong pressure towards academic achievement, but other aspects of the "public school ethos", especially in team games, are not neglected. They are predominantly single-sex; girls' prep schools were gradually established to serve the needs of the girls' public schools, but some boys' prep schools take girls in the junior forms and vice versa.

Pre-Raphaelite Brotherhood A group of 19th-century artists, who looked to Italian painting before Raphael (1483–1520) for their inspiration, in reaction to what they saw as the empty academicism of their contemporaries. The name, originally the nickname of the Nazarenes (1809–30), a group of German

335

PRE-RAPHAELITE BROTHERHOOD Ophelia, *by Millais, 1852. Millais' careful observation of nature and choice of dramatic Shakespearean subject (in this case, Ophelia's drowning, from* Hamlet) *are characteristic of Pre-Raphaelite art.*

painters with similar ideals, was secretly adopted in 1848 by the painters John Everett Millais (1829–96), William Holman Hunt (1827–1910), Dante Gabriel Rossetti (1828?–82), George Stephens (1828–1907), and James Collinson (1825?–81), and the sculptor Thomas Woolner (1825–92). The initials PRB were first used on Hunt's *Girlhood of Mary Virgin*, exhibited in 1849; when their meaning was revealed by Rossetti in the following year the group was widely attacked, particularly for the arrogance of apparently setting themselves above Raphael. Their work is characterized by an intricacy of detail, often resulting from direct observation of nature. An interest in social realism is shown in some of the best-known paintings associated with the movement, for example in Ford Madox Brown's *Work*, and in Millais' *Christ in the House of His Parents*, condemned by many as blasphemous for its portrayal of the Holy Family as Jewish peasants in the house of an impoverished carpenter. The Pre-Raphaelites are also noted for their experiments with rich and sometimes hectic colour. Sentimentality is

a further criticism that has been levelled against them. Most of the Brotherhood took their subject matter from nature or the Bible; Rossetti, however, found more scope for his imagination in Shakespeare, Dante, and Keats, taking his technical inspiration from early Flemish masters. The Brotherhood dissolved after 1853 but not before it had won approval, notably from John Ruskin (1819–1900), art and social critic. Later artists who were influenced by its ideas include Edward Burne-Jones (1833–98) and William Morris (1834–96) (*see* Art and Crafts movement). Fine collections of Pre-Raphaelite works can be found at the Tate Gallery, London, the Ashmolean Museum, Oxford, and the City of Birmingham Art Gallery.

Presbyterian Church of Wales (Calvinistic Methodist Church of Wales) The only truly indigenous Welsh Church, the Presbyterian Church of Wales was founded by Howell Harris (1714–73), a Welsh schoolteacher who, after a spiritual conversion in 1735, became one of his country's most famous revivalist preachers. He was four times refused ordination in the Church of England and remained a lay evangelist, establishing his own religious community at Trevecca in 1752. He later gained the support of the prominent Calvinistic Methodist Selina Hastings, Countess of Huntingdon (1707–91). Although the Calvinistic Methodists had split with the Wesleyan Methodists on doctrinal grounds as early as 1740, Harris wished to remain within the Church of England. However, episcopal pressure forced the Calvinistic Methodists to register their meeting rooms as "dissenting chapels" under the terms of the 1689 Toleration Act. Ministers were first ordained in 1811 and by 1826 the Church was fully constituted in its own right, based on presbyterian government. Today it has 1200 chapels, 180 ministers, and about 75,000 members.

Presbyterians Those who accept the form of church government rediscovered from the apostolic model found in the New Testament by the French theologian John Calvin (1509–64) and others. They held it to be the only permissible form of government and thus permanently binding upon the Church. In Britain, the major Presbyterian Churches are now the *Church of Scotland, the *Presbyterian Church of Wales, and the Presbyterian Church in Ireland. The small Presbyterian Church of England became part of the *United Reformed Church in 1972. Presbyterianism is based on the Calvinist interpretation of the Bible that regards all members of the Church as equal under Christ. Thus, leaders of the Church are elected by the members rather than installed by a hierarchy of bishops, as in the episcopal system. The lowest tier, which runs the affairs of each congregation, is the session (or kirk session in Scotland) comprising the minister and elders of the church. Deacons administer alms and care for the sick, while the business side is dealt with by the trustees. Ministers and elders from all the churches in an area comprise the presbytery, which meets as required to approve the installation of ministers (who are elected by their congregations), to supervise worship in the area, and to act as a court of appeal for matters arising from the congregations. The synod, which is the regional tier and covers several presbyteries, now

has a reduced role. Ultimate authority rests with the General Assembly – the annual meeting of ministers and elders that supervises and directs overall policies. It is presided over by a moderator, who is elected for a one-year term. There are no compulsory forms of service although each church usually has official books for the guidance of ministers.

In England, Presbyterianism reached its zenith during the Long Parliament of the 1640s (*see* Puritans), but by the end of the 18th century had dwindled to only a few congregations. An influx of Scottish Presbyterians during the 19th century caused a partial revival, and in 1876, the Presbyterian Church of England was formed by a merger of the United Presbyterian Church with various other congregations. In Ireland, Presbyterianism came with the English and Scottish Protestant settlers of the 17th century and survived in the face of Catholic hostility and official disfavour. The Secession Church and Reformed Presbyterians emerged in the mid-18th century and both later gave rise to breakaway factions. In 1840 the Presbyterian Church in Ireland was formed from the merger of the Secession Church and the Synod of Ulster, representing Presbyterians in the north. By the time of partition in 1921, most of its members were in Ulster. It is now the largest of the Irish Presbyterian Churches, with 566 congregations, 444 ministers, and over 133,000 members.

Press Council An independent body set up to maintain the fundamental freedom of the British press, monitor its standards, and adjudicate on any complaints made against it. The Council includes representatives from both press and general public; its annual budget (of around £500,000) is raised by levies on all newspapers. In adjudicating complaints, it is empowered to censure the complainant or the journalist or editor concerned. The Council made 133 adjudications in 1984, of which 72 were upheld, 61 rejected, and 20 settled by conciliation. Recent complaints have drawn attention to the use of subterfuge by journalists, voluntary restraints by financial journalists, the reporting of defamatory statements by witnesses, and the need for editors to prevent powerful institutions and vested interests from manipulating their columns. It publishes an annual report, *Press and the People*, and an advisory handbook, *Principles for the Press* (1984), summarizing past decisions.

Prime Minister The head of Her Majesty's government, responsible for the country's policies at home and abroad in conjunction with the *Cabinet. Like the Cabinet, the office of Prime Minister is a creation not of law, but of constitutional convention (*see* British constitution), only receiving formal recognition in 1905. After the accession in 1714 of George I, the first of the Hanoverian kings, the sovereign gradually ceased to attend in person the meetings of the ministers he selected. Sir Robert Walpole, the First Lord of the Treasury (*see* Chancellor of the Exchequer), presided in the king's place from 1721 to 1742 and is therefore often cited as the first Prime Minister. However, Walpole did not choose his ministers, nor was royal intervention a thing of the past. It was only gradually that the modern conventions developed. It is now accepted that the Crown must act only on the advice of Prime Minister and Cabinet; that the Crown must invite the person best able to command a majority in the House of Commons to become Prime Minister, and to form his or her own Cabinet; and (in the 20th century) that the Prime Minister should sit in the Commons rather than the Lords. The role of the Prime Minister within the Cabinet has been traditionally defined as *primus inter pares* (first among equals), although much depends on the personality and ability of the particular incumbent. In the last 30 to 40 years there has been a marked swing towards what is often described as prime ministerial, or presidential-style, government. The post also includes responsibility for a wide variety of appointments (including the Lord Chancellor, the judges, the Ombudsman, as well as the chairman and governors of the BBC), and the creation of peerages and conferring of other honours. The Prime Minister is also head of the civil service, and holds the office of First Lord of the Treasury (though he is free of departmental duties, which fall on the Chancellor of the Exchequer).

Primrose League An organization founded in 1883 by Lord Randolph Churchill and a number of other leading Conservatives to revitalize the party after its defeat in 1880 by the Liberals under W. E. Gladstone. It honoured the memory and principles of Benjamin Disraeli (1804–81; Prime Minister 1868, 1874–80), whose favourite flower was said to be the primrose. Its purpose was to spread basic Conservative principles – "the maintenance of religion, of the constitution of the realm, and of the unity of British Commonwealth and Empire".

Prince of Wales Wales was ruled by a succession of independent princes from the 5th century, when many Britons retreated to the Welsh mountains to defend themselves against the Saxons. Rhodri the Great (r. 844–78 AD) united the petty states into one principality and for the next 400 years a succession of some 18 Princes of Wales defended their country against the incursions of the Saxons, the Danes, and, most persistently, the Normans and the kings of England. Llywelyn ap Gruffudd (r. 1246–82) was the first of these native princes to be officially acknowledged by the English sovereign as the Prince of Wales – a title granted by Henry III (r. 1216–72) in the treaty of Montgomery (1267). However, when Henry's son, Edward I (r. 1272–1307) summoned Llywelyn to Westminster in 1276, Llywelyn refused to comply. Edward thereupon declared him deposed and Llywelyn was finally slain by the English after a battle near Builth in 1282. His brother, Prince Dafydd ap Gruffudd, surrendered and was executed a year later in Shrewsbury. Edward I had finally subdued the turbulent Welsh and by the Statute of Wales enacted at Rhuddlan (1284) "transferred wholly and entirely to the king's dominion the land of Wales and its inhabitants".

On 25 April 1284 Edward Plantagenet (later Edward II) was born to Eleanor of Castile in the castle at *Caernarfon built by his father. According to Welsh legend Edward I immediately presented his infant son to the Welsh chieftains in hypocritical fulfilment of his promise that they should have a prince "who could not speak a word of English". One embellishment of the legend is that Edward, holding the royal baby aloft to the assembled chieftains, proclaimed in Welsh "*Eich dyn*",

literally "This is your man", with the implication that this was to be their countryman and
their king. However, an entirely contradictory
story asserts that the Prince of Wales's motto,
"*Ich dien*" ("I serve"), surmounted by a plume
of ostrich feathers, was first adopted by Edward II's grandson the Black Prince. He
claimed to have found it inscribed below the
plume of ostrich feathers on the helmet of the
king of Bohemia, who was killed on the battlefield at Crécy. (The king of Bohemia was
serving at the time as a volunteer in the French
army.) Whichever of these stories is true, the
motto and the feathers have remained the
symbol of the English Princes of Wales – a
title conferred by tradition, but not by law, on
the sovereign's eldest son. The conferment is
sometimes accompanied, or later followed, by
an investiture at Caernarfon castle. The Queen
conferred the title on HRH Prince Charles in
1958 and he was invested at Caernarfon in
1969.

Princess Royal A prefix often bestowed
on the eldest, or only, daughter of the sovereign, for her lifetime. It is neither a rank nor
precisely a title, but more akin to the prefix
"Right Honourable" used by Privy Councillors. It is bestowed by royal declaration, specifically a warrant under the *sign manual,
and at the discretion of the sovereign. Princess
Mary, daughter of Charles I, was the first
princess known to use the title, but in her case
it was unofficial, possibly introduced to distinguish her from nonroyal European nobles who
bore the title "prince" or "princess"; she is not
thought to have been called Princess Royal
until 1642, when she went to Holland to join
her husband the Prince of Orange. In Britain
the prefix was first officially bestowed on
Princess Louise, daughter of Edward VII, in
1905. There may only be one Princess Royal
at a time, so a daughter of a past sovereign
must die before the daughter of a current sovereign can be declared Princess Royal. The
first daughter born to a reigning sovereign
may become Princess Royal from birth. The
most recent Princess Royal was Princess Mary
(1897–1965), only daughter of George V,
who received the title in 1932.

prisons Buildings for housing convicted
criminals, who are serving sentences or awaiting sentencing, and people who have been re-
manded in custody to await trial. The essential
features of the English prison system to 1857
were separate confinement and hard labour.
The refusal of the British colonies to accept
more convicts led to the introduction of the
system of penal servitude, under which solitary detention covered only the first nine
months of a sentence, and the idea of remission
was brought into practice. A further major
step was the assumption of control of all prisons by central government in 1878. From 1898
hard labour was limited, and prisoners were
separated according to degree and character of
offence. In 1908 young offenders were segregated into *borstals. There are local prisons
and training prisons. The former comprise a
number of 19th-century establishments that
are now used primarily for short-term prisoners and those awaiting sentence or trial, and
they are all "closed" (i.e. physically secure).
Training prisons, mostly modern buildings,
are equipped in varying degrees for the rehabilitation of medium- and long-term prisoners. Most are closed, but some are "open" (i.e.
dependent for their security on the frequency
with which inmates are checked, and the underlying threat of transfer to a closed prison
for abuse of privilege).
The controlling body for prisons is the prison
department of the Home Office, for which the
Home Secretary is answerable to Parliament.
At its head is the director-general of the prison
service, who, subject to agreement by the
Home Secretary, is responsible for overall
prison policy. The day-to-day running of individual prisons is in the hands of prison governors, and their staff.

private Bill *See* Bill.

Private Eye A satirical weekly magazine,
commonly known as the *Eye*, founded
in 1961 by William Rushton (1937–).
Rushton belonged to a generation of accomplished satirists who in the 1960s created
the taste for irreverent, anti-Establishment
wit. Among the *Eye*'s earliest contributors was
the cartoonist Gerald Scarfe (1936–). The
magazine quickly became a cult among the

young, but has nonetheless survived to achieve the status of a national institution, comparable to *Le Canard Enchaîné* in France. In 1963 Rushton resigned the editorship to Richard Ingrams (1937–), who skilfully maintained the *Eye*'s spirit and style, as well as its undergraduate-magazine layout, while adapting to changing circumstances in the 1970s and 1980s. Ingrams, who resigned in 1985, gives "litigation" as his recreation in *Who's Who*, a reflection of the fact that the *Eye* has sometimes seemed about to founder in a sea of libel writs. On these occasions – most famously, the action for criminal libel brought by Sir James Goldsmith in 1976 but withdrawn the next year – devoted readers have sometimes come to its aid with generous donations.

The *Eye* has often proved itself to be extremely well-informed on the political establishment and the world of big business, as well as having a sharp ear for any rumour of scandal among the rich and famous. Some of its witticisms have proved to be remarkably enduring. Prime ministers' spouses have been the target for long-running and popular series: "Mrs Wilson's Diary" and "Dear Bill" (about Denis Thatcher) have been published in book form.

private member's Bill　*See* Bill.

Privy Council　A body that has been in existence for centuries to advise the monarch. Its members are leading public figures and citizens of those Commonwealth countries that retain the monarchy; in this way all British Cabinet members both past and present, the Archbishop of Canterbury, Speaker of the House of Commons, Lords of Appeal, the Lord Chief Justice, retired High Court judges, and high-ranking ambassadors are members. The Privy Council now exercises certain residual advisory and appellate powers. For instance it advises the sovereign to approve Orders in Council, which become valid by virtue of the sovereign's prerogative powers (*see* royal prerogative) as well as under statutory powers. Orders in Council concern such matters as the granting of royal charters of incorporation, and altering the government of a colony. There is a distinction between an Order in Council, made when the sovereign is present, and an order of the Council, which is an order made by the Privy Council in the sovereign's absence. Indeed the Queen is barred from certain Privy Council committees: prerogative committees concerned with such things as legislation in the Channel Islands and Isle of Man, and such statutory committees as those concerned with the universities of Oxford and Cambridge and Scottish universities. The most important committee is the *Judicial Committee of the Privy Council. Special committees may be set up to consider specific matters, such as the one in 1957 on telephone tapping. The Privy Council also plays an advisory role when royal proclamations are made.

The institution originates in the medieval *curia regis* (king's council), which by the 13th century had become the Privy Council, a recognized body whose members were paid for their services. The king was not usually present at its deliberations. It virtually ruled the country when a monarch was weak, but under Henry VII, for example, it merely approved royal policies. With the Tudors it acquired great importance, wielding legislative, executive, and judicial powers in both civil and criminal cases. (The notorious Star Chamber was a Privy Council institution that investigated political offences.) In the 17th century the Privy Council's influence declined (it ceased to exist during the Interregnum of 1649–60). Nevertheless, in the 18th century it was again the chief repository of executive power.

In 1404 it had only 19 members; in the 17th century around 50; today about 380. A quorum is three, however, and most business is discharged by four to six members (usually Cabinet ministers) who meet in the Queen's presence and by tradition stand throughout the session. Privy Council meetings are usually held at Buckingham Palace, but can take place wherever the Queen may be. Privy Councillors carry the prefix "Right Honourable" before their names, usually abbreviated to "Rt. Hon." There is a separate Privy Council for Northern Ireland.

Privy Purse, Keeper of the　An officer of the royal household who deals with the sovereign's expenses. His responsibilities include the maintenance of the royal palaces (interiors only) and private estates, making charitable donations and paying subscriptions, paying the salaries of the royal officers and servants, and corresponding with the sovereign's solicitors, the Crown Estate departments, and the Department of the Environment. He is also responsible for the Queen's thoroughbred studs and Ascot racecourse. A further duty is the administration of the *Duchy of Lancaster revenues and those of the *Duchy of Cornwall in the event of a Duke of Cornwall's minority or nonexistence. Other offices supervised by him are Pages of Honour and *Military Knights of Windsor; he is also the secretary of the *Royal Victorian Order and one of the three royal trustees for the reception of the civil-list monies. In the past he has met any deficits arising from an inadequate civil list. His department consists of the Privy Purse office, the Treasurer's office, and the Royal Almonry. The Keeper of the Privy Purse is the descendant of the medieval sovereign's domestic financial officers. In its modern form the post dates from the early 19th century. At the coronation in 1953 the then Keeper, Lord Tyron, carried a real "Privy Purse", which became his property afterwards. Formerly it would have contained 100 silver coins, which would have been distributed en route as "largesse".

prize court A court established to decide (in accordance with the rules of international law) questions relating to prize, i.e. ships or goods that, in time of war, have been captured by the forces of a belligerent power. Originally, prize courts were specially created during wartime by a royal commission under the Great Seal (*see* Lord (High) Chancellor), but in 1925 the *High Court of Justice was constituted a standing prize court. Its jurisdiction in prize is exercised by the *Admiralty Court, and appeals on questions of prize go from that court to the *Judicial Committee of the Privy Council.

Probate, Divorce, and Admiralty Division *See* High Court of Justice.

probation Placing a person who has been convicted of a criminal offence under the supervision of a probation officer to assist him in re-establishing himself in the community. A court may make a probation order in respect of any offender over the age of 17 convicted of any offence except those carrying a fixed sentence, provided that the offender agrees and that his character, the nature of his crime, and the circumstances of the case make this seem an appropriate course. The system is used particularly for first offenders and for young or elderly offenders who appear to the court to be in need of support. During the period of probation (one to three years) the offender must comply strictly with the conditions specified in the order. These will relate to such standard matters as place of residence and regular reporting to the probation officer; and the order may also impose certain special requirements, such as submission to medical treatment. A person who commits any new offence while on probation may be punished for his original offence; and a person who breaches any condition of his probation may also be punished.

THE PROMS *Sir Henry Wood, conductor at the Promenade Concerts for almost half a century. Drawing by H. Wiener, 1938.*

Proms, the The London Henry Wood Promenade Concerts, a series of concerts held each year in London for which inexpensive tickets are available to people willing to stand. In former times, audiences would stroll about, or "promenade" as they listened to the music at such concerts. The modern Proms date from 1895, when Robert Newman established the series at the Queen's Hall under the baton of Henry Wood, with whom the concerts have continued to be associated. "Proms" had previously been held in London at the former Vauxhall and Ranelagh Gardens in the 18th century, and at the *Royal Opera in the 19th. When the Queen's Hall was destroyed by a bomb in 1941, the Proms moved to the Royal Albert Hall. There, from mid-July to mid-September, a wide range of serious music, old and new, is performed by various orchestras, conductors, and soloists. Every concert is broadcast by the *BBC, and some are also televised. The last night of the Proms, devoted exclusively to the music of British composers, has become a popular British institution. During the second half – which always includes Elgar's "Land of Hope and Glory", Parry's "Jerusalem", and Wood's "Fantasia on British Sea-Songs" – the cavernous Royal Albert Hall resounds to the participation of the enthusiastic audience, especially that of the "promenaders", many of whom queue for days for the privilege of taking part.

prorogation of Parliament *See* Parliament.

Provos *See* Irish nationalism.

public Bill *See* Bill.

public footpaths An extensive network of footpaths and bridleways throughout the country, providing legal rights of way across privately-owned land. Established when the countryside was more populous and most local journeys were made on foot or horseback, these paths are now used largely for recreation. County councils are responsible for opening and closing them, for signposting them, and for maintaining access to them. However, many paths are seldom used and it is left to such groups as the Ramblers' Association to maintain the legal right of way, which can be lost on grounds of disuse. More recently, the closure of some railway lines has provided new routes for footpaths along the abandoned tracks, while on a grander scale, a number of long-distance paths have been opened – 13 in England and Wales and 3 in Scotland. These include the Pennine Way, the *Ridgeway, and *Offa's Dyke. Local authorities work in conjunction with the *Countryside Commission to signpost the routes and to provide route maps and guidebooks.

public house The public house, or pub, developed from the taverns and alehouses of the past. These required a licence from a local magistrate and since the number of such establishments licensed was limited it was possible to make a reasonable living as a tavern-keeper. During the 18th and 19th centuries, however, the availability of cheap gin, the opening of tea and coffee houses, and eventually of beer shops, meant that alehouses and taverns had to keep pace with growing competition. Originally looking like cottages or houses, pubs were forced to imitate the gin shops, with their large windows and welcoming lighting. The removal of the duty on beer in 1830 and the increasing willingness of magistrates to grant licences enabled pubs in grander styles to proliferate around market squares, along main highways, by docks and barracks, and in the new seaside resorts. The old coaching inns usually held the prime sites; however, many of these became hotels, providing only limited drinking facilities. Many others gradually became little more than pubs, sometimes including a restaurant. To attract more customers publicans, or more often the breweries who controlled the pubs, built smoke rooms, parlours, and snugs, as well as large public rooms, later used for music-hall entertainment or meetings, as newspaper rooms, or as billiard saloons. With the rise of working-class living standards in the 1870s, particularly in industrial towns, pubs grew into gin palaces adorned with carved mahogany, gleaming brasswork, engraved mirrors, and tiles and murals, all brilliantly lit by gas.

These days most pubs are tied houses, that is, they are owned by a brewery, which rents the house to a landlord. The brewery is responsible for maintaining the premises and the landlord is obliged to buy most of his stock from the brewery. In some cases tied houses have a manager, who is paid a salary. A few pubs are free houses – the landlord owns the building and can obtain his supplies wherever he chooses. The laws relating to pubs are complicated and strictly applied. The landlord must have an on-licence (as opposed to an off-licence) to sell drink for consumption on the premises. Such licences are granted and renewed at special magistrates' courts (brewster sessions) held every February. In England strict opening hours apply in the middle of the day and in the evening and it is an offence to sell or consume drinks outside these periods. It is also an offence for the licensee not to open during ascribed hours, although he or she does have the right to refuse to serve anyone and does not have to give any reason for this decision. In Wales a few counties are "dry", that is, the pubs are closed on Sundays, and periodically referenda are held to decide whether counties remain "wet" or "dry". In Scotland strict licensing hours have been abandoned. Significantly, this seems to have had an effect in reducing alcoholism and general drunkenness.

Pubs play a significant part in national life, particularly in towns and village centres, and the concept of the traditional English pub – the quaint oak-beamed country inn or the friendly "local" – has become a national institution. In fact there are as many kinds of pub as there are communities – city pubs specializing in lunches for businessmen; large "road houses" providing restaurant-style meals; modern pubs catering for young people, with juke boxes, live music, and electronic games; and there have been significant changes in the character of pubs over the past few years. Once a place where men went to drink beer, the pub has become a more general meeting point and place of entertainment. Women are more willing to go into pubs unaccompanied, rules on the admission of children have been relaxed, and most pubs serve food. Drinking habits have also changed, with a great increase in consumption of lager, cider, wines, vodka, and even bottled water. At the other extreme, the efforts of the Campaign for Real Ale (*see* beer) have also had an effect in halting the

trend towards pressurized keg beer and reintroducing more traditional brews. Despite these changes, the pub remains an essential part of Britain's heritage, although the idea that it is somehow a greater national institution than, say, the French café or the American bar is, perhaps, a national illusion.

Public Record Office (PRO) The national depository of government papers, selected archives, and legal documents to be permanently preserved. It was established by Act of Parliament in 1838 in order to save important government papers, which were then held in damp storerooms and in danger of rotting away (*see* Master of the Rolls). In 1958 the Public Records Act transferred the responsibility of records to the Lord Chancellor's office, with a civil servant, the Keeper of Public Records, as administrative head of the PRO. In 1967 a further Act limited delay of the release of documents to 30 years, with few exceptions. Documents are classified by their source and selected from the government's huge output, firstly by each departmental records officer and subsequently by the inspecting officers of the PRO. The total archive now stretches to some 135 kilometres (84 miles) of material, with 2.5 kilometres (1.5 miles) being added each year. Holders of a reader's ticket may view documents at the London reading rooms in Chancery Lane, Portugal St, and the main centre at Kew. With a budget of £9.3 million in 1984–85 and 400 staff, the PRO carries out skilled conservation work on old documents, such as *Domesday Book.

public schools Certain independent schools providing secondary education for fee-paying pupils in the 13–18 age range. They are privately financed (whereas in other countries the term "public" school indicates a state-funded institution). Many developed from an original status as charitable endowed foundations or grammar schools, establishments open to the public, hence "public schools" – which in earlier centuries were contrasted with "private schools", run as profit-making ventures by their masters or proprietors. The Clarendon Commission (1861), set up to inquire into the country's major endowed schools, recognized nine as "public schools": *Eton, *Harrow, *Winchester, Westminster, St Paul's, Rugby, Shrewsbury, Merchant Taylors', and Charterhouse. The term was already being more broadly applied, however. There are now approximately two hundred, the present criterion being no more than the head's membership of the Headmasters' Conference. They include a number of girls' schools established in the 19th century, for example, **Cheltenham Ladies' College** (founded 1853), **Roedean** (1865), and **Wycombe Abbey** (1896).

Although several public schools had existed for centuries previously, the "public-school system" as it came to be recognized emerged after the mid-19th century, mainly through the example of Thomas Arnold, headmaster of Rugby School (1828–42). Rugby – and its subsequent followers – were to be schools for "Christian gentlemen", and the education of the future leaders of the professions, services, and Church became a matter of character-building as much as teaching. Great emphasis fell on instilling religion and on discipline: the latter was maintained to a large degree by senior pupils themselves, through the **prefect system** which Arnold adopted. The balance of privilege and obligation also included **fagging**, by which junior boys carried out menial duties for their seniors. This has now almost entirely lapsed, along with many of the harsher aspects of former public-school regimes. Competition is still fostered through the house system, numerous school prizes, and team games; and prefects remain, though largely for administrative purposes.

Most public schools remain boarding schools (with the exception of a number in London); and the majority are single-sex, although some boys' schools now have mixed sixth forms (e.g. Charterhouse). While there exist certain assistance schemes and scholarships to gifted children, the fees are generally very high. Opponents of public schools insist that they are socially divisive and a preserve of the wealthy: some advocate depriving them of their charitable status. In their defence it is held that the scope and choice of education is widened by their existence, and that they retain traditions and standards elsewhere often receding.

The phrase and usage of the **old school tie** arose from the loyalty of ex-pupils to their public schools and to one another's interests in working life. This might also be called the **old boy network** (a phrase now used more widely to indicate common assistance among former members of any particular institution). The "old school tie" is far more common as an expression than as an actual item worn; and there are now fewer circumstances than previously in which the indication of public-school membership might be of immediate use.

public sector borrowing requirement (PSBR) *See* national debt.

pub names The names of public houses today still serve the purpose for which they were originally devised: to distinguish between two or more inns or taverns situated in close proximity. They are also an invaluable aid when giving directions and provide a wealth of information about local history and legends. A pub in Uxbridge that was the scene of talks between the royalists and Parliament in 1645 is now known as the **Crown and Treaty**; the **Haycock** at Wansford in Cambridgeshire derives its name from a legend about a local man, Drunken Barnaby, who fell asleep on a haystack and woke up to find himself floating down the River Nene on his impromptu bed. Some pub names crop up in almost every town, notably the patriotic **George and Dragon**. There are those relating to royalty, such as the **King's Head**, the **Crown**, and the **Royal Standard**; many more in this category refer to heraldic emblems such as the **White Hart**, the **Red Lion**, the **Blue Boar**, and the **Rising Sun**. Charles II's escape from the battle of Worcester (*see* Oak Apple Day) is immortalized in the many pubs that go by the name of the **Royal Oak**; the Wars of the Roses, in which the opposing sides selected red and white roses as their emblems, gave us the **Rose and Crown**. Other common inn signs have religious connotations: the **Angel**, the **Seven Stars**, and the **Bell** are all still popular. Sport is another recurrent theme, producing such names as the **Cricketers**, the **Fox and Hounds**, the **Bull** (from bull-baiting). Then there are signs connected with farming, such as the **Plough**, or with a local trade, as in the **Bricklayer's Arms**, or with transport, as in the **Railway**, the **Ship**, and the **Coach and Horses**; the list of associations is endless. The origins of many pub names bear no relation to their present meaning. The **Bag o' Nails** is a corruption of **Bacchanales**, relating to the god of wine Bacchus; the **Pig and Whistle** evolved from a dialect word for a mug or pail (pig) and a drinking toast (wassail); the **Dog and Bacon** at Horsham refers to the nearby Dorking Beacon; and the **Elephant and Castle** is believed to be a corrupted version of the "Infanta of Castille", who was once engaged to Charles I. The publican's sense of humour is sometimes reflected in the picture on his inn sign or in such punning names as **Nobody Inn, Listen Inn**, and **Never Inn**. Some pub names have more than one meaning: the **Greyhound** may refer to sport, a royal emblem, or a fast mailcoach, the **Anchor** has obvious seafaring connections but is also a religious symbol signifying hope, and the ***Green Man** has been taken to represent *Robin Hood, the pagan figure of Jack-in-the-Green, or simply a forester. Other names have lost their meaning with the passage of time: the **Halfway House** may no longer be halfway along the main route between two towns and the **New Inn** may be two or three hundred years old.

Puck *See* Robin Goodfellow.

puisne judge An ordinary judge of the *High Court of Justice ("puisne", pronounced "puny", is from Anglo-French, "born later", i.e. junior). A puisne judge is appointed by the Crown, acting on the advice of the Lord Chancellor, from among barristers of at least ten years' standing. He is knighted on his appointment, but is referred to as "Mr Justice A ... " or (in law reports, etc.) "A . . . , J.". Under the Act of Settlement 1701, a puisne judge holds office for life, unless removed by the Crown in response to an "address" from both Houses of Parliament (and possibly, though this is uncertain, for any serious misconduct not resulting in an address). There is now, however, a compulsory retiring age of 75; and the Lord Chancellor has power to declare a judge's office vacant earlier, on grounds of physical or mental incapacity. The declaration must be supported by medical evidence, and agreed to by the head of the judge's Division. Puisne judges may also be required to sit in the *Court of Appeal.

Punch The oldest and best-known humorous magazine in the English language, first published in 1841. It was jointly conceived by the illustrator Ebenezer Landells (1808–60) and the journalist and playwright Henry Mayhew (1812–87). The latter was coeditor with Mark Lemon (1809–70) and Joseph Stirling Coyne (1803–68) in *Punch's* first year, but then Lemon, whose successful plays were keeping the financially ailing magazine afloat, assumed sole control, which he retained for 29 years. In this time he turned *Punch* into an influential organ with an unrivalled status as a comic periodical free from the violence and coarseness that characterized most early 19th-century humorous journalism. Two early series contributed greatly to *Punch's* popularity: "Mrs Caudle's Curtain Lectures" (1845) by Douglas Jerrold (1803–57) and the "Book of Snobs" (1846–47) by William Makepeace Thackeray (1811–63). A tradition begun in Lemon's day and still maintained is the regular dinner attended by the inner circle of staff and contributors at which the content of the next week's issue is decided. The table around which these deliberations are held bears the carved signatures of many of the great modern humorists.

The name "Punch" is derived from the traditional puppet character. (The second part of the title "or the London Charivari" alludes to a satirical journal published in Paris since 1832.) The famous drawing of Mr Punch by Richard Doyle (1824–83) was adopted as the magazine's cover in 1849 and retained until 1956.

Punch's character in the early 20th century was largely determined by (Sir) Owen Seaman (1861–1936), outstanding writer of light verse, who was editor from 1906 to 1932. A more controversial editorship (1953–57) was that of Malcolm Muggeridge (1903–), who attempted to restore to *Punch* something of its 19th-century role as a leader of opinion. Muggeridge was succeeded by Bernard Hollowood (1910–), whose 11-year editorship

(1957–68) re-established *Punch*'s character as a primarily humorous magazine.

Punch and Judy A puppet show, usually held in the open air, once a common sight on the streets of British towns, but now confined largely to seaside resorts. The hand puppets are manipulated by the puppeteer, or showman, inside a tall, striped canvas booth, with an opening for the stage. The story enacted by Punch and Judy has developed from the resources available – since the puppeteer could handle only two characters at any time – and is full of fighting and beating, to which hand puppets are particularly suited. Punch is a cruel character who still retains his humped back and hook nose. He is merciless to his wife Judy (the name is probably a corruption of 'Joaney'), eventually killing her along with various other victims, such as a baby, who is thrown out of the window. Punch eventually meets his doom, usually by being eaten by a crocodile, hanged, or taken by the Devil (a shadow of earlier *mystery plays). Punch's dog Toby (always a real dog) sits at the side of the booth throughout the performance. When, in 1962, the 300th anniversary of Punch and Judy was celebrated at St Paul's

PUNCH AND JUDY *Spectators watching a show on Weymouth beach, Dorset.*

Church, Covent Garden, London, some 50 showmen attended with their dogs.

punting The propelling of a flat-bottomed square-ended boat of shallow draught by means of a long pole. Punts date back to at least the 15th century when they were used to navigate the fens and marshes of eastern England. Popular as a summer pastime in Victorian England, punting as a sport dates from the late 18th century. A print of 1793 shows Thames watermen holding a punting race in honour of the Prince of Wales's birthday. The Thames Punting Club was formed in 1885 and that same year it organized the first amateur punting championship. It remains the sport's governing body to this day.

The method of propulsion appears deceptively simple: the punter stands at one end of the boat, usually the back, and angles his pole into the river bed. By leaning on it he propels the punt forward. However, this is far from easy to do gracefully and many novices have been faced with the embarrassing choice of abandoning the pole or hanging on to the pole and parting company with the punt!

Racing punts are narrower and longer than those used for leisure. The pole used in racing can be up to 4.3 metres (14 feet) long and has a metal fork on the end. The punting championships are held on the River Thames at Laleham over a measured course of 1.2 kilometres (0.75 miles). They involve passing a post called a ryepeck, reversing round it and getting back to the start. There are singles, doubles, and mixed doubles races. The world speed record, 12.9 kph (8 mph), was set by a Mr Rixon in 1896 and this is likely to remain unbeaten as the condition of most river courses has seriously deteriorated since then.

Punting is not a widespread pastime, being practised almost exclusively on the Thames, and especially on the rivers at Oxford and Cambridge. By tradition, punters stand at the platform end at Cambridge and the opposite end at Oxford.

Puritans A Protestant movement that arose in the 16th century to press for more radical reform of the Church of England, particularly its "purification" by the removal of what they believed to be the survival of Cath-

PUNTING *A popular summer pastime: punting on the Backs, in Cambridge.*

olic practices in reformed churches. Puritans were inspired by the ideas of such European reformers as John Calvin (1509–64). They first came to prominence during the reign of Elizabeth I, whose reforms of the Church (e.g. the 1559 Book of Common Prayer) did not go far enough for some Protestants. Demands for presbyterian government of the Church went unheeded and during the 1570s and 1580s the movement grew in strength. Puritan hopes of reform after the accession of James I in 1603 came to nought; one group of Puritans who went to Holland in 1607 later sailed for America aboard the *Mayflower* to found the

Plymouth Colony on Cape Cod in 1620. Archbishop Laud was staunchly opposed to Puritanism and tried to reintroduce some elements of pre-Reformation liturgy and to enforce uniformity within the Church. This oppression gave Puritanism an increased momentum and with the summoning of the Long Parliament in 1640, the Puritans were seen to have acquired numbers that made them a real political force, which might succeed in imposing some of their ideas on the Anglican Church. The Westminster Assembly, convened in 1643 to reform the English Church, had only partial and short-lived success in introducing presbyterian government, similar to that established in Scotland. But the Puritans were divided, broadly between the Presbyterians and those who favoured congregational church government – the Independents. Cromwell, an Independent with the backing of the army, purged Parliament of Presbyterians in 1648. Thereafter, a variety of more radical religious factions emerged; the Levellers, the Diggers, and the extremist Fifth Monarchy Men soon died out, but the *Quakers survived. After the Restoration of 1660, Puritans of all shades were outmanoeuvred by supporters of less radical principles, and episcopacy was reintroduced. In the 1660s the terms "nonconformist" or "dissenting" were used to describe the various Puritan factions (*see* Nonconformists). Puritan ideals were embodied in many of the Nonconformist churches that later sprang up.

Q

Quakers (Society of Friends)   Members of the worldwide Christian movement, founded in England by George Fox (1624–91), the son of a Leicestershire weaver. In the 1640s and 1650s Fox had several revelations that convinced him of his mission to communicate the "inner light" of Christ's salvation. In his outdoor sermons, he minimized the value of the creeds, sacraments, and other features of the established Church, and was well known for interrupting church services and arguing with the minister. Fox soon drew considerable numbers of followers, who refused to pay tithes or to take legal oaths on the Bible. Fox was imprisoned several times; arraigned at Derby in 1650, he told a judge that he should "quake" at the name of the Lord, and the name "Quaker" was at once given to him. About 450 Quakers died during this period as a result of incarceration. Another famous Quaker, William Penn, left England in 1682 for America, where he founded Pennsylvania. He was assisted by Robert Barclay, whose

Apology (1676) contains a classic exposition of Quaker theology. During the 18th century, Quakers were prominent in pressing for social reforms, such as the abolition of slavery; this tradition was continued in the 19th century by the prison reformer Elizabeth Fry (1780–1845) and others. Quakers maintained their traditional pacifism during the wars of the 20th century, opting instead to organize relief for the victims.

Quaker meetings are not led by a minister but consist of essentially silent fellowship with spoken contributions from members as they feel moved. Administrative meetings dispense with formal officers as far as possible and decisions are arrived at by consensus. Affairs concerning each congregation, or "meeting", are conducted by a "preparative meeting"; certain matters devolve to the regional "monthly meeting", comprising usually between four and eight "meetings". Most of the routine national business is conducted by the monthly Meeting for Sufferings, which is held in London and dates from 1675. The principal governing body is the London Yearly Meeting. The three national subject committees – home service, peace, and social responsibility – consider a range of spiritual topics relevant to Quakers, and wider social issues. There are currently some 444 places of worship, often called meeting houses, and over 18,000 members in Britain.

quango   A shortened form of quasi-autonomous nongovernmental organization. A quango is an advisory, academic, or judicial public agency that functions independently of government but depends on a government department for all or part of its funds. Quangos are set up when it is thought that a specific task is best handled by a panel of salaried experts and interested parties rather than by civil servants and central government. Quangos can exert considerable influence and vary in size from the *United Kingdom Atomic Energy Authority to such tiny bodies as the Inquiry into Human Fertilization. Important new quangos include the eight new bodies that manage the aspects of London's administration remaining after the abolition of the GLC (1986). In 1984 some 1680 quangos were estimated to have spent over £7 billion and to have employed 100,000 people. During the 1980s their numbers have been reduced.

quarter days The days that traditionally mark the quarters of the business year. In England and Wales these are *Christmas Day (25 December), *Lady Day (25 March), *Midsummer Day (24 June), and *Michaelmas (29 September). The Scottish quarter days are *Candlemas (2 February), *Whit Sunday, *Lammas (1 August), and *Martinmas (11 November). Their greatest significance was and still is in contracts between landlord and tenant, being the days on which quarterly rents and other charges become due and on which tenure agreements begin or expire. *Fairs were traditionally held at Michaelmas and Martinmas; they were often the occasions on which farmers hired their servants and labourers for the coming year.

quarter sessions Courts which, until 1972, shared with *assizes the trial of indictable offences (the more serious crimes). They consisted either of the lay magistrates for a county (see justice of the peace) meeting at quarterly intervals under a legally qualified chairman or, in some cities and boroughs, of a barrister sitting alone under the style of *recorder. They were replaced in 1972 by the *Crown Court.

Queen's Bench Division See High Court of Justice.

Queensberry Rules See boxing.

Queen's Birthday The date of the Queen's natural birthday is April 21. The Union flag is hoisted on government and public buildings from 8 am to sunset; it is one of the Red Letter Days when judges of the Queen's Bench Division wear scarlet robes at sittings. The latest Queen's Awards to Industry are also announced on this day.
The Queen's official birthday is a moveable feast but is usually celebrated on a Saturday about the middle of June (before 1958 the second Thursday in June). It is associated with the *trooping the colour ceremony by the Household Division, a ceremony that originally took place on the monarch's natural birthday. Edward VII (r. 1901–10) instituted the tradition of an official birthday in early summer because his own birthday was in No-

vember, when the weather was unlikely to be fine for this colourful event. The Queen's official birthday also sees the issue of the *Birthday honours list, one of the two major such announcements in the year (the other being the *New Year's honours list).

Queen's Counsel (QC) A *barrister or (in Scotland) *advocate who has been appointed one of Her Majesty's counsel by letters patent granted by the Queen on the recommendation of the Lord Chancellor or Secretary of State for Scotland. (When the monarch is male, the rank changes automatically to **King's Counsel** or **KC**). He is also known as a "silk" (and the process of becoming a QC as "taking silk") because he exchanges his gown of stuff for one of silk. QCs are also referred to as leading counsel because they are, by convention, assisted by a barrister who has not taken silk (a "junior", however senior in length of practice). It follows that his work becomes concentrated on the more important cases. The rank originated in England during the 16th century, and entailed appointees in assisting the *Law Officers in Crown work. Since around 1800, however, it has been one purely of eminence, awarded to successful practitioners (of standing and experience). In Scotland, the rank was originally conferred only on the Law Officers and the Dean of Faculty (see Faculty of Advocates), but from 1897 it became available to all advocates. A separate roll for Northern Ireland was created in 1921.

Queen's Flight A pool of aircraft maintained by the Ministry of Defence for the use of the Queen, the Queen Mother, the Duke of Edinburgh, and the Prince of Wales, stationed at RAF Benson in Oxfordshire. Other members of the royal family use the aircraft for certain official duties, as do the Prime Minister, senior ministers, senior officers of the armed forces, and visiting heads of state. The King's Flight (as it then was) was inaugurated by Edward VIII in 1936. The aircraft now used are three Hawker Siddeley Andover passenger transports and two Wessex helicopters. Two of the Andovers were replaced in early 1986 by British Aerospace 146-100 long-range jet aircraft. In the past the Andovers have been used only for internal flights and European trips; a VC 10 has been chartered for longer flights. The aircraft bear a badge consisting of the Crown over a cipher EⁿR in red, with "The Queen's Flight" in white on a blue scroll underneath it. Royal flight routes, called "purple corridors", are planned with extra safety precautions: they are 16 kilometres (10 miles) wide and 1219 metres (4000 feet) deep, all other planes are barred from the route for 30 minutes either side of the royal plane's passage. The Queen and the Prince of Wales, as sovereign and heir apparent, never fly on the same aircraft together.

Queen's Gallantry Medal A decoration instituted in 1974 and conferred on civilians and service personnel of either sex for exemplary acts of bravery.

Queen's Proctor An office (usually held by the *Treasury Solicitor) the duties of which are to protect the public interest in matrimonial proceedings, particularly petitions for divorce. The Proctor may be invited by the court to advise it on points of law arising in the proceedings; and if it appears to him (normally from information given by a member of the public) that material facts have been suppressed, or that there has been collusion between the parties, he may with the leave of the court intervene to prevent a decree being made absolute.

Queen's Remembrancer Originally an officer of the Exchequer (*see* Chancellor of the Exchequer) who recovered debts and penalties due to the Crown. He also had a part in the selection of a *High Sheriff, and the swearing-in of the *Lord Mayor of London. In 1875, on the replacement of the Court of Exchequer and others by the *High Court of Justice, the principal officials of which are known as masters of the Supreme Court, his title and formal functions were transferred to the senior master of the Queen's Bench Division.

Queen's speech *See* state opening of Parliament.

Queen's University of Belfast The older of the two universities in Northern Ireland (the other being the New University of Ulster, founded in 1970). In 1845 the British government made a grant of £100,000 for the building of three Queen's Colleges, at Belfast, Cork, and Galway, to form the Queen's University in Ireland (1850–79). This was strongly opposed by the Catholic bishops who wished all institutions for higher education to be denominational. In a move to pacify the Catholic hierarchy the government suppressed the Queen's University in 1879 and replaced it by the Royal University. This was unsatisfactory, being little more than an examining body to which affiliated denominational colleges could present candidates for degrees. Under the Irish Universities Act 1909, Queen's College was raised to the status of an independent university. New statutes were framed and a new governing body, the Senate, was set up; there followed a rapid growth in student numbers and in the range of courses available. In 1982 a new charter and statutes were granted.

quit rents ceremonies Two ancient ceremonies involving the token payment of rent to the Crown; they are performed by the City Solicitor in the presence of the *Queen's Remembrancer at the Royal Courts of Justice in late October. They date back more than 700 years when the Remembrancer was attached to the royal Court of Exchequer (*see* common law). One ceremony related to a plot of land held by a blacksmith in the parish of St Clement Danes for which he paid a token rent of 6 enormous jousting horseshoes and 61 nails. The *Corporation of London continued to render the quit rent after the smithy was destroyed and the same shoes and nails are solemnly counted out by the City Solicitor in front of the Queen's Remembrancer, whose only comment is "Good number". The other ceremony relates to land in Shropshire, which passed to the City through some liverymen in the 16th century; the quit rent for this involved "two knives to cut a hazel rod, the other to bend in green cheese; and . . . no other service be rendered for the land". Over the years the hazel rod became a bunch of hazel twigs which the City Solicitor attacks first with a billhook (representing the blunt knife), and then successfully with a hatchet (representing the sharp knife); to this the Queen's Remembrancer comments "Good service". The City Solicitor returns to his seat and the implements, the horseshoes, and the nails are put away safely until the following year.

R

RAC (Royal Automobile Club) Britain's oldest motoring organization. Founded in 1897 as the Automobile Club of Great Britain and Ireland, "a society for the protection, encouragement and development of automobilism", it acquired the title "Royal" in 1907 with the patronage of King Edward VII. Originally its members were an elite core of motorists but in 1901 its membership was extended with the formation of the Motor Union. Subsequently the Union broke away and was replaced in 1908 with the Associate Section, which continues to meet the motoring needs of members (numbering some 2.6 million drivers and motorcyclists in 1985). In return for an annual subscription the RAC provides radio-controlled breakdown recovery and "at home" services, route information, legal, technical, insurance and other services, and campaigns to protect motorists' interests. The founding body continues to exist and full members have access to clubhouses in Pall Mall, London, and Woodcote Park near Epsom. A major annual event is the RAC's famous *London to Brighton Veteran Car Run.

RAC Rally, International One of the world's greatest motor rallying events, held annually in November, and covering over 3200 kilometres (2000 miles) in Britain in five days and nights. The RAC Rally began in 1932, following the format of the Monte Carlo Rally with several starting points and all cars converging on a central rendezvous before heading for the finish. This style of rally continued until 1959, with the inclusion of some hill climbs and testing road sessions. Because of the dangers of driving at high speed on public roads, the format of the rally began to change in the 1960s, with "special stages" through difficult wooded roads and on racing

tracks being incorporated; speed on the open road sections became less important. The new form of the rally, together with driving conditions in mid-November, suited the Scandinavian drivers, who have been frequent winners. The Rally has a great following from the public and also the motor trade, which sees it as a vital proving ground for new vehicles, tyres, and components.

RADA *See* Royal Academy of Dramatic Art.

railways Britain's present railway network, comprising some 17,700 kilometres (11,000 miles) owes its existence largely to the skill and enterprise of Victorian engineers, although the system originated much earlier. Wooden tracks were used to carry horse-drawn wagons in mines from the Middle Ages, and by the mid-18th century there was a total of about 160 kilometres (100 miles) of such "tramways", mainly carrying coal from pitheads to nearby iron works or quays. Canal companies built tramways to link their waterways with quarries or mines. The first public railway in the world to carry general freight was the Surrey Iron Railway, opened in 1801 to connect Croydon in Surrey to the Thames at Wandsworth.

During this period the Cornish engineer Richard Trevithick (1771–1833) built the first steam-powered railway locomotive, based on James Watt's (1736–1819) steam engine. This made its inaugural run on the Penydarren Tramroad on 13 February 1804. However, Trevithick's engine was heavy and slow and it was left to colliery engineers in northern England to produce better designs. The most famous was George Stephenson (1781–1848), who opened a locomotive works at Newcastle upon Tyne. Stephenson acted as engineer in the construction of the Stockton and Darlington Railway, built principally to carry coal from the Durham coalfield to the coast. This, the first public railway employing steam locomotion, opened on 27 September 1825 with a train carrying 600 passengers pulled by Stephenson's engine *Locomotion*. In 1829 Stephenson demonstrated his engine *Rocket* to directors of the Liverpool and Manchester Railway, then nearing comple-

RAILWAYS *Navvies working at the Olive Mount cutting, c. 1830. The railway builders overcame great obstacles to complete the Manchester–Liverpool Railway.*

tion. This locomotive set new standards of speed and power, being capable of an unprecedented 56 kph (35 mph).

Stephenson's son Robert carried on his father's pioneering tradition, supervising the construction of the London and Birmingham Railway, a landmark in railway history involving 20,000 navvies; it also required numerous cuttings and embankments as well as Kilsby tunnel, which is two kilometres (one and a quarter miles) long.

However, the greatest of the Victorian railways engineers was Isambard Kingdom Brunel (1806–59). Appointed chief engineer to the Great Western Railway in 1833, he was responsible for more than 1600 kilometres (1000 miles) of railway in total, as well as several bridges, such as the Maidenhead Bridge and the Royal Albert Bridge at Saltash, near Plymouth, built to carry the Cornwall Railway across the River Tamar. One of his innovations, however, did not prove permanent: the "broad gauge" of 7 feet, which he used on the Great Western, did not supersede the standard gauge (4 feet 8.5 inches) used elsewhere.

The railways played a vital role in Britain's industrial growth during the 19th century and also introduced cheap long-distance travel to the mass of its citizens. By 1860, 16,416 kilometres (10,201 miles) of routes had been opened and railways already reached Plymouth, Holyhead, and Aberdeen; by the early 1900s – the golden era of rail – the length of rail had doubled. Thereafter the advent of the internal-combustion engine began to challenge the monopoly of the railways in transporting medium- and long-distance passengers and freight. After World War I, the railway companies regrouped to create four large conglomerates: the London Midland and Scottish Railway (LMS); the London and North Eastern Railway (LNER); the Great Western Railway (GWR); and the Southern Railway (SR). But the slow decline continued until 1947 when they were bought by the state and united under the control of the British Transport Commission. During the 1950s a programme of modernization was introduced using diesel and electric locomotives to replace steam engines. The present British Railways Board was set up in 1962 and the following year its chairman, Dr Richard Beeching, announced plans for a drastic reduction ("the Beeching axe") in the size of the rail network, with the subsequent pruning of some 12,800 kilometres (8000 miles) of branch lines. BR now accepts that it has an obligation to maintain certain services on the grounds of social need, particularly those in remote rural areas, but much of its resources are concentrated on the major inter-city routes and its commuter services around London and the other large cities.

rates A tax on property paid to local authorities. Originating in the Middle Ages, rates were regularized under Elizabeth I to finance the Poor Law (*see* welfare state), and became the means of financing the expanding responsibilities of local government in the 19th century. Rates are assessed by assigning each property a rateable value, based on the notional rent it would provide if it were let. This value takes into account such factors as the type of property, its size and location, and general amenities, such as central heating, number of bathrooms, garage, etc. Rateable values are supposed to be reviewed every five years; in fact, the interval is always longer, except in Scotland. Each year, the local authority states its rate poundage, i.e. the amount in pounds that ratepayers have to pay for each pound of rateable value. Rates have been criticized on several grounds: that they do not take into account the householder's ability to pay, that the system of assessment is too arbitrary, and that they are levied only on the householder; reforms or replacements are therefore frequently proposed. Although government grants have usually provided the majority of local authority income since the 1930s, the rates are defended by some as a guarantee of a little local independence.

real tennis An ancient and complex racket-and-ball game played on an indoor court. It originated in medieval France, possibly from a game played by monks around the edge of covered cloisters. This could explain the galleries round three sides of the court and their sloping roofs. The game was taken up by the French kings and reached the peak of its

REAL TENNIS *The playing area includes the sloping roofs (penthouses) of the galleries, which run round three sides of the court.*

popularity in the 16th century in France and England. In France it has retained its original name of *le jeu de paume*, whereas in England it has become known as "real" tennis (a corruption of "royal" tennis). The game has always had strong links with royalty: both Henry VII and Henry VIII were players and Elizabeth I was a keen spectator. Henry VIII had a court built at Hampton Court Palace, which is still in use today. Charles I played real tennis at Oxford during the Civil War. After a decline in the 18th century real tennis re-emerged with vigour in the 19th century and was introduced to other English-speaking countries. There are now 15 real tennis courts in England, 7 in the USA, 2 in Australia, but only 2 in France.

Received Pronunciation (RP) The standard pronunciation of southern British English, widely accepted throughout Britain and certain other parts of the world as more "correct" or acceptable than other accents.

353

The term "Received Pronunciation" was coined by the English phonetician Daniel Jones (1881–1967), and used by him in the first edition of his *English Pronouncing Dictionary* (1917) to denote "the accent of the public schools". Historically, RP is derived from the Middle English London accent, the language spoken by Chaucer. The desire for conformity and standardization that characterized 18th-century attitudes towards language, and later the rise of the *public schools, where upper- and middle-class children from many different regions were sent to be educated, had the effect of turning this London regional accent into a class characteristic of remarkable uniformity. For two hundred years, until about 1960, RP was the accent of most "educated" Englishmen. At the same time, the working classes in the London region developed their own independent accent (*see* Cockney). **BBC English** was a somewhat artificial diction originally used in radio broadcasting and mistaken by some for a "definitive" pronunciation. BBC announcers now have a variety of accents. RP, in fact, is no longer the only accent of the educated, and indeed, some of the respect for the neutral English of RP has transferred to the broader and more distinctive regional accents. In the meantime, RP has continued more or less unchanged and is invariably used in those dictionaries that provide a phonetic transcription to enable readers to know how to pronounce a word.

recorder A person appointed by the Crown on the advice of the Lord Chancellor to serve part-time as a judge in the *Crown Court and *county courts. He may also be invited by the Lord Chancellor to sit in the *High Court of Justice. A recorder must be a barrister or solicitor of at least ten years' standing. The Recorder of the City of London is, by contrast, a barrister appointed by the Lord Mayor and aldermen of the City to a judicial office that has existed since the 13th century. He has been a judge of the *Central Criminal Court since it was established, sitting originally as a commissioner of *assize, and now as a *circuit judge. *See also* quarter sessions.

redbrick universities Those universities founded in the late 19th or early 20th century

in the large industrial cities. A denigratory comparison was originally implied between the architecture of these institutions, many of which were constructed in red brick, and the largely stone-built colleges of Oxford and Cambridge. Manchester (1880; new charter 1903) was the first of these provincial universities, followed by Liverpool (1903; affiliated to Manchester 1884–1903), Leeds (1904; affiliated to Manchester 1887–1904), Birmingham (1900), Sheffield (1905), and Bristol (1909).

Red Ensign *See* flags.

Reformation The disintegration of the medieval Catholic Church in the 16th cen-

REFORMATION View of the burning of the bodies of Bucer and Fagius and their writings at Cambridge on the 14th of January 1557 before the University and Queen Mary's Inquisition, *from Foxe's* Acts and Monuments. *The persecution of Protestants during Mary's reign was exploited by propagandists like Foxe, helping to create a powerful myth of popular and patriotic Protestantism; the persecution seems to have caused remarkably little trouble at the time.*

tury, which led to all Britain rejecting the authority of Rome and altering many long-held beliefs and practices. In the early 16th century the moral laxity and material corruption of the Church caused resentment throughout Western Europe; its spiritual lassitude failed to satisfy the religious needs of the people. Martin Luther (1483–1546) supplied the spark that lit the fire of reform in 1519, when he attacked both financial and doctrinal abuses in his 95 Theses. The movement quickly snowballed, finding political support among the German princes but no adequate response from the Church; by the middle of the century Europe was irrevocably split between Roman Catholicism and various forms of Protestantism.

In England, Henry VIII (r. 1509–47) at first resisted change; indeed in 1521 he completed a book rejecting some of Luther's assertions, for which the pope rewarded him with the title *Fidei Defensor*, Defender of the Faith (a title still borne by the British monarch). However, in the late 1520s, Henry, already anxious about Queen Catherine of Aragon's failure to produce a male heir, became infatuated with Anne Boleyn and made strenuous efforts to obtain an annulment of his marriage from the pope. For diplomatic reasons the pope was unable to grant this; Henry responded by rejecting papal authority. A series of measures in the 1530s substituted royal for papal power over the English Church, culminating in the Act of Supremacy 1534, which declared the king to be supreme head on earth of the Church of England. It was not the king's aim to create a Protestant Church, and indeed he claimed to be upholding true and uncorrupted Catholicism. Nevertheless, the severance with Rome and the dissolution of the *monasteries (ostensibly on the grounds of laxity and corruption, in fact to bring their wealth to the Crown) invited comparisons with the continental reformation and encouraged reformers. In the late 1530s Henry permitted some Protestant-like reforms, including an English Bible (1539), in order to curry diplomatic favour with German Lutherans. Although this policy was abruptly reversed in 1540, the reformers regained influence at the very end of his reign – a crucial advantage, which placed them in control under the boy king Edward VI (r.

1547–53). Factional rivalry then resulted in a move towards the extreme Protestantism of the French theologian John Calvin (1509–64), a trend reflected in Archbishop Thomas Cranmer's two versions of the *Book of Common Prayer (1549 and 1552). However, there is doubt about how far these changes penetrated to a popular level, for Mary I (r. 1553–58) had little difficulty in re-establishing Catholic doctrine and allegiance to Rome. About 280 people, including Cranmer, were burned as heretics for resisting this and later hailed by Protestant propagandists (such as John Foxe, author of *Acts and Monuments* (1563), popularly known as the "Book of Martyrs") as victims of a vicious persecution; but at the time there was very little resentment, and the scale of this "persecution" was minuscule compared to that in mainland Europe.

Had Mary lived longer or produced an heir, the English Reformation might well have petered out. However, her death brought the moderately Protestant Elizabeth I (r. 1558–1603) to the throne. Her settlement – the reintroduction of the royal supremacy and the 1552 Prayer Book, accompanied by a rather ambiguous definition of faith in the Thirty-Nine Articles (1563) – became firmly established because her long reign provided the time for it to do so. By the end of her reign England was firmly Protestant. The religious elements of the troubles of the 17th century concerned the nature of this Protestantism; a return to Rome was out of the question.

In Scotland the course of the Reformation was crucially affected by the minority of Mary, Queen of Scots from 1542, and her absence in France from 1548. Without a firm guiding hand, rival parties were able to develop. Protestantism flourished in the 1540s, with a vernacular Bible legalized in 1543, but the old faith was not rejected. By the time the Catholic Mary returned in 1561, there were strong Catholic and Protestant parties. The latter had won an important victory in 1560 when the Scottish parliament adopted the Calvinist John Knox's *Confession of Faith*, abolished the mass, and denied papal authority; but the Catholic cause was not lost until Mary's political tactlessness resulted in her deposition and exile to

England (1567). Thus Calvinist Presbyterian Protestantism triumphed in spite of the Crown rather than under it, and in the 17th century the monarchs' attempts to impose their authority on the Church dominated Scottish history; at the same time Catholicism remained strong, especially in the *Highlands. In Ireland Anglican Protestantism was imposed by the English rulers and Scottish Presbyterianism introduced by the 17th-century plantations, while the native Irish stubbornly clung to Roman Catholicism – divisions which contributed greatly to the Irish problem in later years (see Irish nationalism).

Reformed Episcopal Church See Free Church of England.

regalia, Scottish The insignia of Scottish royalty, which includes a crown, sceptre, sword of state, and associated jewels. Known as the "Honours of Scotland", they are older than the present English regalia (see Crown jewels). Part of the existing crown may date back to the coronation of David II at Scone in 1331, earlier ones having been plundered by the English. James V had the medieval crown remodelled and enriched in 1545, using Scottish gold and even some Scottish pearls among the many gems. It consists of a gold band ornamented with fleurs-de-lis and crosses fleury, surmounted by four arches, topped by a globe and cross, and worn over a red velvet and ermine bonnet. He also caused the sceptre, a gift from the Borgia pope Alexander VI to James IV in 1494, to be refashioned. The sword of state was also a papal gift. from Michelangelo's patron Julius II in 1507. It is ornamented with gilded-silver oak leaves and acorns, Julius II's personal emblem, which are repeated in the scabbard and woven-lace sword belt.

By 1585 the regalia was in the charge of the captain of Edinburgh castle and released to Scottish nobles for openings of parliament and coronations. During the turbulent years of Charles I's reign the regalia was seized by the Covenanters (militant Scots Presbyterians) but reappeared for Charles II's coronation at Scone, the last to take place in Scotland, on 1 January 1651. Then, following Cromwell's conquest of Scotland, the regalia was secretly buried under Kinneff church, Kincardineshire (now Grampian Region), for nine years, and only returned to Edinburgh castle at the Restoration. The Act of Union of 1707, by which Scotland ceased to be a separate kingdom, meant that the "Honours" were no longer needed for ceremonial puposes, although a clause added to the 24th article of the treaty made sure they stayed in Scotland, "notwithstanding the Union". Thus the regalia was locked up in an oak chest in the Crown Room of Edinburgh castle and largely forgotten for over a hundred years. Then in 1817, under pressure from Sir Walter Scott, the chest was opened and the regalia rediscovered. In 1818 the items were exhibited, together with the 17th-century Lord Treasurer's mace, which was also found in the chest. In 1830 they were joined by jewels assumed to have been taken by James VII (James II of England) when he fled to France in 1688 (see Glorious Revolution) and later returned to George III. They consist of a collar of the Order of the Garter, a St George jewel, a St Andrew jewel from the Order of the Thistle, and a ruby and diamond ring. All have been on show to the public since then, except for the period of the two world wars, and are currently housed in Edinburgh castle.

regent The person appointed to act in the offices of the monarch if the sovereign is incapacitated, unavailable, or under 18 on succeeding to the throne. A regency remains valid until a written declaration removing the real sovereign's specific disability is made. The regent enjoys full royal powers except the right to approve bills changing the order of succession or repealing the laws that maintain Scotland's religion and Church. The declaration that the sovereign is incapacitated or unavailable must be made by at least three of the following: the sovereign's consort, the Lord Chancellor, the Speaker of the House of Commons, the Lord Chief Justice, and the Master of the Rolls. It is now customary for any regent to be the next heir to the throne provided that he or she is of age. Thus if the Queen were unavailable or incapacitated the Prince of Wales would become regent, but if both the Queen and the Prince of Wales were to die before Prince William of Wales were 18,

Prince Andrew would become regent. Some Commonwealth countries have their own regency acts, which may differ slightly from that in Britain.

The most notable regency in British history was from 1811 to 1820, when the then Prince of Wales (from 1820 George IV) was, owing to his father George III's insanity, given full kingly powers though with certain restrictions on creating peers and granting offices.

Regent's Park *See* royal parks.

registrars of births and deaths Officials responsible for keeping registers of births and deaths in the UK. In England and Wales (the position elsewhere being broadly comparable) a registrar is appointed under the Births and Deaths Registration Act 1953 for a registration subdistrict, births within which must be registered with him within 42 days of their occurring, and deaths within 5. Registration must be effected in person by the parents of a child, or by relatives of a deceased person, and they must supply the registrar with certain details and sign the register in his presence.

Registration subdistricts are grouped into registration districts, each under a superintendent registrar of births, deaths, and marriages, who maintains registers of civil marriages, and to whom registers of births and deaths are given by the registrars when completed. The registration system as a whole is controlled by the Registrar General, whose former General Register Office was merged in 1970 with the Government Social Survey Department to form the Office of Population Censuses and Surveys (*see* Population Censuses and Surveys, Office of) where copies of all original registrations are kept.

Remembrance Day The day on which the British people commemorate those who died in two world wars. Remembrance Day is now held on the Sunday nearest to 11 November, the anniversary of the armistice that ended World War I. Wreath-laying ceremonies take place at war memorials throughout the country. At the Cenotaph in London's Whitehall, the ceremony is attended by the Queen, other members of the royal family, political leaders, representatives of the armed services, ex-servicemen, and members of the public. A two-minute silence is observed from 11.00 am, which ends with the sounding of the last post and the laying of wreaths.

During the preceding weeks, many people subscribe to the Haig Fund, an appeal fund for ex-servicemen started in 1928 in memory of Earl Haig (1861–1928), commander-in-chief of British forces on the Western Front (1915–18), and organized each year by the *British Legion. In return for their donation, people receive a poppy – a symbol of the fields of Flanders, on which so many young men died in World War I.

repertory theatre A theatre company that mounts plays from a repertoire, or stock, of productions. Frank Benson pioneered repertory theatre in seasons at Stratford from 1886 to 1916. The company formed by Miss A. E. F. Horniman at Manchester from 1907 inspired the foundation of a number of "reps", among them the Liverpool Playhouse (1911) and the Birmingham Repertory Theatre (1913). The true repertory system (long regarded as the best training ground for young actors) gave way to one-week, and later two- or three-week, runs of a single play. A period of decline in both the quality and number of reps in the 1940s and 1950s was halted by the emergence of a new generation of regional companies, for example, the Belgrade Theatre, Coventry; the Haymarket, Leicester; the Octagon, Bolton; and the Royal Exchange, Manchester. Both the *National Theatre and the *Royal Shakespeare Company are repertory companies.

reserve forces Forces raised to supplement regular troops in times of national emergency. Modern reserve forces have their roots in local militia, which emerged as separate from the regular Army during the 19th century. In 1907, as part of a general reform of the Army, these local militia were reorganized as the Territorial Force, which was renamed the **Territorial Army** in 1922. In World War II these volunteers merged with the regular Army, leaving the defence of the UK in the hands of the Local Defence Volunteers (later the Home Guard), which drew upon men aged between 17 and 65 who had not been called up, and reached a force of 2,000,000 men in 1944. The Home Guard was finally disbanded in 1957 while the Territorial Army was revived in 1947 (known until 1979 as the Territorial Army Volunteer Reserve). The modern Territorial Army, 72,100 strong, provides potential support for NATO and the professional Army, alongside the Regular Reserve, which consists of about 137,700 ex-regulars. A special reserve force, the **Ulster Defence Regiment (UDR)**, operates in Northern Ireland with a strength of 7000. Other reserve forces include the Home Service Force, which is linked to the Territorial Army and guards civilian and military installations, the Royal Naval Reserve, the Royal Naval Auxiliary Service, the Royal Marines reserve, the Royal Auxiliary Air Force, and the Royal Air Force Volunteer Reserve. A number of cadet forces, with a strength of about 145,000, are also raised.

Restoration (1660)   The re-establishment of the *monarchy after the *Civil War, Commonwealth, and Protectorate. None of the various forms of government tried since the execution of Charles I (1649) had proved enduring; Charles II (r. 1660–85) was therefore crowned amid a general desire to return to normality. His restoration was in theory unconditional; he dated his reign from his father's death. Both the Anglican Church and the House of Lords were restored to their former positions, while the Act of Indemnity and Oblivion 1660 pardoned all concerned with the Civil War, except those who had signed Charles I's death warrant (the "Regicides") and a few others. Fourteen men were executed; the bodies of Oliver Cromwell (1599–1658; Lord Protector, 1653–58) and two others were exhumed and hanged as traitors at *Tyburn.
Whatever the theory, in practice the monarchy's defeat in the Civil War could not be ignored. Charles II was careful not to expose the Crown to danger by extensive use of his powers, being content to achieve his ends by manipulation rather than force. Only at the end of his reign, when faced with the need to purge his enemies after the Exclusion Crisis (1679–81; see Glorious Revolution), did he give rein to his inclinations towards independence, ruling without Parliament, supported by a pension from France (1681–85). His

brother, James II (r. 1685–88), was incapable of such subtlety; he tactlessly paraded the Crown's pretensions and was consequently quickly deposed in the Glorious Revolution.

Restrictive Practices Court   A *superior court of the UK, established by Parliament in 1956. Its functions include the making of orders prohibiting unfair consumer trade practices, and declarations as to the validity or otherwise of restrictive trade practices (*see* Office of Fair Trading). The Court consists of five judges, and up to ten lay members who have knowledge or experience of industry, commerce, or public affairs.

Retail Price Index (RPI)   A number expressing the average price of selected commodities as a percentage of their levels at a fixed base date, issued monthly by the Department of Employment. The commodities surveyed include food, clothing, energy, transport, entertainment, services, rent, and mortgage charges; they are selected to reflect the spending patterns of an average household. The first official index to measure inflation was issued in 1914 as the "cost of living" index; the RPI itself dates from 1947. While it is often argued that other indexes calculated by different rules are more accurate, the RPI is the most respected and is used in wage negotiations. 15 January 1974 is the current base date (RPI = 100).

rhyming slang   A form of *slang, associated chiefly with London's *Cockneys, in which a phrase is used to denote something that rhymes with it. Thus, a "butcher's hook" is a "look"; a "ball of chalk" is a "walk"; a person's "bowl of water" is his "daughter". Rhyming slang is complicated by the fact that the second (rhyming) part of the phrase is often omitted. Thus, "Let's have a butcher's" means "Let me have a look". Occasionally, the term rhymed with is itself a slang term. Thus, a "bubble and squeak" denotes a magistrate (a "beak"). If someone asserts that his neighbour is "lakes", he probably means "Lakes of Killarney", that is, barmy.
This extraordinary linguistic practice originated in London in the late 18th century. It has since spread, not only throughout the British Isles, but to Australia and the United

States. There are many theories about its origins. The most plausible is that it represented yet another variation of thieves' cant: the need to talk in code so that outsiders – in particular the police – could not understand what was being said. On the other hand, the role of sheer linguistic exuberance should not be underestimated. Probably both were contributing factors in the rise of rhyming slang.

Richmond Great Park *See* royal parks.

Ridgeway One of the major long-distance footpaths in Britain, the Ridgeway runs for some 137 kilometres (85 miles) from Beacon Hill, near Ivinghoe, Buckinghamshire, via the chalk ridges of the Chilterns, Berkshire Downs, and Marlborough Downs, to Overton Hill, west of Marlborough in Wiltshire. For much of the Chilterns stretch, the route follows the old *Icknield Way, passing through some beautiful beechwoods, before crossing the Thames at Streatley and reaching the open chalk downs further west. The modern footpath traces the path of the prehistoric trading route known as the Great Ridgeway. This followed upland ridges from Axmouth in Devon to East Anglia and the Wash and was of considerable economic and strategic importance from Neolithic times (4000–1800 BC) onwards. More recently, the Great Ridgeway was used as a drovers' route in the 18th century to avoid tolls on the turnpike roads. The route now provides many traffic-free miles for the walker.

riding Derived from a Danish word meaning "a third", the term riding was introduced by Viking invaders in parts of northern England around 875 AD. Each of the three divisions of the Viking kingdom of York – East Riding, North Riding, and West Riding – were represented in the parliament, or *thing*, that met at York. Smaller subdivisions of each riding were called *wapentakes*. The ridings persisted as official administrative regions until the local government reorganization of 1974 designated the new regions of Yorkshire as North Yorkshire, West Yorkshire, South Yorkshire, and Humberside.

riding the marches An annual ceremony dating back to the Middle Ages that takes place in June, July, or August in a number of towns in southern Scotland, notably Lanark, Linlithgow, Lockerbie, Peebles, and Sanquhar. The Scottish equivalent of *beating the bounds, the ceremony involves riding on horseback around the marches (borders) of the town and inspecting the boundary stones: in the days of the border wars between England and Scotland in the 14th, 15th, and 16th centuries the town boundaries frequently had to be redefined after a destructive enemy attack (such as that on Duns in 1545). The impressive and colourful procession, led by the provost and civic dignitaries, is followed by ceremonies and celebrations in the town centre. In Hawick, Selkirk, Galashiels, and some other Scottish towns the ceremony is known as common riding and takes place in early June. The common ridings of Hawick and Selkirk commemorate incidents around the time of the battle of Flodden in 1513, when thousands of Scotsmen were slaughtered by the English. Young men from both towns are supposed to have captured English banners after the battle; the processions around the boundaries are accordingly led by a standard-bearer, known in Hawick as "the Cornet".

Ripon hornblower A ceremony in the cathedral city of Ripon, Yorkshire, in which the mayor's hornblower, dressed in fawn-coloured livery and a three-cornered hat, stations himself at nine o'clock each evening at the foot of the market cross and blows four long blasts on a magnificent buffalo horn, one at each corner of the cross. A fifth blast is sounded outside the mayor's house. The custom is believed to date back to Anglo-Saxon times: the original horn, first blown in 886 during the reign of King Alfred, can still be seen on ceremonial occasions. In the Middle Ages the horn was sounded by the wakeman – a municipal officer who received an annual toll from the householders of the city in return for his protection during the hours of darkness – at the beginning of his evening vigil. The city motto, inscribed on the town hall, reads: "Unless ye Lord keep ye cittie, ye wakeman waketh in vain." In 1604 the wakeman became the first mayor of Ripon, necessitating the appointment of a mayor's hornblower, an office that has continued to this day.

RIDING THE MARCHES *Common riding at Hawick, Borders.*

RNLI *See* Royal National Lifeboat Institution.

Robert Mayer Concerts for Children An annual series of concerts specially intended for children. They are named after their founder Sir Robert Mayer (1879–1985), a German-born businessman who wished to contribute to Britain's musical life. He was encouraged by his first wife, the soprano Dorothy Moulton, who was particularly impressed by the children's concerts given in the United States by the conductor Walter Damrosch. The first concert was held on 23 March 1923 in Central Hall, Westminster, in London, and conducted by Adrian Boult and Walter Damrosch. In the following year Malcolm Sargent became the very popular conductor of the concerts, and by 1939 similar concerts were held in 30 centres throughout Britain. Mayer also founded Youth and Music, an organization that encourages an interest in music among young people. His hundredth birthday was celebrated by a concert at the Festival Hall attended by the Queen.

Robin Goodfellow (Puck) A mischievous spirit in English folklore, famous for his pranks and practical jokes. The offspring of a male fairy and a young girl, Robin Goodfellow is able to change his form at will: he uses this and his other magical powers to punish the wicked and help the good. As a household spirit he carries out the daily chores in return for a little bread and milk. The character appears in Shakespeare's play *A Midsummer Night's Dream* and in the early 16th-century work *Mad Pranks and Merry Gests of Robin Goodfellow.*

Robin Hood A medieval outlaw and popular English folk hero. The first certain reference to the legendary character appeared in 1377 in William Langland's *Piers Plowman*. The tradition has been kept alive over the centuries through ballads, plays, children's stories, and, more recently, films and television.

Robin Hood is said to have roamed the green-woods of Sherwood forest in Nottinghamshire during the reigns of Richard I (1189–99) and John (1199–1216). Making use of his skill in archery to flout the forest laws and poach the king's deer, he was nonetheless a genial and courteous robber who reputedly stole from the rich in order to give to the poor. His arch-enemy was the cruel Sheriff of Nottingham; his friends and companions included Friar Tuck, Little John, and the rest of his band of "Merry Men", and his wife or mistress Maid Marian. The various elements of the legend deal with archery contests, the adventures of individual characters, Robin's encounters with the Sheriff of Nottingham, and an assort-ment of other episodes.

However, medieval ballads, dating from about 1400, make no mention of many of the themes now associated with Robin Hood: Robin is a yeoman and not of noble birth; there is no ref-erence to Richard I or John, but to Edward II; there is no theme of English resistance to the Norman monarchy; Robin issues no directives to rob the rich to help the poor. He reveres his king and directs his hatred against the clergy and the Sheriff of Nottingham. Much of the action of these, often bloodthirsty, medieval tales takes place around Barnsdale in York-shire. Attempts to find historical models for the characters have proved unsuccessful. Robin was perhaps a member of the Hood family of yeomen who were, from the 13th century, tenants of the manor of Wakefield in Yorkshire, or the "Robert Hod, fugitive" rec-orded in the reports of the 1225 York assizes. Maid Marian is a 13th-century import from France who became associated with Robin in the 15th century via the seasonal plays and dances known as the May Games. Ballads and stories concerning such real-life rebel heroes as Hereward the Wake and Fulk fitz Wain, and such legendary ones as Adam Bell, so influ-enced the Robin Hood stories that most of the Nottingham and Sherwood forest tales were probably derived from them.

The post-medieval stories tell of Robin's death at Kirklees Priory in Yorkshire at the hands of his own aunt, who, on the pretext of letting his blood to cure a minor illness, allows him to bleed to death. Attended by Little John, Robin summons his dying strength and shoots an arrow through the open window, requesting that he be buried wherever it lands: a small mound in Kirklees Park is reputed to mark the site of his grave.

Roedean *See* public schools.

Rolling Stones A rock group that remains one of the most famous in the world more than 20 years after its formation in 1962. Its members in its best years, the 1960s, were: Mick Jagger (1944–), whose sexually ag-gressive and explicit vocal performances gave the Stones their rebellious image; Keith Rich-ard (1943–) and Brian Jones (1944–69), guitarists; Charlie Watts (1941–), drum-mer; and Bill Wyman (1941–), bass. Under the management of Andrew Oldham, the group reached the Top Ten in 1964, with "I Wanna Be Your Man". The hugely suc-cessful "Satisfaction" (1965) took them to number one in the USA. Their anti-establish-ment stance brought the Stones into frequent conflict with the authorities, who often re-acted with an exaggerated estimation of the group's evil influence. The lawless image was reinforced in 1969, when during a perfor-mance at the Altamont Festival in California, a black youth was stabbed to death by a Hell's Angel. In the same year Brian Jones died, and was replaced by Mick Taylor (1941–), who in 1974 was succeeded by Ron Wood (1947–).

The earlier music of the Stones reflected the strong influence of rhythm and blues artists, such as Bo Diddley and Muddy Waters. Though they still draw large audiences on their occasional tours, their work has not per-haps retained its early inventiveness.

Roman Britain Britain from the mid-1st century AD, when Roman armies under the emperor Claudius (r. 41–54 AD) and his leg-ates occupied most of southern Britain, to the mid-5th century AD, when the Romans finally withdrew from British shores.

Pre-Roman Britain was inhabited by tribes of Celtic-speaking peoples, many of whom may have been immigrants from Northern Europe. In about 75 BC, however, parts of southeast Britain were colonized by Germanic Belgae from Gaul, a more sophisticated people who

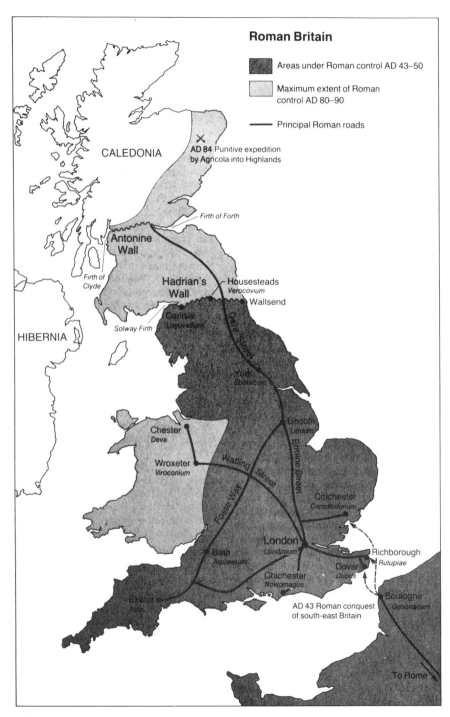

Roman Britain

■ Areas under Roman control AD 43–50

□ Maximum extent of Roman control AD 80–90

━━ Principal Roman roads

CALEDONIA

× AD 84 Punitive expedition by Agricola into Highlands

Firth of Forth

Antonine Wall

Firth of Clyde

Hadrian's Wall

Housesteads
Verocovium

Wallsend

Carlisle
Luguvallium

Solway Firth

HIBERNIA

Dere Street

York
Eboracum

Chester
Deva

Lincoln
Lindum

Wroxeter
Viroconium

Watling Street

Ermine Street

Fosse Way

Colchester
Camulodunum

London
Londinium

Bath
Aquaesulis

Richborough
Rutupiae

Dover
Dubris

Chichester
Noviomagus

Exeter
Isca

Boulogne
Gesoriacum

AD 43 Roman conquest of south-east Britain

To Rome

cleared forests for agricultural purposes. Before Caesar's arrival Britain was known in Latin as Pretannia, a name derived from the Welsh Pretani meaning "painted men", or Picts. Because Caesar mistakenly believed that Pretannia had been colonized by a Gaulish tribe called the Britanni, who lived near Boulogne, he confusingly renamed it Britannia.

Caesar's expeditions in 55 and 54 BC were probably undertaken both to gain prestige for himself (since many Romans regarded "Britain" as a sort of world's end) and to prevent the Belgae in Britain from supporting the restive elements in Roman Gaul, which he had conquered in early 55 BC. Preoccupied with keeping the peace in Gaul, he was forced to leave Britain unconquered although he encouraged British trade with the continent in wheat, cattle, gold, silver, iron, hides, and hunting dogs. Despite its indigenous wealth, no further attempt was made to conquer Britain until Claudius' successful invasion in 43 AD. By this time a powerful new colony of Belgae had taken root in Hampshire, while the rest of the area that is now England was divided between large tribes with a rich material culture and a wealthy aristocracy, each ruled by a king. The most important of these were the Belgae in the south, now united under Cunobelinus (Cymbeline), the Iceni in Norfolk, the Dobuni in the west, and the Brigantes in the northeast. Although some British kings had submitted to Caesar, Claudius met with sustained resistance from several tribes, who were eventually defeated at the battle of the Medway. Their rulers became client kings, under the patronage of the Roman emperor. The future emperor Vespasian led crushing attacks on the south, probably destroying the great *hill fort of Maiden Castle. Then followed the subjugation of Caratacus (Caradog), the son of Cunobelinus, who had gathered a rebel army in Wales. Claudius at once set about the romanization of Britain, a crucial part of which was the building of towns to provide centres for Roman government. He therefore built a new capital at Camulodunum (Colchester), with a huge temple to himself, and set up at Verulam (St Albans) the first British *municipium* (a town with Roman citizenship and therefore voting rights). Londinium (London) had become the commercial centre of Britain following Caesar's invasion and acted as a supply depot for the legions; from it radiated the earliest *Roman roads.

The new province of Britannia was administered by a succession of Roman governors, who were answerable to the emperor. Each governor's term of office lasted about five years. The first appointments were military men, the most famous of whom was Agricola, the father-in-law of the Roman historian Tacitus. The provincial finances were controlled by a procurator independent of the governor. This office was easily and often abused; resentment at the arbitrary treatment meted out by one of them added considerable fuel to a revolt in 61 AD led by Boudicca (Boadicea), queen of the Iceni, in which London and St Albans were destroyed. Boudicca had been deposed by Roman officials, her daughters raped, and the land of all the Icenian aristocracy confiscated. The first to join her revolt were the Belgae of Colchester, who were paying heavy taxes to subsidize the maintenance of Claudius' temple and whose land had been given to retired legionaries. After inflicting heavy casualties on Roman citizens (their towns were unwalled), Boudicca was defeated and the Britons never again revolted. The building of *Hadrian's Wall in the 2nd century AD, however, is an indication of the restlessness of the Picts in the north, who were to overrun Britain 200 years later.

Roman military advisers subsequently played a large part in the design of Romano-British towns, which have a greater resemblance to army camps than the other Roman towns of Europe. They were laid out on a chessboard pattern, with basilicas often big enough to hold twice a town's population, public baths, and amphitheatres. By 275 AD the general economic decline of the Roman empire meant that the towns gradually fell into disrepair, although they continued to function as units of government; the countryside, which had never been throughly romanized, then became the focus of economic activity. Life in the country was organized around the *Roman villas. From the 1st to the 4th centuries these grew in economic importance as the towns declined.

By the mid-4th century Britain was being raided by the Picts and the Scots (inhabitants of Ireland), and the Saxons were settling on the west coast. In 368 AD a Roman army could not save Britain from falling before a concerted attack by the Picts, Scots, Saxons, and Franks. In 400 Theodosius sent the Vandal general Stilicho to liberate Britain, but his success was shortlived. Such was the pressure exerted on all parts of the empire by barbarian incursions that, because the province could support no army of its own, either in terms of manpower or wealth, it became impractical to retain Britain within the empire. By 429 AD the Roman officals had also departed, leaving the Britons to govern themselves. This short period of British freedom was brought to an end in the late 5th century by the Saxon invasion.

Roman Catholic Church in UK Until the 16th century, the Church in Britain was united with the rest of Western Europe in the Catholic Church and acknowledged the authority of the pope in Rome. Henry VIII rejected this authority, and in 1534 declared himself supreme head of the *Church of England (see Reformation); divisions deepened as Protestant doctrines were introduced, especially under Edward VI (r. 1547–53); a Catholic reaction under Mary I (r. 1553–58) failed. In Scotland, the authority of the pope was abolished in 1560 and a Calvinist *Presbyterian Church established (see Church of Scotland). The Irish, however, clung to the old faith, in part as a symbol of opposition to their Anglo-Irish overlords.

The battle between Catholicism and Protestantism dominated Europe in the 16th and early 17th centuries, and in English popular myth Catholicism became associated with plots to subjugate England to foreign tyrants – for example, Philip II of Spain, who launched the Armada against Protestant England in 1588. While the majority of English Catholics were loyal subjects, the few who became involved in the plots of Elizabeth I's reign (1558–1603) and in the Gunpowder Plot (see Guy Fawkes Day) provoked a general hostility towards all Catholics. This feeling was fur-

ther fuelled by the pope's excommunication of Elizabeth in 1570. From 1580 Catholics were singled out for special legal disabilities. Catholic priests were liable to be treated as traitors – a notable early martyr being St Edmund Campion, hanged at Tyburn in 1581. The Stuart kings of the 17th century were generally ambivalent if not sympathetic in their attitude towards Catholics: Charles I (r. 1625–49) had a Catholic wife; Charles II (r. 1660–85) was received into the Catholic Church on his deathbed; and James II (r. 1685–88) was open in his adherence to the faith. For the most part Catholics were not actively persecuted, yet it was politically impossible to allow them more than grudging toleration; James's ill-advised attempts to promote his faith's interests contributed to his overthrow in the *Glorious Revolution, and the Act of Settlement 1701, which barred Catholics from the throne.

In the 18th century religion ceased to be a major issue, except in Ireland. The first Catholic Relief Act was passed in 1778, and nearly all disqualifications were removed by the Catholic Emancipation Act 1829. The Roman Catholic renaissance was helped by the influx of Irish immigrants during the 19th century and by the defection of certain prominent Church of England clergy (see Oxford Movement). The hierarchy of Catholic bishops was established in England and Wales under the Archbishop of Westminster (1850), and in Scotland under the Archbishop of St Andrews and Edinburgh (1878). However, a few obstacles remain: when Prince Michael of Kent married the Catholic Marie-Christine von Reibnitz in 1978, he relinquished his place in the line of succession to the throne.

In mainland Britain there are currently over 5 million Roman Catholics whose children are often educated in Catholic schools. Some are run by local authorities, some by special educational institutes, such as those of the Christian Brothers (a movement founded in 1802 at Waterford, Ireland, whose schools include St Anselm's College, Birkenhead, and St Brendan's College, Bristol), and some by religious orders (e.g. Ampleforth, the public school in North Yorkshire, founded in 1802 and associated with a Benedictine community). Popular prejudice against Roman Catholics was quite significant until recently, especially among *Nonconformist Protestants and in cities with large Catholic communities, such as Liverpool and Glasgow. For example, of the football clubs in these two cities, Everton and Celtic were traditionally Catholic, and Liverpool and Rangers were Protestant (indeed, the latter only took on its first Catholic player in 1986). Even now, it is still considered worthy of comment if a Catholic is appointed to an important position, and leading Catholics (notably the Howard Dukes of Norfolk, whose family never bowed to the Reformation) have a certain prominence as spokesmen for their community.

A completely different situation exists in Northern Ireland, where politics are dominated by the intertwined questions of religion and the maintenance of the union with Britain, a result of over 300 years of struggles between the Catholic native Irish and Protestant immigrants (see Irish nationalism).

The present Archbishop of Westminster is Cardinal Basil Hume. Apart from Westminster, there are four other provinces – Birmingham, Liverpool, Cardiff, and Southwark – each headed by an archbishop. A further 16 bishops are in charge of suffragan sees. The head of the Catholic Church in Scotland is Cardinal Joseph Gray, Archbishop of the province of St Andrews and Edinburgh; the other province is Glasgow. The Roman Catholic Primate of all Ireland is Cardinal Tomas O'Fiaich, the Archbishop of Armagh. The other three Irish provinces are Dublin, Cashel, and Tuam. In England and Wales, the Church's ruling body is the Bishops' Conference, presided over by the Archbishop of Westminster and comprising the diocesan bishops, coadjutant (assistant) bishops, auxiliaries, and titular bishops.

Roman roads A network of usually straight roads on whose course some present-day routes still run. Most were constructed by the Roman army after the invasion of Britain in 43 AD to facilitate conquest, and were maintained subsequently for both military and commercial reasons.

The first three roads built by the Romans radiated from London and reflect the three-pronged advance on British territory made by Claudius' troops in 43 AD. Watling Street led northwest to High Cross in Warwickshire; Ermine Street went north to Lincoln, and a third road led to Silchester (midway between London and Winchester). In 47 AD the governor of Britain, Ostorius Scapula, constructed a road to act as a frontier-line across Britain in order to keep out raiding western tribes. This road he kept garrisoned and patrolled at all times, the friendly tribes behind it having been disarmed. It began in Devon at the headquarters of the second legion and ran in an exceptionally straight line through Bath, Cirencester, and Moreton-in-Marsh, up to High Cross, where it met Watling Street, and then continued via Leicester and Newark as far as Lincoln, where stood the fortress of the ninth legion. This frontier road was called by the Anglo-Saxons the Fosse Way, perhaps because of the drainage ditches, or "fossae", which ran alongside it. Scapula also extended Watling Street to Wroxeter so that he could attack the boundaries of North Wales; it became the great highway of Roman communication from the Channel ports to London and beyond.

Some of the Roman roads that were then built to extend this basic network may have followed prehistoric paths, but an examination of the 5000 miles of known Roman roads shows that the Romans built them by joining two points by a straight line irrespective of what stood between them. The nodal points of the road network were military bases, towns, and tribal capitals, but instead of running along belts of relatively dense population, such as the North or South Downs or the Cotswolds, the main roads cut through them crosswise to traverse as quickly as possible the thick forests that lay between them. They were designed for official, not civil, traffic. More frequent use was made of smaller roads, such as the prehistoric *Icknield Way on the South Downs and the Harroway on the North Downs, or those built by local authorities specifically for civil trade, an example being the White Way in the Cotswolds.

All the main Roman roads were 6–7 metres (20–24 feet) wide, and were constructed on an earth footing, with a layer of small stones in mortar above, on top of which was a hard filling surfaced with stone slabs. Local roads were of lighter construction. After the departure of the Romans in the early 5th century AD, many roads declined and few important new ones were built. The Anglo-Saxons made use of Watling Street and it carried traffic in medieval times; part of it now forms the A5 from St Albans to Telford. Road-building did not take place on anything approaching the Roman scale, however, until the 19th century. Indeed, when Britain's motorway network was begun in the 1950s, the new roads were heralded as the first major trunk roads since those built by the Romans.

Romantic movement A movement in literature and the visual arts in the late 18th and early 19th centuries, which emphasized emotion, individuality, and self-expression, and constituted a reaction to the rationalism of the Enlightenment from which it had evolved. The adoption of a picturesque approach with classical elements was an early

ROMANTIC MOVEMENT *The Bard, by John Martin, 1817. Romantic tendencies are shown in the choice of subject and the dramatic depiction of the solitary bard, dwarfed by the soaring and fantastic rocks.*

manifestation of Romanticism in England, emerging in the landscape gardening of, for example, William Kent, who rebelled against the formality of earlier gardens and strove to effect an apparent spontaneity in his landscapes, as if brought about by time, weather, and nature. A similar espousal of the beauty of nature was found in English Romantic literature, in such works as the *Lyrical Ballads* (1798) by William Wordsworth (1770–1850) and Samuel Taylor Coleridge (1772–1834) who, as two of the *Lake Poets, extolled the landscape of the Lake District in particular. In the second edition of the *Ballads* (1800) Wordsworth supplied a definition of Romanticism as "the spontaneous overflow of powerful feeling". A self-conscious passion for folklore, the supernatural, and a melancholy awareness of the dilemma between imagination and instinct also characterized the poetry of John Keats (1795–1821), P. B. Shelley (1792–1822), and Lord Byron (1788–1824) and the novels of Sir Walter Scott (1771–1832). In *Waverley* (1814) Scott expressed the nationalist fervour, a direct response to the spirit of revolution prevalent throughout Europe and the USA at the time, that also came to be associated with Romanticism.

James Wyatt's Fonthill Abbey (1796–1807) in Wiltshire, built in the medieval gothic manner, is often cited as the most obvious architectural example of Romanticism. When its tower collapsed not long after the building's completion, it became, as a natural ruin, even more "romantic". In painting, Henry Fuseli, with his taste for horror and drama, and William Blake, with his unorthodox mysticism, were true to the Romantic ideal, but J. M. W. Turner (1775–1851) was the supreme Romantic painter in England, in his visionary and atmospheric representation of landscape and weather. The legacy of Romanticism has influenced many subsequent artistic movements, in, for example, the pathos and nostalgia of the *Pre-Raphaelite Brotherhood, and the rebelliousness and emotionalism of futurism and expressionism in the 20th century.

Roman villas Isolated country houses, or groups of houses, with a farm attached. Villas have been found throughout the Roman

ROMAN VILLAS *Mosaic floor at Fishbourne Villa in Sussex. The central medallion shows a winged boy astride a dolphin.*

world, but those in Britain, Germany, and Gaul differ from the rest in design, indicating a preference for Romano-Celtic styles. While villas belonging to important Romans around the Mediterranean were either splendid holiday homes or slave-worked farms, those in Britain were working country houses and farms combined, with tenants and labourers of free or servile status living in smaller outbuildings on the estate.

Some Celtic Britons lived in isolated farmhouses long before the Roman invasion and these served as architectural models for the villas of the Roman period, most of which were developments of an existing Celtic site. The basic type of British villa was the Celtic "barn dwelling", a long aisled corridor partitioned into rooms. Others had additional wings jutting out at either side, while the largest, with 30 or 40 rooms, enclosed a central courtyard. The most splendid so far found in Britain were built in the 3rd and 4th centuries AD. Few are comparable to the magnificent Italian vil-

las of this period, the exception being Fishbourne, a palace built in c. 75 AD and destroyed in c. 280, which originally covered two hectares (six acres). Most late villas in Britain, however, do display sophisticated Roman features, such as hypocausts (underground central heating systems), plaster and stucco wall decoration, gardens, suites of bathrooms, and mosaic floors.

Each of these villas was the centre of a farming estate that produced wheat (Britain's staple cereal), and reared cattle, sheep, goats, and pigs. Workers often made iron and leather goods on site. A villa could be virtually self-sufficient, and the network of *Roman roads enabled villa products to be sold in nearby markets. The villas seem to have been built by wealthy romanized Britons in a style that was strongly influenced by Roman architecture, although conforming to a basic pattern of native, not Roman, origin. Thus the houses owed much of their appearance to the Roman presence, but they continued a Celtic tradition; they were not set up as part of the romanization process begun by Claudius in 43 AD. Built by Britons and producing goods for a local market, they prospered while the empire as a whole declined, but the increasing lack of protection from the Romans left them a rich and easy prey for barbarian invaders. Some, such as Lullingstone, were destroyed by fire in the 5th century, possibly as the result of a Saxon attack; others simply fell into decay after the departure of the Romans in the 420s. About 500 villa sites are known to have existed in Britain, some of which (such as Fishbourne, Lullingstone, Chedworth, and Bignor) are still well preserved.

Romany The language of the *Gypsies. Studies have shown Romany to be North Indian in origin; but, in England, it has been greatly influenced by English and has now become more of a creole, cant, or argot than a language in its own right. A small group of Gypsies in a remote part of North Wales still speak a pure Romany, which has a complex system of inflections. Otherwise, Romany inflections have almost completely died out. Vocabulary is a different matter. Gypsies are careful to ensure that no ordinary English speaker can follow their drift by overhearing their conversation, so words for new technological objects are made up from basic Romany vocabulary elements, rather than borrowed from English. For example, a television is a *dicking muckter* – literally, a "looking box"; a bicycle is a *prastering saster* – a "running iron". English borrowings from Romany are equally rare, although Romany does share a few terms, such as *mush* "man" and *togs* "clothes" with English thieves' cant. In Romany, as in many other cants and argots, the same word (*baulo*) signifies both "pig" and "policeman".

rose rent A single red rose presented annually to the Lord Mayor of London at the Mansion House on Midsummer Day. In 1381 Sir Robert Knollys was ordered to pay the "rose rent" for a connecting gallery constructed between his two properties in Seething Lane. This annual tribute was probably in lieu of payment for a licence for the construction; it has been suggested, however, that the imposition may have been a nominal penalty for constructing the gallery without permission. The rose has been presented on a velvet cushion by the churchwardens of All Hallows, Barking (by the Tower) since the tradition was revived by the vicar of that church in 1924.

Round Tables of Great Britain and Ireland, National Association of A nonpolitical nonsectarian organization for men aged 18–40 founded in Norwich by Louis Marchesi in 1927. There are over 1250 branches with a total membership of more than 30,000 Tablers. Round Tables also exist in some 70 countries, with a worldwide membership of 100,000. Individual Tables are autonomous and provide the opportunity for young men to meet socially, participate in community service through membership of local welfare and other committees, and to raise funds for local, national, and international charities and causes. The name Round Table and the Association's motto, "Adopt, Adapt, Improve" derive from a speech made in 1927 by the then Prince of Wales: "The young business and professional men of this country must get together *round the table, adopt* methods that have proved so sound in the past, *adapt* them to the changing needs of the times and wherever possible *improve* them." The Round Table emblem (adopted in 1929) is an adaptation of the table, said to be King Arthur's, in the Great Hall, Winchester. There is a 41 Club for those who retire from Round Table at 40 and the Ladies Circle, a separate organization, for members' wives.

Royal Academy of Arts A self-supporting body of artists and architects who hold loan exhibitions and an annual show of contemporary art. At their premises at Burlington House, Piccadilly, London, they also run an art school, former pupils of which include Thomas Lawrence, John Constable, and J. M. W. Turner. Founded in 1768, it is the oldest society in Britain devoted solely to the fine arts and consists of 50 Royal Academicians and 25 Associates, all British residents, who elect one of their number as president. The first and most distinguished was Sir Joshua Reynolds (1723–92). The Academy's exhibitions originally occupied a building in Pall Mall, moved to Somerset House in 1771, shared the National Gallery's premises from 1837 to 1868, and then opened at Burlington House. Ever since its foundation each new Academician has presented to the Academy "a Picture, Bas-relief, or other specimen of his abilities", and it has acquired many valuable works in this way as well as receiving gifts from, among others, Turner, Reynolds, Gainsborough, and Stubbs. Its most prized possession is the famous Michelangelo tondo, *The Madonna and Child with the Infant St John.*

By the end of the 19th century the Academy was regarded as the home of academic and conservative artists, a reputation that continues to haunt its annual summer show, open to amateurs and professionals alike: many important contemporary artists in Britain are not associated with the Academy. The annual dinner of the Royal Academy is traditionally attended by the Prime Minister, who uses the occasion to make a significant political speech.

Royal Academy of Dramatic Art (RADA)   A drama school founded by the actor-manager Herbert Beerbohm Tree in 1904. Originally housed in the dome of His (now Her) Majesty's Theatre in London, it moved to its present site in Gower Street in 1905. Here its students appear in public performances of plays in the school's Vanbrugh Theatre, opened in 1954, and named after the actress sisters Irene and Violet Vanbrugh. British actors trained at RADA include Glenda Jackson (1936–   ), Sir Richard Attenborough (1923–   ), Alan Bates (1934–   ), and Margaret Lockwood (1916–   ).

Royal Academy of Music (RAM)   The oldest college of advanced musical training in England. Founded in 1822, with George IV as patron, it received a royal charter in 1830, and moved to its present premises in Marylebone Road, London, in 1912. The RAM confers a degree and a diploma, the GRSM (Graduate of the Royal Schools of Music), and LRAM (Licentiate of the Royal Academy of Music).

Royal Air Force (RAF)   The most recently formed of the three British armed forces. The RAF was officially constituted by Act of Parliament in 1918 when the Royal

Flying Corps (formed in 1912 from the Air Battalion of the Royal Engineers) and the Royal Naval Air Service (formed in 1914) were amalgamated. In the years following World War I the RAF was built up as an independent force and by 1937 had priority for funds over both the Royal Navy and the Army. During World War II RAF fighter pilots, flying Supermarine Spitfires and Hawker Hurricanes, won distinction in the Battle of Britain against the numerically superior German Luftwaffe, whilst the RAF Bomber Command, flying Wellingtons and Lancasters, inflicted considerable damage on German industry. Between 1945 and 1960 radical changes were made in the service, with the introduction of jet aircraft capable of supersonic speeds, electronic guidance systems, missiles, mid-air refuelling, and nuclear weapons. The whole service, organized into Strike and Support Commands, came under the control of the Air Force Board of the Ministry of Defence in 1964, since when it has undertaken important roles in home defence and in NATO. The RAF maintains 12 squadrons in the Federal Republic of Germany, and other garrisons in Gibraltar, Hong Kong, Cyprus, the Falkland Islands, and Belize. The RAF Regiment (formed in 1942) guards RAF installations, while training is organized under the Air Training Corps (formed in 1941). Aircraft used by the RAF in the 1980s include helicopters, strike-attack aircraft, such as Harriers and Tornados, long-range Nimrods, and Hawk jet trainers. The current strength is 91,700 volunteers.

Royal Antediluvian Order of Buffaloes (RAOB)   A philanthropic and charitable organization. The origins of the order are uncertain, though it certainly existed by the early 1820s. It probably began as a breakaway group from a philanthropic society for actors. The first branch is believed to have held its meetings in a public house, the Harp Tavern, probably in Covent Garden. Members were drawn from an organization of theatrical singers and other associates with the theatre, a club known as the Ancient and Honourable City of Lushington. Names of founder members are not recorded. It is not known when the movement adopted its present name, but "buffaloes" is believed to come from a song sung at meetings.

Members give money or service and work together as a fellowship to provide for members and their dependants in need and the dependants of deceased members. Educational grants, family holidays, and convalescent homes at Harrogate and Weston-super-Mare are among the various benefits offered by the RAOB to its members. The Buffaloes are a three-tier organization comprising Minor Lodges, Provincial Grand Lodges, and the Grand Lodge; their four degrees of membership are Brother, Primo, Knight of Merit, and Right Honourable. Membership of countrywide Minor Lodges is open to all adult males regardless of social position, religion, or political belief. Good citizenship and a desire to participate in the work of the Order "to the extent of his power" are the only qualifications for membership.

royal arms The heraldic "achievement" of the Crown: the coat of arms and additional insignia used by the sovereign. It is displayed on flags above buildings in which the sovereign is staying, and on ships when he or she is aboard. It is also on view behind a judge or magistrate in law courts, and in many churches, indicating royal authority over the Anglican Church. Certain schools founded by a monarch use the particular coat of arms of their founder. Tradesmen with royal warrants

ROYAL ARMS

(denoting regular and lengthy patronage by royalty) are permitted to display the royal arms on their shop front or packaging with the words "by appointment" though this practice has long been so widespread as to be unremarkable.

Unlike other coats of arms, the royal arms commemorate the realms the sovereign has come to rule over, rather than family alliances. Thus the present royal arms incorporate three golden lions on a red shield (England), first used by Richard I (1157–99), to which Edward III (1312–77) added a blue background peppered with gold fleurs-de-lis, symbolizing his claim to the French throne. When James I (1566–1625) came to the throne he incorporated the Scottish red lion surrounded by a fancifully decorated red square on a gold background. He also added a gold Irish harp with silver strings on a blue background to denote his sovereignty over Ireland, and replaced the dragon which had supported the shield, opposite the lion, with a unicorn. After the union of Scottish and English parliaments in 1707 the Scottish arms were combined with the English more closely and the French element, though still retained, was separated from the English. The Hanoverians added the arms of their German possessions. At the Act of Union abolishing the separate Irish parliament in 1801 the fleur-de-lis was dropped. When Queen Victoria came to the throne the royal arms became essentially what they are today.

Since Edward III's reign the shield of the royal arms has been surrounded by a Garter belt in blue with the celebrated motto "*Honi soit qui mal y pense*" ("shamed be he who thinks evil of it") inscribed thereon (*see* Garter, Order of the). (The Garter belt is omitted in the Scottish version.) Beneath the shield are the Tudor rose and Scottish thistle. The motto here is "*Dieu et mon droit*" ("God and my right"), first employed by Henry VI (1421–71), but in Scotland this is replaced by "*In Defens*", which is placed above the crest; another motto, "*Nemo me impune lacessit*" ("nobody challenges me and goes unpunished") is sometimes placed below the shield. Above the shield is the helm, on which rests the royal crown, in crimson and gold, studded with jewels, and above this stands the crest, a crowned gold lion, facing towards the onlooker.

When the sovereign is in Scotland the Scottish and English constituent emblems are rearranged to give the former more prominence. The Prince of Wales has a separate coat of arms incorporating specific references to Wales.

royal assent The agreement of the Crown that transforms a parliamentary *Bill into an *Act of Parliament or gives the full force of an Act of Parliament to a measure of the General Synod of the Church of England. Until 1541 the sovereign always attended Parliament to give the assent to a Bill (the ceremony taking place in the House of Lords, with members of the Commons also present), but an Act of that year enabled it to be given by commissioners on behalf of the sovereign, and the Royal Assent Act l967 substituted a simple notification of assent given to each House by its *Speaker. The sovereign still assents in person, however, to Bills submitted for the purpose at the time of prorogation (*see* Parliament). The actual wording of the assent, the date of which is endorsed on the Bill by the clerk of the Parliaments, still follows the Norman French spoken by William the Conqueror and his immediate descendants. For most Bills, it is "*La Reyne le veult*" (the Queen – *Le Roy* in the case of a king – wishes it). There are, however, certain special forms, as for example, in the case of financial Bills, "*La Reyne remercie ses bon sujets, accepte leur benevolence, et ainsi le veult*" (thanks her good subjects, accepts their kindness, and so wishes it). The formula for a refusal to assent is the tactful "*La Reyne s'avisera*" (will consider), although the veto has not been used since the reign of Queen Anne and its exercise would now be highly remarkable (*see* British constitution).

Royal Automobile Club *See* RAC.

Royal Ballet The national ballet company of Great Britain, based at the *Royal Opera House, Covent Garden, in London, but widely known from its regular tours in Britain and abroad. The Royal Ballet originated in the Vic–Wells Ballet, which was founded by Ninette de Valois (1898–) in 1931 and performed at both the Sadler's Wells and Old Vic theatres. Renamed the Sadler's Wells Ballet in 1941, its moved to Covent Garden in 1946, and in 1956 gained a royal charter and its present name. De Valois retired in 1963, to be succeeded by Frederick Ashton (1904–). Ashton gave way to Kenneth MacMillan (1929–) in 1970, and in 1977 Norman Morrice (1931–) became director. The company's repertoire is based on the 19th-century classics, but it also performs ballets created, notably, by Ashton and by MacMillan. The dancers Dame Margot Fonteyn, Rudolf Nureyev, Robert Helpmann, Lynn Seymour, Merle Park, and Wayne Sleep are among those who have made their names in the Royal Ballet. The Royal Ballet School, also founded in 1931, supplies almost all the company's dancers.

Royal British Legion *See* British Legion, Royal.

royal charter A formal document from the sovereign granting certain rights and privileges. In the past royal charters were used to bestow purely commercial benefits, for example, charters to incorporate trading companies for the purposes of foreign expansion, such as the East India Company (1600) and the Hudson Bay Company. Several trading companies were granted charters under Queen Victoria, the most famous of which, the British South Africa Company, was also known as the The Chartered Company. Now royal charters are granted by the Crown to charitable, educational, legal, and professional organizations. The most obvious distinction a royal charter confers in the case of a charity or professional organization is the right to include the word "royal" into the full title. In the past royal charters incorporated boroughs, brought their representatives into the House of Commons, and granted the right to vote to a given class of persons.

Royal College of Music (RCM) One of the principal British musical colleges, founded in 1883, with the Prince of Wales (later Edward VII) as president, and George Grove (editor of *Grove's Dictionary of Music and Musicians*) as its first director. It moved to its present building in South Kensington, London, in

ROYAL BALLET *Anthony Dowell dancing the part of Prospero in* The Tempest, *Covent Garden.*

1894. The RCM trains students to be composers, teachers, or performers, and confers the degree of GRSM (Graduate of the Royal Schools of Music) and the diploma of ARCM (Associate of the Royal College of Music). Former students include Ralph Vaughan Williams and Benjamin Britten.

Royal College of Physicians The oldest and one of the most influential bodies in the medical profession. Besides upholding standards of practice in the profession, the College represents the interests of hospital consultants and specialists, advises the government on health matters, and promotes medical education. The postgraduate diploma, Member of the Royal College of Physicians (UK) (MRCP-UK), awarded in conjunction with the Royal Colleges of Edinburgh and Glasgow, is the standard qualification for medical specialists. In addition to its coveted membership diploma, the College makes its senior members fellows (FRCP) and also offers a licentiate (LCRP) as part of a first degree in medicine.

The College was founded by the physician and humanist Thomas Linacre in 1518 with a charter from Henry VIII. Linacre's intention was to stop the indiscriminate practice of medicine by unqualified people. The terms of the charter gave the College the right to restrict practice within seven miles of London to physicians to whom it had issued licences. In 1523 this right to grant licences was extended to the whole of England. The College was soon the dominant organization in the medical profession with a reputation for jealously guarding its own interests, particularly when the surgeons and apothecaries threatened to usurp the physician's duties. This rivalry declined as the roles of physician, surgeon, and apothecary became more clearly defined with the scientific advances of the 18th and 19th centuries. One of the College's most distinguished presidents was Sir Hans Sloane (1660–1753), under whom the College pressed for curbs on liquor, resulting in the Gin Acts of 1736, 1751, and 1752. Following the Medical Act 1858, the College began awarding diplomas in conjunction with the *Royal College of Surgeons.

In Scotland, the Royal College of Physicians of Edinburgh was founded in 1681 to "promote the science and art of medicine". Glasgow has its own Royal College of Physicians and Surgeons, founded in 1599.

Royal College of Surgeons The principal professional body for surgeons in England and Wales. It is responsible for examining postgraduates who wish to specialize in surgery; to successful candidates it awards the higher diploma of Fellow of the Royal College of Surgeons (FRCS). The origins of the College can be traced to the 15th-century guilds, or "companies", which protected the interests of surgeons and barbers. In 1540 the United Com-

pany of Barber-Surgeons was formed in London with the right to control the practice of surgery within one mile of the City of London. The surgeons increased their links with the apothecaries, who dispensed medicines, and broadened the scope of their activities into more general medicine. The split with the barbers came in 1745 and a separate Surgeons' Company was formed, governed by a Court of Ten Examiners. This new body received its own royal charter in 1800 to become the Royal College of Surgeons of London and later, in 1843, the Royal College of Surgeons of England. After the 1858 Medical Act, the College started to offer diplomas in conjunction with the *Royal College of Physicians.

The College's headquarters at Lincoln's Inn Fields house a library of over 110,000 volumes as well as a museum of anatomical specimens and historical items based on the collection of the famous surgeon John Hunter (1728–93). Many of the original items were lost in the air raids of World War II.

In Scotland, the Incorporation of Surgeons and Barber-Surgeons, formed in Edinburgh in 1505, later became the Royal College of Surgeons of Edinburgh. Glasgow has its own Royal College of Physicians and Surgeons, founded in 1599.

royal commissions A committee of inquiry into a matter of public concern; membership of the committee is not restricted to MPs but includes lawyers and private individuals with a record of public service, thus making possible a measure of public participation in the affairs of government. Founded from the committees of inquiry under the Crown in medieval times, royal commissions became most influential after 1830; the Commission on Children's Employment (1842) and the Commission on the Housing of the Working Classes (1884) were early reports on destitution and have become key social documents of the period. A royal commission is usually disbanded following the publication of its report, although some have become permanent (or standing) commissions, for example, the Royal Commission on Historical Manuscripts (1869). The 1910 committee on royal commissions stated that the device was useful for the "elucidation of difficult subjects which are attracting public attention" but are unsuitable "on subjects as to which there is no reasonable prospect of early legislation".

Royal commissions, which are also used by Commonwealth countries, are appointed about once a year and usually take about two and a half years to complete their deliberations. The commissions accept written and verbal statements, employ research staff, and publish a final report with a list of recommendations. The report, with its ancient preamble in reply to the sovereign's warrant, is sent to the Home Secretary and presented to Parliament, although the government is not bound to accept its recommendations. The procedures of commissions can be very slow; and many reports have been ignored or quietly forgotten.

Royal Company of Archers (Queen's Bodyguard for Scotland) The Queen's ceremonial bodyguard in Scotland. Corps members, who must be Scots, are drawn from the nobility, gentry, and (latterly) professional classes of Scotland. There are some 400 active and 170 nonactive members. Their uniform consists of a dark green tunic and trousers, and a Kilmarnock bonnet (a kind of large beret) with an eagle's feather in it. Officers' bonnets have two feathers; that of the captain-general has three; the secretary's bonnet carries a Himalayan condor's feather, over two feet long. (This was presented to the Company by the Marquess of Dalhousie, governor-general of India in the mid-19th century.) Each Archer carries a bow and three arrows tucked in his belt.

James I (1566–1625) had a personal bodyguard, which some claim is the origin of the Royal Company of Archers. The corps was formed officially in 1676, primarily as an archery club, under its first captain, the Marquess of Athol. Members still compete in archery contests, notably the Musselburgh Arrow (instituted 1603 – the prize is a silver arrow) and the Queen's Prize (instituted 1787). A royal charter was granted in 1704, but it was not until 1822, when George IV visited Scotland, that the Archers offered to act as the sovereign's personal bodyguard as a sign of Scottish reconciliation to the Hanoverian dynasty.

The Archers served overseas on the occasion of the Delhi Durbar of 1911, when they provided George V with a guard, and although without official status in England, ten of them were permitted to attend the Queen's coronation in 1953 as representatives.

Royal Courts of Jersey and Guernsey The courts of the two principal *Channel Islands. Each is presided over by a legally qualified Bailiff, appointed by the Crown, who is not only the Island's chief judge, but also the head of its legislature (known in Jersey as the States, and in Guernsey as the States of Deliberation); and the other members of each, known as jurats, are laymen appointed by an electoral college. The jurisdiction of the Royal Court of Guernsey extends to the hearing of appeals from the courts of Alderney and Sark, which are dependencies of the island (as also are Herm and Jethou, but these have no independent institutions). Appeals from Jersey and Guernsey lie to the *Judicial Committee of the Privy Council.

Royal Exchange A building opposite the Mansion House in the heart of the City of London. Its original purpose was to provide a meeting-place for merchants and bankers to conduct their business, after the model of the 16th-century Bourse in Antwerp. The first building, financed by Sir Thomas Gresham, was completed in 1571 and called the Royal Exchange by order of Elizabeth I. This building was destroyed in the *Fire of London (1666), but rebuilt by 1669. It again burned down in 1838, and the present neoclassical building, designed by Sir William Tite, was opened by Queen Victoria in 1844. The Exchange's original functions ceased in 1939, and it is now mainly used for exhibitions. The outside steps are one of the places where a new sovereign is proclaimed, the others being St James's Palace, Charing Cross, Temple Bar, and Chancery Lane.

royal garden parties Four summer gatherings held by the Queen, three of which take place in July in the grounds of Buckingham Palace and the other a little earlier at *Holyroodhouse in Scotland. The Lord Chamberlain is responsible for the arrangements and up to 10,000 people are invited to each party, either directly or on the recommendation of the Lord-Lieutenants of the counties, ambassadors, heads of the civil service, armed services, industry, and voluntary organizations. Inaugurated in the 1860s, after Queen Victoria had moved to Buckingham Palace from St James's Palace, royal garden parties are one of the few surviving remnants of the formal court functions of the past, such as "drawing rooms" and presentation parties. The latter were discontinued in 1957 although it is still possible for an eldest unmarried daughter over 18 to be included on her parents' garden party invitation (see London season). Guests arrive after 3.15 pm and assemble on the palace lawns where a band plays light music. Men must wear formal dress, morning coats, uniform, or national dress, and women must either wear an afternoon dress with a hat, or national dress. The royal family emerge from the palace at 4 pm and proceed slowly along roped-off lanes towards the tea tents, chatting to their guests as they go; the Queen is introduced to selected guests by the Lord Chamberlain. Important guests and distinguished visitors to the country then join the Queen in the royal tea tent. After the royal family have left the garden, guests are free to stroll around the lake and grounds before leaving. From time to time the Queen holds an additional party to honour a worthy organization, such as the Red Cross.

Royal Geographical Society A society founded in 1830 as the Geographical Society of London, under the chairmanship of Sir John Barrow (1764–1848), to help intending explorers and to accumulate a library of books, maps, and charts. It received a royal charter in 1859. Virtually all major expeditions to leave Britain during the 19th and 20th centuries have had support from the Royal Geographical Society. After some initial financial problems the Society began to mount major expeditions, including Sir John Franklin's ill-fated search for the Northwest Passage in 1845–48. The source of the Nile was the objective of several expeditions sponsored by the Society, and in 1862 John Hanning Speke (1827–64) traced its primary source to the Ripon Falls on Lake Victoria. But uncertainty remained and he was followed by such men as

Sir Samuel White Baker (1821–93), and perhaps the explorer most favoured by the Society, David Livingstone (1813–73). On its return to England, Livingstone's coffin rested in the Society's map room before the funeral in Westminster Abbey. One of the most successful expeditions ever supported by the Society was the British National Antarctic Expedition of 1899–1902, led by Robert Falcon Scott (1868–1912). His team returned with abundant data and Scott received a special medal from the Society. However, his later privately-funded journey to the South Pole (1910–12), to which the Society contributed £850, ended in tragedy. In the 1920s and 1930s, the Society helped to organize several attempts to climb Mount Everest, culminating in the success of Sir Edmund Hillary (1919–) and Tenzing in 1953. Hillary was also a member of the British Commonwealth Trans-Antarctic Expedition of 1955–58, largely organized and financed by the Society, during which Sir Vivien Fuchs (1908–) achieved the first complete crossing of the continent via the South Pole. In recent years, the Society has concentrated on scientific expeditions, such as the ecological survey of Brazil's Mato Grosso in 1967–69 and the comprehensive study of Gunung Mulu National Park in Sarawak (1977–78).

The Society moved into its present South Kensington premises in 1913. These house a collection of some three-quarters of a million maps, charts, and atlases, which the public may consult in the map room. It also has an extensive library of books as well as collections of drawings, paintings, photographs, diaries, and log books. The Society sponsors and organizes lectures, films, and conferences; details of these together with the findings of its expeditions can be followed through its publications, *The Geographical Journal* and *Geographical Magazine*.

Royal Greenwich Observatory Britain's principal astronomical observatory, located until 1990 at the 15th-century castle and estate of Herstmonceux in Sussex. Charles II founded an observatory in Greenwich Park in 1675, to improve knowledge of the stars and so help mariners to navigate at sea. He commissioned Sir Christopher Wren to design a house there (now an astronomical museum) for the first Astronomer Royal, John Flamsteed (1646–1719). His successors included such celebrated men as Edmond Halley (1656–1742) and George Biddell Airy (1801–92). The data collected at Greenwich over the years were invaluable for accurate navigation and time-keeping, and in 1884 the Greenwich meridian was adopted as the Earth's prime meridian (0° longitude). The famous six "pips" of the Greenwich time signal were first broadcast on radio from Greenwich in 1924 by the BBC. The gradual transfer of scientific facilities from Greenwich to Herstmonceux (1948–57) was prompted by the growth of London and the interference in the Observatory's work caused by environmental pollution. "Greenwich" has been retained in its title to commemorate the historical link with the former site.

For still better viewing conditions the major optical telescopes have now been transferred to a new international observatory on La Palma in the Canary Islands where they operate in collaboration with other European countries. One of the latest instruments at Herstmonceux is the satellite laser-ranging telescope, operational since 1983, which provides information for calibration of satellite equipment, earth orientation, geophysics, and geodesic research. The Nautical Almanac Office is responsible for producing the annual *Nautical Almanac* and the *Astronomical Almanac* (in conjunction with US authorities). Until the mid-1980s the Time Department maintained standard times derived from astronomical observations and by using atomic clocks – the basis of Greenwich Mean Time (GMT). However, once the atomic clocks had worn out, Britain was no longer able to supply data to the international time service (based in Paris). In 1986 plans were announced to move the Observatory to Cambridge University in 1990. The Observatory's present director is Professor A. Boksenberg.

Royal Horticultural Society A society founded in 1804 "for the improvement of horticulture". It received its royal charter in 1809. The Society's most famous annual event is the *Chelsea Flower Show, and it maintains one of the world's finest gardens at Wisley in

Surrey. Other activities include shows and competitions, usually held in the Society's own halls in Westminster, London (New Hall in Greycoat Street and Old Hall in Vincent Square), throughout the year. It owns one of the largest horticultural libraries in the world, the Lindley Library, founded in 1868, and through RHS Enterprises Ltd publishes gardening handbooks. As well as admission to shows, lectures, and Wisley Garden, and the use of the library, members receive the Society's monthly journal, *The Garden*, and advice on gardening problems and plant identification.

royal household The collective term for those departments which serve members of the royal family in matters of day-to-day administration (*see* list of departments). Although each married adult royal personage has his or her own household, consisting of equerries, ladies in waiting, secretaries, and chamberlains, the royal household proper is usually thought of as that of the sovereign. It is the remnant of the ancient domestic system of monarchical administration, which crystallized around the early medieval kings and was known as the *curia regis* ("king's court"; *see* common law). No distinction then existed between the sovereign's ministers and personal servants, such as his steward or chamberlain. As the posts of personal servants became hereditary the government of the realm came to be in the charge of appointed officers. A survival of the earlier fusion of posts is still to be found in the titles of government whips, whose formal titles are, for example, Treasurer of the Household, Comptroller of the Household, and Vice-Chamberlain of the Household.

Royal Institution One of Britain's foremost learned scientific societies, founded in London in 1799 by the physicist Benjamin Thompson, Count Rumford (1753–1814), for "diffusing the knowledge and facilitating the general introduction of useful mechanical inventions and improvements". Its laboratories became Britain's first scientific research centre, used by such illustrious scientists as Sir Humphrey Davy (1778–1829) and Michael Faraday (1791–1867). Faraday conducted much of his work on electricity and magnet-

The Royal Household

BUCKINGHAM PALACE

Lord Chamberlain
Lord Steward
Master of the Horse
Mistress of the Robes
Lords-in-Waiting

Captain of the Gentlemen-at-Arms
Captain of the Yeomen of the Guard
Treasurer of the Household
Comptroller of the Household
Vice-Chamberlain of the Household
Ladies-in-Waiting
Equerries

PRIVATE SECRETARY'S OFFICE

Private Secretary and Keeper of the Queen's
Archives
Deputy Private Secretary
Assistant Private Secretary
Chief Clerk

Press Secretary
Two Assistant Press Secretaries
Assistant Keeper of the Queen's Archives
Defence Services Secretary

DEPARTMENT OF THE KEEPER OF THE PRIVY PURSE AND TREASURER TO THE QUEEN

Keeper of the Privy Purse and Treasurer to
the Queen
Assistant Keeper of the Privy Purse
Deputy Treasurer to the Queen
Privy Purse, Chief Accountant

Treasurer's Office, Chief Accountant
and Paymaster
Establishment Officer
Lord High Almoner
Secretary, Royal Almonry
Sandringham Land Agent, Balmoral Resident Factor

MASTER OF THE HOUSEHOLD'S DEPARTMENT

Master of the Household
Chief Clerk
Palace Steward and Chief Housekeeper
Assistant to the Master of the Household
Assistant to the Master of the
Household, 'G' Branch
Assistant to the Master of the
Household, 'F' Branch

LORD CHAMBERLAIN'S OFFICE

Comptroller
Assistant Comptroller
Secretary
Marshal of the Diplomatic Corps
Vice-Marshal of the Diplomatic Corps
Two Assistant Marshals
Surveyor of the Queen's Pictures
Surveyor of the Queen's Works of Art
Librarian, Royal Library
Secretary, Central Chancery of the Orders of Knighthood
Assistant Secretary
Keeper of the Jewel House, Tower of London
Serjeants at Arms
Serjeant at Arms attending the Lord Chancellor
Serjeant at Arms attending the Speaker

Gentlemen-at-Arms
Lieutenant
Clerk of the Cheque and Adjutant

Yeomen of the Guard
Lieutenant
Clerk of the Cheque and Adjutant

Royal Company of Archers
Captain General
Adjutant

Ecclesiastical Household
Clerk of the Closet
Deputy Clerk of the Closet
Dean and Sub-Dean of the Chapels Royal
Domestic Chaplains at Buckingham Palace
Domestic Chaplain at Windsor Castle,
Sandringham, and Balmoral

Medical Household
Physician and Head of the Medical Household
Serjeant Surgeon
Apothecary to the Queen
Apothecaries to the Household
for Buckingham Palace,
Windsor Castle, Palace of
Holyroodhouse, Sandringham,
and Balmoral

Windsor Castle
Constable and Governor
Superintendent

Palace of Holyroodhouse
Hereditary Keeper
Superintendent

CROWN EQUERRY'S DEPARTMENT

Crown Equerry
Superintendent, Royal Mews

ASCOT HOUSE

Her Majesty's Representative
Secretary

ism there, and in 1833 he became the first Fullerian Professor of Chemistry at the Institution. The Davy Faraday Research Laboratory was endowed in 1896 by Ludvig Mond (1839–1909), the chemist and industrialist, in honour of the Institution's famous members. In 1826 Faraday gave the first of the now famous Christmas lectures for young people, held in the Institution's lecture theatre. These remain an important part of the Institution's educational work. Recent research projects have included work on photochemical reactions and their potential as a means of harnessing the sun's energy. The Institution's premises in Albermarle Street also house a library, with many early scientific manuscripts, and a museum. *Proceedings of the Royal Institution* is published annually. Membership currently stands at around 2500. The current Fullerian Professor of Chemistry and the Institution's director is Sir George Porter.

Royal Marines   Regular troops who are trained for action on land, at sea, and in the air. The formation of a "regiment for sea service" was authorized by Charles II in 1664 under the name of the Duke of York and Albany's Maritime Regiment of Foot. By 1756 there were 130 companies of marines in existence, maintaining the discipline of naval crews and providing musketmen and grenadiers for action at sea and for landing parties. Ranks in the Royal Marines correspond with those in the Army, although the regiment has been traditionally administered by the naval establishment. At the suggestion of Horatio Nelson (1758–1805) the force was split into two groups: the Royal Marine Artillery (the "Blue Marines"), who provided gunnery instruction for the fleet, and the Royal Marine Light Infantry (the "Red Marines"). The two branches were merged once more in 1923. The Royal Marine Commando Brigade was formed during World War II as an amphibious striking force to spearhead seaborne attacks, and is now supported by special assault ships carrying helicopters. In recent years the Royal Marines have seen action in the Korean War, Northern Ireland, and the Falklands as well as fulfilling ceremonial roles. The regiment has been a model for similar forces in

other countries, notably the USA. *See also* reserve forces.

Royal Maundy   An annual ceremony that takes place in Westminster Abbey or at a provincial cathedral on Maundy Thursday, the day before Good Friday. The act of distributing alms in Holy Week can be traced back with certainty to the 12th century. Attended by the *Yeomen of the Guard, the sovereign distributes the Maundy Money to the recipients who are carefully chosen for their record of service to the Church and community. Four are selected for reasons of hardship, and there is always one man and one woman for every year of the sovereign's life. Each receives two leather purses: one contains an allowance for clothing and provisions formerly given in kind (from the time of Elizabeth I), and a payment in lieu of the original gift of cloth worn by the sovereign; the other contains the silver Maundy coins – pennies, twopenny, threepenny, and fourpenny pieces, as many pence as the sovereign's years of age. The coins have been specially minted for the occasion since 1662 (during the reign of Charles II), but they are nevertheless legal tender. However, the price that numismatists are prepared to pay for a complete set far exceeds their actual face value.

The word "maundy" is derived from the Latin *mandatum*, referring to Christ's commandment as he washed his disciples' feet after the Last Supper, the origin of this royal act of humility. From the days of Edward I the feet of selected poor people were washed by the monarch himself. James II (r. 1685–88) was the last monarch to give the symbolic dab with a towel and scented water, which was the extent of the ceremony after the mid-16th century. However, the Lord High Almoner (who is usually a bishop) and his assistants are still girded with linen towels and carry the traditional nosegays of herbs in remembrance of this part of the ceremony. During the 18th and 19th centuries, monarchs ceased to attend, but the custom was revived by George V in 1932.

Royal Meteorological Society   A society founded in 1850 as the British Meteorological Society, and becoming the Royal Meteorological Society in 1882. It is open to all with an interest in meteorology or climatology and membership currently stands at around 1400. Topics covered include surface-based remote sensing, the fluid dynamics of air masses, and agricultural meteorology. Apart from the head office in Bracknell, Berkshire, the Society has several branches in Britain and one in Australia. It holds regular meetings and organizes field trips, exhibitions, and conferences, and publishes a *Quarterly Journal*, the *Journal of Climatology*, and *Weather*, a monthly magazine.

Royal Mint The government department responsible for manufacturing metal coins. The London Mint probably dates from 825 AD, and had established an ascendency over other coin-makers by 1300. Since the mid-16th century it has enjoyed a legal monopoly of coinage. It operated in the Tower of London from 1300 to 1810, when it moved to a building on Little Tower Hill. The need for further expansion and the imminent decimalization of the currency led to a move to Llantrisant, South Wales, in 1968. It also manufactures military medals, some foreign coins, and the Great Seal. One famous Master of the Mint (1696–1727) was Sir Isaac Newton who was unusually zealous in tracking down counterfeiters.

Royal National Eisteddfod of Wales (Welsh: Eisteddfod Genedlaethol Frenhinol Cymru) A major competitive festival of Welsh culture held during the first week of every August and staged alternately in North and South Wales (*see* eisteddfod) and arguably the most important cultural event in Wales. The festival organizes and provides prizes for competitions in music, literature, drama, fine arts, and handicrafts; it promotes a full week of evening concerts and plays; and it provides exhibition space for important Welsh organizations, both cultural and commercial. The eisteddfod competitions and ceremonies, conducted entirely in Welsh, take place in a specially erected prefabricated pavilion. The most important highlights of the eisteddfod week are two ceremonies presided over by the Gorsedd of Bards, a pseudo-antique literary and academic circle organized along supposedly druidical lines and dating back only to

1792. In the Chairing Ceremony, the winner of a contest in strict-metre verse composition is called up from the eisteddfod audience and presented amid pageantry and procession with a miniature chair. The Crowning Ceremony is a similar occasion, in which the winner of a free verse competition is enthroned and presented with a crown. The Archdruid of the Gorsedd officiates at both ceremonies.

Modern national eisteddfods began with the Corwen eisteddfod of 1789. The first regular annual national eisteddfod was held at Denbigh in 1860. In 1880 the Royal National Eisteddfod Association took responsibility for the Royal National Eisteddfod of Wales. This association merged with the Gorsedd of Bards in 1937 to become the National Eisteddfod Council, later renamed the Eisteddfod Court. This organization administers the festival and subsidizes a local committee through funds raised from private donations and public grants. *See also* International Musical Eisteddfod.

Royal National Institute for the Blind (RNIB) A charity that promotes all aspects of the education and general welfare of blind people, who number around 120,000 in the UK. It is the largest organization of its kind in the world. The RNIB grew out of the work of the British and Foreign Blind Association, which was founded in 1868 to assist the education and employment of blind people, in particular by establishing a suitable and uniform method for producing books for the blind. The RNIB still produces a wide range of books and periodicals in Braille (and the alternative system, Moon type), publishes music in Braille, and runs a "talking book" library service (begun in 1935). It is also active in providing training and finding employment for the blind, training instructors to work with blind people, and running rehabilitation centres for the newly blind. The institute's London resource centre pioneers aids and specially adapted equipment to make life easier for the blind. The RNIB receives part of its income from the government, the rest from donations.

Royal National Institute for the Deaf A charity set up in 1911 as the National Bu-

ROYAL NATIONAL EISTEDDFOD OF WALES *Bards.*

reau for Promoting the General Welfare of the Deaf. It was founded by Leo Bonn (1850–1929), a wealthy merchant banker who was himself deaf, with the aim of coordinating the efforts of the multitude of local groups already in existence. It is now the country's main association for the deaf or those with impaired hearing, with a number of smaller ones under its aegis (e.g. the British Tinnitus Association). Its headquarters are in London and it has scientific and technical departments in both London and Glasgow, which research aids for the deaf and monitor technical advances. The Institute runs a library and information service, and also has departments dealing with employment and social services for the deaf, offers some residential services, and publishes advisory literature.

Royal National Lifeboat Institution (RNLI) A rescue organization manned by volunteers and financed by voluntary contributions that maintains a round-the-clock service for shipping in distress off British shores. In the early 19th century several lifeboats were maintained by local societies and benefactors, and *Lloyd's of London provided a small fleet. However, the impetus for the creation of a nationwide organization came from an Isle of Man resident, Sir William Hillary (1771–1847), who had witnessed many shipwrecks off the island's coasts. In 1824 he founded the Royal National Institution for the Preservation of Life from Shipwreck; the Institution later changed its name, but is still run on the principles laid down by the founder. Besides maintaining the lifeboat service, Hillary envisaged that an important part of the Institution's work would be caring for the dependants of crewmen who lost their lives. After some initial financial difficulties, the RNLI, helped by royal patronage and growing public awareness of the courage of the boat crews, expanded into a thriving network of lifeboats and experienced crews at key points along the British coast.

The first insubmersible boat was designed in 1785 by a London coach-builder, Lionel Lukin. However, public interest in lifeboat design was only aroused by the wreck of the *Adventure* off the mouth of the River Tyne in 1789, and a competition was held to find the best design. The resulting *Original* became the prototype for other lifeboats, although its principles were not generally adopted until the mid-19th century. At this time the boats were driven by oars; the first steam-powered lifeboat entered service in 1890, the first petrol driven one in 1904. Modern RNLI offshore boats are powerful, self-righting vessels, designed for buoyancy and carrying advanced safety equipment. The RNLI maintains over 250 vessels, including smaller inflatable craft with outboard motors for assisting people in difficulties close to shore (e.g. in pleasure craft). Crews hold regular practice launches and other drills.

Royal Navy (RN) A maritime fighting force that has defended Britain's interests at sea for over a thousand years. Founded in the 9th century by Alfred the Great as a defence against the Danes, the Royal Navy has its roots in Tudor times, its early beginnings signalled by the launching of the *Royal Harry* by Henry VII in 1488. Exploration of the Americas and the challenge of Spanish galleons led to the development of an effective navy that was to remain supreme for 400 years. By the time of the Spanish Armada (1588) Sir Francis Drake (1540–96) could call on 197 ships, 34 of which were Royal Navy warships. In the years of peace that followed, however, the Navy declined somewhat both in power and prestige. Charles I's attempt to raise taxes for the Navy by levying ship money was one of the causes of the English Civil War (1642–51) and not until Oliver Cromwell restored the Navy with victories against the Dutch (1653) did it achieve its former glory. Samuel Pepys, as secretary of the Admiralty, encouraged more professional standards and an improvement in the seamen's notoriously bad living conditions, although punishments with the cat-o'-nine-tails and by keel-hauling were practised into the 19th century. The emphasis upon professionalism increased in the 18th century even though some crews were made up to strength by press ganging until the middle of the 19th century, in spite of an Act of Parliament of 1641 making it illegal. Captain James Cook (1728–79), who rose through the ranks by sheer ability, exemplified the role of the Royal Navy in surveying and exploration with his voyages to Australia, New Zealand, and the Pacific islands. Fresh drinking water as well as fresh fruit and vegetables were introduced to counter scurvy and other diseases in an age when more sailors died from poor nutrition and hygiene than from enemy action. At the turn of the century, mutinies in 1797 at The Nore and at Spithead resulted in an Act being passed to raise the wages of sailors and those mutineers who had not been executed were pardoned. Thus the Navy had a new spirit with which to play its part in the Napoleonic wars with France. Under Horatio Nelson (1758–1805), the "Jack Tars" (as the sailors dressed in their blue jackets and bell-bottomed trousers were known) scored their greatest victories – at the Nile (1798), Copenhagen (1801), and *Trafalgar (1805), where they responded heroically to Nelson's famous signal "England expects that every man will do his duty".

The 19th century saw many changes. Principally, of course, the change from sail to steam. The first screw propeller was used by the Royal Navy in 1840 and ten years later 161 of its 500 vessels were steam-powered. Other major innovations included the launching of the first ironclad battleships (1860), the testing of the submarine (1887), and the introduction of exploding shells and torpedoes. While these changes were taking place, the Navy itself was changing: the Commission of Manning (1858) introduced a new career structure, higher pensions, pay, and a standard uniform. Training schools were opened at Portsmouth (1830), Greenwich (1873), and Dartmouth (1905). By the beginning of World War I the dreadnoughts, new and extremely powerful battleships, had appeared and it was these vessels that fought the only large-scale sea battle of World War I, at Jutland. Developments in World War II included direction-finding by radar, and the development of aircraft carriers. By the end of the war supremacy at sea had passed from the Royal Navy to the US Navy. Since then the Navy has occupied an important role in NATO and has seen active service in the Falklands campaign. The RN's current strength is 72,000 men and women. British nuclear submarines first sailed in 1963, armed with Polaris missiles with a range of 4000 kilometres (2500 miles). *See also* women's services; Royal Marines; reserve forces.

Royal Observatory, Edinburgh Scotland's main astronomical observatory, founded in 1818 on Carlton Hill, Edinburgh, as the university's astronomy department. It received the title Royal Observatory in 1834 with the appointment of the first Astronomer Royal for Scotland, Thomas Henderson (1798–1844). In 1896 the Observatory moved to its present site on Blackford Hill. The Observatory's data is now collected using the UK's 1.2 metre Schmidt telescope at the Siding Spring Observatory in New South Wales, Australia, and the UK infrared telescope in Hawaii. One of the most recent facilities in Edinburgh is COSMOS – a computerized machine for scanning astronomical

photographs. It is the successor to GALAXY, an earlier system developed in Edinburgh during the 1960s.

Royal Observer Corps (ROC) A volunteer force formed for the purpose of reporting any enemy attack on Britain. The 11,000 volunteers and 100 full-time officers form the field force of the United Kingdom Warning and Monitoring Organization, which is administered by the Home Office. Founded in 1925, the Royal Observer Corps was established on the advice of Major General E. B. Ashmore as a successor to the Metropolitan Observation Service of World War I. In 1939 the ROC was rapidly expanded to fulfil the role of spotting incoming German aircraft, and later, flying bombs. In 1940, after the destruction of several radar stations in southern England, the ROC became the principal source of information about forthcoming air attacks. When Rudolf Hess parachuted into Scotland in 1941 he was recognized by Major Graham Donald of the ROC, despite official scepticism. Above all, nearly 7000 lost or damaged Allied aircraft were guided safely to ground by the ROC, which received its "Royal" title from King George VI on 11 April 1941. Its motto is "Forewarned is Forearmed".

The ROC's role today is to monitor the effects of a nuclear attack. It operates in three-man teams from a network of 870 underground bunkers located all over the United Kingdom. Its primary objective is the local assessment of damage caused by nuclear blast, radiation, and fallout.

Royal Opera House, Covent Garden The home of the *Royal Ballet and the Royal Opera, in Bow Street, London. Three successive buildings have occupied the site. The first, the Theatre Royal, opened in 1732 with a performance of Congreve's *The Way of the World* (1700). G. F. Handel was musical director from 1734 to 1737. Destroyed by fire in 1808, it was replaced by Robert Smirke's building, which opened in 1809 with Mrs Siddons and John Kemble (1757–1823) in Shakespeare's *Macbeth*. This theatre, like the first, staged both plays and opera, and also burnt down (1856). The present building, by

E. M. Barry, opened in 1858 (with extensions in 1982) and incorporated a frieze of Tragedy and Comedy by the British neoclassical sculptor John Flaxman, the only fragment of the second theatre to survive. In the mid-19th century, the theatre's lease having been bought by an Italian composer, it was renamed the Royal Italian Opera House, and this was reflected in its repertoire which included the British premières of Verdi's *Rigoletto* (1853), *Il Trovatore* (1855), and *Aida* (1876). In 1892 it became simply the Royal Opera House. In the early decades of the 20th century Thomas Beecham was closely associated with Covent Garden. He introduced the operas of Richard Strauss to London, brought Diaghilev's Ballets Russes here in 1911, briefly owned the theatre (with his father, in 1919–20), and later was artistic director (1933–39). The theatre was used as a dance hall during World War II, but in 1946, with funding from a trust founded by the economist John Maynard Keynes, became the nation's centre of opera and ballet. Since then it has staged performances of the highest quality by artists from all over the world. Among British singers, Yvonne Minton, Gwyneth Jones, and Geraint Evans have made their names at Covent Garden. It has given premières of works by Benjamin Britten, Michael Tippett, Peter Maxwell Davies, and Hans Werner Henze. Beecham's successors as musical director have included Rafael Kubelik, Georg Solti, and Colin Davis.

royal parks London is fortunate in having some of the finest city parks in the world, bequeathed by a long line of British monarchs. Hyde Park, Green Park, St James's Park, and Regent's Park were all originally numbered amongst Henry VIII's game forests (lands often acquired as spoils from his dissolution of the monasteries). The largest is **Hyde Park** which, including adjoining Kensington Gardens (formerly the grounds of Kensington Palace), covers over 255 hectares (630 acres). It was first opened to the public during the reign of James I (1603–25), was briefly sold into private hands during Cromwell's era, but returned to the monarchy with the Restoration (1660). It became a popular place for riding for members of fashionable society until the end of World War I. The Household

Cavalry, stationed at neighbouring Knightsbridge Barracks, are among those who still exercise their horses in the park. A lake was created in 1730 on the instructions of George II's queen, Caroline. The Serpentine sweeps gracefully from Hyde Park, under the bridge built by George Rennie in 1826, to become the Long Water in Kensington Gardens. Running round three sides of the park is the riding track known as Rotten Row, probably a corruption of "*route de roi*", the original route to the Palace. At the centre of the western end is the Round Pond, which attracts model boat enthusiasts. On the southern perimeter facing the Royal Albert Hall, is the Albert Memorial, George Gilbert Scott's tribute to the prince erected in 1864, featuring a canopied bronze statue of the prince holding a catalogue of the 1851 *Great Exhibition, which was staged in the park. At the northeastern extremity of Hyde Park is *Speakers' Corner, where orators of all persuasions traditionally hold forth; and Marble Arch, the site of the former *Tyburn gallows.

St James's Park was also first opened to the public in the early 17th century and by the Restoration possessed formal gardens and a canal in the Dutch style. The present design in the style of a country park was the work of architect John Nash (1752–1835). St James's Palace, built by Henry VIII, and Clarence House, the Queen Mother's residence, stand on London's principal processional way, the Mall. Beyond is Green Park, which stretches as far as Piccadilly.

Nash was also commissioned by the Prince Regent (later George IV) to design the layout of **Regent's Park**, when the Crown regained full rights on the land in 1811. The park is divided by the Inner Circle, a road surrounding Queen Mary's Garden, while the Outer Circle follows the perimeter. The Broad Walk leads northwards from Park Square to skirt the grounds of London Zoo, at the northern end. The park also contains two boating lakes, the former buildings of Bedford College, and the US ambassador's residence. Outside the eastern, southern, and southwestern edges of the park stand Nash's opulent classical terraces.

Away from London's centre and upstream along the Thames, are the wider expanses of

Richmond Great Park. Its 954 hectares (2358 acres) contain fish ponds and roaming deer, although only traces of Henry VII's palace remain. Nearby *Hampton Court is still intact in its own park, while further up river still is the Great Park of *Windsor castle, which remains one of the monarch's official residences.

Royal Pavilion, Brighton   A palace built between 1815 and 1822 for the Prince Regent (later George IV). He first visited the emerging seaside resort of Brighton in 1783; his subsequent patronage transformed the Sussex town into one of the most fashionable resorts in Europe. Henry Holland (1745–1806) rebuilt the Prince's house in 1789 to create the Marine Pavilion with its large central-domed rotunda. This was extended between 1801 and 1804; in 1805, the Prince had the idea of building an opulent palace on the site. He was, however, forced to wait until 1815 when, as Prince Regent, he had sufficient funds to commission the architect John Nash (1752–1835) to transform the shell of the Marine Pavilion into a flamboyant mixture of Indian and Chinese styles, with onion domes, minarets, and fretwork. The interior sustained the oriental theme, with exotic murals, painted ceilings, and ornamentation in the form of palm trees and bamboo. The design, inspired partly by George himself, provoked considerable hostil-

ity: "One would think St Paul's cathedral had come to Brighton and pupped", commented the writer Sydney Smith. Victorian Brighton regarded it as a monument of bad taste, relegating George's pleasure palace to a suitable venue for flower shows and civic functions. Only in the 20th century has it been restored and elevated to a tourist attraction, appreciated as a spectacular folly executed with imagination and style.

Royal Philharmonic Orchestra (RPO) An orchestra founded in 1946 by Thomas Beecham when he returned from the USA after World War II. The RPO gave the annual subscription concerts for the Royal Philharmonic Society (hence the orchestra's name), and Beecham also arranged a number of recording contracts with American companies. It was the resident orchestra at *Glyndebourne (1948–63) and toured the USA under Beecham in 1950. After his death in 1961 the RPO became self-governing. His successors as principal conductor have included Rudolf Kempe, Charles Groves, and Walter Weller.

royal prerogative   The sum of powers remaining with the sovereign in the constitutional monarchy. The rights (and duties) that make up the royal prerogative are not always precisely defined but consist of certain executive powers that are nevertheless circumscribed by constitutional conventions (i.e.

ROYAL PAVILION, BRIGHTON   *A blend of Indian-style domes and pinnacles, with exotic Chinese interiors.*

rules necessary to the function of government but not enforceable in law courts). Most exercises of the royal prerogative are carried out by ministers answerable to Parliament, although parliamentary permission is not necessary for their execution. Parliament can, however, abolish or restrict a prerogative right.

The sovereign has the power to appoint the Prime Minister, and if no political party has a parliamentary majority, or the party with a majority has no leader, the sovereign may consult anyone as to the choice of Prime Minister. The sovereign retains the right to be consulted over any government measure. He or she is head of the executive and the judiciary, commander-in-chief of the armed forces, and supreme governor of the Church of England. The sovereign personally chooses knights of the Orders of the *Garter and the *Thistle and people to be honoured within the Order of *Merit, as well as entrants to the *Royal Victorian Order and recipients of the *Royal Victorian Chain. The Dean of Windsor is also the sovereign's choice. The sovereign can declare war, make peace and treaties, recognize foreign states and governments, and annex or cede territory. He or she also has a prerogative of mercy and, at the instigation of the Home Secretary (or, in Scotland, the Secretary of State for Scotland), may grant a royal pardon to anyone convicted of a crime. Instruments of royal prerogative are Orders in Council (*see* Privy Council); commissions (in the armed services) signed by the sovereign and usually by a secretary of state; and proclamations (*see* royal proclamation), writs, letters patent, and other documents under the Great Seal (affixed by the Lord Chancellor in England, and in Scotland by the Secretary of State for Scotland affixing the Great Seal of Scotland in his capacity as Keeper of the Great Seal).

royal proclamation A formal exercise of the royal prerogative by the Queen in Council (*see* Privy Council). Royal proclamations in effect sanction Cabinet decisions: they announce such matters as declarations of war or neutrality, the making of peace, the summoning, dissolution, or prorogation (adjourning) of Parliament, and also the effecting of powers already conferred on the executive by statute

– for example, the declaration of a state of emergency to deal with serious industrial action, natural disasters, severe weather, etc. Under Henry VIII (r. 1509–47) royal proclamations were for a short time declared to be of equal weight with Acts of Parliament as instruments of legislation. They were increasingly used by Elizabeth I and the Stuart kings until the Civil War. The Crown can legislate by proclamation for a newly conquered country (such powers were exercised during the Boer War, for instance), and in British dependent territories proclamations have frequently brought ordinances into force. Royal proclamations are made under the Great Seal affixed by the Lord Chancellor and countersigned by a secretary of state.

Royal Red Cross A decoration instituted in 1883 and originally bestowed on women nurses. It has two classes. Since 1977 a few awards have been made to male nurses in the Royal Navy and the Royal Air Force.

royal salutes The firing of guns to commemorate each year the birth, accession, and coronation of the sovereign. In the case of the present Queen the dates are 21 April, 6 February, and 2 June respectively. These and the birthdays of the Queen Mother (4 August) and the Duke of Edinburgh (10 June) are marked by a salute of 62 guns, fired from the wharf at the Tower of London. On certain ceremonial or triumphal occasions – for example, the opening, prorogation (adjournment), or dissolution of Parliament by the sovereign in person, or when the sovereign passes through London in procession – a salute of 41 guns is fired. A salute of 41 guns is also fired from Hyde Park and the Tower of London to mark the birth of a royal child.

Royal Scottish Academy of Music and Drama An institution founded in Glasgow in 1890 as the Athenaeum School of Music. A drama school was added in 1950, and an opera school, for which the Academy is best known, in 1968. Well-known former students include the actors Tom Conti and Fulton Mackay, the singer Moira Anderson, and Alexander Gibson of the Scottish National Orchestra. Dame Janet Baker was appointed president in 1983.

Royal Scottish Academy of Painting, Sculpture, and Architecture An institution founded in Edinburgh in 1826 to promote the fine arts in Scotland. The Academy holds two main annual exhibitions – a summer show, and the Festival Exhibition to coincide with the *Edinburgh Festival.

Royal Scottish Museum A museum founded in Edinburgh in 1854. It holds collections of decorative arts of the world, archaeology, ethnography, science and technology, natural history, and geology. Displays range from primitive art to space material, from ceramics to fossils (including a remarkable fossil fish collection), and from birds to working models of a wide range of machines; it also houses Benin bronzes and Egyptian antiquities. The museum's notably cavernous buildings were designed by Fowke and Matheson (1861–66).

Royal Shakespeare Company (RSC) A theatre organization founded with the opening in 1879 in Stratford-upon-Avon, Shakespeare's birthplace, of the Shakespeare Memorial Theatre, by which title it was incorporated under royal charter in 1925. Its artistic directors have included Sir Frank Benson, Sir Anthony Quayle, Sir Peter Hall, Trevor Nunn, and Terry Hands.

The present principal theatre at Stratford, designed by Elisabeth Scott, was opened in 1932 and incorporates the surviving elements of the first theatre, which was largely destroyed by fire in 1926. In 1960, the Shakespeare Memorial Theatre also secured a base in London, at the Aldwych Theatre, under the artistic direction of Sir Peter Hall (later artistic director of the *National Theatre). In 1961 the royal charter was amended to change the name of the corporation and the Stratford theatre from the Shakespeare Memorial Theatre to the Royal Shakespeare Theatre, and the organization adopted the operating style of "The Royal Shakespeare Company" or RSC, the name by which it has come to be known worldwide today. In 1963 the RSC first received grant aid from the *Arts Council. A studio theatre, The Other Place, was opened in Stratford in 1974, and its London equivalent, The Warehouse, in 1977. Since 1977 the

RSC has also presented an annual season of work at the Theatre Royal and the Gulbenkian Studio in Newcastle upon Tyne, and has undertaken regular tours to towns and villages throughout the UK which have little or no access to professional theatre. International tours to Europe, the USA, and Australia are also a regular feature of the RSC's programme, as are television versions of RSC productions and transfers to West End and other commercial theatres. In 1982 the RSC's London operation moved to the *Barbican Centre for Arts and Conferences, where two new auditoria, the Barbican Theatre and The Pit, replaced the Aldwych and Warehouse, respectively. A third Stratford theatre, the Swan Theatre, constructed in the shell of the original 1879 auditorium, opened in April 1986.

The RSC's repertoire is extensive and varied. The Royal Shakespeare Theatre presents almost exclusively the plays of Shakespeare, and most of its productions are eventually transferred to the Barbican Theatre, where plays of other dramatists of all periods are also presented. The Other Place and The Pit present occasional productions of the plays of Shakespeare and other classic writers, but concentrate largely on the work of new writers. The Swan specializes in presenting the rarely-seen plays of Shakespeare's contemporaries and near-contemporaries, concentrating on the period 1570–1750.

Royal Society The oldest and one of the most prestigious scientific institutions in Britain and the oldest in the world to have enjoyed a continuous existence. The Royal Society traces its origins to 1645, when a group of scholars associated with Gresham College, London, began weekly meetings to discuss the "new philosophy" then nascent in Europe's centres of learning. During the Civil War some continued to meet at Wadham College, Oxford, in the rooms of John Wilkins, philosopher and later Bishop of Chester. With the Restoration (1660), meetings in London were resumed and the inaugural meeting – the first to be officially recorded – was held at Gresham College on 28 November 1660. Among the 12 founder members were the chemist Robert Boyle and the architect Christopher Wren. The royal charter was granted by Charles II in 1662. A second charter in 1663 gave its full title as "The Royal Society of London for Improving Natural Knowledge". Members excluded politics or religion from their discussions, and concentrated on discoveries in mathematics, astronomy, physics, chemistry, and biology that were taking place. Samuel Pepys joined in 1664, and in 1671 Isaac Newton became a fellow. Newton later served as president of the Society (1703–27) and used it to full advantage in his disputes with rival scientists, notably the German philosopher Leibniz.

Today, under its current president, Sir Andrew Huxley (1917–   ), the Royal Society has nearly 1000 fellows, some 80 foreign members, and royal fellows, who include its patron, the Queen. Since 1849 it has administered a parliamentary grant for research into all branches of the sciences. It also promotes science education, cooperates with scientific organizations abroad, arranges exchange visits of scientists, and advises the government on science policy. *Philosophical Transactions of the Royal Society* was launched in 1665 to publish the work of fellows, and in 1832 *Proceedings of the Royal Society* began publication. The Society gives a number of awards for outstanding scientific achievement, including the Copley medal and the Davy medal. However, the coveted letters FRS, signifying Fellow of the Royal Society, are in themselves sufficient recognition of merit in the scientific world.

Royal Society for the Prevention of Cruelty to Animals (RSPCA) The main British animal welfare society, founded in 1824. Its principal instigator was the Galway landowner Richard Martin (1754–1834), who was nicknamed "Humanity Martin" by his friend King George IV and who waged a long campaign to have cruel sports banned. This made him so unpopular that he was burnt in effigy by a London mob; nevertheless, shortly after his death, bull-baiting was made illegal (1835).

The RSPCA's headquarters are at Horsham, Sussex, and it has 210 regional branches, as well as animal hospitals and homes. Its work is carried out by 230 uniformed inspectors, who investigate complaints (over 47,000 in 1984) and where necessary institute legal proceedings against offenders (over 1900 prosecutions in 1984, of which nearly 98% resulted in convictions). Many of the million calls received by the RSPCA in 1984 were from pet owners who were unable to continue to care for their animals. From its earliest days, the RSPCA has been active in promoting legislation to protect animals. In recent years it has been involved in controversy over the extent of its support for the animal rights lobby on such issues as battery hens, fur-farming, vivisection, and blood sports. It is also involved in enforcement of legislation relating to wild birds and animals, such as the Wildlife and Countryside Act 1981. In 1984 the most frequent category of RSPCA prosecution was cruelty to dogs (880 cases), followed by offences against wild birds (468 prosecutions).

Royal Society for the Protection of Birds (RSPB) A society formed in Manchester in 1889, initially as a protest movement. It obtained its royal charter in 1904. Its original cause for concern was the trade in plumes for women's hats, which was responsible for the destruction of thousands of egrets, herons, birds of paradise, and other species with the misfortune to have fashionable plumage. Strangely enough, all the Society's first members were women. Other early campaigns were against the use of bird traps, the keeping of caged birds, and the eating of song birds. With the increased concern for conservation in recent decades, its membership has soared from 10,500 in 1961 to around 370,000 in 1984, and it is now one of the country's major conservation bodies, owning over a hundred reserves with a total area of over 48,500 hectares (120,000 acres), including a wide range of habitats from moorland to salt marsh. Either alone or in conjunction with other bodies, such as the British Trust for Ornithology, the RSPB has been responsible for numerous campaigns to promote the welfare of wild birds, including national surveys of breeding species, studies of the effects of toxic seed dressings on bird populations, preservation of the habitats of endangered species, and protection of nesting birds of prey from plunder by unscrupulous suppliers to the falconry market.

The RSPB's headquarters are at Sandy, Bedfordshire, and it also has area headquarters in other regions. It publishes books and magazines, and produces educational films. Its emblem, an avocet, represents one of the Society's successes: the avocet, which was lost to Britain for a century as a breeding species, has, since 1946, begun to nest again near the Suffolk coast.

Royal Standard   *See* flags.

Royal Tournament   A military display held annually at Earl's Court in London. Featuring massed bands, physical training exercises, a popular inter-service field-gun race, and mock battles, the event has changed little since 1880, when, as the Grand Military Tournament, it was first held.

Royal Ulster Constabulary   (RUC) Northern Ireland's police force, which comprises about 7000 full-time officers and some 5000 full- and part-time reservists. Headed by the chief constable, the RUC is assisted by the Army, especially the Ulster Defence Regiment, in coping with the problems of maintaining law and order in the Province (*see* Irish nationalism). An Irish police force was created in 1787, although it was 1822 before a permanent trained force came into being. In 1867 Queen Victoria gave it the title Royal Irish Constabulary, but this was disbanded and was replaced in the north by the RUC after partition in 1922.

Royal Victoria and Albert   A decoration originally intended for Queen Victoria's daughters and other princesses, conferring no rank or title. It was instituted on 10 February 1862 and enlarged to include a second class in 1864, when recipients were to be drawn from senior ladies in waiting at court and nonroyal ladies connected with the royal family. A third and fourth class were subsequently added to include lesser ranks. The last holder was Princess Alice, Countess of Athlone, who died in 1981.

Royal Victorian Chain   A decoration instituted in August 1902 by Edward VII, only bestowed on special occasions. It confers no precedence on its holders, who tend to be foreign sovereigns.

Royal Victorian Order   One of the *orders of knighthood. It was instituted on 21 April 1896 by Queen Victoria and was designed to reward distinguished service to the sovereign. It is often bestowed on members of the royal household, *Court of the Lord Lyon, or *College of Arms. Membership is unlimited and its anniversary is 20 June (the day of Queen Victoria's accession). There are five classes: Knights and Dames Grand Cross (who are called Sir or Dame, and put GCVO after their name); Knights and Dames Commanders (who are called Sir or Dame and put KCVO or DCVO after their names); Commanders (CVO); Lieutenants (LVO); and Members (MVO). The Queen is sovereign of the order, and other senior positions are held by the Grand Master and a chancellor. The motto is "Victoria" and the ribbon is blue with red and white edges.

royal yacht   A vessel which is both the official and private residence of the sovereign and other members of the royal family when on state visits abroad made by sea or when cruising in British waters. The present royal yacht, *Britannia*, was so named after her launching by the Queen at Clydebank in 1953. She weighs 5862 tonnes (5769 tons) and can maintain a constant speed of 21 knots. When not in official use she participates in some naval exercises, and in the event of war can be converted for use as a hospital ship. *Britannia* is thought to be the 75th royal yacht in Royal Naval service. She is the only vessel in the Navy to be commanded by an admiral, who is known as Flag Officer Royal Yachts and is normally, as an extra equerry to the Queen, a member of the royal household. The crew numbers 22 officers and 254 men.

RSPB   *See* Royal Society for the Protection of Birds.

RSPCA   *See* Royal Society for the Prevention of Cruelty to Animals.

rugby   A form of *football played with an oval ball, which may be handled as well as kicked. The game descended from football as played at Rugby School in the early 19th century. Tradition ascribes the introduction of handling to one Willam Webb Ellis who, in

1823, "with a fine disregard for the rules of football as played at his time first took the ball in his arms and ran with it". In 1843 Guy's Hospital Rugby Club was formed, to be followed during the next 40 years by scores of notable clubs in Britain and Ireland. Rugby football split irrevocably with soccer (association football) in 1863, when the newly-formed Football Association outlawed handling. In 1871 the Rugby Football Union was formed and the laws codified. Similar unions were soon established in Ireland, Scotland, and Wales; the first international match took place in 1871 at Edinburgh between England and Scotland. By the 1880s the four home unions were playing each other regularly in the international championship. This competition was later joined by France, who played their first international against England in 1905. The county championship began in 1890–91, but club matches were traditionally "friendly" until 1922, when the RFU introduced a national club competition. Welsh clubs now have a similar cup, and the Scots have highly competitive leagues.

A further schism occurred in the 1890s, when some northern clubs in England began to pay their players. The RFU suspended them in 1893, declaring the game to be exclusively amateur; and in 1895 they formed their own Northern Rugby Football Union, later to become the Rugby League. Subsequent divergence in the rules has led to the emergence of two distinct games: rugby union, played by teams of 15 players, and rugby league, played by teams of 13 players. The professional movement flourished, especially in Lancashire and Yorkshire; but the game has also prospered in its own right, and today there are many amateur clubs. The RFU, however, has maintained an uncompromisingly hostile attitude both to the League and to professionalism. Rugby league is the traditional working-class game in the north, though rugby union also has a considerable following. In both England and Scotland, soccer is far more popular than either code, but in Wales rugby union has become the national game.

Both games have become popular overseas. In addition to France, rugby union spread throughout the British Empire, notably to

Australia, New Zealand, and South Africa. It has also flourished in other places, such as Romania and Argentina, and is now increasing in popularity in Canada, the USA, and Italy. Rugby league has taken root in France, Australia, and New Zealand. (*See also* Twickenham; Cardiff Arms Park.)

Runnymede The site on the south bank of the Thames near Egham, Surrey, where King John set his seal on *Magna Carta in June 1215. The site was acquired by the *National Trust in 1929. At the foot of nearby Cooper's Hill stands the Magna Carta Memorial – a domed classical temple erected by the American Bar Association. A little higher is the John F. Kennedy Memorial, unveiled in 1965 to commemorate the US president, while on the summit of the hill is a memorial to Commonwealth airmen who died in World War II.

rush-bearing An annual festival that survives in a few English towns and villages, notably Grasmere, Ambleside, Warcop, and Great Musgrave in the Lake District. Until the 18th century, when wooden flooring began to be installed, the cold stone flagging or beaten earth of the church floor was traditionally strewn with freshly-cut rushes, grass, or hay. This covering, which kept the feet of the congregation warm and dry, was renewed each year at a ceremony that often coincided with the festival of the church's patron saint, the rushes being carried to the church by a procession of parishioners accompanied by children bearing garlands of flowers. The rush-bearing festival at Ambleside takes place on the Saturday nearest to 26 July (St Anne's Day), when local children, adults, and church officials parade through the town carrying "rush-bearings": two tall pillars of rush and an assortment of wooden frames decorated with rushes in traditional designs. After pausing in the market place to sing the Rushbearer's Hymn the procession moves on to the church for a short service, at the end of which each child receives a piece of gingerbread.

Grasmere's rush-bearing festival now takes place on the Saturday nearest to 5 August (St Oswald's Day), with festivities similar to those of Ambleside. At Warcop and Great Musgrave the festival processions perpetuate the

RUSH-BEARING

garland-bearing tradition rather than that of rush-bearing, although rush crosses are sometimes carried as a symbol of the festival's origins. On the Sunday after 29 June at Wingrave, Buckinghamshire, the floor of the parish church is ceremonially strewn with fresh hay from a nearby field; the same custom is observed at Old Weston, Cambridgeshire, on the Sunday nearest to 15 July.

Ruskin College A college founded at Oxford in 1899 to enable working men to enjoy the benefits of study in the great university city. Its founders, the Americans Walter Vrooman and Charles A. Beard, envisaged it as a practical expression of the social ideals of John Ruskin (1819–1900), who had been Slade Professor of Art in the University of Oxford from 1869 to 1884. Although not part of the university, Ruskin College has close links with it. The men and women who come there, generally on scholarships, many from abroad, pursue a two-year course of study on the Oxford pattern in such subjects as economics and political science.

S

Sadler's Wells Theatre A theatre in London famous as the home of the opera and ballet companies that became the *Royal Ballet and the *English National Opera. Sadler's Wells is on the site of a medicinal well (which can still be seen under a trapdoor at the back of the stalls). Here, in 1673, Thomas Sadler founded a "music house", adding the attraction of entertainment to supplement the therapeutic qualities of the well. In the 18th century the theatre was owned first by a local builder, Thomas Rosoman, who rebuilt it and restored its popularity. On his retirement it was taken over by Tom King, the ex-manager of Drury Lane. Under King's management the clown Joseph Grimaldi (1779–1837) made his infant debut at Sadler's Wells. The theatre subsequently served successively as a skating rink, pickle factory, boxing arena, "house of melodrama", and music hall. The present theatre was built 1927–31 to house the ballet and opera companies founded by Lilian Baylis (1874–1937). Following the removal from Sadler's Wells of first the ballet (1946) and then the opera (1968), foreign and touring companies have continued to use the theatre.

Salvation Army A Christian organization dedicated to evangelical and social work that now operates in over 80 countries. It was founded by William Booth (1829–1912), a former Methodist minister who, together with his wife Catherine, set up their Christian Mission tent in Whitechapel, London, in 1865. Booth was a rousing evangelist and vigorous leader for whom salvation through Christ was a vital step towards alleviating the grinding poverty of the Victorian slums. In 1878 his movement became the Salvation Army and adopted a military style, including uniforms, bands, and a hierarchy of command. "Recruits" to Booth's Army were pledged to teetotalism and other strictures on their behaviour, as well as a total commitment to Christ. From the outset women were treated with equality. *War Cry*, the Army's journal, first appeared in 1879.

In the following decades, the Salvation Army spread to the USA, British colonies, and other countries, and its members were increasingly prominent in social reform, setting up hospitals and hostels for the poor. However, Booth had his critics, both in the Church and in Parliament, and some of his officers encountered physical violence, partly organized by the brewers. His best-selling *In Darkest England and the Way Out* (1890) focused attention on the plight of Britain's poor and advocated reforms that were considered "socialist" at the time. On his death Booth was succeeded as leader by his eldest son Bramwell.

The tradition of social concern is maintained today, with around 125 Army social services

SALVATION ARMY *Men queuing for the labour exchange, soup kitchen, and hostel. The Salvation Army opened and operated the first ever labour exchange in Britain in the 1890s.*

centres in Britain and over 1800 officers engaged in social and evangelistic work. It also operates a missing persons investigation service, which traces some 5000 people each year. Each of the 1044 local corps is commanded by an officer and belongs to a regional division. Worship follows no set liturgy and includes no sacraments, although great emphasis is placed on music and song. This is often taken to the streets by the Army's brass bands and hymn singers.

Samaritans A telephone service for the suicidal and despairing. It was started in 1953 by the Rev. Chad Varah after he had officiated at the funeral of a 13-year-old girl who had committed suicide. It was revealed that her distress arose from the onset of menstruation, something that she did not understand and was too frightened of to talk about. The first Samaritan centre was set up in the crypt of St Stephen Walbrook, the Lord Mayor of London's church. Varah's counselling service was an instant success and the pressure of callers made it necessary for the rector to call in some helpers. These helpers, dispensing coffee and cigarettes to the callers, soon began to listen to their problems. Varah discovered that in most cases the attentive ear and caring response of the helpers was as valuable to the callers as the professional counselling of the trained priest. This discovery led to the foundation of the Samaritan movement, which now has 181 branches throughout the country manned by some 20,000 lay volunteers, who are carefully selected but have no qualifications other than a brief preparation course with the Samaritans. Run as a charity, the Samaritans offer a nonprofessional, confidential, and (if required) anonymous service to anyone in despair or distress. Samaritans will listen for as long as they are needed and the service is free. They offer little advice, believing that their callers will be helped to make their own decisions by talking to someone who cares; counselling is available if it is needed. They help some 350,000 new callers each year.

Sandringham A Norfolk estate, mansion, and village owned by the royal family and used as a country retreat, especially at Christmas. The property, which now extends to some 7900 hectares (19,500 acres), was purchased by Edward, Prince of Wales, in 1862. He employed the architect Albert Jenkins Humbert to rebuild the existing house in mock-Tudor style, work that was completed in 1870. The former coach house and other outbuildings house a museum, which contains a collection of royal cars and mementoes of royal successes in horse racing.

King George VI broadcast his first Christmas message to the nation from Sandringham in 1939. He died there in 1952.

SAS See Special Air Service.

Save the Children Fund (SCF) Britain's largest international children's charity, founded in 1919, and having as its president HRH Princess Anne. It is concerned with the rescue of children from disaster and the longer term welfare of children in need. In the developing world, it provides emergency relief, health services, education, hospitals, and training to promote local care; in the UK, it offers services for deprived children – playgroups, adventure playgrounds, youth projects, toy libraries – as well as a counselling service for parents and intermediate treatment for young people in trouble with the law. A special project since 1979 has been Stop Polio, a campaign for the development of major national immunization schemes, which has now expanded to cover other diseases. These activities cost over £42,000 per day. The SCF's income comes mainly from donations, legacies, and grants, and in addition, its 750 branches in the UK are active in fundraising; Save the Children (Sales) Ltd also provides income from its trading activities. The SCF has close links with similar organizations abroad, especially in the Commonwealth.

SCE See school-leaving examinations.

school-leaving examinations The **General Certificate of Education** (**GCE**) and the **Certificate of Secondary Education** (**CSE**) are public examinations taken by pupils at secondary schools in England and Wales; in Scotland they take the **Scottish Certificate of Education** (**SCE**) examination.

The GCE was introduced in 1951 and replaced the former School Certificate and Higher School Certificate. It is taken at two levels: O (or Ordinary) Level is sat around the age of 16, and A (Advanced) Level is usually taken two years later in fewer subjects, which are studied in greater depth. The eight examining boards have close links with the universities, and A-Level results are the principal determining factor for admission to most universities.

The CSE was introduced in 1965 and was intended as an alternative for pupils who are less academically inclined than those who take the GCE. However, pupils can and do take a combination of GCE and CSE examinations in the various subjects studied. The highest grade in the CSE is accepted as the equivalent of a GCE O Level.

There are plans to replace the GCE and CSE examinations by a single system, the General Certificate of Secondary Education (GCSE), which will obviate pupils having to decide (or have teachers decide for them) at the age of about 14 whether to aim for the GCE or the CSE qualifications.

In Scotland pupils taking the SCE sit papers on a range of subjects at Ordinary Grade at the end of their fourth year and at Higher Grade one year later (compare the two-year gap between GCE O and A Level). Pupils who complete a sixth year of secondary schooling may sit the Scottish Certificate of Sixth Year Studies examination for which they study a maximum of three subjects at some depth. The standard is equivalent to GCE A Level.

Science and Engineering Research Council A body established in 1965 to support fundamental research throughout the range of natural sciences, with the exceptions of agriculture, medicine, and the natural environment, which are covered by specific research councils. Most of its funds are used to support research projects in universities, polytechnics, and other establishments, and the Council has only two laboratories of its own – the Rutherford-Appleton Laboratory and the Daresbury Laboratory, both employed principally in the fields of particle and nuclear physics. It also funds the *Royal Greenwich Observatory and the *Royal Observatory, Edinburgh. The work of the Council is divided into four broad areas, each the responsibility of a separate board: astronomy, space, and radio; engineering; nuclear physics; and science.

Science Museum A museum in South Kensington, London, that houses Britain's most important collection of scientific and technological exhibits. The original collection was separated from the Victoria and Albert Museum in 1909 and has continued to expand ever since: the displays cover the entire spectrum of Britain's industrial and scientific development. On the ground floor, the history of steam engines is traced through early models made by James Watt (1736–1819), Richard Trevithick (1771–1833), and other pioneers of the industrial revolution. Successive galleries are devoted to the internal combustion engine, diesel and gas turbines, and electric motors. The oldest railway locomotive in the world, *Puffing Billy* (1813), and Stephenson's *Rocket* (1829) are housed there. Industrial processes are dealt with on the first floor, with displays of machine tools, iron and steel production, spinning and weaving, farm machinery, and others; many exhibits are working models. Other galleries contain astronomical instruments and early clocks, including the working clock mechanism from Wells cathedral, which dates from 1392 – the second oldest surviving clock in England. Second-floor galleries show advances in chemistry and its applications, and include a large-scale working model of an oil refinery; printing and papermaking are also illustrated. Among the nautical exhibits are models of historic vessels, such as Nelson's flagship *Victory*. Some of the very latest developments in technology are demonstrated in the physics and computer galleries. The history of photography and cinematography are described on the third floor, which also houses a display of optics and optical instruments ranging from early microscopes to holograms. Large areas are also devoted to radio, television, radar, aeronautics, and space technology.

One of the latest additions is the Wellcome Museum of the history of medicine on the fourth floor. This is based on the collections of drug manufacturer and philanthropist, Sir

Henry Wellcome (1853–1936) and covers medical practice from prehistoric times to the present day. Basic scientific principles are explored in the children's gallery in the basement.

The *National Railway Museum was opened in York in 1975 and is an annexe of the Science Museum.

Scotland Yard The headquarters of the *Metropolitan Police (officially, New Scotland Yard) at Broadway, Westminster, though the name is often used for the Criminal Investigation Department (*see* CID). The name Scotland Yard derives from the original site of the headquarters, which was in Whitehall Place, backing onto a lane called Great Scotland Yard. In 1891 it moved to Parliament Street as New Scotland Yard, and it took that name with it when moving to Broadway in 1967.

Scots The English language as traditionally spoken in Scotland. In the 14th–16th centuries it was a major literary and administrative language, used at the court of the Scottish kings and by the poets Robert Henryson (?1430–?1506), William Dunbar (?1465–?1530), and others. It has always been more or less mutually comprehensible with English, although derived independently from the Northumbrian dialect of Old English.

If Scotland had maintained its political and cultural independence, Scots today would without doubt be a language quite distinct from English, just as Swedish and Danish are now distinct although in medieval times they were dialects of the same language. However, the union of the crowns of England and Scotland in 1603 and the Act of Union of 1707 were political events that complemented the desire of Scottish writers to reach the wider (and more lucrative) audience of London and the south. Some Scots, therefore, from the 17th century onwards used standard English as the medium of written communication. The effect on Scots was to create a linguistic situation of great stylistic complexity. Scots writers and speakers have available to them choices, for example, between "know" and "ken", "church" and "kirk", "child" and "bairn", and so on, with a range of connotative and denotative implications unknown in standard southern English. A speaker who says "He gaed ben the hoose" rather than "He went into the best room" may be a genuine speaker of a Scots dialect, but he may alternatively be deliberately choosing this linguistic option as an assertion of his own Scottishness. The use of conscious Scotticisms, though now fashionable, is full of traps for the unwary, however.

Literary Scots was kept alive in the 18th century by Allan Ramsay (1686–1758), who collected and published Scottish medieval poetry as well as using Scots for his own poetry, and above all by Robert Burns (1759–96), the greatest of all writers in Scots. Sir Walter Scott (1771–1832), in *Rob Roy* and elsewhere, wrote dialogue in spoken Scots that still rings true today. In the 1920s the so-called *Lallans movement attempted, with some success, to revive Scots as a language for poetry. The most important of the Lallans poets is Hugh MacDiarmid (1892–1978). A leading modern Scots prose writer, Lewis Grassic Gibbon (1901–35), captured in his novels the characteristic rhythms and idiom of northeastern Scots speech, while avoiding the obscurantism of MacDiarmid and his kind.

Scots Guards *See* Household Division.

Scots law Although Scotland is a constituent of the United Kingdom, for historical reasons there exists there a legal system and professional structure very different from that of England and Wales. The domestic law of Scotland is in some respects the same as that of the rest of the UK and in others markedly different. Roman law (or the civil law) is at the root of many domestic systems, particularly those of France and other continental countries into which it was received at the time of the Renaissance. Many other systems are, by contrast, based on the principles of the *common law and *equity that developed in England with relatively little Roman influence. Scots law occupies an intermediate position. At the union with England in 1707, there existed for Scotland a system drawing from both Roman law and common law together with other sources, such as custom, canon law, and Acts of the Scottish parliament.

Scotland had a separate ruling dynasty until 1603 and an independent parliament until the union, separate courts and judiciary, a separate legal profession with distinct training and qualifications, different procedure and terminology, and on most topics distinct bodies of substantive law: for example, argument within Scottish law usually relies upon the relevant general principle rather than on precedent. Under the Act of Union the system's independent continuance was guaranteed. The legislative authority for Scotland is now the Parliament of the UK (which replaced the Parliament of Great Britain under the Act of Union with Ireland, 1800); thus an Act of that Parliament applies to Scotland unless it expressly states otherwise. If it applies only to Scotland, this is indicated in its title: as, for example, the Local Government (Scotland) Act 1975.

The formal sources of Scots law are legislation, judicial precedent, institutional writings, custom, and equity. The branches of law in which English and Scottish law hardly differ are those (e.g. tax law and company law) that are regulated almost exclusively by Acts of Parliament dating after 1707. Those in which there are major differences include the law of contract, criminal law, and land law. In the law of contract, the English doctrine of consideration (under which, unless it is in a deed, a promise cannot be enforced unless something of value is given for it), is, for example, unknown, and a unilateral promise, if proved by writing, is considered obligatory without acceptance or consideration. In the criminal law, the age of responsibility is eight, and verdicts of "not proven" are permissible; in land law, both the rights capable of existing and the procedures for their transfer are substantially different.

Scotsman Scotland's most prestigious daily newspaper, first published in Edinburgh in 1817. It was founded as an independent weekly by William Ritchie (1781–1831), a solicitor, and Charles Maclaren (1782–1866), a customs clerk. It aimed to promote "impartiality, firmness, and independence" in public life, and in its early years waged a successful campaign against abuses in the Scottish policing system. Its well-known thistle emblem was adopted from the first issue. In 1820 Maclaren became the paper's full-time editor, and in 1823 it began to be published biweekly. On Ritchie's death in 1831 his brother John (1778–1870) assumed the copyright. Maclaren was succeeded as editor in 1845 by Alexander Russell (1814–76), one of the greatest 19th-century newspaper editors.

On the abolition of the Stamp Tax (1855), the *Scotsman* became a daily, and its circulation increased from around 3400 to 6000. In 1868 a London office was opened, and the *Scotsman* led the fight for provincial newspapers to be allowed to have representatives in the parliamentary press gallery, a privilege hitherto reserved for London papers; this was granted in 1881. Due mainly to the energy of its business manager and later coproprietor James Law (1839–1922), the *Scotsman's* circulation climbed steadily, reaching 50,000 by 1877. Law's association with the paper lasted from 1857 to 1922; his descendants, together with those of John Ritchie Findlay (1824–98), grand-nephew of the first John Ritchie, continued to own the paper until 1953.

The first half of the 20th century was spanned by three editors: John P. Croal (1906–24), George A. Waters (1924–44), and James Murray Watson (1944–55). The *Scotsman* continued steadily to build up its reputation as a national paper. In the 1930s it pioneered distribution by air, as James Law had done by rail 70 years earlier.

In the 1950s, despite protest in Scotland, the paper was bought by the Canadian newspaper magnate Roy Thomson, later Lord Thomson of Fleet (1894–1976), who modernized and revitalized it. From 1980 the *Scotsman Colour Magazine* was published monthly, and circulation in the early 1980s was around 90,000.

Scottish Ballet A ballet company founded as the Western Theatre Ballet in 1956 in Bristol. Its first director was Elizabeth West (1927–62), who was succeeded after her premature death in an accident by the ballet's chief choreographer Peter Darrell (1929–). The policy of the company is to present full-length dramatic contemporary works, such as Darrell's *Sun into Darkness* (1966). The company has also presented the work of such choreographers as Maurice Béjart (1928–) and

Kenneth MacMillan (1929–   ). Since moving to Glasgow in 1969 it has also introduced some classical ballets into its repertoire. It took its present name in 1974.

Scottish Certificate of Education (SCE) *See* school-leaving examinations.

Scottish education   The Scottish system of education differs somewhat from that of England and Wales, particularly at secondary level. In Scotland preschool education is neither compulsory nor widespread, although some children attend state or private nursery schools. Pupils enter primary school at or around the age of five, and after seven years they proceed to secondary school, there being no equivalent in Scotland of the middle school existing in some areas of England. Formerly pupils in the last year of primary school took an exam called the "qualifying exam", the equivalent of the English eleven-plus. This determined whether they would proceed to senior secondary school or to a junior secondary school, the latter being designed for less able students who would leave school at the minimum leaving age. The establishment of comprehensive schools did away with the necessity for this selection process.

In the fourth year of secondary school, around the age of 16, Scottish pupils are presented for the Scottish Certificate of Education examinations at O Grade. The more able pupils go on to a fifth year to undertake further exams known as Highers. The Scottish educational system has always prided itself on the breadth of its coverage and although the standard of the individual Higher exams is lower than that of the corresponding A-Level exams in England, the average Scottish pupil sits significantly more Highers than his or her English counterpart does A Levels. Pupils wishing to extend their number of Higher passes or to study further subjects in which they have already gained Higher passes go on to the sixth year. They can then sit the Sixth Year Studies examinations, which are accepted by English universities as being the equivalent of A Levels. The Scottish secondary school system is in the process of being revised: under the proposed scheme the O-Grade exam would be replaced by a Standard-level one, in which continuous

teacher assessment and communicative skills would play a signficant part.

Scottish Episcopal Chuch   The only Scottish member of the *Anglican Communion, having some 66,000 members and around 200 clergy, presided over by seven diocesan bishops, one of whom is elected primus, or head, of the Church. The governing body is a General Synod.

When William of Orange allowed the Presbyterians to seize control of church government in Scotland in 1689, many Episcopalians chose to adhere to their own form of church order. In 1746, as a result of a belief that many Episcopalians might prefer the return of Stuart monarchs (who were expected to reassert episcopacy), the government introduced repressive measures against the Scottish Episcopalians, making it illegal for them to possess churches or chapels and forbidding public services. Indeed, Episcopalian clergy were banned from ministering to a gathering of more than five people at risk of imprisonment or banishment. But the Church survived and in 1784 an upstairs room in Aberdeen saw the consecration of Bishop Samuel Seabury, first bishop of the Protestant Episcopal Church of America. The antiepiscopal laws were repealed in 1792.

Scottish Law Commission   *See* Law Commission.

Scottish National Opera   An opera company founded in 1962 in Glasgow with Alexander Gibson as its artistic director. From its first one-week season, it has come to mount an all-year programme. The company produced the first complete performance anywhere of Berlioz's *The Trojans* in 1969, and the first German-language performance in Scotland of Wagner's *Ring* cycle in 1971. In 1975 it moved into permanent premises at the converted Theatre Royal, originally built in 1867.

Scottish National Orchestra   An orchestra established in Glasgow in 1898 by the amalgamation of the Choral Union Orchestra (founded in 1874) and the Scottish Orchestra (founded in 1891). Its principal conductors have included John Barbirolli (1899–1970), from 1933 to 1936, and Alexander Gibson

(1926–), who became its first Scottish-born conductor (1959–84); its current musical director is Neeme Järvi (1937–). Under Gibson, it gave increased emphasis to Scottish works; and in 1971, in conjunction with Glasgow University, it established Musica Nova, an organization to promote interest in new music. It also holds its own season of promenade concerts.

Scottish National Party A political party that aspires to gain independence for Scotland. It emerged as a major Scottish party in the 1970s, winning seven seats in the House of Commons in the general election of February 1974 and 11 in October of that year. Its policy then was to work towards independence through a preliminary stage of devolution and the establishment of a directly elected Scottish assembly (with limited powers of legislation and of control over the Scottish Office). In March 1979, however, a referendum showed that only one third of the Scottish electorate favoured devolution, at least in the form then proposed by Westminster legislation. In the subsequent election (May 1979), the party's representation in the House fell to two (which is the present number).

Scottish Tourist Board *See* British Tourist Authority.

Scouse A native of Liverpool, or the variety of working-class English spoken by such a person. The term itself is of uncertain origin, but may derive from a kind of stew (lob-scouse) eaten by sailors. Scouse speech is characterized by its flat intonation patterns and somewhat adenoidal delivery. Phonetically, it is a typical Lancashire accent, although several of its vocabulary items have been brought in by immigrants from Ireland. A few examples of current Scouse expressions are "scally" (denoting a street urchin), "woollyback" (a general term of contempt for non-Liverpudlians, especially those from north of Liverpool), and "sly" meaning uncooperative.

Scout Association An international youth movement founded in England in 1908 by Robert Lord Baden-Powell (1857–1941). While in the army, Baden-Powell had written a book about the scouting techniques he

had developed; especially patrolling in small units for reconnaissance purposes. He later learned that the book was being used for training boys and on the basis of the interest shown in its ideas, he organized an experimental camp for about 20 boys on Brownsea Island, in Poole harbour, Dorset, in 1907. He then wrote a proposal for a national movement for scouts, and published *Scouting for Boys* in 1908.

The purpose of the Scout Association is to train boys to use their initiative, to teach them practical skills, and to help them become useful members of society. Open to all, both able-bodied and handicapped, it is a voluntary, nonpolitical organization based on moral principles, such as loyalty (especially to one's country and religion), active participation in society, and responsibility for self-development.

Scout groups, of which there are nearly 12,000 in the United Kingdom, consist of **Cubs** (8–11 years), Scouts (11–16 years), and **Venture Scouts** (open to young men and women of 16–20 years). Specialist groups include Air and Sea Scouts and a pre-Cub group, the Beavers (6–8 years). Activities include sports, bands, camping, community service, and stage work, such as the famous "Gang Shows". Fundraising efforts include Scout Job Week, formerly known as Bob-a-Job Week. Progress is marked by awards, the highest being the Queen's Scout Award. The Scouts have their own shops, magazine, radio stations, and every four years hold a World Jamboree. By the 1980s the world movement comprised more than 16 million Scouts in some 120 countries. Some 200 million people have belonged to the Scouts for a time during their lives.

The **Girl Guides** movement was also started by Baden-Powell, with his sister Agnes, in 1910. His wife Lady Olave St Clair Baden-Powell did much to promote the Guides. Girls aged 7–11 become **Brownie Guides** (or Brownies); they may become Guides at age 10, and Rangers from 14.

SDLP *See* Social Democratic Labour Party.

SDP *See* Social Democratic Party.

Sealed Knot Society The best known of several British historical re-enactment societies. Founded in 1968 by the historian Brigadier Peter Young, who became its Captain General, the Sealed Knot is named after a group of royalists who worked for the restoration of the monarchy when the future Charles II was in exile after the English *Civil War. With a membership of some 5000, the Sealed Knot stages mock battles all over the country, usually in cooperation with local charitable bodies. Its members, who wear period costume and armour, are trained in the use of musket, pike, and artillery and include a small troop of cavalry. A similar organization, the English Civil War Society, also presents "living history" weeks, during which members live as authentically as possible in the manner of the 17th century. Although these are the two largest re-enactment societies in Britain, parallel groups now exist for most periods of the nation's history, including the *Wars of the Roses and the Napoleonic Wars. Inspired by the British example, similar societies have been founded in the USA to commemorate the War of Independence and the American Civil War.

searching the cellars An annual ceremony that takes place at the Houses of Parliament a few hours before the state opening in early November. The tradition is believed to date back to the Gunpowder Plot of 1605: the *Yeoman of the Guard, in full uniform, diligently search every inch of the cellars and vaults for a second *Guy Fawkes or a cache of explosives. They are armed for the purpose with candle-lanterns, disregarding the modern electric lighting. Having assured themselves that all is well, they send a message to the monarch to the effect that the state opening of Parliament may now safely commence. More recent attempts to blow up Her Majesty's ministers have made such searches as much a necessity as a tradition.

seaside resorts For many British people, holidays and the seaside remain inseparable. The popularity of seaside resorts began with the fashion for sea bathing, which began during the 18th century. *Spa towns such as Bath and Buxton had already attracted the wealthy and fashionable; but in the 1730s Scarborough in Yorkshire became the first seaside resort, by offering sea bathing in addition to its medicinal spring. It quickly drew affluent patrons, who as well as "taking the waters" might walk and ride on the coast and enjoy society in the evenings.

Restorative properties were claimed for seawater by an astute Dr Richard Russell in a widely read dissertation published in the 1750s; doctors began to prescribe sea bathing (and even the drinking of seawater). Russell moved his practice to Brighton in 1753, where he soon had numerous patients. Eastbourne, Weymouth, and Margate soon followed this example: but with the patronage of George, Prince of Wales, and later, his unique *Royal Pavilion, Brighton outstripped all competition. However, patronage of the aristocracy and upper middle classes ensured architectural improvements to several resorts, particularly during and after the Regency. Crescents and façades overlooking the sea appeared, and the seafront "promenade" was established.

The 19th century saw a vast expansion in the popularity of the seaside: following the example of Queen Victoria and Prince Albert, middle-class families went to the coast, and it was during this period rather than during the Regency that the habit became established. The railways brought many new visitors after the mid-century and new resorts, such as Blackpool and Southport, grew as the railway reached them. Bank holidays were introduced in 1871; and when paid holidays became more general in British working life in the 1880s, the resorts gained a further increase in their trade. As they vied with one another for attractions, the now familiar features appeared: *piers, winter gardens, bandstands, fairgrounds, and amusement parks. Blackpool Tower was built in 1884. Towards the end of the century, the numbers of visitors caused still more building to take place in many coastal towns: hotels, boarding houses, and homes for the increasing number of residents. At the same time a whole range of seaside paraphernalia developed, to be sold along the front: peppermint rock, novelties, souvenirs, and postcards, photographic and comic.

Throughout the first half of the 20th century, the British seaside holiday flourished. World War II interrupted but did not end its popularity (the late forties were perhaps its Indian summer, when the success of *holiday camps revealed an unexpected British enjoyment of communal fun). However, the rapid development and falling price of holidays on the Mediterranean, especially in Spain, permanently altered the scene. The British climate could not compete, and for some years holidays "at home" became unfashionable. Though the tourist authorities have gradually restored Britain's appeal to holidaymakers, the seaside resorts have been forced to accept a reduced status. Some have relapsed into a pre-Victorian gentility; and for a few of them – notably Bournemouth, Brighton, and Blackpool – the annual season of political party conferences still brings its mixed blessings.

secondary modern school   *See* state education.

secretary of state   A senior *minister of the Crown in charge of one of the major government departments (e.g. Home Office (*see* Home Secretary), Foreign Office (*see* Foreign Secretary), environment, defence, trade and industry, health and social security, education and science, and employment). The office's origins lie with the royal secretary of medieval times, who by the 16th century had become the sovereign's chief minister. From 1540 there were usually two principal secretaries of state, joint holders of the same office. In 1689 their functions, both domestic and foreign, were divided on geographical lines (a northern and southern department); in 1782 the designation was changed to home and foreign affairs. From the late 18th century, more secretaries of state were created: the shortlived secretary of state for the American colonies (1768–1782); war and the colonies (1794, the two functions being separated in 1854); India (1858); and the Royal Air Force (1918). The pre-Union Scottish secretaries of state lapsed in the 18th century; the secretaryship for Scotland was established in the 19th century, but only became a full office in 1926. After World War II the number of secretaries increased greatly and is currently about 15. In law, the secretaries of state are still interchangeable, to the extent that the powers conferred by an Act of Parliament on "the secretary of state" may be exercised by any one of them. Similarly, documents used to be issued simply by "one of Her Majesty's principal secretaries of state"; now they are usually more specific.

Sedgemoor, battle of (6 July 1685)   A battle fought southeast of Bridgwater, Somerset, which ended the Duke of Monmouth's rebellion against James II. James Scott, Duke of Monmouth, was the illegitimate son of Charles II and a nephew of James II, who came to the throne in 1685. When unsuccessful efforts were made to exclude the Catholic James from the succession (1678–81), Monmouth was the Protestant candidate as heir to the throne; and he had been in exile since being implicated in the Rye House Plot to kill Charles and James in 1683. Taking advantage of the strength of feeling against the new king, he landed at Lyme Regis with 150 men in June 1685 and declared James a usurper. He was proclaimed king at Taunton and raised a peasant army. After failing to take Bristol, the rebel army attempted but failed to surprise the royal forces, led by the Earl of Feversham and John Churchill (later Duke of Marlborough – *see* Blenheim Palace), at night, while they were encamped on Sedgemoor. Monmouth's cavalry fled and the foot soldiers failed to cross a ditch separating them from their enemies. In the slaughter that followed the undisciplined and untrained peasants were massacred, while the duke himself was captured and later beheaded on Tower Hill. Up to 320 rebels were executed as a result of the ensuing "Bloody Assizes", when Judge Jeffreys, Chief Justice of the King's Bench, conducted a notoriously unfair and savage circuit of the West Country. In addition, 800 rebels were transported. Three years later James II was deposed in the *Glorious Revolution. Sedgemoor was the last battle fought on English (as opposed to British) soil.

select committee   A committee appointed by either House of Parliament, or the two Houses jointly, to investigate or keep under review some matter of domestic or public interest (*compare* standing committee). Committees concerned with domestic matters include the Committee of Privileges of each House (see parliamentary privilege) and the select committees on procedure that are regularly constituted. A joint committee is that on Statutory Instruments (the Joint Scrutiny Committee), which examines much of the large quantity of delegated legislation (see Act of Parliament) and draws Parliament's attention to any unusual features. Most select committees are, however, committees of the Commons concerned with such matters as government expenditure, the activities of particular government departments, and the policy of the government on particular subjects, or with subjects of particular public concern. The overseeing of government policies and departments began experimentally in 1967 with the appointment of two specialist committees, one on agriculture and one on science and technology. They were not at first a total success, their true constitutional role (especially their standing between ministers and civil servants) taking time to establish, and the committee on agriculture was discontinued in 1969. Further committees were, however, developed (e.g. on race relations and overseas aid) and there have been about 12 in regular operation since the House reorganized and extended them in 1977. A recent example of a committee investigating a matter of public concern is that appointed at the end of 1984 (as a result of public disquiet) to examine the role of the *Special Branch.

Senate of the Inns of Court and the Bar
The governing body of *barristers in England and Wales, formed in 1974 by the merger of the **General Council of the Bar** (also known as the **Bar Council**, which is the name since 1974 of a comparable committee of the Senate) and the Senate of the Four Inns of Court. The General Council was an elected body, established in 1894 to promote and protect the interests of the Bar. It was particularly concerned with the maintenance of professional standards, but by way of guidance only, because disciplinary powers were vested exclusively in the individual *Inns of Court. The Senate of the Four Inns of Court was established in 1966 to coordinate the activities of the Inns and the Council. Consisting of repre-

sentatives of both, it took disciplinary decisions which the individual Inns were obliged to implement, exercised general control over the Council of Legal Education (see Inns of Court), and assumed responsibility for the overall organization of the profession. The Senate of the Inns of Court and the Bar is a greatly enlarged and differently constituted version of the 1966 Senate, consisting of some 90 members who include the *Law Officers, Benchers and other representatives of the Inns, and practitioners directly elected by the Bar. Responsible for policy on all matters formerly dealt with by that Senate and the General Council, it meets four times a year, and operates mainly through standing committees. One of these, consisting of the Law Officers and the elected practitioners and in practice autonomous, is known as the Bar Council and, like the General Council, is particularly concerned with matters of conduct and etiquette. The Senate appoints, where necessary, a disciplinary tribunal to hear charges of professional misconduct.

Serjeant-at-Arms The officer of the House of Commons responsible for maintaining order and for internal administration. He is appointed by the sovereign on the recommendation of the House. In preserving order in the chamber, he is directed by the Speaker, but his authority extends to strangers, whether in the public galleries of the House or elsewhere in the Commons end of the Palace of Westminster. He is responsible for allocating rooms, for the general maintenance of the building, and for providing services to members. He also has certain ceremonial functions, particularly that of carrying the Speaker's mace (symbolizing his authority and the royal protection) in his procession to the Chair at the beginning of each day's business.

shadow cabinet See leader of the opposition.

Shakespearean theatre The strongest and most enduring theatrical tradition in Britain. It is kept alive by the work of the *Royal Shakespeare Company in London and Stratford-upon-Avon, by the *National Theatre, by theatrical companies in some of the larger

SHAKESPEAREAN THEATRE *Indoor playhouse c. 1632, possibly The Cockpit. The spectators are sitting in front of the stage as well as in a high gallery behind, making this true "theatre in the round". The hangings at the back (the arras) conceal a space for hiding actors and props; Polonius is killed in such an area in Hamlet.*

towns, by radio and television, and by the innumerable amateur productions of schools, colleges, and drama societies. As Shakespeare's language is so expressive, his characterization so rich, and the plays so diverse, this tradition has probably contributed to the wealth of acting and directing talent in Britain, and indeed, in most English-speaking countries.

William Shakespeare (1564–1616) is acknowledged as a genius throughout the world, but he might have remained a poet in an age of many poets had there not been a sudden upsurge of theatrical activity that began in his childhood and continued throughout his life. Although Stratford was a relatively long way from London in the 16th century, it was nevertheless a stimulating place in which to live – a bustling market town with a grammar school, close to the medieval castles of Warwick and Kenilworth – and it was regularly visited by travelling players. Although very

little is known of the details of Shakespeare's life, according to one theory he joined such a group and followed it to London. There he found several established open-air theatres outside the City boundaries, each run on a repertory basis and needing between 30 and 40 new plays a year to satisfy its audience. By 1592 he had become an established playwright of histories and comedies, enjoying the patronage of several members of the nobility; in 1594 he joined the Lord Chamberlain's Men and later became a shareholder as well as an actor and playwright in the King's Men. This company soon emerged as the dominant force in the theatre of the time, and in 1599 Shakespeare moved with it from Shoreditch to the Globe on Bankside. Here nearly all his greatest comedies and tragedies were performed, in "the wooden O" (on account of its shape) referred to in *Henry V*. In 1608 the manager Richard Burbage reclaimed Blackfriars Theatre, a private indoor theatre, from the Children of the Chapel Royal (a group of boy actors), and set up another company there, with Shakespeare as one of the partners. It seems likely that his last plays, including *The Tempest*, were put on at the Blackfriars Theatre during the last few winters before he returned to his family and property in Stratford.

That 16 of Shakespeare's plays were pirated for publication in small quarto volumes during his lifetime is an indication of their popularity. Since actors and managers were constantly making alterations in their prompt-books these texts are unlikely to be exactly what Shakespeare wrote; but in view of the liberties that were taken with his plays in later centuries it is fortunate that two of Shakespeare's oldest friends, John Heminge and Henry Condell, brought together both the previously printed plays and the unprinted ones in a corrected folio edition of his collected works. Published in 1623, the folio edition contained 36 plays, (*Pericles* being added in 1664). The 1623 folio was reprinted three times in the 17th century, edited six times in the 18th century, and many more times in the 19th and 20th. Nevertheless it is to the 1623 text that editors, critics, actors, and directors must return.

The Globe was closed by the *Puritans in 1642 and demolished two years later. Theatrical activity did not entirely die out, however, and only a year after the Restoration (1660) Pepys went to see *Hamlet*. There followed a sequence of great actor-managers from David Garrick (1717–79), John Kemble (1757–1823), Edmund Kean (c. 1787–1833), and William Macready (1793–1873), to Sir Henry Irving (1838–1905), nearly all of whom ran seasons at the Drury Lane Theatre. The plays were adapted – sometimes drastically – to suit both their own talents and the tastes of the time; moreover, for certain famous actresses the female parts had to be expanded and made more sentimental. In all these early productions the theatres were cavernous, the scenery unwieldy, and the lighting poor – nevertheless the passions came across, often to the detriment of the verse. "Bardolatry" swept fashionable society (partly in the absence of good contemporary dramatists); John Boydell (1719–1804) commissioned 35 leading artists to paint scenes from Shakespeare for him to turn into popular engravings; and Charles Lamb wrote his *Tales* "for the Use of Young Persons". Stratford turned into a place of pilgrimage. In the 19th century historical detail overwhelmed many productions. However, in the 20th century Gordon Craig (1872–1966) and Harley Granville-Barker (1877–1946) showed that a well-lit stage with simple scenery and swift continuity of action was much closer to the conditions at the original Globe and actually enhanced the drama; moreover, the growth of higher education produced an audience ready to listen to uncut texts. Lilian Baylis's first Shakespeare season at the Old Vic in 1914 at popular prices was a considerable success and led to the revival of several neglected plays; repertory companies in the main provincial towns followed her example and it was here that such actors as Sybil Thorndike, Ralph Richardson, Edith Evans, John Gielgud, Michael Redgrave, Alec Guinness, Laurence Olivier, and Peggy Ashcroft learnt their craft.

The festival at Stratford-upon-Avon had become established from the 1830s, performing plays from the complete canon there in the summer and taking them on tour in the winter. The first Memorial Theatre was built on the banks of the Avon in 1879 thanks to the enthusiasm of Charles Edward Flower, a member of the local brewing family; after being devastated by fire in 1926 it was replaced by the present building. The Royal Shakespeare Company originates productions there before taking them to London to the new Barbican theatre, whose design is in some ways reminiscent of an Elizabethan playhouse. (An Elizabethan stage is being added to Stratford's Memorial Theatre; and the American actor Sam Wanamaker has attempted to form a group to build a replica of the Globe on Bankside.) In spite of nearly 400 years of uninterrupted popularity, Shakespeare's plays are constantly being reinterpreted in the light of new criticism, new philosophies, or new trends in the theatre. It is remarkable that new riches are still being found in them. As the director Peter Brook has written: "in the second half of the 20th century in England we are faced with the infuriating fact that Shakespeare is still our model".

Shelta A cant or jargon used by an ethnic group of itinerants or "travellers" in Britain and Ireland. It is estimated that there are today about 15,000 speakers of Shelta in Britain and 6000 in Ireland. Shelta has a highly distinctive vocabulary, probably derived from *Irish Gaelic and English words distorted in various ways to make them unrecognizable. Its origins are disputed, but it probably arose among Irish tinkers towards the end of the 17th century. Others believe that it contains remnants of an ancient, even a pre-Celtic, language. Certainly some of the supposed distortions are so complex that the proposed origin cannot be held with any certainty. Thus, the Shelta word *skop* "open" is supposed to be derived from Irish *oscailt*. Some English slang words are derived from Shelta, for example *monicker* "name", from Shelta *munik* (which in turn is from Irish *ainm* "name") and *gammy* "lame", from Shelta *gyami*, from Irish *cam* "crooked".

Shelter (National Campaign for the Homeless) A charity founded in 1966 to foster the principle that "everyone has a right to a decent home at a price they can afford". Shelter provides help for those in need, and campaigns to inform the public of their difficulties and influence housing policy. Activities include an advice service and assistance with problems; provision of emergency hostels for the homeless; initiatives to make more housing available; investigations and reports; lobbying government and Parliament; and production of a bimonthly newspaper, *Roof*. Shelter's impact was immediate, with 300 families being housed and over £200,000 being raised in its first year. Its income comes principally from donations.

sheriff An officer of the Crown in Scotland, or of the City of London (*compare* High Sheriff). In Scotland, the sheriff's functions are primarily judicial (*see* sheriff courts) but he also has administrative duties: for example, he acts as returning officer at parliamentary elections. The right of the City of London to elect two sheriffs was granted by royal charter in 1132. They are chosen annually by the Court of Common Hall (*see* Corporation of London), and their duties are now purely ceremonial; they wait on the Lord Mayor on state occasions, and present petitions from the City to Parliament.

sheriff courts Scottish courts exercising a civil and criminal jurisdiction of significant, but not unlimited, extent. (*Compare* *Court of Session and *High Court of Justiciary.) Scotland is divided into six sheriffdoms, each having a sheriff-principal and a number of sheriffs, all legally qualified. Courts presided over by sheriffs exercise a civil jurisdiction broadly comparable to that of the *county court in England and Wales; and courts presided over by either a sheriff-principal or a sheriff exercise a criminal jurisdiction wider than that of *magistrates' courts in England and Wales in that it extends to both summary offences and some offences triable by jury. Civil appeals from a sheriff court lie to the Inner House of the Court of Session (but, in some cases, via an intermediate appeal to the sheriff-principal), and criminal appeals to the High Court of Justiciary. A sheriff court is not a *superior court.

sherry A fortified wine produced originally from the Palomino grape in the area surrounding Jerez de la Frontera in Spain. Sherry has long been Britain's most popular apéritif.

Wine from the Jerez area has been exported to Britain since Elizabethan times when it was known as sack, a term applied to any white wine from southern Europe, or sherris-sack, "sherris" being a corruption of "Jerez". The city of Bristol soon became the English centre of the sherry trade, and it was here that the popular cream sherry (a dark, sweet variety) was first developed. Since the early 19th century sherry has been produced by the *solera* system, in which the casks of maturing wine are repeatedly topped up with younger wines to perpetuate the quality and character of the original. Before the sherry is fortified, it may be blended with wines from different *soleras* to create a sherry of a particular colour and flavour. The distinctive flavour of sherry is due to a secondary fermentation that takes place: if the yeast develops, the wine will be *fino* (pale and dry); if there is little development, it will be *oloroso* (rich and slightly sweet). A true *amontillado*, a medium sherry, is expensive as it is derived from very old *fino*, but most *amontillados* are made by sweetening *fino*. *Manzanilla* is a very dry pale sherry, and cream sherry is a sweetened *oloroso*. Sherry is also produced in Cyprus and in South Africa.

shinty (Gaelic: *camanachd*) The traditional stick-and-ball field game of the Scottish *Highlands. Shinty is played with 12 players to a side, who use a wooden club, known as a *caman*, to attempt to score goals or "hails" with a small hard leather-covered ball. Kicking the ball is not permitted, and only the hail-keeper may handle it. Derived from the Irish game of *hurling, shinty developed as a separate game during the 14th century. It was customarily played on Sundays, despite the restrictions of Sabbath observance; later, it also survived the destruction of Scottish clan society after the battle of *Culloden (1746). Although the game declined in the 19th century, its revival after 1880 led to the formation of the Camanachd Association in 1893 and the drawing up of a uniform code of rules. The major shinty competitions still held are the Challenge Trophy and the Sutherland Cup. An international competition played on alternate years in Scotland and Ireland was inaugurated in 1972, using special rules that compromise between shinty and hurling.

shire An administrative area dating from Anglo-Saxon times. The shires, on which many of the modern counties are based, probably arose as territorial units based either on early kingdoms (for example Kent and Sussex) or on traditional tribal regions surrounding a major town (for example Dorset, centred on Dorchester). In Wessex, by the 9th century, shires had evolved into administrative units of local government and with the expansion of Wessex during the 10th century the system was extended to the Midlands. These new shires often ignored traditional boundaries for the sake of convenience so that the principal town lay more or less in the centre of its region. The judicial and administrative affairs of the early shires were conducted in the shire court, presided over by the *ealdorman* (chief man), who was appointed by the king, with the local bishop in attendance to safeguard the interests of the Church. By the 10th century, each *ealdorman* was responsible for a group of three or four shires and jurisdiction over individual shire courts was delegated to a shire-reeve (later corrupted to sheriff). The shires were subdivided into districts known as hundreds, each superintended by a royal reeve, who presided over a hundred court. Its equivalent in areas still under Danish influence was known as a *wapentake* (*see* riding). Many of the traditions of this early system have survived into modern times, including the titles *alderman, *earl, and *sheriff.

shove-ha'penny A board and table game requiring manual dexterity, probably a miniature adaptation of the deck game shuffleboard. It has long been a popular game in public houses where the name first appeared in the 1840s. Today the game is often played in leagues by teams representing different pubs and clubs. A normal board is made from polished mahogany, marble, or slate and measures 2 feet by 1 foot 3 inches. It has nine transverse bands, 1.25 inches wide, known as "beds". The game is played with discs, originally halfpennies (or ha'pennies), polished smooth on one side. Five of these are pushed forward one by one by placing the coin on the edge of the board and tapping it sharply with the palm of the hand. The object is to bring each coin to rest completely within a bed. Players try to get three discs in each bed and the scores are recorded in chalk at the side of the board. Should a coin come to rest on the dividing line between two beds it may be pushed forward by the next one. Powdered chalk is used to make the surface of the board smoother so that the discs slide easily.

show jumping An equestrian event in which horse and rider jump over a series of fences, often against the clock. Show jumping competitions became popular at the end of the 19th century, especially at agricultural shows. The first major event in Britain was the International Horse Show held at Olympia in 1907, and over the years British riders have been successful in Olympic and world championship competitions. The two main show jumping competitions in Britain are the Royal International Horse Show and the Horse of the Year Show, both held at Wembley. The principal contests at the Royal International Horse Show in the summer are the King George V Gold Cup for men and the Queen Elizabeth II Cup for ladies. The Horse of the Year Show, which was inaugurated in 1949 and takes place in October each year, is considered by many to be the climax of the show jumping year. Riders compete in various competitions, such as the Foxhunter Novice championship and the Leading Show Jumper of the year contest, and spectators see a wide range of show-class animals, including hunters, police horses, shire horses, and ponies.

Shrovetide football An annual contest that takes place on Shrove Tuesday in various English towns, notably Ashbourne, Derbyshire. Shrovetide football has been played for many hundreds of years, although several attempts to ban this boisterous and potentially dangerous sport were made in the 19th century. The Ashbourne game begins at two o'clock on the afternoon of Shrove Tuesday and now officially ends at ten o'clock; in earlier years it was not unknown for the game to be still in progress on Ash Wednesday morning. There are no boundaries or official rules; the goals are situated some two miles apart and the players are divided into two teams: Uppards (those born above Henmore Brook, which runs through the town) and Downards

SHROVETIDE FOOTBALL *Ashbourne, Derbyshire.*

(those born below Henmore Brook). The heavy leather ball, made by a local craftsman, is retained as a trophy by anyone who manages to score a goal; most of the game, however, consists of violent and muddy struggles in and around Henmore Brook. Similar contests are held at Alnwick in Northumberland, Sedgefield in Durham, and Atherstone in Warwickshire.

Shrove Tuesday The eve of the first day of Lent (Ash Wednesday), which falls in February or early March and is popularly known in Britain as Pancake Day. "Shrove" derives from the verb "to shrive", referring to the confession and absolution of sins before the beginning of Lent: in some towns and villages the "pancake bell", which once summoned people to church, is still rung on Shrove Tuesday morning. The making of pancakes on Shrove Tuesday provided a useful way of using up eggs and butter, forbidden foods during the Lenten fast, and the popularity of the pancake has ensured the survival of the custom. Pancake-tossing forms an integral part of such

traditions as the Pancake Greaze at Westminster School, London, and the Olney *pancake race. The Pancake Greaze takes place at eleven o'clock on Shrove Tuesday morning in the school hall, when the cook tosses a pancake over an iron bar some 5 metres (16 feet) high: there follows a violent scramble for it among the boys, the winner receiving one *guinea. *See also* Shrovetide football; hurling the silver ball.

sign manual The monarch's signature, used to express the royal will in the administration of affairs of state, such as on letters of appointment for ambassadors, royal charters, free pardons, the Queen's speech (*see* state opening of Parliament) and many other formal documents. The earliest example of this use of the royal signature dates from the reign of Edward III (r. 1327–77) who is, in fact, the first English sovereign after the Norman conquest known to have been fully literate. From the reign of Richard II (r. 1377–99) to that of Henry VIII (r. 1509–47) the sign manual was increasingly used as an instrument of everyday

405

government. However, this tendency was checked after 1535 owing to resentment at its use to bypass the royal seals.

Silverstone A motor racing circuit created from a disused airfield near Towcester, Northamptonshire. Silverstone was opened in 1948 and is the fastest circuit in the world. The British Grand Prix is held every other year, alternating with *Brands Hatch. Silverstone is controlled by the British Racing Drivers Club.

simnel cake A fruit cake topped with a layer of marzipan, traditionally baked in mid-Lent or at Easter. Simnel cakes were once made by servant girls to take home to their families on *Mothering Sunday: the word "simnel" originally meant a kind of biscuit dating back to Roman times, made from fine wheat flour (*simila*). The simnel cake mixture is similar to that of the traditional Christmas cake (*see* Christmas fare). The topping of almond paste is decorated with twelve marzipan balls to represent the twelve apostles; sometimes only eleven balls are present, symbolizing the exclusion of Judas Iscariot.

Sinn Fein *See* Irish nationalism.

skittles A target game in which a ball or bowl (called a "cheese" in some areas) is thrown at a set of wooden pins to knock them over. The game has been played in various forms for centuries, and was well established throughout Europe by the Middle Ages. At various times laws were passed prohibiting the playing of skittles because it encouraged men to spend their time in taverns and diverted them from more desirable pastimes, such as archery. Henry VIII, a noted sportsman in his day, is said to have enjoyed the game of skittles, and even purchased equipment for use in Westminster Palace. After this, it was virtually impossible to suppress the sport. It is almost exclusively associated with public houses, mostly in southwest England, London, South Wales, and parts of Scotland.

slang Those words and phrases that are regarded as specially informal, vulgar, rude, or nonstandard in some other way. English slang differs from *dialect in that dialect speakers typically use their dialect for all their communicative needs; slang is used by speakers of standard as well as regional English, but only occasionally, in informal circumstances or for special effects. Varieties of slang are often associated with particular activities or places: there are slangs connected with gambling, horse racing, boxing, card-playing (and card-sharping), and with the armed forces, prison, and public school. There is also a huge number of slang expressions for sexual and excretory activities; the only ways of referring to such matters, very often, are either to use slang or to resort to technical medical jargon.

Slang is often metaphorical ("one-eyed trouser snake" for a penis) and enjoys short-lived vogues: 19th-century slang expressions, such as a "pug" for a pugilist, or Oscar Wilde's "the boy" for champagne, are entirely obsolete. Slang terms need to be used with care, for logic is not a sound guide to idiomatic usage. "Breadbasket" is a slang term for the stomach, but while you might hit someone in the breadbasket, to complain that your breadbasket is empty (meaning that you are hungry), though logical enough, would be quite unnatural. The meaning of slang expressions tends to be unstable. To Shakespeare, a "punk" was a prostitute. In the 1920s it denoted a worthless person, and was especially associated with American gangster movies. In the 1970s it came to denote the cult of personal worthlessness as an attempted art form. Some expressions hover uneasily between slang and the standard language. To Dr Johnson, "clever" was a "low word, scarcely ever used but in burlesque or conversation; and applied to anything a man likes, without a settled meaning." He defined it in his *Dictionary of the English Language* (1755) as "1. dextrous; skilful; 2. just; fit; proper; commodious; 3. well-shaped; handsome". Although Johnson's first sense at least has now passed into the standard language, the word has acquired new slang extensions, for example the meaning "sensible" or "wise", usually used with a negative. Slang terms may receive an altered meaning if they pass into the standard language. In the 18th century a "scamp" was a slang term for a highwayman: it later became an affectionate term in standard English for a mischievous child. Thieves' slang has always been influential. In Shakespeare's time, a "gull" was a fool or simpleton, ripe for duping – hence the standard word gullible. A magistrate has been a "beak" since at least the 18th century; in the 19th century the term was borrowed into public-school slang to denote a master. To some people, slang is a type of language to be avoided; for others, it is the area of the language where it is at its most vital and interesting. See also rhyming slang.

slavery In common with most early societies, slavery was practised in *prehistoric Britain; the estate worked by slaves was also the economic basis of the early Roman Empire. From the later Roman period, the emergence of the "unfree" peasant and the *manor led to a decline in the number of slaves. Nevertheless, *Anglo-Saxon Britain was involved in a significant slave trade with Ireland. In *Domesday Book, 9% of the population were described as slaves; but the emergence of the well-defined status of villein in the 13th century absorbed both slaves and many peasants, and slavery all but vanished in England.

The next phase of British involvement in slavery began in the 1560s, when John Hawkins broke into the Spanish monopoly of trade (including trade in slaves) with her New World colonies. In the 17th century slaves formed the labour force of the sugar-growing islands of the West Indies and the southern colonies on the American mainland. The wealth of 18th-century Bristol and Liverpool was founded on a triangular trade: British manufactures were traded in West Africa for slaves, who were transported to America and traded for goods (such as sugar and tobacco) with a market in Britain. However, in 1772 slavery in Britain was declared illegal by judicial decision. In the later movement, which aimed at complete abolition, William Wilberforce (1759–1833) was prominent. The slave trade was abolished in the *British Empire in 1807, but slavery itself was not abolished until 1833.

small claims courts See county court.

smallholdings Any small farm units, including those let to people making a start in farming. Since 1892 there have been a number of Acts of Parliament under which local authorities have acquired farmland to let as smallholdings. The original Smallholdings Act

of 1892 was passed in an attempt to counter the disappearance of small private farms and the resultant decline in rural population following the laws of *enclosure and the industrial revolution. The Quaker reformer and politician John Bright (1811–89) was one of its proponents. The Act empowered county councils to create smallholdings and provide them with a farmhouse and buildings. A 1908 Act gave councils the option (now rescinded) of compulsory purchase to meet the demand for smallholdings, and after World War I, an Act of 1919 gave a further boost to the movement in an attempt to settle returning soldiers. Unfortunately, many of the new smallholders lacked farming experience, causing a large number to go bankrupt or simply to give up. In the light of this experience, a further Act (1947) after World War II insisted on agricultural experience as a qualification for a smallholding tenancy; the 1970 Agriculture Act demanded even higher qualifications – at least five years' full-time experience – bringing a change in emphasis toward larger, more commercially viable units. A commercial unit is now regarded as being able to support two people working full-time and is typically an intensive dairy farm with some 20–24 hectares (50–60 acres) of land. Smallholdings are now the chief means of entry into farming for people with no family connections in the profession.

snooker A table game derived from *billiards, played with 22 balls of various colours on a billiard table. It was probably invented at Kabul in 1875 by Colonel Sir Neville Chamberlain, an Indian army officer, when he added extra balls to the normal three used for billiards. Gradually the rules evolved and in 1891 the modern scoring system was adopted. Snooker was not immediately popular and it was only in 1926 that the Billiards Association and Control Council organized the first world professional snooker championship. It was won by Joe Davis (1901–78), a top billiards player, who recognized the possibilities of snooker as an entertaining contest. He went on to dominate the game as world champion, unbeaten from 1927 until his retirement in 1946. No-one of the same stature emerged as replacement and the game declined somewhat in the 1950s and 1960s until coverage on television, particularly colour television, attracted large audiences and enabled the payment from sponsorship of huge prizes. In the 1980s world professional snooker is dominated by English players, who number more than 50 among the world's 120 professionals, with Ireland, Wales, and Canada also producing world champions. Snooker clubs are common in Britain, and the game has a thriving popular base. The annual world championship, now held at Sheffield's Crucible Theatre, has become a national institution, being followed on television by enormous audiences, even into the early hours of the morning.

Snowdonia A mountainous area in Gwynedd, northwest Wales. The highest peak of Mount Snowdon itself, Yr Wyddfa, rises 1085 metres (3560 feet) above sea level and is the highest mountain in Wales. To this region of high passes, rocky crags, and sheer precipices overlooking deep valleys, the Welsh gave the name Eryri, "place of eagles". It has been inhabited since the Bronze Age (c. 1800–500 BC), and has formed a natural fastness against invaders. As the core of the principality of Gwynedd, it was not penetrated by the Norman Marcher lords (*see* Welsh Marches), and only fell to a royal invasion by Edward I (1277). The area is still a stronghold of the Welsh language, with about two-thirds of the population being active speakers.

The most important economic activities are hill farming and tourism. Slate quarrying, which grew up in the early 19th century to provide tiles for workers' houses built during the industrial revolution, has long been in decline, but its legacy is still visible: for example, the landscape of Blaenau Ffestiniog is dominated by the refuse of the quarries. Recently, the quarries and the caverns produced by mining have been developed as tourist attractions. An offshoot of the slate industry, the Ffestiniog railway (constructed in 1836 to link Blaenau with Portmadoc on the coast, closed in 1946, and reopened in 1955 for passengers) now carries over 200,000 people every year. Other leisure activities include walking, climbing, pony-trekking, fishing, and sailing. The many castles, especially those built by Edward I (*see* castles of Wales), also attract many

408

visitors. The name Snowdonia is also applied to the *national park, designated in 1951, that encompasses 2189 square kilometres (845 square miles), including Snowdonia proper and a large part of Gwynedd as far south as the River Dovey.

social class Britain has often been called the most class-ridden country in the western world, not infrequently by its own people. Although this implies a preoccupation with class membership, a definition of class structure in the late 20th century is elusive. The old popular classification, which divided the nation into "aristocracy", "gentry", "middle class" (by profession), "lower middle class" (by trade), and "working class", is now not always workable, if only because the distribution into these strata is no longer what it used to be. For instance, what might once have been termed the proletariat was progressively eroded by the reduction of labour, firstly in agriculture, and more recently in the old heavy industries. Again, the social structures which maintained the so-called "squirearchy" no longer exist: its remnants pursue occupations largely identical to those of the erstwhile "middle class" – a term which is itself now of almost no practical value save as cant abuse. The traditional professions of law, the armed forces, the Church, and medicine were rapidly overtaken in numbers by the proliferation of a "managerial" class (now very heterodox in nature), representing the administrators and accountants of the service industries, new business, new local government – a group that continues to grow. Political allegiance, equating Conservatives with wealth and Labour with manual workers, is also less straightforward, a situation further obscured with the formation of the *Alliance. Well within living memory, most British people were "placed" by very many aspects of their lives and persons: speech, manners, and dress were the most obvious. Much of this great code of class indicators has simply vanished, and in contemporary society generally, descent matters much less and money much more (though some concern about the source of the money persists). Accent and clothes have (in theory) less significance than before, and social deference is less apparent. Class barriers still exist everywhere,

ANGLESEY

COLWYN BAY

BEAUMARIS

CONWY

BANGOR

MENAI STRAIT

BETHESDA

Carnedd
Llywelyn
1064m
△

Llyn
Eigiau

CAERNARFON

LLANBERIS

LLANWRST

△ Glyder Fawr 999m

Snowdon
Mountain Railway

BETWS-Y-COED

Snowdon
1085m

△

Carnedd Moel
Siabod 872m

Moel Hebog
782m △

Moelwyn Mawr
770m △

BLAENAU
FFESTINIOG

Llyn Celyn

Ffestiniog Railway

PORTMADOC

PORTMERION

Llyn
Trawsfynydd

Arenig Fawr
854m

△

BALA

Bala Lake

ABERHIRNANT
FOREST

HARLECH

Aran Fawddwy
905m △

DOLGELLAU

BARMOUTH

CARDIGAN BAY

△
Cader Idris
893m

DOVEY
FOREST

**Snowdonia
National
Park**

Tal-y-Llyn
Railway

MACHYNLLETH

0	5	10 miles
0	5	10	15 km

although they may be less obtrusive and easier to cross than ever before. A currently favoured scapegoat is education: the grammar schools having been largely dismantled, what remains speciously resembles a two-tier system, divided between public schools and the state sector. The legacy is much more complex, and features much of the same fragmentation and compromise that have characterized every other social institution of such size. Snobbery, it is claimed, still diverts talent away from the areas where it would benefit the country economically, and into "professions" with traditional social approval; still operates to spread discord at every level of the educational system; still encourages a petty inquisition into matters of "background", if no longer of "breeding". The preoccupation remains intense – almost more real, at times, than what it seeks to identify, excoriate, or praise.

Social Democratic and Labour Party (SDLP) A political party, founded in Northern Ireland in 1970 by a group of moderate Catholics, including Gerry Fitt (the party's first leader; now Lord Fitt), John Hume, Paddy Devlin, and Austin Currie. Fitt left the SDLP in 1979 and leadership passed to his deputy, Hume. In the 1983 general election, Hume was the only successful SDLP candidate, being elected MP for Foyle. (He is also a Member of the European Parliament.) The SDLP has sought to appeal to those Catholics who reject the use of violence in pursuit of their political objectives. In recent years the party has been identified very much with Hume, who has constantly urged the renewal of political links between Northern Ireland and the Republic of Ireland.

Social Democratic Party (SDP) A British political party formed in March 1981 by ,four former *Labour Cabinet ministers, the so-called "gang of four". They were: Roy Jenkins (a former deputy leader of the Labour Party and at the time president of the European Commission in Brussels); Shirley Williams (not at that time an MP but a member of Labour's national executive); and David Owen and William Rodgers (both MPs). They had earlier issued the "Limehouse Declaration" calling for a realignment of British

politics; they were joined in the launch of the SDP by 12 other Labour MPs and one Conservative. The party has both a leader and president. The leader (currently David Owen), is elected by its MPs and heads its parliamentary party. The president is elected by postal ballot of the entire membership and leads the party through the Council for Social Democracy. The representation of the SDP in the House of Commons is small (six members in the 1983 election) but it works towards government in alliance with the Liberal Party (*see* Alliance).

social security The system of state benefits, about 80 in number, designed to offer security against the hardships of poverty, disease, and unemployment. Social security, governed by the provisions of the Social Security Acts of 1973, 1975, and 1980, is administered by the Department of Health and Social Security (DHSS) through a network of 550 local offices, with records held at its central office in Newcastle. Its noncontributory benefits include basic pensions (plus Christmas bonuses); war pensions; supplementary benefit for 3.5 million people; child benefit; housing benefit (through local authorities); allowances for one-parent families, disability, maternity, and mobility; and rent allowances and rebates. Its contributory benefits under the *national insurance scheme include unemployment and sickness benefits; retirement and widows' pensions; and grants for invalidity, industrial injury, and maternity. Although many social insurance schemes were in existence prior to the 1942 Beveridge Report (a widely supported document proposing the introduction of a unified scheme of social insurance to abolish "want, sickness, squalor, ignorance, and idleness"), social security on a comprehensive scale did not come into existence until 1948 (*see* national insurance; National Health Service). The social security scheme that has evolved since then has relied upon the addition of special benefits as the need for them became apparent; this has resulted in a system of great complexity (the DHSS benefits manual has 16,000 paragraphs of instructions). Family income supplement was introduced in 1971 and the state earnings related pensions scheme (SERPS) was established in 1978 in order to compensate for the low level of the basic pension.

The British economy has at the same time suffered from a shrinking industrial base and has had to support the ever-increasing cost of the social security scheme. This has caused attention to be focused upon better management of available resources, the simplification of benefits, and the computerization – and possible union – of tax and social security administrations. The total cost of all social security benefits in 1984 was £35 billion. *See also* welfare state.

social services A network of special care services run by the social services departments of each local authority, which is answerable to the director of social services and the local social services committee, as stipulated by the Local Authority Social Services Act 1970. The statutory duties of these departments include support for the handicapped, mentally ill, elderly, and young children, through the provision of residential homes, home helps, community care, day-care centres, and general assistance. The main work is carried out by professional social workers, who are trained by the Central Council for Education and guided by a code of ethics (adopted 1975). The social services must also assess the status of children in deprived or dangerous circumstances, acting in their best interests in the juvenile courts and providing foster homes or adoption when appropriate.

Some of the services now provided by the state were formerly offered piecemeal by a variety of different charitable and religious organizations. The Local Government Act 1929 made the local authorities responsible for the poor; and the National Assistance Act 1948 finally replaced the Poor Law system, which had offered the absolute minimum of relief for the able-bodied poor and semi-penal workhouse accommodation for those unable to fend for themselves (*see* welfare state). The services now provided are funded partly by local authority revenues (rents and rates) and partly by central government through the rate-support grant (now reduced to 40% of local spending). The voluntary services unit of the Home Office, set up in 1971, coordinates the work of voluntary organizations. The esti-

mated expenditure by local authorities on personal social services in 1985–86, totalled £2260 million.

Society for Promoting Christian Knowledge (SPCK) The oldest surviving missionary society of the Church of England, founded in 1698 by the parson Thomas Bray (1656–1730), and four laymen, to promote the establishment of charity schools in England and Wales and the dissemination of Christian literature both at home and overseas. Today it has its own publishing house with three imprints and operates a chain of Church and college bookshops. Religious books are distributed to clergy and lay helpers throughout the world. One of its main tasks now is the provision of financial and technical help to churches overseas in setting up their own publishing and distribution facilities. The Archbishop of Canterbury serves as its president.

Society of Friends *See* Quakers.

Soho A district of the City of Westminster bounded by Regent Street, Oxford Street, Charing Cross Road, Coventry Street, and Piccadilly Circus, famous until recently for its restaurants and cosmopolitan atmosphere. Farmland during the Middle Ages, the area acquired its name from an ancient hunting cry ("so-ho!") that used to be heard when it was a royal park attached to Henry VIII's Whitehall Palace. Building began in the 17th century when several large mansions were erected. The first of many immigrants, mostly French Huguenots, arrived in the 1670s and 1680s. The rise in population eventually led to overcrowding and cholera, a serious outbreak of which in 1854 resulted in the departure of the last of the wealthier residents. The district then became widely known as a centre of entertainment, with theatres and music halls opening, and numerous prostitutes on the streets. Many artists and intellectuals, including William Blake, William Hazlitt, and Karl Marx also took up residence, thus adding to the area's colourful reputation. Kettner's, the first of many famous restaurants, appeared in 1868, but it was not until after World War I that Soho became celebrated for its eating places. During World War II it became the closest thing to an artistic Bohemia that London has possessed. Since that time, however, the resident population has dwindled and it has declined into a somewhat sleazy red-light district of sex shops and strip clubs, in spite of the City of Westminster's attempts to clean it up.

solicitor A member of the legal profession in the UK, enrolled as a solicitor by the *Law Society, the Law Society of Scotland, or the Incorporated Law Society of Northern Ireland. Solicitors constitute one branch of the profession (the junior, though larger, branch) and *barristers, or in Scotland *advocates, the other. Many solicitors are employed in central or local government, or in commerce. Those who engage (alone or in partnership) in private practice must hold a practising certificate, issued by their Law Society and renewable annually. As practitioners, they undertake a certain amount of work before the courts and other tribunals; but they have in general no right of audience in the *superior courts (*compare* barrister; advocate) and are mainly concerned with giving advice and carrying out legal transactions (e.g. the drafting of conveyances, mortgages, and land leases; the making of wills and settlements, and the administration of estates on death; the establishment of trusts; and the formation of companies and partnerships). Solicitors have hitherto enjoyed a monopoly over conveyancing, but the Administration of Justice Act 1985 ends this in England and Wales by allowing the service to be offered also by licensed conveyancers under the aegis of a supervisory council. They are subject to rules of conduct laid down by their societies, through whom clients' complaints are handled.

In Scotland, many solicitors, though enrolled and governed by the Law Society there, belong to one of many local societies that exist. The best known of these is the Edinburgh-based Society of Writers to the Signet, founded in 1532, whose members are entitled to the letters "WS" after their names.

Solicitor General The second law officer of the Crown in England and Wales, appointed by the government to assist the *Attorney General. A barrister (never, despite his

name, a solicitor) and usually a member of the House of Commons, he holds ministerial office not of Cabinet rank, and is customarily knighted. The Law Officers Act 1944 authorizes him to discharge any function that the Attorney may delegate to him, and to act generally for the Attorney when the latter is incapable through illness or absence. The Solicitor General often succeeds the Attorney General. Like the Attorney General he could, until 1895, engage in private practice; he is now remunerated by salary. There is also a Solicitor General for Scotland, whose function is to assist the *Lord Advocate, but the office has never existed in Northern Ireland.

Solicitor General for Scotland *See* Lord Advocate.

South Bank The South Bank of the River Thames in central London – usually a specific reference to the group of buildings devoted to the arts, by the Hungerford and Waterloo bridges. The earliest of these was the Royal Festival Hall, built as the permanent aspect of the *Festival of Britain (1951). In addition to this, there are now the Queen Elizabeth Hall and Purcell Room (further concert halls), the *Hayward Gallery, and the *National Film Theatre. The *National Theatre is located nearby, just east of Waterloo Bridge.

spa towns A number of towns throughout Britain that possess thermal or mineral springs. The generic name originated in the 16th century from the town of Spa in Belgium, and some English counterparts prospered in the 17th and 18th centuries on account of the reputed beneficial effects of their waters. Centuries earlier the Romans had enjoyed thermal baths at Bath and Buxton. In the Middle Ages, many natural springs and wells became religious shrines, where pilgrims took the healing waters associated with the saints. Buxton had its St Anne's Well while Walsingham in Norfolk had two wells associated with the cult of the Virgin Mary. Following the Reformation of the 1530s and 1540s, such shrines were proscribed. But increasingly, physicians commended the healing waters to their patients and by the early 16th century, Harrogate, Tunbridge Wells, and Epsom had joined Bath and Buxton as established spas. The patronage

SPA TOWNS *The Royal Crescent in Bath, Avon.*

of Charles II (r. 1660–85) ensured the early prosperity of Tunbridge and it soon became a resort of fashionable society, offering such amusements as gaming, dancing, and bowling. Others followed suit, although Epsom's original spring had run dry by the early 18th century and its popularity dwindled thereafter. Other places around London once noted for their wells or springs include Islington, Streatham, and Clerkenwell.

Bath was also popular, but its evolution into the pre-eminent spa resort began in the early 18th century under the auspices of two men: its master of ceremonies Richard "Beau" Nash (1674–1762) and the speculator Ralph Allen. The latter employed the architect John Wood the Elder (c. 1705–54) to transform the town's appearance with a series of new squares, thoroughfares, and crescents. John Wood the Younger (d. 1782) later completed many of his father's schemes, including the elegant Royal Crescent. Meanwhile, Richard Nash acted as supreme arbiter of Bath's social life, establishing a disciplined etiquette and an aura of respectability. Buxton lagged somewhat behind until the Duke of Devonshire commissioned architect John Carr to design a crescent that would rival the Georgian splendour of Bath. Completed in 1784, it marked the start of a resurgence in Buxton's popularity.

By the late 18th century the inland spas were facing competition from the newly emerging *seaside resorts. Indeed, as early as the 1730s, Scarborough was offering sea-bathing as well as a mineral spring. In the 20th century changing tastes and scepticism about the benefits of well water have necessitated alternative attractions. Many traditional spas now hold summer arts festivals and boast of conference centres and other facilities.

SPCK *See* Society for Promoting Christian Knowledge.

Speaker The presiding officer of the House of Commons. The first recorded Speaker of the Commons, Peter de la Mare, was chosen by the Commons in 1376, in the reign of Edward III, to represent their views to the Crown during a particularly stormy session. The office was firmly established by the end of the century. Although an agent of the Commons, Speakers had to be acceptable to the Crown, and were frequenty royal servants. In practice, they were a useful channel of communication – a sometimes dangerous role, as the execution of several early Speakers shows. Especially under the Tudors and Stuarts, however, their primary loyalty lay to the monarch, leading the Commons to devise ways to evade their authority (such as the committee of the whole House, which dates from the early 17th century; *see also* Ways and Means). The Speaker presides in person or through his deputy over all debates and other proceedings of the House, except proceedings in committee when his place is taken by a chairman, and is responsible for their proper conduct. His duty is to apply the rules and traditions of the House impartially, with regard for the rights of all members. He selects speakers from the MPs who rise to catch his eye, decides on amendments to be discussed, calls divisions, grants or refuses emergency debates, and rules on points of order. He is also responsible (with the assistance of the *Serjeant-at-Arms) for

good behaviour by MPs and the public in the House. If a member persistently disobeys him, he may resort to the sanction of "naming". When **naming a member** the Speaker rises and says "I must name the Honourable Member for A . . . , Mr X, for disregarding the authority of the Chair". A government member then moves that the offending member be suspended, and the suspension lasts for 5 days for a first offence, 20 days for the next, and indefinitely thereafter. The Speaker is elected by the House at the beginning of every new Parliament, the majority party attempting to put forward a candidate acceptable to all. Formerly the seat of a reigning Speaker was not contested at a general election, but there have been departures from this practice in recent years.

The equivalent of the Speaker in the House of Lords is the *Lord Chancellor.

Speakers' Corner A venue for public speaking, usually of the more eccentric type, that lies in the northeastern corner of Hyde Park in London. Speakers' Corner has its origins in a demonstration that took place there in 1855, when 150,000 people gathered to protest against Lord Robert Grosvenor's Sunday Trading Bill. At that time there was no legal right of assembly and the authorities attempted to arrest the speaker at the meeting. However, the orator had already left when the police arrived, and since 1872, when the right of assembly was formally recognized, Speakers' Corner has been a traditional site of open-air public speaking. The orator may declaim upon any subject, provided that he is not obscene, does not blaspheme, or does not incite a breach of the peace. It is still the gathering point for large rallies or demonstrations that have marched through London.

Special Air Service (SAS) A specialist division of the British Army. The SAS was formed in 1942 under Colonel David Stirling as a flexible assault unit for use against the Germans in North Africa. The force was revived in 1952 and has seen service in, among other critical areas, Malaya, Aden, and Northern Ireland. Organized from its headquarters in Herefordshire, the SAS is a unit whose members and activities were long kept from

SPEAKERS' CORNER *Hyde Park, London.*

public attention. However, since its successful action in releasing hostages held in the Iranian embassy in London (1980), the SAS has acquired an aura of mystery and professionalism with the British public. The motto of the unit is "Who Dares Wins", shown on the cap badge under a winged dagger.

Special Branch The branch of a police force concerned primarily with political security. There is such a branch in every force, but by far the largest is that of the *Metropolitan Police, which numbers nearly 400 officers out of some 1250 for the whole of England and Wales. Forming part of the *CID, it was established in 1883 as the Irish Special Branch, specifically to respond to a wave of Irish bombings, and continued under its present name when these ended a few years later. In common with its counterparts in other forces it is concerned with all forms of subversive activity, but it still bears national responsibility for Irish terrorism on mainland Britain; the Special Branch also undertakes national protection duties for royalty, politicians, diplomats, and others at special risk.

special hospital A hospital for dangerous mentally disordered people who have to be confined, for which the Home Secretary is ultimately responsible. Mental disorder is defined by legislation to cover any mental illness or disability, including arrested development of the mind and any psychopathic disorder resulting in abnormally aggressive or irresponsible behaviour. The majority of patients in special hospitals have been sent there on conviction of a criminal offence. A magistrates' court or the Crown Court may authorize the detention of a convicted person in any specified hospital (not necessarily a special one) if that seems the most suitable solution to his case. There are four special hospitals: **Broadmoor** (the prototype in Crowthorne, Berkshire, originally referred to as a "criminal lunatic asylum", which has lent its name to the generic description "Broadmoor institutions"); Rampton; Moss Side; and Park Lane, near Liverpool (which is the most recent and only purpose-built one).

special schools Schools catering for the needs of those in the 2–19 age range who are identified as suffering from a degree of mental

415

or physical handicap that would make them unable to benefit from education in ordinary schools. The Education Act 1944 laid the basis for the provision of special schools for children with various disabilities. Recently there has been a tendency to integrate these children where possible into ordinary schools and make special provision for them there, the theory being that contact between the handicapped and their nonhandicapped contemporaries is beneficial to both. Nonetheless, in 1981, when a revised framework for special education was introduced, there were over 120,000 children attending special schools.

Spectator, The A weekly magazine founded in 1828 under the editorship of the Scottish journalist Robert Stephen Rintoul (1787–1858). The paper set out to follow its short-lived early-18th-century predecessor, *The Spectator*, edited by Richard Steele and Joseph Addison, in its emphasis on literary and social affairs. However, it soon took up advocacy of the Great Reform Bill (*see* Great Reform Act (1832)), and during Rintoul's 30-year editorship was in the forefront of every major social and political debate as the acknowledged voice of educated radicalism. In 1860 Meredith Townsend (1831–1911) bought *The Spectator* and the following year offered a half share and joint editorship to Richard Holt Hutton (1826–97); this arrangement lasted until just before Hutton's death, with Townsend responsible for the political side and Hutton the literary. Despite incurring initial unpopularity through backing the northern states in the American Civil War (1861–65), *The Spectator* under their editorship grew steadily in prestige. In 1898 Townsend relinquished editorial control to John St Loe Strachey (1860–1927), under whose editorship *The Spectator* became the principal Unionist journal. Another long editorship (1932–53) was that of Wilson Harris (1883–1955), who imbued the paper with his own moral seriousness and patriotism while its politics moved from a position somewhat left of centre towards the right. In the post-World War II period, the influence of *The Spectator* as a shaper of opinion, along with that of other surviving periodicals, dwindled under competition from radio and television. Its circulation, even in its heyday, was never large, but it retained sufficient appeal to its traditional readership (politically centrist and highly educated) to enable it to continue. Much of its space is devoted to reviews of books and the arts, and it still attracts distinguished writers and reviewers.

speech day An annual event at many British schools at which merit prizes are presented by a distinguished guest, and the school's head and the head boy or girl give an account of the past year's activities to the assembled parents and visitors. In certain schools the ceremony is known by other names, for example, "Apposition" at St Paul's. *See also* sports day.

Spital sermon An annual service dating back many centuries, which is attended by the Lord Mayor and his escort as well as by sheriffs and aldermen of the City of London. It is now held in mid-May at the church of St Lawrence Jewry, but its origin lies in Easter week when three sermons on the theme of the Resurrection were preached on three consecutive days from an open-air pulpit in the churchyard of the 12th-century priory church of St Mary Spital (hence the name Spitalfields), which looked after the poor and afflicted. The Lord Mayor and his retinue used to sit at the windows of the house opposite to listen to the sermons, which were sometimes of great length. The pulpit was destroyed in the Civil War but the sermons were revived in St Bride's, Fleet Street, after the Restoration, and then moved to Christ's Church, Newgate Street, before becoming a single annual sermon at St Lawrence Jewry, conveniently adjacent to the Guildhall.

Sporting Life, The Britain's premier racing newspaper, published daily. It was founded in 1859 as *Penny Bell's Life* and has absorbed several other sporting papers, such as the *Sporting Telegraph* and the *Sportsman*. Although it carries a form guide and results service for *grey-hound racing and items on other sports, it is primarily devoted to *horse racing, both on the flat and over jumps, with a comprehensive guide to the form of runners at every race meeting in the British Isles. It is a familiar sight in betting shops and at racecourses, and in the early 1980s had a circulation of around 70,000.

Sports Council An independent body set up in 1972 to promote sport in Britain by encouraging participation and developing sports facilities. Rising living standards, more leisure time, and an increased awareness of the importance of regular exercise for good health, have all contributed to the demand for more centres for sport and recreation. There are three councils, serving England, Scotland, and Wales: the Sports Council of Northern Ireland is an advisory body only, and is not empowered to make grants. The councils work in co-operation with local authorities and voluntary organizations, providing grants and loans for improved facilities and encouraging contacts with sports organizations overseas. There are now nearly one thousand local sports centres, as well as ten national sports centres, such as those at Crystal Palace, Lilleshall, and Cardiff, throughout the UK.

sports day An annual event at many schools at which the pupils compete against each other in sporting and other competitions, watched by parents and visitors. They were originally intended to promote the spirit of sporting competition and fair play, and to provide a visible expression of this working through the "house" system.

squash rackets A racket-and-ball game for two (occasionally four) players, which originated at Harrow School around 1830. It is derived from the game rackets but is played with a softer ball on a smaller, enclosed court. It is claimed that the Harrow schoolboys, waiting to play rackets, would practise in a confined space near the rackets court. As the area was so small, a slower ball that could be squashed in the hand was used: hence the name "squash". There were many variations of the game in the 19th century, but by the early 20th century it had become established in its present form and in 1920 L. R. Read became the first professional champion. In 1929 the Squash Rackets Association was formed to organize tournaments; after World War II it became the world governing body for squash. The game was taken to other parts of the world by the British Army, for which it provided excellent concentrated exercise in a small space in places where outdoor sport was not possible. Many of the best players have emerged from the Middle East, India, and Pakistan. The British Open, for many years the world's leading tournament, dates from 1930. It was won seven times by Pakistan's Hashim Khan in the 1950s, and three times by Egypt's Abu Taleb in the 1960s. The British game was revived in the late 1960s and the 1970s by Jonah Barrington, who organized the first international tournament circus. Barrington was the world's leading player for some time before the Australian Geoff Hunt overtook him. In the women's game the outstanding star has been the Australian Heather Mackay, world champion for more than 15 years from the late 1960s to the early 1980s.

For many years a game for the upper and middle classes, squash is now very popular with thousands taking part in regular leagues and tournaments at clubs and leisure centres. Spectator interest has been limited until recently when some courts were given a clear perspex back wall and there are now a few courts made entirely from perspex.

stag hunting A sport traditionally associated with royalty and the landed aristocracy. It is now almost totally restricted to the west of Scotland and to Ireland as a result of overhunting in the past and the clearing of forests. The stag hunting season runs for six weeks in April and early May and from 10 August to 10 October. A stag is located and forced out into the open by a few well-trained hounds and then chased by the main pack and the horsemen before being killed by gunshot. Some stags, however, are "carted", which means that they are imported, chased, and then recaptured rather than slain. In addition to the shortage of stags to be hunted, animal protectionists and agitators against blood sports have contributed to the decline of the sport.

stamp duties *See* tax system.

standing committee A committee that gives detailed consideration to a *Bill during its passage through the House of Commons, unless it is important enough to warrant consideration by a committee of the whole House. There are frequently up to eight committees at work, constituted ad hoc for each Bill, despite the name "standing", and having between 16 and 50 members each. They are distinguished by letters of the alphabet (standing committee A, B, and so on). Their members are nominated by a selection committee appointed by the House, with the chairman drawn from a panel appointed by the *Speaker. While nominations take account of the specialist qualifications of members, they must, above all, reflect the political complexion of the House.

St Andrew The patron saint of Scotland, Andrew was one of the 12 apostles of Jesus of Nazareth. He and his brother Peter were fishermen from Capernaum and it was Andrew, a follower of John the Baptist, who brought Peter to Christ. According to legend Andrew later preached in Greece and was crucified at Patras in Achaia around 60 AD. A major cult developed in both the East and West and his feast day was celebrated universally from the 6th century. The legend continues with St Rule (St Regulus), a 4th-century monk from Patras, who was instructed by an angel to convey Andrew's relics to a place in the far northwest. He travelled until the angel told him to stop at a site on the Fife coast of Scotland, where he founded the settlement of St Andrews. A more prosaic but possibly authentic version is that the 7th-century abbot of Hexham and later bishop of York, St Wilfrid (634–709), brought back some of the saint's supposed relics from a trip to Rome, and his successor, Acca, possibly sold or gave them to the Scots king Angus MacFergus. The relics were then installed at St Andrews to enhance the prestige of the new bishopric.

St Andrew is said to have been crucified on a saltire cross, hence St Andrew's cross, which appears as a white saltire on blue in the Scottish flag and is also one of the elements of the Union Jack (*see* flags). It is said that in a vision, the Pictish king Angus was promised victory over the Anglian king Athelstan by St Andrew. Following this, a saltire cross appeared in the sky, so terrifying Angus's opponents that the prophesy was fulfilled. Many churches are dedicated to St Andrew. His feast day (30 November) is still widely celebrated in Scotland. He is also the patron saint of Greece, Romania, and the USSR.

St Andrew's University The oldest university in Scotland. It originated in a school of higher studies founded at St Andrew's in 1410 and recognized by the pope as a *studium generale* in 1413. Modelling itself upon the constitution of the university at Orléans in France, the university was under the supervision of the bishop of St Andrew's (for many years the ex officio chancellor) and a rector, in charge of administration. The chapel and college of St John the Evangelist (1419) were the earliest university buildings, and the first fully endowed college, St Salvator's, was founded in 1450; the latter's chapel is still the university's main place of worship. Further colleges followed in the 16th century, and in 1579 the university and its colleges were granted a fresh foundation. The university library (1612) was founded by James VI (James I of England). The Senatus Academicus, comprising college principals, professors, and "regents", first appeared in the mid-17th century as the university's supreme authority, although the Universities (Scotland) Act 1858 transferred some of its functions to the newly created university court. In 1892 women were admitted as students. Another major milestone was the affiliation in 1897 of the university college of Dundee (founded 1881), which became St Andrew's medical faculty. In 1972 the college of St Leonard, first founded in 1512, was re-established as a college for postgraduates.

In line with the general Scottish practice, first degree courses at St Andrew's take four years and the first degree in the arts faculty is the MA. According to their year of study, students are called bejants, semis, tertians, and magistrands. The university year has three terms: Martinmas, Candlemas, and Whitsunday. Undergraduates wear a distinctive scarlet academic gown; graduates wear a black gown with a violet cross of St Andrew. The university celebrates its past with the Kate Kennedy procession in April, a historical pageant named after the niece of a 15th-century benefactor; she is said to have made provision for free oatmeal to be given to poor students.

Star of India An order of chivalry, having the designation "Most Exalted", admission to which was conferred on princes or chiefs of India (who were invariably advanced imme-

ST ANDREW'S UNIVERSITY *St Salvator's Quadrangle.*

diately to the senior class, that of Knight Grand Commander) and on British subjects for services to the Indian Empire. The second class of Knights Commanders and third class of Companions were awarded for a minimum of 30 years in the department of the Secretary of State for India. The order was instituted by Queen Victoria in 1861 and subsequently en-larged on many occasions. The order will eventually become defunct as no appointments have been made since 1947 after the British withdrawal from India. Its motto is "Heaven's Light Our Guide".

state education   The system of education provided by the state that has evolved in Brit-

419

ain beside the *independent schools (*see* public schools; preparatory schools). Direct state intervention in education began in 1870 and was extended in the subsequent Education Acts of 1902, 1918, and 1944. Before 1870 governments had been reluctant to interfere with children's education. The belief then held was that education was a matter either for a child's family or for his church: the end of education was not to impart knowledge or communicative skills except insofar as they made a good Christian. The result was that at this time some 69 out of 70 children did not attend a secondary school of any kind. Having established a dual system of voluntary and local authority elementary schools under the Elementary Education Act 1870, the government encouraged the *Local Education Authorities (LEAs) to set up (1902) many more **grammar schools** to provide secondary education on a strongly academic curriculum for children aged 11–18. These were based on existing grammar schools, founded in late medieval or Tudor times, which were funded by endowments and fees, and intended to teach boys grammar (which then meant Latin) as a preparation for the professions or for university. In 1918 the school-leaving age was fixed at 14 and the Burnham Committee (under Lord Burnham) was set up to negotiate teachers' salaries. By 1939 some 400,000 children were attending grant-aided grammar schools, but still this figure, combined with the children at independent secondary schools, meant that only 14% of the children eligible were receiving a secondary education.

The 1944 Education Act for the first time introduced free universal secondary education, and placed the national system of education under the control of the Department of Education and Science. The elementary schools were abolished and state education was henceforward regarded as a continuous process beginning with primary schools (nursery schools, 3–5 years old; infant schools, 5–7; and junior schools 7–11), passing through secondary schools (11–18), on to further education (18 upwards). State secondary education was initially a three-part system in England and Wales, with grammar schools taking the academic pupils, **technical schools** taking those with a bent for practical skills, and the **secondary modern schools** taking the rest. Selection for grammar schools was by eleven-plus exam, taken at age 11 or 12 years. Under most LEAs the eleven-plus exam has now been dropped and a widespread system of large **comprehensive schools** introduced to merge the three ranges of pupils into one school. However, the extent to which pupils should be segregated on the basis of ability at secondary-school level remains a controversial issue. In some LEAs a middle school (8–12 or 9–13 years) has been introduced, as recommended by the Plowden Report (1967). Under other LEAs pupils over the age of 16 continue their studies in separate sixth-form colleges. *See also* Scottish education.

stately homes *See* country houses.

state opening of Parliament The opening of a new *Parliament, or a new session of Parliament, normally by the sovereign. It is an elaborate occasion, preceded, in commemoration of the Gunpowder Plot (*see* Guy Fawkes Day), by the ritual of *searching the cellars performed by the *Yeomen of the Guard. The ceremony itself, parts of which date back to the 16th century, begins at Buckingham Palace, from which the sovereign rides in a state coach to the Palace of Westminster, accompanied by other members of the royal family. On their arrival, the King's Troop of the Royal Horse Artillery fire a salute. The royal party proceeds to the robing room and then to the Lords chamber, where the Queen ascends her throne, the peers of the realm take their seats, and the Commons assemble at the Bar of the House, having been summoned there by the Gentleman Usher of the *Black Rod. The central feature is the speech from the throne (the **Queen's speech**), outlining the government's aims, for the session, which is subsequently debated by each House for some six days, technically on a motion of thanks. The text of the gracious speech, as it is called, is handed to the Queen by the *Lord Chancellor from the purse that symbolizes his office as Keeper of the Great Seal, after which he descends the steps to the throne backwards to return to his place in the House. Parliament is on occasion opened by commissioners on behalf of the sovereign, in which case the speech is read by the Lord Chancellor.

Statesman's Year-Book, The A reference work containing statistical and historical information on the countries of the world and international organizations, published annually since 1864. The founder-editor was the writer Frederick Martin (1830–83); Benjamin Disraeli (Prime Minister 1868, 1874–80) considered the book so useful that he granted Martin an annual pension of £100 in 1879. After Martin's death *The Statesman's Year-Book* was taken over by (Sir) John Scott Keltie (1840–1927), who edited it until 1926. After him there were only two other editors before Dr John Paxton (1923–   ), who took over in 1969. The book falls into two sections, the first listing international organizations such as the United Nations (with its different agencies), the Commonwealth, the World Council of Churches, and smaller, regional or special interest groupings such as EFTA, OPEC, CARICOM, and NATO; while the second section comprises an alphabetically arranged survey of the nations of the world covering history, area and population, constitution and government, defence, economy, industry and trade, communications, religion, and education.

steeplechase Horse racing that involves jumping a number of fences, ditches, and streams. Chasing, meaning hunting, had been popular for many centuries before the idea of racing across country was thought of. The usual reason for a cross-country race was to settle an argument about the relative merits of two horses. It was necessary to have starting and finishing points that were visible to all and church steeples were considered suitable markers, hence the name. (In its modern form steeplechasing takes place at racecourses.) The first such race was held at Bedford in 1810; by the mid-19th century steeplechasing was well established. Every steeplechase must have at least twelve fences in the first two miles and six every mile after that. The height of all jumps is standardized. Steeplechasing in England takes place under National Hunt rules, which are now administered by the *Jockey Club. Certain steeplechases are restricted to horses that are normally hunters rather than racehorses

and such races are limited to amateur jockeys. The most famous steeplechase of all is the *Grand National, held at Aintree, while the National Hunt Festival held in March makes Cheltenham the main centre of English steeplechasing.

sterling The British currency, the unit of which is the pound sterling. The term probably originated from the Old English *stearling*, an early Norman coin with a star (*steorra*) on one face. Valued at a penny, 240 were made from a pound of silver – hence "pound of sterlings", which later became "pound sterling". Pennies were the only coins in circulation until the late 13th century; larger units were used only in accounting. Trade expansion led to the introduction of the first gold coin, the noble worth six shillings and eight pence, in 1344. The first pound coin, called the sovereign because it bore the image of an enthroned king, was minted in 1489.

The value of a pound was measured in silver until the 18th century, and thereafter in gold. From 1817 to 1925, the standard coin was the new sovereign, with paper notes being redeemable in gold until 1914. Large issues of paper money to finance World War I made it impossible to resume convertibility and paper money thereafter became legal tender. An attempt in 1925 to reattach the pound's value to gold led to overvaluation, which contributed to economic depression; the gold standard was finally abandoned in 1931. Since 1972 the pound's value has been allowed to float against other currencies, being determined by market forces. In 1971 Britain replaced its traditional system of pounds, shillings, and pence by the decimal system.

St George The patron saint of England, who is thought to have been a Christian martyred by the Roman emperor, Diocletian, at or near Lydda (now Lod in Israel), around 303 AD. His cult was celebrated throughout Christendom from the 6th century and he is mentioned in the martyrology compiled by St Bede (c. 673–735). However, he assumed special symbolic importance in England as a result of Richard the Lionheart's crusade to Palestine (1189–92), during which the English king restored to Christian hands the church at Lydda containing St George's relics. Richard adopted the saint as his army's patron (St George is still the patron saint of soldiers). Also dating from around this time is the famous legend of St George and the dragon, which was probably based on the Greek myth of Perseus' rescue of Andromeda from a sea monster. According to this legend a dragon with poisonous breath terrorized the region. After it had exhausted the supply of sheep given by the people to placate it, it started to demand human offerings. The hapless victims were drawn by lot, until the turn of the king's daughter arrived. Dressed in her bridal gown, she was led to her fate. However, the intrepid St George intervened, attacked the dragon with his lance and when he had cornered it, offered to destroy it on condition that the people converted to Christianity. In the Middle Ages George became the embodiment of Christian chivalry and accordingly the crusaders sported St George's Cross on their tabards. Venice, Genoa, Portugal, and Catalonia made him their patron saint and churches were dedicated to him throughout Europe. In c. 1347 Edward III (r. 1327–77) founded the Order of the *Garter, with St George as its patron, and St George's Chapel adjacent to *Windsor castle was built during the reign of Edward IV (1461–83). While his popularity later dwindled elsewhere, St George remained prominent in England. St George and the dragon is a common heraldic symbol and the George ensign – a red cross on white – is incorporated into the national flag, the Union Jack. His feast day, 23 April, is, however, largely ignored.

Stirling castle A castle set high on a rocky crag overlooking the town of Stirling in central Scotland, and commanding the principal route between the *Highlands and *Lowlands. This strategic site was occupied by a castle before the 11th century and changed hands many times, especially during the wars of independence fought against the English (1297–1314); the castle was won in 1314 by Robert the Bruce following the battle of *Bannockburn nearby. However, most of the existing structure dates from the 15th century, when Stirling was used as a royal palace by the Stuart kings of Scotland. The turreted gate-house, curtain walls, and towers that defend the inner citadel were erected by James III (1452–88), who also built the great hall to house his parliament and as a place in which to hold state ceremonies. The Renaissance palace was built for James V in the early 16th century; James VI built the chapel royal for the christening of his eldest son Prince Henry in 1594. Near the castle gates is the church of the Holy Rood, scene of the coronation of Mary, Queen of Scots, in 1543. After James VI became King James I of England in 1603, Stirling reverted to its role as a garrison or, at times, prison. It was besieged, unsuccessfully, by the Jacobites during the Forty-five (see Jacobite rebellion).

St James's Palace One of the principal royal palaces in London until the mid-19th century. St James's Palace stands in the Mall, overlooking St James's Park, in central London. It was built by Henry VIII, but only parts of the original Tudor palace remain, notably the gatehouse (c. 1532). The chapel royal also dates from Tudor times and still retains the original painted ceiling. Charles I spent his final days at St James's before his execution in Whitehall in 1649. After Whitehall Palace was destroyed by fire in 1698, St James's became the main royal residence in London and remained so until the purchase and extension of *Buckingham Palace. Many of the state rooms date from this time, although a fire in 1809 caused considerable damage. Foreign ambassadors to Britain are still accredited to the Court of St James, although they are received by the sovereign at Buckingham Palace, and the accession of a new sovereign is proclaimed first at St James's. Much of the palace is now used as offices for the Lord Chamberlain's staff or as accommodation for members of the royal household.

St James's Park See royal parks.

St John Ambulance Association and Brigade A charitable organization, founded in 1877, whose unpaid volunteers provide emergency first-aid cover at public gatherings and sporting events. They wear a black uniform with a white Maltese cross emblem that indicates their connection with the medieval religious order of the Knights of St John of Jerusalem (also known as the Knights Hospitallers), founded to assist and nurse pilgrims to the Holy Land. The brigade section of the organization began in 1888 and in 1982 numbered about 32,000 adult members and 40,000 cadet members. It was famous for its outstanding medical work in the field during the two world wars.

St Leger *See* Classics.

St Michael and St George, Order of An order of chivalry having the designation "Most Distinguished", admission to which is conferred on those who have held high office or have rendered distinguished nonmilitary service in colonial or foreign affairs. In practice most members belong to the *diplomatic service. The order was founded in 1818 and subsequently enlarged and extended on many occasions. There are three classes: up to 120 Knights and Dames Grand Cross (who are called Sir or Dame and add GCMG after their names); up to 390 Knights and Dames Commanders (who are called Sir or Dame and add KCMG or DCMG after their names); and up to 1775 Companions (CMG). Senior positions in the order include the sovereign, a Grand Master (the Duke of Kent), a chancellor, a King of Arms, and a Gentleman Usher of the Blue Rod. The order's chapel is in St Paul's cathedral.

Stock Exchange The institution providing a centralized market for trading in stocks and shares and for raising capital for industry. The London Stock Exchange originated in dealings conducted in coffee houses from the late 17th century. In 1773 a group of brokers bought a building in Threadneedle Street and allowed anyone to trade there for sixpence per day. After this was closed in 1801, a private exchange opened on the present Capel Court site in 1802 with 550 members. The first rule book dates from 1812; the present constitution was laid down in 1875. The current building, which incorporates computer technology, was opened in 1972.

Only members of the Stock Exchange (numbering about 4200) and clerks are admitted to the dealing floor. Until 1986 members were divided into two classes, jobbers and brokers, in a system unique to Britain. Jobbers dealt in shares, deciding prices according to supply and demand, and dealing only with other members of the Stock Exchange. Brokers acted as agents for members of the public for whom they bought and sold securities by striking bargains with jobbers. The broker–jobber division is now abolished, and shares can now be bought and sold directly through a broker or dealer. The Stock Exchange is governed by a council of 46 elected members and 5 outsiders, which has wide powers to ensure fairness and honesty both between members and towards the public. For example, taking advantage of inside information from a company is forbidden. The London Stock Exchange has a tradition for trading by word of mouth on the floor of the Exchange, which is reflected in their motto "My word is my bond".

stone circles Prehistoric monuments found in most parts of Britain, but almost nowhere else in Europe. They are a type of "henge" monument, the generic name for a ceremonial site delimited by a circular bank and internal ditch, with one or two entrances. Circles of regularly spaced standing stones are found in only a few on these. As well as the circle itself, most have single standing stones (monoliths) outside them, in some case apparently aligned with the rising or setting sun at midsummer or midwinter. Such hypothetical alignments with landmarks or astronomical bodies have suggested various theories for the purpose of stone circles, the most likely being a religious involvement with celestial bodies. The first stone circles were constructed some time before 3000 BC, but the most impressive examples, such as *Avebury and *Stonehenge, date from around 2000 BC or later. No circles seem to have been erected after the late second millenium BC.

Stonehenge A megalithic ruin of prehistoric origin that stands on Salisbury Plain in Wiltshire. The best-known prehistoric monument in Europe, it was a ceremonial or religious centre for over a thousand years, although its precise significance is unknown. Salisbury Plain is a vast chalk plateau from which radiate the chalk ridges that formed the areas of original settlement in lowland Britain: *the Icknield Way, running through the

STONE CIRCLES *Ring of Brodgar on Mainland, Orkney. The towering stones of this site form a vast circle with a diameter of about 104 metres (340 feet).*

Chilterns to the Wash; a ridge through the South Downs to Beachy Head; another running southwest to the Dorset coast, landing-place for many immigrants of the pre-Roman period; and the ridge that forms the Cotswolds. These areas of chalk and limestone had the only fertile and naturally-drained soil in lowland Britain. Later, farmers learned how to drain richer, loamy soils elsewhere, but at that time these areas provided habitable land where a civilization could develop, and its obvious centre was Salisbury Plain.

The first phase of building at Stonehenge began in about 2500 BC when a single ring of stones was erected and encircled by a ditch and embankment. (All *stone circles with embankments are known today as "henge monuments" after this one. The -henge element of the name seems to be connected with the verb "to hang" (henges were probably stones that were supported, or "hanging" in the air) and presumably refers to the later characteristic trilithons at Stonehenge – two standing stones that support another laid horizontally across them, forming a rudimentary arch.) At this early stage the site also included the huge Heelstone at the entrance and a ring of 56 pits, later used for the burial of cremated bodies, which are now known as the Aubrey Holes after their discoverer, the 17th-century diarist John Aubrey.

STONEHENGE *On Salisbury Plain, Wiltshire.*

The second stage of construction began in about 2100 BC after the arrival from Northern Europe of the people known as the Beaker Folk, who take their name from the distinctive cups found in their graves. Also responsible for the many barrows on Salisbury Plain and the stone circle at *Avebury in Wiltshire, they erected at Stonehenge a circle of huge bluestones, dressed with bronze tools and transported from the Prescelly hills in Wales. This extraordinary feat, like the building of the pyramids, reflects the great religious importance that has been attributed to the site. They also added an earthwork approach, now known as the Avenue, which, with the double circle, was apparently orientated toward the summer solstice sunrise. Later in the Bronze Age (1800–500 BC), the area became rich through foreign trade and farming, and a much larger stone circle and trilithons were added. The great *hill forts raised in the area by the newly-arrived Celts during the Iron Age, which began in the 6th century BC, suggest that Stonehenge continued to play an important role in British life until the beginning of *Roman Britain.

Stonehenge has long been a ruin. In the past much of its stone was removed for building, or broken up by those who considered it a pagan symbol. It is now the responsibility of *English Heritage and is fenced off to protect it from vandalism, espically by hippies and others who gravitate to the ruin at the summer solstice. The Druidic Order, which was formed in the 20th century, have used it for religious purposes, although historians do not connect it with the ancient *druids. Certain of the stones are so positioned that at the summer solstice the rays of the rising sun are caught between them, evidence of the remarkable building skills of the Bronze Age Britons.

stone of Scone A piece of sandstone, known also as the "stone of destiny" or "fatal stone", on which Scottish kings were ceremonially enthroned. It was originally located at the ancient Pictish capital of Scone (now a small village near Perth) until its removal by King Edward I of England, in 1296. Legend held that the stone was "Jacob's Pillow" or "Columba's Pillow" and was brought to Scotland by Gaythelus – one of the fabled founders of the Scots' pedigree. How it came into Pictish hands is unknown, but it was said that "wherever the stone should rest, a king of Scots would reign". By the 13th century it had been fitted with carrying rings, of which Edward presumably took full advantage. He placed it in the care of Westminster Abbey, and commissioned Walter of Durham to design an oak chair to fit over it. This is known as the Coronation Chair, and most monarchs have been crowned seated upon it. The stone was briefly taken back to Scotland in 1950 as a protest by Scottish nationalists, but was later returned.

Stormont A suburb of Belfast in which are situated Parliament House (built in 1932 to house the parliament of Northern Ireland, and now the home of the *Northern Ireland Assembly and certain government offices), Stormont House (formerly the official residence of the Prime Minister of Northern Ireland), and Stormont Castle (the home of further government offices).

St Patrick The patron saint of Ireland, who lived c. 390–461 AD. St Patrick is a major figure in the development of Christianity in Britain. Many details of his life and works are derived from his own *Confession* and his letter (*Epistola*) to a certain Coroticus. Patrick was born in mainland Britain, the son of a local councillor (*decurio*) and the grandson of a priest, at a place he refers to as Bannavem Taburniae, the location of which still baffles historians. Captured by Irish pirates at the age of 16, he spent six years in slavery in Ireland, which he converted to Christianity before finally escaping back to Britain. Patrick tells of his experiences in a strange land, perhaps Gaul, but it is thought that he received his Christian education in Britain and went to Ireland around 435 as a missionary. Establishing his see at Armagh in the north, he embarked on a vigorous evangelical crusade to combat paganism and sun worship and to convert the Irish to Christianity.

On the evidence of his own writings he was by no means an accomplished scholar, although he was undoubtedly a champion of the faith. Nevertheless not even Patrick could have converted all the Irish singlehanded or driven all the snakes from the country – the two chief legendary stories told about him. There are many churches dedicated to him in Ireland and among expatriot Irish communities – New York's St Patrick's cathedral, for instance. His feast day on 17 March is celebrated by the wearing of shamrock, the three-leafed clusters which are said to have helped Patrick explain the Trinity to his flock.

St Paul's cathedral   *See* cathedral.

strangers' gallery   The gallery in the House of Lords or House of Commons to which members of the public are admitted during debates and other proceedings (except daily prayers, which are private). The gallery in the Commons formerly had an area partitioned off for ladies, but segregation ended in 1918. Each House has the unchallengeable right to exclude the public from any proceedings, and the clearing of the Commons gallery is signalled by the cry "I spy strangers", in response to which the Speaker must put to the vote, without debate, the motion "that strangers do withdraw".

Stratford–upon–Avon   *See* Shakespearean theatre.

St Swithin's Day   15 July, the feast day of St Swithin, who must surely be the unofficial patron saint of Britain's weather. An old proverb runs:
"St Swithin's Day, if thou dost rain,
For forty days it will remain;
St Swithin's Day, if thou be fair,
For forty days, 'twill rain na mair."
Swithin was bishop of Winchester from 852 and was noted for his acts of charity and energetic church-building. On his death in 862, he was buried outside the walls of the cathedral, in accord with his wishes. But on 15 July 971 his relics were removed to a more fitting shrine inside the cathedral, an occasion apparently marked by miracles and heavy rainfall, hence the proverb. His remains were moved again, to the new Norman cathedral, in 1093, but his shrine was destroyed during the Reformation and the relics disappeared. The shrine was restored in 1962.

St Valentine's Day   14 February, the day on which greeting cards are sent, usually anonymously, by admirers to those whom they admire. The association of St Valentine's Day with lovers probably derives from a whole group of traditions associated with the onset of spring. It has very little to do with the historical figures of either of the two St Valentines martyred by the Romans. However, the roots of the custom do appear to reach back to the Roman fertility festival, the Lupercalia, which was celebrated on 15 February; the Roman respect for their goddess of motherhood, Juno, was also part of the tradition. At about this time of the year, a lottery was held in her name, in which the boys in the community drew from an urn the names of their sweethearts for the following year. This tradition is echoed in the English belief (mentioned by Chaucer, in the 14th-century poem *The Parliament of Fowls*) that birds choose their mates on 14 February. By the 17th century Samuel Pepys was also referring to Valentines being chosen by lottery and he recorded that notes were passed between potential lovers, bearing endearments and enticements. By the 19th century commercial Valentine cards had appeared: in 1874 over one and a half million were handled by the Post Office. In recent years the personal columns of the daily newspapers have become a popular means of sending Valentine's Day messages.

suffragette   *See* women's movements.

Sunday school   Many churches and chapels run voluntary classes on Sundays to provide children with basic instruction about Christianity and its application in the world. Sunday schools were started in 1769, at the height of the evangelical revival, by the Methodist Hannah Ball. But the idea was fully developed by an Anglican layman, Robert Raikes (1735–1811), who in 1780 organized Sunday schools in Gloucester in an effort to combat the illiteracy then almost universal among the poor by combining religious instruction with basic reading skills. This example prompted other philanthropists to set up both Sunday and weekday schools for poor children and represents one of the roots of the movement that eventually resulted in free education for all. The Church of England's Sunday School Society was founded in 1786 by clergyman

William Richardson. The interdenominational Sunday School Union was set up in 1803 to promote Sunday schools in London; achieving national status in 1903, it became the National Christian Education Council in 1966.

superior court Any court whose decisions on points of law are, under what is known as the doctrine of judicial precedent, binding on courts lower in the system. Of the ordinary courts in the UK, the superior courts are: throughout the UK, the *House of Lords; for England and Wales, the *Court of Appeal, the *High Court of Justice, and the *Crown Court; for Scotland, the *Court of Session and the *High Court of Justiciary; and for Northern Ireland, the Court of Appeal, the High Court, and the Crown Court there (*see* Supreme Court of Judicature of Northern Ireland. A few courts of special jurisdiction are also superior courts (e.g. the *Employment Appeals Tribunal and the *Restrictive Practices Court), but these are the exception rather than the rule.

Supreme Court of Judicature A court established for England and Wales by the Judicature Act 1873. The inconvenience of having numerous courts was marked, as there were conflicts of jurisdiction, different bodies of law, different procedures, and difficulties therefore in discovering the appropriate court in which to sue. After several legislative attempts at improvement, the Judicative Commission proposed the unification of jurisdictory law and procedure in what is now the Supreme Court of Judicature. It is in fact made up of three courts: since its inception, the *High Court of Justice and the *Court of Appeal (which together replaced the inconveniently large number of superior courts then in existence, with the exception of the *House of Lords and the *Judicial Committee of the Privy Council); and today, the *Crown Court also. Rules of the Supreme Court (RSC) govern practice and procedure in the High Court and Court of Appeal, and are published with annotations in *The Supreme Court Practice* ("the White Book"). There are distinct Crown Court Rules.

Supreme Court of Judicature of Northern Ireland A court in Northern Ireland corresponding to the *Supreme Court of Judicature of England and Wales. Established in 1920, its component courts, the High Court of Justice, the Court of Appeal, and a Crown Court (since 1978), likewise corresponded to those of the latter. At the head of all three is, however, the Lord Chief Justice of Northern Ireland; and terrorist offences are triable in a Crown Court without juries. The difficulty experienced in obtaining convictions for such offences led to a recommendation to this effect by a commission under Lord Diplock (a *Lord of Appeal in Ordinary) and courts sitting without juries are frequently referred to as Diplock courts. Appeal lies from the Court of Appeal to the *House of Lords. The civil servants responsible for servicing the courts are known as the Northern Ireland Courts Service.

surnames The names borne by members of the same family, passed down from father to children. There are four main sources of English surnames: names of local features such as Hill and Ford; occupational names such as Smith and Baker; nicknames such as Short and Wild; and personal names such as Peters and Martin. The earliest surnames in English originated from places in Normandy: followers of William the Conqueror and his successors in the 12th century identified themselves by reference to the estates in Normandy from which their families came – Robert de Crequer's family was from Crèvecoeur in Calvados; Ralph de Sentcler's came from one of several places called Saint-Clair in northern France. From these developed the modern surnames Crocker and Croaker, and Sinclair. There are several hundred modern English surnames derived in this way from places in Normandy.

Within 200 years of the Norman conquest most citizens of any substance in England and English-speaking Scotland bore a surname, many of which were derived from place names. Two kinds of "local" surname may be distinguished: habitation names and topographic names. Habitation names are those taken from the name of a town or village. Often, but by no means always, these were associated with lordship of the manor in medieval times. Thus, somebody called Beresford had an ancestor who was lord of the manor of the village of Beresford in Staffordshire. On the other hand, surnames such as Darby and Darbyshire imply no more than that the original bearer came from the town or county of Derby. As a general rule, the larger the unit referred to, the further the bearer had moved: someone called Scott, France, or Pettingale (from Portugal) had moved right away from his native land.

Another kind of local name derives from the actual topography: someone called Hill or Ford had an ancestor living by such a place and the surname could have been acquired any time between the 12th and the 17th centuries (though probably earlier rather than later). Sometimes it is impossible to say which kind of local name is in question. Is someone called Bradford to be associated with one of the many towns and villages of this name, or did he merely have an ancestor living by a "broad ford"?

Similar imponderables occur with "nickname" surnames. One interesting example arises with the names Black and Blake. Ostensibly, they were nicknames for a dark-haired or dark-skinned person, from Old English *blaec* "black". However, they have become inextricably confused with derivatives of another Old English word: *blāc*, which means "bright", "pale", or "blond". It would be an oversimplification to say that the surname Black is from the first and Blake from the second. The truth is that both forms can have either origin, and since we know nothing about the appearance of the original bearers, we are unable to choose between them. Many "nickname" surnames refer to physical characteristics: Smollett ("small head"), Brown (in hair or dress), and Armstrong. Others refer to moral characteristics: Noble, Hardy, Quant (from Middle English *coint* "neat"), and Bragg ("lively") were all originally complimentary nicknames. Some surnames are based on fancied resemblance to a creature: Sparrow, Fox, and Buck are examples. Others are derived from obscene nicknames: Wagstaff and Shakespeare may well be among these, although we cannot be certain what it was that

was wagged or shaken. The surnames King, Duke, and Prince do not denote aristocratic ancestry; they, too, are nicknames. Names such as Nunn, Bishop, and Monk may or may not refer to the occupation of the bearer, since in view of the supposed celibacy of the clergy before the Reformation they should not have become hereditary surnames on a wide scale. They could have been nicknames for sanctimonious individuals.

Those in minor orders were allowed to marry, however, so Clark is an example of a common hereditary occupational name, derived from "cleric". Other specialized occupational names include Skinner and Tanner (leather workers), Wright (a carpenter), and Potter. Some occupational names denote keepers of animals: Shepherd, Coward (cow herd), and Herd or Hurd itself. The popularity in the Middle Ages of field sports is attested by the frequency of such names as Hunter, Faulkner and Falconer, Fowler, Forster, and Forrester. In many cases, different names were used in different regions for an occupation. The word for a weaver provides an interesting example: Webster, like many other names ending in -ster (Brewster, Baxter, etc.), is typically East Midland and Norfolk. Webb, like Brewer and Baker, is the usual southern form. Weaver itself is chiefly West Midland; Webber is commoner in Devon and Somerset. Some surnames did indeed denote rank: Reeve and Sherriff both refer to medieval administrative officials. Stewart and Butler, originally words for servants, came to denote very high-ranking and powerful officials.

The last of the four classes of surnames are those derived from *Christian names. These often show an enormous variety of forms, in particular derivatives of medieval pet forms. Typically, surnames from Christian names end in -s or, especially in the north, -son. Thus, from Robert, we find not only Roberts, Robarts, Robertson, Robbs, Robson, and Robeson, but also Hobbs, Hobson, Hopkins, and Hopkinson (from the medieval pet form Hobbe and its derivative Hopkin).

Most Celtic surnames are derived from personal names. Welsh Probert is from Robert with the patronymic prefix *ap*; Bevan is similarly derived from Evan or Ieuan, the Welsh form of John. Many Scottish and Irish Gaelic names are distinguished by the prefix Mac ("son of"), and Irish ones by O' ("descendant of"). Irish names often go back to pre-Christian personal names. Callaghan, for example, goes back to a personal name Ceallach ("strife"), borne by a 10th-century king of Munster. Under English rule, many Irish names became distorted almost beyond recognition, in some cases being changed to look as if they were of English origin. Thus, Begley, which looks like an English local name, is actually from the Irish *beag laoch* "the small hero".

Sutton Hoo A village in Suffolk famous for the discovery (1939) of an undisturbed Anglo-Saxon ship burial, dating from about 625 AD. It was the habit of the earlier Anglo-Saxons, like the Norsemen, to inter their deceased kings in some martial context; but unlike the Norsemen they tended to prefer burial to incineration. Found in one of a group of 16 burial mounds, the vessel measured about 24 metres (80 feet) in length and contained military equipment, gold jewellery, silver dishes, and many other fine artefacts, including many originating on the continent, and even a bronze Coptic bowl from Egypt. Probably one of the most important archaeological finds from this period, the discovery both provided useful confirmation of literary sources (one helmet is almost identical to one described in the epic poem *Beowulf*), and also greatly influenced ideas on the wealth and contacts of 7th-century England. No body was found, probably destroyed by the acid soil; but the burial is usually associated with King Raedwald of East Anglia (d. 625), one of the seven *bretwaldas* ("overkings") listed by the Venerable Bede (*see* Anglo-Saxon Britain). The ship is now housed in the British Museum.

swan-upping An annual ceremony that takes place on the River Thames to establish the ownership of the swans that live on it and record their numbers. Swans were believed to have been introduced into Britain in the 12th century by Richard I (r. 1189–99). Ever since then they have received royal protection; no-one but the monarch could own swans without a licence and one of the conditions for holding such a licence was that every bird should bear an ownership mark (*cygninota*) on its beak. Originally the licence was only available to the owners of large freehold lands but since the middle of this century these regulations have been relaxed and some 900 swan marks are recognized by the Royal Swanmaster throughout the kingdom.

The custom of marking swans gradually died out in the 18th century and today it is observed only by the Companies of the Dyers and the Vintners (*see* City livery companies), who continue to mark their swans on the Thames, whereas the royal swans are unmarked. On the Monday of the third week in July, the Queen's swan keeper and representatives of the Dyers' and Vintners' Companies meet at Temple Steps, Blackfriars, and move up river in skiffs as far as Henley, marking and establishing the ownership of the swans as they go. Cygnets are marked according to the marks of their parents and their wings are pinioned to prevent them from flying far afield. The process, known as swan-upping, or sometimes swan-hopping, continues for four days.

sword dance A dance performed in various towns of northern England, notably Flamborough, Grenoside, and North Skelton in Yorkshire. The dancers carry long flexible swords made of wood or steel, with which they perform a set pattern of movements and manoeuvres culminating in the "lock": a complicated interweaving of the swords into a star-shaped pattern that is then held aloft by the leader. The dance is accompanied by a play, similar to the *mummers' play, at the climax of which a character known as the Fool puts his head inside the locked swords. As the swords are withdrawn he falls to the ground, apparently decapitated, to be revived by Besom Betty or the Doctor. This ritual of death and resurrection is believed to symbolize the death of the old year and the rebirth of nature and suggests the ancient origins of the dance.

A sword dance known as the Gillie Chalium, quite different from those of northern England, is performed in Scotland. A solo dance, it consists of a number of intricate steps executed over and around two crossed Highland broadswords. The Gillie Chalium dates back at least

429

to the mid-18th century and may originally have been a victory dance.

syllabub A rich cold dessert made from double cream whipped up with wine, lemon juice, and sugar, sometimes with the addition of beaten egg-whites, brandy, or nutmeg. Syllabub was originally a 17th-century drink consisting of sweetened or spiced white wine, cider, or fruit juice with a frothy head produced by squirting a jet of milk or cream into the bowl. By the 18th century the more solid cream syllabub, often laced with brandy, had become a popular dessert dish and was sometimes used as the topping for an early form of trifle.

Synod of the Church of England *See* General Synod of the Church of England.

T

Tate Gallery A gallery at Millbank, London, housing the nation's chief collection of British art and modern foreign art. It was opened in 1897 to accommodate a collection of British art given to the nation in 1890 by Sir Henry Tate (1819–99), a wealthy sugar merchant, and a series of earlier bequests, including the Turner Bequest (1856) of 282 paintings and 19,000 watercolours, which the cramped *National Gallery had been unable to display. Originally conceived as a gallery for modern British art, the Tate came to specialize in paintings showing its long development, Hogarth, Blake, and the *Pre-Raphaelites, as well as Turner, being particularly well represented in the Tate's collection. Its collection of foreign works received an early boost from the creation in 1923 by Samuel Courtauld of a fund for the purchase of modern French paintings. At first subordinate to the National Gallery, the Tate became administratively autonomous after 1915 and fully independent in 1955.

Tatler An illustrated society magazine founded in 1901 as a weekly and now published ten times a year. The title originated in the periodical begun by Richard Steele (1672–1729) in 1709 and continued with the collaboration of Joseph Addison (1672–1719) until 1711. Its promise to carry reports of "gallantry, pleasure, and entertainment" is fulfilled in the general bias of its 20th-century namesake, the principal section of which displays photographs of the wealthy and fashionable at such functions as debutantes' balls, society weddings, and charity premieres. It also contains gossipy articles on society life and personalities, and features on such topics as fashion, restaurants, and property.

tax system Levies by the state on various aspects of national activity to provide its income. All taxes are voted annually by Parliament in the Finance Act and fall into two categories: direct (levies on income, profits, or wealth), principally income tax, corporation tax, inheritance tax (replacing capital transfer tax), and capital gains tax; and indirect (surcharges on goods or services), mainly customs and excise duties, value added tax, petroleum revenue tax, and stamp duties. The proportions of total tax revenue they yield (based on 1983–84) are: income tax 39.5%, corporation tax 7.6%, capital transfer tax 0.8%, capital gains tax 0.8%, customs 1.4%, excise 21.5%, value added tax 19.2%, petroleum revenue tax 7.6%, and stamp duties 1.4%.

Customs duties on goods entering or leaving the country are the oldest surviving form of taxation, originating in 1275 with a levy on the export of wool and leather. They provided a major part of state revenues until the 19th century, when they were recognized to be harmful to trade. Between 1824 and 1864 they were largely abolished, and subsequent arguments in their favour and short-term general revivals (e.g. 1932) have centred around the manipulation of trade rather than raising revenue. **Excise** was introduced by Parliament in 1643 to finance its effort in the Civil War (1642–51), and was confirmed at the Restoration (1660). It is a surcharge on selected commodities, the main targets being petrol, tobacco, alcoholic drink, and vehicle licensing (*see also* Customs and Excise). **Stamp duties,**

levies on certain legal documents such as house conveyances and Stock Exchange transactions, date from 1690. The oldest surviving direct tax is **income tax**, introduced in 1797 to pay for the wars against revolutionary and Napoleonic France (1793–1815). It was abolished in 1816, but renewed in 1842 to cover the fall in customs revenue. A progressive element (taxing higher incomes at higher rates) was introduced in 1909. Since 1944 income tax has been deducted where possible by the employer when wages are paid, a system known as **PAYE** (pay-as-you-earn). The basic rate (which was 7% in 1842), is currently 29%. Company profits were subject to income tax and an additional profits tax until 1966, when a separate **corporation tax** was introduced. Other capital gains (increases in the value of capital assets outside the normal course of business) were first subjected to income tax in 1962, and to a separate **capital gains tax** from 1965. A general capital transfer tax on gifts of wealth was introduced in 1974, extending the previous duties which applied only at death. This was replaced by an inheritance tax in 1986. **Value added tax** was imposed in 1973 to bring Britain into line with the EEC. It is effectively a surcharge on the price of most goods and services; but its method of collection, while ensuring that the net is spread widely but fairly, is complex and places unwelcome administrative burdens on the taxpayer. The newest major tax is the petroleum revenue tax, dating from 1975 and designed to exploit the earnings of North Sea oil.

The balance between the various taxes is a constant topic of political and economic debate. In general, the Labour Party tends to prefer direct taxes, because they distinguish between levels of income; whereas the Conservatives favour indirect taxes, which distinguish between the uses to which income is put.

tea   A light meal eaten between lunch and dinner, usually in mid-afternoon and traditionally between four and five o'clock. The light meal of afternoon tea was devised in the mid-17th century to bridge the gap between a large breakfast (or insubstantial lunch) and a late dinner, which was then served at about eight o'clock in the evening. Its invention is attributed to the wife of the 7th Duke of Bedford in 1840. The tea was traditionally poured by the lady of the house and accompanied by bread and butter, delicately cut sandwiches, cakes, scones, and pastries. The afternoon tea party, essentially a female affair, has largely died out with changes in eating habits and the increasing number of women who go out to work, but afternoon tea is still enjoyed in many homes on nonworking days and in tea shops and cafés throughout the country. Certain regions have their own specialities, notably the clotted cream teas of Devon and Cornwall. High tea is a more substantial meal, usually including a cooked dish, that is served around six o'clock after a day in the open air. Tea is also a working-class name given to the evening meal.

Tea, the beverage, was brought to Europe by the Dutch at the beginning of the 17th century. From Holland, it was brought to England by Lord Ossory and Lord Arlington in 1666, although Samuel Pepys recorded his first cup of tea in 1660. It then became fashionable among the gentry, replacing coffee and chocolate; during the last half of the century tea shops and tea gardens began to open in and around London and the other big cities. In 1669 the East India Company first began to import tea from India, an exclusive privilege they held until 1830, when tea auctions began in Mincing Lane in the City of London. These sales still continue. In the middle of the 18th century, as tea became cheaper and more plentiful in Britain, it came to be the most popular beverage for all social classes. By 1830 it was reported in the House of Commons that Great Britain was consuming some 30 million pounds of tea, while the rest of the world consumed only 22 million pounds. By the turn of the 19th century British consumption had increased tenfold.

technical school   *See* state education.

tennis   A racket-and-ball game for two or four players, more correctly known as lawn tennis to distinguish it from the much older game of *real tennis. Lawn tennis evolved in England in the 1870s as an open air version of the old game, and rules were drawn up by the *All-England Lawn Tennis and Croquet Club in Wimbledon for their first ever lawn tennis tournament in 1877 (*see* Wimbledon). There have been only minor alterations to this code. By the 1880s a game recognizably similar to that now seen was being played. The growth in popularity amongst both men and women led to the formation in 1888 of the Lawn Tennis Association. The game soon spread abroad, and took hold in the USA and Australia particularly. In 1900 there were sufficient countries playing to a good standard to lead to the creation of the Davis Cup competition between national men's teams. Women players had to wait until 1923 for their first international team event, the Wightman Cup between England and the USA.

After World War II increasing numbers of top players turned professional, but the International Lawn Tennis Federation insisted that championships remain for amateurs only. This situation was ended in 1967 when the LTA voted for an "open" Wimbledon, and the ILTF capitulated the following year. Since then the game has been entirely open to amateurs and professionals and has enjoyed a worldwide boom.

Territorial Army *See* reserve forces.

Test and Corporation Acts Several statutes passed under Charles II that were intended to restrict most public offices to members of the Church of England. The Corporation Act (1661) was one of a series of statutes, the "Clarendon Code", that sought to strengthen the position of the Anglican Church after the *Restoration. It required all municipal office holders to take various oaths of loyalty to the Crown, to renounce Puritanism, and to have taken Anglican Communion within the previous year. It was aimed primarily at Protestant dissenters, but also affected Roman Catholics. The reverse was the case with the Test Act (1673). In 1672 the pro-Catholic Charles II suspended nearly all religious disabilities by the Declaration of Indulgence. This proved so unpopular that it had to be withdrawn the next year; and Parliament insisted that the Test Act be passed, which excluded all Catholics and most Protestant dissenters from civil and military office, by requiring holders to take oaths of loyalty

and Anglican Communion and to repudiate the Catholic doctrine of transubstantiation. A second Test Act (1678) excluded all Catholics from Parliament (excepting only the future James II). These laws endured until the 19th century, although indemnities to the Corporation Act were passed annually from 1727. The Corporation Act was repealed in 1828; the Test Acts were rendered inoperative in practice at the same time, though they were not formally repealed until later.

In Scotland, an Act of 1567 made holding public office conditional on a profession of the reformed (i.e. Protestant) faith. A further Act was passed in 1681, and religious tests were not finally abolished until 1889.

theatre in education (TIE) The work of theatre groups in schools. TIE groups are sponsored by Local Education Authorities and drama departments at colleges and universities. The movement developed after World War II out of children's theatre, such as Bertha Waddell's Scottish Children's Theatre (1927–69), Esmé Church's Northern Children's Theatre (1947–58), and Caryl Jenner's Unicorn Theatre (1962–) in London. The Pear Tree Players (1945–47), founded by the pioneer of TIE, Peter Slade, was probably the first company set up specifically to play in schools. The *repertory theatres, notably the Coventry TIE at the Belgrade Theatre since 1965, have also helped to foster the movement. The purpose of theatre in education is primarily to involve children in an imaginative process. They are encouraged to participate in the performance of a visiting company, which will present fairy tales, for example, to younger children, or specially devised scenes in which older children explore different situations. Sometimes a specific skill, such as road safety, is taught by the enactment of relevant dramas.

Thistle, Order of the A Scottish order that is the second oldest order of chivalry in Britain. Although extravagant claims for its antiquity have been made, it was probably instituted by James III of Scotland (r. 1460–88). After a lapse it was revived by James VII of Scotland and II of England in 1687 only to lapse again the next year. Queen Anne restored the order once more in 1703, together with its traditional designation of "The Most Ancient and Most Noble". Members are only 16 in number under the sovereign, although additional royal knights (e.g. the Duke of Edinburgh and the Prince of Wales) and other knights may be admitted by special statutes. Among the rank and file is the former Prime Minister, Lord Home of the Hirsel. The motto of the order is *Nemo me impune lacessit* ("No one provokes me with impunity").

Three Choirs Festival An annual six-day festival mainly of choral music, which is based in turn at Gloucester, Worcester, and Hereford cathedrals. When it began in the early 18th century only liturgical music and anthems were performed in the cathedral; secular concerts, mainly of Handel oratorios, were held in the town. Until the mid-19th century the festival was known as the Gloucester (or Worcester or Hereford) Music Meeting. Its scope widened in the 20th century, when Edward Elgar (1857–1934), who was born in Worcestershire, was closely associated with the festival. It has also presented first performances of works by, for example, Ralph Vaughan Williams (1872–1958), Gustav Holst (1874–1934), and Malcolm Williamson (1931–).

Times, The Britain's oldest surviving daily newspaper. It was founded in 1785 as the *Daily Universal Register* by John Walter (1739–1812). In 1788 he changed the title to *The Times*. His son John Walter II (1776–1847) established *The Times* as the country's leading newspaper, independent of government subsidies and with its own news-gathering service. Its reputation and influence continued to grow under the editorship (1817–41) of Thomas Barnes (1785–1841), under whom the paper acquired its nickname of "The Thunderer", and under his successor John Thaddeus Delane (1817–79), who edited the paper until 1877.

During the editorship (1884–1912) of George Earle Buckle (1854–1935) *The Times* suffered severe damage to its finances and prestige by its publication of the forged Parnell letters (1889). Its circulation dwindled and in 1908 Lord Northcliffe (1856–1922) acquired the ailing paper. The first editorship of Geoffrey

Dawson (1874–1944) ran from 1912 to 1919, until he quarrelled with Northcliffe, and during World War I *The Times* regained much of its former prestige and political influence. On Northcliffe's death Dawson returned as editor (1922–41) and exercised considerable influence, particularly on Stanley Baldwin (Prime Minister 1924, 1925–29, 1935–37), although his espousal of appeasement in the period leading to World War II brought considerable discredit upon the paper. Under Dawson's successor, Robin Barrington-Ward (1891–1948) who edited the paper until his death, it advocated a pro-Russian policy. From 1922 until 1966 the paper was owned by the Astor family; it was then acquired by Lord Thomson of Fleet (1894–1976). In 1981 in the wake of four years of industrial problems and strikes, the Thomson Organization sold *The Times* to Australian newspaper proprietor Rupert Murdoch (1931–).

For much of its existence *The Times*'s leaders have had a significant influence upon British political life, but other aspects of the paper have also contributed to its unique status as a British institution: the ingenious crossword (introduced in 1929), the letters page, the law reports, the obituaries, and the personal column. Its pre-eminence in reporting foreign news dates from the time of John Walter II, the first man to publish news of the battle of *Trafalgar (1805); other famous scoops include its reporting of the capitulation of Paris during the Franco-Prussian War (1870), accounts of General Gordon's desperate plight at Khartoum (1884), descriptions of the siege of Peking during the Boxer rebellion (1900), the discovery of Tutankhamen's tomb (1922), and the ascent of Everest (1953). *The Times* has carried book reviews since its inception; since 1902 it has also published a weekly literary supplement (*TLS*); more recent innovations are the supplements on education (*TES*) and higher education (*THES*).

Until 1974 *The Times* was published from its original site in Printing House Square, Blackfriars, London. Under Lord Thomson it moved to Gray's Inn Road and more controversially under Rupert Murdoch to Wapping, east London. On the technical front, *The Times* has often been an innovator. In 1929 the distinguished typographer Stanley Morison (1889–1967) was called upon to improve the typography of the paper and designed the Times New Roman typeface, first used in 1932 and a lasting success. The conservatism of *Times* readers, however, means that change often meets with protest, as in 1966 when news items first appeared on the front page, displacing the personal column. One famous feature that has not survived is the "fourth leader", a humorous piece following the serious leaders, which was dropped in 1967.

Toc H An interdenominational Christian movement dedicated to making faith an active force in the community through service and Christian fellowship. It began in 1915 with the opening of a rest-house for troops in the Ypres Salient, Belgium, by an Anglican army chaplain, the Rev. P. T. B. ("Tubby") Clayton (1885–1972). It was called Talbot House after Gilbert Talbot, son of the Bishop of Winchester, who was killed in action that year. In 1920 Clayton opened another Talbot House in London and launched a movement "to teach the younger generation class-reconciliation and unselfish service". The society was henceforth known as Toc H, from the military signallers' jargon for the initial letters; it was incorporated by royal charter in 1922. In the same year Clayton was appointed vicar of All-Hallows-by-the-Tower in the City of London, and soon after, Toc H undertook the Tower Hill Improvement scheme (1926) as its first major project. Clayton travelled all over the world on behalf of Toc H and hundreds of branches were established, initially with a high proportion of ex-servicemen members, but latterly taking in any adult fired by the spirit of Christian social service.

Tolpuddle Martyrs Six farm labourers from Tolpuddle in Dorset, who were transported to Australia in 1834 for organizing trade-union activities. The leaders of the group, George and James Loveless, had established the Friendly Society of Agricultural Labourers at Tolpuddle in 1833 in an attempt to improve their inadequate wages. Although trade unions had been legalized nine years earlier, the government was still uneasy lest the increasing demands of organized bands of dis-

contented workers should get out of hand. The Loveless brothers and four others were accordingly held up as examples and accused of administering illegal oaths, found guilty, and sentenced to seven years' transportation. The subsequent outcry from those sympathetic to the cause, such as the *Chartists, eventually resulted in a free pardon, but not before they had served the first two years of their sentence. In the meantime they became popular heroes, and are still regarded as pioneers of the trade-union movement.

Tolzey Court *See* Bristol Tolzey Court.

Tory *See* Conservative Party.

Tower Bridge The easternmost bridge over the River Thames, which can open to allow large ships in and out of the Pool of London. By the middle of the 19th century a third of London's population lived east of London Bridge and there was growing public demand for a new bridge, which the construction of the Dartford tunnel under the river in 1870 did little to satisfy. Various designs were suggested and in 1885 Parliament finally approved Horace Jones's scheme for a bascule bridge with towers clad in granite and Portland stone, to harmonize with the nearby Tower of London. John Wolfe Barry was appointed as the engineer to supervise its construction. The sight of the bridge roadway splitting and lifting for the first time, at the opening ceremony in 1894, caused considerable pride to Londoners. Thereafter it opened and closed up to 50 times a day, an operation which took just over five minutes. Hydraulic power to lift each bascule leaf was provided by two 360 horsepower steam pumping engines lodged in the two towers. With the decline of shipping in the Pool of London, Tower Bridge has to open less often; the bascules are now operated (by electricity) only two or three times a week, and so the heavy flow of traffic over the bridge is seldom interrupted. Visitors can still see the original boilers, steam and hydraulic engines, and accumulators in the towers, as well as a fine view of London from the upper walkways.

Tower of London A castle started by the Normans that ranks among the most famous

TOWER BRIDGE *In the background is the White Tower.*

in the world, both for its size and its prominent place in English history. At its centre is the White Tower, begun by order of William the Conqueror in 1078 as a palace for the Norman rulers and a fortress to dominate London. The site chosen was by the River Thames within the old Roman city wall where a Norman timber castle had stood since 1066–67. The great stone keep contained two suites of residential rooms, the grander for the royal family, with St John's Chapel – a fine example of Norman architecture – adjoining it. Over the next 200 years the castle was augmented

until in Edward I's reign (r. 1272–1307) it became a concentric fortress with two lines of massive walls and towers surrounded by a moat. None of the subsequent attempts made to besiege it was ever successful. Meanwhile a new palace had been built outside the White Tower and was richly adorned by Henry III (r. 1216–72); he also had the White Tower whitewashed, hence its name. From Richard II to Charles II nearly 300 years later, almost every sovereign proceeded to his or her coronation from the Tower and the coronation regalia is still kept there (*see* Crown jewels).

435

Tower of London

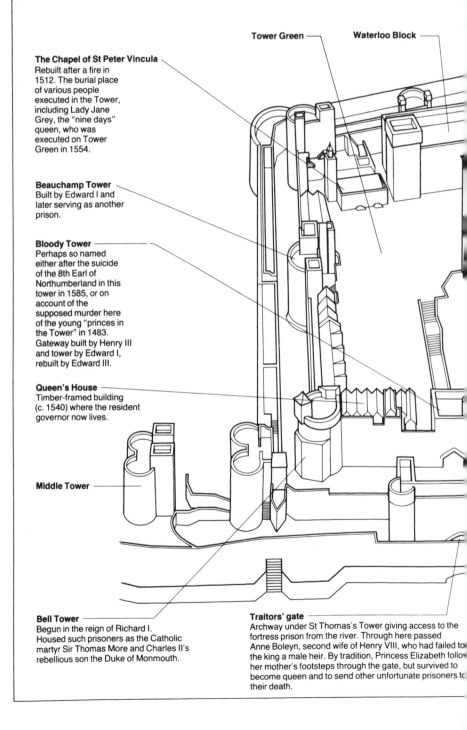

Tower Green

Waterloo Block

The Chapel of St Peter Vincula
Rebuilt after a fire in 1512. The burial place of various people executed in the Tower, including Lady Jane Grey, the "nine days" queen, who was executed on Tower Green in 1554.

Beauchamp Tower
Built by Edward I and later serving as another prison.

Bloody Tower
Perhaps so named either after the suicide of the 8th Earl of Northumberland in this tower in 1585, or on account of the supposed murder here of the young "princes in the Tower" in 1483. Gateway built by Henry III and tower by Edward I, rebuilt by Edward III.

Queen's House
Timber-framed building (c. 1540) where the resident governor now lives.

Middle Tower

Bell Tower
Begun in the reign of Richard I. Housed such prisoners as the Catholic martyr Sir Thomas More and Charles II's rebellious son the Duke of Monmouth.

Traitors' gate
Archway under St Thomas's Tower giving access to the fortress prison from the river. Through here passed Anne Boleyn, second wife of Henry VIII, who had failed to give the king a male heir. By tradition, Princess Elizabeth followed her mother's footsteps through the gate, but survived to become queen and to send other unfortunate prisoners to their death.

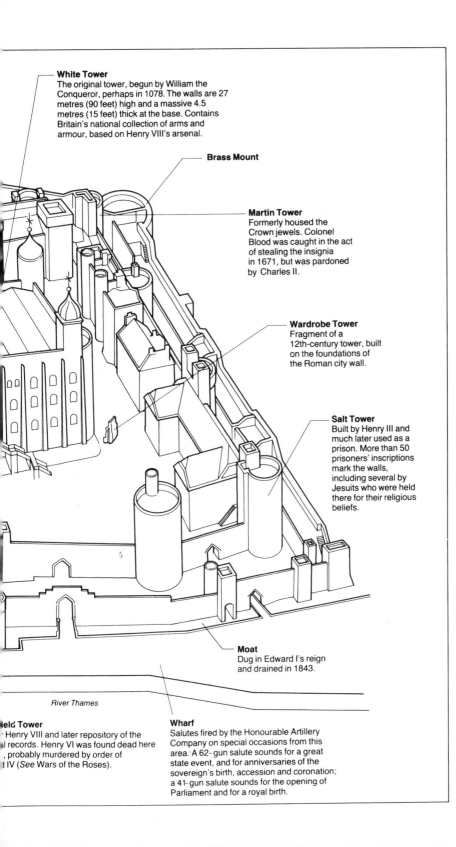

White Tower
The original tower, begun by William the Conqueror, perhaps in 1078. The walls are 27 metres (90 feet) high and a massive 4.5 metres (15 feet) thick at the base. Contains Britain's national collection of arms and armour, based on Henry VIII's arsenal.

Brass Mount

Martin Tower
Formerly housed the Crown jewels. Colonel Blood was caught in the act of stealing the insignia in 1671, but was pardoned by Charles II.

Wardrobe Tower
Fragment of a 12th-century tower, built on the foundations of the Roman city wall.

Salt Tower
Built by Henry III and much later used as a prison. More than 50 prisoners' inscriptions mark the walls, including several by Jesuits who were held there for their religious beliefs.

Moat
Dug in Edward I's reign and drained in 1843.

River Thames

ield Tower
Henry VIII and later repository of the records. Henry VI was found dead here, probably murdered by order of IV (*See* Wars of the Roses).

Wharf
Salutes fired by the Honourable Artillery Company on special occasions from this area. A 62-gun salute sounds for a great state event, and for anniversaries of the sovereign's birth, accession and coronation; a 41-gun salute sounds for the opening of Parliament and for a royal birth.

From the 15th century onwards the Tower became notorious as a state prison. Its darkest associations began with the *Wars of the Roses (1455–85) and the murder of Henry VI (1471; *see* Lilies and Roses, ceremony of); and were reinforced by the mysterious fate of the boy king Edward V and his brother Richard of York, who disappeared there in 1483 and are generally thought to have been killed by orders of their uncle, Richard III. Many famous figures of Tudor and Stuart times were prisoners there, often before public execution on Tower Hill outside the castle. Sir Thomas More (1535), Thomas Cromwell (1540), and Archbishop Laud (1645), were all beheaded there. Women, including Anne Boleyn (1536), Catherine Howard (1542), and Lady Jane Grey (1554) were executed within the walls on Tower Green. Some of the prisoners left touching memorials by carving their names in the wall of their prison. What had been a utilitarian water-gate under St Thomas's Tower became known as Traitor's Gate, because it was a convenient landing-place for prisoners who had been tried at Westminster. The Garden Tower, through similar association, became the Bloody Tower. Prisoners were few after the 18th century. (The last to be held in the Tower was Rudolf Hess in 1941.) The disused palace buildings were demolished to make room for vast store-houses, and the Tower, already a great arsenal, began to display its historic arms and armour, attracting the first tourists. Today the Tower Armoury is the national museum of arms and armour; perhaps its most outstanding exhibits are the armour of Henry VIII and others made in the royal workshops at Greenwich. Until the mid-19th century the Tower also housed the *Royal Mint, some government records, and an army garrison. The royal menagerie, predecessor of London Zoo, was also lodged there from the 13th century until 1834. It is now Britain's most popular tourist attraction, drawing more than two million visitors a year. A history gallery, an oriental gallery, a wall walk, and various towers have been opened up for special displays, and tourists can be conducted around the outside by Yeoman Warders wearing their picturesque uniforms (*see* Yeomen of the Guard). As in its earliest

days, a whole community lives within the Tower: mainly Tower officers and the families of the Yeoman Warders, a detachment of soldiers for guard duty, and six ravens, whose presence in the Tower, according to an old superstition, guarantees the kingdom from destruction.

town and country planning A statutory system that controls land and building development to ensure that it is not contrary to the public interest. It is administered primarily by local authorities or (e.g. in the Lake and Peak districts) joint boards of local authorities, but the Secretary of State for the Environment has very considerable supervisory powers.

Town and country planning is a phenomenon of the 20th century. In the previous century, public health and housing Acts had given local authorities certain powers of intervention (e.g. to prevent the erection of dwellings without proper sanitation or ventilation, and to clear slums), but no power to control development as a whole, as by preventing the building of a factory in a residential area. Overall control began with the Housing, Town Planning, etc. Act 1909, which gave limited powers of planning to urban authorities; the modern system was established in 1947 and subsequently amended by the Town and Country Planning Act 1971.

There are three key ingredients in town and country planning: development plans, planning permission, and enforcement.

1) Development plans are prepared by the local planning authorities and consist of structure plans and local plans. A structure plan sets out the authority's general planning policy for the area, taking into account such factors as size, economy, distribution of population, and communications, and must be approved by the Secretary of State for the Environment. A local plan indicates the authority's detailed proposals for the development and use of land within the framework of the structure plan. It must be copied to the Secretary of State, but does not require his approval.

2) Planning permission is required for *every* development of land, from building work, engineering, mining, etc., to changes in the use of any buildings or land. (Exceptions are works that do not affect the external appearance of a

building, and changes of use that fall within a class of use specified by the Secretary of State.) Planning permission for certain types of development (e.g. limited home improvements) has been granted as "permitted development" by a general development order of the Secretary of State, who may also issue special development orders in certain cases. Normally, however, the grant or refusal of permission is for the local planning authorities to decide in the light of the relevant development plan, although an applicant has the right of appeal to the Secretary of State.

3) Enforcement of planning control is primarily in the hands of the local planning authorities. If someone develops land without permission, or breaches any condition attached to a permission, the authority may serve an enforcement notice on him requiring remedial steps to be taken within a specified time. Failure to comply renders him liable to prosecution, and the authority may do the work itself at his expense. Appeal against an enforcement notice lies to the Secretary of State, who also has power to issue such a notice on his own initiative.

The general system of town and country planning is supplemented by a number of special controls: for example, the display of outdoor advertisements is controlled by strict regulations made by the Secretary of State; it is necessary to obtain planning permission and a site licence, to which particularly stringent conditions are liable to be attached, in order to set up a caravan site; buildings of special architectural or historic interest are listed by the Secretary of State, and may not be demolished or altered without special "listed building consent"; tree preservation orders may be made by the authority, preventing the felling of trees without consent. Finally, a local authority may designate part of the locality a "conservation area", thereby attracting special planning rules, and causing virtually all buildings and trees to be treated as if they were listed or subject to preservation orders.

town crier A civic office that originated in the Middle Ages as a means of conveying information to the inhabitants of a town. The town crier, dressed in livery and carrying a handbell, would station himself at some point in the town to make his announcement, ringing his handbell to attract the attention of passers-by and nearby residents, and crying "Oyez! Oyez!": an Old French word meaning "Hear ye!". With the advent of more sophisticated means of mass communication and increased literacy, town criers eventually became superfluous; the tradition is still carried on, however, in a number of British towns. Each year in August the national town criers' championship is held at Hastings in Sussex: contestants arrive from all parts of the country, wearing a variety of picturesque and historic costumes and carrying the traditional handbell, to compete for the challenge cup. Each declaims his test-piece in stentorian tones before a panel of judges, the trophy being awarded to the contestant with the most powerful and impressive voice. Other factors, such as dignity of bearing, are also taken into consideration and there are usually additional prizes for costume.

Toynbee Hall The first university settlement (institutions through which university men can live and work in deprived city communities), founded in Whitechapel, east London, in 1884. It was named after the social reformer and economist Arnold Toynbee, who, with Canon S. A. Barnett, later first warden of Toynbee Hall (1884–96), dedicated himself to improving the quality of life of the urban poor Guided by Toynbee's ideals, Toynbee Hall became the prototype for similar institutions in Britain and elsewhere. Today, it offers many welfare services, including a citizens' advice bureau, legal advice, playgroups, and a housing association, as well as some accommodation for the elderly. It is also used as a base by independent groups.

trade unions Workers' organizations that uphold the rights of employees and negotiate with employers on their behalf. Britain is the birthplace of modern trade unionism, a movement that since the 19th century has achieved a dramatic improvement in the rights and conditions of workers and given them a political voice in the form of the *Labour Party. An urgent need for trade unions was created by the effects of the *industrial revolution, which in the 18th and 19th centuries transformed the country's social and economic life at the cost of often atrocious working conditions.

The origins of trade unions are traced to craftsmen's clubs of the 18th century, which were set up locally to defend their members' interests. But the government, alarmed by the French Revolution, regarded workers' associations as a threat and legislated against them with the Combination Acts of 1799 and 1800, which defined trade unions as criminal conspiracies. In spite of persecution by both employers and the state, however, unions continued to operate until, in 1824, the Combination Acts were repealed and the law was relaxed slightly. The movement suffered a further setback in 1834 when six members of a farmworkers' union from Tolpuddle in Dorset were sentenced to penal servitude in Australia for administering unlawful oaths. The *Tolpuddle Martyrs, who were pardoned in 1836, exemplified the often bitter struggle to secure trade-union rights and are still regarded as heroes of the labour movement. The year 1834 also saw the collapse of Robert Owen's Grand National Consolidated Trades Union, formed the previous year. The Amalgamated Society of Engineers, formed in 1851, was the first union effectively to represent a single trade throughout the country; it set new standards by offering its members a range of benefits and by regulating apprenticeships in the engineering profession. In 1868 the **Trades Union Congress (TUC)** was formed to represent the interests of the trade-union movement, although legal status for unions was not achieved until the passage of the Trade Union Act 1871. As suffrage was extended during the 19th century, the political aspirations of trade unionists increased; in 1900 members of the TUC were among the founders of the Labour Representation Committee, which in 1906 changed its name to the *Labour Party. The unions helped to provide financial support for the new party by means of a political levy collected from their members, thus giving both individual members and the unions themselves a political voice. In the decade that included World War I, trade-union membership trebled to over eight million, although by 1933 it had slumped to just half that number after a period of economic depression and ris-

ing unemployment. Moreover, the collapse of the 1926 General Strike, called by the TUC in support of the miners' refusal to accept a cut in wages, shook the confidence of the movement. The government pressed home its advantage by making sympathy strikes illegal and forcing members to "contract in" in order to pay the political levy – that is, to state positively that they wished to pay (as opposed to "contracting out", where the burden of action is placed on those who do not wish to pay). This measure, financially damaging to the Labour Party, was reversed by the 1945 Labour government.

Since World War II the unions of traditional industries, such as iron and steel, shipbuilding, agriculture, textiles, and mining have lost members, while recruitment to the "white-collar" unions, representing clerical workers, civil servants, and others in the service industries, has grown. Many of the older craft unions have amalgamated to form so-called industrial unions, such as the National Union of Mineworkers, which represent well-defined sections within a single industry. The so-called general unions, which represent workers in many different industries, include Britain's biggest union, the Transport and General Workers Union (TGWU). Since the mid-1970s, union membership has again been hit by worsening unemployment, so that by 1982 total membership had fallen from its 1979 peak of 13.5 million to 11.7 million.

Although there are over 450 trade unions in Britain, only about 100 are affiliated to the TUC. Nevertheless, the TUC is by far the largest trade-union association in the country, representing some 90% of union members. The TUC's principal officer is the general secretary, who implements the decisions of the general council. This comprises members from a wide spectrum of industries and trades, who are elected by delegates sent by affiliated unions to the TUC's annual congress. Apart from congress, much of the TUC's work is done by its various committees and through its participation in such national bodies as the *National Economic Development Council and the *Manpower Services Commission.

Individual unions all have their own rules, but are usually run by an elected executive, with either the general secretary or president acting as chief officer. Members are organized into local branches, which send delegates to the union's annual conference. Trades councils, which began to appear in the first half of the 19th century and were instrumental in establishing the TUC, consist of representatives drawn from local branches of various trade unions. They also have their annual conference and most are recognized by the TUC. The Scottish TUC, established in 1897, is an organization of Scottish trade unions, Scottish branches of British trade unions, and trades councils, with about one million affiliated members. Most of the major unions operating in Northern Ireland are affiliated to the Northern Ireland Committee of the Irish Congress of Trade Unions, based in Dublin. Traditionally, agreements between Britain's trade unions and employers have not been enforceable in law, and unions have been protected against claims for damages arising out of breach of contract in pursuance of a trade dispute since 1906. However, this position of relative freedom has been eroded by legislation passed by recent Conservative governments, particularly the Employment Acts of 1980 and 1982. These sought to restrict picketing and enable employers to sue unions for damages in certain cases, notably sympathy strikes. The Trade Union Act 1984 required that before a strike is called, a union must demonstrate the support of a majority of its members by means of a secret ballot if it is to retain its legal immunities. Thus the trade-union movement retains its traditional strong links with the Labour Party, in the hope that a sympathetic Labour government will tilt the legislative balance once more in its favour.

Trafalgar, battle of (21 October 1805) The major naval battle of the Napoleonic Wars. Fought west of Cape Trafalgar, between Cadiz and Gibraltar, the battle was the greatest of Admiral Horatio Nelson's victories and established the supremacy of the British navy. Having delivered his famous signal "England expects that every man will do his duty" from his flagship, HMS *Victory, Nelson led his fleet of 27 ships of the line into battle at right angles to the line of the combined French and Spanish fleet, which was under the command of Admiral Villeneuve. This tactic – "breaking the line" – subjected the enemy ships after the break to murderous fire, whilst those in front could not, in the age of sail, turn around quickly enough to be of real assistance. Of the enemy's 33 ships, about 18 were captured or destroyed and 4300 casualties resulted. Although no British vessels were lost, 454 English seamen died, including Nelson himself, struck down by a sniper's bullet. The victory ensured England's safety from invasion by Napoleon and has remained a lasting symbol of British heroism. Memorials to it include Nelson's Column, 44 metres (145 feet) high, in Trafalgar Square, and the *Victory* herself, preserved at Portsmouth.

Treasury *See* Chancellor of the Exchequer.

Treasury Counsel A small group of barristers, nominated by the Attorney General, who undertake important prosecutions at the Central Criminal Court (the Old Bailey) on the instructions of the Director of Public Prosecutions. There are currently 16 such Counsel, 8 of them senior and 8 junior (though the former, despite their title, are junior barristers rather than Queen's Counsel; *see* barrister). Barristers are invited to become Treasury Counsel after they have shown themselves to be successful as prosecuting counsel; thereafter, although theoretically free to accept other briefs, they often appear almost exclusively for the Crown.

Treasury Solicitor The head of the legal civil service. His department is responsible for the legal work of the Treasury (*see* Chancellor of the Exchequer) and also for that of the smaller government departments without their own solicitor's branch. He instructs counsel to appear in civil disputes affecting the Crown (*compare* Treasury Counsel) and himself acts also as *Queen's Proctor. Between 1883 and 1908, his office was combined with that of the *Director of Public Prosecutions, but the two are now quite separate.

Tribune A radical socialist weekly paper founded in 1937 and closely associated with the left wing of the Labour Party. The paper has given its name to the Tribune Group of Labour MPs, who are sympathetic to its critical view of capitalism and its conviction that socialism is the only route to freedom and happiness for the individual. *Tribune* was founded under the editorship of William Mellor (1888–1942) with Michael Foot (1913–) as assistant and the prominent Labour politicians Stafford Cripps (1889–1952) and Aneurin Bevan (1897–1960) as leading contributors. Foot subsequently edited *Tribune* (1948–52, 1955–60), as did Bevan (1942–45), when the paper was used to attack Churchill's conduct of the war, and most radical Labour MPs have at some time contributed to it, including party leaders from Clement Attlee (1883–1967) to Neil Kinnock (1942–). Contributors eminent in other fields include the authors George Orwell (1903–50) and Doris Lessing (1919–), the dramatist Arnold Wesker (1932–), and the geneticist J. B. S. Haldane (1892–1964).

Tribune's pugnacious voice in radical issues quickly won it a healthy circulation (30,000 per week by spring 1939). It was vehemently antifascist and anti-appeasement in politics, and strongly supportive of the trade-union movement, but it also dealt with domestic social issues, such as the role of women in society. At its foundation it had strong links with the Left Book Club, founded in 1936 by Victor Gollancz (1893–1967). The *Tribune* activists suffered a certain amount of disillusionment when Labour came to power in the postwar period: the paper lost readers and was forced for a short period in the early 1950s to appear only fortnightly (the period of the famous *Tribune* pamphlets). In 1958 it espoused the cause of the newly formed *CND, which won it renewed popular support. Under its longest-serving editor (1961–82), Richard Clements (1928–), *Tribune* continued in its appointed role as scourge of the Tories and irritant to the more complacent members of the Labour movement.

Trinity House, Corporation of An ancient chartered organization with sole responsibility for providing navigational aids – 92 lighthouses, 21 light-ships, 700 radio beacons and buoys – around Britain's coasts, and for the organization of the 640 licensed members of the pilot service in London and 39 other districts. Trinity House also performs charit-

able works for seamen and their dependents in financial distress. It was founded by Sir Thomas Spert in 1512 as an association for piloting ships; it was incorporated two years later when it received its royal charter from Henry VIII. By the 17th century it was an important maritime body, responsible for the certification of pilots. Every year since, Trinity House has been rededicated to the Church of England, its name reflecting its religious associations. Trinity House retains many ancient traditions: its senior management, who take oaths upon appointment, are known as the elder brethren, and hold an annual court. They are elected annually by the 300 master mariners, who are known as younger brethren. The Corporation has the privilege of escorting the monarch during sea voyages through Trinity House districts, and the Master of Trinity House is always a member of the royal family, at present HRH the Duke of Edinburgh. The Corporation is also responsible for the marking of shipping lanes in the Straits of Dover and the installation of large automatic buoys. Its work is funded from shipping levies for pilot services.

tripe The stomach lining of ruminant animals, such as cows and sheep, used as food. Introduced to British cookery by the French after the Norman conquest, tripe was once popular in London and the Midlands and is the basic ingredient of a classic northern dish, tripe and onions. The tripe is cleaned and partly cooked before being sold; it is then cut into small pieces and simmered in milk with onion and seasonings to produce an inexpensive and substantial meal. Tripe can also be fried with bacon, combined with other ingredients in a stew, or prepared according to traditional French recipes.

tripos The examination for an honours degree at *Cambridge University. Originally, the tripos was the three-legged stool used by the bachelor of arts who examined candidates for degrees at the now abolished Cambridge ceremony of Commencement; by extension the man himself became known as the tripos. The name attached itself to the humorous verses, which he traditionally published along with the list of successful candidates in the mathematics examination – which in turn began to be called the tripos list. By a further extension, firstly the mathematics examination itself, and eventually those for all subjects, became known as the tripos. It is now divided into two stages (Part I and Part II).

trooping the colour An annual ceremony on Horse Guards Parade to celebrate the Queen's official birthday on a Saturday morning in June. The Queen is Colonel-in-Chief of each of the seven regiments of her personal guard, the *Household Division of the Army: this consists of two mounted regiments – the Life Guards and the Blues and Royals – and five regiments of foot guards – the Grenadiers, the Coldstream Guards, and the Scots, Irish, and Welsh Guards. Each year the regiments of the foot guards take it in turn to troop their Queen's colour, in memory of the time when a soldier's effectiveness on the battlefield might depend on rallying to his unit's flag or colour. Colours used to be trooped at the end of the day in garrisons all over the world, as a reminder of a regiment's *esprit de corps*. The form of the present ceremony goes back to 1805 and involves about 1500 men.
The Queen arrives at 11 o'clock from Buckingham Palace, riding side-saddle and wearing the uniform of the regiment whose colour is being trooped. She is followed by other members of the royal family, usually the Duke of Edinburgh and the Prince of Wales, and attended by the sovereign's escort of the Household Cavalry. As she reaches the saluting base the *national anthem is played and a royal salute fired. She inspects the guards, drawn up along two sides of Horse Guards Parade in a double line, with the colour posted to one side, and then returns to the saluting base for the trooping, which consists of many separate and complex drill movements. The massed bands salute the colour and then the escort for the colour advances to receive it. It is then trooped between the stationary lines of the guards to the tune of "The Grenadiers' March". A march past the Queen, first of the foot guards in slow and quick time – the colour being dipped as it passes the Queen – and then of the Household Cavalry, is followed by a second rendering of the national anthem. The Queen then precedes the guards back to Buckingham

Palace to the music of their bands, or pipes and drums; she finally takes the salute at the gates. The entire royal family subsequently appears on the balcony, and an RAF fly-past takes place if the weather permits.

Trustee Savings Bank *See* banks.

TT Races, Isle of Man A motorcycle racing competition held each year on the Isle of Man. The races were first held in 1905; in 1907 the Auto-Cycle Club of the *Royal Automobile Club staged the first Tourist Trophy (TT) races. These took place over a mile course for one- and two-cylinder machines, the riders setting off in pairs at regular intervals and completing ten laps. In 1911 the course was extended to 38 miles, taking in Snaefell (620 metres, 2034 feet), and in 1920, 250, 350, and 500 cc classes were introduced. Over the years the roads improved and the speeds increased. Alec Bennett won in 1924 at 60 mph and Frederick Frith won in 1937 at 90 mph. Since 1945 speeds of 100 mph and over have become normal on the TT circuit. In the modern era James Redman and John Surtees have been notable TT winners; but the most successful ever was Mike Hailwood, with 14 victories (1961–79). Some of the top riders are now reluctant to compete as their machines are capable of speeds they consider unsafe on the island's narrow twisting roads with their ordinary metalled surfaces, and the course is too long to have proper safety cover throughout. Indeed there have been a number of deaths and serious injuries in practice and in races. Nonetheless, the Isle of Man TT Races continue to be a popular motorcycling event with competitors and the public.

Turpin, Dick An English highwayman, born in Hempstead, Essex, in 1706 and hanged at York in 1739. The son of a butcher, Turpin followed his father's trade for some years before embarking on a life of crime. He was involved with a gang of house-robbers in the mid-1730s and soon became a wanted man, one of his accomplices having turned king's evidence: Turpin managed to avoid capture and became a notoriously successful highwayman, robbing travellers in the forests around London. The murder of a forest keeper's servant in Epping, however, increased the price on Turpin's head and he was forced to work his way north under a false identity. Four years later in York, where he had set himself up as a horse-dealer under an assumed name, he was arrested for horse-stealing, recognized as the infamous Dick Turpin, and hanged. By this time Turpin had become something of a celebrity; curious visitors flocked to the prison to take a look at the man who had succeeded in evading justice for so long. Turpin's legendary image as a gallant rogue, however, owes much to Harrison Ainsworth's novel *Rookwood*, published in 1834. Ainsworth also describes in vivid detail Turpin's famous ride from London to York on his mare Black Bess; this meteoric flight from the law has no historical foundation in the life of Dick Turpin and is probably based on a similar feat performed (in an attempt to establish an alibi for a robbery) by the highwayman John Nevison, who was hanged at York in 1685.

Twickenham The headquarters of the Rugby Football Union, the governing body of rugby union in England (*see* rugby), and the venue for the England team's home matches. The ground was first used for rugby in 1909 and the first international match there took place in 1910 between England and Wales in front of 18,000 spectators. The largest crowd ever to attend a game at Twickenham was 75,500 to see England v. Wales in 1950. The ground is also the venue for the annual match between *Oxford and *Cambridge universities, the English Club and County Championship Finals, and the world famous Middlesex Seven-a-side Tournament.

Two Thousand Guineas Stakes *See* Classics.

Tyburn The principal place of execution in London from 1388 until 1783. Tyburn took its name from a stream which used to flow through the site of Marble Arch. The first permanent triangular gibbet was erected in 1571, by which time a number of traditions regarding the business of execution were widely recognized. The condemned man, for instance, was customarily given a last mug of ale at St-Giles-in-the-Fields and presented with a nosegay of flowers as his cart passed the gates of St Sepulchre's, Holborn. The body of a

hanged man was also believed to have certain beneficial medicinal qualities and huge crowds would gather at an execution in order to view the spectacle (hanging days were usually made public holidays) or to touch the corpse. 200,000 people were reported to have attended the execution of the highwayman Jack Shepherd in 1714. In 1660 the exhumed body of Oliver Cromwell was gibbeted at Tyburn by a vengeful mob, whilst other notable victims of the Tyburn gallows include Perkin Warbeck, pretender to the throne under Henry VII (1499), and Oliver Plunket, the last English martyr (1681). The precise location of the gibbet is now marked by a stone in the traffic island at the northeastern corner of Hyde Park.

Tynwald The legislature of the *Isle of Man, which is not part of the UK, but belongs to the Crown as Lord of Man. The UK assumes responsibility for the island's defence and foreign relations, and the Westminster Parliament is empowered to legislate for it on any matter; however, in practice the Tynwald (from the Old Norse for "assembly" and "field") has exclusive powers to legislate on all domestic matters. It comprises two chambers: the **House of Keys** and the legislative council. The House of Keys has 24 elected members, 13 from the 6 "sheadings" into which the Isle is divided, 7 from Douglas (the capital), 2 from Ramsey, and 1 each from Castletown and Peel; the council has 3 ex officio members (the lieutenant-governor, the attorney general, and the Bishop of Sodor and Man) and 8 members elected by the Keys. An Act of Tynwald takes effect only with royal approval, signified by an order of the Privy Council.

Tynwald Day 5 July, the day when the officers of the Isle of Man parliament assemble as the ancient *Tynwald Court in an open-air ceremony on Tynwald Hill, St John's, that dates from the time of Norse control over the island (9th–13th centuries). After meeting the dignitaries in St John's Chapel, the lieutenant-governor (who represents the Queen) leads them to the ancient three-tiered mound which is said to consist of soil from all 17 Manx parishes. He takes his seat on top with

<small>TYBURN</small> *The gallows at Tyburn, from an engraving by Hogarth, 1747.*

the deemsters, or judges, and members of the legislative council before him. Beneath them sit the 24 members of the House of Keys, and beneath them in turn sit the clergy and captains of the parishes. The Court is ceremonially "fenced" with the reading of a proclamation forbidding any disturbance. The main business of the Court is the reading of the English titles of all Acts passed by the English Parliament since the previous 5 July. The process is repeated in the Manx language, whereupon the Acts officially become part of Manx law.

U

UDR *See* reserve forces.

UKAEA *See* United Kingdom Atomic Energy Authority.

Ulster Defence Regiment (UDR) *See* reserve forces.

undersecretary A senior rank in the administrative grade of the civil service (*see* permanent secretary). In some government de-

partments, there is also a junior ministerial rank of undersecretary of state (*see* minister).

Union Jack *See* flags.

Unitarianism A religious movement that rejects the doctrine of the Trinity and the divinity of Christ, believing in the oneness of God and that Christ was a religious teacher; Unitarians also reject orthodox Christian teaching on the original sin and atonement. In Britain the founder of the movement was John Biddle (1615–62), who only narrowly escaped execution for his views, which were considered blasphemous, even by other Nonconformists. Unitarianism was excluded from the 1689 Toleration Act, which legitimized other denominations, and remained illegal until 1813. The movement remained a collection of believers until 1774, when Theophilus Lindsey (1723–1808) opened the first Unitarian church, Essex Chapel in London. Also prominent was the chemist and theologian Joseph Priestley (1733–1804), who emigrated to America in 1794 after his house and laboratory were burnt by a mob. During the 19th century James Martineau (1805–1900) urged a more intuitive and emotional approach, in contrast to the scripture-based rationality of Priestley and others. This caused a schism between the older scriptural wing and the new spiritual wing, who called themselves Free Christians. Unity was restored in 1928 with the formation of the General Assembly of Unitarian and Free Christian Churches. The 20th century has been marked by the increasing prevalence of radical and humanistic doctrines.

British Unitarians have a congregational form of government, that is, one that devolves on individual churches. There are currently some 95 ministers and 250 chapels and other places of worship in Britain.

United Kingdom Atomic Energy Authority (UKAEA) A body established under the terms of the Atomic Energy Authority Act 1954, and responsible for Britain's programme of research and development in atomic energy and other aspects of atomic and nuclear physics. Most of this work is undertaken at the Authority's own research establishments, the largest of which is at Harwell in Oxfordshire, where efforts are currently focused on reactor development and materials research.

The major part of the Authority's work is done at the various nuclear power development laboratories. The two projects currently receiving most attention are the prototype fast reactor at Dounreay in Scotland and the development of fuel systems for both thermal and fast reactors at Windscale in Cumbria, adjacent to the Sellafield nuclear power station. The development and safety of advanced gas-cooled reactors and of pressurized water reactors are the other important nuclear power projects. The centre for research in nuclear fusion and plasma physics, run by the Authority at Culham in Oxfordshire, is also the site of the Joint European Torus (JET) – a collaborative venture under the Euratom treaty, which began operating in 1983. Research into the hazards of handling and storing radioactive materials is conducted at various sites, particularly Winfrith in Dorset and at Culcheth, near Warrington. The other main UKAEA research establishments are at Risley, near Warrington, and Springfields, near Preston. The UKAEA is funded by the Department of Energy.

United Reformed Church A Church formed in 1972 by the union of the Congregational Church in England and Wales and the Presbyterian Church of England (*see* Presbyterians). The United Reformed Church is based on the congregational form of government in which each local church is autonomous and decides its own forms of service and administration. Most of the congregationalist churches that declined union are members of the independent Congregational Federation. In 1981 the United Reformed Church was joined by the Association of Churches of Christ of Great Britain and Ireland.

Congregationalists have their origins in the small groups of dissenting Protestants, known as Independents, who preferred to practise their faith outside the Church of England in the wake of the *Reformation. Many were persecuted during the reign of Elizabeth I for their separatist tendencies and some, led by Robert Browne (1550–1633), fled to Holland. Under the Protectorate of Oliver Cromwell, the Independents became firmly established and achieved positions of power. This was reversed with the *Restoration in 1660. The 1662 Act of Uniformity persecuted Independents and Presbyterians alike in an effort to eradicate Nonconformist sects (*see* Nonconformists) until their right to exist was secured by the 1689 Toleration Act. After a period of relative quiescence, the Congregationalists found new strength from the evangelical revival of the 18th century, and they were largely instrumental in founding the London Missionary Society in 1795. In 1966 this merged with the Commonwealth Missionary Society to form the Congregational Council for World Mission (now the Council for World Mission). The formation of county associations of congregational churches in the early 19th century was followed by the creation of a Congregational Union of England and Wales in 1832.

Congregationalists have always stressed the central importance of scripture to Christian faith and have upheld the freedom of separate groups and churches to worship as they see fit. Services are conducted by a minister and all members are expected to help run their church's affairs. Each of the 12 provinces in

England is supervised by a provincial moderator. The governing body is the General Assembly, presided over by the Moderator. In 1984 the United Reformed Church had some 132,000 members, 1250 ministers, and 1078 lay preachers. The Congregational Church has been much less prominent in Scotland, arising during the 19th century and combining with the Evangelical Union in 1896.

unit trusts Investment trusts introduced into the UK from America in 1931, and designed especially for the small investor. The trust is run by managers with an expertise in stock-exchange investments, who build up a portfolio of investments in a hundred or more companies, according to detailed rules. The total holding is divided into units, which are sold to members of the public at a price based on the market value of the whole portfolio. The managers will repurchase units from the public at any time at slightly less than the current sale price. Dividends on the trust holdings are pooled and paid out, pro rata, to the holders of units.

The advantage of unit trusts to the small investor is that he has a much wider spread for his investments than he would secure on his own, that he has the benefit of the expertise of the managers, and that his holding can always be quickly liquidated.

universities The 47 institutions of higher education in the United Kingdom (37 in England and Wales, 8 in Scotland, 2 in Northern Ireland). Historically they fall into three main categories: the ancient universities of *Oxford and *Cambridge and their Scottish counterparts (*St Andrew's, Glasgow (1451), Aberdeen (1495), and Edinburgh (1583)), the *redbrick universities, and the new universities.

Despite their different characters, British universities are alike in being self-governing bodies that award their own degrees (*compare* *polytechnics*). They receive most of their funding from the government through the University Grants Committee (UGC), a body of academics and administrators established in 1919. (An exception is the independent University of Buckingham, set up in the 1970s.) The governing bodies of the universities usually have a chancellor as honorary head, and a vice-chancellor who is responsible for administration. Undergraduate admission to the universities (with the exception of the *Open University) is through the Universities Central Council on Admissions (UCCA), which matches the would-be student's qualifications and requirements with the places available. The usual pattern of study is a three-year course leading to a bachelor's degree, with further courses open to students wishing to proceed to a master's degree or to a diploma in an area of specialist study.

The increased demand for tertiary education in the years after World War II led to the creation of several new universities. Most of these were designed as "campus universities" on integrated sites (unlike the older universities whose buildings tend to be scattered around

UNIVERSITIES *Distinctive pyramid-shaped student residence blocks, designed by Denys Lasdun in the 1960s, at the University of East Anglia.*

UP-HELLY-AA *Celebrations at Lerwick, Shetland Islands.*

town centres), and made extensive and not always successful use of such modern building materials as concrete and laminated glass. Keele (1950) was the first; others established since then include Sussex (near Brighton), East Anglia (Norwich), Warwick, York, Lancaster, Kent (Canterbury), Exeter, Hull, and Stirling. Aston and Salford were former colleges of advanced technology raised to university status in the mid-1960s, following the recommendations of the Robbins Report (1963), which emphasized the development of technical studies. More recently, financial considerations have caused extensive reappraisal of the universities' role in education, and they are under pressure to tailor their courses and student numbers to economic criteria rather than the pursuit of purely "academic" goals.

Up-Helly-Aa An annual fire festival that takes place in the former Viking stronghold of Lerwick in the Shetland Islands on the last Tuesday in January. The festival was originally celebrated on January 29 to mark the official end of the pagan Yuletide festivities and to welcome the returning sun: blazing tar-barrels were dragged through the streets and bands of people in fancy dress (called "guizers") went from house to house bringing

good luck for the year ahead. The tar-barrels were banned as too dangerous in 1874, and since then the focal point of the festival has been the burning of a Norse galley, possibly symbolizing the ancient practice of dispatching dead Viking chiefs to Valhalla in a blazing longship. In the days preceding Up-Helly-Aa the galley, which is 9 metres (30 feet) long and has its bow traditionally fashioned in the form of a dragon's head, is built and decorated; and the chief guizer (the Guizer Jarl) composes a "proclamation", a collection of lighthearted satirical comments about local people and events, which is displayed near the market cross on the morning of the festival. In the evening the Guizer Jarl, wearing Viking armour, takes up his position at the helm of the galley; several hundred torch-bearing guizers follow the ship as the procession moves off to the accompaniment of local bands. On reaching the chosen site the guizers form a circle around the galley and fling their burning torches into it: as the galley blazes they give a hearty rendering of the song "The Norseman's Home".

Urdd Gobaith Cymru (Welsh League of Youth) A nationalist and social organization for children in Wales. It was founded in 1922 by Sir Ifan ab Owen Edwards (1895–1970), with the aims of serving Christ, fellow men, and Wales. Each child who becomes a member of the Urdd makes a pledge to remain faithful to these ideals. The movement, whose name literally means "the Order of the Hope of Wales", is the most extensive youth movement in Wales, having some 40,000 members by the beginning of the 1980s. The Urdd's most important activity is fostering the Welsh language and to this end it stages *eisteddfods and organizes such events as summer camps where non-Welsh-speaking youngsters can learn Welsh. It also arranges sports meetings, quizzes, and other competitions for children. The symbol of the Urdd Gobaith Cymru is a triangle in white, red, and green – Wales's national colours.

V

V & A *See* Victoria and Albert Museum.

VAT (value added tax) *See* tax system.

Venture Scouts *See* Scout Association.

verge *See* Board of Green Cloth.

vicar-general Originally, an official (usually lay) appointed by a bishop or archbishop of the Church of England to assist him in the administration of his diocese or province. In the dioceses, the office gradually merged with that of the chancellor, a lawyer appointed to exercise the bishop's judicial functions in the *consistory court. There are still, however, provincial vicars-general, for both Canterbury and York.

Victoria and Albert Museum (V & A) A museum of fine and applied arts, created after the *Great Exhibition of 1851 and intended for "the improvement of public taste in design" and "the application of fine art to objects of utility", one purpose of which was to increase the competitiveness of British products in world markets. The core of the museum was formed by objects of applied art bought from the Great Exhibition together with the collection of the Government School of Design (now the Royal College of Art). Under the directorship of Sir Henry Cole, with Prince Albert the chief inspiration behind both the Great Exhibition and the V & A, it opened in 1852 in Marlborough House as the Museum of Manufactures. In 1853 it was renamed the Museum of Ornamental Art, and four years later moved to its present site in South Kensington. In 1899 Queen Victoria laid the foundation stone of the present building, by Sir Aston Webb; and she asked that the museum be renamed the Victoria and Albert. When the new building was opened in 1909, the science collection was moved to the nearby *Science Museum. The V & A's wide-ranging exhibits include post-classical sculpture, silverware, pottery, and miniatures.

Victoria Cross The highest decoration for valour. It is awarded "for conspicuous bravery in the face of the enemy". The Victoria Cross was instituted by Queen Victoria on 29 January 1856, but awarded retrospectively to 1854, thus acknowledging heroism during the Crimean War. In 1902 it was decreed that the decoration could be conferred posthumously, and in 1911 Indian soldiers were made eligible, making it the first decoration for which all ranks could be considered. In 1920 nursing staff and civilians of either sex working for the armed services were made eligible. As yet, however, no woman has received it. The Victoria Cross is made of bronze (from guns captured from the Russians in the Crimean War, and now in the Royal Armouries at the Tower of London), in the shape of a Maltese cross. It is worn on the left breast and takes precedence over all other decorations. The ribbon is crimson, although before 1918 members of the Royal Navy wore theirs on a blue ribbon. Holders may add VC after their names and are entitled to a £100 tax-free annuity.

Victory Nelson's flagship at the battle of *Trafalgar in 1805. The *Victory*'s keel was laid in 1759 and the finest materials were used in her construction: oak trees over one hundred years old were used for the ribs. By the time of her launch in 1765, she was the most magnificent three-decked ship of her class, carrying just over 100 guns and a crew of 844 men. On the Trafalgar voyage, somewhat surprisingly, the crew consisted of 50 boys (the youngest being ten years old) and many nationalities, including Americans, Dutch, and West Indians. Nevertheless, the battle resulted in a decisive victory over the French navy, marred only by the death of Nelson. The *Victory* is now preserved and open to the public at Portsmouth, having survived a collision with the ironclad *Neptune* in 1903, while being towed out of Portsmouth harbour.

Viking invasions *See* Anglo-Saxon Britain.

villages The typical village, as it is popularly imagined, is largely characteristic of the more populous rural parts of England. Grouped around an old church, and probably an open green area, will be a few streets of

449

houses in the vernacular style, with one or two small shops and pubs, a school, and perhaps at a slight remove, a larger "manor house" – all surrounded by fields and farms. Though this picture may occasionally be realized in the less hospitable northern and western extremes of England, and in Scotland and Wales, settlement in those parts was far more scattered, and subject to different landscapes and social formations than the essentially Anglo-Saxon pattern that has formed the traditional vision. The structure had emerged by the 10th century, and was imposed upon, rather than fundamentally altered by, the Norman conquest. Villages in this time were socially static for long periods: travel was difficult, and for the vast majority of people life was bounded by the annual agricultural cycle of work. It is this static element that provided continuities unbroken even by the industrial revolution.

The oldest building in a village is frequently the church, of which some 10,000 are of medieval origin and some even predate the Norman conquest. Every village church is of the greatest significance for the history of its locality and for a long time was almost the only repository of records. Outside, the village cross may have stood either in the churchyard or on the green: but most were destroyed during the 16th and 17th centuries. There is now more likely to be a war memorial or perhaps a village sign, featuring a coat of arms or some picture relevant to the district. The green itself may be a little triangle where the principal roads meet, or several acres of common, once – and still, in some cases – grazing land. The larger ones will often be used for cricket, and may originally have been central enclosures for livestock, or spaces for setting up fairs. Of the size of the village itself there is no precise definition and their variety is immense. Each has houses of different periods and degrees of importance (except where occasionally a whole village has been "moved" and wholly rebuilt by a local landowner – as at Milton Abbas in Dorset). The uses of local stone – such as the granites of Cornwall and the extreme north, the limestones of the southwest, Cotswolds, and Midlands, and East Anglian flint – have in recent decades been widely repopularized. Perhaps most pleasing are local elements, such as the patterned plasterwork (pargeting) of Suffolk and Essex.

The expansion of industry in the 19th century initially had a more drastic effect on villages in the north and north Midlands than elsewhere. What had been close groups of villages rapidly turned into manufacturing towns. Although the cities drew many people from rural life, it was not until the mechanizing of agriculture that the numbers employed on the land, and therefore the backbone of village population, began to fall sharply. World War I also had a severe impact on rural society, as is evident from the war memorials of even quite small villages.

In the 20th century many British people continue to prize the village ideal, even when it may no longer seem appropriate: the "village character" of formerly separate places long since absorbed into cities is often insisted upon. The improvement of transport has meant that many villages, especially in the southeast, are predominantly inhabited by commuters who can afford to restore often crumbling properties to a habitable state, but who take little part in the life of the community. Recent decades have seen a general pattern of withdrawal of services from villages, especially the most remote. Rail and bus networks have contracted; many local stores, particularly if not part of a chain, have closed; and small sub-post offices are now following. Village schools are threatened by any fall in the numbers of children, as well as by economic stringencies. Churches now frequently form units of large parishes served by "team ministries", where population and churchgoing may both be declining. Vandalism has caused many churches to be locked outside service hours. Even the village pub has not been untouched and in lonelier regions some have closed. However, although the sum of different changes may present a bleak picture, village life is not wholly altered, nor yet a thing of the past; changing patterns of employment may yet demonstrate its powers of regeneration.

viscount The fourth highest title of honour in the *peerage or the courtesy title of the eldest son of an earl or marquess (or duke, in the single case of the Duke of Manchester). It was the last degree of peerage to appear in England, the first viscount, created in 1440, being Viscount Beaumont. The word comes from the Latin *vice-comes*, meaning deputy of a count. In the early Middle Ages on the continent of Europe, it developed from an official post to become a hereditary title, and after the conquest of 1066, the Normans identified the Anglo-Saxon sheriffs with the officials they knew as viscounts. The premier viscount in the entire peerage is Viscount Hereford (created 1550), but the title of the premier viscount in the peerage of Ireland, Viscount Gormanston, is of greater antiquity, dating from 1478. A viscount is styled Right Honourable and his children take the prefix Honourable. A viscountess is normally the wife of a viscount, although viscountesses in their own right have been created: for example, Viscountess Bayning of Foxley in 1674, whose peerage was conferred for life only. It used to be customary for retiring senior ministers and the Speaker of the House of Commons to be made viscounts; although this practice is now less frequently adopted, in 1983 the retiring Speaker, George Thomas, was created Viscount Tonypandy.

Voluntary Service Overseas (VSO) A London-based charity founded in 1958 to send volunteers to work for a period in developing countries. VSO was started by Alexander Dickson, who, during his time spent with a UNESCO education team in Iraq, had come to realize that highly paid experts were not necessarily the most effective teachers of poor and backward communities. His original idea was to form an international student volunteer force to work in areas of extreme poverty, but his proposals met with no response. He decided therefore to begin in Britain: as an initial experiment six young men volunteers left for Sarawak in September 1958, and the first two women were posted (to Sarawak and Kenya) in 1959. Such was the success of the first volunteers that demand for such helpers increased rapidly. Many of the original volunteers were young people eager to combine work in a good cause with foreign travel in the year between leaving school and starting university, but VSO now seeks to recruit older people with some specific expertise to work for a two-year period. Much of the work is English language teaching, but volunteers also teach other subjects, help develop agricultural or technical projects, or improve medical services. VSO has around a thousand volunteers in 40 countries; it briefs them and provides them with air fares and a grant, while the host government provides a living allowance and accommodation.

wakes week An annual holiday in some industrial areas of northern England, particularly Yorkshire and Lancashire, when factories and shops in a town close, workers take a summer vacation, and local celebrations often take place. Wakes week was originally devised to avoid the inconvenience to employer and employee of staggered holidays and to permit the overhaul of factory machinery; the dates of the holiday vary from town to town and may coincide with the feast day of the patron saint of the local parish church. The eve of this day was once the occasion of a vigil or "wake" in churches throughout the land; the name was later applied to the games, feasts, and other festivities that took place at this time. The wake, or patronal festival, is known as the "revel" in the west country and the "feast" elsewhere. Until the end of the 19th century it was the high point of the village year. Surviving traditions associated with the wake include the *rush-bearing ceremonies of the Lake District and and a number of *fairs, notably St Giles' Fair in Oxford.

Wales Tourist Board *See* British Tourist Authority.

Wallace Collection A museum of paintings, furnishings, and other *objets d'art* at Hertford House, Manchester Square, London. The collection was created by successive Marquesses of Hertford, especially the 4th, who, while living in Paris, acquired a superb group of 18th-century French paintings. At his death in 1871, he left the collection to his natural son and constant companion Sir Richard Wallace, whose widow bequeathed it to the nation in 1897. A fire in 1874 destroyed part of the collection, leaving mainly 17th- and 18th-century *objets d'art*. Wallace then added Italian maiolica and Renaissance goldwork, bronzes, and armour. Put on display at Hertford House (built by the 4th Duke of Manchester in 1776 and acquired by the 2nd Marquess of Hertford in 1797), the Wallace Collection was opened to the public in 1900. Among its treasures are works by Fragonard, Boucher, Poussin, and Watteau as well as Velazquez's *Lady with a Fan* and the famous "Laughing Cavalier" by Frans Hals.

Wars of the Roses (1455–85) A period of political unrest and short periods of military conflict between the houses of Lancaster and York in England. The name was coined by Sir Walter Scott, who based it on the traditional badges of the two houses, which were in fact rarely used in the 15th century: the white rose of York, and the red rose adopted by the Tudors, the heirs of Lancaster. These symbols were immortalized in Shakespeare's famous scene (*1 Henry VI*, II. iv), where rival nobles declared their allegiance by plucking red or white roses.

The dynastic issue was simple: the Lancastrians, who had occupied the throne since 1399, were heirs of Edward III through his fourth son, John of Gaunt; while the Yorkists were also heirs, descended from his third son, Lionel of Clarence, through the female line, as well as from Edmund of York (fifth son) in the male line. However, this issue did not surface until contemporary politics made it a convenient peg on which to hang opposition to Henry VI (r. 1422–61). The cause of the troubles were Henry's failings as a king; he was unsuccessful

WARS OF THE ROSES Edward V and the Duke of York in the Tower. *The mysterious disappearance of "the Princes in the Tower" captured the imagination of the 19th-century artist Delaroche. The painter has reproduced the historical detail in the clothing and furnishings with great care.*

in war, he was outmanoeuvred in diplomacy, his finances were chaotic, but most seriously he allowed himself to be dominated by a clique, which failed to provide consensual government and ruthlessly exploited its position for personal advantage. This group of favourites inevitably gave rise to an opposing faction, prominent in which was Richard, Duke of York (1411–60), second in line to the throne after Henry's infant son Edward (1453–71). A crisis arose in 1453, when the king began to suffer from intermittent bouts of madness. When he became unfit to rule, York became protector and turned out the courtier faction; when Henry recovered, they were restored. This happened twice in two and a half years. The medieval political system and constitution were not designed to stand such instability and in 1455 violence between the opposing sides broke out at the first battle of St Albans (22 May). This was more than simple political rivalry, but was armed resistance to the king, and therefore treason. Moreover, blood feuds between some of the most powerful families in the realm were involved. The royalists, led by the forceful Queen Margaret, and the Yorkists manoeuvred for position until 1459, when compromise again failed and open war broke out. After an initial Yorkist success by the Earl of Salisbury at Blore Heath (22 September), York was routed at Ludford Bridge (13 October). He fled to Ireland, and he and his followers were condemned as traitors. His response was logical: when Richard, Earl of Warwick ("the Kingmaker") captured the king at the battle of Northampton (10 July 1460), York claimed the throne. The House of Lords received this demand coolly, but the fortunes of war forced their hands. York was killed at the battle of Wakefield (30 December 1460) and Warwick was defeated at the second battle of St Albans (17 February 1461), where Henry VI was freed, but York's son Edward assumed the throne (4 March 1461) as Edward IV and routed the Lancastrians at Towton (29 March).

Edward reigned until 1483, apart from an extraordinary lapse in 1470. In 1469, the ambitious and discontented Warwick and Edward's wayward brother George of Clarence, put out by their inadequate share of power,

had rebelled unsuccessfully. Forming an alliance of convenience with the Lancastrians under Margaret, they surprised Edward and forced him to flee the country. Henry VI, whom Edward had captured in 1465 and imprisoned in the Tower of London, was briefly restored (October 1470 to May 1471); but Edward regained the throne after victories at the battles of Barnet (14 April 1471), where Warwick was killed, and Tewkesbury (4 May). On the day of his triumphal entry into London (21 May), Henry VI was killed in the Tower (see Lilies and Roses, ceremony of).

Edward's reign saw a recovery of the power of the monarchy and the firm establishment of the Yorkist dynasty. However, in 1483 he died, leaving a child heir, Edward V. The situation was complicated by the hatred between his surviving brother, Richard of Gloucester, and his queen Elizabeth Woodville and her family. Richard pursued the logical course mapped out by his family's experiences: he seized the throne for himself, partly no doubt out of ambition, partly because a child king was an undeniable national liability, and partly to protect himself from the Woodvilles. In all probability he followed the lesson learned by his brother, and had Edward V and his brother Richard (the "princes in the Tower") killed. Whatever the truth, the widespread rumour of this deed disgusted many people, and, more importantly, split the Yorkist affinity. Richard's favouring of northerners further alienated the south of the kingdom. An uneasy reign punctuated by rebellion was ended when Henry Tudor, the Lancastrian claimant (though through an illegitimate line), killed Richard at the battle of *Bosworth Field (22 August 1485), and took the throne as Henry VII.

This was the end of the Wars of the Roses, because Henry succeeded in holding the throne against Yorkist pretenders, subduing the nobility, and exacting obedience to the Crown (see monarchy). However, the legacy of bitterness and insecurity lasted for many years: it was dangerous to be connected with the house of York, and by 1541 most of its descendants had been executed on various pretexts.

WARWICK CASTLE

It is unfortunate that the most widely known account of the Wars of the Roses is that of Shakespeare, who had to conform to the requirements both of dramatic impact and the interpretation of history acceptable to the Tudors. In particular, his treatment of Richard III is very wide of the truth. Shakespeare does, however, capture the decline in political morality to the point at which a man should feel it necessary to kill the nephews he had sworn to protect.

Warwick castle One of the finest and best-preserved medieval fortresses in Europe. Dramatically situated on a curve of the River Avon, the castle dominates the town of Warwick in the English Midlands. The first fortification at this strategic site was built on a mound at the orders of Ethelfleda (d. 989), daughter of Alfred the Great, to ward off Danish attacks. A more substantial castle was raised in 1068 and was later given to the Beaumont family by Henry II (r. 1154–89). The present structure dates largely from the 14th and 15th centuries although the original motte and bailey (*see* castles of England) are still visible. Surrounded on three sides by a dry moat and on the fourth by the River Avon, the castle features a tall central gatehouse flanked by

two large and well-preserved towers, Caesar's Tower and Guy's Tower, the latter being 39 metres (128 feet) high. Richard III altered the curtain wall to take artillery (1483–85), while Fulke Greville, who was granted the castle in 1604, refurbished the interior of the spacious living quarters that were originally erected in the 14th century, and converted the castle into a private mansion. It was never the scene of any major conflict. The castle, which now houses many classical paintings and an important collection of arms and armour, stands in extensive grounds laid out by "Capability" Brown in 1753.

wassailing An annual ceremony performed on 17 January (Old Twelfth Night) in a number of apple-growing areas, notably Somerset. The word "wassail" derives from the Anglo-Saxon equivalent of "Good health!" Toasts were traditionally drunk from a wassail bowl on New Year's Eve and Twelfth Night; the custom of wassailing the apple trees to ensure a good crop of fruit in the coming year was a natural extension of this tradition. The wassailers form a circle around the largest apple tree in the orchard, pour cider into its roots, and drink its health with a traditional wassailing song. Sometimes a piece of toast soaked in cider is placed in the fork of the tree, supposedly for the robins and other birds that will watch over the tree in the year ahead. Shots are fired into the branches to frighten away any evil spirits and to awaken the god or goddess of the tree. At Carhampton in Somerset the apple trees of a certain orchard were still regularly wassailed on Old Twelfth Night in the mid-1970s; the custom now survives in only a few West Country villages.

Waterloo, battle of (18 June 1815) The final battle of the Napoleonic Wars, fought near the Belgian village of Waterloo between the army of imperial France, under the Emperor Napoleon (1769–1821), and a combined British, Dutch, and German force, commanded by the Duke of Wellington (1769–1852). The battle was the culminating conflict of over 20 years of warfare against Revolutionary and (from 1799) Napoleonic France. Napoleon had been defeated in 1814 and exiled to Elba; but he returned to France in March 1815, overthrew the restored monarchy, and began his second reign, known from its duration as the "Hundred Days". Two indecisive battles at Ligny and Quatre-Bras on 16 June resulted in Napoleon being able to isolate Wellington's force of 68,000 at Waterloo and launch a direct attack with his own army of 72,000. The fighting was concentrated around the farmhouses of Hougoumont and La Haye-Sainte. However, despite all the efforts of the imperial army, the allies resisted stubbornly until 45,000 Prussians under Marshal Blücher arrived to put the French to flight. About 25,000 Frenchmen died and 9000 were taken prisoner; the British lost 15,000 and the Prussians 8000. Four days later Napoleon finally abdicated and was exiled to St Helena, where he died. The victory is commemorated in such names as Waterloo Station, Waterloo Bridge, and Waterloo Place in London.

Watling Street *See* Roman roads.

WAYLAND THE SMITH *The entrance to Wayland's Smithy, Oxfordshire. The burial chamber associated with the legendary blacksmith is believed to date from c. 3500 BC. The burial place lies upon an earthen long barrow of even greater antiquity.*

Wayland the Smith A legendary master smith and sword-maker in northern European folk tales. Wayland the Smith is reputed to have forged magic swords for the heroes of ancient mythology and was referred to in the writings of Alfred the Great. According to the legend recounted in the 13th-century Icelandic *Edda*, the Swedish king Nidudr captured Wayland and forced him to work in the royal smithy, having taken the precaution of laming his prisoner so that he could not escape. In revenge, Wayland murdered Nidudr's two

sons (making drinking bowls of their skulls which he sent to their father), raped his daughter, and flew to freedom on feathered wings, or by the magical power of a gold ring. At an ancient burial chamber near White Horse Hill in Oxfordshire, known as Wayland's Smithy, an invisible smith is alleged to shoe the horses of passing travellers in exchange for a coin, on condition that the customer looks away from the forge while the work is being done. Two iron bars found at the site, once thought to be Iron Age currency bars but now believed to be of medieval origin, have been associated with the legend.

Ways and Means A committee formed by the whole House of Commons, up until 1968, to discuss matters relating to taxation (the ways and means of raising revenue), particularly the budget proposals. When sitting in committee, the House is not presided over by the *Speaker. The Chair is vacated, the mace removed, and proceedings take place under an elected chairman seated at the table. The Ways and Means procedure was adopted to enable finance to be discussed freely in former days when Speakers were royal nominees, and frequently also royal informants. Committees of Ways and Means have now been abandoned, money matters being discussed in the normal way by the House, but the title Chairman of Ways and Means is still held by the deputy Speaker.

WEA *See* Workers' Educational Association.

welfare state The popular name for the range of state programmes concerned with the health and social welfare of the British population since World War II. The first is covered by the *National Health Service, the second by two parallel schemes: *social security, which is a noncontributory, often means-tested, system of state benefits for the needy; and *national insurance, a compulsory scheme of contributory unemployment and sickness benefits combined with retirement and widows' pensions. In 1984 42% of government expenditure was devoted to the welfare state.
In the Middle Ages, any assistance for the poor came mainly from the Church: in the 16th century various ad hoc measures, including

several Acts of Parliament, attempted to deal with the growing numbers of paupers. The prevailing attitude was that able-bodied people were only destitute through some fault of their own: an Act of 1531 ordered that "sturdy beggars" should be whipped, sent back to their own parish, and ordered to set themselves to work at some honest occupation. Under an Act of 1536, second offences were punishable by mutilation. This same Act, however, authorized the collection of alms for the sick and disabled. It was not until 1601 that the Poor Law Act established a regular administration of relief, based on the parish and financed by local *rates. Its intention was to provide the able-bodied poor with work, in special workhouses if necessary, while supporting the incapacitated with money payments. In 1782 parishes were permitted to provide subsidies to the able-bodied poor and in 1795 the Berkshire justices, spurred by the effects of inflation, the war with France, and a bad harvest, established the "Speenhamland system" of topping up wages, which rapidly spread to much of the south and east of England. The same pressures, and fear of revolution, led the Prime Minister, William Pitt, in 1796 to advocate its expansion into a national scheme, with additional schemes for rudimentary old-age pensions and for training children in a craft or trade. However, the proposal was widely opposed, and, when the better 1796 harvest relieved the immediate pressure, it was dropped. The trend towards "outdoor" relief through monetary payments was reversed by the Poor Law Act 1834: to keep costs down, relief would only be provided in the workhouses, which were deliberately made as harsh as possible to deter people from "going on the parish". More positive assistance was left to philanthropic social reformers, such as Lord Shaftesbury (1801–85) – who among other achievements established lodging homes for the poor – and the socialist manufacturer Robert Owen (1771–1858), who established a model community for his workers at New Lanark (1800) with humane working conditions and good housing.

The modern concept of a welfare state stemmed from the work of late 19th-century investigation, pioneered by Charles Booth with *Life and Labour of the People in London* (1891–1903) and B. Seebohm Rowntree with *Poverty: a study of Town Life* (1901), which both revealed the deleterious effects of low and irregular wages and showed that the influence of moral factors was negligible. The Liberal administration elected in 1906 was the first to introduce state-run schemes for relief, beginning in 1908 with old-age pensions. Further schemes were based upon the principle, borrowed from the 19th-century friendly societies and trade unions, of insurance by the individual against his own future needs. These measures enabled the range of services to be expanded beyond the basic relief provided by the Poor Law while keeping down costs. In 1911 compulsory sickness insurance was established, financed by contributions from employers, employees, and the state (*see* national insurance). This was expanded to provide more extensive old-age pensions in 1925. In 1942 a committee under William Beveridge (later Lord Beveridge) produced a report that proposed the expansion of these schemes into a comprehensive system of welfare insurance. This formed the basis of the measures enacted by Clement Attlee's postwar Labour government (1945–51) that made the welfare state a reality: the Family Allowances Act 1945, the National Health Service Act 1946, and the National Assistance Act 1948. The last provided basic relief, superseding the Poor Law, which was finally abolished.

Since the Labour government introduced the welfare state no subsequent government, Labour or Conservative, has felt it has had a mandate to diminish the security provided by those Acts. The example set by Britain and the Scandinavian countries has frequently been followed elsewhere in the developed world. *See also* social security.

well-dressing An annual ceremony that takes place in Derbyshire and also (to a lesser extent) in Staffordshire and Shropshire. Believed to have originated in the Derbyshire village of Tissington, possibly as a thanksgiving for the village's five wells that remained uncontaminated during the *Black Death (1348), well-dressing soon became a religious ceremony. In Tissington the five wells are dressed for Ascension Day by differ-

WELL-DRESSING *Well at Tideswell, Derbyshire.*

ent groups of villagers, who compete to make the most ornate designs. Each well is surmounted by a large wooden frame, which is plastered with soft clay; natural materials such as flowers, berries, and pebbles, are then pressed into the clay to build up a picture, which usually bears a religious theme. Following the Ascension Day service the clergy and the congregation move in procession from well to well, blessing each one as they go. Other Derbyshire villages in which similar ceremonies are performed include Barlow, Wirksworth, Youlgreave, and Tideswell.

Welsh The ancient language of Wales, a *Celtic language of the southern or Brythonic group. It is the direct descendant of the vernacular spoken in Britain in Roman times (1st to early 5th centuries AD). Nowadays over 500,000 people claim to speak Welsh, although all of them can also speak English. In the normal course of events, such bilingualism would lead to the demise of the minority language. However, in the 20th century, Welsh has, for the time being at least, stemmed its own decline. It has considerable cultural and

symbolic importance for the inhabitants of Wales and for Welsh nationalism (*see* Plaid Cymru), and many non-Welsh speakers (including immigrants from England and else-

WELSH *Map shows greater familiarity with the Welsh language to the west.*

457

where) have made a deliberate effort to learn to speak and use the language (*see* Welsh Language Society; Welsh Language Service). It is used not only in a robust popular culture, of which the *eisteddfod is only one manifestation, but also for everyday conversation, and is a medium of instruction in some schools. Welsh literature dates back to the 6th century AD, the period of four great *bards, Aneurin, Taliesin, Myrddin (or Merlin), and Llywarch Hen. Much early Welsh poetry is heroic or elegiac, and concerns pre-Christian heroes and their exploits. The *Mabinogion*, a prose work written in about 1060, records legends about Celtic gods and heroes. Welsh literature had a profound influence in medieval Europe, as it is the source both of *Arthurian legend and that of the Holy Grail (*see* Arthurian legend). From the 15th century onwards classical Welsh literature declined, partly because it was overtaken by a kind of stilted formalism, and partly because of the encroachment of English as a result of the anglicization of the Welsh gentry.

Welsh spelling, unlike that of Irish and Gaelic, is more or less phonetic. The most characteristic speech sound other than those found also in English is the lateral fricative represented in spelling by -ll-, as in the place name Llanelli. The normal word order of Welsh sentences, like those of other Celtic languages, in verb-subject-object. The most striking aspect of Welsh grammar is the system of "mutations", a feature common to all Celtic languages. The initial consonant of a word can take up to four forms, the choice of form being determined by a complex set of syntactic and collocational rules. Thus, the noun *ci* "dog" is also found as *gi* (*dy gi* "your dog", *dau gi* "two dogs"), *nghi* (*fy nghi* "my dog"), and *chi* (*ei chi* "her dog", *tri chi* "three dogs").

Welsh Development Agency A government-funded organization that aims to promote the development of industry and commerce in Wales. Set up in 1976, the agency took over some of the functions of the Welsh Office, and is empowered to provide finance through loans, loan guarantees, and equity capital for the expansion and modernization of industry. The agency, whose headquarters are at Treforest, near Pontypridd, Mid Gla-

morgan, in the industrial heartland of southeast Wales, rents or leases factories to new businesses, gives grants for the reclamation of derelict land, and provides financial aid for small firms and rural industries. It has been active in its efforts to attract new industries to the country, a policy necessitated by the recent decline of Wales's traditional economic activities of metal production, mining, and quarrying. With the agency's help, new industries, such as vehicle production, light engineering, and microelectronics, as well as service occupations, have begun to fill the vacuum left by the heavy industries.

The Development Board for Rural Wales, also established in 1976, operates in central Wales – Powys, northern Dyfed, and southern Gwynedd – where it is responsible for economic and social development in this mainly rural area and in the new town of Newtown. It also acts as an agent for the Welsh Development Agency in the provision of financial aid to industry in Mid Wales.

Welsh Folk Museum An important museum of Welsh culture and crafts, at St Fagans, South Glamorgan, on the northern outskirts of Cardiff. The Welsh Folk Museum was first developed in the 1940s and is a branch of the *National Museum of Wales. It is housed in a beautiful Elizabethan mansion, standing in formal terraced gardens, on the site of the medieval castle of St Fagans. The house contains period furniture, and in the grounds are buildings brought from all regions of Wales, representing many different periods and styles and furnished accordingly. There are demonstrations of traditional country crafts, and collections devoted to costume and agriculture.

Welsh Guards *See* Household Division.

Welsh Language Service (S4C) The bilingual television network, Sianel Pedwar Cymru, broadcasting on the fourth channel in Wales. The service operates under the control of the *Independent Broadcasting Authority (IBA) and is the Welsh equivalent of Channel Four, Independent Television's second national service. S4C is administered on behalf of the IBA by the Welsh Fourth Channel Authority and is funded by advertising and through subscriptions levied on independent television companies and finance provided by the British Broadcasting Corporation (*BBC). It transmits English-language items from the national Channel Four service as well as programmes in Welsh made by the BBC and by Harlech Television (the independent television company serving Wales and the west of England). The BBC and Harlech together provide about 22 hours of Welsh-language material each week, much of it being screened during the peak viewing period between 7 pm and 9 pm. S4C, the only service in the Welsh language, came into being in response to demands from *Plaid Cymru and the *Welsh Language Society for a Welsh-language television service. Set up in 1980, S4C commenced transmission on 1 November 1982. Its existence means that the majority of people living in Wales who normally speak English (about 80% of the population, according to the 1981 census) now have an all-English service on Harlech Television and BBC Wales, while Welsh speakers are catered for by S4C. However, the network also claims an increasing proportion of English-speaking viewers for its Channel Four material.

Welsh Language Society (Welsh: Cymdeithas yr Iaith Gymraeg) An organization seeking improved status for the Welsh language in Wales in an attempt to halt its decline (see Welsh). The society's activities are generally viewed within the context of Welsh nationalism, but its first aim has always been the advancement of the Welsh language. It was formed in 1962 and throughout the next decade its largely middle-class membership conducted a well-publicized campaign of protest, civil disobedience, and lawbreaking in pursuit of its goals. Its demands included the provision of bilingual official forms and road signs, and a separate television channel for Welsh-language programmes. Demonstrations were accompanied by deliberate infringements of the law, such as nonpayment of licence fees. The more militant of the society's 4000 members damaged property, notably television transmitters. The court appearances of those responsible inevitably raised demands for trials to be conducted in Welsh. The activities of Cymdeithas yr Iaith Gymraeg – especially the painting-out of English roadsigns –

caused a mixture of anger and sympathy in Wales. The society has achieved some success: under the Welsh Language Act 1967, bilingual forms have become widely available; in the early 1970s a government committee supported the introduction of bilingual roadsigns; special simultaneous translation facilities were first introduced into Welsh law courts in 1973; and Welsh is now taught in all schools, with some lessons being conducted in Welsh in certain areas. A television channel entirely devoted to Welsh-language programmes is not yet a reality, but Sianel Pedwar Cymru (S4C), a bilingual network separate from the other channels, went on the air in 1982 (see Welsh Language Service).

Welsh male-voice choirs Choirs consisting exclusively of men (tenors and basses) and not including boys. Male-voice choirs originated in South Wales during the period of rapid industrialization in the 19th century. The Welsh valleys attracted many immigrants seeking work in the new coalmines, steelworks, and other heavy industries. Many newcomers came from England, but a large number came from western and central Wales, bringing with them their own musical traditions, influenced by such institutions as the *eisteddfod and by the church music of nonconformist religion. The Rhondda Valley was particularly affected by the influx from the west. The Treorchy Male Choir, from the Rhondda, was in existence before the 1880s: the earliest record of it commemorates its victory at a local eisteddfod at Treorchy in 1884, and it performed before Queen Victoria at Windsor castle in 1895. Like other choirs in South Wales, it suffered a decline during the depression of the 1920s and 1930s. It was relaunched in 1945 and has since won worldwide acclaim through concert tours and recordings. The Morriston Orpheus Choir, from near Swansea, has acquired a similar international reputation. Although male-voice choral singing is largely a phenomenon of South Wales, there are some notable male choirs from North Wales, the most famous perhaps being the choir from Rhosllanerchrugog, in Clwyd.

Many male-voice choirs are large, numbering well over a hundred singers, who are always amateurs. Choristers are often recruited from local rugby clubs and join the choir after they have given up active participation in the sport. Consequently, they are predominantly middle-aged, the average age range being between 40 and 60 years old. The typical repertoire of the male-voice choir consists of large-scale arrangements of hymns, such as "Aberystwyth", grand showpieces, such as the "Martyrs of the Arena", such popular songs as "Myfanwy", and, rarely, contemporary pieces, such as William Matthias's "Y Sipsiwn" ("The Gypsy"). A male-voice choir competition is held each year at the *Royal National Eisteddfod.

Welsh Marches The territory on either side of the border between England and Wales. (The word "march" derives from the Old French *marche*, "border", and is related to the German *mark*, and to the title "marquess".) Following the Norman conquest of England (1066), William I granted the barons holding lands on the border special rights as a defence against the Welsh, and successive kings acquiesced in their private conquest of much of Wales. Though held in feudal tenure, these lands were not part of England, and matters of justice, finance, military service, and administration were in the hands of the barons. When Edward I conquered the remainder of Wales (1276–84), he left these territories untouched, while extending the English *shire system to his new acquisitions (the former counties of Anglesey, Caernarvon, Merioneth, Cardigan, and Carmarthen; *see* Norman Britain for map), and Flintshire (created out of existing royal lands). Deprived of their frontier role, the Marches (as the area was known to distinguish it from the royal Principality of Wales) became a powerbase for their lords during political strife in England, notably during the *Wars of the Roses. By the 16th century, most Marcher lands had fallen to the Crown, either through inheritance (both the Lancastrian and Yorkist families had previously held border territories) or by forfeiture (during the Wars of the Roses or under the early Tudors). In 1536 Wales was united with England, the special status of the Marches was abolished, and the land was divided into shires. The Council in the Marches of Wales, which had administered the Principality and Crown lands since the 1470s, was constituted by statute in 1543, with authority over all of Wales and the border counties of England. It was abolished in 1689, after the *Glorious Revolution.

The term "Welsh Marches" is now used only in an informal geographical sense, denoting the westernmost parts of the English counties of Cheshire, Shropshire, Hereford and Worcester, and Gloucestershire and the easternmost parts of the Welsh counties of Clwyd, Powys, and Gwent. The dominant economic activity of the area is agriculture, but some light industries and tourism are also important.

Welsh national anthem The patriotic song "Hen Wlad Fy Nhadau" ("Land of My Fathers") that serves as Wales's national song on many official occasions. The Welsh words were written by Evan James (1809–93), and the music was composed by James James (1832–1902), for the national *eisteddfod at Llangollen in 1868, where the song was first performed. Lacking the antiquity of the British anthem "God save the Queen", "Hen Wlad Fy Nhadau" has only gradually been accepted as an official national anthem outside Wales, but within the Principality it is sung at many events, from concerts to international rugby matches. "Hen Wlad Fy Nhadau" celebrates the bardic traditions, language, and scenic beauty of Wales and tells how these assets – especially the language – have survived against considerable odds.

Welsh Nationalist Party *See* Plaid Cymru.

Welsh National Opera (WNO) Wales's chief national musical organization devoted to the professional performance of opera. WNO was conceived in 1943 and emerged as the Welsh National Opera Company in the following year. It became a fully professional company in 1973 and adopted its present name in 1977. It inaugurated a training scheme for young singers in 1962. In Cardiff WNO stages its performances at the New Theatre but has no permanent opera house of its own. It undertakes tours throughout Wales and England, and has made international tours to many European countries. The company has achieved a great deal of artistic success during its existence. Apart from the traditional repertoire it has done much to popularize the works of Janáček and Martinů; and it is the first British opera company to have taken Wagner's *Ring* on tour. Since 1973 its musical director has been Richard Armstrong (1943–).

Welsh valleys The valleys of the South Wales coalfield, principally those of the rivers Taff, Rhondda Fach, Rhondda Fawr, and Rhymney, and the Neath and Swansea valleys, which extend into the mountains behind the coastal urban centres of Cardiff, Newport, and Swansea. Until the advent of heavy industry, the valleys were sparsely populated and thickly wooded, with the main occupation being sheep and cattle farming. Industrialization began in the early 19th century with iron smelting, for example at Merthyr Tydfil, followed by coal mining, which transformed the valleys, as the demand for coal increased to supply industry, railways, and ships. As late as 1836, the traveller Thomas Roscoe praised the beauty of Rhondda Fawr. By mid-century, the Rhondda valleys dominated coal production, and massive immigration in the following years led to extensive urban development (between 1861 and 1921, the Rhondda's population increased from 4000 to 166,000). Constricted by the narrow valley floors, housing was pushed up the sides, resulting in rows of terraced houses strung out along the valleys, overshadowed by mounting hills of waste. Until World War I Welsh coal was exported all over the world; but thereafter the increasing use of alternative fuels led to a decline in demand. The last pit in the Rhondda closed in the mid-1980s and of the major steel works only Port Talbot remains. For many years, the valleys have faced economic and social dislocation as traditional industries have declined, the gaps being only partly filled by newer light industries. On the other hand, the environment has improved significantly in recent years.

The distinctive culture of the valleys developed in the 19th century, based on the twin pillars of religious nonconformity, with its peculiarly Welsh musical traditions (brought by immigrants from west Wales), and the Welsh language. The latter was later eroded by the influx of English immigrants and through official disapproval; but the chapel was still a dominant social force well into the 20th century, and the musical tradition is flourishing, especially in brass and silver bands, and the world-famous *Welsh male-voice choirs.

The valleys have maintained a tradition of political radicalism, which produced solid support for the Liberal Party until about World War I, and Labour thereafter, with the miner's union playing a significant role. In 1900 Keir Hardie became one of the first Labour MPs when he was elected at Merthyr Tydfil; former miners' leaders Aneurin Bevan and James Griffiths were members of Attlee's postwar Labour government; and two recent Labour leaders (Michael Foot and Neil Kinnock) both represent constituencies in the Welsh valleys.

Wembley Stadium One of the most famous *football stadiums in the world. It was built in 1923, the year that the British Empire Exhibition was held at Wembley in northwest London, and hosted its first FA *Cup Final in that year. The attraction of the new stadium, the presence of King George V, a London team, and fine weather led nearly 200,000 people to attend the match. So great was the crush that the crowd spilled onto the pitch before the match, delaying the start by 40 minutes. Since then admission has been by ticket only and spectators limited to 100,000. The stadium has staged England international matches since 1924 and the Rugby League Cup Final since 1929, as well as international hockey, speedway, greyhound racing, and even American football. Two of Wembley's most celebrated occasions were the 1948 Olympic Games and the 1966 football World Cup Final, appropriately won by England.

Wesleyan Reform Union A breakaway faction of the Methodist Church (*see* Methodists). It originates from the expulsion of the Wesleyan Reformers from the main movement in 1849 and follows a congregationalist approach to government, that is, determined by each congregation. Concentrated in the Midlands and north of England, it now has some 130 chapels and about 3400 members.

Wessex The kingdom of the West Saxons, a Teutonic people who migrated from Frisia in northern Europe. It emerged from obscure origins in the 6th century AD as a relatively small area of the country surrounding the upper Thames basin south of Mercia, with its chief settlements at Dorchester and Wallingford. It disappeared 500 years later with the Norman conquest. In those 500 years Wessex became the leading Anglo-Saxon kingdom, and its royal house provided all the Anglo-Saxon kings of England up to the conquest.

Expanding in the late 6th century under King Cealwin into what is now Wiltshire, the West Saxons were soon forced by Anglian Mercia to abandon newly won Buckinghamshire and Gloucestershire and their old homeland, and they moved southwestwards into Somerset, Dorset, and Devon. Adopting new capitals at Winchester and Oxford, they were for two centuries dominated by Mercia until King Egbert gained political independence (825). In 877, after a decade of Danish onslaught on England, Mercia fell to the Danes and the West Saxon king, Alfred, became the only surviving English king. Acknowledged ruler of all Englishmen outside the Danelaw, he routed the Danes the following year at the battle of Edington. Believing that the Danes had been sent as divine retribution for English neglect of learning, Alfred made Wessex a centre of education; the Anglo-Saxon Chronicle was begun in his reign. A man of exceptional courage and tenacity, his victory enabled his son to reconquer Danish territory, and his grandson Aethelstan became the first king of all England when he annexed Northumbria. Wessex was now an earldom, administered by its own law.

The Wessex dynasty lasted until Edmund Ironside, the son of Aethelred the Unready, gave way to the Dane Canute in 1016. Harold II, who fell at Hastings, though not of Alfred's line, was an Earl of Wessex and the last Anglo-Saxon king.

Today, southwest England from Hampshire to Devon is still sometimes known as Wessex, and it has gained modern fame through the writer Thomas Hardy, who gave its name to his native Dorset, the setting for most of his major novels. *See also* Anglo-Saxon Britain.

West End, London The area of central London, west of the City, in which the most prestigious of the capital's hotels, restaurants, theatres, cinemas, and department stores are to be found. Much of the district, which includes six *royal parks covering 2400 hectares (5900 acres), was originally owned by the Duke of Westminster. Mayfair has long been London's most exclusive residential area, in which trading was prohibited until the 1920s. Areas such as Belgravia (where many foreign embassies are situated) and parts of Chelsea are also noted for their elegance. Many houses in St James's Street, once the residence of such men as Byron, Louis Napoleon (Napoleon III of France), and Haydn, are now occupied by some of the oldest of the *London clubs. Famous department stores, such as Selfridges in Oxford Street, Harrods in Knightsbridge, and Fortnum and Mason in Piccadilly attract shoppers from all over the world (*see* London shops), while Christie's and Sotheby's, the main art auctioneers, have made London the art centre of the world.

The West End also boasts many fine hotels and restaurants and is renowned as a centre of the fashion world. It is perhaps best known, however, as the heartland of British theatre (*see* West End theatre).

West End theatre Perhaps the most famous area of theatrical activity in the world, so called because it developed in fashionable areas to the west of the City of London. After the *Restoration of the monarchy in 1660, two companies were allowed to start up in new theatres in Lincoln's Inn Fields and Drury Lane. Her Majesty's, briefly under the management of Sir John Vanbrugh (1664–1726) and William Congreve (1670–1729), opened in 1705, and the Haymarket opposite in 1720; they staged opera, pantomime, and contemporary plays. Covent Garden theatre opened in 1732 and followed Drury Lane in performing plays by Shakespeare under the great actor-managers (*see* Shakespearean theatre), before becoming exclusively an opera house (*see* Royal Opera House).

The theatres of the West End area – in and around Shaftesbury Avenue, Aldwych, St Martin's Lane, Charing Cross Road, and the Strand – were not built until the theatrical boom of the late 19th and early 20th centuries. Here were performed the Savoy operas, the revues of C. B. Cochran, the Aldwych farces of Ben Travers, such long-running musicals as *Chu Chin Chow* and *No, No, Nanette*, as well as the work of Wilde, Pinero, Granville-Barker, Galsworthy, Barrie, Shaw, Priestley, Coward, Novello, Rattigan, Maugham, and hundreds of playwrights now forgotten. Plays set in drawing rooms with elegantly attired stars were their staple fare until the 1950s, when John Osborne, Arnold Wesker, and the other "angry young men" introduced the so-called "kitchen-sink" drama to the West End from the English Stage Company under George Devine at the Royal Court Theatre. The Society of West End Theatre (SWET) – started in 1908 – represents the owners and managers of some 45 member theatres, some as far away as Sloane Square (Royal Court), south of the Thames (Old Vic), or in Regent's Park and Islington (Open Air Theatre and Sadler's Wells). Although often criticized for offering middle-brow commercial entertainment for tourists in the shape of musicals, thrillers, and farces (Agatha Christie's *The Mousetrap* has run for over 35 years, and *No Sex Please, We're British* for more than 12), SWET has subsidized several of its member theatres, enabling them to take over serious productions from the National Theatre and Royal Shakespeare Company, from the provinces, and from the "fringe", as well as originating their own. Recently, the theatres have supported a centralized cheap ticket system operating on the day of performance from a kiosk in Leicester Square, so that students and the less well-off can continue to go to the theatre, despite the high price of seats (in the past they had to queue up outside individual theatres to buy seats in the gallery known as "the gods").

Outside SWET are the so-called *fringe theatres, usually in the inner suburbs (Shepherd's Bush, Greenwich, Hampstead, Mile End, Stratford East, etc.) but also in the West End, in the back rooms of pubs or in multipurpose halls. Their willingness to experiment and the ever-present possibility of successful shows transferring to the West End has often had a revitalizing effect on SWET. For the past ten years SWET has been presenting its own awards (now the Laurence Olivier Awards) to recognize the outstanding creative achievements of each year in theatre, opera, and dance.

Westminster Abbey The collegiate church of St Peter in Westminster, more popularly known as Westminster Abbey. It has a very special importance in the history of England, having been the scene of the coronation of all English monarchs except Edward V (and Edward VIII, who was never crowned) since William I was crowned there on Christmas Day, 1066. It also serves as a national shrine, with many memorials to those who have shaped the country's history. The *stone of Scone, stolen from the Scots by Edward I, forms part of the coronation chair, which has featured in the *coronation ceremony since the 13th century.

The abbey's origins are obscure. According to legend, a monastic community and church were founded in the 7th century by Sebert, king of the East Saxons, on the instructions of St Peter, who paid a miraculous visit to the consecration ceremony. It does seem that by 785 AD a community dedicated to St Peter had been established on an island in the Thames called Thorney, which later became known as Westminster. The abbey received a new and impressive abbey church, which was consecrated in 1065. Eight days later Edward the Confessor died and was buried at the foot of the altar. Edward's canonization in 1139 enhanced the abbey's prestige and successive monarchs favoured it with gifts and privileges. In 1245, under Henry III, work started on the construction of a new abbey on the same site. The design, a splendid example of early English gothic architecture, was conceived by Henry of Reims, but after the king's death in 1272, progress was slow; work on the nave was not completed until the early 16th century. Henry VII's chapel, with its exquisite fan vaulting in stone, is the work of mason Robert Vertue and a major feature of the abbey. In 1540 the monastery was dissolved and part of its revenues were transferred to St Paul's cathedral (hence the phrase "robbing Peter to pay Paul"). The abbey then became the cathedral of a new but short-lived diocese of Westminster. The monastery was restored by Mary I (r. 1553–58) and subsequently abolished by Elizabeth I (r. 1558–1603). During the Civil War, Cromwell billeted his army in the abbey.

In 1698 Sir Christopher Wren was appointed surveyor and he carried out some restoration and designed twin west towers, which were modified by his pupil Nicholas Hawksmoor, who completed the work in 1745.

George II was the last monarch to be buried in Westminster Abbey, where lie many of his predecessors, including Henry III and Henry V. Many famous statesmen, scientists, engineers, explorers, and others are also buried there or are honoured with memorials. Poets' Corner contains the mortal remains of Chaucer, Ben Jonson, Dryden, Samuel Johnson, Browning, and Tennyson. In the nave is the tomb of the Unknown Soldier, the body of a soldier, who died in Flanders during World War I, chosen at random by a blindfolded senior officer from a number of unidentifiable corpses, and who lies in soil brought from the battlefield.

In 1973 a major restoration programme was started to repair and resurface the abbey's stonework which had been damaged by atmospheric pollution. The work, which has been described as the biggest job of restoration since the time of Sir Christopher Wren, is due to be completed in the 1990s at a cost of more than £10 million.

Westminster cathedral See cathedral.

Westminster, Palace of A royal palace at Westminster, first built by King Canute (r. 1016–35). On his accession in 1066, William I (the Conqueror) began to replace it on a grander scale, but it was under his son William II (r. 1087–1100) that the new palace really began to take shape. He was responsible for the construction, between 1097 and 1099, of Westminster Hall, the only part still to survive. The rest, developed and embellished over the centuries, was destroyed by fire in 1834. The present neogothic palace, the work of architect Sir Charles Barry (1795–1860) and designer Augustus Pugin (1812–52), was begun in 1839, and, though not completed until 1870, was first occupied by both Houses for a state opening in 1852 (see also Big Ben).

Which? The monthly magazine of the Consumers' Association. The Consumers' Association was founded in 1956 with Michael D. Young (1915–   ) as its first chairman (1956–65); financed by its members' subscriptions, it is independent of both government and industry and aims to raise the standard of goods and services supplied to the public. The results of the Association's research are published in *Which?*, which tries to establish the "best buy" in a given range of items, whether life insurance or washing machines. In addition to the monthly issues of *Which?*, there are quarterly supplements on motoring, money and investment, DIY supplies, and holidays, and a separate survey of drugs and pharmaceutical goods for doctors.

whips Members of a party in Parliament appointed to manage their fellow supporters. Their name derives from the hunt, where whippers-in prevent straying in the field, and their functions range from promoting good relations between the party leaders and backbench MPs to securing the attendance of members for important debates and divisions. They also discipline disobedient members. The weekly agenda that they send out is also known as a whip, and underlines items of business once, twice, or three times, according to their importance. A one-line whip merely requests attendance; a two-line whip particularly requests it, but attendance is excused if a member has been officially "paired" with an opposition absentee; a three-line whip says that attendance is essential, and disobedience may result in loss of party recognition for the future (withdrawal of the whip). Government whips are all government ministers. In the House of Commons, the chief whip is the Parliamentary Secretary to the Treasury, and his assistants are the vice-chamberlain of the royal household (see Lord Chamberlain), its comptroller and treasurer, and the junior lords of the Treasury (see Chancellor of the Exchequer). In the Lords, the chief whip is the captain of the Gentlemen at Arms, his deputy is the captain of the Yeomen of the Guard, and the others *lords in waiting.

whisky A spirit distilled from malted barley or other grain in Scotland and Ireland. The name "whisky" or "whiskey" – the latter spelling being used for the Irish liquor – derives from the Gaelic *uisge beatha*, meaning "water of life". The traditional Scotch malt whisky is made entirely from malted barley, yeast, and the pure clear water of Scotland's lochs and burns, and is matured in oak casks for a number of years. Malt whisky is generally divided into four categories: Highland, Lowland, Islay, and Campbeltown; within each group the flavour of the liquor varies considerably from region to region and from distillery to distillery. Most of the Scotch whisky consumed in England is blended from a combination of malt and grain whiskies: as many as 50 types of whisky may be used in a single blend.

The production of Irish whiskey dates back at least to the 15th century, although it has been suggested that Irish monks were distilling the spirit as early as the 10th century (*see* poteen). Irish whiskey differs from Scotch in that the malted barley is mixed with other unmalted cereals before fermentation. It is also stronger and purer, since it passes through an extra stage of distillation, but lacks the characteristic flavour imparted to Scotch whisky by the peat fires over which the malt is dried. Like Scotch whisky, it is matured for a period of five to fifteen years before bottling. Both Scotch whisky and Irish whiskey are drunk neat, diluted with water or soda, or used in the preparation of a variety of drinks and cocktails. Toddy is a traditional mixture of Scotch whisky, hot water, and sugar, drunk for pleasure or for medicinal purposes; Irish or Gaelic coffee is sweetened coffee laced with Irish whiskey and topped with a floating layer of cream; whisky nog is a restorative made by mixing whisky, milk, raw egg, and sugar.

Whitaker's Almanack An annual reference book first issued for the year 1869 by the London publisher Joseph Whitaker (1820–95). Described by Whitaker in his preface to the first edition as a "household book", it contained information about the calendar, astronomical phenomena, the British constitution, parliamentary proceedings, the legal system, the Church, the armed forces, scientific events, trade and industry, and foreign countries. It was an immediate success, over 36,000 copies being subscribed before publication. The format, layout, and presentation of the *Almanack* have remained virtually unchanged, although its range has been increased considerably, to include information on such subjects as income tax and social security benefits, and curiosities, such as the list of holders of the office of Master of the King's (Queen's) Music.

white horses *See* chalk hill figures.

white paper *See* command papers.

Whit Sunday The seventh Sunday after Easter is known in the Christian Church as Whit Sunday and celebrates the feast of Pentecost, when the Apostles received the Holy Ghost (Acts 2.1). Pentecost is the Jewish harvest festival of Weeks, held 50 days after the start of Passover. It became a favoured day for Christian baptisms and the name was probably derived from the white robes worn by the newly baptized. The ensuing days of Whitsuntide were a popular time for May fairs, feasts, and village parties. Whit Monday was formerly a public holiday but this has now been replaced by the spring bank holiday, fixed on the last Monday in May, which does not necessarily coincide with Whit Monday.

Whittington, Richard (Dick) A wealthy English merchant, three times Lord Mayor of London; the hero of popular *pantomime and children's story. The early life of the legendary Dick Whittington bears little resemblance to that of the historical figure. Born into a well-established Gloucestershire family in the mid-14th century, the young Richard Whittington was apprenticed to a London merchant and went on to become a prosperous and successful mercer in his own right. He supplied textiles to royalty and the aristocracy and is known to have made substantial loans to Henry IV and Henry V. In 1397 he was elected Lord Mayor of London for the first time. He became known for his generous benefactions, such as endowing almshouses and libraries, and restoration work; these were perpetuated after his death in 1423 through a charitable trust set up in accordance with his will.

The legend of Dick Whittington and his cat first appeared in 1605 in a London play called *The History of Richard Whittington*. Unlike the historical figure, Dick Whittington is a poor orphan boy who travels to London to make his fortune, believing the streets are paved with gold. Employed as a scullion in the house of a rich London merchant, his existence is so wretched that he decides to run away back to his native Lancashire; upon reaching Highgate Hill he is halted by the distant sound of the bells of Bow church, which seem to be saying, "Turn again Whittington, thrice Lord Mayor of London". He returns to the city and ventures his beloved cat on one of his master's merchant ships: the cat proves to be such an exceptional mouser that it is bought by the ruler of one of the trading countries for a considerable sum. Dick's wealth is thus assured, and, having married his master's daughter, he becomes Lord Mayor of London three times. Although there is no historical evidence for the cat, it seems likely that this element of the legend comes from a similar Persian or Italian folk tale. Such was the popular appeal of the animal that when the 17th-century engraver Renold Elstracke published a portrait of Whittington, his hand resting on a skull as a symbol of man's mortality, he found himself obliged by public demand to reissue the print with the figure of a small cat in place of the skull. Whittington Hospital in Highgate Hill is named after this historical figure and the Whittington Stone, marking the spot at which he is reputed to have stopped at the sound of Bow bells, stands at the foot of the hill.

Who's Who An annual reference book of contemporary biography, published in its present form since 1897. It started life in 1849 as a mere list of titled notables, but when the publishing house of A. & C. Black purchased the copyright for £30 in 1896 they widened the scope of the book to include biographical details and people other than public office-holders. They also initiated the system of sending out questionnaires to enable people to write their own entries with the stipulation that inclusion was strictly by invitation and could not be bought. The first edition contained around 5000 entries; in the early 1980s the number had risen to around 26,000. The questionnaire system accounts for much of the fascination of the book, unearthing facts about people's hobbies and interests. In some cases it may diminish its usefulness as a reference work, when people suppress dates of birth, previous marriages, or other facts they prefer to forget. Periodically, biographies removed on account of death are published in a volume entitled *Who Was Who*, the first of which, covering the period 1897–1915, appeared in 1920.

WI *See* Women's Institute.

Wildfowl Trust A charitable trust devoted to the study and conservation of wildfowl, founded in 1946 by (Sir) Peter Scott (1909–). Its headquarters are at Slimbridge, Gloucestershire, on the eastern side of the estuary of the River Severn, where thousands of migrant swans, geese, and ducks congregate during the winter months. The Trust runs a research unit for scientific and conservation studies, concentrating upon what can be done to preserve threatened species. It also aims to educate the public regarding wildfowl, running lectures, films, field study courses for schools, and exhibitions. Besides Slimbridge, the Trust has 150 hectares (360 acres) of marshland at Martin Mere, Lancashire; a refuge of 400 hectares (1000 acres) at Caerlaverock, Dumfries and Galloway; a refuge at Washington New Town, Tyne and Wear, in which many North American species are kept to emphasize the local links with George Washington's family; a waterfowl garden at Peakirk near Peterborough; a refuge at Welney, Norfolk; and a landscaped site of 22 hectares (55 acres) at Arundel, Sussex. Through his fine paintings of wildfowl and his writings on ornithological subjects, Peter Scott, honorary director of the Trust since its inception, has done much to bring its work to the notice of the public.

Wimbledon The home of lawn *tennis championships since 1877, the oldest and most important of tennis tournaments. The championships are organized by the *All-England Lawn Tennis and Croquet Club, in conjunction with the Lawn Tennis Association. At first there was only a men's singles tournament; men's doubles and women's singles were incorporated in 1884, and the women's and mixed doubles in 1913. In the early years of the championships British players were dominant, but since the Australian Norman Brookes became the first overseas player to win the men's singles in 1907, only A. W. Gore (1908–09) and Fred Perry (1934–36) have won the title for Britain. British women have done rather better, most recently with Ann Jones winning the singles title in 1969 and Virginia Wade winning in Wimbledon's centenary year (1977). Since 1968 the championships have not been restricted to amateur players, and now large sums in prize money are at stake (some £130,000 for the men's singles winner in 1985). Wimbledon ranks as one of the world's four great tournaments, which, with the French, Australian, and US Open championships, constitute the "grand slam" of professional tennis titles. It is certainly one of the sporting and social highlights of the English summer, taking place in the last week of June and the first week of July. Afternoon tea with champagne and strawberries and cream are traditionally part of a day's visit to Wimbledon. Tickets are difficult to obtain, especially for the Centre and No. 1 courts where the top matches are played. The royal family has its own box and trophies for the championship are presented by the Duke or Duchess of Kent, the former being president of the All-England Club.

Winchester College The oldest English *public school, founded at Winchester, Hampshire, in 1382 by William of Wykeham (1324–1404), Bishop of Winchester and twice Lord Chancellor of England. The school

WINCHESTER COLLEGE *Scholars at Winchester. In the background are the individual cubicles known as "toys", which are used as studies. Many aspects of the traditional lifestyle and the spartan surroundings still survive.*

educated boys up to the age of about 16, when they transferred to New College, Oxford, also established by William of Wykeham in 1379. Both colleges produced men fit for the service of Church and state at a time when their numbers had been depleted by the *Black Death (1348–49). Wykehamists, as the school's pupils are called, still honour the six-century-old tradition of learning, but the school's motto, "Manners makyth man", reminds them that mere bookishness is not enough. The buildings around Chamber Court were erected by the founder to house his 70 "poor scholars", their warden, head master, second master, and accompanying clerks and fellows. Ten "commoners", fee-paying pupils from the nobility or gentry, were also admitted. The growth in the number of commoners over the centuries necessitated a reorganization of the school into "tutors' houses" during the 1860s, although the ancient distinction between "College men" and "Commoners" remained. Elements of the prefect system, often seen as a quintessential part of public-school life, existed even in the 14th century, when William of Wykeham ordained that certain senior boys should have authority to supervise others.

Windsor castle The largest of England's castles, Windsor castle was founded by William the Conqueror (r. 1066–87) after the typical Norman design of motte and bailey, and is sited on a chalk cliff beside the River Thames. First used as a royal residence by Henry I (r. 1100–35), the original wooden structures were replaced by stone during the reign of Henry II (1154–89), who constructed the Round Tower – still one of the most prominent features of the castle. The castle stands on the edge of Windsor Great Park, formerly a popular hunting ground of kings, which is now open to the public. St George's Chapel, a masterpiece in the perpendicular style, was begun by Edward IV in 1475 and has long served as the last resting place of sovereigns. The process of converting Windsor from a fortress into a palace began in the 16th century and continued in the 17th when Charles II commissioned Hugh May (1621–84) to refurbish the royal apartments with lavish decor. From 1826, at the wish of

George IV, Sir Jeffry Wyatville (1766–1840) remodelled a substantial part of the building. Prince Albert died at Windsor in 1861, and to commemorate her husband Queen Victoria dedicated the chapel built by Henry VII as the Albert Memorial Chapel. More recently, Edward VIII made his famous abdication broadcast from Windsor in 1936.

Windsor, House of The name of the royal dynasty was changed by George V from that of Saxe-Coburg and Gotha (family name Wipper or Wettin) in 1917, when anti-German sentiment as a result of World War I rendered palpably Teutonic antecedents embarrassing. Windsor was suggested as a substitute by George V's private secretary, Lord Stamfordham, who recalled that Edward III had on occasion been known as Edward of Windsor. George V took the name of Windsor by proclamation for Queen Victoria's descendants in the male line who were British subjects (other than females who married). In 1952 the present Queen declared that she and her children should be known as the House and Family of Windsor and that her descendants in the male line (other than married females) should be called Windsor. In 1960 the Queen reserved Windsor to herself and her children but declared that her descendants, other than those entitled to style themselves HRH, Prince, or Princess, and married females and their children, should take the family name Mountbatten-Windsor.

Wisden Cricketers' Almanack The best-known reference book of cricket statistics, published annually since 1864 and regarded by cricket lovers worldwide as the authoritative source for facts and figures of the game. It was the brainchild of Sussex cricketer John Wisden (1826–84), who retired from first-class competition in 1863 and began publishing the *Almanack* from his sports shop in London. At first it contained extraneous, noncricketing information, but it soon began to incorporate the essential ingredients of cricket records, a full list of batting and bowling averages for the past season (first published in 1887), biographies and obituaries of leading cricketers, and scores of test, county, and other first-class

The Royal House of Windsor

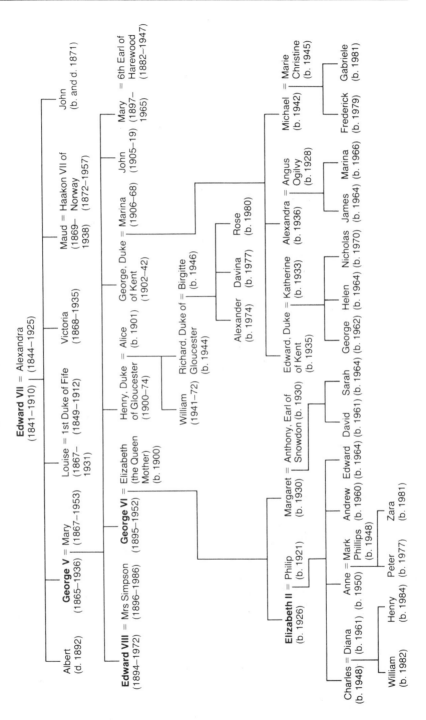

games. Match reports were introduced in 1870, written mainly by the sporting journalist W. H. Knight, who compiled the *Almanack* for a number of years until his death in 1879. Continuity was ensured in 1880 with the formation of the Cricket Reporting Agency; its associates edited *Wisden* from 1887 to 1933. While retaining its small, single-volume format, *Wisden* has in recent times expanded to incude new developments such as the John Player League, Benson & Hedges Cup matches, and women's cricket.

witches Women who are alleged to possess supernatural powers as a result of a pact with the devil. The idea that some women are witches is ancient and virtually worldwide; the belief reached its strongest influence in the Christian world during the 16th and 17th centuries, when witch-hunts took place throughout Europe and in New England (1650–1710) on the strength of the Old Testament injunction (Exodus 22, 18) "Thou shalt not suffer a witch to live". The first major witch-hunt took place in Switzerland in 1427. In England witchcraft became a capital offence in 1542 (1563 in Scotland), and subsequently for more than 150 years, supposed witches of all ages were persecuted, tortured, and put to death on evidence, much of which came from confessions extracted under torture. The witches' supposed supernatural powers included the ability to fly, traditionally astride a broomstick; to have as servants demons in the form of animals, often a cat; and to bring about suffering and death by casting spells or placing curses on those they wished to harm. Organized groups or covens of witches were believed to hold regular orgies of devil-worship known as sabbats at which new members would be initiated. The idea of the sabbat dates only from 1400, when the Inquisition began investigating witchcraft.

The laws concerning the incrimination and punishment of witches were uncompromising

WITCHES *Ducking a suspected witch, from a woodcut of 1612. The accused was lowered into the water with thumbs tied to opposite big toes.*

and widely abused. Witch-hunting was particularly virulent during the reign of James I (r. 1603–25; Scotland, 1567–1625) and from 1645 to 1647, the years of the Long Parliament, when Matthew Hopkins, self-styled "Witch Finder General", sent 200 women to their deaths in the eastern counties of England before he was discredited. In addition to confessions under torture, witches were identified by a "witch-mark", a small insensitive spot that did not bleed when pricked: a retractable pin was often used by the more zealous "witch-prickers", particularly Hopkins, to obtain the desired results. A second test, known as ducking, involved throwing the supposed witch into the river: if she sank she was proved innocent, if she floated she was proved guilty, for water was thought to reject anyone who had rejected baptism. The punishment was often the death sentence; in England this usually took the form of hanging, but in Scotland witches were commonly burnt at the stake or submitted to more horrific ordeals. The last judicial execution for witchcraft in England took place in 1712. By 1736, when many of the laws against witchcraft were finally repealed, about 2000 women, many of whom were guilty of no more than having earned the hatred and suspicion of their neighbours, had been condemned and executed in Britain as witches.

Woburn Abbey The home of the Dukes of Bedford for over three hundred years, situated near Leighton Buzzard in Bedfordshire. The original Cistercian abbey was founded in 1145 and given to the Russell family by Henry VIII in 1540 at the dissolution of the monasteries. The present house was constructed around the quadrangle of the old abbey; the west side was transformed by Henry Flitcroft (1697–1769) and dates from 1747–61, and the south side is the work of Henry Holland (1745–1806) in the 1780s and 1790s. The eastern block was demolished in 1950 because of dry rot. The interior is richly furnished and decorated and contains a priceless collection of paintings by such masters as Velazquez, Reynolds, Teniers, and Holbein. The grounds feature a maze, which has a Chinese pavilion at its centre; by the lake is the Chinese dairy, built by Henry Holland. The deer park, land-scaped by Humphry Repton (1752–1818) in the early 19th century, now has the world's largest breeding herd of the rare Père David's deer. The abbey, which is open to the public, also has a safari park.

Women's Institute (WI) Branches of the National Federation of Women's Institutes, Britain's largest women's voluntary organization. The movement was started in Canada in 1897 by a farmer's wife, Adelaide Hoodless, as a means of providing classes in domestic science and homemaking, believing that the death of one of her babies had been due to her own ignorance of hygiene and childcare. The WI began in Britain in Anglesey, in 1915, and was originally a rurally-based organization, though now its members come from all areas. It works "to improve the quality of life, to enhance the position of women and to influence decision makers locally, nationally and internationally". In England, Wales, the Channel Islands, and the Isle of Man it has 354,000 members in some 9200 Institutes grouped in 71 county federations.

The WI maintains international connections and is affiliated to the Associated Countrywomen of the World, which provides links with the United Nations. Involvement in the European Community includes members serving on a variety of committees. It offers training locally in many subjects and has its own residential adult education college near Oxford (Denman College), its own publishing company (WI Books), and produces a monthly magazine, *Home & Country*. There are over 500 WI markets throughout the country selling high-quality home-produced goods.

Women's Land Army *See* women's services.

women's movements The demand for equal opportunities for women goes back to the late 18th century when Mary Wollstonecraft first applied egalitarian principles to women in *A Vindication of the Rights of Women* (1792). She had no interest in women's suffrage, however, as relatively few men at that time had the vote either; it took another century for an awareness of the disadvantages women endured, both inside and

WOMEN'S MOVEMENTS Defiance: removing a grille and the suffragette chained to it, in the House of Commons, *from* The Illustrated London News, *1913.*

outside marriage, to be linked with a belief that the vote would strengthen their position. A flurry of activity occurred in the late 1860s when, during the debate on the Second Re-

form Bill, John Stuart Mill moved an unsuccessful amendment to give votes to women. This led to the formation of the first of several suffrage organizations. Restricted to genteel

WOMEN'S MOVEMENTS *Munition workers in an English shell-filling factory, 1914–18. The two world wars had a dramatic impact on women's social and economic role, bringing them out of the home and into munitions factories and onto farms.*

lobbying, these achieved little success, although the situation of middle-class women, at least, began to improve. By the end of the century there was some legislation, and education for women began to expand. However, it was the **suffragette** Mrs Emmeline Pankhurst (1858–1928), the widow of the radical Richard Pankhurst, who realized that public opinion needed to be aroused, even scandalized, if real progress was to be made. She founded the Women's Social and Political Union (WSPU) in 1903, in loose alliance with the Labour Party, and continued to dominate it with her two daughters, Christabel and Sylvia. The next 11 years saw a steady escalation in their campaigns of civil disobedience. Starting with disruptive behaviour at meetings, harassment of politicians, and mass marches with banners, they eventually moved on from mere words to sticks and stones, with which they attacked property, breaking windows, and

sometimes setting light to buildings, including churches. Some of Mrs Pankhurst's more drastic tactics alienated even her own supporters who formed the nonviolent Women's Freedom League; they did, however, achieve their purpose of embarrassing the government, especially when their provocations led to police reprisals and a number of hunger strikes in prison by several leading suffragettes. Herbert Asquith, the Liberal leader, appeared sympathetic to the women's cause. They soon realized, however, that he was not going to put a new Act before Parliament to give women the vote and was merely proposing an amendment to his bill giving votes to all men. (Part of Asquith's resistance to the notion of women's suffrage stemmed from his conviction that if the female franchise were restricted on the same property basis as the male, there would be a massive gain to the Conservatives.) The suffragettes reacted to the disappointment

473

with increasing violence (by this time women in Australia, New Zealand, and some states of America already had the vote); Emily Davison threw herself in front of the king's horse at Epsom, wearing the purple, white, and green colours of the suffragette movement, and the Rokeby Venus in the National Gallery was slashed. These dramatic gestures might well have illicited some concessions, but when war broke out in Europe, the suffragette movement came to an end as patriotism took precedence over feminism. After the war women's war work, partly organized by the suffragette groups, was rewarded by women over 30 being given the vote. In 1928 women were given complete equality with men at last: the right to vote at 21.

Politicians' fears that women would vote for women proved to be groundless. In spite of the emancipation of women, they continued to be grossly under-represented in Parliament and, indeed in most institutions and professions also. In 1980 the 300 Group was formed to "awaken, encourage, and train women to participate in all aspects of public life" – the figure being the approximate number of female MPs required to produce a balance of the sexes in the House of Commons. However, the main thrust of the women's liberation movement in Britain, which followed that of the USA in the late 1960s, is both more radical and more private; it questions the whole basis of society. Unlike the suffragette movement it has no strong central organization, but consists of small groups throughout the country, run informally by and for women, not only to raise their political consciousness but also to increase their personal fulfilment.

Women's Royal Air Force (WRAF)   *See* women's services.

Women's Royal Army Corps (WRAC) *See* women's services.

Women's Royal Naval Service (WRNS) *See* women's services.

Women's Royal Voluntary Service (WRVS)   A service founded in 1938, closely linked with local authority community work but run mainly through part-time unpaid helpers, many of them housewives. It has nearly 1300 branches in England and Wales, and over 180 in Scotland. The Women's Voluntary Services for Air Raid Precautions was set up by Stella, Dowager Marchioness of Reading (1894–1971), at the request of Home Secretary Samuel Hoare (1880–1959), to draw women into civil defence as the threat of war increased. The following year the phrase "for Air Raid Precautions" was dropped and "for Civil Defence" substituted, and throughout World War II the Service did invaluable work in this role, mustering over a million volunteers by 1942. Among their numerous tasks were helping with evacuee children, running social events for servicemen on leave, providing and altering clothing for civilians and servicemen, and organizing soup kitchens for people whose homes had been bombed. Their grey-green and burgundy-red uniforms became a familiar feature of the wartime scene. After the war the phrase "for Civil Defence" was dropped and the government proposed to keep the Service in existence for two more years to carry on with rehabilitation work. By 1947, however, the value of the WVS's work was so apparent that it was decided to maintain it indefinitely.

The WVS's role in peacetime is principally supplementing the social services provided by government and local authorities. They had already pioneered the first home-help scheme (1944) and this spread throughout the country. They run the meals–on–wheels service for the housebound elderly, staff day centres for pensioners and the handicapped, organize children's holidays and playgroups, visit prisoners and their families, do nonmedical work in hospitals, and provide drivers for rural transport. In 1955 the WVS set up a housing association to provide and convert flats for the elderly. It became the Women's Royal Voluntary Service in 1966.

women's services   Organizations in which women operate alongside servicemen in all three British armed services. The formation of such forces is a relatively recent development, having its roots in the **Women's Land Army** (1917–50), which mobilized women for work in agriculture and industry during World War I. By 1938 there were various women's corps in existence; in that year they were amalgamated to create the Women's Voluntary Service, which was of particular value during air raids on Britain during World War II. It was renamed the *Women's Royal Voluntary Service in 1966. Women also enlist as auxiliaries in the regular forces, chiefly fulfilling support roles, although some are trained to bear arms for defensive purposes. The three separate corps for women in the regular services are the **Women's Royal Naval Service (WRNS,** popularly known as the "Wrens"), formed in 1917 for two years and permanently in 1939, the **Women's Royal Air Force (WRAF)**, formed in 1918 and known as the Women's Auxiliary Air Force (WAAF) from 1939 to 1948, and the **Women's Royal Army Corps (WRAC)**, formed in 1949 to replace the Auxiliary Territorial Service (ATS). Women also serve as nurses in Queen Alexandra's Army Nursing Corps and Naval Nursing Service, and, for the RAF, in Princess Mary's Nursing Service.

wool churches During the 15th century, wool and cloth merchants used their new wealth to finance the construction of exceptionally fine parish churches. These so-called wool churches are still a notable feature of the former sheep-rearing regions of England, par-ticularly Norfolk, Suffolk, and the Cotswolds. Cirencester in Gloucestershire has the largest of the Cotswold wool churches, built in the 15th and early 16th centuries. Other examples include Chipping Campden and Fairford. In Northleach church the merchant benefactors are depicted on brasses with their feet resting on a sheep or woolsack. Stoke-by-Nayland is one of the finest Suffolk wool churches. The brick-built tower was financed by local cloth merchants and erected between 1440 and 1460.

Woolsack *See* Lord (High) Chancellor.

Woolwich A district on the south bank of the Thames, known for its docks and ordnance works. Occupied since Roman times, Woolwich was established as a ferry crossing of the Thames in the Middle Ages. In 1512 it became the site of Henry VIII's royal dockyard, where such ships as the *Great Harry* (1512) and the *Sovereign of the Seas* (1637) were built. In the 19th century the dockyard was converted for building steamships, but was finally closed down in 1869. The town was also the site of England's first salt-glazed stoneware kiln, built in the early 17th century, and the Woolwich Arsenal, which was built as

WOOL CHURCHES *The church at Long Melford, a product of lavish benefactions in the 15th century, reflects the former prosperity from the wool trade of this small Suffolk town.*

the royal laboratory in 1694. In 1716 the Arsenal became the home of two regiments of artillery and, also in 1717, of the main government foundry, thus becoming the oldest and largest centre for the manufacture of arms in Britain. The Royal Military Academy was also attached to the Arsenal (1808) before being moved to Woolwich Common, where such soldiers as Lord Kitchener, General Gordon, and Orde Wingate were trained. Many of the guns made at the Arsenal are now housed in John Nash's Rotunda (1822), also built upon Woolwich Common. Since World War II, when up to 40,000 workers were employed at the Arsenal, activity in the ordnance works and on the riverside has declined and the area is now awaiting extensive redevelopment. The Arsenal itself has been reduced considerably in size to make room for new housing. (Arsenal football club, founded here in 1886, is now based in Highbury, north London.)

Workers' Educational Association (WEA) An organization primarily dedicated to advancing the cause of adult education. It was founded in 1903 by Albert Mansbridge to give direction to the demand for adult education at the end of the 19th century. It is a nonsectarian and non-party-political movement that has been successful in promoting the education of trade unionists. Its work is recognized by the Department of Education and Science and Local Education Authorities give administrative grants to its 900-plus branches.

working men's clubs Clubs founded to provide education, relaxation, and recreation for working men. They were the idea of the Rev. Henry Solly, who felt that workers needed an alternative to the *public house as a place of recreation. The first clubs, founded in the 1850s, were and still are nonpolitical, and initially did not serve alcohol – an idea that quickly proved impractical and was largely dropped in the 1860s. The National Working Men's Club and Institute Union was created in 1862 under Solly's inspiration. The limitations of transport and communication made its administration difficult in the early years. It was during the secretaryship (1893–1929) of

B. T. Hall that branch organization and cooperation in the regions developed, to be followed by nationally coordinated activity. Hall was also responsible for the regular production of the national journal, which had hitherto only appeared intermittently, and for the opening of convalescent homes for club members.

The Club and Institute Union had some 4400 member clubs and four million members in 1985, making it the largest recreational body in the world. The clubs are important local social centres, particularly in the north of England.

World Service The *BBC radio service that broadcasts 24 hours a day in English to about 25 million overseas listeners. Beginning as the Empire Service in 1932, the service expanded considerably during World War II, when it began a number of foreign language transmissions to ensure that Britain's position was understood elsewhere in the world. The World Service forms part of External Services, which are funded by an annual grant from the Treasury. Of the World Service's total output, broadcast from Bush House in London, 42% consists of news, talks, and current affairs, 14% of light music; and the remainder includes reviews, concerts, major sports events, and a substantial number of magazine programmes. Having established a reputation for integrity and impartiality, the news department of the World Service is relied upon by millions of listeners overseas for information during international crises; to this end, the style of news presentation is deliberately plain and uncoloured. Many features of the World Service – its theme tunes, such as *Lillibulero*, the chimes of Big Ben, the familiar voices of its presenters – are recognized all over the world. The old system of relaying signals transmitted from Britain through a network of short-wave booster transmitters is slowly being superseded by satellite communications.

WRAC *See* women's services.

WRAF *See* women's services.

WRNS *See* women's services.

WRVS *See* Women's Royal Voluntary Service.

Wycombe Abbey *See* public schools.

Y

Yeomen of the Guard, Queen's Bodyguard of the The oldest and most famous of the four corps of the sovereign's personal bodyguard (*see also* Gentlemen at Arms, Honorable Corps of; Royal Company of Archers; Military Knights of Windsor). They were officially founded in 1485 for the coronation of Henry VII, composed of men who had formed a private bodyguard of loyal followers during his exile, and protected him at the battle of *Bosworth Field. They continued to ensure the monarch's personal safety in battle for a further 250 years and also guarded the inside of the royal palaces. Here they had to taste the royal food (hence their popular name – **beefeaters**) and check the royal bedchamber for threats to the sovereign's life. It is they who discovered Guy Fawkes in the cellars of Westminster Palace preparing to blow up king and Parliament (1605; *see* Guy Fawkes Day), and one of their ceremonial duties is still to search the cellars before a state opening of Parliament (*see* searching the cellars).

The Yeomen of the Guard's basically Tudor uniform was modified under the Stuarts and again in the 18th and 19th centuries. It consists of a flat black round-brimmed Tudor bonnet encircled with red, white, and blue rosettes, a ruff and full-length scarlet tunic with black and gold bands, white gloves, and scarlet knee breeches and stockings decorated with rosettes at knee and foot. A Tudor rose, a thistle, and a shamrock flanked by the sovereign's initials and surmounted by a Tudor crown are embroidered on the tunic, which is crossed with a belt that once carried an arquebus (a 15th-century long-barrelled gun). A sword and a ceremonial halberd (spear with an axe head), called a partisan, complete the uniform.

By the 19th century the Yeomen of the Guard had ceased to live in the royal palaces and were

then, as now, only called out for special duties – such as attendance on the monarch at coronations and state funerals, at investitures, state visits, the state opening of Parliament, and other traditional ceremonies involving the sovereign (*see* Royal Maundy). Numbering about 60, they are under the command of six officers who wear conventional army dress uniform with a cocked hat; they are often former members of the *Household Division although retiring members of other regiments and services can apply to join.

Still doing a full-time job are the **Yeoman Warders of the Tower of London** (*see* Tower of London), who were designated "Extraordinary Yeomen of the Guard" in 1550 and allowed to wear the same uniform, except for the cross-belt. There had been warders guarding the Tower and its prisoners

YEOMEN OF THE GUARD

for years, but it seems that Henry VIII left some of his personal bodyguard behind when he abandoned the Tower as a residence in 1509, and later replacements were drafted in as the numbers of distinguished prisoners grew. The Warders' position was anomalous until the Duke of Somerset took up their case after a period in their care in 1549. Today they no longer guard prisoners but guide tourists round the Tower, attend the gates, and live there with their families until retirement. Like the Yeomen of the Guard they were formerly noncommissioned officers in the services. The Yeoman Warders usually wear a dark blue tunic and trousers with scarlet stripe, plus a cloak and dark blue bonnet. This uniform is donned for ceremonies of the Tower, such as the installation of the Constable, beating the bounds, for royal and state visits to the Tower itself, for the three Church holidays, and for family weddings within the Tower. On days of royal salutes that mark royal birthdays, state visits, and the state opening of Parliament they wear their red tunic over trousers, and the Tudor bonnet. The only time they are all on parade at the same time as the Yeomen of the Guard is for a coronation. On formal occasions the Chief Yeoman Warder carries a mace surmounted by a silver image of the White Tower, and the Yeoman Gaoler a ceremonial axe. This used to be carried in front of a prisoner on his way to trial at Westminster with the blade pointing away from him; if he was sentenced to death the blade would be turned towards him on the way back to show the public what the verdict had been. Other senior officers among the Yeoman Warders are the Yeoman Clerk and the Yeoman Raven Master, who is responsible for feeding the Tower's six ravens.

Yeomen Warders of the Tower of London See Yeomen of the Guard, Queen's Bodyguard of the.

YMCA See Young Men's Christian Association.

York Minster See cathedral.

Yorkshire pudding A batter pudding, made from eggs, milk, flour, and water, served throughout the country with roast beef. The pudding is traditionally cooked in a large baking tin below the roasting joint so that the juices of the meat drip into the batter as it cooks, but in modern homes and restaurants it is often more convenient to serve individual Yorkshire puddings cooked in a tin above the meat. In its native county, Yorkshire pudding may be eaten with any roast meat and is often served with gravy before the main course, a custom originally intended to take the edge off the family's appetite; in other northern counties the pudding was sometimes sprinkled with sugar and eaten at the end of the meal. The same batter is often used to make the traditional toad-in-the-hole, a baked dish consisting of sausages encased in a batter pudding.

Young Farmers' Clubs An organization started in Devon in 1921 with the purpose of fostering education in agricultural subjects. The first club was founded after encouragement from the newspaper proprietor Lord Northcliffe (1865–1922), his *Daily Mail* newspaper, and United Dairies Ltd. In 1929 the National Association of Young Farmers' Clubs came into being under the auspices of the National Council for Social Services. This was superseded in 1932 by the National Federation of Young Farmers' Clubs with Lord Burghley, the Olympic athlete, as its first president and Major Morton Hiles as secretary. Membership ranges from 10 to 26 years of age; it is open to men and women. As well as agricultural education, clubs organize environmental projects and a variety of social functions. International links are maintained through competitions, exchange visits, and study tours, as well as through active participation in various committees and agricultural organizations in the European Community.

Young Men's Christian Association (YMCA) A charity founded in 1844 that aims to promote the spiritual, social, and physical welfare of boys and young men. Its founder was George Russell Williams (1821–1905), who formed the first club among the employees of a London drapery business in which he worked, and who remained closely associated with the YMCA for the rest of his life. He became president after the death of the Earl of Shaftesbury

(1801–85), who was president from 1851 and did much to help the Association in its formative years. The so-called Exeter Hall lectures (1845) were an early and successful move to publicize the YMCA's work. The movement expanded rapidly and in 1855 Williams presided over the first international YMCA conference in Paris, attended by representatives from Europe and North America, which established a World Alliance of YMCAs with headquarters in Geneva. In the 1980s the YMCA was active in over 90 countries, with around 10,000 centres and 23 million participants in its activities. Its hostels provide inexpensive accommodation for young men and women and it also runs educational and recreational courses. In 1976 the YMCA opened a new multistorey building in Great Russell Street, London, incorporating a hotel, club, and residence.

Young Women's Christian Association (YWCA) A charity founded in 1855 to care for the spiritual, social, and physical wellbeing of girls and young women, particularly those living and working away from home. Its headquarters are in Weymouth Street, London. It grew from two separate organizations: a prayer union founded in 1855 in Barnet, London, by Emma Roberts (d. 1877) and a home in Great Charlotte Street, London, founded in 1855 by (Lady) Mary Jane Kinnaird (1816–88) for nurses en route to and from the Crimean War. These organizations united in 1877 under the presidency of the Earl of Shaftesbury (1801–85), who also became president of the first national YWCA organization in 1884. The movement spread to the USA (1866) and then to many other countries, with a world organization being set up in 1892. It now runs social, educational, and recreational facilities in over 80 countries and its hostels provide inexpensive accommodation for young women.

youth custody centre A place of custody to which a young offender aged 15 to 20 may be sent for training, instruction, and work in preparation for his release into society. His offence must have been one punishable by imprisonment in the case of a person aged 21 or more, and the court must be satisfied that a custodial sentence is necessary either to protect the public or reflect the gravity of his offence, or because he seems unwilling to respond to a noncustodial penalty. The minimum sentence is normally four months, and the maximum is that for which he could have been sent to prison if over 21. *Compare* detention centre.

Youth Hostels Association (YHA) An organization providing low cost accommodation for young people. The movement originated in Germany in 1910, and spread to other European countries during the 1920s. Founded in the early 1930s, the YHA was specifically designed to promote a greater interest in the countryside by enabling young people of limited means to visit places of natural beauty. There are 260 hostels in England and Wales, some 80 in Scotland, and many more in similar organizations abroad to which the YHA is affiliated as a member of the International Youth Hostels Federation (1932). Typically they concentrate on providing warmth, shelter, and good basic food, and hostellers are expected to observe a few basic rules: they may only stay for three days at any one hostel; they must do their share of the domestic chores; and they must be in bed by ten o'clock, with all lights out one hour later. Sleeping accommodation is usually in single-sex rooms or dormitories. In the mid-1980s, however, the YHA announced plans to do away with the somewhat severe image of hostels and to begin a programme of modernization. Many hostels are situated in splendid locations, often in areas popular for walking or climbing.

YWCA *See* Young Women's Christian Association.

SELECTED BIBLIOGRAPHY

ART

G.A. Bawden, (ed.), *The Oxford Companion to Film*, (Oxford University Press, 1976).

J. Buxton, *Elizabethan Taste*, (Sussex, Harvester Press, 1963).

T.D. Kendrick, *Anglo-Saxon Art to A.D. 900*, (London, Methuen, 1970).

D. Piper, (ed.), *The Genius of British Painting*, (London, Weidenfeld & Nicolson, 1975).

R. Strong, (ed.), *Tudor and Jacobean Portraits*, (London, H.M.S.O. National Portrait Gallery, 1969).

E. Walker, *A History of Music in England*, (London, Da Capo, Plenum Publishing, 1978).

E.K. Waterhouse, *Painting in Britain 1530–1790*, 3rd edn (Harmondsworth, Penguin, 1969).

BUILDINGS

N.B.L. Pevsner et al., *The Buildings of England*, 46 vols, (Harmondsworth, Penguin, 1951–74).

A. Rowan et al., *The Buildings of Ireland*, (Harmondsworth, Penguin, 1979).

N. Craig, *The Architecture of Ireland*, (London, Batsford, 1982).

G. Cobb, *English Cathedrals: forgotten centuries – restoration and change from 1530 to the present day*, (London, Thames & Hudson, 1980).

A. Clifton-Taylor, *The Cathedrals of England*, (London, Thames & Hudson, 1967).

A. Clifton-Taylor, *English Parish Churches as Works of Art*, (London, Batsford, 1974).

D. MacGibbon & T. Ross, *The Castellated and Domestic Architecture of Scotland*, (Mercat Press, 1971).

B. Fletcher, *A History of Architecture*, 18th edn (London, Athlone Press, 1975).

J. Summerson, *Architecture in Britain 1530–1830*, (Harmondsworth, Penguin, 1969).

J. Summerson, *Victorian Architecture*, (New York, Columbia University Press, 1970).

H.M. & J. Taylor, *Anglo-Saxon Architecture*, (Cambridge University Press, 1965).

E. Mercer, *English Vernacular Houses*, (Royal Commission on Historical Monuments, 1975).

J.B. Lowe, *Welsh Industrial Workers Housing 1775–1875*, (National Museum of Wales, 1977).

S. Muthesius, *The English Terraced House*, (Yale University Press, 1982).

J. Burnett, *A Social History of Housing*, (London, Methuen, 1980).

CEREMONIES

E.J. Hobsbawm & T. Ranger (eds.), *The Invention of Tradition*, (Cambridge University Press, 1983).

J. Luciani (ed.), *The Times Guide to the House of Commons*, (London, Times Books, 1983).

J. Whaley (ed.), *Mirrors of Mortality: Studies in the Social History of Death*, (London, Europa, 1981).

CUISINE

E. Ayrton, *The Cookery of England*, (Harmondsworth, Penguin, 1977).

I. Beeton, *The Book of Household Management*, (London, Cape, 1961).

J. Burnett, *Plenty and Want: a social history of diet in England*, (London, Methuen, 1978).

C. Driver, (ed.), *The Good Food Guide*, (annual), (Kent, Hodder & Stoughton).

F.M. McNeill, *The Scots Kitchen*, (St Albans, Mayflower, 1974).

F.M. McNeill, *The Scots Cellar*, (St Albans, Mayflower, 1981).

A.C. Wilson, *Food and Drink in Britain*, (Harmondsworth, Penguin, 1984).

CUSTOMS

C. Hole, *Dictionary of British Folk Customs*, (St Albans, Paladin, 1978).

I. & P. Opie, *Children's Games in Street and Playground*, (Oxford University Press, 1969).

S. Piggott, *Druids*, (London, Thames & Hudson, 1975).

EDUCATION

E. Blishen, *Uncommon Entrance*, (London, Hamish Hamilton, 1974).

A.M. Carr-Saunders, *The New Universities Overseas*, (1961).

G.E. Davie, *The Democratic Intellect: Scotland and her universities in the 19th century*, (Edinburgh University Press, 1964)

J. Lawson & H. Silver, *A Social History of Education in England,* (London, Methuen, 1973).

A.S. Neill, *Summerhill: a radical approach to education*, (Harmondsworth, Penguin, 1970).

L. Stone, (ed.), *The University in Society*, (Oxford University Press, 1975).

FINANCE

H.D. Berman, *The Stock Exchange: an introduction for investors*, 6th edn (London, Pitman, 1971).

A.E. Feaveryear, *The Pound Sterling*, 2nd edn (Oxford University Press, 1963).

R.G. Hawtrey, *The Art of Central Banking*, (London, F. Cass, 1970).

P.L. Payne, (ed.), *Studies in Scottish Business History*, (London, F. Cass, 1967).

R.S. Sayers, *The Bank of England 1891–1944*, (Cambridge University Press, 1976).

R.S. Sayers, *Central Banking after Bagehot*, (Greenwood Press, 1982).

GEOGRAPHY

M. Aston & J. Bond, *The Landscape of Towns*, (London, Dent, 1976).

H.C. Darby (ed.), *A New Historical Geography of England Before 1600*, (Cambridge University Press, 1978).

L. Fleming & A. Gore, *The English Garden*, (London, Michael Joseph, 1982).

T.W. Freeman, *A Hundred Years of Geography*, (London, Duckworth, 1971).

W.G. Hoskins, *The Making of the English Landscape*, (Harmondsworth, Penguin, 1970).

R. Muir, *Shell Guide to Reading the Landscape*, (London, Michael Joseph, 1982).

M.L. Parry & T.R. Slater (eds.), *The Making of the Scottish Countryside*, (London, Croom Helm, 1980).

A.A. Tait, *Landscape Garden in Scotland 1735–1835*, (Edinburgh University Press, 1980).

C.C. Taylor, *Fields in the English Landscape*, (London, Dent, 1982).

B. Trinder, *The Making of the Industrial Landscape*, (London, Dent, 1982).

HISTORY

Books on British history are even more numerous than those on the other subjects of this book. This section of the bibliography is therefore devoted to (a) further bibliographies (b) general surveys.

(a)

J.L. Altholz, *Mind and Art of Victorian England*, (Minnesota, University of Minnesota Press, 1976).

L.M. Brown & I.R. Christie, *A Bibliography of British History 1789–1861*, (Oxford University Press, 1976).

G. Davies, *A Bibliography of British History: the Stuart Period, 1603–1714*, ed. M.F. Keeler, (Oxford Univeristy Press, 1970).

C. Gross, *A Bibliography of English History to 1485*, ed. E.B. Graves, (Oxford University Press, 1975).

D.J. Guth, *Late-medieval England 1377–1485*, (Cambridge University Press, 1976).

H.J. Hanham, *A Bibliography of British History 1851–1914*, (Oxford University Press, 1976).

(b)

A.A.M. Duncan, R. Nicholson, G. Donaldson & W. Ferguson, *The Edinburgh History of Scotland*, (Edinburgh, Oliver & Boyd, 1965–78).

H.P.R. Finberg, (ed.), *The Agrarian History of England and Wales*, (Cambridge University Press, 1972).

C. Haigh, (ed.), *The Cambridge Historical Encyclopedia of Great Britain and Ireland*, (Cambridge University Press, 1985).

T.W. Moody, F.X. Martin & F.J. Burne, (eds.), *A New History of Ireland*, Oxford University Press, 1976–82).

D.S. Thomson, (ed.), *The Companion to Gaelic Scotland*, (Oxford, Blackwell, 1983).

R.K. Webb, *Modern England*, 2nd edn (London, Allen & Unwin, 1980).

LANGUAGE

A. Burgess, *Language Made Plain*, (Glasgow, Collins, 1984).

W. Empson, *The Structure of Complex Words*, (London, Chatto, 1969).

H.W. Fowler, *A Dictionary of Modern English Usage*, (Oxford University Press, 1983).

H.W. & F.G. Fowler, *The King's English*, (Oxford University Press, 1973).

E. Gowers, *The Complete Plain Words*, (Harmondsworth, Penguin, 1970).

W.B. Lockwood, *Languages of the British Isles Past and Present*, (London, Deutsch, 1975).

M. McLennan, *Gaelic Dictionary: Gaelic-English English-Gaelic*, (Aberdeen University Press, 1979).

W.F.H. Nicolaisen, *Scottish Place Names*, (London, Batsford, 1976).

H. Orton & N. Wright, *A Word Geography of England*, (Seminar Press, 1975).

E. Partridge, *Usage and Abusage*, (Harmondsworth, Penguin, 1979).

T.F. O'Rahilly, *Irish Dialects*, (Dublin Institute for Advanced Studies, 1972).

M.F. Wakelin, *Language and History in Cornwall*, (Leicester University Press, 1975).

LAW

A.G. Chloros, *Bibliographical Guide to the Law of the U.K., the Channel Islands and the Isle of Man*, (University of London Institute of Advanced Legal Studies, 1973).

E.A. Martin (ed.), *A Concise Dictionary of Law*, (Oxford University Press, 1983).

F. Pollock & F.W. Maitland, *History of English Law Before the Time of Edward I*, 2nd edn (Cambridge University Press, 1968).

D.M. Walker, *The Oxford Companion to Law*, (Oxford University Press, 1980).

MONARCHY

W. Bagehot, *The English Constitution*, (London, Fontana, 1963).

G. Battiscombe, *Queen Alexandra*, (London, Constable, 1969).

C. Hibbert, *The Court at Windsor*, (Harmondsworth, Penguin 1982).

L.F. Hobley, *The Monarchy*, (London, Batsford, 1962).

R.R. James, *Albert, Prince Consort*, (London, Hamish Hamilton, 1983).

H.G. Nicolson, *King George V*, (London, Constable, [no date]).

P. Rose. *George V*, (London, Weidenfeld & Nicolson, 1983).

MONUMENTS

A. Burl, *The Stone Circles of the British Isles*, (Yale University Press, 1976).

J. Harvey, *Medieval Craftsmen*, (London, Batsford, 1973).

A.H.A. Hogg, *Hill Forts of Britain*, (London, Hart-Davis MacGibbon, 1975).

T.D. Kendrick, *The Druids*, (London, F. Cass, 1966).

D.F. Renn, *Norman Castles in Britain*, (London, J. Baker, 1973).

A.S. Robertson, *The Antonine Wall*, (Glasgow Archaeological Society, 1973).

M.W. Thomson, *Ruins: their preservation and display*, (London, British Museum Publications, 1979).

J. Wacher, *The Towns of Roman Britain*, (London, Batsford, 1975).

POLITICS

S.H. Beer, *Modern British Politics*, 3rd edn (London, Faber & Faber, 1969).

R. Blake, *The Conservative Party from Peel to Thatcher*, (1985)

D. Butler et al, *The British General Election of 1955*, (London, F. Cass).

D. Butler & D. Stokes, *Political Change in Britain: the evolution of electoral choice*, 2nd edn (London, Macmillan, 1975).

J.G. Kellas, *The Scottish Political System*, 3rd edn (Cambridge University Press, 1984).

H.M. Pelling, *A Short History of the Labour Party*, 5th edn (London, Macmillan, 1985).

R. Rose, *Politics in England*, (London, Faber & Faber 1980).

ORGANIZATIONS AND SOCIETIES

B. Abel-Smith, *Value for Money in Health Services: a comparative study*, (London, Heinemann, 1976).

W.E. Baugh, *Introduction to the Social Services*, (London, Macmillan, 1983)

T.A. Critchley, *A History of the Police in England and Wales*, (London, Constable, 1978).

E.N. Gladden, *A History of Public Administration*, (London, F. Cass, 1972).

W.M. James, *The Naval History of Great Britain, Index*, (London, Conway Maritime Press, 1971).

I. Pinchbeck & M. Hewitt, *Children in English Society*, (3 vols, London Routledge & Kegan Paul, 1969–73).

M. Cowling, *Religion and Public Doctrine in Modern England*, (Cambridge University Press, 1980).

RELIGION

O. Chadwick, *The Victorian Church*, (2 vols., London, Black, 1966–70).
J.D. Gay, *The Geography of Religion in England*, (London, Duckworth, 1976).
P. Collinson, *Mirror of Elizabethan Puritanism*, (Dr William's Trust, 1964).
I.B. Cowan, *The Scottish Reformation: Church and Society in 16th Century Scotland*, (London, Weidenfeld & Nicolson, 1982).

SPORT

D. Brailsford, *Sport and Society: Elizabeth to Anne*, (London, Routledge & Kegan Paul, 1969).
P.E. Cunnington & A. Mansfield, *English Costume for Sports*, (London, Black, 1969).
J.W. Hills, *A Summer on the Test*, (London, Deutsch, 1983).
U.A. Titley & R. MacWhirter, *Centenary History of the Rugby Football Union*, (Rugby Football Union, 1971).

ACKNOWLEDGEMENTS

Nigel Luckhurst 5, 63, 89, 347, 372;
The British Library 12(Harl. MS 502.f.32),
177(Stowe MS 549.f.7v), 245(Egerton MS
618.f.74);
By courtesy of Birmingham Museums and Art
Gallery 17;
South East England Tourist Board 18, 68, 384;
Scottish Tourist Board 22, 181, 204, 210;
The Master and Fellows of Corpus Christi
College, Cambridge 24;
Northern Ireland Tourist Board 30, 70, 78,
123, 165;
BBC Hulton Picture Library 32, 33, 54, 117,
233, 472;
Doc Rowe 33, 87, 106, 146, 207, 210, 304,
390, 405, 415, 457, 477;
Paul Harvey 34;
Cambridge University Collection: copyright
reserved 39, 81, 205;
Allsport 41, 139, 185, 248, 329;
Stephanie Boyd 41;
Cambridgeshire Collection, Cambridgeshire
Libraries 56, 354;
Photographs by Britain On View
Photographic Library (BTA/ETB) 59, 77,
168, 171, 195, 196, 202, 252, 254, 260, 267,
315, 322, 325, 346, 360, 413, 435, 448;
Wales Tourist Board 62, 73, 116, 380;
Highlands and Islands Development Board 71,
131, 335, 424;
By kind permission of Country Life 72, 122;
Royal Commission on the Historical
Monuments of England 76, 279, 475;
Trustees of the National Portrait Gallery,
London 103, 188, 193, 219, 341;
Patrick Eagar 130;
By permission of the Controller of Her
Majesty's Stationery Office, Crown
copyright 133;
The Trustees of the Imperial War Museum,
London 138, 473;

Reproduced by kind permission from the
Phillimore edition of Domesday Book
(General Editor, John Morris), volume 1
Kent (County Editor, Philip Morgan),
published in 1983 by Phillimore and Co.
Ltd., Shopwyke Hall, Chichester,
W. Sussex 143;
British Crown Copyright Reserved 153;
The Provost and Fellows of Eton College 159;
C.S. Middleton 163;
Courtesy of Southampton City Museums 175;
Guildhall Library, London 182, 445;
Museum of London 187, 247, 317;
John Tarlton 192;
The Mansell Collection Ltd 208, 284, 312;
Reproduced by gracious permission of Her
Majesty the Queen 226;
Geoffrey Berry 235;
J. Sainsbury Plc. 250;
The Heart of England Tourist Board 265;
By permission of the Master and Fellows,
Magdalene College, Cambridge 266;
Bodleian Library 280(MS Auct.F.4.32, fol.1
recto);
© National Railway Museum, York 291, 352;
The Tate Gallery, London 336;
The Tennis and Rackets Association 353;
From the collection at the Laing Art Gallery,
Newcastle upon Tyne, reproduced by
permission of Tyne and Wear Museums
366;
Fishbourne Roman Palace/Sussex
Archaeological Society 367;
The Salvation Army 391;
University of St. Andrews 419;
The Automobile Association 424;
University of East Anglia 447;
Reproduction by permission of the Trustees,
The Wallace Collection, London 452;
John Wright Photography of Warwick 454;
Jeff Saward/Caerdroia 455;
Dr R.S. Shorter 467